Business
Accounting

BUSINESS ACCOUNTING

An Introduction to Financial and Management Accounting

Jill Collis, Andrew Holt and Roger Hussey

Third edition

 palgrave

First edition 2007, Second edition 2012 published by
Palgrave Macmillan.

Third edition published 2017 by
PALGRAVE

Palgrave in the UK is an imprint of Macmillan Publishers Limited, registered in England, company number 785998, of 4 Crinan Street, London, N1 9XW.

Palgrave® and Macmillan® are registered trademarks in the United States, the United Kingdom, Europe and other countries.

ISBN: 978–1–137–52149–1 paperback

A catalogue record for this book is available from the British Library.

A catalog record for this book is available from the Library of Congress.

Table of contents

List of figures

List of tables

Preface

Accounting information lies at the heart of business, irrespective of the size of the company and regardless of whether the user of the information is the owner, the manager or an external party. Therefore, it is not surprising that accounting is a core subject on programmes that include the study of business.

Now in its third edition, *Business Accounting* has been developed specifically for the needs of non-specialist students studying accounting. It provides an introduction to financial and management accounting in an accessible, non-technical style and is suitable for undergraduate and postgraduate students. The active-learning approach seeks to convey an understanding of the subjectivity inherent in accounting and the ability to evaluate financial information for a range of business purposes.

The book provides clear and concise coverage of financial and management accounting principles and practice, set in a business context. The chapters are presented in a logical teaching sequence and each chapter has a clear structure with learning objectives, key definitions and activities within the text to illustrate principles, encourage reflection and introduce the next learning point. There is a wealth of worked examples, recurring case studies and recent company data to ensure that learning relates to business reality.

At the end of each chapter there are discussion questions and exam-style practice questions that test the learning outcomes. Answers to these questions, together with additional materials, PowerPoint slides and interactive quizzes for use in a virtual learning environment are available on the companion website (see p. xxiv). A unique feature of the book is the addition of suggested topics for dissertation students at the end of each chapter, with potential research questions and preliminary reading.

Part I of the book sets the scene with two chapters that introduce the student to the world of accounting and finance in a business context, while Parts II and III cover the key aspects of financial and management accounting respectively. Part IV focuses on capital investment appraisal techniques. In addition to the traditional syllabus, there are chapters on contemporary accounting issues such as corporate governance, stewardship, social responsibility and integrated reporting, as well as strategic management accounting and environmental accounting.

The wide range of topics offered allows the lecturer to select those that are relevant to the syllabus and the level of study. On some programmes, the two main branches of accounting are studied at different stages (for example, in consecutive semesters for Master's and MBA students, or consecutive years for undergraduate students); on other programmes, the topics are drawn from both branches (for example, introduction to accounting in year 1 and a follow-up module as a core or elective in years 2 or 3). The use of the book on consecutive modules offers the advantage of continuity as well as cost savings for students.

Suggested teaching syllabus

Example 1. Two branches of accounting are taught separately

Module 1
Financial accounting
Part I The world of accounting and finance
1 Introduction to business accounting
2 The importance of cash

Part II Financial accounting
3 The accounting system
4 The regulatory framework for financial reporting

5 The conceptual framework for financial reporting
6 The statement of profit or loss and other comprehensive income
7 The statement of financial position
8 The statement of cash flows
9 Consolidated financial statements
10 Financial statement analysis
11 Corporate governance, stewardship, social responsibility and integrated reporting

Example 2. Both branches of accounting are taught together

Module 1
Introduction to accounting

Part I The world of accounting and finance
1 Introduction to accounting
2 The importance of cash

Part II Financial accounting
3 The accounting system
4 The regulatory framework for financial reporting

5 The conceptual framework for financial reporting
6 The statement of profit or loss and other comprehensive income
7 The statement of financial position
8 The statement of cash flows

Part III Management accounting
12 The importance of cost information
13 Costing for product direct costs
14 Costing for indirect costs

Acknowledgements

We would like to acknowledge the invaluable feedback on this book and its associated learning resources given to us by our students over the years. We are also grateful to the anonymous reviewers for their thoughtful suggestions and comments.

We are indebted to a number of friends and colleagues, who have given us the benefit of their experience: Rachel Jones and Bian Tan in relation to the first edition; Mark Farmer and Geoffrey George in connection with the second edition; and Robin Jarvis and Lawrence Wu with regard to the third edition. Thanks are also due to our editorial team at Palgrave and our copy-editor, Ann Edmondson, whose support has been invaluable.

Acronyms

AADB	Accountancy and Actuarial Discipline Board
ABC	activity-based costing
ACCA	Association of Chartered Certified Accountants
AGM	annual general meeting
AIA	Association of International Accountants
AICPA	American Institute of Certified Public Accountants
AIM	Alternative Investment Market
APB	Auditing Practices Board
ARR	accounting rate of return
ASAF	Accounting Standards Advisory Forum
ASB	Accounting Standards Board
ASC	Accounting Standards Committee
BBB	British Business Bank
BEP	breakeven point
b/f	brought forward
BIS	(Department for) Business, Innovation and Skills
BSC	balanced scorecard
BVCA	British Private Equity & Venture Capital Association
CA 2006	Companies Act 2006
CAI	Chartered Accountants Ireland
CE	capital employed
c/f	carried forward
CGMA	Chartered Global Management Accountant
CIMA	Chartered Institute of Management Accountants
CIPFA	Chartered Institute of Public Finance and Accountancy
CSR	corporate social responsibility
DCF	discounted cash flow
ECB	European Central Bank
ECGI	European Corporate Governance Institute
EEA	European Economic Area
EEC	European Economic Community
EFAA	European Federation of Accountants and Auditors
EFRAG	European Financial Reporting Advisory Group
EMA	environmental management accounting
EMS	environmental management system

EPS	earnings per share
ERP	enterprise resource planning
EU	European Union
FASB	Financial Accounting Standards Board
FCA	Financial Conduct Authority
FIFO	first in, first out
FRC	Financial Reporting Council
FRS	Financial Reporting Standard
FRSSE	Financial Reporting Standard for Smaller Entities
GAAP	generally accepted accounting principles
GHG	greenhouse gas
HMRC	HM Revenue and Customs
HP	hire purchase
IAASB	International Auditing and Assurance Standards Board
IAS	International Accounting Standard
IASB	International Accounting Standards Board
IASC	International Accounting Standards Committee
ICAEW	Institute of Chartered Accountants in England and Wales
ICAS	Institute of Chartered Accountants in Scotland
ICSA	Institute of Chartered Secretaries and Administrators
IESBA	International Ethics Standards Board for Accountants
IFAC	International Federation of Accountants
IFRIC	International Financial Reporting Interpretations Committee
IFRS	International Financial Reporting Standard
IIRC	International Integrated Reporting Council
IoD	Institute of Directors
IOSCO	International Organization of Securities Commissions
IPO	initial public offering
<IR>	Integrated Reporting
IRR	internal rate of return
ISA	International Standard on Auditing
ISD	Investment Services Directive
ISO	International Organization for Standardization
JIT	just-in-time
JO	joint operation
LLP	limited liability partnership
LSE	London Stock Exchange
Ltd	Limited
MEP	member of the European Parliament
MOA	market-orientated accounting

NCF	net cash flow
NCI	non-controlling interest
NGO	non-governmental organization
NPV	net present value
NRV	net realizable value
OAR	overhead absorption rate
OCI	other comprehensive income
OECD	Organisation for Economic Co-operation and Development
P2P	peer-to-peer
PBIT	profit before interest and tax
PCAOB	Public Company Accounting Oversight Board
P/E	price/earnings or price-earnings
PIR	Post-Implementation Review
PLC	Public Limited Company
PPE	property, plant and equipment
PRC	People's Republic of China
PV	present value
QCA	Quoted Companies Alliance
ROCE	return on capital employed
ROE	return on equity
SCI	strategic cost index
SEC	Securities and Exchange Commission
SIC	Standard Interpretations Committee
SMA	strategic management accounting
SMEs	small and medium-sized entities
SWOT	strengths, weaknesses, opportunities, threats
TQM	total quality management
UCITS	Undertakings for Collective Investment in Transferable Securities
UEAPME	European Association of Craft, Small and Medium-sized Enterprises
UK	United Kingdom [of Great Britain and Northern Ireland]
UKBAA	UK Business Angels Association
UK CG Code	UK Corporate Governance Code
UN	United Nations
USA	United States of America
WAC	weighted-average cost
WBCSD	World Business Council for Sustainable Development
WIP	work-in-progress
WRI	World Resources Institute

Tour of the book

- **Learning objectives**: Each chapter starts by setting out the main topics you should be able to master after studying the chapter

Learning objectives

When you have studied this chapter, you should be able to:

- Explain the theory of a finance gap for small and medium-siz
- Describe and classify potential sources of business finance
- Explain the need for cash flow information
- Prepare and interpret a cash flow forecast and a cash flow st
- Describe the principles for monitoring and controlling cash

- **Worked examples**: An abundance of easy-to-follow worked examples, recurring case studies and recent company data ensure your learning reflects business reality

Your forecast should look like this:

Candlewick Ltd

Draft cash flow forecast for January–June 2018

	January £	February £	March £	April £	May £	June £	Total £
Cash inflows							
Capital	10,000	0	0	0	0	0	10,000
Revenue (cash sales)	2,000	2,000	2,500	2,800	3,000	3,000	15,300
Revenue (credit sales)	0	0	6,000	6,000	7,500	8,400	27,900
	12,000	2,000	8,500	8,800	10,500	11,400	53,200
Cash outflows							
Purchases	0	6,000	6,000	7,500	8,400	9,000	36,900
	0	6,000	6,000	7,500	8,400	9,000	36,900
Net cash flow	12,000	(4,000)	2,500	1,300	2,100	2,400	16,300
Cumulative cash b/f	0	12,000	8,000	10,500	11,800	13,900	0
Cumulative cash c/f	12,000	8,000	10,500	11,800	13,900	16,300	16,300

- **Activities within the text**: Illustrate the principles, encourage reflection and give you a chance to apply what you have been shown before you move on to the next learning point.

Activity

During the month of August, a car deal purchased at the beginning of the mon car, but has not yet received the cash fi tion at the end of August?

- **Key definitions**: Each chapter contains clear and authoritative definitions of key terms for easy learning and quick revision

Key definition

Financial accounting is the branch of accounting concern measuring and recording the economic transactions of an established principles, legal requirements and accounting concerned with communicating a true and fair view of the financial position of an entity to external parties at the en

- **Figures and tables**: Figures help you visualize processes and structure, while tables illustrate layouts for presenting financial statements and other financial information

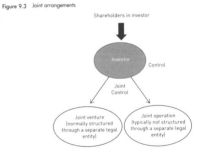

Figure 9.3 Joint arrangements

Table 5.1 Set of financial statements under IAS 1

IASB terminology	Traditional UK terminology
Statement of profit or loss and other comprehensive income	Profit and loss account
Statement of financial position	Balance sheet
Statement of changes in equity	Statement of recognized gains an
Statement of cash flows	Cash flow statement

- **Common problems to avoid**: Tips and advice help you improve your grades by avoiding common mistakes

 Common problems to avoid

Common mistakes students make when constructing an invente

- Forgetting to include the unit of measurement or the currenc column headings
- Forgetting to show the date of each receipt or issue of mater
- Failing to show the opening balance of inventory (if applicab
- Treating opening inventory as a receipt of materials
- Forgetting the formula for calculating the weighted-average

- **Discussion questions**: Give you an opportunity to debate in class or write essays on key issues covered in the chapter

 Discussion questions

1 Discuss the reasons why students studying business or about cash flow management.

2 Discuss the obstacles that start-up and early stage comp access to finance.

3 Define finance and discuss the extent to which alternati finance gap for small companies.

- **Practice questions**: Allow you to test your skills and knowledge as you work through progressively challenging exam-style questions

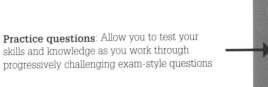 **Practice questions**

3 Rex Wellworth started Wellworth Fencin his uncle. On 1 June he opened a bank a capital he has invested in the business. cheques to buy a lorry for £16,000, to pay £4,500 for three months' rent on premise business cheques: £5,400 to pay for equi als from Timber Supplies; and £420 to pa the business bought a further £120 of fer Supplies Ltd.

- **Suggested research topics**: Ideal for dissertation students and those undertaking a research project, these offer potential research questions on accounting topics, together with helpful pointers to preliminary reading

 Suggested research questions

Students interested in costing for product dire more of the following research questions:

- What are the factors that affect the choice country]?
- Are the cost accounting tools based on a la SMEs?
- Is underperformance in SMEs due to their costing tools?

Digital support for lecturers and students

A companion website for this edition (www.palgravehighered.com/collis-ba3e) features the following resources.

For lecturers:

- PowerPoint presentation for each chapter in the book
- A new digital test bank of questions and problems developed chapter by chapter, perfect for creating quizzes to assess your students' progress with quick spot-check tests or mid-term assignments
- All of the materials above can be readily integrated into your existing VLE in a seamless way to support your course design and delivery. Contact your Palgrave representative to obtain access to the website resources and find out how you can integrate them into your VLE
- Lecturer's Answer Book with answers to the end-of-chapter practice questions

For students:

- Student's Workbook to support the exercises in the PowerPoint presentations
- Progress tests give you the opportunity to test your progress at your own pace. Now with automated grading, each chapter offers a range of questions with feedback supplied when you answer incorrectly, helping you to navigate back to the book to improve your mastery of key skills and knowledge
- Ted Baker Annual Report – the full annual report and accounts referred to in the book is provided for ease of reference

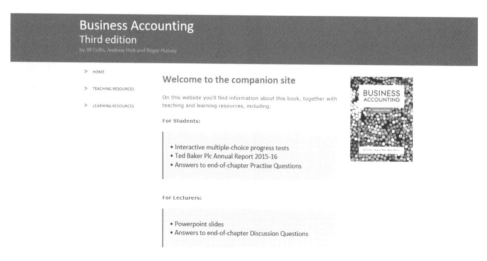

PART I

The world of accounting and finance

1 Introduction to business accounting

Learning objectives

When you have studied this chapter, you should be able to:

- Compare different types of business entity
- Explain the concept of limited liability
- Discuss the advantages and disadvantages of a code of ethics for accountants
- Explain the nature and purpose of accounting
- Distinguish between management accounting and financial accounting

1.1 Introduction

This book focuses on accounting in a business context. Everyone knows that business is about trying to make money and in this chapter we will start by looking at the different types of business entity. Whether you decide to start your own business when you complete your studies, or you find a job in a large, small or medium-sized entity, you will need a basic understanding of accounting. In this chapter we provide an overview of the different types of business entity and draw attention to the economic importance of small and medium-sized entities. We also explain the role of the accountancy profession and the need for a code of ethics for professional accountants. This leads to a discussion of the nature and purpose of accounting and an overview of the two main branches of accounting.

1.2 Types of business entity

Most businesses are set up with a view to making a profit. The sector of the economy in which they operate is known as the private sector. The private sector can be distinguished from the public sector (entities under state control) and the voluntary sector (public benefit entities such as charities and other not-for-profit entities). Accountants can work in any of these sectors, but we are going to focus solely on the private sector. Before we look at the work of the accountant, we are going to examine the different types of business entity as this will help you understand the context in which business accounting takes place.

In the UK the legal form of businesses in the *private sector* can be classified into three main types:

- sole proprietorships
- ordinary partnerships
- limited liability partnerships, companies and other incorporated entities.

At the start of 2016, the number of private sector enterprises in the UK was a record 5.5 million. Figure 1.1 shows how they were dispersed among the three main categories.

Figure 1.1   UK private sector enterprises by legal status

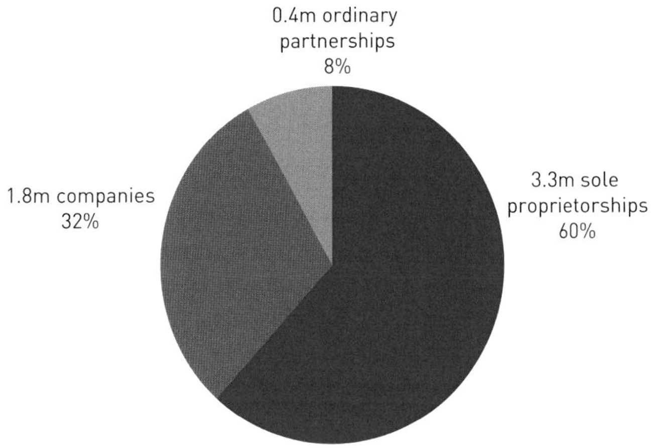

0.4m ordinary
partnerships
8%

1.8m companies
32%

3.3m sole
proprietorships
60%

Source: Adapted from BEIS, 2016, p. 2.

The size of private sector enterprises ranges from very small businesses, such as a sole proprietorship or a one-person company with no employees, to a large international company with thousands of owners and employees. Of the total of 5.5 million businesses in the UK, 99.9% were small (fewer than 50 employees) or medium-sized (fewer than 250 employees). In addition to providing a living for their owners, these small and medium-sized enterprises (SMEs) contributed to the economy by providing 15.7 million jobs (60% of private sector employment) and producing a combined annual turnover of £1.8 trillion (47% of private sector turnover) (BEIS, 2016, p. 1). In the European Union (EU), SMEs make up 99.8% of all enterprises. In 2015, just under 23 million SMEs in the EU employed 90 million people (providing two-thirds of jobs) and generated €3.9 trillion of value added (just under three-fifths of value added) in the non-financial business sector (European Commission, 2016). Not surprisingly, they are considered to be the backbone of the European economy.

The majority of smaller entities are owner-managed and family-owned (Collis, 2008 and 2012), but family ownership may become fragmented over time (ICAEW, 2015). In larger businesses, it is more likely that ownership and control will become separated, and the owners will appoint managers to run the business on their behalf. Businesses also differ in terms of their legal status and in the groups of people who are likely to be interested in financial information about them.

To a large extent, the range of users of the financial information depends on the size of the business. For example, financial information relating to a small shop is likely to be used only by the owner-manager and the tax authorities, whereas financial information relating to a large international company will be of interest not only to managers within the business but also to investors, lenders, suppliers, customers and other external parties, such as competitors. Each user group needs financial information for a different purpose. For example, a manager working in a division of a large company is likely to require detailed information in order to run the department, a bank lending officer contemplating lending £1 million to a business is likely to need information for assessing the lending risk and a supplier will need information for assessing the risk of supplying goods and/or services on credit to the business.

Accounting provides important financial information that helps businesses achieve their objectives. All entities strive to ensure that the income generated and the costs incurred are at acceptable levels, but what is considered to be an acceptable level varies. In the private sector, the economic objective of some business owners is to maximize their wealth by following profit maximization strategies. Others simply want to make sufficient profit to maintain a certain lifestyle and can be described as following satisficing strategies. Therefore, the owners of small businesses do not necessarily have plans to grow the business, but may be motivated by lifestyle factors (Fraser et al., 2015). Research suggests that around 56% of smaller businesses intended to grow in 2016 (BBB, 2016). Although we are looking at accounting in a business context, you should be aware that the economic objective of organizations in the public sector and the voluntary sector is to break even. This means that their managers focus on generating enough income to cover costs and thus avoid making a profit or a loss.

1.2.1   Sole proprietorships

The majority of businesses are *sole proprietorships*. At the start of 2015, there were 3.3 million sole proprietorships in the UK (62% of the total number of private sector enterprises). A sole proprietorship is an unincorporated entity[1] owned by one person, who is in business with a view to making a profit. The business may be providing a service (for example, a window cleaner, hairdresser or business consultant), trading goods (for example, a newsagent, florist or grocer) or making goods (for example, a cabinet maker, potter or dress designer). Alternatively, it may have activities in the

---

1. This means it has not been incorporated as a company.

primary sector (agriculture, forestry or fishing). The owner may run the business alone or employ staff.

The owner of a sole proprietorship has *unlimited liability*, which means that he or she is personally liable for any debts the business may incur. This liability extends beyond any original investment and could mean the loss of personal assets. There are no legal formalities to set up this type of business, but an entrepreneur wanting to start a sole proprietorship may experience difficulty in obtaining finance, as the capital is restricted to what he or she has available to invest, supplemented by what he or she can borrow. The owner must keep accounting records, but there is no obligation to disclose financial information to the public.

1.2.2 Ordinary partnerships

An *ordinary partnership* is also an unincorporated entity. It is created when two or more people join together in business with a view to making a profit. At the start of 2015, there were 436,000 ordinary partnerships in the UK (8% of the total number of private sector enterprises). There has been no restriction on the maximum number of partners since 2002. The partners own the business and may run it alone or employ staff. The partners have joint and several liability, which means they have unlimited liability for each other's acts in terms of any debts the business may incur. This liability extends beyond any original investment and could mean the loss of personal assets. The capital is restricted to what the partners have to invest, supplemented by what they can borrow. The *Business Names Act 1985* requires the names of the partners to be shown on business stationery, but they need not be used in the business name. The partners must keep accounting records, but there is no obligation to disclose financial information to the public.

The relationship between partners should be formalized in a partnership agreement, which is a deed of contract relating to the agreement to form a partnership.

Activity

What sort of financial matters do you think partners ought to agree before forming an ordinary partnership?

The most obvious points on which they should reach agreement are:

- How to divide the profit
- How much money (capital) each partner will invest in the business
- Whether any of the partners will be entitled to a salary
- Whether any interest will be payable on the capital invested by the partners
- Whether any interest will be payable on any loan made to the partnership by any of the partners.

In the absence of a partnership agreement, or if the agreement does not cover a point in dispute, the *Partnership Act 1890* provides the following rules:

- Partners share equally in the profits or losses of the partnership
- Partners are not entitled to receive salaries
- Partners are not entitled to interest on their capital
- Partners may receive interest at 5% per annum on any advances over and above their agreed capital
- A new partner may not be introduced unless all the existing partners consent
- A retiring partner is entitled to receive interest at 5% per annum on his or her share of the partnership assets retained in the partnership after his or her retirement
- On dissolution of the partnership, the assets of the firm must be used first to repay outside creditors, second to repay partners' advances, and third to repay partners' capital. Any residue on dissolution should be distributed to the partners in the profit-sharing ratio (equally unless specified otherwise in the partnership agreement).

You may think that the partners do not need an agreement, because the Partnership Act 1890 sets out the relationship in case of dispute. However, this means the rules of a standard agreement would be applied, which may not be appropriate to the circumstances.

Activity

Indicate which of these characteristics apply to the following types of business:

	Sole proprietorship	Ordinary partnership
(a) The entity is an unincorporated business	❑	❑
(b) There is only one owner	❑	❑
(c) There is no maximum number of owners	❑	❑
(d) There are no formalities involved when starting the business	❑	❑
(e) There should be a contract of agreement	❑	❑

What sole proprietorships and ordinary partnerships have in common is their unincorporated status, which means their owners have unlimited liability for any debts or losses incurred by the business. Of course, there is only one owner of a sole proprietorship, who is solely responsible, whereas the responsibility is shared in a partnership. A partnership can also raise more capital than a sole proprietorship because there it has at least two owners (there is no maximum number of partners). For the same reason, a greater range of skills is likely to be available in a partnership. There are no formalities involved in setting up a sole proprietorship, but the relationship between partners should be formalized in a partnership agreement. All businesses, regardless of legal status, must keep accounting records.

1.2.3 Limited liability partnerships

One of the major disadvantages of an ordinary partnership is the financial risk to individual partners due to the actions carried out by other partners in the normal course of business. In other words, if you are a partner and one of the other partners is incompetent and incurs large debts, you will have responsibility for those debts even if it means bankruptcy. If the partnership has only two or three partners it may be possible to monitor the activities of all partners, but this would be impossible in a large international firm with hundreds of partners spread throughout the world. Moreover, it would not be very agreeable to accept personal liability for their actions. This issue is resolved by allowing a partnership to obtain limited liability by incorporating as a *limited liability partnership (LLP)*.

LLPs were introduced in the UK by the *Limited Liability Partnership Act 2000* and the *Limited Liability Partnership Regulations 2001*. They are a popular form of business for professional firms offering services, such as accountants, doctors, dentists and solicitors. All LLPs must be registered at Companies House, which is part of the Department for Business, Innovation and Skills. LLPs are allowed to organize themselves internally in the same way as an ordinary partnership, but the regulations that apply to them are similar to the requirements for companies. If one of the partners dies, his or her shares can be transferred to someone else and the business continues. On the other hand, when a partner in an ordinary partnership dies, the partnership ceases. If the remaining partners want the business to continue, they need to form a new partnership, with or without additional partners.

An important advantage of an LLP is that each partner's liability for the debts and losses incurred by the business is limited to the amount of his or her investment in the business. There are two main exceptions to this limited liability:

- If a partner of an LLP is personally at fault, he or she may have unlimited liability if he or she accepted a personal duty of care or a personal contractual obligation.
- If an LLP becomes insolvent, the partners can be required to repay any property withdrawn from the LLP (including profits and interest) in the two years prior to insolvency. This applies where it is reasonable that the partner could not have concluded that insolvency was likely.

> **Key definition**
>
> Limited liability refers to the extent to which members of a limited company or LLP are liable for payment of the debts of the business.

1.2.4   Limited companies

The majority of limited liability entities are *limited companies*. A limited company is a business that through the process of incorporation acquires a legal status that is separate from that of its owners. Historically corporation status was achieved by royal charter or letters patent (a chartered company), by Act of Parliament (a statutory company) and since 1844 by registration (a registered company). Under the various Companies Acts since that time, registration has become the most common form of incorporation and today nearly all commercial companies are registered companies. Like LLPs, all limited companies in the UK must be registered at Companies House, which is part of the Department for Business, Innovation and Skills. Figure 1.2 shows an extract from a page in the Company Register for 1862.

Figure 1.2   Entries in the Company Register for 1862

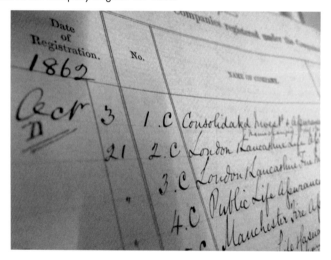

Source: Companies House.

The capital invested in the business is raised by selling shares to investors (hence the term *shareholder*), who are known as members. The capital invested in any type of business can be supplemented by loans and other forms of finance, such as trade credit from suppliers. Trade credit does not provide additional cash, but allows money already in the business to be used for other purposes until it is needed to pay creditors. Members have limited liability, which means that even if the business goes into liquidation owing significant amounts to lenders and creditors, the owners' liability for those debts is limited to the capital they have invested. Figure 1.3 explains the concept of limited liability in more detail.

Figure 1.3 The concept of limited liability

'The Limited Liability Act 1855 was the first to establish the principle of limited liability subject to certain safeguards, but it was only in force a few months before the Joint Stock Companies Act 1856 superseded it and became the first in the line of statutes which culminated in the concept of limited liability as we know it today.

The concept of limited liability relates to the members of a company being liable to contribute towards payment of its debts only to a limited extent. The amount of members' liability is determined by the liability clause contained in a company's memorandum of association, and differs in its nature according to whether the company is one which is limited by shares, limited by guarantee, or unlimited.

The vast majority of companies registered under the Companies Act are companies "limited by shares". This means that the shareholders or members have a limited liability to pay the debts of the company. When new shares are issued by a company the person who takes the shares must agree to pay for them. Usually payment will be made immediately but sometimes shares will be issued "unpaid" or "partly paid", in which case payment must be made later. If the company goes into liquidation and is insolvent, the members are liable to pay for their shares in full if they have not already done so ...

Complementary to the concept of limitation of the members' liability is the notion that the company is a separate "legal person" distinct from the members and the directors. It is the company that buys and sells, owns land, employs workers, makes profits or losses, and not the individuals who make up the company. The company itself is owned by the members, and its directors act on its behalf, but the debts are the debts of the company and the only assets which can be used to satisfy those debts are the assets owned by the company...These complementary rules of limited liability and legal personality, therefore, combine to confer enormous advantages on the sole proprietor who turns his [or her] business into a company.'

Source: Mallet and Brumwell, 1994. Reproduced with permission of House of Words Ltd.

The need for limited companies developed in the eighteenth century when the Industrial Revolution in Europe began to change many countries from rural economies to urban economies and the new industrialists needed investors to fund their entrepreneurial endeavours. In the nineteenth century new commercial and industrial technologies, such as engineering and applied science, and industrialization spread to other continents through the colonial activities of the more powerful European nations as they competed for raw materials, new markets and political advantage. In the UK the *Joint Stock Companies Registration and Regulation Act 1844* was important because not only did it introduce incorporation by registration, but it also introduced the requirement that companies present a balance sheet to shareholders. Figure 1.4 summarizes these developments.

Figure 1.4 Development of incorporated entities in the UK

The *Companies Act 2006 (CA 2006)* defines a company as a *limited company* if the liability of its members is limited by its constitution. The company may be limited by shares or by guarantee:

- It is limited by shares if the members' liability is limited to the amount (if any) unpaid on the shares held by them.
- It is limited by guarantee if the members' liability is limited to such amount as they undertake to contribute to the assets of the company in the event of it being wound up (when all the assets are sold to pay the creditors, any remaining assets are distributed to the owners and the business is dissolved).

Limited companies can be divided into *public companies* and *private companies*. A public company is a company limited by shares or limited by guarantee and having share capital. A private company is any company that is not a public company. Of the population of 1.8 million companies on the register in 2015–16, 99.98% were private companies and the remainder (0.02%) were public limited companies (Companies House, 2016). Most companies are started as private limited companies and, if they are successful and grow large, their owners may decide to convert them into a public company under the re-registration procedure in CA 2006. They can then obtain a listing on a stock exchange and make an *initial public offering (IPO)*. This allows public companies to raise large amounts of capital to fund their activities. Public limited companies often have familiar names and a higher public profile than private companies. They can also pay high salaries to attract the best staff and negotiate favourable terms with lenders and suppliers because of their size and status. It is an offence for a private limited company to offer its shares to the public.

The main differences between a public company and a private company are:

- A public company must state in its memorandum of association that it is a public company.
- A public limited company's name must end with the words 'Public Limited Company' or the abbreviation 'PLC', whereas a private limited company's name must end with the word 'Limited' or the abbreviation 'Ltd'. Omitting the relevant ending or using an unauthorized abbreviation when filing the registration document will result in the document being rejected.

- A public limited company can advertise its shares for sale to the public and, if it has a listing on a stock exchange, its shares can be traded in the stock market. However, a private limited company's shares can only be offered for sale privately.

The shares of a UK public limited company are listed on the *London Stock Exchange (LSE)* and may also be listed on any of the international stock exchanges. Investors can buy and sell shares in person, through a broker, a bank, a share shop or on the Internet. When shares are issued, an advertisement is placed in the newspapers in the form of a prospectus and application coupon. Most investors take professional advice before buying shares, since all investments carry some risk as well as the possibility of financial rewards. Because limited companies are so important to the economy, information about them, particularly public companies, is readily available. This is because all companies must comply with the regulatory framework for financial reporting which requires them to publish an annual report and accounts. We discuss this in Chapter 4.

Activity

What do you think are the advantages of a private company over a public company?

One of the advantages you may have thought of is that the formalities for setting up a private limited company are somewhat easier than for a public company. In addition, private companies are not obliged to comply with stock exchange regulations and the majority of small private companies do not have to disclose as much financial information as public companies.

Figure 1.5 summarizes the different types of business entity we have described.

Figure 1.5 Types of business entity

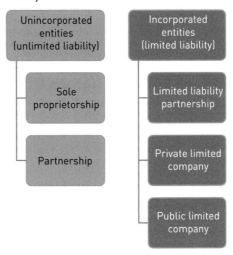

1.3   The accountancy profession

A professional accountant in the UK or the Republic of Ireland must pass a number of rigorous examinations set by one of the recognized accountancy bodies and pay an annual subscription to become a member of that body. The examinations cover a wide range of topics such as business and finance, financial and management accounting, financial reporting, auditing, taxation, law, business strategy and financial management. Once qualified, accountants can set up in practice on their own or with partners, or seek employment in an existing accountancy practice. Others may choose to work as accountants in industry and commerce, or in the public or voluntary sectors. Some accountants qualify with a view to working in the family business, and those with entrepreneurial ideas may choose to start a new enterprise.

1.3.1   Accountancy bodies in the UK and Ireland

Table 1.1 shows the worldwide membership (including students) of the six chartered accountancy bodies, plus one other body that offered a recognized audit qualification, at the start of 2016. Combined membership of these seven accountancy bodies continues to grow steadily with 497,674 members worldwide by 2015 (up 3.2% since 2011) and 342,000 members in the UK and Ireland (up 2.4% since 2011). ACCA, CIMA and CAI showed the strongest growth in worldwide membership since 2011, with compound annual growth rates of 3.6%, 3.2% and 3.6% respectively. However, worldwide membership of AIA and CIPFA declined during the same four-year period.

Table 1.1   Worldwide membership of UK and Irish accountancy bodies (as of end 2015)

Accountancy body	Number	%
Association of Chartered Certified Accountants (ACCA)	183,386	37
Institute of Chartered Accountants in England and Wales (ICAEW)	145,746	29
Chartered Institute of Management Accountants (CIMA)	102,942	21
Chartered Accountants Ireland (CAI)	24,496	5
Institute of Chartered Accountants in Scotland (ICAS)	20,709	4
Chartered Institute of Public Finance and Accountancy (CIPFA)	13,640	3
Association of International Accountants (AIA)	6,755	1
Total	497,674	100

Source: FRC, 2016, p. 11. © The Financial Reporting Council Limited (FRC). Adapted and reproduced with the kind permission of the Financial Reporting Council. All rights reserved.

ACCA is the largest chartered accountancy body in terms of total membership and has the highest proportion of female members (45%) and the highest proportion of female students (54%). ACCA also has the highest proportion of students based outside the UK and the Republic of Ireland (79%).

An accountant in a professional practice is likely to be a member of ACCA, ICAEW, ICAI or ICAS. Membership of CIMA would be most appropriate for a management accountant in industry. Membership of ACCA or CIPFA would be appropriate for a treasurer in a local authority, or an accountant in the National Health Service or other public sector organization with funding from national or local government. The American Institute of Certified Public Accountants (AICPA) and CIMA have formed a joint venture to establish the Chartered Global Management Accountant (CGMA) to promote the profession of management accounting. The CGMA designation can be held by Certified Public Accountants in the USA with qualifying management accounting experience or associate or fellow members of CIMA.

Large businesses are likely to have sufficient resources to employ a number of accounting and finance specialists, whereas medium-sized entities may employ one accountant who is responsible for all financial and management accounting functions, supported by other staff, such as a credit controller and bookkeeper. Small entities often find it more cost effective to employ an external accountant to provide most of their accounting needs.

1.3.2   Code of ethics for professional accountants

The preparation of statutory financial statements is the responsibility of the directors of the company, but it is likely that they will employ a qualified accountant to do it on their behalf. They may also appoint an independent professional accountant to audit the financial statements. The auditor examines the financial systems and records in order to give an opinion on whether the statutory financial statements give a true and fair view. We will examine this in more detail later on in this chapter. The point we want to make here is that because accountants are involved in the preparation and auditing of published financial information, they have a duty to serve the public interest. The work of professional accountants and auditors is guided by a code of ethics. *Ethics* refers to moral principles that underpin what is considered right and wrong in society, and how people should behave.

Activity

How ethical are you? Imagine you came out of a restaurant and found that the waiter had not charged you for your dessert. Would you go back and tell him?

You have to ask yourself whether you would be happy to tell everyone (not just your friends, but your family and your teachers or boss) and how you would defend your actions if you were challenged. An ethical person would go back and tell the waiter or the manager, so the correct answer is 'Yes'. The important thing to realize is that ethics are not always about what other people might do, but about honesty and personal integrity.

Key definition

Ethics are the moral principles that guide behaviour. They may form a code of conduct for a specific group.

The need for high values and consistent, ethical behaviour across the accountancy profession led to the development of an international code of ethics by the International Ethics Standards Board of Accountants (IESBA). The *Code of Ethics for Professional Accountants* (the IESBA Code) is published by the *International Federation of Accountants (IFAC)*, which is an association of professional bodies of accountants throughout the world. IFAC was founded in 1977 and now has 172 members and associates in 129 countries and jurisdictions, representing approximately 2.5 million accountants (including those in Table 1.1).

The IESBA Code requires a professional accountant to comply with five fundamental principles (IESBA, 2015, para 100.5):

(a) Integrity – to be straightforward and honest in all professional and business relationships.

(b) Objectivity – to not allow bias, conflict of interest or undue influence of others to override professional business judgments.

(c) Professional Competence and Due Care – to maintain professional knowledge and skill at the level required to ensure that a client or employer receives competent professional service based on current developments in practice, legislation and techniques and act diligently and in accordance with applicable technical and professional standards.

(d) Confidentiality – to respect the confidentiality of information acquired as a result of professional and business relationships, and, therefore, not disclose any such information to third parties without proper and specific authority, unless there is a legal or professional right or duty to disclose, nor use the information for the personal advantage of the professional accountant or third parties.

(e) Professional Behavior – to comply with relevant laws and regulations and to avoid any action that discredits the profession.

Source: This text is an extract from *Code of Ethics for Professional Accountants* of the International Ethics Standards Board for Accountants (IESBA), published by the International Federation of Accountants (IFAC) in May 2015, and is used with permission of IFAC.

Activity

What are the advantages and disadvantages of the IESBA Code of Ethics for Professional Accountants?

You may have thought of some of the following advantages:

- It provides explicit guidance to accountants and aids their understanding of the expectations placed upon them in terms of their ethical behaviour.
- It lets clients know what they can expect from their professional accountants.
- It provides a standard for disciplining professional accountants who adopt poor accounting practices.
- It enhances the reputation of professional accountants.
- It promotes a commitment to best practice within the profession.
- Abiding by a code may decrease the legal liability of professional accountants from inappropriate actions.
- It provides users of the accounts with a standard against which they can compare the ethical behaviour of their professional accountants and complain about poor accounting practice.

The disadvantages are:

- Without proper guidance and enforcement, different accountants may interpret the code differently.
- The code may raise public expectations to a level that some professional accountants may be unable to achieve.

A survey of mainly European professional accountants (EFAA, 2017) found that 64% had been put under pressure to act contrary to their professional ethics or to tax and/or accounting legislation. Most commonly the pressure was to:

- understate costs and expenses by postponing their recognition
- manipulate the value of inventory
- categorize personal expenses incurred by employees, directors or shareholders as company expenses
- overstate expenses by accounting for fictional expenses or accounting for expenses early.

The following activity allows you to apply the IESBA Code in a situation where fraudulent activity is suspected.

Activity

Steve Goodchild is an accountant at VAPE Ltd. He recently noticed a steep rise in the price of one of the materials used in the production process, and this coincided with a change of supplier. When he tried asking the purchasing manager, Jon Schneider, about it, he was more or less told to mind his own business. Jon concluded by saying, "I've known the managing director of this new supplier for years and, in any case, it's my job to decide which suppliers we use!" Around this time, Steve also noticed that Jon had started driving an expensive new car. He suspects that the two events are connected, which might indicate fraud. Should he (a) turn a blind eye, (b) challenge Jon further, or (c) discuss the matter with another senior manager?

The facts are that the cost of materials has risen as a result of changing the supplier and Jon is responsible for the decision. Steve has an ethical dilemma because he is concerned about Jon's dismissive response, weak justification for the change in supplier, and luxurious new car. He suspects fraud and wonders what the best action would be. To ensure that he behaves with integrity, objectivity and professional competence, he should take action (b) followed by (c) if necessary.

It may be necessary to take the matter to the highest level (the board of directors). If the matter cannot be resolved following this consultation, the accountant may wish to seek advice on the ethical issue, without breaching confidentiality, from the accountancy body of which he or she is a member. The reporting of this potentially fraudulent activity to the relevant authorities may breach the professional accountant's responsibility to respect confidentiality, so legal advice is essential to determine whether there is a requirement to report. If the ethical conflict remains unresolved after exhausting all these avenues, the accountant should refuse to remain associated with the matter creating the conflict and may consider it appropriate to resign from the employing organization.

1.4   Nature and purpose of accounting

We are now ready to examine the nature and purpose of accounting. In its broadest form, we might say that accounting is a service provided to those who need financial information. In everyday language, *accounting* for something means giving an explanation or reporting on something, and this lies at the heart of the subject. As explained by Nobes and Kellas (1990), historically, it was the duty of stewards to keep records and periodically give an account to the lord of the land. The term *audit* comes from the time when the account was given orally and the lord would listen to the account of how the steward had collected and used the lord's money. This accountability or stewardship role still applies, and the main *purpose* of accounting is still to communicate financial information to interested parties. 'Today, the owners of companies (the shareholders) expect to see an account from their stewards (the directors), which has already been audited by independent accountants (the auditors)' (Nobes and Kellas, 1990, p. 10).

The following definition describes accounting in a business context.

Key definition

Accounting is the process of identifying, classifying, measuring, recording and communicating the economic transactions of the entity.

The term *economic transactions* refers to the money-making activities of the business that are concerned with creating wealth for the owner(s). We will now examine each stage in the accounting process.

- *Identifying* economic transactions in most cases is fairly straightforward. Examples include selling goods and services to customers, paying employees, purchasing inventories (goods for resale) and buying equipment (for use in the business) from suppliers. It is also important to distinguish between the economic transactions of the business and the personal economic transactions of the owner(s) and manager(s).
- *Classifying* the economic transactions of the business requires grouping them into categories, such as purchases, sales revenue and salaries.
- *Measuring* economic transactions is done in monetary terms. This convention began when more people learned to read and write, and society moved from a bartering system in which goods and services were exchanged without using money. For example, a farmer might have exchanged 10 pigs for 1 dairy cow and recorded the sale in those very simple quantitative terms. Under a monetary system, the farmer might sell 10 pigs at £20 each, recorded as revenue of £200; 1 cow purchased at £200 would be recorded as purchases of £200. Not only is a monetary system convenient for suppliers and customers, but measuring transactions in monetary terms makes it easier to aggregate, summarize and compare financial transactions.
- *Recording* economic transactions is essential. Traditionally transactions were recorded in handwritten books of accounts known as ledgers, but today most businesses record transactions in a computerized accounting system. Small businesses may be able to use a relatively simple accounting system based on spreadsheets, but larger businesses with a wider range and volume of transactions will need to use sophisticated accounting software. We will look at this in more detail in Chapter 3.

- *Communicating* economic transactions is achieved by generating a variety of financial statements from the records in the accounting system. These are presented in a format that summarizes a particular financial aspect of the business. We will be looking at the layout and content of the main financial statements in Part II.

The next activity allows you to carry out the basic accounting procedures of identifying, measuring and recording the economic transactions involved in building some office shelves.

Activity

A business buys 5 litres of paint, 20 metres of timber and employs a carpenter for two days to build shelves in an office. Paint costs £4 per litre, timber costs £2.50 per metre and the carpenter charges £50 per day. What is the total cost of the shelves?

The cost can be calculated in a number of stages. You need to multiply the cost of paint per litre by the amount used. You also need to multiply the cost of timber per metre by the amount used. Finally, you need to calculate the cost of employing the carpenter by multiplying his daily rate by the number of days. The order in which you work out the figures does not matter, as long as you arrive at three figures which, when added together, make up the total cost of the job:

	£
Cost of paint (£4 × 5 litres)	20
Cost of timber (£2.50 × 20 metres)	50
Cost of labour (£50 × 2 days)	100
Total cost of the shelves	170

In more complex examples it is not so easy to identify and measure the economic events in monetary terms. We will be looking at some of these problems in subsequent chapters.

You have seen from the definition of accounting that it is a process that results in the communication of financial information. There are two main branches of accounting: financial accounting, which is concerned with providing financial information to external users (those not involved in managing the business), and management accounting, which is concerned with providing financial information to internal users.

1.5   Overview of financial accounting

As you can see from the following definition, the *purpose* of *financial accounting* is to provide financial information to meet the needs of external users.

> **Key definition**
>
> Financial accounting is the branch of accounting concerned with classifying, measuring and recording the economic transactions of an entity in accordance with established principles, legal requirements and accounting standards. It is primarily concerned with communicating a true and fair view of the financial performance and financial position of an entity to external parties at the end of the accounting period.

The term *true and fair view* implies that the financial statements produced at the end of an accounting period (usually one year) are a faithful representation of the entity's economic activities. The financial statements of limited liability entities are drawn up within a regulatory framework and are prepared using a number of accounting principles which have been established as general principles. We examine these topics in Part II. Generally, an entity's financial statements are considered to give a true and fair view if they comply with the regulatory framework and accounting principles. However, in a few cases, the preparers may have to ignore specific rules to ensure that the financial statements give a true and fair view and do not mislead the users.

1.5.1 Importance of financial reporting to external parties

The *annual report and accounts* is a comprehensive source of financial information on a limited liability entity and includes narrative reports as well as the annual financial statements. The publication of general purpose financial information by limited liability entities to external parties is known as *financial reporting*. According to the *Conceptual Framework for Financial Reporting* (IASB, 2015), the objective of financial reporting is to provide information that is useful to users.

> **Key definition**
>
> Financial reporting refers to the statutory disclosure of general purpose financial information by limited liability entities via the annual report and accounts.
>
> Source: IASB (2015). Reproduced with permission from the IFRS Foundation.

The following activity will help you understand the importance of financial information to external parties in the context of a small business.

Activity

For some years Sally Lunn has owned and managed a small coffee shop which is a limited company. List the various external parties who might find financial information about the business useful and how they would use it.

You may have started by thinking about the bank that provides Sally's business banking needs. These are likely to include a current account with overdraft facilities, debit and credit cards and even a small loan or a mortgage on the business premises. The bank and other lenders are likely to be interested in detailed financial information about Sally's business in order to assess and monitor their lending risk. In addition, you may have thought of suppliers and trade creditors who supply goods or services to the business who will want to assess their credit risk. Of course, the tax authorities will need financial information about the business in order to assess how much tax needs to be paid and Companies House will be interested in whether the annual report and accounts has been filed on time (there is a penalty for late filing).

You may also have thought of competitors as being interested parties, but they would have to rely on the information filed at Companies House which is available on the website for a small fee. If Sally's business had been set up as a sole proprietorship, competitors would find it difficult to obtain any financial information about the business, since only limited liability entities have a statutory obligation to publish annual financial statements. The primary users of financial information published by limited liability entities are:

- existing and potential investors
- lenders and other creditors.

We will look at the information needs of these users in Part II.

1.5.2   Role of the financial accountant

Financial accounting can be divided into a number of specific activities, such as the following:

- *Bookkeeping* focuses on the recording of business transactions. Some small businesses keep a simple cash-based system, but the majority of businesses record transactions using an accounting system known as *double-entry bookkeeping*, which provides an arithmetical check on the accuracy of the records. Most small businesses use spreadsheets or standard accounting software, while large businesses are more likely to need tailor-made accountancy software.
- *Accounts preparation* involves the compilation of *general purpose financial statements* by limited liability entities that must be registered at Companies House and sent to members. Special purpose financial statements are required for the tax authorities. Detailed sets of special purpose financial statements may also be prepared for lenders, suppliers and customers.
- *Auditing* involves a thorough examination of the entity's financial systems and records, tangible assets, management and employees, suppliers, customers and other business contacts. Auditors conduct compliance tests to assess the effectiveness of the systems of financial control and substantive tests to assess the completeness, ownership, existence, valuation and disclosure of the information in the accounting records and financial statements.

In addition to providing accounting and auditing services, firms of accountants may offer general advice on running the business. They may also provide specialist advice on taxation, raising finance, insolvency, investment, pension planning, treasury management, IT and human resource management.

Activity

A financial accountant can give advice on the following matters (*tick the appropriate box*):

		True	False
(a)	How to arrange financial affairs so that the least amount of tax is incurred	❏	❏
(b)	The best way to borrow money for a specific project	❏	❏
(c)	The likely profit to be made on a music festival	❏	❏
(d)	Carrying out financial transactions in foreign currencies	❏	❏
(e)	Deciding on the best way to provide for a pension	❏	❏
(f)	Calculating the amount to be paid to the tax authorities	❏	❏
(g)	Trading in stocks and shares	❏	❏

You may have been puzzled by some of these statements, but you would be right if you said that they are all the concern of the financial accountant. However, as in other professions, there are specialists who may concentrate on specific areas within financial accounting.

1.6   Overview of management accounting

The *purpose* of *management accounting* is to provide managers with financial and other quantitative information to help them carry out their responsibilities, which focus on planning, controlling and decision making. Unlike financial accounting, management accounting focuses on meeting the needs of internal users and is not governed by the regulatory framework. In management accounting the emphasis is on providing information that will help the business achieve its financial objectives.

Key definition

Management accounting is the branch of accounting concerned with collecting and analyzing financial and other quantitative information. It is primarily concerned with communicating information to management to help effective performance measurement, planning, controlling and decision making.

Performance measurement involves developing financial and non-financial indicators of progress towards the organization's goals and regularly reviewing progress. Non-financial measures might include delivery time, customer retention and staff turnover. *Planning* includes developing budgets for future activities and operations and *controlling* involves using techniques for highlighting variances once the actual figures are known and ensuring that costs fall within acceptable levels and revenue targets are achieved. Costing techniques provide information that will help management set the selling prices of products and services.

Activity

Imagine you are a manager and decide whether you would require the following information for planning, controlling or decision making:

(a) The amount claimed for taxi fares by staff last month
(b) The prices charged by a new supplier for services or materials
(c) The cost of running the office photocopier
(d) The cost of employing subcontracted staff, compared with your own employees
(e) The cost of making a component, compared with buying it from a supplier

Items (d) and (e) should be easy to define because in both circumstances you are choosing between alternatives and therefore you are making decisions. With items (a) and (c) you are mainly concerned with controlling costs, although you might want the information to make plans for future expenditure. Item (b) could be concerned with planning future costs or you may be about to decide whether to change to another supplier. This decision may have arisen because you are trying to control costs. Although the boundaries between planning, controlling and decision making are blurred, financial and statistical information has a very important role to play and it is the management accountant who provides this information.

Management accounting offers a number of general advantages, such as helping the business to become more profitable.

Activity

What other advantages do you consider management accounting information offers to managers? Draw up a list of the ways in which management accounting information can be used by managers under the headings of planning, controlling and decision making.

Your list may include some of the following advantages:

Planning

- the selling price of products or services
- the number of employees and what they should be paid
- the quantity of each product or service that must be sold to achieve the desired level of profit.

Controlling

- unnecessary expense and waste
- the amount of investment in machinery or equipment
- the cost of running different departments.

Decision making

- whether to make or buy a particular component
- whether it is worth investing in new technology
- which products or services to offer if there is a shortage of materials or skilled labour.

1.6.1 Importance of financial information to internal parties

To understand how financial information can be useful to internal parties, we need to identify the uses to which it can be put. One way of doing this is to define the responsibilities involved in a particular job or activity.

Activity

Here is a list of the responsibilities of Sally Lunn, who is the owner-manager of a small coffee shop:

- ordering and controlling inventories of food and drink to sell in the shop
- supervising two full-time and two part-time staff
- ensuring the security of premises
- keeping cash records and daily banking
- general display and maintenance of the shop
- serving customers
- dealing with customers' complaints.

Think of your current job or one you have had in the past and jot down a list of your responsibilities. If you have not had any work experience, think about any voluntary job you may have done, such as helping in a charity or organizing a student event.

No matter what work you are describing, it is likely that your responsibilities can be classified under one of the following major activities:

- *Planning* – Without plans and policies a business has no sense of direction or purpose. Financial information allows plans and policies to be formulated and helps people in the organization understand the targets and standards it intends to achieve. For example, a manager needs to know what profit it is hoped the business will make; on a personal level you need information in order to plan holidays, whether you need to take a weekend job, etc.
- *Controlling* – A large number of responsibilities at work are concerned with ensuring that the organization makes progress towards its objectives. For control to be effectively maintained, financial information is required on such matters as the cost of products and processes, monitoring labour efficiency and identifying the sources and purpose of all expenditure. Similarly, for social activities, such as organizing a student ball, information is needed to ensure that a loss is not made.
- *Decision making* – In establishing plans, it is necessary to decide which of the various courses of action should be taken. We need to know the financial implications of our actions in order to select the most appropriate plan. In business, a manager may need to make a decision between using machinery and labour on an activity; on a personal level we may need to make a decision between buying a car and using public transport.

Activity

Consider any financial information you currently receive and classify it according to whether it helps you in controlling, planning or decision making. The information can be financial information you receive at work or at home, such as your bank statement, household bills, etc. You may find that some types of information help with more than one activity.

Once you have completed your list, compare it with the one you drew up for the previous activity. The information should match. For example, if you decided that most of your responsibilities are concerned with controlling, then most of the information you receive will be ticked under that heading in your list. On the other hand, you may have identified financial information that you need but do not currently receive, or financial information you receive but cannot use because you do not understand it. In subsequent chapters we will look at different types of financial information and identifying those that are most relevant to your responsibilities.

1.6.2 Role of the management accountant

A management accountant is concerned with identifying why the information is required so that the most appropriate technique can be used to supply information to managers. Managers need this information to enable them to plan the progress of the business, control the activities and understand the financial implications of any decisions they may take.

Management accounting can be divided into the following main activities:

- *Cost accounting* focuses on techniques for recording costs that help managers ascertain the cost of cost units (such as products and services) and cost centres (such as departments for which costs are collected). This allows management to make important decisions, such as setting selling prices, production/sales targets, and deciding which products or services are the most profitable to produce/sell. Another important aspect of cost accounting is establishing budgets and standard costs, and comparing them with the actual costs incurred. Large organizations may employ a cost accountant; smaller businesses may use the services of an external accountant. Cost accounting provides the cost and expenditure figures that are needed by the financial accountant when the business prepares its annual financial statements.
- *Managerial accounting* focuses on the processing and reporting components of management accounting. Although most small businesses are owner-managed, the large majority use monthly or quarterly management accounts and budgets in addition to cash flow information and bank statements to help them manage the business (Collis and Jarvis, 2002).

To illustrate the difference between financial accounting and management accounting we will return to the example of the office shelves we used earlier in the chapter.

- A financial accountant would be interested in the total cost of £170 so that it can be recorded as the economic transaction.
- A management accountant would be more concerned with informing managers how much the individual elements cost, such as the paint, the timber and the labour. A management accountant would also want to calculate how much the shelves actually cost and compare it with the budgeted figure that represented the estimated cost.

Activity

Classify the following accounting activities (*tick the appropriate box*):

	Financial accounting	Management accounting
(a) Auditing the accounting systems and records of a business	❑	❑
(b) Managing the tax affairs of a business	❑	❑
(c) Analyzing the financial implications of management decisions	❑	❑
(d) Preparing financial statements at the end of the financial year	❑	❑
(e) Ensuring compliance with legal and other regulations	❑	❑
(f) Providing financial information for managers	❑	❑
(g) Keeping the accounting records of the business	❑	❑

By now you are probably more confident about deciding which activities involve financial accounting and which can be classified as management accounting. With the exception of (c) and (f), all the above activities are concerned with financial accounting.

Although accounting can be divided into financial and management accounting, you should not be misled into thinking that there is no relationship between these two activities, since they both draw on the same data sources. However, there are some important differences, which relate to the level of detail and timing of the information produced.

Financial accounting operates on the basis of an annual reporting cycle and, as you will see in Part II, the preparation of the financial statements of limited liability entities is highly regulated to ensure that external users receive high quality, reliable information. However, the annual report and accounts are not published until some months after the end of the financial year. By contrast, management accounting is not regulated at all, which means the information can be provided to internal users in the form they want it and as often as they want it. In both large and small businesses, detailed management accounting information for each activity in each part of the business is produced on a weekly, monthly or quarterly basis. If the periodic management accounts for the different parts of a business were aggregated, the totals would be very similar to the figures in the financial accounts, but there would be some differences. For example, the financial accounts would contain information on finance costs (e.g. interest on loans) and taxation, whereas the management accounts are likely to contain more estimated figures.

1.7   Conclusions

In this first chapter we have drawn attention to the economic importance of small and medium-sized entities, and we have examined the main characteristics of two types of unincorporated business (sole proprietorships and ordinary partnerships) and two types of incorporated business (limited liability partnerships and limited liability companies). We have also compared and contrasted some of the key features of private limited companies with those of public limited companies. This has allowed us to highlight the financial implications resulting from the choice of business form, with a particular focus on raising capital and disclosure of financial information.

You have now been introduced to the role of the accountant in business and in practice, and the reasons why there is a code of ethics for professional accountants. Our discussion of the nature and purpose of accounting distinguished between the two main branches of accounting. Our discussion of the importance of management accounting in providing financial information to internal users led to the general conclusion that it aids managers in their responsibilities for planning, controlling and decision making. Our discussion of the importance of financial accounting in providing financial information to external users led to the general conclusion that financial reporting needs to be regulated to ensure that the financial statements provide a true and fair view to those not involved in managing the business.

References

BBB (2016) *Small Business Finance Markets Report 2015-16*, British Business Bank. Available at: http://british-business-bank.co.uk/research/small-business-finance-markets-report-201516/ (Accessed 8 February 2016).

BEIS (2016) *Statistical Release*, BEIS/16/34, 13 October. Available at: www.gov.uk/government/collections/business-population-estimates (Accessed 27 November 2016).

Collis, J. (2008) *Directors' Views on Accounting and Auditing Requirements for SMEs*, London: BERR. Available at: http://webarchive.nationalarchives.gov.uk/20090609003228/http:/www.berr.gov.uk/files/file50491.pdf (Accessed 27 November 2016).

Collis, J. (2012) 'Determinants of voluntary audit and voluntary full accounts in micro- and non-micro small companies in the UK', *Accounting and Business Research*, 42(4), pp. 1–28.

Collis, J. and Jarvis, R. (2002) 'Financial information and the management of small private companies', *Journal of Small Business and Enterprise Development*, 9(2), pp. 100–110.

Companies House (2016) *Companies Register Activities 2015–2016*. Available at: www.gov.uk/government/statistics/companies-register-activities-201516 (Accessed 27 November 2016).

EFAA (2017) *Accounting and Ethics: Pressure Experienced by the Professional Accountant*, European Federation of Accountants and Auditors for SMEs.

European Commission (2016) *Annual Report on European SMEs 2015/2016*. Available from: https://ec.europa.eu/growth/smes/business-friendly-environment/performance-review-2016_en#annual-report (Accessed 27 November 2016).

Fraser, S., Bhaumik, S.K. and Wright, M. (2015) 'What do we know about entrepreneurial finance and its relationship with growth?' *International Small Business Journal*, 33(1), pp. 70–88.

FRC (2016) *Key Facts and Trends in the Accountancy Profession*, June. Available at: www.frc.org.uk/Our-Work/Publications/Professional-Oversight/Key-Facts-and-Trends-2016.pdf (Accessed 23 September 2016).

IASB (2015) *Exposure Draft Conceptual Framework for Financial Reporting*, ED/2015/3, London: IFRS Foundation.

ICAEW (2015) *SME Accounting Requirements: Basing Policy on Evidence*, Public policy paper.

IESBA (2015) *Code of Ethics for Professional Accountants*, New York: International Ethics Standards Board for Accountants. Available at: www.ethicsboard.org/system/files/publications/files/2015-iesba-handbook.pdf (Accessed: 8 February 2016).

Mallet, N. and Brumwell, J. (1994) 'The concept of limited liability', *Credit Control*, 15(10), pp. 6–9.

Nobes, C. and Kellas, J. (1990) *Accountancy Explained*, London: Penguin Books.

Discussion questions

1 Discuss the reasons why students studying business and management should learn about accounting.

2 Discuss the concept of limited liability and the advantages of a company over an unincorporated business.

3 Discuss the reasons why the accountancy bodies issue codes of ethics for their members.

4 Debate the advantages and disadvantages of the IESBA Code of Ethics for Professional Accountants.

 ## Practice questions

5 Define the term *accounting* and explain the difference between the two main branches.

6 Compare and contrast the advantages and disadvantages of public and private companies.

7 Describe the fundamental principles in the IESBA Code of Ethics for Professional Accountants.

8 You are a qualified accountant and a member of one of the UK accountancy bodies. You are employed by a firm of accountants in the town where you live and expect to be a partner in this accountancy practice soon. Five years ago you introduced an important client to your firm, someone with whom you regularly play golf. After your most recent game, the client asks if you will 'modify' the revenue estimate in the financial statement recently prepared by your firm as part of a forthcoming initial public offering (IPO) when shares of your client's company will be offered for sale for the first time on the stock exchange. Your client makes it clear that he believes that the revenue estimate is too low.

Required

Discuss the following questions:

a) Is there is an ethical issue for you in this scenario?

b) The IESBA Code of Ethics states that 'a professional accountant shall not knowingly be associated with reports, returns, communications or other information where the professional accountant believes that the information … contains a materially false or misleading statement' (IESBA, 2015, para 110.2). If you agree to increase the revenue estimate, would the financial statement contain a materially false or misleading figure?

c) How likely is it that you will associate yourself with this client's income statement if he insists on increasing the revenue? (Circle the number closest to your view.)

	Likely				Unlikely
I would associate myself with the financial statement	5	4	3	2	1

 Suggested research questions for dissertation students

Students interested in ethics may wish to investigate one or more of the following research questions:

- Why do professional accountants need a code of ethics?

- What are the most common ethical dilemmas faced by accountants?

- Do the ethical dilemmas faced by accountants working for small or medium-sized businesses (or with SME clients) differ from those faced by accountants working for large businesses (or with large business clients)?

- What are the advantages and disadvantages of the IESBA Code of Ethics for accountants, their employers or clients, and the users of accounting information?

- How effective is the ethical code for professional accountants in [country]?

Preliminary reading

IFAC (2006) *Code of Ethics for Professional Accountants*. Available at: http://web.ifac.org/publications/international-ethics-standards-board-for-accountants/code-of-ethics (Accessed 8 February 2016).

Jackling, B., Cooper, B.J., Leung, P. and Dellaportas, S. (2007) 'Professional accounting bodies' perceptions of ethical issues, causes of ethical failure and ethics education', *Managerial Auditing Journal*, 22(9), pp. 928–944.

Pflugrath, G., Martinov-Bennie, N. and Chen, L. (2007) 'The impact of codes of ethics and experience on auditor judgments', *Managerial Auditing Journal*, 22(6), pp. 566–589.

Velayutham, S. (2003) 'The accounting profession's code of ethics: Is it a code of ethics or a code of quality assurance?' *Critical Perspectives on Accounting*, 14(3), pp. 403–503.

2 The importance of cash

Learning objectives

When you have studied this chapter, you should be able to:

- Explain the theory of a finance gap for small and medium-sized enterprises
- Describe and classify potential sources of business finance
- Explain the need for cash flow information
- Prepare and interpret a cash flow forecast and a cash flow statement
- Describe the principles for monitoring and controlling cash

2.1 Introduction

In Chapter 1 we explained that the objective of some business owners is to maximize their wealth, whereas others simply want to make enough money to maintain a certain lifestyle. Before an owner can start making money, he or she needs to have enough capital to set up or acquire a business, and enough cash to run the business. Irrespective of whether it has been set up as a sole proprietorship, partnership or company, once the business has started, the cash position must be monitored closely. There are many reasons why businesses close and they are not all associated with failure. For example, the owner may have simply decided to sell the business or retire. The main reason for failure is that the business does not have sufficient cash or credit to continue as a going concern. Typically, the business will have fallen behind with payments for goods or services received, leading to supplies being cut off. In addition, it may not be able to pay interest on any bank overdraft or loan, leading to demand for immediate repayment. Insufficient cash also means that employees cannot be paid and must be laid off. Thus, cash is crucial to the survival of the business.

Because of the importance of cash, would-be entrepreneurs and the owners and managers of existing businesses need information about the current and future cash position. This allows them to check that there will be sufficient finance in terms of cash or credit facilities to meet the needs of the business and also allows them to plan the investment of any surplus cash. In this chapter we describe the main sources of finance in the UK for small and medium-sized enterprises (SMEs) and discuss the difficulties entrepreneurs may face in seeking finance to start and develop a business. We also introduce you to a simple financial statement known as a cash flow forecast and how it can be used.

2.2   The finance gap

In general, the term *finance* refers to the management of money and this is a subject that may form part of your future studies. There are two further ways in which the term can be used, which we will examine next.

Key definition

Finance is:

1   The money involved in a project, especially the capital needed to start a business.
2   A loan of money for a particular purpose, especially a loan provided by a bank or other financial institution.

You can see from the above definitions that finance is not used to refer to small amounts of money, such as the cost of £170 for the materials and labour used to make a set of office shelves (the example we looked at in Chapter 1). Instead, it refers to large sums of money, such as the amount invested in the business by the owner(s) or borrowed from a financial institution such as a bank, or from some other provider of finance for the purpose of buying land, premises, vehicles, equipment, etc. From this we can deduce that one of the key considerations when planning a business is to ensure that the owner has sufficient finance in place to launch the enterprise and allow it to grow to the desired size.

Unfortunately, some entrepreneurs who have an idea for a new business or want to expand an existing business cannot raise sufficient finance. The situation where a business has profitable opportunities, but is unable to raise the funds to exploit them can be described as a *finance gap* (Jarvis and Schizas, 2012). Figure 2.1 gives further details.

The main argument supporting the notion of a finance gap is that because the majority of SMEs are sole proprietorships, partnerships and private companies, they cannot raise equity finance by selling shares to the public. In other words, there is no capital market for privately held businesses, as only public listed companies can raise capital on a stock exchange. This aspect of the finance gap is sometimes referred to as the *equity gap*.

Figure 2.1 The finance gap

'Historically, the existence of a "finance gap" was formally recognised 80 years ago. In 1931 the government-sponsored Macmillan Committee reported that the financing needs of small business were not well served by the then existing financial services institutions. The committee consisting of such eminent academics as John Maynard Keynes and politicians such as Ernest Bevin illustrates the importance given to the subject of financing small firms by government in the 1930s. Since then this criticism of financial institutions has been echoed by other important inquiries (e.g. Bolton, 1971; Wilson, 1979). In response to this criticism successive governments have introduced a number of initiatives with varying success. For example, the Enterprise Finance Guarantee (formerly Small Firms Loan Guarantee) is a guarantee scheme for firms which can only offer limited security as collateral for bank loans... In recent years financial services institutions have broadened their scope and for commercial reasons have introduced new products that have made access to funds easier for smaller firms. It has been argued that if a finance gap still exists, it has been substantially narrowed because of these initiatives and subsequent responses by the market since the 1930s (Deakins, 1996). However, others dispute this claim on both empirical and theoretical grounds (for example, Harrison and Mason, 1995)... A particular problem for policymakers wishing to support growth firms is the low levels of supply and take-up of equity capital (HM Treasury and Department for Business, Innovation and Skills, 2010). The problem is that businesses can only increase loan capital in proportion to assets held and the equity interest prevailing. Therefore, these firms are effectively constrained in accessing debt finance and the only way the firm can increase capital is through injections of equity.'

Source: Jarvis and Schizas, 2012, pp. 364–365, 367. Reproduced with permission from Pearson Education Limited.

Activity

In addition to the equity gap, there are a number of other reasons why smaller entities may have difficulty in accessing finance when they need it. Draw up a list of other possible explanations.

Some of the explanations you may have thought of relate to the start-up stage when there is no evidence of:

- the quality of the business idea
- the entrepreneur's management skills
- a financial track record that demonstrates ability to service a loan (pay the interest and repay the amount borrowed) or pay suppliers for goods and services provided on credit.

At any stage there may be obstacles such as:

- the cost of borrowing when interest rates are high
- an information gap due to insufficient knowledge of potential sources of finance
- lack of skills to present a convincing proposal to investors or lenders
- lack of collateral to offset risk, which may be particularly relevant in the service sector.

During times of recession, access to appropriate finance is the key to ensuring that small and growing businesses are able to survive and expand, and in 2011 access to finance was considered as one of the most important problems for SMEs in Europe (UEAPME, 2011). In view of their importance to the economy, governments have conducted consultations and commissioned studies to suggest remedies. In the UK, one such remedy was to set up the *Business Growth Fund* in 2011. This £2.5 billion fund helps companies struggling to find long-term growth finance in amounts ranging from £2 million to £10 million. The fund seeks sound investments where it can make minority investments and build long-term positive relationships with the companies it helps. A second remedy was to establish a mentoring programme to provide SMEs with free access to bankers and others in their locality with the skills and experience to help them grow. The mentor can help the business make the most of the relationship with the bank and give advice on where to find further financial and business support. These funding, mentoring and information schemes for SMEs are supported by the British Bankers' Association and a dedicated website (www.betterbusiness finance.co.uk) provides a 'one-stop shop' to address the information gap.

To put the finance gap into perspective, it is useful to look at the other problems faced by SMEs. A survey on access to finance by the European Central Bank (ECB, 2015) examined the needs of SMEs in the euro area in 2015 and found that the most important concern was finding customers (25%), followed by lack of availability of skilled labour, increases in the costs of production and labour, competitive pressures and the regulation. Access to finance (11%) was the least important problem.

When interpreting the results of surveys examining the problem of access to finance, you need to remember that the respondents are likely to be owners or managers of existing businesses and may not include entrepreneurs who could be having difficulty in obtaining start-up finance. In addition, businesses require finance for particular purposes and therefore owners and managers seek finance on a contingency basis. Consequently, unremitting or regular problems, such as poor sales, may be considered to be a more important problem during times of economic recession.

2.3   Main sources of finance

The cash invested by the owner to start a business is known as *capital*. Sources include money from savings, redundancy, inheritance, investments, winnings, etc. Once the business is established, the capital can be increased by retaining some of the profit (earnings) in the business. You will also see capital referred to as owners' equity.

Key definition

Capital is the money contributed by the owner(s) of the business to enable it to function.

If these internal sources are not sufficient, the owner or manager may need to consider external sources of finance. These sources can be classified according to the length of time the finance is required, which relates to the purpose for which it is required. Figure 2.2 shows this classification.

Figure 2.2 Main sources of finance by term and purpose

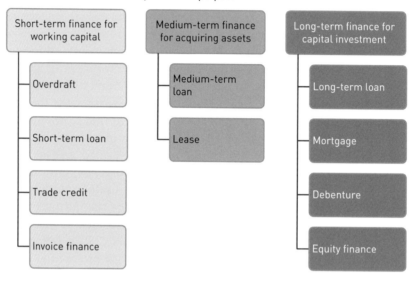

The survey of SMEs in the euro area we mentioned earlier (ECB, 2015) shows that the main types of finance used by small and micro-entities are bank overdrafts, short-term loans and credit cards, followed by long-term bank loans, trade credit and leasing. Debentures and other debt instruments are mainly used by large companies, and we discuss this type of finance later in the chapter. The two most important purposes for which SMEs require finance are to acquire assets (such as property, plant and equipment) and to provide working capital (including inventory). Loans from family, friends or related companies were important sources of financing for 21% of SMEs.

Little is known about the support provided by *family and friends*, but a survey of unincorporated small and micro-businesses in the UK (Lloyds Bank, 2015) found that 64% of micro-entities rely on support from family and friends, who put in an average of 6 hours a week helping the business to stay afloat. To give you an idea of the importance of this help, 10% of the 502 business owners taking part in the study said that the business would not survive without the support of family and friends. The support they give includes helping to make business decisions (40%), completing practical tasks (34%), running errands (29%), managing social media (10%) and helping with childcare (8%). Although 41% of respondents pay their family and friends an average of £14 per hour, 51% said this help is unpaid. Most of the support is provided by the owner's spouse/partner (43%) and children (19%), with 29% receiving support from friends (Lloyds Bank, 2015, p. 3).

2.3.1 Short-term finance

Short-term finance is used to provide the *working capital* needed to fund the day-to-day activities of the business. For example, cash is needed to purchase inventory that is sold and turned back into cash, and used to buy more inventory. Thus, short-term finance is required for periods of less than a year. We will now discuss the traditional sources of this type of finance.

An *overdraft* is a form of bank loan that is set up for a short period (usually one year and renegotiated annually) to cover the possibility of a cash deficit up to an agreed amount. This situation would arise if there was insufficient cash in the bank account to cover the cash going out. An authorized overdraft is arranged with the bank in advance with an agreed borrowing limit, whereas an unauthorized overdraft is when the customer goes over the limit or spends more than there is in the bank account without agreeing it in advance. The cost of an overdraft can be very high and usually comprises interest plus a daily, weekly or monthly fee. An overdraft facility is an 'on demand' form of borrowing. This means the bank can withdraw the facility or demand immediate repayment of the overdrawn amount together with any interest fees and charges due.

If the business needs money for a fixed period of time (of less than a year), a *short-term loan* from a bank, family or friends may be more appropriate. Banks may charge a setting-up fee. Interest is charged at a rate that varies according to the risk, which is often measured by a credit rating score. Loans are repaid in instalments or at the end of the term according to the loan agreement. Banks normally require some form of collateral or personal guarantee from the owner(s) to provide security for a loan, so that the bank can recover any amounts outstanding should the business default on the loan agreement. Lack of collateral is often a problem for SMEs, particularly for firms in the service sector that have few assets that can be used as security. From the lender's perspective, small firms represent high risk, as many start-ups do not survive the first five years.

Trade credit is finance provided by a *trade creditor*. Amounts owed by trade creditors are known as *trade payables*. A trade creditor is a supplier from whom the business has purchased goods or services on credit. This means that the business does not need to pay for the goods or services until the end of the *credit period*. This is a specified length of time after they have been received (typically between 30 and 90 days) and is dependent on the purchaser's credit rating. Discounts may be offered for prompt payment on the due date. Trade credit does not provide additional cash, but allows money already in the business to be used for other purposes until it is needed to pay the trade creditors.

Invoice finance can be divided into two main types. *Factoring* is finance provided by a factor (usually a bank or other financial institution) which buys the trade debts of the business. Trade debts are known as *trade receivables*. They are the amounts owed by customers to whom the business has sold goods or services on credit but who have not yet paid. The factoring firm assesses the creditworthiness of the debtors and collects the debts in return for a fee that represents the risk. The advantage to the business is that it can receive a large proportion of the value of the invoices imme-diately (depending on the terms agreed) and a further sum after the debt has been collected. Factoring is useful for a business that does not have collateral to support a bank loan because the factor is primarily interested in the creditworthiness of the firm's customers and the validity of the invoices, rather than the firm's credit history or assets. *Invoice discounting* is where the business sells its invoices at a discount to a factoring company for immediate cash.

2.3.2   Medium-term finance

Medium-term finance is used to provide assets that are expected to generate cash for the business in the medium term, such as fixtures and fittings, equipment and vehi-cles. Since the finance is secured on an asset, this type of finance can be referred to as *asset-based finance*. We will now discuss the traditional sources of this type of finance.

A *medium-term loan* from a bank, government scheme, friends or family is used to fund the purchase of an asset over a fixed period of time that is linked to the economic life of the asset. The conditions of the loan are similar to those described for short-term loans.

A *lease* is a contract that conveys the right to use an asset for a period of time in exchange for a consideration (lease payments). The lessee has control of the asset, but ownership of that asset remains with the leasing company (the lessor). The main advantage is that it allows the asset to be used immediately with minimum initial out-lay. There are two main types of lease. Some leases are essentially rental agreements for the temporary use of an asset (usually referred to as *operating leases*). In this case, the lessee hires the asset from the lessor for a period of time that is normally substan-tially shorter than the life of the asset, but ownership of the asset remains with the lessor. This type of lease is commonly used for assets where technological advances are rapid (such as office equipment), where there is extensive wear and tear on the asset (such as fleet vehicles) or the asset is required for a particular job (such as plant and machinery for a specific construction project). Other types of lease are essentially finance agreements (sometimes referred to as *finance leases*) and ownership of the asset passes to the lessee once the final lease payment has been paid. *Hire purchase (HP)* is an example of a hybrid of these two types of lease. IFRS 16, *Leases* (IASB, 2016), which applies from 2019, removes the distinction between operating and finance leases in terms of the accounting treatment. The default position will be that all leases will give rise to an asset, and the depreciation of the asset and the finance cost will be associated with the corresponding liability.

2.3.3   Long-term finance

Long-term finance is used to provide assets that are expected to provide economic benefits to the business in the long term. Long-term finance can be divided into *debt finance* and *equity finance*. We will start by looking at the main sources of debt finance.

A *long-term loan* is a suitable form of finance for capital investment in assets that are not acquired for trading purposes but intended to be kept in the business in the long term, such as investment in plant and machinery. A *mortgage* is a long-term loan for purchasing land or premises. Mortgages are usually supplied by financial institutions, such as banks and building societies, for a specified number of years (e.g. 25 years) at a fixed or variable rate of interest. Repayment may be by instalments or at the end of the term.

A *debenture* is a type of debt instrument that can only be issued by a company. It is not secured by physical assets or collateral and is backed only by the general creditworthiness and reputation of the issuing company. Debentures are typically issued to raise capital for expansion and are usually repayable at a fixed date. They are sometimes referred to as revenue bonds because it is expected that they will be paid from the proceeds of a new business project. The debenture holder (the investor) normally receives a fixed rate of interest. Debentures involve less risk to the investor than equities and can be sold on a stock exchange.

Equity finance refers to finance raised from the sale of ordinary shares as opposed to preference shares.[1] This type of finance is only available to companies and LLPs. Public listed companies (PLCs) can raise capital by offering their shares for sale on the main market of the *London Stock Exchange (LSE)*. Small, fast-growing PLCs can obtain access to the market at an earlier stage in their development through a listing on the *Alternative Investment Market (AIM)*, which was set up as a subsidiary market in 1995. The listing rules for the AIM are less onerous and, therefore, less expensive. Both markets are open to UK and international companies. To give you some idea of size, at the end of 2015 there were 919 companies listed on the LSE with a market value of £2,183,680.9m and 1,004 companies on the AIM with a market value of £73,076.6m (LSE, 2015).

Private equity and *venture capital* are types of finance where the private equity company or the venture capital company (the investor) provides equity finance for around 3–8 years in return for shares. Private equity companies focus on investing in under-performing private companies with potential for high growth. The investor works closely with management to improve performance and develop strategy. If successful, the investor receives a return when the company is sold (usually via an initial public offering (IPO) on the stock exchange or to a strategic buyer). Venture capital companies focus on investing in companies at the concept stage, where they provide seed finance for research and development before the company is set up, start-up finance (within three years of the company starting) and early stage finance for development. They typically provide expertise in the development of new products and technologies, such as clean technology, digital media, life sciences and the Internet. Private equity and venture capital companies have financed well-known businesses in the UK, such as Alliance Boots, Centre Parcs, Odeon & UCI Cinemas and Spotify (BVCA, 2016).

---

1. Holders of preference shares are entitled to a fixed percentage dividend rather than a variable dividend and receive preference over ordinary shareholders if the company goes into liquidation.

Informal venture capital from *business angels* is also a valuable source of equity finance. Business angels are wealthy individuals or syndicates of angel investors who wish to provide equity finance over a period of 3–8 years in return for shares. Angel investors focus on start-up and early stage companies and often join the board of directors or take another role where they use their knowledge and experience to help the company grow. If a syndicate of angels has provided the finance, a leading angel will take this role. Businesses seeking angel investors often rely on accountants and other professional advisers to introduce them to investors. The UK Business Angels Association connects all those involved in the angel investment market. Members include angel networks, syndicates, individual investors, early stage venture capital firms, equity crowdfunding platforms, professional advisers and intermediaries (UKBAA, 2016).

2.3.4   Alternative finance

Alternative finance is a general term that refers to a number of innovative financing models that supply finance via online platforms or websites and connect those seeking finance directly with those willing to supply finance. Alternative finance provides new opportunities for entrepreneurs, SMEs and not-for-profit entities to raise debt or equity finance from a collection of lenders or investors which, in many cases, they would not otherwise be able to obtain. Table 2.1 gives details of main financing models in the alternative finance market in 2014.

Table 2.1   **Top four alternative finance platforms by volume**

	Average amount raised	Average number of funders
Debt–based securities	£730,000	587
Equity crowdfunding	£199,095	125
P2P business lending	£73,222	796
Invoice trading	£56,075	7

Source: Zhang et al., 2014, p. 14.

Debt-based securities represent a relatively new model of alternative finance. A debt security is any debt instrument that can be bought or sold between two parties and has basic terms defined, such as notional amount (amount borrowed), interest rate and maturity/renewal date. Lenders receive a non-collateralized debt obligation (no assets to act as security for the debt), which is typically paid back over an extended period of time. Investors in debt–based securities generally invest relatively large amounts in single or very few projects. In 2014, the average investment in debt-based securities was £1,243 (Zhang et al., 2014).

Equity-based crowdfunding is where a company raises finance by issuing shares to a number of investors (the 'crowd'). It is mainly used by early stage companies for seed finance, start-up capital or growth. Equity-based crowdfunding fundraisers come from a diverse range of sectors, from high-tech and healthcare to consumer products. Investors are motivated by potential high returns and a diversified portfolio. In 2014, the size of the average portfolio was £5,000 (Zhang et al., 2014). Equity-based crowdfunding tends to be high risk/high return. Like banks and other financial institutions in the UK, those operating crowdfunding platforms are subject to minimum capital requirements and must comply with the rules issued by the *Financial Conduct Authority (FCA)* which cover the conduct of business, client protection and dispute resolution (Brookes and Davies, 2014).

Peer-to-peer (P2P) business lending is where the business (usually an SME) interested in a loan for a particular purpose completes the platform's online application form. The platform quickly assesses the risk using online data and technology, determines the applicant's credit rating and assigns an interest rate. Successful applicants receive offers in minutes and can evaluate their options. P2P business lending allows cash-rich individual or institutional lenders to select applicants to whom they wish to lend, and earn monthly returns. In 2014, borrowers tended to be businesses in the manufacturing, professional business services, construction or retail sectors and were seeking capital for growth or working capital (Zhang et al., 2014). Although some P2P lending platforms have developed funds to compensate lenders if a borrower defaults, lenders are still at risk because loans are generally unsecured.

Invoice trading is where firms sell their invoices at a discount to a pool of individual or institutional investors in order to receive funds immediately rather than waiting for invoices to be paid. The average invoice auction takes 8 hours and the average invoice value is £56,075. Invoice trading is funded mainly by institutional investors and high-net-worth individuals (Zhang et al., 2014).

Activity

Classify the following sources of finance into debt finance, asset-based finance and equity finance (*tick the appropriate box*):

		Debt finance	Asset-based finance	Equity finance
(a)	Share capital	❏	❏	❏
(b)	Debenture	❏	❏	❏
(c)	Hire purchase	❏	❏	❏
(d)	Invoice finance	❏	❏	❏
(e)	Leasing	❏	❏	❏
(f)	Mortgage	❏	❏	❏
(g)	Crowdfunding	❏	❏	❏
(h)	Trade credit	❏	❏	❏
(i)	Venture capital	❏	❏	❏
(j)	P2P lending	❏	❏	❏

You can check your answers against Figure 2.3 which summarizes the main sources of external finance.

Figure 2.3 Main sources of finance by type

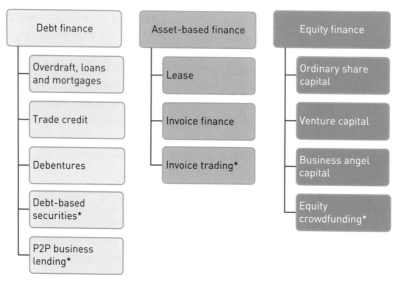

*Alternative finance

A study by the British Business Bank (BBB, 2016) reports that flows of debt and equity finance to SMEs grew in 2015, showing that overall the finance market has improved. Asset-based finance continued to grow strongly and, for the first time in several years, net bank lending to smaller businesses increased. Although less than 3% of gross lending, alternative finance business lending grew by 75% to £1.26bn in 2015. However, there is still cause for concern about a finance gap for small firms despite these improvements. 'Evidence suggests a material portion of smaller businesses who apply for finance are still rejected as a result of problems in small business finance markets. This reflects the likelihood of information asymmetries between borrowers and lenders where it may be costly or difficult for lenders to secure the information they need to make an informed investment decision, as well as other structural issues. It applies to small businesses at all stages of development, whether they are starting-up, scaling-up or seeking finance to stay-ahead in their particular area of the market' (BBB, 2016, p. 5).

2.4 Need for cash flow information

Since business is about money, information about cash is very important. Without sufficient cash an individual or organization may become insolvent, which in many cases leads to a state of *bankruptcy* for an individual or *liquidation* for an organization. In business, economic transactions are based on the immediate payment of cash (a cash transaction) or payment after an agreed period (a credit transaction). The term *cash* refers to all money, whether in the form of coins, notes, cheques or any other way of making payment that does not involve the use of credit. Businesses need to keep a careful record of all the cash receipts and payments in order to keep track of the money. These records are kept as part of the accounting system we describe in Chapter 3.

Activity

Imagine you have £200 cash that you use to buy a computer from another student. You are a bit of an opportunist and see a chance to make some money. You decide to advertise the computer for sale, which costs £10, and you sell the computer for £300 cash. You have no other business transactions. Calculate the cash position of your business at the end of the month.

You should have found the answer by deducting all the cash outflows for the month from all the cash inflows for the month; something you might have been able to do in your head. However, you will not have arrived at the correct answer of £290 if you overlooked the recording of the capital of £200, which was the amount you invested in your business at the start. The following simple statement shows how we arrived at the correct answer.

	£
Your business	
Cash flow statement for the month	
Cash inflows	
Capital	200
Revenue	300
	500
Cash outflows	
Purchases	200
Advertising	10
	210
Net cash flow (500 – 210)	290

Starting at the top of the statement, you see the term *capital* which we have already explained is the term used to describe the money contributed by the owner to enable the business to function. *Revenue* is cash flowing into the business from sales to customers and *purchases* is cash flowing out of the business to suppliers for goods that are purchased for resale. Advertising represents cash flowing out of the business when that expense is paid.

Activity

Using the same example, imagine that this time you agreed to sell the computer on credit, but a few days later you receive a letter from your telephone service provider that you will be disconnected unless you pay an overdue invoice. Which of the following actions do you think is the best one to take and which is the worst? Give your reasons.

(a) Allow the connection to be cut and have it reconnected after you have received the cash from the sale of the computer.
(b) Use your savings to pay the bill.
(c) Take out a loan to pay the bill.
(d) Ask the person who bought the computer to pay you immediately.

You may be able to think of other courses of action, but all the alternatives have advantages and disadvantages. If the connection is disconnected, it is likely to prevent you from carrying out your business activities. Although using your savings remedies the situation, you will lose any interest your investment might be earning. Borrowing money would also prevent the connection being cut, but you would incur interest charges and have to repay the loan. You may think that the best solution is to ask the buyer to pay you immediately, but he or she may not be able to do so. From this example you can appreciate that not only do we require a record of what has happened to cash in the past, but also information that will show us what is likely to happen to cash in the future.

2.5 Preparing a cash flow forecast

A financial statement that shows what is likely to happen to cash in the future is known as a *cash flow forecast* and is used for the following *purposes*:

- To plan capital requirements at the start-up stage, where it helps establish whether the proposed capital will be sufficient to finance the activities of the new business.
- To plan a forthcoming accounting period in an existing business, where it helps anticipate the need for additional finance if the cash going out of the business is expected to exceed the cash in the business (a *cash deficit*) and the investment of cash if the cash in the business is expected to exceed the cash going out (a *cash surplus*).

A cash flow forecast shows the predicted movement of cash over a specified accounting period (usually one year, but it could be six months or a quarter). It is divided into months, with a total column at the end to provide a summary for the period. It predicts as accurately as possible the amount of cash that is expected to come in and go out of the business, and when the movements are expected to take place.

The expected timings of the cash transactions might be monthly, quarterly or annually. We will use an example to examine this in more detail.

Sarah Wick is planning to set up a company selling candles on 1 January 2018. She has £10,000 capital to invest in the business, which she is going to register as Candlewick Ltd. She will buy candles from a local supplier and sell them via a market stall and the Internet. She will work from a small unit on an industrial estate near her home. She plans to purchase the candles for £15 per box and sell them at £20 per box. Her supplier will allow her one month's credit. Sales revenue from the market stall will represent 25% of total sales revenue and these customers will pay cash. The remaining 75% of sales revenue will come from the mail order part of the business, where customers will be given two months' credit.

The following table shows the number of candles Sarah expects the business to purchase at £15 each during the first six months of trading. It also shows the amount of cash she expects to pay each month, taking into account that her supplier allows one month's credit.

	January	February	March	April	May	June	Total
Quantity	400	400	500	560	600	600	3,060
Cost of purchases	£0	£6,000	£6,000	£7,500	£8,400	£9,000	£36,900

Having looked at the expected purchases, we can now look at the sales figures Sarah hopes Candlewick Ltd will achieve. The next table shows the number of candles Sarah expects the business to sell at £20 each during the first six months of trading. It also shows the anticipated amount of cash received each month, taking into account that 25% of customers will pay cash and the remaining 75% will be given two months' credit.

	January	February	March	April	May	June	Total
Quantity	400	400	500	560	600	600	3,060
Revenue (cash sales)	£2,000	£2,000	£2,500	£2,800	£3,000	£3,000	£15,300
Revenue (credit sales)	£0	£0	£6,000	£6,000	£7,500	£8,400	£27,900

The movements of cash are given specific names and it is important to use them to avoid confusing them with other terms you will learn in connection with other financial statements that we will be looking at in Part II.

- *Cash inflows* are cash transactions that bring money into the business. They are described as *positive cash flow*. They include capital, loans, revenue and interest received. The forecast cash inflows for Candlewick Ltd are the capital Sarah plans to invest and the expected revenue.
- *Cash outflows* are cash transactions that take money out of the business. They are described as *negative cash flow*. They include purchases of inventory and

overheads such as wages, rent, electricity, telephone, insurance, finance costs (such as interest on loans), and cash payments made in connection with loans, HP and leasing agreements. At this stage we know that the forecast cash outflows for Candlewick Ltd are what Sarah expects to pay for purchasing candles.

- *Net cash flow* is the difference between the cash inflows and the cash outflows. If the net cash flow is a *cash deficit*, it is shown in brackets.
- The *cumulative cash brought forward (b/f)* refers to the cash surplus or deficit at the start of the month (the first day of the month). It is the cash position that has been brought forward from the last day of the previous month. In the first month of a new business there is no cash to bring forward so this is always zero.
- The *cumulative cash carried forward (c/f)* refers to the cash surplus or deficit at the end of the month. It consists of the cumulative cash brought forward from the previous month plus the net cash flow that has taken place during the month. It shows the *cash position* at the end of the month, which is carried forward to become the *cumulative cash brought forward* at the start of the next month.

Activity

The following cash flow forecast has been partially completed using the predicted figures for purchases and revenue that we calculated above. Calculate the subtotals for cash inflows and outflows and use them to work out the expected net cash flow each month and the cumulative cash position at the start and end of each month.

Candlewick Ltd

Draft cash flow forecast for January–June 2018

	January £	February £	March £	April £	May £	June £	Total £
Cash inflows							
Capital	10,000	0	0	0	0	0	10,000
Revenue (cash sales)	2,000	2,000	2,500	2,800	3,000	3,000	15,300
Revenue (credit sales)	0	0	6,000	6,000	7,500	8,400	27,900
Cash outflows							
Purchases	0	6,000	6,000	7,500	8,400	9,000	36,900
Net cash flow							
Cumulative cash b/f							
Cumulative cash c/f							

Your forecast should look like this:

Candlewick Ltd
Draft cash flow forecast for January–June 2018

	January £	February £	March £	April £	May £	June £	Total £
Cash inflows							
Capital	10,000	0	0	0	0	0	10,000
Revenue (cash sales)	2,000	2,000	2,500	2,800	3,000	3,000	15,300
Revenue (credit sales)	0	0	6,000	6,000	7,500	8,400	27,900
	12,000	2,000	8,500	8,800	10,500	11,400	53,200
Cash outflows							
Purchases	0	6,000	6,000	7,500	8,400	9,000	36,900
	0	6,000	6,000	7,500	8,400	9,000	36,900
Net cash flow	12,000	(4,000)	2,500	1,300	2,100	2,400	16,300
Cumulative cash b/f	0	12,000	8,000	10,500	11,800	13,900	0
Cumulative cash c/f	12,000	8,000	10,500	11,800	13,900	16,300	16,300

You may find the following points helpful:

- The total column shows the cash receipts and cash payments for the entire six months. If we deduct the expected payments for the six months, which total £36,900, from the expected receipts, which total £53,200, you can see that there is a forecast cash surplus of £16,300.
- The figures shown in brackets in the cash flow forecast represent cash deficits.
- In a continuing business, the total column should also show any cumulative cash b/f at the beginning of the accounting period (in a new business, such as this, it is nil).
- The cumulative cash c/f in the total column should agree with the equivalent cumulative cash c/f at the end of the last month of the accounting period. This acts as a crosscheck on the accuracy of the calculation of the cash position.

Key definitions

Cash inflows are the cash receipts of a business.

Cash outflows are the cash payments made by a business.

Net cash flow is the difference between the cash inflows and the cash outflows.

A cash surplus describes the cash position when the accumulated cash in the business exceeds the cash outflows.

A cash deficit describes the cash position when the cash outflows exceed the accumulated cash in the business.

Cumulative cash brought forward (b/f) is the cash surplus or deficit at the start of the accounting period that has been brought forward from the previous period.

Cumulative cash carried forward (c/f) is the cash surplus or deficit at the end of the accounting period that is carried forward to the next period.

It may have occurred to you that the purchase of candles is not the only cost the business will incur. This is why the heading refers to the forecast as a draft forecast. Accountants use the term 'purchases' to mean the purchase of goods that will be sold as part of the trading cycle. Other costs incurred are given specific names. The other costs Candlewick Ltd is expected to incur are as follows:

- Office and other equipment will be bought for £13,000 on 1 January, but will not be paid for until February, as Sarah will make use of the one month's interest free credit period on the business credit card.
- Rent will be £150 per month, payable by the end of each month.
- Advertising will be £250 per month, payable one month in arrears.
- Telephone and Internet expenses will be £450 per quarter, payable at the end of each quarter.
- Printing, postage and stationery, which include packaging, are estimated at £600 per month. Suppliers will give one month's credit, so the cost for January will be paid in February and so on.

We now have all the information we need to complete the cash flow forecast for Candlewick Ltd.

Candlewick Ltd

Cash flow forecast for January–June 2018

	January £	February £	March £	April £	May £	June £	Total £
Cash inflows							
Capital	10,000	0	0	0	0	0	10,000
Revenue (cash sales)	2,000	2,000	2,500	2,800	3,000	3,000	15,300
Revenue (credit sales)	0	0	6,000	6,000	7,500	8,400	27,900
	12,000	2,000	8,500	8,800	10,500	11,400	53,200
Cash outflows							
Purchases	0	6,000	6,000	7,500	8,400	9,000	36,900
Equipment	0	13,000	0	0	0	0	13,000
Rent	150	150	150	150	150	150	900
Advertising	0	250	250	250	250	250	1,250
Telephone & Internet	0	0	450	0	0	450	900
Printing, postage & stationery	0	600	600	600	600	600	3,000
	150	20,000	7,450	8,500	9,400	10,450	55,950
Net cash flow	11,850	(18,000)	1,050	300	1,100	950	(2,750)
Cumulative cash b/f	0	11,850	(6,150)	(5,100)	(4,800)	(3,700)	0
Cumulative cash c/f	11,850	(6,150)	(5,100)	(4,800)	(3,700)	(2,750)	(2,750)

Most accountants adopt the layout we have illustrated when preparing a cash flow forecast, but you may come across other variations. Do not let this confuse you because the principles are exactly the same. The main points to remember are:

- The heading should state the name of the business and the accounting period to which the forecast refers.
- The columns should be labelled with the months to which they relate and the currency. You should include a total column at the end to provide summary figures for the whole period.
- The cash inflows are itemized separately under that heading and subtotalled.
- Next, the cash outflows are itemized separately under that heading and subtotalled.
- The subtotal for the cash outflows are deducted from the subtotal for the cash inflows to give the net cash flow. If this represents a predicted cash deficit (a negative figure), it is shown in brackets.
- The next row shows the cumulative cash brought forward (b/f) at the start of each period.

- The final row calculates the cumulative cash carried forward (c/f) at the end of each period. This is the 'bottom line' that shows whether a cash deficit (shown in brackets) or a cash surplus is predicted at the end of each month. The last figure in this row shows the predicted cash deficit or surplus at the end of the whole period and should be the same as the cumulative cash c/f at the end of the last month of the period.

Once you have learned the layout for a cash flow forecast, you should be able to construct one manually (with the aid of a calculator or using mental arithmetic) or using a spreadsheet. The only difference is that negative figures are entered with a minus sign rather than in brackets and formulae are entered to perform the arithmetic. We used Microsoft® Excel to prepare the forecast for Candlewick Ltd and Figure 2.4 shows you the formulae we used.

Figure 2.4 Cash flow forecast formulae

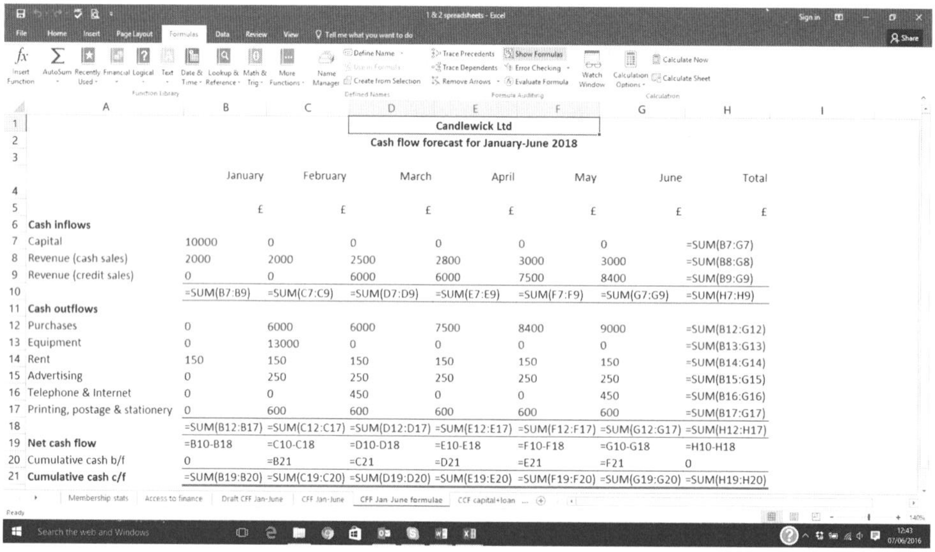

2.6 Planning capital requirements

The first step for anyone thinking of starting a new business is to consider how much finance is needed and the source(s) of that finance; in other words, to plan the capital requirements of setting up the enterprise. We already know that Sarah is planning to invest £10,000 of her own money in Candlewick Ltd when it starts on 1 January, but the cash flow forecast shows that by the end of February this will turn into a cash deficit as the cumulative cash position is negative. Based on these predictions, Sarah would go out of business by February and it is clear that she must make some plans to avoid this before starting the business.

Activity

Sarah has decided she needs to look for external finance to ensure the company is solvent for the first six months. How much cash does the business need to borrow to ensure there is no cash deficit in any month?

(a)   £18,000
(b)   £6,150
(c)   £5,100
(d)   £4,800
(e)   £3,700

The correct answer is that Sarah needs £6,150 to give her sufficient cash to start the business and ensure that it does not have a deficit during the first six months. Her main choices are:

- to obtain a bank overdraft or loan
- to allow only one month's credit to the mail order customers
- to see if her supplier will allow two or three months' credit
- to lease some of the equipment or buy it on HP
- to control the cash expected to go out on telephone and Internet, printing, postage and stationery
- to look for a cheaper unit to rent
- a combination of these solutions.

After discussing her cash flow forecast with the bank lending officer, Sarah takes out a bank loan for £6,500 over two years and arranges a £2,500 overdraft facility for short-term cash deficits. The loan has a fixed rate of interest of 7.4% for the first six months which works out at £40 per month. Having made these arrangements, Sarah prepares the following revised cash flow forecast.

It is difficult to make general rules about interpreting a cash flow forecast, because it depends on the particular business. The checklist in Figure 2.5 includes questions you need to consider.

Candlewick Ltd

Revised cash flow forecast for January–June 2018

	January £	February £	March £	April £	May £	June £	Total £
Cash inflows							
Capital	10,000	0	0	0	0	0	10,000
Loan	6,500	0	0	0	0	0	6,500
Revenue (cash sales)	2,000	2,000	2,500	2,800	3,000	3,000	15,300
Revenue (credit sales)	0	0	6,000	6,000	7,500	8,400	27,900
	18,500	2,000	8,500	8,800	10,500	11,400	59,700
Cash outflows							
Purchases	0	6,000	6,000	7,500	8,400	9,000	36,900
Equipment	0	13,000	0	0	0	0	13,000
Rent	150	150	150	150	150	150	900
Advertising	0	250	250	250	250	250	1,250
Telephone & Internet	0	0	450	0	0	450	900
Printing, postage & stationery	0	600	600	600	600	600	3,000
Finance costs	40	40	40	40	40	40	240
	190	20,040	7,490	8,540	9,440	10,490	56,190
Net cash flow	18,310	(18,040)	1,010	260	1,060	910	3,510
Cumulative cash b/f	0	18,310	270	1,280	1,540	2,600	0
Cumulative cash c/f	18,310	270	1,280	1,540	2,600	3,510	3,510

Figure 2.5 Checklist for interpreting cash flow information

- Is all the cash due to the business being collected as early as possible? Although it may be necessary to give credit to customers, the credit period should not be so long as to result in cash flow problems for the business. Alternatively, can invoice finance be arranged?

- Are all payments being made by the due date and not before? To pay sooner than necessary represents poor cash management, but to pay too late runs the risk of not being allowed credit in future and/or being sued for non-payment.

- Can credit agreements be arranged with suppliers who are being paid immediately, or can longer credit periods be agreed that will further delay payments?

- Can hire purchase or leasing be arranged to spread the cost of acquiring large items, such as equipment and vehicles?

- Is there sufficient cash to ensure that the business does not become insolvent?

- Have overdraft facilities been arranged to cover relatively small amounts of cash deficit?

- Has a decision been made to invest any cash surplus where it will receive interest?

2.7 Preparing a cash flow statement for management

A simple *cash flow statement* for management shows the actual movements of cash. The financial information provided can be used to help make decisions about whether to revise planned activities and this helps make the cash flow forecast more realistic. Having realistic plans increases the chance that the business will be successful in meeting its economic objectives, whether the business is pursuing profit maximization or satisficing strategies. Since events seldom turn out exactly as predicted, it is important to establish control of the cash on a regular basis by comparing the actual movements of cash against the predicted movements. If things are not turning out as planned, corrective action can then be taken. Without this comparison of the actual results with the plan, there will be no control.

The following simple cash flow statement shows the actual cash flows for Candlewick Ltd for the first six months. As this is being prepared for management, there are no rules about how it should be constructed. The following layout is one used by accountants and reflects the layout for the cash flow forecast, but note that the heading reflects the fact that it is now a statement of the (actual) cash flows rather than a forecast.

Candlewick Ltd
Cash flow statement for January–June 2018

	January £	February £	March £	April £	May £	June £	Total £
Cash inflows							
Capital	10,000	0	0	0	0	0	10,000
Loan	6,500	0	0	0	0	0	6,500
Revenue (cash sales)	1,600	1,800	2,000	3,500	4,100	4,500	17,500
Revenue (credit sales)	0	0	4,800	5,400	6,000	7,800	24,000
	18,100	1,800	6,800	8,900	10,100	12,300	58,000
Cash outflows							
Purchases	0	6,000	6,000	7,500	8,400	9,000	36,900
Equipment	0	13,000	0	0	0	0	13,000
Rent	500	500	500	500	500	500	3,000
Advertising	50	50	50	50	50	50	300
Telephone & Internet	0	0	450	0	0	450	900
Printing, postage & stationery	0	100	100	100	100	100	500
Salaries	0	500	500	500	500	660	2,660
Finance costs	40	40	40	40	40	40	240
	590	20,190	7,640	8,690	9,590	10,800	57,500
Net cash flow	17,510	(18,390)	(840)	210	510	1,500	500
Cumulative cash b/f	0	17,510	(880)	(1,720)	(1,510)	(1,000)	0
Cumulative cash c/f	17,510	(880)	(1,720)	(1,510)	(1,000)	500	500

As you can see, things have not turned out entirely as planned: the revenue from cash sales is slightly higher than planned, but revenue from credit sales is lower than anticipated. In addition, the rent is much higher because she had underestimated the cost, and it looks as though Sarah is paying the company's advertising expenses in the month in which they are incurred, rather than taking the one month's credit allowed. However, they are much lower than expected. You may also have noticed that the business has only paid £100 per month for printing, postage and stationery since February instead of the predicted figure of £600, as these expenses were lower than predicted. In addition, Sarah took on a part-time employee in February to help with packing and dispatching the orders and this employee receives a salary of £500 per month, rising to £660 in June.[2] Despite introducing £10,000 capital and taking out a loan for £6,500 you can see that the cumulative cash position at the end of February shows a cash deficit of £880 and by the end of March it has gone up to £1,720. This reduces over the next three months and by the end of June there is a cash surplus of £500. Fortunately, the business has not gone into liquidation because the cash deficits between February and May were covered by the overdraft Sarah arranged with the bank.

Activity

Sarah must revise her plans for the next six months. Suggest what actions she might take.

You may think that Sarah would be in a better position if she compared her actual cash flow with her plan on a monthly basis, instead of waiting for six months. Certainly, control is improved with frequency and most businesses carry out this sort of exercise every month. Given the position Sarah is now in, you should have suggested the following:

- She introduces more capital than planned.
- She revises her planned sales figures for the next six months to reflect the level of sales she achieved in the first six months and any variations she expects during the forthcoming festive season.
- She revises the number of candles she will purchase to reduce the amount of inventory.
- She takes up the offer of one month's credit on advertising.
- She revises the planned spending on printing, postage and stationery to reflect the mail order sales more closely.
- She tries to negotiate more favourable terms from the suppliers of candles and packaging.
- She looks for a cheaper unit to rent.

2. Sarah will wait until the end of the financial year before deciding whether to take any money from the business. If the business is sufficiently profitable, she will pay herself cash and this is known as a dividend.

If Sarah revises the cash flow forecast, she may decide it is not worthwhile continuing the business. We have not yet allowed for the interest that must be paid on the overdraft or the fact that she will need to draw cash out of the business to provide herself with a living. Cash flow statements sometimes show unpleasant information, but are essential to the effective running of a business.

Cash flow information is useful in a number of ways. You have seen that planned cash flow information can be used to prepare what is called a *cash flow forecast* that predicts the monthly cash flows for the first accounting period (usually one year) for a new business. Exactly the same construction is used by existing businesses for subsequent periods, but it is usually called a *cash flow budget*. A cash flow budget is prepared in advance of the accounting period and predicts the cash flows for the following year as accurately as possible. Once that year starts, the actual figures in the *cash flow statement* are compared with the budgeted figures to check that the business is meeting its targets. If targets are not being met, the owner or manager can take whatever action is necessary to make sure the business meets its economic objectives. We will be looking at budgets in more detail in a subsequent chapter.

Preparing cash flow forecasts and statements, and making revisions to plans can be very tedious if done by hand. The task is made considerably easier and more efficient if you use a spreadsheet. Nevertheless, it is important to remember that even if it is prepared using a spreadsheet, a cash flow forecast is only as good as the quality of the predicted figures it contains.

Activity

Using your own bank statement, prepare a cash flow forecast for yourself for the next six months using a spreadsheet. When you have completed your forecast, reflect on the decisions you need to make using the checklist given in Figure 2.5 as a guide.

2.8   Conclusions

In this chapter we have considered the importance of cash and the need all businesses have for finance. We have discussed the theory of a finance gap for SMEs, examined some of the evidence and classified the potential sources of traditional and alternative finance. We have also looked at the need for financial information in a business at the start-up stage and beyond. We have introduced you to a financial statement known as a cash flow forecast/budget, which uses estimated or budgeted figures to predict the cash position at the end of a future accounting period. Once that accounting period has started, a cash flow statement using the actual figures can be prepared to show the actual cash position at the end of an accounting period.

Cash flow information aids planning, control and decision making. In particular, it helps owners and managers:

- ensure that the business has sufficient cash to carry out planned activities
- anticipate the need for additional finance if a cash deficit is forecast
- plan the investment of any cash surplus
- control cash flows by comparing actual figures against the plan or budget
- take decisions to modify activities to ensure the business remains solvent and has enough cash to pay its debts when they fall due.

References

BBB (2016) *Small Business Finance Markets Report 2015–16*, British Business Bank. Available at: http://british-business-bank.co.uk/research/small-business-finance-markets-report-201516/ (Accessed 8 February 2016).

Bolton, J.E. (1971) *Report of the Committee of Inquiry on Small Firms*, Cmnd. 4811, London: HMSO.

Brookes, S. and Davies, C. (2014) 'FCA moves ahead on crowdfunding regulation', *Accountancy*, May, p. 59.

BVCA (2016) *Private Equity Explained*, British Private Equity and Venture Capital Association. Available at: www.bvca.co.uk/PrivateEquityExplained.aspx (Accessed 8 February 2016).

Deakins, D. (1996) *Entrepreneurs and Small Firms*, Maidenhead: McGraw-Hill.

ECB (2015) *Survey on the Access to Finance of Enterprises in the Euro Area April to September 2015*, European Central Bank, December. Available at: www.ecb.europa.eu/pub/pdf/other/accesstofinancesmallmediumsizedenterprises201512.en.pdf?2c146594df6fe424c7adb001e1306c73 (Accessed 8 February 2016).

Harrison, R. and Mason, C. (1995) 'The role of informal venture capital in financing the growing firm', in Buckland, R. and Davis, E.W. (eds), *Finance for Growing Enterprises*, London: Routledge.

HM Treasury and Department for Business, Innovation and Skills (2010) *Financing a Private Sector Recovery*, London: The Stationery Office, Cm 7923.

IASB (2016) IFRS 16, *Leases*, London: IFRS Foundation.

Jarvis, R. and Schizas, E. (2012) 'Finance and the small firm', in Carter, S. and Jones Evans, D. (eds) *Enterprise and Small Business: Principles, Practice and Policy*, 3rd edn, Harlow: Pearson Education.

Lloyds Bank (2015) *Big Issues for Small Businesses*. Available at: www.lloydsbankinggroup.com/globalassets/documents/media/media-kit/final-approved-report.pdf (Accessed 4 December 2016).

LSE (2015) *Main Market Factsheet*, London Stock Exchange Group, December, Table 8. Available at: www.londonstockexchange.com/statistics/historic/main-market/main-market-factsheet-archive-2015/dec-15.pdf (Accessed 8 February 2016).

Macmillan Committee (1931) *Report of the Committee on Finance and Industry*, Cmnd 3897, London: HMSO.

UEAPME (2011) *SMEs' Access to Finance*. Available at: www.ueapme.com/spip.php?rubrique46 (Accessed 8 February 2016).

UKBAA (2016) *About UK Business Angels Association*. Available at: www.ukbusinessangelsassociation.org.uk/about (Accessed 8 February 2016).

Wilson Committee (1979) *The Financing of Small Firms: Interim Report of the Committee to Review the Functioning of the Financial Institutions*, Cmnd 7503, London: HMSO.

Zhang, Z., Collins, L. and Baeck, P. (2014) *Understanding Alternative Finance: The UK Alternative Finance industry Report 2014* (Nesta). Available at: www.nesta.org.uk/publications/understanding-alternative-finance-uk-alternative-finance-industry-report-2014 (Accessed 23 September 2016).

Discussion questions

1 Discuss the reasons why students studying business or management should learn about cash flow management.

2 Discuss the obstacles that start-up and early stage companies face in obtaining access to finance.

3 Define finance and discuss the extent to which alternative finance bridges the finance gap for small companies.

Practice questions

4 Explain the theory of the finance gap.

5 Compare and contrast the potential sources of long-term finance available to an unincorporated business such as a sole proprietorship or traditional partnership.

6 Francesca Diva is planning to start a shoe shop called Dudes & Divas Ltd on 1 July 2018 with £25,000 she has inherited. She is going to be a sole proprietor and plans to open a small shop in the town centre. She has found suitable premises and has arranged for professional shop fitters to refurbish them. The new fixtures and fittings will cost £30,000, but will not have to be paid for until September. In addition, she estimates the following transactions will take place during the first three months of trading.

Revenue (cash sales)	£10,000 per month
Revenue (credit sales)	£2,000 per month (customers will have one month's credit)
Purchases	£5,000 per month (suppliers will give two months' credit)
Overheads	£5,000 per month
Salaries	£1,500 per month

Required

(a) Prepare a cash flow forecast for Dudes & Divas Ltd for the three months, 1 July to 30 September 2018.

(b) Interpret the cash flow forecast you have prepared and comment on the cumulative cash position at 30 September 2018.

7 Phil Trigg is the owner of Trigg Electronics Ltd. He has negotiated with two manufacturers of electric circuit boards to carry out assembly work for them and anticipates assembling the following numbers of circuit boards for each manufacturer during his first year (2018).

	Jan	Feb	Mar	Apr	May	Jun	Jul	Aug	Sep	Oct	Nov	Dec
Customer A	120	130	130	150	140	140	160	160	170	140	140	120
Customer B	200	240	240	240	220	220	220	270	270	270	230	210

Customer A has agreed to pay £6.60 for each board assembled and Customer B will pay £6.50. Customer A will pay two months after the work has been done, but Customer B will pay one month after the work has been done. Phil anticipates the following expenses.

Rent	£6,000 per annum, payable at the beginning of each quarter
Lighting and heating	£120 per month, payable one month in arrears
Telephone and Internet	£50 per quarter, payable at the end of each quarter
Printing, postage and stationery	10% of sales revenue, payable the month after the cash for the sale is received
General expenses	£25 per month
Equipment	£2,500 in January, £1,000 in February and £500 in March

Required

(a) Prepare a cash flow forecast for Trigg Electronics Ltd for the six months ended 30 June 2018.

(b) Calculate the amount of capital Phil needs to invest in the business to prevent a cash deficit at any time during the six months.

8 David Green has recently graduated from horticultural college and is going to start an ecologically-friendly gardening company called Urban Green Ltd. He plans to invest £5,000 in the business on 1 July 2019 and has provided estimates of his cash inflows and outflows so that you can help him prepare a cash flow forecast for his business plan.

David does not need any business premises, but on 1 July the business will need to spend £2,000 on office and gardening equipment. He is planning to buy the equipment on the company's credit card, which he will pay in full in August without incurring any interest. The business needs a small truck and David has found a hybrid vehicle for £15,000 which he will pay for out of the capital he has invested in the business. He will acquire the truck on 1 July, but the dealer has given him three months' credit so he will not have to pay for it until 30 September.

David expects cash sales from landscaping jobs of £9,000 per month for the first quarter, rising to £10,000 per month thereafter. He has maintenance contracts starting on 1 July with two corporate customers. They will be given one month's credit and the total credit sales from these two customers will be £1,000 per month. He will buy organically produced plants and garden products for his customers. These purchases will amount to £3,000 per month and the wholesaler will give him two months' credit. All sales and purchases are assumed to take place evenly over the month. Distribution costs will be £750 per month and administrative expenses will be £8,000 per month.

Required

(a) Prepare a cash flow forecast for Urban Green Ltd for the six months ended 31 December 2019.

(b) Interpret your cash flow forecast by stating the amount of additional finance that will be needed to avoid a bank overdraft during the first six months.

(c) Describe three sources of medium-term finance that David should consider as alternatives to paying cash for the truck. Conclude with a recommendation, giving your reasons.

(d) Help David further by explaining the benefits and limitations of cash flow forecasts.

 Suggested research questions for dissertation students

Students interested in issues related to access to finance may wish to investigate one or more of the following research questions:

- How do SMEs meet their need for finance at the start-up stage and beyond?

- How do SMEs wishing to grow meet their need for finance?

- What financial strategies did SMEs follow to survive the most recent economic recession in [country]?

- What are the main sources of advice on access to finance used by SMEs at the start-up stage and beyond?

- How effective is alternative finance in bridging the finance gap for small companies?

Preliminary reading

BBB (2016) *Small Business Finance Markets Report 2015–16*, British Business Bank. Available at: http://british-business-bank.co.uk/research/small-business-finance-markets-report-201516/ (Accessed 8 February 2016).

Beck, T. and Demirguc-Kunt, A. (2006) 'Small and medium-size enterprises: Access to finance as a growth constraint', *Journal of Banking & Finance*, 30(11), pp. 2931–2943.

Berger, A.N. and Udell, G.F. (2006) 'A more complete conceptual framework for SME finance', *Journal of Banking & Finance*, 30(11), pp. 2945–2966.

Cumming, D., Guariglia, A., Hou, W., Lee, E. and Newman, A. (2014) 'Introduction: Exploring entrepreneurial activity and small business issues in the Chinese economy', *International Small Business Journal*, 32(6), pp. 603–609.

ECB (2015) *Survey on the Access to Finance of Enterprises in the Euro Area April to September 2015*, European Central Bank, December. Available at: www.ecb.europa.eu/pub/pdf/other/accesstofinancesmallmediumsizedenterprises201512.en.pdf?2c146594df6fe424c7adb001e1306c73 (Accessed 8 February 2016).

Jarvis, R. and Schizas, E. (2012) 'Finance and the small firm', in Carter, S. and Jones Evans, D. (eds) *Enterprise and Small Business: Principles, Practice and Policy*, Harlow: Pearson Education.

McGuinness, G. and Hogan, T. (2016) 'Bank credit and trade credit: Evidence from SMEs over the financial crisis', *International Small Business Journal*, 34(4), pp. 412–445.

PART II

Financial accounting

3 The accounting system

Learning objectives

When you have studied this chapter, you should be able to:

- Describe the fundamental accounting principles
- Explain the accounting equation
- Apply the principles of double-entry bookkeeping
- Balance the ledger accounts and prepare a trial balance
- Discuss the limitations of a trial balance

3.1 Introduction

All individuals and businesses are required to keep accounting records in order to provide financial information to the tax authorities. In addition to filing tax returns, limited liability partnerships and companies must file a copy of their annual report and accounts at Companies House. Keeping the records and preparing financial statements are part of the work done by a financial accountant. In this chapter we start by introducing you to the fundamental accounting principles that guide financial accountants in these tasks.

In order to generate financial information, a business needs to establish an efficient accounting system for collecting and storing accounting data. The nature of the system depends on the size and type of business, but there are common features since procedures must be established to allow all economic transactions and events to be recorded. These procedures involve raising source documents, such as invoices, purchase orders and credit notes, so that those responsible in the business are made aware that a transaction has taken place and the details of the transaction can be recorded. The most commonly used accounting system is known as double-entry bookkeeping. In this chapter we describe a simple double-entry bookkeeping system and explain how the records are used to construct a trial balance. Although it is not necessary for students who are not specializing in accounting to learn about bookkeeping in depth, it is useful to understand something about the accounting system that generates the financial information they are likely to use as the entrepreneurs and/or managers of the future.

3.2   Accounting principles

You will remember from Chapter 1 that the *purpose* of *financial accounting* is to provide financial information to meet the needs of external users as shown in the following definition.

> **Key definition**
>
> Financial accounting is the branch of accounting concerned with classifying, measuring and recording the economic transactions of an entity in accordance with established principles, legal requirements and accounting standards. It is primarily concerned with communicating a true and fair view of the financial performance and financial position of an entity to external parties at the end of the accounting period.

The requirement to give a *true and fair view* implies that the financial statements produced at the end of an accounting period (usually one year) are a faithful representation of the entity's economic activities. The financial statements of limited liability entities are drawn up within a regulatory framework and are prepared using a number of established general accounting principles. It is important to remember that accounting has its roots in best practice from which a number of *accounting principles*[1] developed. Many of the fundamental accounting principles are still in use today and some of them are incorporated in the conceptual framework for financial reporting, which we examine in Chapter 5.

> **Key definition**
>
> Accounting principles are the basic theoretical concepts that guide financial accounting.

3.2.1   Going concern principle

We are going to start our examination of the fundamental accounting principles by looking at the principle of going concern. An underlying assumption is that the reporting entity is a going concern. In other words, it is assumed that the entity will

---

1. Also known as accounting concepts or accounting conventions.

continue in operation for the foreseeable future and has neither the intention nor the need to liquidate or cease trading. Therefore, the financial statements will be prepared on an ongoing basis. However, if the assumption of going concern is not valid, the financial statements may have to be prepared on a different basis. If so, the basis used must be disclosed in the financial statements (IASB, 2015). For example, the financial statements will show the assets of the business at their break-up value and any liabilities that are applicable on liquidation. The going concern assumption is confirmed by IAS 1, *Presentation of Financial Statements* (IASB, 2014), which requires management to look at least 12 months ahead to assess this. If there is significant doubt over the entity's ability to continue as a going concern, those uncertainties must be disclosed, together with the basis used.

Activity

A company bought a machine for the production department at the beginning of the year for £3,000. It is estimated that the machine will contribute to the profits of the business for the next ten years. Six months later the chief accountant finds out that if the machine had to be sold, it would be worth only £2,000. Using the going concern concept, which of these two amounts should be shown in the accounts?

The clue to answering this question lies in understanding what we mean by a going concern. As we have already seen, a going concern is a business that will continue to operate for the foreseeable future. In other words, the business does not have to sell its machine and it will be shown in the accounts at £3,000, as it is anticipated that it will continue to contribute to the profits of the business.

Next we consider what situation a business might be in if it were not a going concern. You are probably aware of the consequences of a business closing or going into liquidation. The activities of the business cease, the workforce is made redundant and any assets the business owns, such as buildings, vehicles, equipment and so on are liquidated. This means that they are sold and the proceeds are used to pay any outstanding debts. If the business is a going concern, the correct figure for the machine is the price which was paid for it: £3,000. If the business is not a going concern, the figure would be the estimated market value of the machine: £2,000. However, if there was no going concern concept, either of these figures might be used, which would be very confusing for the users of the financial information.

When a business is closing down it needs to prepare the financial statements on a *break-up basis*. Essentially, this means all assets (what the business owns) and liabilities (what it owes) will be classified as current in the sense that they do not relate beyond the next accounting year. In addition, all the assets will be valued at their net realizable value (the disposal value less any direct selling costs), which is likely to be substantially lower than the carrying amount under historical cost accounting.

A wide range of stakeholders in the company will be interested in whether it is a going concern. For example, if it is intending to close down or significantly reduce its activities:

- Existing investors would try to sell their shares and potential investors would be deterred from investing in the company.
- Existing lenders would demand repayment of loans, increase interest rates on overdraft facilities or even withdraw such facilities.
- Suppliers would be unwilling to supply goods and services on credit.
- Customers would be anxious about the continuity of supply of goods and services and switch to alternative providers. They would also be concerned if they have bought goods that are still under warranty or those that require specialist replacement parts.
- Employees will be concerned about their job security, remuneration and future benefits.

3.2.2 Accrual principle

A second underlying assumption is that, apart from cash flow information, the annual financial statements of limited liability entities are prepared using the accrual basis of accounting. The *accrual principle* requires that revenue and costs are recognized as they are earned and incurred not as cash is received or paid (the *realization concept*), and they are matched with one another (the *matching concept*) and dealt with in the statement of profit or loss for the period to which they relate (the *time period concept*). Thus, the effects of economic transactions and events are shown in the period in which those effects occur, even if the resulting cash receipts and payments occur in a different period. Accrual accounting can be contrasted with cash accounting, which recognizes transactions and events only when cash has been received or paid.

Activity

During the month of August, a car dealer sold a vehicle for £7,500 that he had purchased at the beginning of the month for only £6,000. He paid cash for the car, but has not yet received the cash from the buyer. What is his financial position at the end of August?

Using the accrual principle, we can calculate the profit he has made as revenue minus purchases:[2]

	£
Revenue	7,500
Purchases	(6,000)
Profit	1,500

---

2. Note that we are using brackets to indicate figures that will be subtracted in the calculation.

However, that is only part of the story. At the end of the month he has £6,000 less than he had at the start of the month because he has paid for the car, but has not yet received the cash from the buyer. We can show his cash position as follows:

	£
Cash at the start of the month	6,000
Purchases	(6,000)
Cash at the end of the month	0

It is because of the accrual principle that we need to use more than one financial statement to give a complete picture of the financial performance and wealth of a business.

3.2.3   Other accounting principles

Other fundamental accounting principles you need to learn include the following:

- *Business entity* – the principle that the financial statements reflect the economic activities of the entity and not those of the owner(s). This means that the accounting records for the business must be kept separately from the personal accounting records for the owner.
- *Monetary measurement* – the principle that transactions are only recognized in the financial statements if they can be measured in monetary terms. For example, rather than recording the number of haircuts in a year, the owner-manager of a hair salon must record the value of the haircuts. Thus, 1,500 haircuts at £50 each becomes revenue of £75,000. Related to this concept is the assumption that currency is stable and holds its value over time (for example, there is no inflation or deflation and no fluctuations in foreign exchange rates).
- *Materiality* – the principle that only items of information that are material (significant) are included in the financial statements. An item of information is material if its omission or misstatement could influence the economic decisions of those using the financial statements. We will look at this again in Chapter 5.
- *Historical cost* – the principle that the values of assets are based on their original acquisition cost, unadjusted for subsequent changes in price or value. This presents some problems. For example, four years ago a business may have had to pay £50 for a box of printed stationery, but due to advances in printing technology the business would only have to pay £45 today. On the other hand, the business may have paid £2,500 for office furniture four years ago, but replacing it might cost £3,250 due to higher manufacturing costs. Some assets, such as property in a prime location, increase in value over time. Historical cost is widely used, but it is usually combined with *fair value*. The four main bases of fair value are current cost, net realizable value (selling price less costs of selling), value in use and replacement cost. We will refer to this again in subsequent chapters.

- *Consistency* – the principle that there is consistency in the accounting treatment of items of a similar nature within each accounting period and from one period to the next.
- *Prudence* – the principle that caution should be exercised when making judgements under conditions of uncertainty. This means that assets and income are not overstated or understated and liabilities and expenses are not understated or overstated, because such misstatements can lead to the overstatement of income or the understatement of expenses in future periods.

Figure 3.1 summarizes the accounting principles we have discussed. Although you may find the accounting principles fairly difficult to understand at this stage, they lie at the heart of financial accounting and you need to become familiar with them. We will show you how some of them are applied in this chapter.

Figure 3.1 Fundamental accounting principles

Business entity

Money measure-ment

Prudence

Assumptions:
Going concern
Accrual basis

Materiality

Consistency

Historical cost

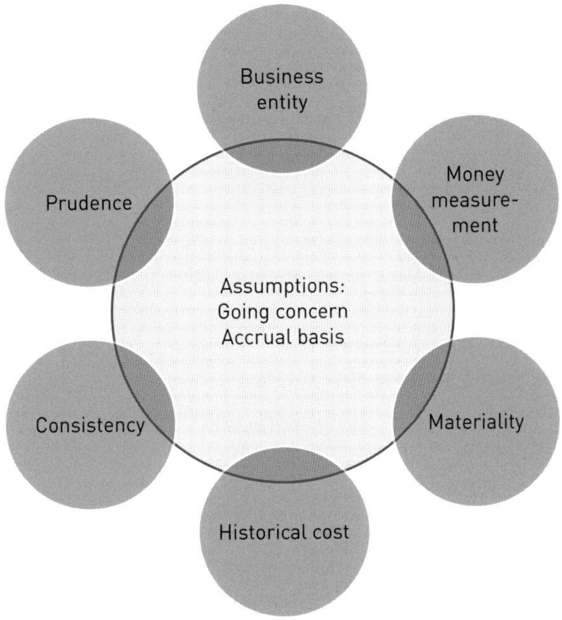

3.3 Accounting information systems

Irrespective of size and whether they are unincorporated entities (sole proprietorships and partnerships) or incorporated entities (limited liability partnerships, private companies and public companies), all businesses are required to keep accounting records so that they can provide financial information to the tax authorities. Incorporated entities must also prepare financial statements to meet their statutory financial reporting obligations. Therefore, owners and managers need an accounting information system for recording the economic transactions and events of the business and aiding the preparation or generation of financial statements which summarize the accounting information.

Large organizations have a wide range of activities and carry out thousands of transactions every day. Therefore, they need sophisticated computerized accounting systems, which may be part of an *enterprise resource planning (ERP) system* that integrates the finance function with other areas such as purchasing, inventory, sales, marketing and human resource management. On the other hand, small businesses have a narrower focus and relatively few transactions. Therefore, most small businesses use spreadsheets such as Microsoft® Excel or standardized accounting software such as SAGE. Many small businesses use *cloud accounting*, which means they are no longer keeping their software and data on a computer hard drive or on a server, but on an Internet platform that makes them accessible online at any time and from any device. This addresses some of the problems of traditional accounting software:

- The data in the system may not be up to date and the most recent data may be kept on a USB drive until it is entered into the system, which is highly risky.
- The software may not be up to date and it may only be available on one computer.
- Typically, only one person has user access and thus key people do not have access to the latest financial and customer information at all times.
- It can be expensive and complicated to keep back-ups of the data (if done at all).
- It is costly and time-consuming to upgrade the software, and customer support may also be expensive.

Research suggests that the majority of micro-businesses in the UK use inefficient methods to manage their accounting records (International Accountant, 2015). Just over half of those surveyed (54%) use pen and paper or a spreadsheet, 23% spend more than one working day per month personally managing their accounts and a further 8% spend at least three days each month on this part of the business. Whether the accounting system is manual or computerized, it is normally based on the principles of double-entry bookkeeping and the bookkeeper will apply the relevant fundamental accounting principles we described in the previous section.

3.3.1 Source documents

Some business transactions are for immediate cash, but many business transactions are credit transactions. Therefore, owners and managers need a system for recording both types of transaction and documents that give details of the transactions made. Such documents are known as *source documents* and are the foundation on which the financial records of the business are built. The main documents that provide the data recorded in the accounting system can be summarized as follows:

- sales orders, delivery notes, invoices paid by customers and credit notes issued for goods returned by customers
- purchase orders, invoices received from suppliers and credit notes received for goods returned to suppliers
- payroll information, inventory records, banking records and other documents.

3.3.2 The accounting process

We will now look at the process of raising source documents in more detail. In many businesses, goods are purchased on credit and a number of external and internal documents are produced to record these activities. First, the business purchasing the goods issues a *purchase order* and sends it to the supplier. This document specifies the quantity, type and price of the goods ordered. When the purchaser receives the goods, they are examined to ensure that they match the items on the purchase order and a *goods received note* is raised. Copies of the goods received note are sent to the accounts department, the purchase department and the stores department. When the stores department receives the goods, the details are recorded on an *inventory record card* so that the manager of the stores has a record of the goods available. Goods are released by the stores department only on receipt of a properly authorized *stores requisition*, the fourth document in this chain. When goods are issued, the *inventory record card* is adjusted to show the decrease in inventory.

On receipt of the purchase order, the supplier sends the goods to the purchaser with an accompanying *delivery note*. The purchaser signs the delivery note and returns it to the supplier as proof of receipt. Next, the supplier issues an *invoice* showing the amount the purchaser will have to pay. If the purchaser is dissatisfied with any of the goods and returns them, the supplier issues a *credit note*. This shows the value of the goods returned, which the purchaser will not have to pay. If the supplier receives many orders from the same purchaser, rather than requiring payment of each invoice individually, the supplier may issue a monthly statement summarizing the invoices and credit notes during the month and showing the balance due.

In addition to recording transactions for goods, a business must record labour costs. In the manufacturing industry it was traditional to use *clock cards* to record the time spent at work by employees and *job cards* to record the amount of time spent on each job. The job cards were then reconciled with the clock cards. The wages office then prepared the *payroll* by calculating the wages from the time clock cards for the workers paid on a time basis and from the job cards if there was an incentive scheme. Today the information is likely to be recorded in a computerized information system. In the service industry, *time sheets* may be used to record how much time has been spent on each job so that clients can be charged for the time spent on their work.

Activity

Design a flow diagram to illustrate the external and internal movement of source documents that are raised when a business purchases goods from a supplier on credit.

In constructing your diagram, you will have experienced some of the difficulties in establishing and maintaining business information systems. It is necessary to ensure that each stage of the process is monitored, that the appropriate personnel are kept informed and that the records are correctly referenced and dated. The system needs to be designed so that if there is an error or a query, the appropriate source document can be traced and the problem resolved.

Figure 3.2 provides an overview of the accounting process. You are already familiar with the first stage from the definition of accounting you learned in Chapter 1. In this chapter we will cover the second and third stages of recording the economic transactions and preparing a trial balance. We will explain how the different financial statements are prepared in the chapters that follow.

Figure 3.2 Overview of the accounting process

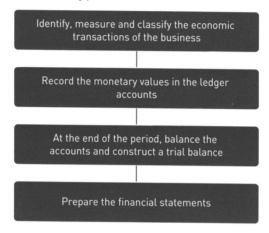

3.3.3 Double-entry bookkeeping

Some small entities keep a simple cash-based accounting system, but many businesses record transactions using a system known as *double-entry bookkeeping*. A double-entry bookkeeping system is based on the principle that every financial transaction involves the simultaneous receiving and giving of value. Therefore, every transaction needs to be recorded at least twice in the accounting system. This reflects the dual nature of economic transactions and ensures that an arithmetical check is made on the accuracy of the records. It is widely used because it is the most efficient and effective method for recording financial transactions in a way that allows financial statements to be prepared easily. The financial statements summarize the transactions that have taken place during a particular period of time.

Key definition

Double-entry bookkeeping is an accounting system based on the principle that every financial transaction involves the simultaneous receiving and giving of value and therefore needs to be recorded in at least two accounts.

History of double-entry bookkeeping

According to Nobes and Kellas (1990), the use of double-entry bookkeeping dates from the early fourteenth century when records show that it had been adopted by Italian merchants in Provence, London and the city of Genoa. It became known as the 'Italian method', and was brought to a wider audience when Luca Pacioli published his highly influential book, *Summa de arithmetica, geometria, proportioni e proportionalità*, in Venice in 1494. The double-entry system of debits and credits described by Pacioli underpins the double-entry booking system we use today.

In order to understand accounting and the principles of double-entry book-keeping, you need to remember that the business is a separate entity from its owner(s) when it carries out transactions. Therefore, it can have dealings with the owner(s). All businesses need resources and these are known as *assets*. Assets are what the business owns, such as premises, machinery, vehicles, equipment, inventory and cash. *Liabilities* are what the business owes to others apart from the owners, such as money owed to lenders and suppliers. What remains once the liabilities are subtracted from the assets is known as *equity*. Equity represents the owners' interest in the business and can be divided into the capital invested in the business by the owner(s) plus retained earnings (profits left in the business to help it grow). These explanations will help you understand the formal definitions below.

Key definitions

An asset is a present economic resource controlled by the entity as a result of past events.

An economic resource is a right that has the potential to produce economic benefits.

A liability is a present obligation of the entity to transfer an economic resource as a result of past events.

Equity is the residual interest in the assets of the entity after deducting all its liabilities.

Source: IASB, 2015 [4.4]. Reproduced with permission from the IFRS Foundation.

The relationship between the assets, liabilities and equity forms what is known as the *accounting equation*:

$$\text{Assets} = \text{Equity} + \text{Liabilities}$$

The accounting equation reflects the dual nature of business transactions by stating that the assets of the entity are always equal to the claims against them: the equity and other liabilities. The point about any equation is that it balances; in other words, the total of the values on each side of the equation are equal. The accounting equation lies at the heart of double-entry bookkeeping.

Activity

A business has capital of £20,000 and assets of £20,000. It then borrows £10,000 from the bank to finance the purchase of some new office equipment. How does this affect the accounting equation?

In this case the business has assets of £20,000 which will increase by £10,000 (the new equipment), making total assets of £30,000. At the same time, it will increase its liabilities by £10,000 (the bank loan) while the equity, representing the capital of £20,000, remains unchanged. The accounting equation still balances as shown below:

Assets	=	Equity	+	Liabilities
£		£		£
20,000		20,000		10,000
10,000				
30,000		20,000		10,000

You need to remember that in double-entry bookkeeping, every economic transaction of the business is recorded twice to keep the accounting equation balanced. This provides an arithmetical check on the records, which enables the business to be controlled. If a manual system is kept, the bookkeeper records the business transactions in the *ledgers*, which are books of accounts (hence, the term *bookkeeping*). Accounts for each different type of transaction are kept on separate pages in the ledger. The bookkeeper records every transaction as a *debit* entry in an account that receives the value of the transaction and as a *credit* entry in an account that gives the value of the transaction. The following illustration of one page shows the layout.

Name of the account

Date	Details of debit entries	£ Amount	Date	Details of credit entries	£ Amount

As you can see, the page is divided into two, with three columns on each side. Debit entries are shown on the left-hand side of the account and credit entries on the right. On each side there is a column for the date, details of the transaction and the amount involved. Because of their layout, ledger accounts are often referred to as *T accounts*.

3.4 Recording economic transactions

3.4.1 Recording assets and liabilities

The double-entry bookkeeping system provides rules for recording each different type of transaction in the ledger accounts. The rules for recording transactions concerning assets and liabilities are as follows:

- To show an increase in an asset account, debit the account.
- To show a decrease in an asset account, credit the account.
- To show an increase in a capital or liability account, credit the account.
- To show a decrease in a capital or liability account, debit the account.

To illustrate these rules, we will use an example. Mulch Garden Design Ltd was set up on 1 January this year. The owner, Nick Mulch, has invested £5,000 in the company. His girlfriend, Louise, has given the business a loan of £2,000. All the money is kept in the bank. To record these transactions, we need to open three accounts: a *capital account* for the money invested by the owner; a *loan account* for the loan; and a *bank account* to show the bank transactions. There are two transactions to record: the amount invested by Nick and the loan given by Louise. Each transaction will require a debit entry to be made to one account and a corresponding credit entry of the same amount in another account.

Capital account

		£			£
			1 January	Bank	5,000

Loan account

		£			£
			1 January	Bank	2,000

Bank account

		£			£
1 January	Capital	5,000			
1 January	Loan	2,000			

If you study these accounts, you can see that the rules for recording transactions have been stringently applied. The investment of £5,000 by the owner has been shown as a credit in the capital account. Because the assets of the business have increased by this amount, the corresponding debit entry is in the bank account. When Louise gave the £2,000 loan to the business, its liabilities increased, so the loan account was credited with this amount. The corresponding debit entry is in the bank account, since the loan means an increase in the assets of the business. As you can see, for each transaction you need to record the date, the name of the account where the corresponding entry is made and the amount. This allows you to trace it at a later date if you have any problems with the records.

We will now look at the transactions made on 2 January. Using the company's cheque book, Nick pays £3,000 for the premises, £1,000 for machinery and £500 for office equipment. The bank account is already open, but we need to open three new asset accounts to record these transactions:

Bank account

		£			£
1 January	Capital	5,000	2 January	Premises	3,000
1 January	Loan	2,000	2 January	Machinery	1,000
			2 January	Equipment	500

Premises account

		£			£
2 January	Bank	3,000			

Machinery account

		£			£
2 January	Bank	1,000			

Office equipment account

		£			£
2 January	Bank	500			

These records reflect the transactions that have taken place. For example, the bank account is an asset account. When the business received the investment of £5,000 from Nick and the loan from Louise, these amounts were debited to the bank account to show the increase in assets represented by the amount of money held at the bank. When the business paid for items such as the machinery, the bank account was credited. If you take the total of all the debit entries in the bank account and deduct the total of all the credit entries, the resulting figure is £2,500, which is the amount of money the business now has left at the bank.

Activity

Mulch Garden Design Ltd repays £1,500 of the loan to Louise on 3 January and on the same day returns £250 worth of faulty equipment to the supplier and receives a refund. Nick pays the refund into the bank. Enter these transactions in the ledger accounts.

The updated accounts should look like this.

Bank account

		£			£
1 January	Capital	5,000	2 January	Premises	3,000
1 January	Loan	2,000	2 January	Machinery	1,000
3 January	Equipment	250	2 January	Equipment	500
			3 January	Loan	1,500

Loan account

		£			£
3 January	Bank	1,500	1 January	Bank	2,000

Office equipment account

		£			£
2 January	Bank	500	3 January	Bank	250

3.4.2 Recording revenue and expenses

A business also needs ledger accounts for recording *revenue* and *expenses*. Revenue is the income the business receives from the sale of goods or services to customers. However, the business may also receive non-sales revenue, such as interest and dividends on investments or rents received. Expenses are the monetary value of the costs and other expenditure incurred by the business in order to obtain its income. You need to learn the formal definitions for these terms.

Key definitions

Income is defined as increases in assets or decreases in liabilities that result in increases in equity, other than those relating to contributions from holders of equity claims.

Expenses are defined as decreases in assets or increases in liabilities that result in decreases in equity, other than those relating to distributions to holders of equity claims.

Source: IASB, 2015 [4.4]. Reproduced with permission from the IFRS Foundation.

The double-entry bookkeeping rules for recording transactions involving revenue and expenses are as follows:

- To show an increase in an expense account, debit the account.
- To show a decrease in an expense account, credit the account.
- To show an increase in a revenue account, credit the account.
- To show a decrease in a revenue account, debit the account.

As required in double-entry bookkeeping, every transaction will involve making a credit entry to one account and a debit entry to another account. We will start by explaining what is meant by an increase in an expense account and an increase in a revenue account.

On 4 January Mulch Garden Design Ltd spends £200 on advertising in the form of printed leaflets and £20 on posting them to potential customers. Prior to this date the company has not incurred any expenses, so the monetary value was nil. Now it has incurred some expenses and we need to show the increase in the appropriate accounts.

Bank account

		£			£
1 January	Capital	5,000	2 January	Premises	3,000
1 January	Loan	2,000	2 January	Machinery	1,000
3 January	Equipment	250	2 January	Equipment	500
			3 January	Loan	1,500
			4 January	Advertising	200
			4 January	Postage	20

Advertising account

		£			£
4 January	Bank	200			

Postage account

		£			£
4 January	Bank	20			

As the business has paid for the advertising leaflets and postage, its cash assets at the bank must have decreased by the amount of these expenses. Therefore, these two transactions resulted in debit entries to the expense accounts and both were credited to the bank account.

Activity

On 5 January Mulch Garden Design Ltd pays £50 for the cleaning of the premises. On 6 January the company allows its display gardens to be used as a venue for a wedding reception and receives £350 in rent. Make the necessary entries in the appropriate revenue and expense accounts.

You should not have had too much difficulty with this activity. The cleaning expenses were a pair of straightforward entries. The receipt of rent may have caused you to think because we have not illustrated any similar transactions. However, as long as you remembered the rule that you show an increase in revenues by crediting the revenue account (in this case, rent received), the corresponding entry had to be to debit the bank account to show an increase in cash assets of £350. The updated accounts should look like this.

Bank account

		£			£
1 January	Capital	5,000	2 January	Premises	3,000
1 January	Loan	2,000	2 January	Machinery	1,000
3 January	Equipment	250	2 January	Equipment	500
6 January	Rent received	350	3 January	Loan	1,500
			4 January	Advertising	200
			4 January	Postage	20
			5 January	Cleaning	50

Cleaning account

		£			£
5 January	Bank	50			

Rent received account

		£			£
			6 January	Bank	350

3.4.3 Recording purchases, sales and inventory

In a trading business, it is not much use advertising goods for sale unless the business has purchased goods to sell and it is necessary to open a *purchases account*, where purchases are recorded as a debit entry. However, when the business sells the goods they are not shown as a credit entry in the purchases account for two reasons. First, they will not be sold at the price for which they were purchased, as the business adds a mark-up in order to make a profit and therefore we do not want to lose this information. The second reason is that at the end of an accounting period it is likely that there will be some *inventory* (unsold goods). This inventory requires special treatment which we shall be describing at the end of this section.

Instead of crediting sales to the purchases account, a sales account is opened. If the goods are sold to customers for cash, the sale is shown as a credit in the sales account and the corresponding entry is a debit in the bank account. The latter entry reflects the increase in cash assets held at the bank.

We need to look at a new example to show how this is done. Katey Burton opened a boutique called Kool Kate Ltd on 1 July 2017 by investing £10,000 in the business. On that day the business buys equipment costing £1,000, purchases of inventory costing £4,000 and pays £500 in advertising expenses. On 2 July she makes sales amounting to £2,800 and buys a second-hand car for business use for £4,000. On 3 July she makes sales totalling of £3,500 and purchases further inventory for £2,000. The entries in the accounts are shown below.

Capital account

		£			£
			1 July	Bank	10,000

Bank account

		£			£
1 July	Capital	10,000	1 July	Equipment	1,000
2 July	Sales	2,800	1 July	Purchases	4,000
3 July	Sales	3,500	1 July	Advertising	500
			2 July	Vehicles	4,000
			3 July	Purchases	2,000

Equipment account

		£			£
1 July	Bank	1,000			

Advertising account

		£			£
1 July	Bank	500			

Purchases account

		£			£
1 July	Bank	4,000			
3 July	Bank	2,000			

Sales account

		£			£
			2 July	Bank	2,800
			3 July	Bank	3,500

Vehicles account

		£			£
2 July	Bank	4,000			

In this example we have referred to the goods that the business is buying and selling as *inventory*. However, we will not use an inventory account until the end of the accounting period, as we will explain in a moment. Instead, the purchases and sales of goods have been recorded in separate accounts: the *purchases account* and the *sales account*. Accountants use the term *purchases* to refer only to the purchase of goods for resale in a trading business or to the purchase of materials used to produce goods for sale in a manufacturing business. Do not confuse this with the acquisition of other assets, such as vehicles and equipment, which are not intended for resale but will stay in the business in the long term to help generate revenue.

There is one final aspect of the purchase and sale of goods that we need to consider. Sometimes a business purchases goods, but has returned some of them to the supplier because they are faulty, or for other reasons. Alternatively, a customer sometimes returns goods to the business. The first transaction requires a *returns outward account* (also known as a *purchases returns account*) to be opened. The second transaction requires a *returns inward account* (also known as a *sales returns account*) to be opened.

The following example illustrates the returns outward account. On 1 July Kool Kate Ltd purchases goods from a supplier, but later a £200 suit was found to be faulty. It was returned to the supplier on 12 July and a refund of £200 was received the same day. These transactions are recorded as follows:

Bank account

		£			£
1 July	Capital	10,000	1 July	Equipment	1,000
2 July	Sales	2,800	1 July	Purchases	4,000
3 July	Sales	3,500	1 July	Advertising	500
12 July	Returns outward	200	2 July	Vehicles	4,000
			3 July	Purchases	2,000

Returns outward account

		£			£
			12 July	Bank	200

As you can see, the bank account has been debited to show the increase in cash assets due to the cash refund by the supplier, but rather than crediting the purchases account to record the goods which were returned, a returns outward account has been opened and this provides an accurate record of what has happened.

Activity

The same principles are applied if one of the customers returns goods. Show how the transactions would be recorded in the ledger accounts if a customer returns £500 worth of goods to Kool Kate Ltd on 14 July and is given a refund the same day.

The transactions would be recorded as shown below.

Bank account

		£			£
1 July	Capital	10,000	1 July	Equipment	1,000
2 July	Sales	2,800	1 July	Purchases	4,000
3 July	Sales	3,500	1 July	Advertising	500
12 July	Returns outward	200	2 July	Vehicles	4,000
			3 July	Purchases	2,000
			14 July	Returns inward	500

Returns inward account

		£			£
14 July	Bank	500			

3.4.4 Credit transactions

All the receipts and payments in the examples we have used so far have been for cash. However, many economic transactions are *credit transactions* and the receipt or payment of cash does not take place until a later date. This requires accounts to be opened for *trade receivables* to record the amounts owed by customers who have bought goods or services on credit and who owe the business money. Accounts also need to be opened for *trade payables* to record the amounts due to be paid to suppliers from whom the business has bought goods or services on credit and to whom the business owes money. Trade receivables are classified as assets of the business and trade payables are classified as liabilities. Therefore, the rules of double-entry book-keeping for making entries in asset and liability accounts apply to trade receivables and trade payables respectively.

First, we will consider an example where a customer has been sold goods on credit. Suppose the clothes sold by Kool Kate Ltd for £2,800 on 2 July were credit sales to a customer called Pippa Merton. The entry in the sales account will still be a credit, but instead of debiting the bank account to show an increase in cash assets, we need to open an account for Pippa Merton and debit that account to show an increase in the trade receivables asset. The entries in the accounts are as follows.

Sales account

		£			£
			2 July	Pippa Merton	2,800

Pippa Merton account (trade receivables)

		£			£
2 July	Sales	2,800			

Because Pippa Merton is a trade receivable account, we have followed the rules for all asset accounts. Before 2 July, Pippa owed the company nothing, but after the sales transaction on that date, she owed Kool Kate Ltd £2,800. The increase in trade receivables is shown by debiting the Pippa Merton account. The trade receivables account has been opened in Pippa Merton's name so that a record can be kept of who owes money to Kool Kate Ltd.

Activity

On 20 July Pippa Merton pays £750 of the money she owed to Kool Kate Ltd. Show how this transaction will be recorded in the accounts.

The accounts will be amended as follows.

Bank account

		£			£
1 July	Capital	10,000	1 July	Equipment	1,000
3 July	Sales	3,500	1 July	Purchases	4,000
12 July	Returns outward	200	1 July	Advertising	500
20 July	Pippa Merton	750	2 July	Vehicles	4,000
			3 July	Purchases	2,000
			14 July	Returns inward	500

Pippa Merton account (trade receivables)

		£			£
2 July	Sales	2,800	20 July	Bank	750

As you can see, cash assets have increased by £750 and the asset of trade receivables has decreased by the same amount. Note that in the bank account there is no entry on 2 July for sales of £2,800 because Pippa Merton did not pay cash but took the goods on credit. Therefore, the debit entry is to the Pippa Merton account and the sales account remains unchanged.

Next, we consider a case where the business has not paid cash but has obtained goods or services on credit. In such a case the business has acquired a liability and you will need to use the double-entry rules for increasing and decreasing liability accounts. On 26 July Kool Kate Ltd purchases goods for £1,500 on credit from a supplier, Patel & Co. On 28 July Kool Kate Ltd pays the amount in full. The transactions are recorded as shown below.

Purchases account

		£			£
1 July	Bank	4,000			
3 July	Bank	2,000			
26 July	Patel & Co	1,500			

Patel & Co account (trade payables)

		£			£
28 July	Bank	1,500	26 July	Purchases	1,500

Bank account

		£			£
1 July	Capital	10,000	1 July	Equipment	1,000
3 July	Sales	3,500	1 July	Purchases	4,000
12 July	Returns outward	200	1 July	Advertising expenses	500
20 July	Pippa Merton	750	2 July	Vehicles	4,000
			3 July	Purchases	2,000
			14 July	Returns inward	500
			28 July	Patel & Co	1,500

While working through the activities in this chapter, you may have noticed how easy it is to make a mistake and enter a transaction on the wrong side of an account. Although you may have found the process somewhat tedious, the activities help you understand the principles of double-entry bookkeeping, which can be summarized as follows:

- A transaction that represents an increase in purchases, expenses or assets is recorded as a debit entry on the left-hand side of the ledger account.
- A transaction that represents an increase in revenue, liabilities or sales is recorded as a credit entry on the right-hand side of the ledger account.

The pearls of wisdom shown in Figure 3.3 have been passed on by students across the decades. They will help you remember the rules of double-entry bookkeeping:

Figure 3.3   Pearls of wisdom

PEA | RLS

This mnemonic is set out as a T account and reminds you that an increase in Purchases, Expenses or Assets is a debit entry shown on the left-hand side, while an increase in Revenue, Liabilities or Sales is a credit entry shown on the right-hand side.

The illustrations in Figure 3.4 show how you would keep the accounting records for Kool Kate Ltd for the month of July using Excel.

Figure 3.4   Excel accounting records for Kool Kate Ltd

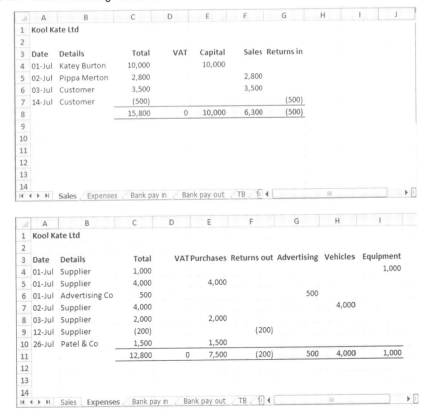

	A	B	C	D	E	F	G	H	I	J
1	Kool Kate Ltd									
2										
3	Date	Details	Total	Capital	Sales	Returns out				
4	01-Jul	Katey Burton	10,000	10,000						
5	02-Jul	Pippa Merton	750		750					
6	03-Jul	Customer	3,500		3,500					
7	12-Jul	Supplier	200			200				
8			14,450	10,000	4,250	200				
9										
10										
11										
12										
13										
14										

Sales / Expenses / **Bank pay in** / Bank pay out / TB

	A	B	C	D	E	F	G	H	I	J
1	Kool Kate Ltd									
2										
3	Date	Details	Total	Purchases	Returns in	Advertising	Vehicles	Equipment		
4	01-Jul	Company	1,000					1,000		
5	01-Jul	Supplier	4,000	4,000						
6	01-Jul	Advertising Co	500			500				
7	02-Jul	Supplier	4,000				4,000			
8	03-Jul	Supplier	2,000	2,000						
9	14-Jul	Customer	500		500					
10	28-Jul	Patel & Co	1,500	1,500						
11			13,500	7,500	500	500	4,000	1,000		
12										
13										
14										

Sales / Expenses / Bank pay in / **Bank pay out** / TB

3.5   Preparing a trial balance

At the end of the accounting period the ledger accounts are balanced and the balances are used to construct a trial balance, which lists the debit balances in one column and the credit balances in the other.

3.5.1   Balancing the accounts

The rules for balancing the ledger accounts are very straightforward:

1 If the total amounts on each side of the account are equal, they are double underlined to close the account. This means that there is no outstanding balance on the account at the end of the accounting period. Kool Kate Ltd's trade payables account for Patel & Co is an example of this.

Patel & Co account

		£			£
28 July	Bank	1,500	26 July	Purchases	1,500

2 If the account contains only one entry, insert the figure required to make the account balance on the opposite side and label it *carried forward* (or the abbreviation *c/f*). Insert the same balancing figure on the same side as the original entry to start the next period, labelling it *brought forward* (or the abbreviation *b/f*). Kool Kate Ltd's vehicle account provides an example of this. We are still complying with the rules of double-entry bookkeeping since, as you can see, for every debit entry there is a corresponding credit entry. Therefore, to balance the account, we have credited the account with a closing balance of £4,000 and debited the account an opening balance of the same amount.

Vehicle account

		£			£
2 July	Bank	4,000	31 July	Balance c/f	4,000
1 August	Balance b/f	4,000			

3 If the account contains a number of entries, add up both sides. If both sides are the same, insert the totals and double underline them. This means that there is no outstanding balance on the account. An extension of Kool Kate Ltd's trade receivable account for Pippa Merton provides an example of this.

Pippa Merton account

		£			£
2 July	Sales	2,800	20 July	Bank	750
5 July	Sales	200	28 July	Bank	2,550
12 July	Sales	300			
		3,300			3,300

4 If both sides are not the same when you add them up, use the larger figure as the total for both sides and then insert the balancing figure to the side that originally had the smaller total. Complete the entry by bringing forward the balancing figure on the opposite side to become the opening balance for the next accounting period. Kool Kate Ltd's bank account is an example of this.

Bank account

		£			£
1 July	Capital	10,000	1 July	Equipment	1,000
3 July	Sales	3,500	1 July	Purchases	4,000
12 July	Returns outward	200	1 July	Advertising	500
20 July	Pippa Merton	750	2 July	Car	4,000
28 July	Pippa Merton	2,550	3 July	Purchases	2,000
			14 July	Returns inward	500
			28 July	Patel & Co	1,500
			31 July	Balance c/f	3,500
		17,000			17,000
1 August	Balance b/f	3,500			

You can see that the balance c/f refers to the balance at the end of the accounting period (in this case, at the end of July) and the balance b/f refers to the balance at the start of the next period (in this case, the start of August).

Activity

Calculate the closing balances of the remaining accounts for Kool Kate Ltd. These are the capital account, the sales account, the purchases account, the equipment account, the returns inward account, the returns outward account and the advertising account.

You should not have had too much difficulty with this activity if you followed the rules. You can check your answer in the next section where the closing balances are used to construct the trial balance.

When all the ledger accounts have been balanced off, some of them will have been closed completely and will show no balance brought down to commence the next accounting period, whereas others will show either a debit or a credit balance. The debit balances normally represent the assets and expenses of the business and the credit balances normally represent the capital, revenue and liabilities of the business. The list of balances at a particular point in time is known as a *trial balance*.

Key definition

A trial balance is a list of the balances on all the accounts in a double-entry bookkeeping system that shows the debit balances in the left-hand column and credit balances in the right-hand column. If the principles of double-entry bookkeeping have been followed and the records are accurate, the totals of each column should be the same.

If you have made a debit entry for every credit entry and vice versa, the total of the debit balances should be equal to the total of the credit balances; in other words, your trial balance should balance. If they are not the same, you will need to look for the cause by checking the bookkeeping entries in the ledger accounts. It may require a number of trials to get the two columns to balance. When you have achieved this, you will have evidence of the arithmetical accuracy of the record keeping. Some adjustments to the trial balance figures may be necessary to take account of closing inventory, accruals, prepayments, depreciation and doubtful debts, after which the figures are used to prepare the financial statements. We will explain how this is done in subsequent chapters.

Continuing to use the example of Kool Kate Ltd, we can now calculate the closing balances for the accounts at the end of the month and construct a trial balance. As you can see, if the balance b/f on the account is a debit balance, it is shown in the debit column in the trial balance; if the balance b/f on the account is a credit balance, it is shown in the credit column in the trial balance.

Kool Kate Ltd

Trial balance as at 31 July 2017

	Debit £	Credit £
Capital at 1 July 2017		10,000
Revenue		6,800
Purchases	7,500	
Cash at bank	3,500	
Vehicles	4,000	
Equipment	1,000	
Returns inward	500	
Returns outward		200
Advertising	500	
	17,000	17,000

Note: Inventory at 31 July 2017 was £4,000

You will see that at the end of the trial balance there is a note stating that the business has *closing inventory* of £4,000 at 31 July. This is not surprising because the business needs to have a certain amount of inventory on the last day of the accounting period ready to sell on the first day of the next accounting period. Thus, closing inventory at the end of one period becomes the *opening inventory* at the beginning of the next period.

In order to value closing inventory, a physical count of goods is carried out (usually at the year end or on a random basis throughout the year) to compare the quantities counted with the records. This is referred to as *inventory counting*. Once the quantity of each type of goods in stock is known, the value of this inventory can be calculated by multiplying the quantity by the original purchase price. This complies with the *historical cost concept*. However, some goods may be worth less than their original cost due to changes in taste, technological obsolescence or other factors that have reduced market demand. In such cases the goods should be valued at the *net realizable value*. The net realizable value is the price the business expects to get for the inventory less any costs incurred in selling it. We look at this again in Chapter 6.

Activity

A business purchased 100 items at £2 each with a view to selling them at £2.40 each. At the end of the year 20 items remained unsold. Due to a decline in demand, the business can now sell them for only £1.50 each. Calculate the value of the closing inventory.

You may have calculated the closing inventory as 20 items at £2 each (£40) but the value of the closing inventory is 20 items at £1.50 each (£30) because this represents the net realizable value, which is lower than the original cost.

3.5.2   Other transactions

You will remember that Kool Kate Ltd was started on 1 July and we drew up the trial balance at the end of the first month's trading on 31 July. We are now going to extend that simple example and prepare a trial balance at the end of the first six months of trading. This allows us to introduce a number of other transactions. Instead of drawing up separate accounts using double-entry bookkeeping, we are going to focus on the nature of the transaction. However, the principles of double-entry bookkeeping still apply.

- *Carriage inward* and *carriage outward* – The business may have to pay delivery charges for raw materials or goods, and this is sometimes referred to as *carriage inward*. It is an expense of the business and therefore appears in the debit column of the trial balance. Carriage inward is regarded as part of the cost of purchasing the raw materials or goods. Sometimes the business has to bear the cost of delivery of its goods to customers, and this is known as *carriage outward*. This is also an expense and appears in the debit column of the trial balance.
- *Discounts allowed* and *discounts received* – When a business purchases goods it may be able to negotiate a trade discount and pay slightly less than the normal price. In such a case only the net price (the price after discount) is entered into

the accounts. Another form of discount sometimes available is a cash discount to encourage customers to pay promptly. When a business offers a cash discount to customers it is referred to in the supplier's accounts as discounts allowed. It is treated as an expense of the business and appears in the debit column of the trial balance. When a business receives cash discounts from its suppliers they are referred to in the customer's accounts as discounts received and appear in the credit column of the trial balance.

- *Petty cash* – As well as maintaining a bank account, a business may keep a very small amount of cash on the premises, known as petty cash. This is used to pay miscellaneous expenses, such as window cleaning, travelling expenses or the milk bill. A cash account must always appear in the debit column of the trial balance because it is an asset. The balance shown on a ledger account for bank transactions appears in the debit column of the trial balance if the

Activity

On 31 December 2017, after the first six months of trading, Kool Kate Ltd has 180 items that cost £20 each and can be sold for £45 each, and 200 items that cost £14 each and can be sold for £16 each. The account balances at 31 December 2016 were as follows.

	£
Capital at 1 July 2017	10,000
Revenue	52,400
Salaries	14,400
Purchases	38,700
Cash in hand	300
Bank overdraft	2,800
Vehicles	4,000
Equipment	1,000
Returns inward	900
Returns outward	800
Advertising	3,400
Carriage inward	960
Discounts allowed	1,200
Discounts received	680
Telephone	600
Shop overheads	1,220

Prepare a trial balance for Kool Kate Ltd at 31 December 2017.

business has cash at the bank, as it is an asset. However, if the business has an overdraft, the balance appears in the credit column of the trial balance because it is a liability.

- *Non-sales revenue* – In addition to revenue arising from the sale of goods and services, a business may have income in the form of interest, dividends, royalties, rent, etc. It is important that these items are recorded separately. You will remember that all revenue is shown in the credit column of the trial balance.

We have already mentioned that the inventory account is somewhat special and that separate accounts are maintained for purchases and revenue. When constructing a trial balance, it is usual to show the figure for *closing inventory* as a footnote because it will be needed for preparing the financial statements.

Your completed trial balance should look like this:

Kool Kate Ltd

Trial balance at 31 December 2017

	Debit £	Credit £
Capital at 1 July 2017		10,000
Revenue		52,400
Salaries	14,400	
Purchases	38,700	
Cash	300	
Bank		2,800
Vehicles	4,000	
Equipment	1,000	
Returns inward	900	
Returns outward		800
Advertising	3,400	
Carriage inward	960	
Discounts allowed	1,200	
Discounts received		680
Telephone and Internet	600	
Shop overheads	1,220	
	66,680	66,680

Note: Inventory at 31 December 2017 was £6,400

If you had any difficulty with this activity, you may find it useful to think of the mnemonic PEARLS again.

The illustration in Figure 3.5 shows how you would generate the trial balance for Kool Kate Ltd for the month of July using Excel. As you can see, you simply need to add the post trial balance adjustments to arrive at the adjusted figures.

Figure 3.5 Excel trial balance for Kool Kate Ltd

	A	B	C	D	E	F	G	H	I	J	K	L
1	Kool Kate Ltd											
2												
3		Opening balance		Movement		Closing balance		Adjustment		Adjusted balance		
4		Dr	Cr	Dr	Cr	Dr	Cr	Dr	Cr	Dr	Cr	
5	Equipment			1,000		1,000						
6	Vehicles			4,000		4,000						
7	Bank			14,450	13,500	950						
8	Receiveables			6,300	4,250	2,050						
9	Payables											
10	Sales				6,300		6,300					
11	Returns in				(500)		(500)					
12	Purchases			7,500		7,500						
13	Returns out			(200)		(200)						
14	Advertising			500		500						
15												
16	Capital				10,000		10,000					
17												
18		0	0	33,550	33,550	15,800	15,800	0	0	0	0	
19												
20												

Sales / Expenses / Bank pay in / Bank pay out / TB

3.6 Limitations of a trial balance

A trial balance can only detect arithmetical errors as it is simply a list of the debit balances and credit balances on the ledger accounts at the end of the accounting period. If the principles of double-entry bookkeeping have been followed with a debit entry for every credit entry, the sum of the debit column in the trial balance will be the same as the sum of the credit column. If they do not balance, checks must be made to identify the reasons for any discrepancies. A common error is to transpose numbers; for example, writing £320 instead of £230. To find out whether this is the reason for your trial balance not balancing, calculate the difference between the total of the debit and credit columns on the trial balance. If this figure is divisible by 9, you have probably transposed a number somewhere and you should check for this error.

Activity

If the trial balance balances, it does not necessarily mean that the figures are correct. What other mistakes could have been made in the recording of transactions that would not be revealed by a trial balance?

You may have thought of the following errors that are not revealed in a trial balance:

- Omission – the transaction has not been recorded in the accounts at all.
- Wrong account – the transaction has been recorded in the wrong account (for example, in the vehicles account instead of the equipment account or in an asset account instead of a liability account).
- Wrong amount – the transaction has been recorded in the correct accounts, but the wrong amount was entered.
- Reverse entry – the transaction has been recorded in the correct accounts, but on the wrong side of both accounts.

The accuracy of the records in the accounting system is important as the balances shown in the trial balance are used as the basis for the financial statements that are prepared at the end of the accounting period. In a new business, it is likely that an external accountant will have given advice on an appropriate accounting system and may have supplied other services such as bookkeeping and accounts preparation. Even in a small business, the accounting system should incorporate internal controls to minimize opportunities for fraud and theft. Examples include requiring more than one signature on key documents, use of passwords for access to computer files and keeping control accounts that act as a crosscheck on the accuracy of subsidiary records. Larger businesses are likely to have an internal audit function that carries out checks to ensure that its internal controls are operating satisfactorily.

3.7   Conclusions

This chapter has introduced you to the fundamental accounting principles that underpin financial accounting. Large organizations carry out thousands of transactions every day and need sophisticated, computerized accounting systems. Most small and medium-sized businesses use spreadsheets, such as Microsoft® Excel, or an accounting package, such as SAGE. Whether the system is computerized or manual, it is normally based on the principles of double-entry bookkeeping. This is the most efficient and effective method for recording transactions and events in a way that allows the balances on each ledger account to be summarized in a trial balance at the end of the accounting period.

The trial balance acts as a check on the mathematical accuracy of the record keeping. However, there are some limitations to the trial balance because it does not show other errors that might have occurred. Once all errors have been checked and corrected and the two columns agree, the figures in the trial balance are used as the basis for preparing the financial statements. After we have given you an overview of the regulations and theoretical concepts that underpin financial reporting in the next two chapters, we will show you how to prepare the financial statements.

References

IASB (2014) IAS 1, *Presentation of Financial Statements* (as amended at January 2014), London: IFRS Foundation.

IASB (2015) *Exposure Draft Conceptual Framework for Financial Reporting*, ED/2015/3, London: IFRS Foundation.

International Accountant (2015) 'Small businesses still using inefficient accounting methods', *International Accountant*, September/October, p. 5.

Nobes, C. and Kellas, J. (1990) *Accountancy Explained*, London: Penguin Books.

Discussion questions

1 Discuss the two underlying assumptions that underpin financial accounting: the accrual principle and the going concern principle.

2 Discuss the advantages of a double-entry bookkeeping system and the limitations of a trial balance.

Practice questions

3 Rex Wellworth started Wellworth Fencing Ltd with £50,000 he inherited from his uncle. On 1 June he opened a bank account for the business and paid in the capital he has invested in the business. On the same day he wrote business cheques to buy a lorry for £16,000, to pay £1,400 to insure the lorry and to pay £4,500 for three months' rent on premises in advance. On 2 June he wrote three business cheques: £5,400 to pay for equipment; £850 to pay for fencing materials from Timber Supplies; and £420 to pay for advertising expenses. On 4 June the business bought a further £120 of fencing materials on credit from Timber Supplies Ltd.

Required

Write up the ledger accounts for Wellworth Fencing Ltd.

4   Mrs Lawley owns a gift shop business called Lavender & Lace Ltd. On 4 July the company's cash account looked like this:

Cash account

		£			£
1 July	Opening balance	500	1 July	Postage	25
2 July	Cash sales	138	1 July	Window cleaning	10
3 July	Cash sales	192	1 July	Stationery	15
			1 July	Parking	2
			1 July	Stationery	36
			1 July	Petrol	18
			2 July	Parking	2
			2 July	Postage	31
			2 July	Purchases	104
			3 July	Parking	2
			3 July	Petrol	18
			3 July	Purchases	89

Required

Write up the ledger accounts for Lavender & Lace Ltd to show the corresponding entries.

5   The following bank account shows transactions for the bookshop owned by Burton & Son Ltd for the month of October.

Bank account

		£			£
1 October	Balance b/f	6,400	2 October	Purchases	750
12 October	Sales	1,800	3 October	Advertising	1,120
15 October	Jones Ltd	950	16 October	Purchases	2,300
18 October	Jones Ltd	950	18 October	Davies Ltd	780
30 October	Revenue	1,450	25 October	Purchases	3,400

Required

Balance the account at 31 October and show the balance c/f at 1 November.

6   The following account is that of Lambrook Ltd, a credit customer of Burton & Son Ltd.

Lambrook Ltd				
		£		£
2 November	Sales	850		
12 November	Sales	1,650		
18 November	Sales	260		
21 November	Sales	400		
25 November	Sales	640		

Required

On 30 November Lambrook Ltd pays 50% of the amount due. Record this transaction and balance the account.

7 The following list of balances at 30 June 2017 is taken from the accounts of Hampton Health Food Ltd.

Hampton Health Food Ltd	
	£
Revenue	26,200
Purchases	?
Returns inward	900
Returns outward	460
Discounts allowed	720
Discounts received	620
Equipment	2,000
Bank	1,500
Salaries	1,600
Rent	1,400
General expenses	390
Capital at 1 July 2016	18,000

Required

Calculate the figure for purchases and prepare a trial balance at 30 June 2017 for Hampton Health Food Ltd.

8 During the year ending 31 December 2017, Country Furniture Ltd achieved sales that were three times higher than total purchases. Operating expenses were 25% of total purchases. On 31 December 2017 the business had £4,000 in the bank and this was half the amount it had incurred in operating expenses. Premises were acquired for £75,000 and one-third of this was financed by a mortgage. Inventory at the beginning of the year was the equivalent of two months' revenue from sales.

Required

Calculate the figure for capital at 1 January 2017 and prepare a trial balance for Country Furniture Ltd at 31 December 2017.

 ## Suggested research questions for dissertation students

Students interested in accounting information systems may wish to investigate one or more of the following research questions:

- How does the accounting system of a business benefit from the systematic use of business process management practices?

- Can business process management improve the accuracy of predicting future states of the business in management accounting practice?

- What are the economic and operational benefits to the business of using a cloud-based accounting information system?

- Does the increased level of data integration provided by a cloud-based accounting system help make existing business networks more successful and/or help generate new networks?

Preliminary reading

Aguilar-Saven, R.S. (2004) 'Business process modelling: Review and framework', *Journal of Production Economics'*, 90(2), pp. 129–149.

Hepp, M. and Roman, D. (2007) 'An ontology framework for semantic business process management', *Proceedings of Wirtschaftsinformatik 2007*, 28 February–2 March, Karlsruhe.

Romney, M.B. and Steinbart, P.J. (2015) *Accounting Information Systems, Global Edition*, 13th edn, Harlow: Pearson Education.

4 The regulatory framework for financial reporting

Learning objectives

When you have studied this chapter, you should be able to:

- Explain the need for a regulatory framework for financial reporting
- Describe the key elements of UK GAAP
- Explain the need for international harmonization and convergence
- Discuss the advantages and disadvantages of little GAAP
- Explain how UK GAAP contributes to harmonization and convergence

4.1 Introduction

In Chapter 1 we explained that financial accounting is the branch of accounting concerned with classifying, measuring and recording the economic transactions of an entity in accordance with established principles, legal requirements and accounting standards. It is primarily concerned with communicating a true and fair view of the financial performance and financial position of an entity to external parties at the end of the accounting period. Financial reporting is a key part of financial accounting and refers to the statutory disclosure of general purpose financial information by limited liability entities via the annual report and accounts.

In this chapter we focus on the regulatory framework for financial reporting in the UK. We examine the need for regulation and the historical reasons for international differences in accounting practices. We also describe the harmonization of company law in Europe and wider international convergence of accounting practice through the use of International Financial Reporting Standards (IFRSs). The latter have a major influence on financial reporting since they specify how particular economic transactions and events should be accounted for by large entities in around

150 countries worldwide. However, we also discuss the need for regulatory relaxation for smaller entities and examine the development of differential reporting in the UK from the 1980s to the three-tier regime in place today.

4.2 Need for a regulatory framework for financial reporting

Although financial accounting is guided by established accounting principles based on convention and best practice (see Chapter 2), over the years it has been found that a regulatory framework is needed to guide financial reporting. The *regulatory framework for financial reporting* ensures that the financial statements are prepared in a standard way and that they provide high quality, reliable information for external users. You will remember from Chapter 1 that financial reporting is a key part of financial accounting and refers to the statutory disclosure of general purpose financial information by limited liability entities via the *annual report and accounts*. A reporting entity is an entity that is required to prepare *general purpose financial statements* or chooses to do so.

4.2.1 The annual report and accounts

The *annual report and accounts* contains narrative reports (such as a report from the directors that explains the entity's activities and operations throughout the year and the auditor's report) and the accounts (the financial statements). It is the most useful source of financial information issued by reporting entities. A *reporting entity* is an entity that is required to prepare general purpose financial statements or chooses to do so. Limited liability partnerships (LLPs), private companies, public companies and group companies are examples of reporting entities. Many public limited companies in the UK are well-known high street names such as Boots Alliance, Marks & Spencer, J Sainsbury, Tesco, HMV, WHSmith, Barclays, Lloyds TSB, Halifax, HSBC and NatWest. Because of the economic importance of public limited companies in terms of employment and the monetary value of goods and services they produce, information on them is by far the easiest to obtain. If you look in the business sections of newspapers such as the *Financial Times, Guardian, The Independent*[1] or *The Times,* you will find news on the financial performance and share prices of major public limited companies and articles about their directors.

---

1. Online only.

Key definition

A reporting entity is defined as an entity that chooses, or is required, to prepare general purpose financial statements. It is not necessarily a legal entity and can comprise a portion of an entity, or two or more entities.

Source: IASB, 2015a [3.11].

All incorporated entities (except some unlimited companies) are required by CA 2006 to register their annual report and accounts at Companies House. Once filed, the information is available to the public. Anyone can download copies of annual reports and accounts from www.gov.uk/government/organisations/companies-house. The annual reports and accounts of public limited companies are also available from their websites.

Activity

Download a copy of the latest annual report and accounts for Ted Baker Plc from www.tedbakerplc.com/investor-relations and look at the information disclosed.

This company makes an interesting case study of how a small company can grow. The entrepreneur behind Ted Baker is designer, Ray Kelvin, who left school at the age of 18 and started a business manufacturing menswear. After supplying the high street retailer, Burton, for ten years, Ray sold his business to the management team in 1997 and founded Ted Baker with a partner. That year they opened a shirt store in Glasgow. The business has flourished and today Ted Baker Plc is a global brand. It has a range of lifestyle products distributed via the company's own and licensed retail outlets, leading department stores and selected independent stores in Europe, North America, the Middle East, Asia and Australasia. Figure 4.1 shows the contents page of Ted Baker's annual report and accounts for 2015/16. You will see that it contains a wide range of narrative reports in addition to the financial statements.

To allow shareholders to appreciate the activities of the entire group, Ted Baker's financial statements not only show information for the parent company, but also for the group. The information from the individual financial statements of the parent and its subsidiaries is adjusted and combined in a process called consolidation and the resulting *group accounts* are presented as those of a single economic entity. This might sound very complicated, but we will show you how it is done later, in Chapter 9.

Figure 4.1   Contents page from Ted Baker Plc Annual Report and Accounts 2015/16

❦ CONTENTS ❦

Registered Office: The Ugly Brown Building, 6a St. Pancras Way, London NW1 0TB
Company Secretary: Charles Anderson ACMA
Financial Advisers and Sponsor: Liberum Capital Limited, 25 Ropemaker St, London EC2Y 9LY
Auditors: KPMG LLP, 15 Canada Square, Canary Wharf E14 5GL
Bankers: Barclays Bank Plc, 1 Churchill Place, London E14 5HP
                                           The Royal Bank of Scotland Plc, 62-63 Threadneedle Street, London EC2R 8LA
Registrars: Capita Asset Services, 34 Beckenham Road, Beckenham, Kent BR3 4TU

Ted Baker Plc - Registered in England number: 03393836

Source: Ted Baker Plc Annual Report & Accounts 2015/16 p. 1. Reproduced by permission.

Because companies differ in their activities and the amount of information they volunteer, no two annual reports are identical. Voluntary disclosures may include information about the company's products, employees and environmental and social responsibilities. There is some debate over the extent to which some of this information clutters the annual report and obscures relevant information, making it harder for users to find the main points about the performance of the business and its future prospects. *Environmental and social reporting* focuses on the communication of the social and environmental effects of organizations' economic activities. It extends the accountability of reporting entities beyond the traditional role of providing financial reports to investors and is based on the assumption that companies have wider responsibilities than creating returns for their shareholders.

Key definition

Environmental and social reporting is the process of communicating the social and environmental effects of organizations' economic activities to particular interest groups within society and to society at large.

Source: Gray et al., 1987, p. ix.

The *Companies Act 2006 (Strategic Report and Directors' Reports) Regulations 2013* requires quoted companies to report on greenhouse gas emissions for which they are responsible in their annual report and accounts. In addition, they must report on environmental matters to the extent necessary for an understanding of the company's business, including key performance indicators (where appropriate). If this information is not disclosed, the annual report must point out the omissions. However, it can be argued that separate financial, environmental and corporate responsibility reports within the annual report and accounts can only provide a partial picture of how the entity adds economic, social, environmental value. This has led to demand for an *integrated report* capable of giving a holistic view in a concise, comparable format. The *purpose* of Integrated Reporting (<IR>) is to improve the quality of information available to investors with a view to enabling a more efficient and productive allocation of capital. We discuss this in more detail in Chapter 11.

Key definitions

Integrated Reporting (<IR>) promotes a more cohesive and efficient approach to corporate reporting and aims to improve the quality of information available to providers of financial capital to enable a more efficient and productive allocation of capital.

An integrated report is a concise communication about how an organization's strategy, governance, performance and prospects, in the context of its external environment, lead to the creation of value in the short, medium and long term.

IIRC, 2013, pp. 4 and 7. © December 2013 by the International Integrated Reporting Council ('the IIRC'). All rights reserved. Used with permission of the IIRC.

Financial reporting is a dynamic and expensive activity. As new issues of public interest arise, companies must attempt to address them in their annual report and accounts, either voluntarily or as required by the regulations. There is a considerable cost for public listed companies in complying with the regulatory framework for financial reporting, and some companies choose to spend a lot of extra money on publishing additional material in their annual report and accounts. Both factors have resulted in the annual report and accounts of major companies expanding greatly. 'In 1996, the average length of the annual report of a listed company was 44 pages. By 2000 it was 56 pages. In 2005, the average was 71 pages, increasing to 85 in 2006. From there, it increased steadily to 99 pages in the 2009 survey. It is now 101 pages. Yes, that's a 250% increase in the number of pages in an average annual report over a 14 year span!' (Deloitte, 2010).

It is interesting to look at some specific examples. In 2008 the length of Ted Baker's annual report and accounts was 68 pages compared with 104 pages in 2016; in 2008 the length of HSBC's annual report and accounts was 454 pages and weighed 1.5 kg. It was so heavy that Royal Mail had to restrict the number of HSBC reports a postman could carry for health and safety reasons. More recently, there has been a move away from traditional print to pdf and other digital formats as there is a sustainability benefit in not producing paper copies.

4.2.2 Accountability and stewardship

Small private companies are often owner-managed, but investors in large private and public companies have no day-to-day involvement in the business and appoint directors to manage the company on their behalf. This separation of ownership and control leads to an *agency relationship* in which there is information asymmetry between the directors (the agents), who are *accountable* to the investors (the principals), who have delegated authority to the directors for managing the resources they own. Some monitoring is necessary since it cannot be assumed that the directors will always act in the best interests of the investors. The annual report and accounts supports the agency relationship between the directors and the investors by providing financial and other information. Not only is the annual report and accounts an important source of information about the company for existing and potential investors, it is also of interest to other user groups such as existing and potential lenders and creditors. Investors, lenders and creditors rely on the integrity and judgement of the directors to provide high quality information and we will discuss their information needs in the next chapter.

The annual report and accounts allows users to assess the financial performance, financial position and changes in financial position of the entity. In companies that are not owner-managed, the directors are accountable to the investors and the information in the annual report and accounts allows the investors to assess the *stewardship* of the directors; in other words, the information helps investors assess how effectively and efficiently the directors have discharged their responsibilities in managing the business on their behalf.

Key definitions

Accountability refers to a duty or obligation to give an account.

Stewardship is the responsible management of resources entrusted to the care of an agent (such as a company director) and the obligation to provide relevant and reliable financial information to the principal (such as an investor in a company).

One way in which the investors can trust that the financial statements the directors have prepared are a fair representation of the economic activities of the entity is to have the accounts audited. The auditor's report must include an opinion as to whether or not the financial statements give a *true and fair view* of the company's profit or loss for the accounting period and of its state of affairs at the end of the period. There is no legal definition of the term, but essentially 'true' means the financial statements are in accordance with the facts (accurately reflect the underlying transactions) and 'fair' means they are not misleading.

The auditor's report must also state whether the financial statements have been prepared consistently using appropriate accounting policies that are in accordance with company law and accounting standards. In addition, it must state whether there is adequate disclosure of information relevant to the proper understanding of the financial statements. The auditor can issue a qualified or adverse opinion if he or she is not satisfied. It is an offence under CA 2006 for an auditor to knowingly or recklessly cause an auditor's report to contain a statement that is misleading, false or deceptive or cause that report to omit a statement relating to problems with the accounts.

Key definition

An audit is an independent examination of the accounting systems and records, and the subsequent expression of opinion on whether the financial statements give a true and fair view of an organization.

Activity

Look at the auditor's report in your copy of the latest annual report and accounts for Ted Baker Plc.

The process of auditing is guided by *International Standards on Auditing (ISAs)* which are developed by the *International Auditing and Assurance Standards Board (IAASB)* of the *International Federation of Accountants (IFAC)*. These are referred to as the Clarified ISAs because they are written using a new drafting convention called the 'clarity format' to make them clear, consistent and easy to understand. The UK's *Auditing Practices Board (APB)* has not adopted *Clarified ISA 700, Forming an Opinion and Reporting on Financial Statements*, but has issued a clarified version of *ISA (UK and Ireland) 700, The Auditor's Report on Financial Statements* which reflects the requirements of company law and provides a more concise auditor's report. This does not prevent the auditor from being able to assert compliance with the Clarified ISAs.

Having a regulatory framework gives guidance to the directors and reduces the choice of accounting policies the company can adopt. It also allows the auditors to point out the relevant regulations if they consider the directors' choices are inappropriate. Without a regulatory framework, directors might choose unsuitable accounting policies and auditors might be reluctant to raise objections since they risk losing future business if the directors decide not to recommend their reappointment.

4.3   Key elements of UK GAAP

Although the words stem from a time when financial accounting was guided by principles drawn from best practice, today the term *Generally Accepted Accounting Practice (GAAP)* refers to the regulatory framework for financial reporting that applies in a particular jurisdiction. The three main elements of UK GAAP are as follows:

- Company law provides general rules which are codified in the Companies Act 2006 (CA 2006) and subsequent statutory instruments. Company law is developed by government and sanctioned by Parliament.
- Accounting standards provide more detailed regulation and guidance. They are issued by an independent (non-government) organization.
- Stock exchange rules apply only to public companies with a listing on the London Stock Exchange and are issued by an independent regulator.

A detailed discussion of stock exchange rules is beyond the scope of this book. It is sufficient for you to know that the London Stock Exchange (LSE) is regulated independently by the *Financial Conduct Authority (FCA)*. Public companies must meet stringent requirements to obtain a listing on the LSE and these are contained in the *Stock Exchange (Listing) Regulations* and the *Admission of Securities to Listing*. Less information is required for a listing on the *Alternative Investment Market (AIM)*, which is a subsidiary market for small, growing public companies. Private companies and unlisted public limited companies do not need to comply with stock exchange rules.

> **Key definition**
>
> UK GAAP refers to the regulatory framework for financial reporting in the UK, which contains three main elements: company law, accounting standards and stock exchange rules.

We will now look at company law and accounting standards in more detail.

4.3.1 Company law

We noted in Chapter 1 that the regulatory framework for financial reporting in the UK is rooted in accounting principles based on best practice and early company law in the form of the *Joint Stock Companies Registration and Regulation Act 1844*, the *Limited Liability Act 1855* and subsequent Companies Acts. Modern company law is embodied in the *Companies Act 2006 (CA 2006)*, the development of which is the responsibility of the Department for Business, Energy and Industrial Strategy (BEIS).

In 1973, the UK became a member of the European Union (EU) and, at the time of writing, there is some uncertainty over how long this membership will continue. Under the terms of the Treaties of Rome, the governments of all Member States must incorporate EU Directives in their national legislation (see section 4.4.2). These Directives are issued by the European Commission and approved by the elected members of the European Parliament (MEPs). Directives on accounting and auditing affect company law. They are issued with a view to removing barriers between Member States and harmonizing financial reporting in the EU. Although the original Directives represented a more prescriptive European approach, the UK's influence on their development meant that other Member States had to adopt the true and fair concept which lies at the heart of UK GAAP.

The current Directives are the *Accounting Directive (Directive 2013/34/EU)* and the *Audit Directive (Directive 2014/56/EU)*. One of the requirements of the Accounting Directive continues to be that reporting entities must make their accounts available at a registry. The rationale for publishing the accounts is that anyone dealing with a limited liability company should be able to see the financial statements. This stems from the publicity doctrine that asserts that the publication of the annual report and accounts is part of the price companies pay for having limited liability. In the UK, the official Registrar of Companies operates under the name of *Companies House*, which is an executive agency of BIS. Companies House has responsibility for incorporating and dissolving limited companies, examining and storing company information delivered under the Companies Act 2006 (CA 2006) and related legislation, and making that information available to the public.

According to CA 2006, the general characteristics of a company limited by shares[2] are as follows:

- The company has a legal identity separate from its members.
- It has perpetual existence because it continues to exist even though a member may die or sell his or her shares to another individual or institutional shareholder.
- It can sue and be sued and, on liquidation, members have limited liability for its debts (limited to the amount they have invested).
- Members of the company appoint the directors (one vote per share).

On formation the company must register three documents:

- The *memorandum of association* defines the company's constitution and provides a record of facts at the time of incorporation. There is no need to state the objects of the company; hence no restriction on its activities.
- The *articles of association* is a document that gives details about the internal regulation of the business, including the voting rights of shareholders, how shareholders' and directors' meetings will be conducted and the powers of management. This is the core document approved by members that gives directors their operational parameters.
- The *statement of capital* provides information on the number of shares issued and the company's share capital.

CA 2006 sets the general regulatory framework for financial reporting. We will now examine some of the main requirements. In a one-member company there must be at least one 'natural person' who must be aged 16 or over, which gives ultimate accountability to a human being. Companies must keep adequate accounting records to show and explain the company's transactions, to disclose with reasonable accuracy the financial position of the company and to enable the directors to ensure that any accounts required to be prepared comply with CA 2006 and International Financial Reporting Standards (IFRS), where applicable. The directors must prepare annual accounts comprising a statement of financial position (referred to in CA 2006 as a balance sheet) and a statement of profit or loss and other comprehensive income (referred to in CA 2006 as a profit and loss account) for the period, with *group accounts* as appropriate. Additional information must be disclosed in the notes to the accounts and the form and content of the financial statements must comply with the provisions. There are simplifications for most non-publicly accountable entities, which we will discuss in the next section.

The statutory accounts must be accompanied by a *directors' report*, signed by a director or company secretary. The directors must not approve the accounts unless they are satisfied that they give a *true and fair view* of the assets, liabilities, financial position and profit or loss. The requirement to present a true and fair view in

---

2. See Chapter 1 for an explanation of the difference between a company limited by shares and a company limited by guarantee.

financial statements is enshrined in EU and UK law. 'In the vast majority of cases a true and fair view will be achieved by compliance with accounting standards and by additional disclosure to fully explain an issue. However, where compliance with an accounting standard would result in accounts being so misleading that they would conflict with the objectives of financial statements, the standard should be overridden' (FRC, 2014, p. 1). If departure from the standard is necessary, the directors must disclose the reason and the effect of the departure in the notes to the accounts.

In addition, the statutory accounts must be accompanied by an *auditor's report*, signed by the auditor. Unless the company qualifies for exemption from statutory audit, external auditors must be appointed to audit the accounts and their report consists of an opinion on whether the accounts show a true and fair view of the financial performance and position of the business. Exemption from statutory audit is offered to qualifying small non-publicly accountable entities.

All companies must file their statutory accounts with Companies House every year. They must prepare annual accounts for their tax return to the tax authority, HM Revenue and Customs (HMRC). Advances in technology, the desire to reduce costs and administrative burdens led to the introduction of mandatory e-filing by small, audit-exempt companies. These small companies can choose to file their statutory accounts and tax returns together using HMRC's online service or accounting software. This is known as joint filing. Alternatively, small companies can send their accounts to Companies House online and send their tax returns separately to HMRC using HMRC's online service or accounting software.

Public companies are required to hold an *annual general meeting (AGM)* for members. A 21-day notice period is required. The main items are the presentation of the annual report and accounts, the recommendations of the payment of dividends, the election of directors, and the appointment and remuneration of the auditors. Private companies do not need to hold an AGM, but members can demand one if it is required by at least 10% of shareholders (5% in certain circumstances) and a 14-day notice period is required. Public companies must submit their annual reports and accounts to Companies House and lay them before members at an AGM within six months of the year end.[3] Private companies must submit their annual reports and accounts to Companies House and distribute them to members within nine months of the year end.

Public companies must appoint a *company secretary*, who is required to have certain qualifications. His or her duties include the submission of the annual report and accounts to Companies House and keeping the minutes of meetings. Private companies may choose to appoint a company secretary if they wish. The company's website can be used to transmit all corporate documentation once approved by members. Electronic communications, including emails and websites, must include the company's name, number, registered office and other particulars (as business letters are required to do).

---

3. Stock exchange rules require a listed company to reduce this period to four months.

Figure 4.2 compares some of the main features of company law for public and private companies.

Figure 4.2 Key features of company law for public and private companies

Public limited companies (<1%)	Private companies (99.98%)
• Name must end with 'Public Limited Company' or 'PLC' • Can offer shares on LSE or AIM • Must have at least one natural person not under 16 as a director • Must have a company secretary (person or corporate) and hold AGM with members to pass resolutions • Must publish an annual report and accounts within six months of the accounting year end • Extensive financial disclosure	• Defined as a company that is not a public company • Name must end with 'Limited' or 'Ltd' or Welsh equivalent • Shares can be offered for sale privately but not publicly • No need for a company secretary or AGM with members • Must publish an annual report and accounts within nine months of the accounting year end • Extent of financial disclosure depends on size and public interest

The *size thresholds* in CA 2006 stem from the Accounting Directive (Directive 2013/34/EU), which specifies the size criteria and maximum thresholds[4] that Member States can set. It also places a restriction on the disclosures that Member States can require small companies to provide in their annual accounts. Since 2004, the UK has contributed to EU harmonization by adopting the EU maxima. From 1 January 2016, unless the entity is excluded for reasons of public interest,[5] it generally qualifies for a particular size category if it does not exceed two or more of the three size criteria shown in Table 4.1 in its first year. In a subsequent financial year, the entity must qualify or satisfy the size tests in that year and the preceding year.

Table 4.1 Size thresholds for accounting and auditing in the UK

Criteria	Micro	Small	Medium
Turnover	£0.632m	£10.2m	£36m
Balance sheet total	£0.316m	£5.1m	£18m
Average number of employees	10	50	250

Source: Companies House, 2016.

---

4. Thresholds are revised periodically to take account of indexation (monetary and economic trends).
5. Under the Companies Act 2006, 'an entity is excluded from the small companies regime if it is a public company, a company that is an authorised insurance company, a banking company, an e-money issuer, an ISD investment firm or a UCITS management company, or carries on insurance market activity, or is a member of an ineligible group' (c. 46, Part 15, Chapter 1, p. 178).

The Accounting Directive introduced a new requirement that all companies, regardless of size, must state in their individual accounts:

- the part of the UK in which the company is registered
- the company's registered number
- whether the company is a public company or a private company, and whether it is limited by shares or by guarantee
- the address of the company's registered office
- whether the company is being wound up (only if applicable).

Other changes to company law resulting from the Accounting Directive include the following:

- Large and medium-sized companies must make full disclosure about their subsidiaries and other significant investments in their accounts. Disclosure must include the address of the registered office of all related undertakings, whether inside or outside the UK. Small companies are exempt from these disclosures.
- Auditors have new reporting responsibilities in relation to the directors' report and strategic report.
- Where no reliable estimate of life is possible, the maximum useful life of goodwill and intangible assets is set at ten years.
- Abbreviated accounts for small and medium companies are abolished, but small companies can prepare abridged accounts for shareholders and for filing at Companies House.
- Disclosure requirements for small company accounts are simplified significantly.
- Small company thresholds for accounting purposes and audit exemption are raised substantially.

4.3.2 Accounting standards

Since the *Companies Registration and Regulation Act 1844* introduced the first requirement that companies present a balance sheet to shareholders, there has been a steady pressure on companies to increase the amount of information they disclose. Prior to 1970 the regulation of financial reporting in the UK was relatively light. It was governed solely by company law, with additional rules laid down by the Stock Exchange for listed companies. The Companies Acts of 1948 and 1967 provided general requirements in connection with the preparation, distribution and filing of financial statements, but the detail was left to the practices of accountants.

There was little concern with developing standards on accounting until the Institute of Chartered Accountants in England and Wales (ICAEW) began drafting pronouncements on accounting principles in 1942. Between 1942 and 1969 a total of 29 guidance statements were issued. They had been subjected to a complex exposure process among ICAEW members and had to be approved by an overwhelming majority of its Council, which meant that the ICAEW held considerable influence over accounting practices. However, this basic framework was widely considered to be inadequate for achieving a satisfactory standard of financial reporting. The main problems were the amount of flexibility permitted to companies in the way that they could account for transactions and the minimum amount of information they could disclose. In the 1960s there were a number of major financial scandals involving companies reporting misleading profit figures,[6] which could be attributed in part to perceptions of the inadequacy of accounting regulations. Similar problems were experienced in other jurisdictions and some of the wealthier countries addressed them by setting *accounting standards* which gave detailed guidance on how a particular type of economic transaction or event should be reflected in the financial statements.

In 1970 the *Accounting Standards Committee (ASC)* was established as the first standard setter in the UK, with the objective of reducing flexibility by requiring all members of the accountancy bodies to apply accounting standards or face disciplinary action. Over the next 20 years, the ASC issued 25 accounting standards known as *Statements of Standard Accounting Practice (SSAPs)*. The ASC did much to improve the quality of financial reporting, but it did not have the authority or resources to deal with all the problems. Following recommendations made by the Dearing Committee (Dearing, 1988), the ASC was replaced by the *Accounting Standards Board (ASB)* in 1990 under the control of an independent regulator, the *Financial Reporting Council (FRC)*. The ASB immediately adopted all the SSAPs issued by the ASC and began issuing *Financial Reporting Standards (FRSs)*, some of which replaced earlier standards.

Key definition

An accounting standard is an authoritative statement on how a particular type of transaction or other event should be reflected in the financial statements. In the UK, compliance with accounting standards is normally necessary for the financial statements to give a true and fair view.

The work of the FRC has evolved since the 1990s and it has been restructured to reflect its much wider remit. Today, the FRC is not only responsible for setting standards for financial reporting, but also for setting standards for auditing and actuarial practice. In addition, the FRC sponsors the UK Corporate Governance Code (for companies) and the Stewardship Code (for investors) which we examine in Chapter 11. The FRC is also responsible for other activities that promote high quality corporate reporting, including monitoring, oversight, investigative and disciplinary functions.

---

6. Two examples include the collapse in 1964 of Rolls Razor Ltd after publishing 'clean' accounts, and the difference between AEI's profit forecast for 1967 and the large loss reported after it was taken over by GEC Plc (partly due to the use of different accounting principles).

Activity

What are the advantages and disadvantages of accounting standards?

Looking first at the advantages, accounting standards offer a number of benefits to the preparers and users of accounts:

- Preparers have an authoritative guide to the most appropriate method for accounting for many of the important activities undertaken by companies.
- Users have additional financial information to that required by legislation alone, as well as information about the basis on which the accounts have been drawn up. This allows comparison of a company's results with other companies and between one year and another.

The main disadvantages are:

- They impose additional costs for the company, but to some extent this is offset by the availability of accounting software.
- Standard setters must decide which accounting methods are appropriate for all companies in all industries and in all circumstances.

4.4 International harmonization and convergence

Historically, many countries have developed their own regulatory frameworks for financial reporting; hence the terms Australian GAAP, French GAAP, German GAAP, Indian GAAP, Japanese GAAP, People's Republic of China (PRC) GAAP, UK GAAP, US GAAP, etc. Not surprisingly, this has resulted in significant differences in accounting practices which mean that a company can show one figure of profit when the financial statements are drawn up under one country's rules and a completely different figure when drawn up under another country's rules. These differences are important when a company is seeking a listing on a stock exchange in another country. For example, if a UK company wanted its shares to be traded on the New York Stock Exchange as well as on the London Stock Exchange, it would prepare two sets of accounts: one set complying with US GAAP and the other complying with UK GAAP. The US is one of the few countries that does not permit domestic public companies to use IFRSs. Nevertheless, IFRSs are used by nearly 500 large foreign companies trading securities in the US as well as thousands of foreign subsidiaries, associates, and joint ventures owned by US companies.

4.4.1 Reasons for international differences

It is difficult to summarize the complex social, economic and cultural reasons for international differences in accounting practices and the regulation of financial reporting.

Activity

What do you think are the main reasons for the development of different regulatory frameworks for financial reporting in different countries?

There is a general consensus that one important factor is the *legal system*.[7] In some countries the legal system is based on the Roman laws of the sixth century. This tends to result in a rules-based approach to the regulation of financial reporting with detailed 'codified' rules (e.g. France, Germany, Italy and Spain). Requirements are more likely to be controlled by the government, but there may still be some contribution from the accountancy profession (e.g. the Netherlands). In other countries the legal system may be based on the English common law system whereby a limited number of statutes are interpreted by the courts to produce supplementary case law. This tends to result in a principles-based approach to the regulation of financial reporting with minimal legal requirements supported by accounting principles (e.g. Australia, India, UK and USA). Therefore, the accountancy profession plays a key role in developing requirements and the regulations can be changed more frequently. Of course the size and strength of the accountancy profession in a particular country also has a bearing on its ability to contribute to the regulatory framework. Therefore, a large, strong profession is associated with countries where there is a requirement for the financial statements to be audited.

A country's regulatory framework for financial reporting is likely to consist of accounting practices that have evolved over time and legal requirements that are added to from time to time. These legal requirements arise on a contingency basis as a response to an unusual event such as a financial scandal, or to a change in the economic environment. Of course, countries are not likely to experience the same unusual events and, if they do, the events are not likely to occur at the same time or lead to the same changes in legal requirements. There are also differences due to different attitudes to the law. In some countries it is taken for granted that a law should be obeyed, whereas in other countries there is a subtle understanding about which laws are obeyed and the degree to which they are obeyed. Hence, the famous standard setters' joke shown in Figure 4.3.

Figure 4.3 International understanding on rules

International understanding on rules is very difficult because the rules have different meanings. In Germany everything is forbidden unless it is explicitly allowed by the law, whereas in England everything is allowed except what is explicitly forbidden in the law. In China, on the other hand, everything is forbidden, even though it is allowed by the law, whereas in Italy everything is allowed, especially if it is forbidden.

---

7. This discussion draws on Haller and Walton (2003) and Alexander and Nobes (2010).

A second factor that contributes to international differences in financial reporting practices stems from differences in the objective of financial reporting. In some countries the focus of financial reporting is on meeting the needs of investors for decision making, but in other countries it is on the provision of financial information for creditor protection and taxation. This difference arises because in some countries the main source of finance is the equity finance raised on the stock market (e.g. the UK and the USA) and in others it is debt finance supplied by banks and other financial institutions (e.g. Germany). A further complication is that in some countries there are separate rules for financial reporting and tax purposes (e.g. the UK and the USA) and this requires two sets of financial statements to be prepared. However, in other countries there is one set of rules for both purposes and therefore a single set of financial statements is sufficient. Figure 4.4 summarizes the various reasons we have discussed.

Figure 4.4 Reasons for international differences in GAAP

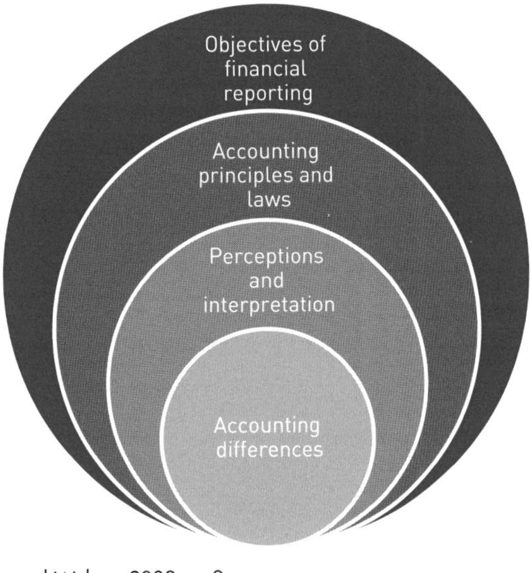

Objectives of financial reporting

Accounting principles and laws

Perceptions and interpretation

Accounting differences

Source: Adapted from Haller and Walton, 2003, p. 2.

4.4.2 Harmonization in the European Union

Over the years, many companies like Ted Baker have become larger and increasingly international in their ownership and activities. This internationalization began to escalate in the 1970s and 1980s when the reduced cost of computer hardware and software helped bring about a revolution in the use of information technology. By the mid-1990s many entities had created websites on the Internet, thus creating a global market place. Another significant influence on the internationalization of business in Europe were the *Treaties of Rome (1957)*, which created the European Economic Community (EEC) and laid the foundation for a common market to stimulate economic development and prevent recurrence of war through closer co-operation. This developed into the European Union (EU), which in 2016 had 28 members (see Figure 4.5).

Figure 4.5   Members of the European Union (EU-28), 2016

Year	Country
1958	France, Federal Republic of Germany, Italy, Belgium, the Netherlands, Luxembourg
1973	UK, Ireland, Denmark
1981	Greece
1986	Spain, Portugal
1990	East Germany
1995	Austria, Finland, Sweden
2004	Cyprus, Malta, Hungary, Poland, Slovakia, Latvia, Estonia, Lithuania, Czech, Republic, Slovenia
2007	Romania, Bulgaria
2013	Croatia

Note: The unification of East and West Germany means that Germany is only counted once.

Key definition

Harmonization refers to the bringing together of practices and regulations in EU Member States.

4.4.3   Need for international accounting standards

In addition to the increasing size of the EU, the establishment of international capital markets for raising finance meant that instead of operating in local or national markets, many businesses now operate in a global economy. Indeed, some have become large conglomerates with complex activities and international operations that were unimaginable in the days when transactions were based on simple bartering. The internationalization of business and the capital markets raises problems because some countries in the developing world have minimal financial reporting regulations, while other countries, such as the USA, have highly developed and prescriptive systems. Clearly this imbalance is highly unsatisfactory today in the context of increased cross-border integration of markets and politics. In addition, the prevailing view in some countries is that the responsibility for controlling accounting should rest with the accountancy profession rather than government and this view became more apparent among the early members of the EU. This led to demand for international accounting standards to bring about *convergence* by reducing differences in financial reporting due to the variation in accounting practices.

> **Key definition**
>
> Convergence refers to the bringing together of financial reporting internationally, especially as a result of the use of International Financial Reporting Standards (IFRSs) issued by the International Accounting Standards Board (IASB).

An important step towards this goal took place in 1973 when the *International Accounting Standards Committee (IASC)* was set up through an agreement made by professional accountancy bodies from Australia, Canada, France, Germany, Japan, Mexico, the Netherlands, the UK and Ireland, and the USA. By 1982, the sponsors of the IASC comprised all of the professional accountancy bodies that were members of the International Federation of Accountants (IFAC). The IASC's objective was to develop *International Accounting Standards (IASs)* that would be internationally acceptable.[8] However, IASC had no power to impose the standards and countries with their own accounting standards were reluctant to relinquish them. In addition, the IASC found it difficult to agree standards that would be appropriate for all companies, in all countries and in all circumstances.

In 2001 the IASC was replaced by the *International Accounting Standards Board (IASB)*, which was set up with an independent oversight organization, which is now known as the *IFRS Foundation*. The IASB adopted all the IASs issued by its predecessor and began issuing new *International Financial Reporting Standards (IFRSs)*, some of which replaced earlier standards. IFRSs set out the procedures and methods for the measurement, valuation and disclosure of an accounting transaction or event (IFRS is the term used to refer to any of the accounting standards issued by the IASB since 2001). The principal objectives of the IFRS Foundation are:

- to develop a single set of high quality, understandable, enforceable and globally accepted international financial reporting standards through its standard-setting body, the *International Accounting Standards Board (IASB)*;
- to promote the use and rigorous application of those standards;
- to take account of the financial reporting needs of emerging economies and small and medium-sized entities (SMEs);
- to bring about convergence of national accounting standards and IFRSs to high quality solutions.

Figure 4.6 shows how the IFRS Foundation is structured. Governance and oversight of the IFRS Foundation rests with a geographically and professionally diverse body of trustees, who are publicly accountable to a monitoring board of public capital market authorities. One crucial element in establishing the IASB was that it would have sufficient resources to carry out its responsibilities. The task of securing those

---

8. It was no coincidence that 1973 was also the year that the UK joined what became the EU. In the same year, the USA established its own standard setter, the Financial Accounting Standards Board (FASB).

funds rests with the IFRS Foundation and is achieved through mandatory levies for listed and non-listed companies in a growing number of countries.

Figure 4.6 Structure of the IFRS Foundation

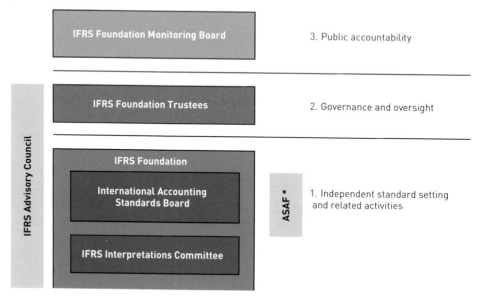

* Accounting Standards Advisory Forum (representative of the international standard-setting community)

Source: IFRS Foundation, 2016a. Reproduced with permission from the IFRS Foundation.

The IASB is responsible for the development and publication of IFRSs and for approving the interpretations of those IFRSs given by the IFRS Interpretations Committee. The IASB engages closely with stakeholders around the world, including investors, analysts, regulators, business leaders, accounting standard setters and the accountancy profession. The task of the IFRS Interpretations Committee is to review widespread accounting issues relating to current IFRSs and provide authoritative guidance. The Committee's interpretation of an IFRS is known as an IFRIC (interpretation of an IAS created by the IASC is known as a SIC). The IASB is required to conduct a Post-Implementation Review (PIR) of each new IFRS about two to three years after it becomes effective.

The IASB's *standard-setting process* (see Figure 4.7) includes the publication of consultative documents on the accounting issue for public comment. These usually take the form of discussion papers and exposure drafts. This is a lengthy procedure to ensure wide consultation and full consideration of problems and alternative solutions. After all comments have been examined and field tests have been conducted, the IASB publishes an *exposure draft* for public comment. The exposure draft takes the same form and content as the proposed standard. Once all the comments have been considered and any amendments made, the IASB issues the IFRS. This process means that the IASB engages closely with stakeholders around the world, which include the following:

- European Commission
- European Financial Reporting Advisory Group (EFRAG)
- International Organization of Securities Commissions (IOSCO)
- International Federation of Accountants (IFAC)
- Financial Accounting Standards Board (FASB) in the USA
- Securities and Exchange Commission (SEC) in the USA
- Public Company Accounting Oversight Board (PCAOB) in the USA.

It is worth noting that EFRAG plays an important role by providing proactive advice to the IASB and advising the European Commission on the acceptability of a particular IFRS with a view to its endorsement for use in the EU. In addition, EFRAG advises the European Commission on any resulting changes to be made to the Accounting Directive.

Figure 4.7   The IASB's standard-setting process

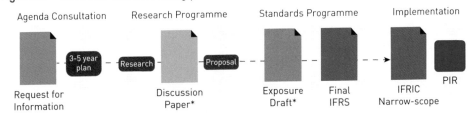

*Published for public comment.

Source: IFRS Foundation, 2016b. Reproduced with permission from the IFRS Foundation.

4.5   Differential reporting

Differential reporting is concerned with the idea that different reporting entities should follow different accounting regulations. Differential reporting is not a new idea in the UK. Prior to 1967 financial reporting requirements only applied to public companies and private companies were exempt. However, The Companies Act of 1967 abolished exempt private company status and brought about a state of universality whereby all companies were subject to the same regulations: the general requirements of company law plus a relatively small number of UK accounting standards.

Key definition

Differential reporting refers to the idea that different reporting entities should follow different accounting regulations.

Differential reporting developed because as circumstances and environments change, accounting practices evolve and adapt. GAAP is a dynamic concept, which is not restricted to the requirements of accounting standards and company law, and is continually responding to change.

Prior to 1981, all companies in the UK were governed by identical financial reporting and disclosure requirements, regardless of size, industry or public interest. However, after the ASB was established in 1990, the volume and complexity of accounting standards increased the burden of compliance. The expansion of the regulatory framework had been primarily in response to what the regulators perceived as the reporting needs of public limited companies. Consequently, some commentators argued that a separate regulatory framework should be developed to meet the accounting requirements of small private companies. The underlying argument was that GAAP imposed a heavy burden on them in relation to the value they receive from the information in the annual accounts, since most small companies are owner-managed. This developed into the *big GAAP/little GAAP debate*, which focused on whether smaller reporting entities should be exempt from some aspects of GAAP on the grounds of their size and lack of public interest in their financial statements. At the heart of the debate was the difficulty in determining the criteria that should be used to exempt companies and widespread concern that accounts that did not comply with accounting standards would not present a true and fair view of the company's activities. We will now examine the main arguments for and against little GAAP.

4.5.1   The case for little GAAP

In public companies, the main *purpose* of financial reporting is investor protection, since the shareholders are external investors. However, in most private companies the shareholders are owner-managers so investor protection is not important. In both public and private companies, a second purpose is creditor protection and general purpose financial statements are probably sufficient for suppliers, but lenders may require more. Employees, customers, government agencies and the public have no specific financial reporting requirements. These similarities and differences are linked to the arguments about users and uses.

- *Users and uses* – There was widespread agreement that the accounts of large companies have a much broader range of users than those of small companies. In addition, the main user groups differ. The primary users of the financial statements of large companies are existing and potential investors, whereas in small companies the investors are typically the owner-managers of the business. There are also differences among other user groups. For example, the role of analysts is very restricted in small private companies, as their shares cannot be traded publicly. In addition, lenders, trade creditors and employees are likely to have close contact with the proprietor and therefore will rely less on public information.

- *Intensity of use* – Related to the above point was the view that the financial statements of large companies are used for a wider range of decisions than the financial statements of small companies. Therefore, the intensity of use by different groups of users is likely to differ between small private companies and large public companies.
- *Comparability* – It was argued that as the users of small company accounts are predominantly different kinds of people with different needs from users of large companies' accounts, it follows that there is no practical need for comparability.
- *Complexity* – Another common argument was that large companies have complex transactions and they provide highly aggregated information needing sophisticated analysis. On the other hand, small companies have fewer and less complex transactions.
- *Costs and benefits* – It was widely held that compliance with GAAP imposed a disproportionate burden on small companies relative to their income. Related to this point of view was the belief that new differential reporting requirements could be developed that would reduce compliance costs and better meet the needs of owner-managers.

4.5.2   The case against little GAAP

Both sides of the debate cite user needs. The other main arguments for one GAAP focus on the notion of 'one size fits all', as can be seen from the following analysis:

- *Users and uses* – In the case against little GAAP, the contention is that if the needs of users are similar for both small and large companies, public interest demands the same GAAP for all companies. However, the counter-argument is that few small companies have external investors or public accountability, and therefore there is no need for the same GAAP.
- *Universality* – The universality argument focuses on the assumption that compliance with GAAP leads to a true and fair view. Therefore, the statutory accounts cannot give a true and fair view if there are different accounting rules for companies of different sizes. It was also argued that any distinction in size would involve an arbitrary cut-off, which would be hard to defend. However, subsequent legal advice confirmed that there could be a different true and fair view for large and small companies.
- *Comparability* – Part of the universality argument is that accounting standards are intended to enhance comparability and reliability of financial statements. The need for equivalence is easier to justify where there is a significant public interest in the entity, but small companies have little or no public accountability. In addition, comparison is important for large entities because they operate in major industries, but this is unlikely to be the case for small companies which often occupy niche markets.

- *Publicity doctrine* – The publicity doctrine asserts that producing and preparing published accounts is part of the price paid by companies for having limited liability status. However, historically, limited companies tended to be formed where there was a separation of ownership and control, and it is a more recent phenomenon for small businesses to be incorporated. Therefore, many owner-managed companies became subject to regulations that were not developed for them.
- *Two-tier profession* – There was some concern that differential reporting could lead to the creation of a two-tier system of reporting (big GAAP and little GAAP) and hence a two-tier profession.

Figure 4.8 summarizes some of the main arguments we have discussed.

Figure 4.8 Main arguments in the little GAAP debate

Factor	PLCs	SMEs
Main user	Investors (external)	Investors (often owner-managed)
Intensity of use	High	Much lower as fewer users
Public accountability	High public interest	No public interest
Reliance on disclosure	High reliance on public disclosure	Most users are likely to have close contact with the directors
Comparability	Very important as PLCs operate in major industries	Less important and some SMEs occupy niche markets
Complexity	Complex activities	Simpler activities
Cost burden	Low relative to revenue	Much higher relative to revenue

4.6 Development of little GAAP in the UK

Traditionally, UK company law had provided a broad framework only. However, in 1973 when the UK joined what was to become the EU, there was a significant increase in the complexity of company law due to the need to incorporate the requirements of EU Directives. This also changed the UK's regulatory focus on financial reporting by large companies because the Directives included options that simplified requirements for small and medium-sized entities.[9] Another influence on the development of little GAAP in the UK was the effort made by the UK's ASB to address the burden of compliance placed on smaller entities by the increase in

---

9. In this context the term *entities* refers to single-entity companies or group companies.

volume and complexity of accounting standards. Today, the three main elements of little GAAP are:

- abridged accounts for small companies and micro-entities;
- audit exemption for small companies and micro-entities;
- an accounting standard for micro-entities: FRS 105, *The Financial Reporting Standard applicable to the Micro-entities Regime*.

We will now examine each element in more detail.

4.6.1   Abridged accounts

From 1981 to 2014, UK company law allowed reporting entities that qualified as small or medium to file less detailed *abbreviated accounts* at Companies House, but prepare full accounts for shareholders. In the case of small entities, this option meant they only had to file an abbreviated balance sheet and related notes.[10] Although drawn from the full accounts, abbreviated accounts could not give a true and fair view because it was deemed that they omitted financial information necessary to giving a true and fair view.

As a result of embodying the Accounting Directive in CA 2006 in 2015, abbreviated accounts for small and medium companies were abolished. However, single entity small companies (but not groups) can now prepare *abridged accounts* for filing at Companies House and for their shareholders. Abridged accounts omit the third (most detailed) level of headings in the balance sheet (statement of financial position), which is otherwise most commonly included in the notes to the accounts. In addition, the figure for turnover (revenue) is not disclosed and some headings in the profit and loss account (statement of profit or loss) are combined into a single heading, 'Gross profit or loss'. A small company can choose to prepare an abridged profit and loss account or an abridged balance sheet, or both. However, all shareholders must give their consent for the choice.

An important development in little GAAP was the Accounting Directive on micro-entities (Directive 2012/06/EU), which affects 5.325 million (75%) of 7.1 million companies in the EU. It was incorporated into CA 2006 by the *Small Companies (Micro-Entities' Accounts) Regulations 2013* (SI 2013/3008). It applies to 1.56 million micro-companies in the UK and allows them to prepare an abridged balance sheet and statement of profit or loss (with abridged notes) for shareholders. Like small companies, they are exempt from the requirement to file a profit and loss account (statement of profit or loss). This development stems from a 'think small first' approach, which rests on the assumption that the requirements of the previous Accounting Directives were an administrative burden, the reduction of which would boost Europe's economy. We refer to micro-entities again in section 4.6.3.

---

10. Abbreviated accounts for medium-sized entities require a higher level of disclosure.

Activity

What are the advantages and disadvantages of filing abridged accounts?

The main advantage of abridged accounts is:

• Abridged accounts reduce the disclosure of financial information about the company that might be useful to competitors. This helps the company if it has activities in competitive markets rather than a niche market.

The main disadvantages are:

• Users of the financial statements may think the company has something to hide.
• Users will find inter-company comparison is difficult, as fewer figures are available for analysis.

4.6.2 Audit exemption

To comply with the original Audit Directive, from 1994, UK company law has allowed a qualifying small company to forgo the statutory audit. However, if audit is required by shareholders holding at least 10% of issued share capital, the company cannot choose audit exemption. When the concessions were first introduced in the UK, the size thresholds for defining a small entity were set lower than the EU maxima and the turnover threshold was set lower for audit exemption than for abbreviated accounts. Subsequently the UK thresholds were raised in steps until in 2004 they had been standardized for all accounting and auditing options and harmonized with the EU maxima.

Activity

What are the advantages and disadvantages of audit exemption?

The main advantages of audit exemption are:

• Audit exemption reduces cost burdens because there will be no auditor's fee to be paid.
• In addition, there will be no working time lost or inconvenience because no auditor will come to the business to conduct compliance tests (to assess the effectiveness of the systems of financial control) and substantive tests (to assess the completeness, ownership, existence, valuation and disclosure of the information in the accounting records and financial statements).

The main disadvantages are:

• There will be no independent assurance for external users of the financial statements. An independent audit gives users confidence that the financial statements give a true and fair view and this is particularly important to external investors and to lenders and creditors for making economic decisions.

- In addition, there will be no assurance for management since audit provides an independent check on the accounting systems and records, which helps prevent material error and acts as a deterrent to fraud.

4.6.3 FRS 105 The Financial Reporting Standard applicable to the Micro-entities Regime

A major development in little GAAP in the UK took place in 1997 when the ASB issued the *Financial Reporting Standard for Smaller Entities (FRSSE)* to reduce the financial reporting burden on non-publicly accountable small companies. It drew together in a single document all the guidance from the full range of UK accounting standards in force at that time that were most likely to be relevant to a small company. The measurement bases were the same as or a simplification of those in the accounting standards used in big GAAP. In 2005, the relevant require-ments of the Companies Act were added, making it a 'one-stop shop' for small companies.

The FRSSE was withdrawn when FRS 105, *The Financial Reporting Standard applicable to the Micro-entities Regime* (2015) became effective in 2016. FRS 105 applies to non-publicly accountable micro-entities. It can be used by micro-entities (as defined by CA 2006) that choose to apply the micro-entities regime introduced in UK company law in November 2013. Despite the fact that micro-entities only have to provide the minimum disclosures required by law, financial statements prepared in accordance with the legal requirements of the micro-entities regime are presumed to give a true and fair view. Unlike the FRSSE, FRS 105 does not reproduce all the reporting requirements from company law applicable to micro-entities at present, but it does include those relating to the financial statements. We refer to FRS 105 again in section 4.7.2.

4.7 Convergence with IFRSs

The European Commission supports the work of the IASB and since 2005 all pub-lic companies listed on an EU stock exchange (approximately 8,000) have been required to use EU-adopted IFRSs for preparing their consolidated (group) financial statements. In addition to the 28 EU Member States, this requirement also applies to the European Economic Area (EEA) which comprises the EU Member States plus Iceland, Liechtenstein and Norway. Although Switzerland is not an EEA member, most large companies in that country also use IFRSs. This is a big step forward in the harmonization of financial reporting in Europe. A convergence project between IFRS and US GAAP has been started, but the USA has yet to make a decision about adopting IFRSs.

Activity

What are the advantages and disadvantages of IFRSs

The following pros and cons are drawn from Ball (2006), who was analyzing the issues in the run-up to the adoption of IFRSs for listed group entities in the EU in 2005. The so-called 'European experiment' was watched with great interest, not least by Ball and others in the USA, but also by policy makers in other major economies outside Europe. Ball analyzed the pros of IFRSs into direct and indirect advantages as follows.

Direct advantages:

- IFRSs provide more accurate, comprehensive and timely financial statement information relative to the national standards they replace in many countries.
- There are reduced costs arising from being informed in a timely fashion (mainly benefits small investors who, unlike investment analysts, do not have access to other sources of information).
- The cost of processing financial information is reduced, since no adjustments are needed for differences in GAAP. This benefits institutions creating standardized financial databases and should increase the efficiency with which the stock market incorporates the information in equity prices (shares or other securities).
- Most assets can be reported using fair value accounting (e.g. replacement cost, market value, net realizable value, value in use), which contains more information than historical cost accounting.
- Companies can compete for capital on equal terms since there are reduced compliance costs for multinational companies, which only need to prepare one set of accounts.
- Transparency is achieved through the use of one global accounting language, which aids inter-company comparison and reduces information costs and information risk to investors, but only if IFRSs are implemented consistently.

Indirect advantages:

- The cost of equity capital is reduced due to higher information quality reducing the risk to investors.
- The cost of debt capital is reduced due to more efficient contracting in debt markets, particularly due to timelier loss recognition.
- Corporate governance (the system by which companies are directed and controlled) is improved due to greater transparency. In particular, timelier loss recognition increases the incentives of managers to attend to existing loss-making investments and strategies more quickly and to undertake fewer unprofitable investments (e.g. pet projects and trophy acquisitions).

Ball divided the cons of IFRSs into immediate and longer-term disadvantages as follows.

Immediate disadvantages:

- It is hard to agree on a global accounting language and whether it should be based on principles or rules. It will mean that national models of best practice may be lost.
- There will be initial training costs for preparers, auditors and enforcers.
- Fair value accounting leads to volatility and may reflect estimation noise or managerial manipulation.
- Despite some regulatory co-ordination, political and economic forces will lead to inconsistency in implementation.

Longer-term disadvantages:

- Allowing all countries to use the IFRS brand name discards information about reporting quality differences. There may also be free rider problems where low-quality countries may adopt IFRSs in name only.
- Competition encourages innovation and discourages complacency and bureaucracy, and imposing global standards is risky centralization.
- At present IFRSs have a strong common law orientation, but over time the IASB risks becoming a politicized, bureaucratic UN-style body.

Research evidence on the improvement in the quality of financial reporting through convergence with IFRSs has been inconclusive. This may be because some of the obstacles to genuine comparability and convergence are deeply cultural (Zeff, 2007). Nevertheless, approximately 140 countries had adopted, adapted or permitted the use of IFRSs by 2015.

4.7.1 The IFRS for SMEs

Initially the IASB focused on designing a full range of IFRSs for large, listed companies, but in 2009 it issued the *IFRS for SMEs*, which was subsequently revised in December 2015. The IFRS for SMEs is a self-contained standard in a single document, designed to meet the needs and capabilities of small and medium-sized entities (SMEs), which are estimated to account for over 95% of companies around the world (IFRS Foundation, 2016c). Although the standard is based on IFRSs, it is less complex than full IFRSs and simpler than many national GAAPs. It is available for any jurisdiction to adopt, irrespective of whether it has adopted full IFRSs. Any jurisdiction deciding to adopt the *IFRS for SMEs* can decide which non-publicly accountable entities should use it. The IASB states that it must not be used by listed companies or financial institutions.

The main ways in which the IASB has reduced complexity in the *IFRS for SMEs* are:

- Topics not relevant for SMEs are omitted (e.g. earnings per share, interim financial reporting, and segment reporting).
- Where full IFRSs allow accounting policy choices, the *IFRS for SMEs* allows only the easier option (e.g. no option to revalue property, equipment, or intangibles;

a cost-depreciation model for investment property unless fair value is readily available without undue cost or effort; no 'corridor approach' for actuarial gains and losses).

- Many principles for recognizing and measuring assets, liabilities, income and expenses in full IFRSs are simplified (e.g. amortize goodwill; expense all borrowing and R&D costs; cost model for associates and jointly-controlled entities; no available-for-sale or held-to-maturity classes of financial assets).
- Significantly fewer disclosures are required (roughly 300 versus 3,000).
- The standard has been written in clear, easily translatable language (published in approximately 50 languages).
- To reduce costs for preparers, it was initially decided that revisions will be limited to once every three years. After the revised version was published in 2015, the IASB agreed that revisions would take place every five or six years, with a request for information triggering the process two years after the implementation date of the previous update.

Activity

What are the advantages and disadvantages of the *IFRS for SMEs*?

Apart from contributing to international convergence, some of the advantages you may have thought of are:

- The *IFRS for SMEs* reduces the financial reporting burden where full IFRSs or full national GAAP are required (e.g. developing countries and transition economies).
- It reduces information costs and information risk to users.
- It improves access to capital.
- It aids comparison if it is applied consistently.
- In some jurisdictions it improves the quality of financial reporting compared to national GAAP.
- It reduces the risk of many different national GAAPs for SMEs, all loosely based on full IFRSs.
- It allows easy transition to full IFRSs if the company grows, as it is based on the same principles.

The main disadvantages are:

- It is hard to agree a definition of an SME that is appropriate and acceptable throughout the developed and developing world, in both market economies and in transition economies (those that have only recently moved to market economies).
- It is based on full IFRSs, which have been designed for large, listed companies.
- The unique features of any little GAAP in a particular jurisdiction may be lost.

- There will be initial training costs for preparers, auditors and enforcers, although implementation guidance released with the standard includes illustrative financial statements, presentation and disclosure checklist, guidance in the form of Q & A and free training materials in many languages.

As anticipated by the IFRS Foundation, some of the countries using full IFRSs or the IFRS for SMEs are those in the developing world or in emerging market economies which do not have national accounting standards. The IFRS for SMEs has not been adopted for use in the EU due to relatively minor conflicts with the Accounting Directive. In addition, there has been a return to the little GAAP debate and the argument that it does not meet the needs of very small reporting entities. Therefore, there is growing pressure on the IASB to develop a simpler set of standards for micro-entities (Cairns, 2011).

4.7.2 Convergence with IFRSs in the UK

In the past, the UK had developed a large number of national financial reporting standards, but they have all been withdrawn (including the FRSSE). Today's standards are entirely IFRS-based:

- FRS 100, *Application of Financial Reporting Requirements* (2012) determines which reporting framework applies to which entities. Listed group entities and other publicly accountable entities have been required to use EU-adopted IFRSs since 2005.
- FRS 101, *Reduced Disclosure Framework* (2012) allows subsidiaries in a listed group to apply the same accounting as in the group accounts, but with fewer disclosures.
- FRS 102, *The Financial Reporting Standard Applicable in the UK and Republic of Ireland* (2013) is based on the IFRS for SMEs with a number of modifications. It is applicable to large, medium and small non-publicly accountable entities.
- FRS 105, *The Financial Reporting Standard applicable to the Micro-entities Regime* (2015) applies to non-publicly accountable micro-entities. The recognition and measurement requirements are based on FRS 102 with a number of significant simplifications. These include exempting micro-entities from having to account for complex transactions such as equity-settled share-based payments, defined benefit pension schemes and deferred tax. Micro-entities need only provide the minimum disclosures required by law.

The new regime has led to tiers (see Figure 4.9). The bottom tier is for incorporated and unincorporated micro-entities; the second tier is for non-publicly accountable entities, regardless of size; and the top tier is for publicly accountable entities (with reduced disclosure for subsidiaries). The financial reporting requirements of each regime are progressively more complex and comprehensive in each tier to reflect the increasing size and complexity of the entities most likely to apply that regime.

Figure 4.9   Three tiers with increasing complexity

A number of benefits arise from taking a tiered approach. The main advantage is that the burden of compliance is reduced by applying the principle of proportionality. In addition, the IFRS-based approach throughout the tiers should aid transition for entities moving between categories. Entities in the lower tiers can use the regime for a higher tier if they wish (for example, if they are close to the threshold or planning an IPO). As the three tiers are all based on IFRSs, the approach also provides a high level of consistency for preparers, auditors and users. However, one disadvantage is that international comparability is slightly impaired in respect of entities using FRS 102 because the UK has had to adapt the IFRS for SMEs slightly to avoid minor conflicts with the Accounting Directive.

4.8   Conclusions

The regulatory framework for financial reporting in the UK has three main elements: company law, accounting standards and stock exchange rules. The latter only apply to listed companies, which are the most stringently regulated businesses due to the extensive public interest in their financial statements. Listed companies are important because they make a substantial contribution to the economy. They are also important because the accounting practices they follow have been shaping financial accounting and reporting for all businesses for many years. The regulatory framework ensures that the annual report and accounts are prepared in a standard way and provide high quality, reliable information for external users. All public and private companies in the UK must file their annual report and accounts with Companies House, where they are available to the public.

We have examined the regulation of financial reporting in the context of the historical reasons for national differences in accounting practices, the need for harmonization among EU Member States and wider international convergence. We have looked at some of the advantages and disadvantages of accounting standards in general as well as the pros and cons of full IFRS and the IFRS for SMEs. We have also evaluated the arguments for and against differential reporting and discussed the development of little GAAP in the UK in terms of concessions in company law and simplified financial reporting standards.

The large number of jurisdictions adopting, adapting or permitting the use of IFRSs is a very important development and this chapter has provided an overview of the way in which the IASB sets IFRSs. In the next chapter we will examine the conceptual framework that provides the principles the IASB follows when setting an accounting standard.

References

Alexander, D. and Nobes, C. (2010) *Financial Accounting – An International Introduction*, 4th edn. Harlow: Pearson (FT Prentice Hall).

Ball, R. (2006) 'International Financial Reporting Standards (IFRS): pros and cons for investors', *Accounting and Business Research*, International Accounting Policy forum, pp. 5–27.

Cairns, D. (2011) 'Financial reporting by micro-entities', *Accountancy*, November, p. 57.

Companies House (2016) *Changes to Accounting Standards and Regulations*, 29 February. Available at: https://companieshouse.blog.gov.uk/2016/02/29/changes-to-accounting-standards-and-regulations/ (Accessed 30 June 2016).

Dearing, R. (1988) *The Making of Accounting Standards*, Report of the Review Committee (The Dearing Report), London: ICAEW.

Deloitte (2010) *Swimming in Words – Surveying Narrative Reporting in Annual Reports*. Available at: www.iasplus.com/en/binary/uk/1010ukswimmingin words.pdf (Accessed 5 December 2016).

FRC (2014) *FRC publishes 'True and Fair' statement*, PN 33/14, 4 June. Available at: www.frc.org.uk/News-and-Events/FRC-Press/Press/2014/June/FRC-publishes-%E2%80%98True-and-Fair%E2%80%99-statement.aspx (Accessed 11 August 2016).

Gray, R., Owen, D. and Maunders, K. (1987) *Corporate Social Reporting: Accounting and Accountability*, Harlow: Prentice Hall.

Haller, A. and Walton, P. (2003) 'Country differences and harmonization', in Walton, P., Haller, A. and Raffournier, B. (eds), *International Accounting*, 2nd edn, London: International Thomson Business Press.

IASB (2015a) *Exposure Draft Conceptual Framework for Financial Reporting*, London: IFRS Foundation.

IASB (2015b) *IFRS for SMEs*, London: International Accounting Standards Board.

IFRS Foundation (2016a) *How We are Structured*. Available at: www.ifrs.org/About-us/Pages/How-we-are-structured.aspx (Accessed 8 February 2016).

IFRS Foundation (2016b) *How We Develop Standards*. Available at: www.ifrs.org/How-we-develop-standards/Pages/How-we-develop-standards.aspx (Accessed 8 February 2016).

IFRS Foundation (2016c) *About the IFRS for SMEs*. Available at: www.ifrs.org/IFRS-for-SMEs/Pages/IFRS-for-SMEs.aspx (Accessed 8 February 2016).

IIRC (2013) *The International <IR> Framework*, International Integrated Reporting Council, December.

Ted Baker (2016) *Ted Baker Plc Annual Report and Accounts 2015–16*. Available at: www.tedbakerplc.com/investor-relations/results-and-reports/2016 (Accessed 11 May 2016).

Zeff, S.A. (2007) 'Some obstacles to global financial reporting comparability and convergence at a high level of quality', *The British Accounting Review*, 39, pp. 290–302.

Discussion questions

1   Debate the need for the regulation of financial reporting.

2   Discuss the historical reasons why one country's GAAP could develop differently from another.

Practice questions

3   Define the term *financial reporting* and explain the purpose of the regulatory framework.

4   Explain the acronym GAAP and describe the key elements of the regulatory framework for public and private companies in the UK.

5   *Pros and cons of IFRS*

Write a short essay on the above title. You should briefly explain what an accounting standard is and the principal objectives of the IFRS Foundation. The main focus should be an evaluation of the advantages and disadvantages of IFRS. Draw conclusions from your analysis.

6   *The big GAAP/little GAAP debate*

Write a short essay on the above title. You should briefly explain what is meant by 'differential reporting'. The main focus should be an evaluation of the arguments for and against little GAAP. Draw conclusions from your analysis.

7   *Harmonization of financial reporting in Europe*

Write a short essay on the above title. You should briefly explain what financial reporting is. The main focus should be a discussion of how developments in company law and accounting standards have contributed to harmonization in the EU. You may wish to use the UK as an example. Draw conclusions from your analysis.

8   *Concessions for small companies*

Write a short essay on the above title. You should explain how a small company is defined. You may wish to use the UK as an example. The main focus should be a discussion of the advantages and disadvantages of abridged accounts and audit exemption for small companies. Draw conclusions from your analysis.

Suggested research questions for dissertation students

Students interested in the effects of IFRS adoption may wish to investigate one or more of the following research questions:

- Has the adoption of IFRS been beneficial to users of financial information?
- What are the costs of IFRS adoption?

Preliminary reading

Armstrong, C., Barth, M., Jagolinzer, A. and Riedl, E. (2010) 'Market reaction to the adoption of IFRS in Europe', *The Accounting Review*, 85(1), pp. 31–61.

Ball, R. (2006) 'International Financial Reporting Standards (IFRS): Pros and cons for investors', *Accounting and Business Research*, International Accounting Policy forum, pp. 5–27.

Houqe, N., Van Zijl, T., Dunstan, K.L., Karim, A.K.M.W. (2012) 'The effect of IFRS adoption and investor protection on earnings quality around the world', *International Journal of Accounting*, 47(3), pp. 333–355.

Nobes, C. (2006) 'The survival of international differences under IFRS: Towards a research agenda', *Accounting and Business Research*, 36(3), pp. 233–245.

Nobes, C. (2015) 'International differences in IFRS adoptions and IFRS practices', in Jones, S. (ed.), *The Routledge Companion to Financial Accounting Theory*, pp. 167–196.

Walker, M. (2010) 'Accounting for varieties of capitalism: The case against a single set of global accounting standards', *The British Accounting Review*, 42, pp. 137–152.

Zeff, S.A. (2007) 'Some obstacles to global financial reporting comparability and convergence at a high level of quality', *The British Accounting Review*, 39, pp. 290–302.

Students interested in accounting quality may wish to investigate one or more of the following research questions:

- Does accounting quality improve after adoption of IFRS?
- What is the impact of institutional factors on accounting quality?
- Which firm-specific characteristics affect accounting quality?

Preliminary reading

Barth, M., Landsman, W. and Lang, M. (2008) 'International Accounting Standards and accounting quality', *Journal of Accounting Research*, 46(3), pp. 467–498.

Christensen, H., Lee, E. and Walker, M. (2008) 'Incentives or Standards: What determines accounting quality changes around IFRS adoption?' *AAA 2008 Financial Accounting and Reporting Section (FARS) Paper (SSRN.com)*.

Dechow, P., Ge, W. and Schrand, C. (2010) 'Understanding earnings quality: A review of the proxies, their determinants and their consequences', *Journal of Accounting & Economics*, 50(2/3), pp. 344–401.

Paananen, M. and Lin, H. (2009) 'The development of accounting quality of IAS and IFRS over time: The case of Germany', *Journal of International Accounting Research*, 8(1), pp. 31–55.

Schipper, K. and Vincent, L. (2003) 'Earnings quality', *Accounting Horizon*, Supplement 17, pp. 97–110.

Students interested in the IFRS for SMEs may wish to investigate one or more of the following research questions:

- What are the pros and cons of the IFRS for SMEs or its equivalent to preparers, auditors and users in [country]?

- What is the impact of introducing the IFRS for SMEs (or an adaptation of it) in [country]?

- What are the pros and cons of developing an international accounting standard for micro-entities?

Preliminary reading

Collis, J., Jarvis, R. and Skerratt, L. (2017) 'The role and current status of IFRS in the completion of national accounting rules: Evidence from the UK', *Accounting in Europe*, Special Issue.

Di Pietra, R., Evans, L., Chevy, J., Cisi, M., Eierle, B. and Jarvis, R. (2008) 'Comment on the IASB's Exposure Draft "IFRS for Small and Medium-Sized Entities"', *Accounting in Europe*, 5(1–2), pp. 27–47.

Evans, L., Gebhardt, G., Hoogendoorn, M., Marton, J., Di Pietra, R., Mora, A., Thinggard, F., Vehmanen, P. and Wagenhofer, A. (2005) 'Problems and opportunities of an International Financial Reporting Standard for Smaller Entities. The EAA FRSC's comment on the IASB Discussion Paper', *Accounting in Europe*, 2, pp. 23–45.

Kaya, D. and Koch, M. (2015) 'Countries' adoption of the International Financial Reporting Standard for Small and Medium-sized Entities (IFRS for SMEs) – early empirical evidence', *Accounting and Business Research*, 45(1), pp. 93–120.

Mkasiwa, T.A. (2014) 'SMEs' financial and differential reporting – A review of publications', *International Journal of Accounting and Financial Reporting*, 4(2), pp. 82–103.

Pacter, P. (2009) 'An IFRS for private entities', *International Journal of Disclosure and Governance*, 6(1), pp. 4–20.

Pacter, P. (2014) 'The IFRS for SMEs', in van Mourik, C. and Walton, P. (eds), *The Routledge Companion to Accounting, Reporting and Regulation*, pp. 411–434.

Students interested in the accounting and assurance needs of small private companies may wish to investigate one or more of the following research questions:

- What are the pros and cons of the abridged accounts for preparers and users of the financial statements of small companies?

- What are the pros and cons of exemption from statutory audit for preparers and users of the financial statements of small companies?
- What is the impact of raising the size thresholds for small companies on the services offered by accountants in [country]?

Preliminary reading

Collis, J. (2012) 'Determinants of voluntary audit and voluntary full accounts in micro- and non-micro small companies in the UK', *Accounting and Business Research*, 42(4), pp. 1–28.

Collis, J. (2010) 'Audit exemption and the demand for voluntary audit – a comparative analysis of the UK and Denmark', *International Journal of Auditing*, 14(2), pp. 211–231.

Collis, J. (2008) *Directors' Views on Accounting and Auditing Requirements for SMEs*, London: BERR. Available from: http://webarchive.nationalarchives. gov.uk/20090609003228/http:/www.berr.gov.uk/files/file50491.pdf (Accessed 8 February 2016).

Collis, J., Jarvis, R. and Skerratt, L. (2004) 'The demand for the audit in small companies in the UK', *Accounting and Business Research*, 34(2), pp. 87–100.

5 The conceptual framework for financial reporting

Learning objectives

When you have studied this chapter, you should be able to:

- Explain the need for a conceptual framework for financial reporting
- Describe the objective and users of general purpose financial statements
- Discuss the qualitative characteristics of useful financial information
- Define the elements of financial statements and explain the recognition and measurement criteria
- Explain the concepts of capital and capital maintenance

5.1 Introduction

In Chapter 4 we explained that financial accounting is primarily concerned with providing a true and fair view of the activities of a business to external parties. Financial statements are prepared in accordance with a regulatory framework, which in many countries comprises company law, accounting standards and stock exchange rules for listed companies. However, we noted that there are likely to be national differences in how the regulation of financial reporting developed due to social, economic and legal factors. In addition, there may be differences as a result of national regulators focusing on the needs of different user groups. This means that the regulators in different jurisdictions may have based their accounting standards on different theoretical principles.

In this chapter we will explain how the development of the International Financial Reporting Standards (IFRSs) issued by the International Accounting Standards Board (IASB) is underpinned by a conceptual framework. We are focusing on the IASB's Conceptual Framework for Financial Reporting, because around 150 countries worldwide have adopted or permit the use of IFRSs. This chapter is important because the principles contained in the conceptual framework help improve the quality of financial reporting and are reflected in the IFRSs we examine in the next few chapters. We start by looking at the need for such a framework and then discuss some of the key principles and definitions.

5.2   Need for a conceptual framework

Prior to the 1970s, the way in which accountants in the USA and UK had tried to achieve consistency in financial accounting was to take an inductive approach, which was based on rationalizing what happened in practice. However, this was criticized because problems were only dealt with as they arose, which caused overlaps, contradictions and loopholes. Policymakers then tried a deductive approach, which was based on theoretical assumptions, but this was considered to be unrealistic because it challenged best practice. This led to demand for a *conceptual framework*.

Activity

In the context of financial reporting, what do you understand by the term 'conceptual framework'?

A conceptual framework for financial reporting is a theory of accounting prepared by a policymaker, such as a standard-setting body, that is intended to guide financial accounting and reporting. It provides a set of coherent underlying principles that addresses questions such as:

- What is the objective of financial reporting?
- Who are the users of the financial statements?
- What information does each group of users need?
- What type of financial statements will best satisfy users' needs?
- What are assets, liabilities, equity, income and expenses, when should they be recognized and how should they be measured, presented and disclosed in the financial statements?

Key definition

A conceptual framework for financial reporting is a statement of the theoretical principles that underpin the development and interpretation of accounting standards.

In the USA, the Financial Accounting Standards Board (FASB) published *Concept Statements* between 1978 and 2000. These were a strong influence on developments at the international level, and in 1989 the *International Accounting Standards Committee (IASC)* issued the *Framework for the Preparation and Presentation of Financial Statements*, which was subsequently adopted by its successor, the IASB. This sets out the theoretical principles that underpin the development and interpretation of IFRSs, which guide financial accounting and reporting to external users.

Although the *Framework for the Preparation and Presentation of Financial Statements* had been useful, there were some gaps and deficiencies that needed addressing. For example:

- It provided very little guidance on measurement or presentation and disclosure.
- The guidance on when assets and liabilities should be recognized was out of date.
- It was unclear what role measurement uncertainty should play in the definitions of assets and liabilities and in decisions about their recognition and measurement.

Therefore, a joint project was started with FASB to revise the IASB's *Framework for the Preparation and Presentation of Financial Statements* and led to the publication of a partly revised version in 2010 under a new title: *Conceptual Framework for Financial Reporting*. In 2011, the IASB carried out a public consultation on its future agenda and many respondents identified the Conceptual Framework as a priority project. Consequently, the IASB restarted its Conceptual Framework project and in 2015 published an Exposure Draft (ED/2015/3) of the fully revised *Conceptual Framework for Financial Reporting*. The final version is due to be published in 2017, which is after this book goes to print. Therefore, we are going to focus on the Exposure Draft, which we will refer to as the draft Conceptual Framework. You can keep up to date on developments by checking the IASB's website www.ifrs.org/Current-Projects/IASB-Projects/Conceptual-Framework/Pages/Conceptual-Framework-Summary.aspx. In the following text, numbers in square brackets refer to the paragraph number in the Draft.

Activity

What are the advantages of having a conceptual framework for financial reporting?

You might start by thinking about the deficiencies in the inductive and deductive approaches taken previously, and then go on to consider who will benefit from a conceptual framework. The main advantage of a conceptual framework is that it clarifies the conceptual underpinnings of accounting standards and allows standard setters to develop accounting standards on a consistent basis. It also assists preparers, auditors and users of financial statements to understand the approach to standard setting, and the nature and function of the financial information reported. Another advantage is that it gives guidance to preparers resolving accounting issues that are not specifically addressed by an existing IFRS or interpretation.

The draft Conceptual Framework is important because it shapes the decisions that the IASB makes when developing future Standards. The introduction to the draft Conceptual Framework [IN1] explains that its *purpose* is to:

(a) assist the IASB to develop Standards that are based on consistent concepts;
(b) assist preparers to develop consistent accounting policies when no Standard applies to a particular transaction or event, or when a Standard allows a choice of accounting policy; and
(c) assist all parties to understand and interpret the Standards.

As you can see, the IASB uses the generic term 'Standard' which covers International Accounting Standards (IASs), International Financial Reporting Standards (IFRSs), the IFRS for SMEs and any other Standard aimed at a particular group of entities that it may issue in the future. It is important to note that the draft Conceptual Framework is not a Standard and does not override any specific Standards.

Looking at the content page for the draft Conceptual Framework, you will see that there are eight chapters:

CHAPTER 1—THE OBJECTIVE OF GENERAL PURPOSE FINANCIAL REPORTING
CHAPTER 2—QUALITATIVE CHARACTERISTICS OF USEFUL FINANCIAL INFORMATION
CHAPTER 3—FINANCIAL STATEMENTS AND THE REPORTING ENTITY
CHAPTER 4—THE ELEMENTS OF FINANCIAL STATEMENTS
CHAPTER 5—RECOGNITION AND DERECOGNITION
CHAPTER 6—MEASUREMENT
CHAPTER 7—PRESENTATION AND DISCLOSURE
CHAPTER 8—CONCEPTS OF CAPITAL AND CAPITAL MAINTENANCE

We will examine the main principles contained in these chapters next.

5.3 Objective and users of general purpose financial statements

The draft Conceptual Framework is a set of principles that underpins the preparation of *general purpose* financial statements intended to meet the needs of a range of external users. General purpose financial statements can be distinguished from *special purpose* financial statements, such as those prepared specifically for share offerings, borrowing or tax purposes.

5.3.1   Objective

Chapter 1 of the draft Conceptual Framework states that the *objective of general purpose financial reporting* is to provide information about the reporting entity that is useful to existing and potential investors, lenders and other creditors in making decisions about providing resources to the entity. Those decisions involve buying, selling or holding equity and debt instruments and providing or settling loans and other forms of credit [1.2]. This principle forms the foundation of the Conceptual Framework and other aspects of the Conceptual Framework flow logically from the objective.

5.3.2   Users and their needs

You can see from the objective that the draft Conceptual Framework defines the primary users of general purpose financial reports as existing and potential investors, lenders and other creditors. These users require financial information for economic decision-making purposes.

- *Existing and potential investors* need financial information to help them make investment decisions such as buying, selling or holding equity and debt instruments. These decisions depend on the investment risks and returns. Returns might include dividends payable on shares, principal and interest payments or market price increases in equity and debt instruments.
- *Existing and potential lenders* need financial information to help them make lending decisions. These decisions depend on the lending risks and returns. They need to assess whether loans can be repaid and whether the interest they expect to receive will be paid when it is due. As expectations depend on their assessment of the amount, timing and uncertainty of payments, they need information that will help them assess the prospects for future net cash inflows to an entity.
- *Existing and potential creditors* need financial information to help them make credit decisions. These decisions will depend on the credit risks and returns. The latter usually take the form of interest payments. As in the case of lenders, their expectations depend on their assessment of the amount, timing and uncertainty of receiving the amounts owed to them and therefore they need information that will help them assess the prospects for future net cash inflows to an entity.

We can conclude from this discussion that one of the main *purposes* of financial reporting is to provide information to help users make *economic decisions*. However, users also need relevant and reliable financial information to assess the *stewardship* of management. The draft Conceptual Framework explains that in order to assess an entity's prospects for future net cash inflows, users need information about the resources of the entity, claims against the entity, and information on how efficiently and effectively the entity's management has discharged its responsibility for the entity's resources [1.4]. Figure 5.1 summarizes the primary users and their needs.

Figure 5.1 Primary users of general purpose financial reports

The draft Conceptual Framework acknowledges that general purpose financial reports cannot meet all the information needs of the primary users, many of whom are not in a position to demand special purpose financial reports. Therefore, users will also need to obtain information from other sources such as reports on general economic conditions and expectations, political events and political climate, and industry and company outlooks [1.6]. For example, if you were an investor, you could make use of information supplied by investment analysts or conduct your own analysis of the economy from International Monetary Fund reports. You could analyze the industry from market reports and compare the entity's performance against that of its competitors or industry benchmarks using data from trade associations or financial databases.

You need to remember that general purpose financial reports are not designed to show the value of a reporting entity. The draft Conceptual Framework points out that these financial reports are intended to provide information to help existing and potential investors, lenders and other creditors estimate the value of the reporting entity. Although these primary user groups have different, and possibly conflicting, information needs, when developing Standards the IASB will seek to provide information that will meet the needs of the maximum number of primary users. However, focusing on common information needs does not prevent the entity from including additional information in its financial reports that is most useful to a particular subset of primary users [1.7–1.8].

Activity

The Conceptual Framework focuses on the primary user groups. Who do you think are the other significant users of general purpose financial reports and what are their information needs?

You may have thought of the following groups:

- Employees need information for assessing any immediate financial benefits, such as bonuses based on the company's results, or for pay bargaining. They are also interested in information that helps them assess any risk to their job security, future prospects or future benefits, such as private health insurance and retirement pension.
- Customers are interested in information about the continued existence of the business and its ability to supply goods and services, especially if there are product warranties or specialized replacement parts involved.
- The government and its agencies are interested in the allocation of resources and the effect of their economic and fiscal policies. Therefore, they need information for regulatory purposes, assessing taxation and compiling statistics.
- The public in general are interested in information that is relevant to how they are affected by the company. For example, the contribution it makes to the local economy by providing employment or using local suppliers; its involvement in the community; its contributions to political and charitable groups; its sustainability policies and impact on the environment.

The Framework notes that the needs of *management* are not considered because managers can obtain the information they need internally. Although other external parties, including *regulators* (e.g. prudential and market regulators) and members of the *public* may also find general purpose financial reports useful, such reports are not directed at meeting their specific needs [1.9–1.10].

Activity

What do you think would be the effect on users if a large company did not supply full information about its financial position, financial performance and changes in financial position to the primary user groups?

One way to tackle this question is to remember that existing and potential investors need financial reports in order to assess investment risk and return, and to assess the stewardship of management. The other primary user group comprises existing and potential lenders and other creditors. You may have thought of some of the following factors:

- Investors will be suspicious that the directors had something to hide and are running the company for their own benefit rather than in the best interests of investors. Therefore, existing and potential investors would be unwilling to invest in the business.
- Lenders would be unable to assess and monitor the lending risk. Therefore, they might withdraw existing sources of finance, raise the interest rates, shorten the term of the loan or ask for personal guarantees from the directors. The company would find it harder to obtain access to new sources of finance.

- Suppliers would also be unable to assess risk and might refuse to give credit terms to the company or require the company to insure against the risk of being unable to pay for goods and services supplied on credit.

Investors, lenders and other creditors have a common interest in information about the entity's economic resources and the claims against the reporting entity. This information is shown in the *statement of financial position*. They are also interested in information about the effects of transactions and other events that change a reporting entity's economic resources and claims. This is shown in the *statement of profit or loss and other comprehensive income*. Finally, they have a common interest in the changes in the entity's cash flows, which are presented in the *statement of cash flows*. However, one point of difference is that while lenders and major suppliers have the economic power to demand special purpose financial statements, investors have no such power and must rely on general purpose financial statements.

The draft Conceptual Framework asserts that information about the nature and amounts of the entity's economic resources and claims can help users identify its financial strengths and weaknesses. This can help users assess the entity's liquidity and solvency, its needs for additional finance and how successful it is likely to be in obtaining that finance. That information can also help users assess management's stewardship of the entity's resources. Information about priorities and payment requirements of existing claims helps users predict how future cash flows will be distributed among those with a claim against the business [1.13].

5.3.3 Qualitative characteristics of useful financial information

Chapter 2 of the draft Conceptual Framework focuses on what makes financial information useful. It starts by explaining that financial reports provide information about the reporting entity's economic resources, claims against the reporting entity and the effects of transactions and other events and conditions that change those resources and claims. Some financial reports also include explanatory material about management's expectations and strategies for the reporting entity and other types of forward-looking information [2.2]. The *qualitative characteristics* of useful financial information apply to financial information provided in financial statements, as well as to financial information provided in other ways. The draft Conceptual Framework acknowledges that there are cost constraints on the entity's ability to provide such useful financial information, but contends that the considerations in applying the qualitative characteristics and the cost constraint may be different for different types of information. For example, applying them to forward-looking information may be different from applying them to information about existing economic resources and claims and to changes in those resources and claims [2.3].

The qualitative characteristics that are likely to make the financial information useful to users are divided into *fundamental* and *enhancing* characteristics. The fundamental qualitative characteristics are [2.5–2.19]:

- *Relevance* – Relevant financial information is capable of making a difference to users' decisions. Financial information is capable of making a difference to decisions if it has predictive value and/or confirmatory value. These two are interrelated. *Materiality* is an entity-specific aspect of relevance based on the nature or magnitude (or both) of the items to which the information relates in the context of an individual entity's financial report. The *materiality concept* is the principle that only items of information that are material (significant) are included in the financial statements. Information is material if its omission or misstatement could influence the economic decisions of the primary users of general purpose financial reports. Materiality depends on the size of the item or error and the circumstances of its omission or misstatement (for example, an omission of revenue of £10 versus an omission of £10,000). One factor affecting the relevance of financial information is the level of *measurement uncertainty*. This arises when a measure for an asset or a liability cannot be observed directly and must be estimated. The use of estimates is an essential part of the preparation of financial information and does not necessarily undermine its relevance, but the estimate needs to be properly described and disclosed.
- *Faithful representation* – General purpose financial reports represent economic phenomena in words as well as numbers. To be useful, financial information must not only represent relevant phenomena, but it must also faithfully represent the phenomena that it purports to represent. A faithful representation provides information about the substance of an economic phenomenon instead of merely providing information about its legal form. Providing information only about a legal form that differs from the economic substance of the underlying economic phenomenon would not result in a faithful representation. Ideally, a faithful representation would be complete, neutral and free from error. A complete depiction includes all information necessary for a user to understand the phenomenon being depicted, including all necessary descriptions and explanations. A neutral depiction is without bias in the selection or presentation of financial information. Neutrality is supported by the exercise of *prudence*. Prudence requires caution when making judgements under conditions of uncertainty. The exercise of prudence means that assets and income are not overstated and liabilities and expenses are not understated. Equally, prudence does not allow for the understatement of assets and income or the overstatement of liabilities and expenses, because such misstatements can lead to the overstatement of income or the understatement of expenses in future periods. 'Free from error' does not mean perfectly accurate. For example, an estimate of an unobservable value cannot be perfectly accurate, but it is a faithful representation if it is clearly described as being an estimate and the nature and limitations of the estimating process are explained, and no errors have been made in selecting and applying an appropriate process for developing the estimate.

Subject to the effects of enhancing characteristics and the cost constraint, the draft Conceptual Framework suggests that the most efficient and effective process for applying the fundamental qualitative characteristics would usually be [2.21]:

1. Identify an economic phenomenon that is capable of being useful to users of the entity's financial information.
2. Identify the type of information about that phenomenon that would be most relevant if it is available and can be faithfully represented.
3. Determine whether that information is available and can be faithfully represented. If so, the process of satisfying the fundamental qualitative characteristics ends at that point. If not, the process is repeated with the next most relevant type of information.

We will now examine the enhancing qualitative characteristics [2.22–2.35]:

- *Comparability* – The information is more useful if it can be compared with similar information for the entity in other periods, or similar information for other entities. A comparison requires at least two items. Consistency helps achieve comparability and refers to the use of the same methods for the same items, either from period to period within a reporting entity or in a single period across entities.
- *Verifiability* – The financial information is more useful if it is verifiable. Verifiability helps to assure users that the information is a faithful representation. It means that different knowledgeable and independent observers could reach consensus, although not necessarily complete agreement, that a particular depiction is a faithful representation.
- *Timeliness* – The financial information is more useful if it is timely. Timeliness means that information is available to users in time to be capable of influencing their decisions.
- *Understandability* – The financial information is more useful if it is readily understandable. Classifying, characterizing and presenting information clearly and concisely makes it understandable. While some phenomena are inherently complex and cannot be made easy to understand, to exclude such information would make financial reports incomplete and potentially misleading. Financial reports are prepared for users who have a reasonable knowledge of business and economic activities and who review and analyze the information with diligence.

The draft Conceptual Framework states that enhancing qualitative characteristics should be maximized to the extent possible. However, either individually or as a group, the enhancing characteristics cannot make information useful if that information is irrelevant or is not faithfully represented. Applying the enhancing qualitative characteristics is an iterative process that does not follow a prescribed order [2.36–2.37].

Figure 5.2 summarizes the qualitative characteristics of useful financial information we have discussed.

Figure 5.2 Qualitative characteristics of useful financial information

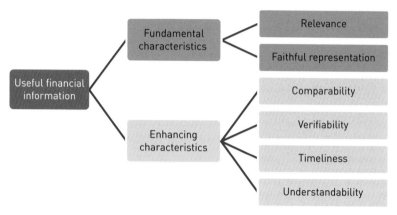

Although you may find some of the principles difficult to understand at this stage, the importance of the concepts will become clearer as you progress through the next few chapters. The following activity will help you think about some of the main qualitative characteristics that make financial information useful.

Activity

Think about your bank statements or credit card statements and answer the following questions:

	Yes	No
(a) Is any item insignificant or irrelevant?	❏	❏
(b) Does the information help you make spending or borrowing decisions?	❏	❏
(c) Is the information a faithful representation of your transactions?	❏	❏
(d) Is the information timely enough to make spending or borrowing decisions to stop you inadvertently incurring additional costs?	❏	❏
(e) Is the information prepared consistently so that you can compare it with corresponding information for previous periods?	❏	❏
(f) Assuming the information is relevant, is it easy to understand?	❏	❏

Of course, cost is a key constraint on the information that can be provided by financial reporting and it is important that the costs are justified by the benefits. In applying the cost constraint, the IASB seeks qualitative and quantitative information from providers of financial information, users, auditors, academics and others about the expected nature and quantity of the benefits and costs of that standard in relation to financial reporting generally. That does not mean that assessments of costs and benefits always justify the same reporting requirements for all entities [2.38–2.41]. As you will remember from the previous chapter, the *IFRS for SMEs* (IASB, 2015b) demonstrates that differences may be appropriate because the reporting applies to a different type of entity (non-publicly accountable entities), different ways of raising capital (only privately), different users' needs or other factors.

5.4   Financial statements and their elements

Chapter 3 of the draft Conceptual Framework covers the role of the financial statements and the boundary of the reporting entity, while Chapter 4 defines the elements of financial statements.

5.4.1   Role of financial statements

The draft Conceptual Framework explains that general purpose financial reports provide information about the reporting entity's economic resources, claims against the entity and changes in those economic resources and claims. General purpose financial statements are a particular form of general purpose financial report in which the financial effects of transactions and other events are classified into assets, liabilities, equity, income and expenses. Financial statements provide information about the financial effects of economic transactions and events of a specified period. Those transactions and events give rise to changes in the entity's assets, liabilities and equity. When combined with the effects of transactions and events from previous periods, those changes give rise to the entity's assets, liabilities and equity at the end of the period [3.2–3.5].

The *objective of financial statements* is to provide information about an entity's assets, liabilities, equity, income and expenses that is useful to users of financial statements in assessing the prospects for future net cash inflows to the entity and in assessing management's stewardship of the entity's resources. It is important to remember that financial statements are prepared from the perspective of the entity, not from the perspective of a particular group of investors, lenders or creditors [3.4–3.9].

The draft Conceptual Framework is based on the assumption that the reporting entity is a *going concern* and will continue in operation for the foreseeable future. It is assumed that the entity has neither the intention nor the need to liquidate or cease trading. If such an intention or need exists, the financial statements may have to be prepared on a different basis and the basis used must be disclosed [3.10]. This important assumption underpins the accrual basis of accounting, which we discussed in Chapter 3 of this book.

> **Key definition**
>
> A reporting entity is defined as an entity that chooses, or is required, to prepare general purpose financial statements. It is not necessarily a legal entity and can comprise a portion of an entity, or two or more entities.
>
> Source: IASB, 2015a [3.11]. Reproduced with permission from the IFRS Foundation.

Financial statements provide information about the assets, liabilities, equity, income and expenses generated by the set of economic activities that lie within the boundary of the reporting entity. When one entity (the parent) has control over another entity (the subsidiary), it would be possible to determine the boundary of the reporting entity using either:

(a) direct control only; or
(b) both direct control and indirect control [3.11–3.14].

We look at the concept of control more closely in Chapter 9 of this book.

5.4.2 Elements of financial statements

Before we look at the elements of financial statements in detail, we need to have an overview of what constitutes a set of financial statements. Guidance on the presentation of general purpose financial statements is contained in IAS 1, *Presentation of Financial Statements* (IASB, 2014). A complete set of financial statements comprises:

- a statement of financial position at the end of the period
- a statement of profit or loss and other comprehensive income for the period
- a statement of changes in equity for the period
- a statement of cash flows for the period
- notes, comprising a summary of significant accounting policies and other explanatory notes
- comparative information for the previous period in respect of all amounts reported in the financial statements and in the notes, unless another Standard requires otherwise. Comparative information is provided for narrative and descriptive content if it is relevant to understanding the financial statements of the current period.

Table 5.1 compares the IASB's terms with those traditionally used in the UK. When looking at the annual report and accounts of UK companies, you need to remember that reporting entities are not obliged to use the IAS 1 titles for their financial statements, but many do.

Table 5.1   Set of financial statements under IAS 1

IASB terminology	Traditional UK terminology
Statement of profit or loss and other comprehensive income	Profit and loss account
Statement of financial position	Balance sheet
Statement of changes in equity	Statement of recognized gains and losses
Statement of cash flows	Cash flow statement

An entity must present a complete set of financial statements at least annually, with comparative information for the previous period. The following items must be identified:

- The reporting enterprise.
- Whether the statements are for a single entity or a group.
- The date or period covered.
- The presentation currency and the level of precision (thousands, millions, etc.).

Each material class of items must be presented separately in the financial statements and dissimilar items may be aggregated only if they are individually immaterial. For consistency, the presentation and classification of items in the financial statements should stay the same from one period to the next, unless a change is justified by a change in circumstances or a new IFRS.

We are now ready to consider the *elements* of the financial statements. Chapter 4 in the draft Conceptual Framework explains that the financial effects of transactions and other events that are reported in general purpose financial statements are classified into *assets, liabilities, equity, income* and *expenses*. These are the elements that form the basic building blocks from which financial statements are constructed. The presentation of these elements in the statement of financial position and the statement of profit or loss and other comprehensive income involves a process of sub-classification in order to present the information in a way that is useful to users. The statement of cash flows reflects elements in the statement of profit or loss and other comprehensive income, and some changes in the elements in the statement of financial position.

Financial position is concerned with the economic resources the entity controls, its financial structure, its liquidity and solvency and its ability to adapt to changes in the business environment. Users need information on the entity's financial position to help them assess its ability to generate future cash flows and evaluate how those cash flows will be distributed among stakeholders. In addition, users need information to evaluate the entity's ability to raise any finance that might be needed and to meet financial commitments when they fall due. The elements that relate to the entity's financial position are shown in the statement of financial position. These elements are:

- assets
- liabilities
- equity.

> **Key definition**
>
> An asset is a present economic resource controlled by the entity as a result of past events.
>
> An economic resource is a right that has the potential to produce economic benefits.
>
> A liability is a present obligation of the entity to transfer an economic resource as a result of past events.
>
> Equity is the residual interest in the assets of the entity after deducting all its liabilities.
>
> Source: IASB, 2015a [4.4]. Reproduced with permission from the IFRS Foundation.

Under IAS 1, assets and liabilities must not be offset against each other, unless expressly required or permitted by an IFRS. The IFRS for SMEs does not allow off-setting either.

Activity

In the following scenarios decide whether you should classify the item as an asset or a liability.

	Asset	Liability
(a) Your taxi business, Parker Cars Ltd, provides a warranty to all contract customers that their chauffeur will arrive on time.	❑	❑
(b) Parker Cars Ltd has acquired a licence that cost £25,000 that allows you to operate your business close to the two main London airports. This will save you £5,000 in motoring costs over the next four years.	❑	❑
(c) Parker Cars Ltd has paid Autoshop Ltd £5,000 towards setting up a workshop that will give priority to any maintenance or repairs needed by your vehicles.	❑	❑

Answers: (a) Liability (b) Asset (c) You might have been tempted to classify this as an asset, but it is not an asset because the resource is not controlled by Parker Cars Ltd. In addition, the argument that there are future economic benefits is weak.

Financial performance is concerned with the profitability of the entity. Users need information on the entity's financial performance to assess potential changes in its economic resources and its capacity to generate cash from its resources. In addition, users need information to evaluate how effectively any additional resources might be used. The elements that relate to the measurement of financial performance are shown in the statement of comprehensive income and the statement of changes in equity. These elements are:

- income
- expenses.

Key definition

Income is defined as increases in assets or decreases in liabilities that result in increases in equity, other than those relating to contributions from holders of equity claims.

Expenses are defined as decreases in assets or increases in liabilities that result in decreases in equity, other than those relating to distributions to holders of equity claims.

Source: IASB, 2015a [4.4]. Reproduced with permission from the IFRS Foundation.

Income and expenses include amounts generated by transactions and other events, including changes in the carrying amount of assets and liabilities. Note that under IAS 1, income and expenses may not be offset against each other unless expressly required or permitted by an IFRS.

5.5 Recognition and measurement of elements

Chapter 5 of the draft Conceptual Framework covers the recognition and derecognition of assets, liabilities, equity, income and expenses, while Chapter 6 discusses their measurement.

5.5.1 Recognition

Recognition is the process of capturing, for inclusion in the statement of financial position or the statement(s) of financial performance, an item that meets the definition of an element. It involves depicting the item (either alone or as part of a line item) in words and by a monetary amount, and including that amount in totals in the relevant statement [5.2]. Recognition links the elements, the statement of financial position and the statement(s) of financial performance as follows [5.4]:

(a) in the opening and closing statements of financial position, total assets less total liabilities equal total equity;

(b) recognised changes in equity during the period comprise:
   (i) income less expenses recognised in the statement(s) of financial performance; plus
   (ii) contributions from holders of equity claims, less distributions to holders of equity claims.

The recognition criteria are based on the qualitative characteristics of useful financial information. An entity recognizes an asset or a liability (and any related income, expenses or changes in equity) if such recognition provides users of financial statements with the following [5.9]:

(a) relevant information about the asset or the liability and about any income, expenses or changes in equity;
(b) a faithful representation of the asset or the liability and of any income, expenses or changes in equity; and
(c) information that results in benefits exceeding the cost of providing that information.

These criteria may not be met if one or more of the following applies [5.13]:

(a) it is uncertain whether an asset or liability exists;
(b) there is only a low probability of future inflows (outflows) of economic benefits from the asset (liability); or
(c) the level of measurement uncertainty is so high that the resulting information has little relevance.

5.5.2   Derecognition

Derecognition is the process of removing all or a part of an asset or a liability from an entity's statement of financial position. The draft Conceptual Framework provides guidance on derecognition aimed at providing a faithful representation of [5.26]:

(a) the assets and liabilities retained after a transaction or other event that led to derecognition (including any asset or liability acquired, incurred or created a part of the transaction or other event); and
(b) the change in the entity's assets and liabilities as a result of that transaction or other event.

Normally decisions about derecognition are straightforward, but they can be more difficult when these two aims are in conflict.

5.5.3   Measurement

Chapter 6 of the draft Conceptual Framework defines *measurement* as the process of quantifying, in monetary terms, information about an entity's assets, liabilities, equity, income and expenses. It explains that consideration of the objective of financial reporting, the qualitative characteristics of useful financial information and the cost constraint is likely to result in the selection of different measurement bases for different assets, liabilities and items of income and expense [6.2–6.3]. The measurement bases are divided into two categories:

• *Historical cost* – Measures based on historical cost provide monetary information about assets, liabilities, income and expenses using information derived from the transaction or event that created them. You will remember that this was one of the fundamental accounting principles we described in Chapter 3 of this book. The historical cost measures of assets or liabilities do not reflect changes in prices. However, they do reflect changes such as the consumption or impairment of assets and the fulfilment of liabilities [6.6]. We will look at this in more detail in subsequent chapters.

- *Current value* – Measures based on current value provide monetary information about assets, liabilities, income and expenses using information that is updated to reflect conditions at the measurement date. Because of the updating, current values capture any positive or negative changes, since the previous measurement date, in estimates of cash flows and other factors included in those current values [6.19]. Current value measurement bases include the following:
    - *Fair value* is defined as the price that would be received to sell an asset, or paid to transfer a liability, in an orderly transaction between market participants at the measurement date [6.21].
    - *Value in use* for assets and *fulfilment value* for liabilities are entity-specific values. Value in use is the present value of the cash flows that an entity expects to derive from the continuing use of an asset and from its ultimate disposal. Fulfilment value is the present value of the cash flows that an entity expects to incur as it fulfils a liability [6.34]. We will explain the concept of present value in Chapter 22 of this book.

We will look at a simple example to illustrate the importance of having guidance on how assets should be measured.

Activity

In Chapter 2, we introduced Sarah Wick who was planning to set up a company selling candles called Candlewick Ltd. Imagine that she started the business on 1 January 2018. On that day the company bought a box of candles for £15 and by the end of the year the box of candles had been sold for £20. Imagine that the general rate of inflation during 2018 was 1%, but the cost of a box of the same type of candles had increased by 10%. What is the potential profit on the box of candles that has been sold?

a) £5
b) £3.50

Answer (a) is based on the historical cost: selling price £20 – £15 historical cost = £5 profit. On the other hand, answer (b) is based on the replacement cost: selling price £20 – £16.50 replacement cost = £3.50 profit. You do not need to take account of inflation in this case because the replacement cost is higher than the rate of inflation. As you can see, the measurement base makes a big difference to the potential profit, and that is why accounting standards stipulate which methods are allowed for different assets, liabilities and items of income and expense.

For information provided by a particular measurement basis to be useful to users of the financial statements, it must reflect the qualitative characteristics of useful financial information. As cost constrains the selection of a measurement basis, the benefits of the information provided by presentation and disclosure must be sufficient to justify the cost of providing it [6.49–6.50]. Historical cost is the most commonly used measurement base, but it is usually combined with others. We will look at specific examples when we examine specific IFRSs in subsequent chapters.

5.6 Presentation and disclosure

Chapter 7 of the draft Conceptual Framework discusses the objective and scope of financial statements, presentation and disclosure as communication tools, and information about financial performance.

5.6.1 Objective and scope of financial statements

The scope of financial statements is determined by their objective, which is to provide information about an entity's assets, liabilities, equity, income and expenses that is useful to users of financial statements in assessing the prospects for future net cash inflows to the entity and in assessing management's stewardship of the entity's resources. That information is provided [7.2]:

(a) in the statement of financial position and the statement(s) of financial performance, by recognising items that meet the definition of an element;
(b) in other parts of the financial statements, including the notes to the financial statements, by providing information about:
   (i) recognised items that meet the definition of an element;
   (ii) items that meet the definition of an element but that have not been recognised;
   (iii) cash flows; and
   (iv) contributions from, or distributions to, holders of equity claims.

The information provided in the notes to the financial statements includes [7.3]:

(a) information about the nature of both recognised and unrecognised elements and about the risks arising from them; and
(b) the methods, assumptions and judgements, and changes in those methods, assumptions and judgements, that affect the amounts presented or disclosed.

Forward-looking information about likely or possible future transactions and events is included in the financial statements only if it provides relevant information about an entity's assets, liabilities and equity that existed at the end of, or during, the period (even if they are unrecognized) or income and expenses for the period. For example, if an asset or a liability is measured by estimating future cash flows, information about the estimates of those future cash flows may be needed in order to understand the reported measures. Other types of forward-looking information are sometimes provided outside the financial statements, for example, in management commentary [7.4–7.5].

5.6.2 Presentation and disclosure as communication tools

The draft Conceptual Framework explains that financial statements present, in the statement of financial position and the statement(s) of financial performance, information about recognized assets, liabilities, equity, income and expenses. They also disclose additional information about those recognized elements and other information that is relevant to users. Efficient and effective communication of that information improves its relevance and contributes to a faithful representation of the assets, liabilities, equity, income and expenses. Such communication also enhances the understandability and comparability of information in financial statements. Efficient and effective communication includes [7.8]:

(a) classifying information in a structured manner that reports similar items together and reports dissimilar items separately;
(b) aggregating information so that it is not obscured by unnecessary detail; and
(c) using presentation and disclosure objectives and principles instead of rules that could lead to purely mechanistic compliance.

As cost constrains decisions about presentation and disclosure, the benefits of the information provided by presentation and disclosure must be sufficient to justify the cost of providing it [7.9].

5.6.3 Information about financial performance

In order to communicate information about financial performance more efficiently and effectively, income and expenses in the statement(s) of financial performance are classified into either [7.19]:

(a) the statement of profit or loss, which includes a total or subtotal for profit or loss; or
(b) other comprehensive income.

The draft Conceptual Framework asserts that the purpose of the statement of profit or loss is to [7.20]:

(a) depict the return that an entity has made on its economic resources during the period; and
(b) provide information that is helpful in assessing prospects for future cash flows and in assessing management's stewardship of the entity's resources.

Therefore, income and expenses included in the statement of profit or loss are the primary source of information about an entity's financial performance for the period. The total or subtotal for profit or loss provides a highly summarized depiction of the entity's financial performance for the period. Many users incorporate that total or subtotal in their analysis of the entity's financial performance for the period and in their analysis of management's stewardship of the entity's resources, using it either as a starting point for further analysis or as the main indicator of the entity's financial performance for the period. Nevertheless, understanding an entity's financial performance for the period requires an analysis of all recognized income and expenses (including income and expenses included in other comprehensive income), as well as an analysis of other information included in the financial statements [7.21–7.22].

For the first time, the draft Conceptual Framework provides conceptual guidance on whether to present income and expenses in profit or loss or in other comprehensive income. It asserts that because the statement of profit or loss is the primary source of information about an entity's financial performance for the period, there is a presumption that all income and all expenses will be included in the statement of profit or loss. That presumption cannot be rebutted for [7.23]:

(a) income or expenses related to assets and liabilities measured at historical cost; and

(b) components of income or expenses related to assets and liabilities measured at current values if the components are separately identified and are of the type that would arise if the related assets and liabilities were measured at historical cost. For example, if an interest-bearing asset is measured at a current value and if interest income is identified as one component of the change in the carrying amount of the asset, that interest income would need to be included in the statement of profit or loss.

The presumption that all income and all expenses will be included in the statement of profit or loss can only be rebutted if [7.24]:

(a) the income or expenses (or components of them) relate to assets or liabilities measured at current values and are not of the type described in paragraph 7.23(b); and

(b) excluding those income or expenses (or components of them) from the statement of profit or loss would enhance the relevance of the information in that statement for the period.

When this is the case, those income or expenses (or components of them) are included in other comprehensive income.

5.7   Concepts of capital and capital maintenance

Chapter 8 of the draft Conceptual Framework provides two concepts of capital [8.1]:

- Under a *financial concept of capital*, such as invested money or invested purchasing power, capital is synonymous with the net assets (assets minus liabilities) or equity of the entity.
- Under a *physical concept of capital*, capital is regarded as the productive capacity or operating capability of the entity (for example, as measured in units of output per day).

The choice should be based on user needs and most reporting entities adopt a financial concept of capital when preparing their financial statements [8.2].

These concepts of capital give rise to corresponding two concepts of *capital maintenance*, which provide the point of reference by which profit is measured [8.3]. You may find it helpful to start with the notion that capital is maintained if the capital at the start of the accounting period is equal to the capital at the end of the period.

(a) Under the *financial capital maintenance concept*, a profit is earned only if the financial amount of the net assets (assets minus liabilities) at the end of the period is higher than the amount of the net assets at the start of the period, after excluding any distributions from holders of equity claims during the period. Financial capital maintenance can be measured in either nominal monetary units or units of constant purchasing power.

(b) Under the *physical capital maintenance concept*, a profit is earned only if the physical productive capacity (or operating capability) of the entity (or the resources or funds needed to achieve that capacity) at the end of the period exceeds the physical productive capacity at the beginning of the period, after excluding any distributions to, and contributions from, holders of equity claims during the period.

The revaluation or restatement of assets and liabilities gives rise to increases or decreases in equity. While these increases or decreases meet the definition of income and expenses, they are not included in the income statement under certain concepts of capital maintenance. Instead, these items are included in equity as capital maintenance adjustments or revaluation reserves [8.10].

The following activity will help you understand the concepts of capital and capital maintenance.

Activity

Last year Joe Cash won £5 million in the national lottery which he used to start a business called Joe Cash Ltd. At the start of the year, the company had £5 million capital and £5 million cash. During the year, the company purchased inventory. By the end of the year, all the inventory had been sold for £6.25 million. Assume there were no other transactions.

(a) Calculate the profit for the period under the financial capital maintenance concept.
(b) Joe finds out that it would cost £5.65 million to replace the inventory at the end of the year in terms of its operating capacity. Calculate the profit for the period under the physical capital maintenance concept.

Check your answer against the calculations below.

	Financial capital maintenance £m	Physical capital maintenance £m
Assets at the end of the year	6.25	6.25
Assets required at the end of the year to maintain capital		
(a) Financial capital maintenance	(5.00)	
(b) Physical capital maintenance		(5.65)
Profit for the period	1.25	0.60

This question is not as difficult as it might look. You just needed to remember the principles of the two capital maintenance concepts that explain how profit is earned. Under the financial capital maintenance concept, profit or loss is the difference between the capital at the end of the accounting period (£6.25 million) and capital at the start of the period (£5 million). In this simple exercise, there are no distributions to or contributions from the owner that need to be considered. Under the physical capital concept, the profit or loss is the difference between its operating capability at the end of the period (£6.25 million) and its operating capability at the start of the period (£5.65 million).

5.8   Conclusions

In this chapter we have examined the need for a conceptual framework for financial reporting and discussed the advantages and disadvantages in the context of dissatisfaction with the inductive and deductive approaches that had been taken in the past by national standard setters in different jurisdictions. Because of the widespread use of IFRSs around the world, we have focused on the draft Conceptual Framework for Financial Reporting (IASB, 2015a). As the Exposure Draft is still under consultation, you will need to be vigilant in checking when the final version is published from www.ifrs.org/Current-Projects/IASB-Projects/Conceptual-Framework/Pages/Conceptual-Framework-Summary.aspx.

It is important to note that the draft Conceptual Framework is not a Standard and does not override any specific Standards. The Conceptual Framework has eight chapters and we have examined some of the key principles each chapter contains. The main principle focuses on the objective of general purpose financial reporting. This led us to examine the primary users of financial reports and the fundamental and enhancing qualitative characteristics of useful financial information. We then discussed the role of financial statements and defined the reporting entity. We have drawn your attention to the elements of financial statements and the main features of the recognition, derecognition and measurement criteria. Finally, we discussed the principles guiding the scope, presentation and disclosure in the financial statements, and the concepts of capital and capital maintenance. We noted that in all financial reporting areas, the draft Conceptual Framework indicates that decisions should be guided by the qualitative characteristics of useful financial information. As there are always cost constraints, one of the principles is that the benefits of the information provided must be sufficient to justify the cost of providing it.

A set of financial statements under IAS 1 comprises a statement of profit or loss and other comprehensive income, a statement of financial position, a statement of changes in equity and a statement of cash flows. We will examine each of these statements in the next four chapters.

References

IASB (2014) IAS 1, *Presentation of Financial Statements*, London: IFRS Foundation.

IASB (2015a) *Exposure Draft Conceptual Framework for Financial Reporting*, London: IFRS Foundation.

IASB (2015b) *IFRS for SMEs*, London: IFRS Foundation.

IASC (1989) *Framework for the Preparation and Presentation of Financial Statements*, London: International Accounting Standards Committee.

Discussion questions

1 Debate the advantages and disadvantages of the IASB's Conceptual Framework for Financial Reporting.

2 Compare and contrast the information needs of the three primary user groups identified in the IASB's Conceptual Framework for Financial Reporting.

3 In Chapter 3 we explain that the prudence principle requires caution when making judgements under conditions of uncertainty. In this chapter we explain that a faithful representation ideally requires neutrality. Discuss the potential conflict between these two principles.

Practice questions

4 Explain what a conceptual framework is and describe the fundamental and enhancing qualitative characteristics of usefulness in the latest issue of the IASB Framework.

5 Define the three elements of financial position and the two elements of financial performance in the Conceptual Framework (IASB, 2015a).

6 Explain the general recognition criteria relating to the elements of financial statements and outline the four measurement methods mentioned in the latest issue of the IASB Framework. In addition, explain the financial capital maintenance and physical capital maintenance concepts.

7 Explain when assets, liabilities, equity, income and expenses should be recognized and how they should be measured, presented and disclosed.

8 Measurement is the process of quantifying information about an entity's assets, liabilities, equity, income and expenses in monetary terms. Discuss the factors that should be considered when selecting a measurement basis.

 Suggested research questions for dissertation students

Students interested in the objectives and qualitative characteristics of financial reporting may wish to investigate one or more of the following research questions:

- Why do standard setters such as the IASB need to keep revising their conceptual frameworks?

- Is there a trade-off between relevance and reliability?

- Is there a conflict between economic reality and principal social constructs of income and capital?

Preliminary reading

Bence, D. and Fry, N. (2004) 'The International Accounting Standards Board's search for a general purpose accounting model', *Journal of Financial Reporting, Regulation and Governance*, 3(1), pp. 1–29.

Booth, B. (2003) 'The Conceptual Framework as a coherent system for the development of Accounting Standards', *ABACUS*, 39(3), pp. 310–324.

Hines, R. (1989) 'Financial accounting knowledge, conceptual framework projects and the social construction of the accounting profession', *Accounting, Auditing & Accountability Journal*, 2(2), pp. 72–92.

Lee, T.A. (2015) 'Accounting and the decision usefulness framework', in Jones, S. (ed.), *The Routledge Companion to Accounting Theory*, pp. 110–128.

Tweedie, D. (2015) 'Standard setting politics and change management', in Jones, S. (ed.), *The Routledge Companion to Accounting Theory*, pp. 147–166.

Students interested in fair value accounting may wish to investigate one or more of the following research questions:

- What are the pros and cons of fair value accounting?
- Did fair value accounting contribute to the 2008 financial crisis?

Preliminary reading

Cairns, D. (2014) 'Fair value and financial reporting', in van Mourik, C. and Walton, P. (eds), *The Routledge Companion to Accounting, Reporting and Regulation*, pp. 128–143.

Lee, T.A. (2015) 'Accounting and the decision usefulness framework', in Jones, S. (ed.), *The Routledge Companion to Accounting Theory*, pp. 110–128.

Penman, S.H. (2007) 'Financial reporting quality: Is fair value a plus or a minus?' *Accounting and Business Research*, Special Issue: International Accounting Policy Forum, pp. 33–44.

Power, M. (2010) 'Fair value accounting, financial economics and the transformation of reliability', *Accounting and Business Research*, 40(3), pp. 197–210.

Ramanna, K. (2008) 'The implications of unverifiable fair-value accounting: Evidence from the political economy of goodwill accounting', *Journal of Accounting and Economics*, 45(2), pp. 253–281.

Rayman, R. (2007) 'Fair value accounting and the present value fallacy: The need for an alternative Conceptual Framework', *The British Accounting Review*, 39, pp. 211–225.

Reis, R. and Stocken, P. (2007) 'Strategic consequences of historical cost and fair value measurements', *Contemporary Accounting Research*, 24(2), pp. 557–584.

Ryan, S.G. (2008) 'Accounting in and for the subprime crisis', *The Accounting Review*, 83(6), pp. 1605–1638.

Veron, N. (2008) 'Fair value accounting is the wrong scapegoat for this crisis', *European Accounting Review*, 5(2), pp. 63–69.

Walton, P. (2014) 'Recognition and measurement', in van Mourik, C. and Walton, P. (eds), *The Routledge Companion to Accounting, Reporting and Regulation*, pp. 113–127.

Whittington, G. (2015) 'Fair value and IFRS', in Jones, S. (ed.), *The Routledge Companion to Accounting Theory*, pp. 217–235.

6 The statement of profit or loss and other comprehensive income

Learning objectives

When you have studied this chapter, you should be able to:

- Explain the purpose of the statement of profit or loss and other comprehensive income
- Differentiate between accruals and prepayments
- Calculate depreciation using the straight-line method
- Differentiate between bad debts and doubtful receivables
- Prepare a statement of profit or loss

6.1 Introduction

All businesses are required to keep accounting records so that they can provide financial information to the tax authorities. Incorporated entities must also prepare financial statements to meet their financial reporting obligations. Therefore, owners and managers need an efficient and effective accounting information system for recording the economic transactions and events of the business and aiding the preparation or generation of financial statements which summarize the accounting information. Whether the accounting system is manual or computerized, it is normally based on the principles of double-entry bookkeeping. At the end of the accounting period, a trial balance is generated which is a list of all the debit and credit balances on the accounts. This forms the basis of the financial statements.

In Chapter 4, we explained that financial reporting refers to the statutory disclosure of general purpose financial information by limited liability entities via the annual report and accounts. All limited liability entities in the UK are required to register their annual reports and accounts at Companies House, where they are made available online to the public. This makes the annual report and accounts the main source of financial information about a reporting entity for external users. Under IAS 1, *Presentation of Financial Statements* (IASB, 2014a) and the *IFRS for SMEs* (IASB, 2015b), a full set of financial statements includes a statement of profit or loss and other comprehensive income. This important financial statement is the focus of this chapter.

6.2 Purpose of the statement of profit or loss and other comprehensive income

Users of general purpose financial statements (see Chapter 5) have a common interest in information about the effects of transactions and other events that change a reporting entity's economic resources and claims. This is shown in the *statement of profit or loss and other comprehensive income*. The *purpose* of the statement of profit or loss and other comprehensive income is to provide information to external users on the financial performance of the reporting entity over the accounting period (usually one year). As its name suggests, the main focus is on the amount of the profit or loss the business has made during the period. Because it is retrospective, it is sometimes referred to as a 'financial history book'. The elements that relate to the measurement of financial performance are *income* and *expenses*. The following definitions explain the meaning of all the terms used in defining these two important elements.

Key definitions

Income is defined as increases in assets or decreases in liabilities that result in increases in equity, other than those relating to contributions from holders of equity claims.

Expenses are defined as decreases in assets or increases in liabilities that result in decreases in equity, other than those relating to distributions to holders of equity claims.

An asset is a present economic resource controlled by the entity as a result of past events.

An economic resource is a right that has the potential to produce economic benefits.

A liability is a present obligation of the entity to transfer an economic resource as a result of past events.

Equity is the residual interest in the assets of the entity after deducting all its liabilities.

Source: IASB, 2015a [4.4]. Reproduced with permission from the IFRS Foundation.

Essentially, a profit or loss is the difference between the income earned and the expenses incurred over the accounting period. One of the most important things to remember is that a profit or loss can be made whether the transactions of the business are for cash or on credit. If this sounds familiar to you, it is because the statement of profit or loss and other comprehensive income is prepared on an accrual basis. On the other hand, cash accounting is based on the principle that transactions and events are recognized when cash has been received or paid.

Key definition

Accrual accounting is based on the principle that revenue and costs are recognized as they are earned and incurred irrespective of when cash (or its equivalent) is received or paid (the *realization principle*), and they are matched with one another (the *matching principle*) and dealt with in the statement of profit or loss of the period to which they relate (the *period principle*).

Activity

You may recall doing this activity in Chapter 2. Imagine that you have £200 cash that you use to buy a computer for resale. You decide to advertise the computer, which costs £10, and you sell it for £300 cash. You have no other business transactions. Calculate your cash position at the end the month and your profit for the month.

It is likely that you have been able to work out the cash position and the profit in your head, but you may have decided to use the layout for a simple cash flow statement prepared for management that we illustrated in Chapter 2 where you deduct all the cash outflows from the total cash inflows to arrive at the net cash flow. To calculate the profit, you need to deduct all the costs you incurred during the month from the value of the sale. It does not matter at this stage how you calculated the figure, as long as you understand the principles involved. The layout of the following statement of profit or loss is typically used by accountants for a simple business.

Your business Cash flow statement for the month	£
Cash inflows	
Capital	200
Revenue	300
	500
Cash outflows	
Purchases	200
Advertising	10
	(210)
Net cash flow	290

Your business Statement of profit or loss for the month	£
Revenue	300
Cost of sales	
Purchases	(200)
Gross profit	100
Expenses	
Advertising	(10)
Profit for the period	90

As you can see, the cash position is a cash surplus of £290 and you have made a profit of £90. You need to remember that the statement of profit or loss does not tell us anything about cash. For example, it does not tell us about the £200 capital or whether cash has been received for the sale of the computer; nor does it tell us whether the costs have actually been paid or merely incurred. To emphasize the difference between profit and cash we will make the example slightly more complex.

Activity

The information is the same as in the previous activity. You have £200 that you use to buy a computer. You advertise the computer, which costs £10, and sell it for £300. You have no other business transactions. However, the buyer is not able to pay you straight away, so you give him one month's credit. Calculate your cash position at the end of the month and your profit for the month.

Your business Cash flow statement for the month	
	£
Cash inflows	
Capital	200
Cash outflows	
Purchases	200
Advertising	10
	(210)
Net cash flow	(10)

Your business Statement of profit or loss for the month	
	£
Revenue	300
Cost of sales	
Purchases	(200)
Gross profit	100
Expenses	
Advertising	(10)
Profit for the period	90

Looking at the terms we have used in this simple cash flow statement, *capital* describes the money contributed by the owner to enable the business to function. *Purchases* refers to the cash flowing out of the business to suppliers in respect of goods bought for resale, and advertising represents cash flowing out of the business when that expense is paid. However, in the statement of profit or loss we have illustrated, *revenue* refers to all sales made to customers during the accounting period, irrespective of whether cash has changed hands.[1] In the statement of profit or loss, the term *purchases* refers to the cost of goods that have been purchased from suppliers for resale, irrespective of whether cash has changed hands; and *advertising* refers to that expense, irrespective of whether cash has changed hands.

---

1. In some companies, the terms 'sales' or 'turnover' are used to describe revenue.

If you have calculated the net cash flow correctly, the cash position is now a cash deficit of £10. This may have misled you into thinking that you have now made a loss of £10 (the cost you have incurred) or a loss of £300 (the amount owing to you). Neither figure is correct. The answer is still a profit of £90. It is very important to remember that profit is not the same as cash and that the statement of profit or loss is not a record of cash flows in and out of the business. When we calculate profit we are concerned with the intentions of the parties and the transactions they have entered into, regardless of whether any cash has changed hands. In other words, the figures for revenue, cost of sales and expenses do not take into account whether you have paid the supplier for the computer, whether your customer has paid you for the computer or whether you have paid the newspaper for your advertisement. This is because you are using the principles of accrual accounting when calculating the profit or loss for the period.

In Chapter 2 we constructed a simple cash flow statement for the first six months of trading of Candlewick Ltd, the company started by Sarah Wick on 1 January 2018. This showed that after Sarah had invested £10,000 capital and the company had borrowed £6,500 from the bank, the business had a cash surplus of £500 at 30 June 2018.

Activity

Do you consider the company's financial performance was satisfactory? Draw up a list of questions you would like to ask Sarah to find out whether she thinks the first six months were a financial success.

You may have thought of the following questions:

- Did Sarah think the cash surplus of £500 was a satisfactory cash position, considering the money, time and effort she put into the business?
- How much profit did she hope to achieve for the first six months?
- How much profit did she actually make?
- Did she think the profit she made was satisfactory, considering the money, time and effort she put into the business?
- Were her achievements typical for her type of business?
- Would she have been better off using her money, time and effort in some other enterprise?
- Has she built up a business that is worth something in terms of the assets it has acquired (such as cash or inventory) or its potential to generate profit?

This is a challenging list of questions and you may think that answering them will be very difficult. Although the simple cash flow statement we demonstrated in Chapter 2 provides some answers, we need to prepare a statement of profit or loss and other comprehensive income before we can answer the others.

6.3   Preparing a draft statement of profit or loss and other comprehensive income

In order to communicate information about financial performance efficiently and effectively, income and expenses are classified either into the statement of profit or loss or into other comprehensive income. Under IAS 1 and the *IFRS for SMEs*, reporting entities can choose to prepare:

- a single *statement of profit or loss and other comprehensive income* in which profit or loss and other comprehensive income are presented as two consecutive sections; or
- the same information presented as two separate, but consecutive statements: a *statement of profit or loss* and a *statement of other comprehensive income*.

Regardless of which format is adopted, the statement of profit or loss is the primary source of information about an entity's financial performance and the profit or loss summarizes the financial performance for the period.[2] The business can analyze expenses by nature or by function, whichever provides information that is relevant and more reliable. If expenses are analyzed by function, information by nature must be disclosed in the notes to the financial statements. If the entity is preparing a separate statement of other comprehensive income, it must begin with the amount of profit or loss for the period and classify the line items for amounts of other comprehensive income by nature. The format we are going to illustrate presents a single statement of profit or loss and other comprehensive income as two consecutive sections and we will demonstrate the classification of expenses by function and also by nature.

Key definitions

Profit or loss is the total of income less expenses, excluding the components of other comprehensive income.

Other comprehensive income (OCI) comprises items of income and expense (including reclassification adjustments) that are not recognised in profit or loss as required or permitted by other IFRSs.

Total comprehensive income is the change in equity during a period resulting from transactions and other events, other than those changes resulting from transactions with owners in their capacity as owners.

Source: IAS 1, IASB, 2014a [1.7].

The first thing to determine when preparing a *statement of profit or loss and other comprehensive income* is the accounting period over which the profit or loss will be

---

2. Smaller businesses may not have any other comprehensive income to report.

calculated (the maximum being one year). As this financial statement is prepared on an accrual basis, all sources of income for the period need to be included regardless of whether the transactions were for cash or on credit and irrespective of whether cash has been received. This income is then matched with the expenses incurred during the period in order to earn the income, irrespective of whether cash has been paid yet. The calculation of profit is based on the following equation:

Income – Expenses = Profit or loss for the period

Users of the financial statements of a trading business, like Candlewick Ltd, need detailed information about the profit made on buying and selling goods, which is known as the *gross profit*. This is calculated as the difference between the *revenue* for the period and the *cost of sales*. The cost of sales is the cost of the goods that have been sold during the period.

Revenue – Cost of sales = Gross profit

Then *distribution costs* (such as packaging, postage, transport costs and insurance of goods in transit), *administrative expenses* (such as office rent and the cost of administrative salaries, heating and lighting, cleaning, telephone and stationery) and *other expenses* are deducted to calculate the *operating profit*. The distribution costs, administrative expenses and other expenses are known collectively as *revenue expenditure*.

Gross profit – Revenue expenditure = Operating profit

Next, any finance income (such as interest received from investments) is added and any *finance costs* (such as interest paid on loans) are deducted to calculate the *profit before tax*. Finally, income tax expense is deducted to arrive at the *profit for the period*. Then any items of *other comprehensive income* are added to give the total comprehensive income for the year.

We are now ready to see whether Candlewick Ltd has made a profit or a loss over the first six months of trading. Here is a reminder of the main facts:

- Office and other equipment was acquired on 1 January, but did not have to be paid for until February, as Sarah made use of the one month's interest-free credit period on the business credit card.
- Rent was payable every month.
- Advertising was payable one month in arrears.
- Telephone and Internet expenses were payable at the end of each quarter.
- Printing, postage and stationery, which include packaging costs, are paid one month later because suppliers give one month's credit.
- Employees' salaries are paid monthly.

We need to look more closely at the actual sales and purchases for each month shown in the simple cash flow statement we constructed in Chapter 2. For ease of reference this is reproduced below.

Candlewick Ltd

Cash flow statement for January-June 2018

	January £	February £	March £	April £	May £	June £	Total £
Cash inflows							
Capital	10,000	0	0	0	0	0	10,000
Loan	6,500	0	0	0	0	0	6,500
Revenue (cash sales)	1,600	1,800	2,000	3,500	4,100	4,500	17,500
Revenue (credit sales)	0	0	4,800	5,400	6,000	7,800	24,000
	18,100	1,800	6,800	8,900	10,100	12,300	58,000
Cash outflows							
Purchases	0	6,000	6,000	7,500	8,400	9,000	36,900
Equipment	0	13,000	0	0	0	0	13,000
Rent	500	500	500	500	500	500	3,000
Advertising	50	50	50	50	50	50	300
Telephone & Internet	0	0	450	0	0	450	900
Printing, postage & stationery	0	100	100	100	100	100	500
Salaries	0	500	500	500	500	660	2,660
Finance costs	40	40	40	40	40	40	240
	590	20,190	7,640	8,690	9,590	10,800	57,500
Net cash flow	17,510	(18,390)	(840)	210	510	1.500	500
Cumulative cash b/f	0	17,510	(880)	(1,720)	(1,510)	(1,000)	0
Cumulative cash c/f	17,510	(880)	(1,720)	(1,510)	(1,000)	500	500

When preparing a statement of profit or loss and other comprehensive income, we are interested in the value of the economic transactions that took place over the accounting period. To calculate these figures, we need to focus on the months when the transactions took place, rather than when cash was received or paid. The cash flow statement shows the lag of one month between the purchase of candles and the payment of cash, and the lag of two months between credit sales and receipt of cash. The other point to note is that although Candlewick Ltd purchased the same number of boxes of candles as planned, the actual sales were lower than forecast. This means the company will have unsold goods at the end of the accounting period, which is known as *closing inventory*. A business needs to have a certain amount of goods in stock on the last day of the accounting period to be able to sell them on the first day of the next period. Therefore, the closing inventory at the end of the period is the *opening inventory* at the start of the next period.

In order to value closing inventory, at the end of the accounting period, a physical count of goods is carried out to compare those quantities with the records. This is referred to as *inventory counting*. Once the total number of items in stock is known, the value is calculated by multiplying the number of items by the original cost of the item.

Activity

A garden centre purchased 100 plants at £2 each with a view to selling them at £2.40 each. At the end of the year 20 plants remained unsold. Because the plants are no longer in flower, the business will have to drop the price to £1.50 each. Calculate the value of the closing inventory.

You may have calculated the closing inventory as £40 (20 × £2), but the value the business must use is £30 (20 × £1.50) because these plants were worth less than the price that was paid for them. Apart from seasonal factors, other factors that may reduce demand for goods and services include changes in taste and fashion or advances in technology. IAS 2, *Inventories* (IASB, 2003) and the *IFRS for SMEs* require inventory to be valued at the lower of cost or *net realizable value (NRV)*. Cost includes purchase cost, conversion cost (materials, labour and overheads) and other costs (excluding foreign exchange differences) to bring inventory to its present location and condition. Net realizable value is the estimated selling price in the ordinary course of business less the estimated costs of completion and the estimated costs necessary to make the sale. We will be looking at the valuation methods permitted under IAS 2 in Part III.

Key definitions

Inventory refers to the unsold goods in a trading business, or the raw materials, components, work-in-progress and finished goods in a manufacturing business. Net realizable value (NRV) is the sales value of the inventory minus any additional costs likely to be incurred in getting it to the customer.

Returning to the example of Candlewick Ltd, the following table summarizes the quantities and values of the purchases and sales over the six-month period.

Date	Purchases		Cash sales		Credit sales	
	Quantity	£	Quantity	£	Quantity	£
January	400	6,000	80	1,600	240	4,800
February	400	6,000	90	1,800	270	5,400
March	500	7,500	100	2,000	300	6,000
April	560	8,400	175	3,500	390	7,800
May	600	9,000	205	4,100	410	8,200
June	600	9,000	225	4,500	425	8,500
Total	3,060	45,900	875	17,500	2,035	40,700

Activity

(a) What was the revenue for the period?

(b) How many boxes of unsold candles did Candlewick Ltd have at the end of June and what was the total cost of that closing inventory?

Taking the information from the preceding table, the first calculation is:

Working 1

	£
Cash sales	17,500
Credit sales	40,700
Revenue	58,200

There are several ways in which you can calculate the answer to the second question. The quantity of closing inventory is calculated as:

Quantity of opening inventory + Quantity purchased – Quantity sold

Candlewick Ltd had no opening inventory because this is the first six months of trading, so check your figures against the following calculations.

Working 2

	Quantity
Purchases	3,060
Cash sales	(875)
Credit sales	(2,035)
Closing inventory	150

The cost of sales is calculated as:

Value of opening inventory + Purchases – Closing inventory

For the reason already mentioned, Candlewick Ltd had no opening inventory, so we simply need to subtract the value of closing inventory from purchases.

Working 3

	£
Purchases (£15 x 3,060)	45,900
Closing inventory (£15 x 150)	(2,250)
Cost of sales	43,650

We can now draft the trading section of the statement of profit or loss.

Candlewick Ltd

Draft statement of profit or loss for six months ending 30 June 2018

	£
Revenue (W1)	58,200
Cost of sales (W2 and W3)	(43,650)
Gross profit	14,550

As you can see, the company made a gross profit of £14,550 during the six months and we can crosscheck this by doing a small calculation. We know that the business buys each box of candles for £15 and sells them for £20 per box, thus making a gross profit of £5 per box. As 2,910 candles have been sold in the period, the gross profit is £5 x 2,910 = £14,550. In a more complex business, you could not carry out these simple calculations.

The *cost of sales* figure reflects the cost of the goods sold. In this example we deducted the cost of the closing inventory from the cost of the goods purchased during the period. This is because we are preparing this financial statement on an *accrual* basis and want to match the revenue to the cost of purchasing the candles actually sold during the period. We are ignoring the movement of cash.

The term *gross* is used to describe the profit at this stage because this is the larger figure of profit before any of the expenses have been deducted. If the business had any other operating income, such as interest received on investments or rent received from lettings, it would be shown after the figure for gross profit.

The cost of sales is not the only expense incurred by the business and we need to deduct the operating expenses before we can calculate the operating profit. We then need to consider any other expenses, such as the income tax that Candlewick Ltd will have to pay. Sarah has decided to employ a part-time accountant who estimates that this tax would be approximately £2,085. As Candlewick Ltd has no other income or gains, we now have everything we need to complete the draft statement of profit or loss for the six months ended 30 June 2018.

Candlewick Ltd

**Draft statement of profit or loss
for six months ended 30 June 2018**

	£
Revenue (W1)	58,200
Cost of sales (W2 and W3)	(43,650)
Gross profit	14,550
Expenses	
Rent	(3,000)
Advertising	(300)
Telephone and Internet	(900)
Printing, postage and stationery	(500)
Salaries	(2,660)
	(7,360)
Operating profit	7,190
Finance costs	(240)
Profit before tax	6,950
Income tax expense	(2,085)
Profit for the period	4,865

The draft statement of profit or loss shows that the business has made a profit of £4,865 during the first six months of trading. If the total expenses were greater than the total income, the final figure would be negative and you would label it 'loss for the period'. Under the *IFRS for SMEs*, if an entity has no items of other comprehensive income in any of the periods for which financial statements are presented, it is allowed to present a statement of profit or loss[3] alone, which is what Sarah has done here. We have called it a draft statement because later on in this chapter we will explain how to prepare the annual statement of profit or loss with post trial balance adjustments.

6.4 Difference between cash and profit

To review the difference between cash and profit we need to look at the events that took place during the year. On 1 January 2018 Sarah invested £10,000 capital in Candlewick Ltd and borrowed £6,500 from the bank. After six months' trading, the simple cash flow statement prepared for management shows that the business has a cash surplus of £500 and the statement of profit or loss for the same period shows a profit of £4,865. There seems to be a discrepancy of £4,365 (£4,865 − £500).

---

3. At the time of writing (2016), the *IFRS for SMEs* still uses the older term 'income statement'.

Activity

List the items that you think caused the difference between the cash and the profit by comparing the items in the cash flow statement with the items in the statement of profit or loss.

The items causing the apparent discrepancy are as follows:

- Sarah has allowed two months' credit to her credit customers. From the cash flow statement we can see that cash received from credit sales totalled £24,000, but that does not include the credit sales of £8,200 for May and £8,500 for June which combined represent £16,700 in trade receivables. This brings the value of credit sales to £40,700, to which we then add the cash sales of £17,500 to give us the total revenue figure shown in the statement of profit or loss of £58,200. Therefore, the difference in total revenue stated in the two financial statements is £16,700.
- On the other hand, Sarah has negotiated one month's credit from the supplier from whom she buys her candles. We can see from the cash flow statement that the cash paid for purchases totalled £36,900, but to calculate profit we need to include the purchases of £9,000 incurred in June, which represents £9,000 in trade payables. This brings the value of purchases to £45,900, which is the figure shown in the statement of profit or loss.
- At 30 June the business had 150 candles in stock. These cost £15 each and this is how they have been valued in the trading section of the statement of profit or loss: £15 x 150 = £2,250. This figure is not included in the cash flow statement.
- Sarah did not take up the offer of credit for the advertising expenses and none was available for the telephone and Internet expenses or the rent, so there is no discrepancy between cash and profit here.
- The cash flow statement shows all cash income and all the cash expenditure. It includes cash inflows from the capital Sarah invested in the business and the loan made by the bank. It also shows the cash outflows on buying the equipment and Sarah's drawings. None of these items are shown in the statement of profit or loss, so here is another difference between the two financial statements.
- The final difference is that because the income tax expense has not yet been paid, it is not shown in the cash flow statement, but it is included in the statement of profit or loss.

In order to make the position clear, we will divide the information into good news and bad news. The good news is where Candlewick Ltd has assets and the bad news is where the business has incurred liabilities.

	£
Good news (assets)	
Equipment (at cost)	13,000
Cash owed by customers (trade receivables)	16,700
Closing inventory (at cost)	2,250
	31,950
Bad news (liabilities)	
Equity (owner's capital)	(10,000)
Loan owed to the bank	(6,500)
Cash owed to supplier (trade payables)	(9,000)
Cash owed to tax authorities	(2,085)
	(27,585)
Difference	4,365

As you can see, this analysis shows a difference between the assets and the liabilities of £4,365, which explains the apparent discrepancy between the profit of £4,865 for the period and the cash surplus of £500 (£4,865 – £500 = £4,365). There are a number of important lessons to be learned from the principle that cash is not the same as profit, and these can be used to run a business more efficiently:

- Giving credit to customers may have the advantage of increasing sales and thus potential profit, but results in a delay before the sales value is realized in the cash flow. In extreme cases this means that an organization can make a good profit, but at the same time risks failure due to lack of liquidity (insufficient cash for its activities).
- Building up inventory to an unnecessarily high level can have an adverse effect on cash flow. Managers who take advantage of bargains, such as special discounts, often forget this; perhaps because they consider that cash flow is the concern of the accountant and not of the organization as a whole.
- Taking credit from suppliers is one way of improving cash flow and is a form of free finance. However, if an organization takes more time than the agreed credit period, it runs the risk of losing this advantage, the supplier refusing to provide any more goods or services and difficulty in obtaining credit in future.
- Both the cash flow statement and the statement of profit or loss analyze financial information retrospectively over the accounting period. However, the past is not an accurate guide to the future. From a management point of view, planned or budgeted financial information should be compared frequently with actual information to ensure that the business is meeting its financial objectives.

So far we have only prepared a draft statement of profit or loss using cash information. We will now explain how the statement of profit or loss is prepared from a trial balance. Although the records in the accounting system may be fully up to date, there are always a number of *post trial balance adjustments*[4] that must be made to conform with the *accrual principle*.

---

4. *Post* is Latin for 'after', so this phrase refers to adjustments that are made after the trial balance has been generated.

As we are interested in financial reporting, we will look at the trial balance at 31 December 2018, which marks the end of the first year of trading for Candlewick Ltd. Note that the proportionately higher finance cost for the whole year compared with the first six months, reflects rising interest rates on the loan in the second half of the year.

Candlewick Ltd
Trial balance at 31 December 2018

	Debit	Credit
	£	£
Revenue		173,200
Purchases	113,400	
Equipment (at cost)	13,000	
Trade receivables	27,500	
Trade payables		15,000
Cash and cash equivalents	26,150	
Salaries	14,500	
Rent	6,000	
Advertising	600	
Telephone and Internet	1,960	
Printing, postage and stationery	1,100	
Interest paid on loan	490	
Loan		6,500
Share capital at 1 January 2018		10,000
	204,700	204,700

In practice, all the post trial balance adjustments would be entered in the ledger accounts and a revised trial balance would be generated. However, we will show the post trial balance information as notes because this is the way you are likely to encounter it in your assessments.

6.5 Inventory, accruals and prepayments

6.5.1 Inventory

In a trading business, *inventory* refers to unsold goods, but in a manufacturing business, it comprises raw materials, work-in-progress and finished goods. We introduced the adjustments for inventory earlier in this chapter. IAS 2, *Inventories* (IASB, 2003) and the *IFRS for SMEs* require closing inventory to be valued at the lower of cost or net realizable value (NRV). As we have already noted, the closing inventory at the end of the period is the figure used as the opening inventory at the start of the next period. In the statement of profit or loss, the adjustments for opening and closing inventory are incorporated in the cost of sales calculation.

Activity

Total purchases during the year ending 31 December 2018 were £113,400 and at the end of the year the annual inventory count showed that Candlewick Ltd had 50 boxes of candles in stock which had cost £15 each. What are the figures for closing inventory at 31 December 2018 and the cost of sales for the year ending 31 December 2018?

You should have found this straightforward. Closing inventory is cost (£15) × quantity (50) = £750. The cost of sales is purchases (£113,400) − closing inventory (£750) = £112,650 and this adjustment is shown in the statement of profit or loss for the year ending 31 December 2018.

Activity

Imagine that £500 of inventory was stolen during the year, so that the figure for closing inventory is overstated in the statement of profit or loss. What impact would there be if the true figure were substituted?

The greatest impact would be on the profit because the gross profit would decrease by £500. If a business has inventory stolen or it has deteriorated so that the value is less, it should be noticed during the inventory count. The loss is borne by the business and the reduced figure for closing inventory should then be shown in the financial statements. Because of the impact of closing inventory on profit, this is an area where fraud can be perpetrated if adjustments are not made to take account of lost or damaged goods. Therefore, inventory is one of the key checks made by the auditors. The following table illustrates the impact of overstated inventory on profit.

| | Overstated inventory | | Correct inventory | |
	£	£	£	£
Revenue		173,200		173,200
Cost of sales				
Purchases	113,400		113,400	
Closing inventory	(750)	(112,650)	(250)	(113,150)
Gross profit		60,550		60,050

6.5.2 Accruals

When the ledger accounts are closed at the end of the accounting period, some expenses incurred for goods and services used during the period may not have been recorded because the business has not yet received an invoice from the supplier. For example, perhaps the business has had the use of telephone and Internet services during the final quarter of the year, but the provider has not yet sent the invoice. The business needs to estimate the amount of any accrued expense or liability, and add the *accrual* to the trial balance figure for that expense because it belongs to the accounting period for which the financial statements are being prepared.

Key definition

An accrual is an estimate of a liability that is not supported by an invoice or a request for payment at the time the accounts for the period are being prepared.

Candlewick Ltd has three accruals:

- The trial balance shows telephone and Internet expenses of £1,960, but these only cover the first 11 months and the accountant Sarah has employed estimates that a further £200 is owed for December. This means that the expense shown in the statement of profit or loss should be £1,960 + £200 = £2,160.
- The accountant knows from the invoices for advertising that the total amount paid was £600, but during December Sarah took out extra advertisements to promote sales over the festive season. The company will not be invoiced for these advertisements until January, but the accountant estimates the amount will be £100. This means that the expense shown in the statement of profit or loss should be £600 + £100 = £700.
- On 1 July 2018 the interest rate on the company's loan increased to 9.23%, which is £50 per month. The total interest for 2018 was £540, but only £490 has been paid as the company pays one month in arrears. This means that the finance cost in the statement of profit or loss should be £490 + £50 = £540.

6.5.3   Prepayments

Another situation that commonly arises is when part of the amount paid for an expense in the current accounting period covers goods or services that will not be received until the next period. The amount of this payment in advance is known and the *prepayment* needs to be deducted from the trial balance figure for that expense.

Key definition

A prepayment is a payment made for goods or services that will be received in the next accounting period.

Candlewick Ltd has one prepayment. Sarah has recorded printing, postage and stationery expenses of £1,100 in the accounts, but at the end of December she realizes that she has accumulated a small surplus of these items that the business will not use until January. The cost of these items was £100. This means that the expense shown in the statement of profit or loss should be £1,100 − £100 = £1,000.

6.6 Depreciation of property, plant and equipment

IAS 16, *Property, Plant and Equipment* (IASB, 2014b) and the *IFRS for SMEs* give guidance on the accounting treatment of most types of property, plant and equipment so that users of the financial statements have information about an entity's investment in its property, plant and equipment and the changes in such investment. Property, plant and equipment (PPE) are defined as tangible items that:

(a) are held for use in the production or supply of goods or services, for rental to others, or for administrative purposes; and

(b) are expected to be used during more than one period.

You will remember that an asset is a present economic resource controlled by the entity as a result of past events. A *tangible asset* is non-monetary in nature and has a physical substance. The above definition of PPE makes it clear that the focus is on *non-current tangible assets* because it refers to tangible items that are expected to be used for more than one accounting period. Examples include freehold and leasehold land, buildings, fixtures and fittings, machinery, equipment and delivery vehicles.[5] Non-current tangible assets can be distinguished from *non-current intangible assets* which do not have a physical form, such as goodwill, patents and trademarks.

> **Key definition**
>
> Property, plant and equipment are tangible assets that are held for use in the production of supply of goods or services, for rental to others, or for administrative purposes, and are expected to be used during more than one period.
>
> Source: IAS 16, IASB, 2014b [16.6]. Reproduced with permission from the IFRS Foundation.

All items of PPE with a finite life must be depreciated. *Depreciation*[6] is the systematic allocation of the cost or revalued amount of a non-current tangible asset, less any residual value, over its useful life. Thus, depreciation represents the consumption of the economic benefits embodied in the asset.

Residual value refers to the estimated amount that the entity would currently obtain from disposal of the asset, after deducting the estimated costs of disposal if the asset were already of the age and in the condition expected at the end of its useful life.

---

5. IAS 16 does not apply to property, plant and equipment where another Standard requires or permits differing accounting treatments (for example, assets held for sale; biological assets related to agricultural activity; and mineral rights and mineral reserves such as oil, natural gas and similar non-regenerative resources).

6. Depreciation is sometimes referred to as amortization.

The *depreciable amount* is the cost of an asset, or other amount substituted for cost (assets may be revalued in subsequent years), less its residual value.

The asset's *useful life* is an estimate of the number of years the asset is expected to be available for use by the entity or the number of production or similar units expected to be obtained from the asset by the entity. Some assets, such as fixtures and fittings or vehicles will be worn out after a period of time; others, such as machinery or equipment, are likely to become obsolete through advances in technology. On the basis of materiality, some entities write off low value items to expenses in the year of purchase (e.g. equipment that cost £250 or less).

With large items of PPE, such as a ship or an aircraft, each significant component must be depreciated separately, but components can be grouped together if they have the same length of useful life and the same depreciation method is used. Although land and buildings are often acquired together, they must be accounted for separately. Buildings are always depreciated, but freehold land is not usually depreciated because it normally has an infinite life. An exception would be land held for coal mining or quarrying stone, where the useful life of the asset is depleted as the resources are extracted.

Key definitions

Depreciation is the systematic allocation of the depreciable amount of an asset over its useful life.

The depreciable amount is the cost of an asset, or other amount substituted for cost, less its residual value.

Residual value is the estimated amount that an entity would currently obtain from disposal of the asset, after deducting the estimated costs of disposal, if the asset were already of the age and in the condition expected at the end of its useful life.

Useful life is the period over which an asset is expected to be available for use by an entity ... or the number of production or similar units expected to be obtained from the asset by the entity.

Source: IAS 16, IASB, 2014b [16.6]. Reproduced with permission from the IFRS Foundation.

The cost of acquiring or producing the asset (e.g. buying components and building a new computer system), or enhancing an existing asset (e.g. extending or refurbishing a factory or office building) is classified as *capital expenditure*. An *allowance for depreciation* is made for each category of PPE in order to match the revenue the asset has helped generate during the accounting period to an estimate of the cost that has been consumed during the year.

The cost of an item of property, plant and equipment is recognized as an asset only if:

(a) it is probable that future economic benefits associated with the item will flow to the entity; and

(b) the cost of the item can be measured reliably.

Under the *IFRS for SMES*, initial recognition is at cost. In subsequent years, recognition is at cost less any accumulated depreciation and any accumulated impairment losses. Under IAS 16, the initial measurement is also at cost, but in subsequent years two measurement models are offered:

- The *cost model*, where the asset is carried at cost less accumulated depreciation and accumulated impairment losses (the same as under the *IFRS for SMEs*); or
- The *revaluation model*, where the asset is carried at a revalued amount, being its fair value at the date of revaluation less subsequent accumulated depreciation and impairment, provided that fair value can be measured reliably.

The model chosen must be applied consistently across the class of assets (e.g. all equipment).

Table 6.1   Examples of fair value

Asset	Example of fair value
Buildings	Market-based evidence of fair value determined by professionally qualified valuer
Plant and equipment	Market-based evidence of fair value
Specialized items of PPE that are rarely sold	Fair value based on replacement cost as there is no market-based evidence

Candlewick Ltd has one tangible fixed asset, which is the equipment that was bought on 1 January 2018 at a cost of £13,000. Sarah needs a method that will measure the proportion of the benefits that have been used up during the accounting period in order to make an allowance for depreciation on equipment. She estimates that the equipment has four years of useful life before technological advances mean it will become redundant. Nevertheless, at the end of four years she thinks the business will be able to sell it in the second-hand market for £1,000.

Activity

What do you consider it would be fair to charge as an expense in the statement of profit or loss for the use of the equipment for the year ending 31 December 2018?

The clue to the correct figure is the word 'fair'. You might argue that the equipment has a historical cost of £13,000 and this is the figure that should be used. Alternatively, you might think that the equipment has a residual value of £1,000 and therefore the answer should be £12,000. However, that cost covers four years' use and it would not be fair to charge the full amount against only one year's trading. Therefore, you may have rightly concluded that £3,000 is a fair figure as this takes all these factors into consideration. It would certainly not be fair to charge £1,000 as an expense for the year, as this is the estimated second-hand value of the asset at the end of four years.

The accountant has suggested that the company uses the *straight-line method* of depreciation, which spreads the cost (or revalued amount) evenly over the life of the asset. It is calculated using the following formula:

$$\frac{\text{Cost - Residual value}}{\text{Useful life}}$$

The first step is to deduct the estimated residual value from the cost and then divide the result by the estimated useful life:

$$\frac{£13,000 - £1,000}{4 \text{ years}} = \frac{£12,000}{4 \text{ years}} = £3,000 \text{ per annum}$$

Sarah can now add an allowance for depreciation on equipment of £3,000 to the other administrative expenses listed in the trial balance at 31 December 2018. We know that the cost of the asset was £13,000 and the equipment was bought on the first day of the accounting period (which for convenience we will call Year 0). At the end of the first year (Year 1), this figure will be reduced by the annual depreciation charge made in the statement of profit or loss. This means that the cost of £13,000 will reduce by £3,000 each year for four years, and at the end of this time there will be a residual value of £1,000.

6.7   Bad debts and doubtful receivables

Candlewick Ltd has a combination of cash sales and credit sales, and Sarah may not realize that some customers she has allowed to buy on credit may never pay for their candles. There are several reasons for this. For example, the customer may have died without leaving enough money to pay for any outstanding debts, or the customer may have become bankrupt or moved away without any trace. In such cases, as soon as Sarah finds out the money is irrecoverable, she would need to consider the amount owed as a *bad debt*, which would be an expense the business has to bear. She would need to write it off as a charge against profit or against an existing *allowance for doubtful receivables* in the statement of profit or loss. Occasionally news of a bad debt is not received until after the trial balance has been constructed, which means that the accountant will have to make a post trial balance adjustment.

Fortunately, Candlewick Ltd has not had any bad debts, but Sarah has been giving customers two months' credit and so far she has included all credit sales when calculating the total revenue for the year. Her accountant advises her that she should be prudent and make some provision for the possibility that some customers may not pay by making an allowance for doubtful receivables.

Key definitions

A bad debt is an amount owed to the entity that is considered to be irrecoverable. It is written off as a charge against profit or against an existing allowance for doubtful receivables.

An allowance for doubtful receivables is an amount charged against profit and deducted from receivables to allow for the estimated non-recovery of a proportion of debts.

The allowance for doubtful receivables can be based on specific debts where there is documentary evidence to suggest that the debts will not be paid. Another method that is used in some jurisdictions is based on the general assumption that a certain percentage of receivables are doubtful. However, it is not acceptable to the tax authorities in the UK.

Activity

The trial balance at 31 December 2018 shows that revenue for the year was £173,200 which comprised cash sales of £63,750 and credit sales of £109,450. Trade receivables were £27,500. If Candlewick Ltd makes an allowance for doubtful receivables of 10%, which of the following figures is the correct amount?

(a) £17,320

(b) £6,375

(c) £10,945

(d) £2,750

The first amount is 10% of the total sales revenue, but this includes cash sales so this answer is wrong because they have been paid for. The figure of £6,375 is 10% of the cash sales, but this is wrong for the same reason. The amount of £10,945 is 10% of credit sales for the year, but this too is wrong because the business has received payments from some of these customers. It is only the last two months' credit sales that are outstanding, so the allowance for doubtful receivables should be based on the trade receivables of £27,500:

$$£27,500 \times 10\% = £2,750$$

The allowance for doubtful receivables of £2,750 will be an additional expense to those listed in the trial balance. Consistency enhances comparability, so Sarah will use the same method every year unless there is good reason to change it.

Supposing the company has trade receivables of £25,000 in Year 2 because Sarah has improved the credit control system and she continues to make a 10% allowance for doubtful receivables. The calculation will be:

$$£25,000 \times 10\% = £2,500$$

This represents a decrease of £250 on Year 1 (£2,500 in Year 2 minus £2,750 in Year 1). Therefore, the allowance for doubtful receivables in Year 2 will decrease expenses by £250. If trade receivables in Year 3 are £26,000, the allowance for doubtful receivables will be:

$$£26,000 \times 10\% = £2,600$$

This is an increase of £100 on Year 2 (£2,600 in Year 3 minus £2,500 in Year 2). Therefore, the allowance for doubtful receivables in Year 3 will increase expenses by £100.

6.8   Finalizing the statement of profit or loss and other comprehensive income

Sarah's accountant has explained that classifying the company's expenses by function rather than by nature would reduce disclosure of information about costs that may be useful to competitors. This means that instead of listing the individual expenses, they are grouped into three categories: distribution costs, administrative expenses and finance costs. The guiding principle is that the classification should result in information that is relevant and reliable.

We now have all the information we need to finalize the statement of profit or loss and other comprehensive income for Candlewick Ltd for the year ending 31 December 2018. In practice, all the post trial balance adjustments would be entered in the ledger accounts and a revised trial balance would be generated. However, we have shown the post trial balance information as notes because this is the way you are likely to encounter it in your assessments.

Additional information available at 31 December 2018:

- Closing inventory is valued at £750.
- Rent, printing, postage and stationery, and salaries are allocated 50% to distribution costs and 50% to administrative expenses.
- Advertising is classified as a distribution expense.
- Telephone and Internet are classified as administrative expenses.

Candlewick Ltd
Trial balance at 31 December 2018

	Debit £	Credit £
Revenue		173,200
Purchases	113,400	
Equipment (at cost)	13,000	
Trade receivables	27,500	
Trade payables		15,000
Cash and cash equivalents	26,150	
Salaries	14,500	
Rent	6,000	
Telephone and Internet	1,960	
Printing, postage and stationery	1,100	
Advertising	600	
Interest paid on loan	490	
Loan		6,500
Share capital at 1 January 2018		10,000
	204,700	204,700

- There are accruals of £100 for advertising, £200 for telephone and Internet, and £50 for interest on the loan because December's interest of £50 will not be paid until 1 January 2019.
- Printing, postage and stationery include a prepayment of £100.
- The equipment is expected to have a useful life of four years, and an estimated residual value of £1,000. Depreciation on equipment will be charged 50% to distribution costs and 50% to administrative expenses.
- An allowance for doubtful receivables will be based on 10% of trade receivables. This allowance will be charged 100% to administrative expenses.
- Estimated income tax, to be paid by 31 January 2019, is £8,970.
- Sarah is the sole shareholder of the company and shareholders normally expect to receive a return from their investment. However, Sarah has decided to leave all profits in the company to help it grow.
- The company has no other comprehensive income.

Activity

Using the relevant items listed in the trial balance and all the additional information provided for the post trial balance adjustments, prepare a statement of profit or loss for Candlewick Ltd for the year ending 31 December 2018.

You will find it useful to start by drawing together all the calculations we have made in connection with the post trial balance adjustments at 31 December 2018. These can be summarized as follows.

Working 1

	£
Purchases	113,400
Closing inventory	(750)
Cost of sales	112,650

Working 2

$$\text{Depreciation on equipment} = \frac{£13,000 - £1,000}{4 \text{ years}} = £3,000$$

Working 3

Allowance for doubtful receivables = £27,500 × 10% = £2,750

Working 4

	Amount (£)	Distribution costs (£)	Administrative expenses (£)	Finance costs (£)
Rent	6,000	3,000	3,000	
Advertising (600 + 100)	700	700		
Telephone and Internet (1,960 + 200)	2,160		2,160	
Printing, postage and stationery (1,100 − 100)	1,000	500	500	
Interest on loan (490 + 50)	540			540
Salaries	14,500	7,250	7,250	
Depreciation on equipment (W2)	3,000	1,500	1,500	
Doubtful receivables (W3)	2,750		2,750	
Total	30,650	12,950	17,160	540

Your completed financial statement should look like this.

Candlewick Ltd

**Statement of profit or loss and other comprehensive income
for the year ended 31 December 2018**

	£
Revenue	173,200
Cost of sales (W1)	(112,650)
Gross profit	60,550
Distribution costs (W2, W3, W4)	(12,950)
Administrative expenses (W2, W3, W4)	(17,160)
Operating profit	30,440
Finance costs (W4)	(540)
Profit before tax	29,900
Income tax expense	(8,970)
Profit for the period	20,930
Other comprehensive income	–
Total comprehensive income for the period	20,930

As it is the company's first year of trading, it is not possible to provide comparative figures for the previous year, and this is a fairly simple financial statement because Candlewick Ltd does not have any other comprehensive income.

Because the statement of profit or loss is the primary source of information about an entity's financial performance, there is a presumption that all income and all expenses will be included in the statement of profit or loss. This is the case when:

(a) income or expenses related to assets and liabilities are measured at historical cost; and

(b) components of income or expenses related to assets and liabilities are measured at current values if the components are separately identified and are of the type that would arise if the related assets and liabilities were measured at historical cost. For example, if an interest-bearing asset is measured at a current value and if interest income is identified as one component of the change in the carrying amount of the asset, that interest income would need to be included in the statement of profit or loss.

Income or expenses (or components of them) are included in other comprehensive income if:

(a) the income or expenses (or components of them) relate to assets or liabilities measured at current values and are not of the type described above; and

(b) excluding the income or expenses (or components of them) from the statement of profit or loss would enhance the relevance of the information in that statement for the period. For example, if a current value measurement basis is selected for an asset or a liability for the statement of financial position and a different measurement basis is selected for determining the related income and expenses in the statement of profit or loss.

If income or expenses are included in other comprehensive income in one period, there is a presumption that it will be reclassified into the statement of profit or loss in some future period. That reclassification occurs when it will enhance the relevance of the information included in the statement of profit or loss for that future period.

Other comprehensive income (OCI) comprises items of income and expense (including reclassification adjustments) that are not recognized in profit or loss as required or permitted by other IFRSs. Examples of such items include:

- Changes in revaluation surplus where the revaluation method is used under IAS 16, *Property, Plant and Equipment* and IAS 38, *Intangible Assets*.
- Remeasurements of a net defined benefit liability or asset recognized in accordance with IAS 19, *Employee Benefits*.
- Exchange differences from translating functional currencies into presentation currency in accordance with IAS 21, *The Effects of Changes in Foreign Exchange Rates*.
- Gains and losses on remeasuring available-for-sale financial assets in accordance with IAS 39, *Financial Instruments: Recognition and Measurement*.
- The effective portion of gains and losses on hedging instruments in a cash flow hedge under IAS 39 or IFRS 9, *Financial Instruments*.
- Gains and losses on remeasuring an investment in equity instruments where the entity has elected to present them in other comprehensive income in accordance with IFRS 9.
- The effects of changes in the credit risk of a financial liability designated as at fair value through profit and loss under IFRS 9.

You will find it useful to learn the following layout for the statement of profit or loss and other comprehensive income.

Name of entity
Statement of profit or loss and other comprehensive income
for the year ended (date)

	This year £	Last year £
Revenue	X	X
Cost of sales	(X)	(X)
Gross profit	X	X
Other income	X	X
Distribution costs	(X)	(X)
Administrative expenses	(X)	(X)
Other expenses	(X)	(X)
Operating profit	X	X
Finance costs	(X)	(X)
Profit before tax	X	X
Income tax expense	(X)	(X)
Profit for the period	X	X
Other comprehensive income		
Xxx	X	X
Xxx	(X)	(X)
Total comprehensive income for the period	X	X

6.9 Conclusions

The statement of profit or loss and other comprehensive income is one of the four financial statements that are prepared by reporting entities at the end of the accounting period. Its purpose is to measure the financial performance of the business over the accounting period, which is usually one year. In this chapter we have described how to prepare a statement of profit or loss for a simple trading business which does not have any other comprehensive income.

If the business keeps cash records, after some adjustments these figures can be used as the basis for preparing the statement of profit or loss, as we have demonstrated in this chapter. If the business uses a double-entry bookkeeping system, the figures are taken from the trial balance, which summarizes the economic transactions that have been identified, measured and recorded in the accounting system. We have examined some of the post trial balance adjustments that must be made before the statement of profit or loss can be finalized.

 ## Common problems to avoid

Common mistakes students make when preparing a statement of profit or loss are:

- Not showing the name of the business
- Not stating the period covered by the financial statement
- Forgetting to include the currency symbol
- Confusing opening inventory with closing inventory
- Not making all the post trial balance adjustments
- Forgetting that it is only the final figure that is double underlined
- Forgetting to show all workings

References

IASB (2003) IAS 2, *Inventories*, London: IFRS Foundation.
IASB (2014a) IAS 1, *Presentation of Financial Statements*, London: IFRS Foundation.
IASB (2014b) IAS 16, *Property, Plant and Equipment*, London: IFRS Foundation.
IASB (2015a) *Exposure Draft Conceptual Framework for Financial Reporting*, London: IFRS Foundation.
IASB (2015b) *IFRS for SMEs*, London: IFRS Foundation.

Discussion questions

1 Discuss the general purpose of the statement of profit or loss and other comprehensive income and the meaning of the terms *income* and *expenses* as defined by the Conceptual Framework for Financial Reporting (IASB, 2015a).

2 Discuss the accrual basis of accounting and the principles involved, taking the example of the cost of sales adjustment in the statement of profit or loss.

Practice questions

3 Insert the missing figures in the following examples, remembering that some items will be added and others will be subtracted.

	(a) £	(b) £	(c) £	(d) £	(e) £
Opening inventory	100	?	1,020	?	14,960
Purchases	?	680	?	1,924	?
	500	730	?	2,156	?
Closing inventory	(50)	?	(1,550)	(150)	(18,815)
Cost of sales	?	520	9,680	?	159,715

	(f) £	(g) £	(h) £	(i) £	(j) £
Revenue	10,000	?	17,000	18,150	?
Cost of sales	(6,000)	(450)	?	?	(24,590)
Gross profit	?	150	3,500	17,470	3,160
Expenses	(3,500)	?	?	?	?
Profit for the period	?	50	250	2,100	740

4 Salma Ibrahim set up a company called Uplights Ltd selling lights and started trading on 1 January 2017. Her brother is studying for his accountancy exams and helps her by doing the bookkeeping and managing the inventory. At the end of the first year of trading, he generates the following trial balance from the accounting records.

Uplights Ltd
Trial balance at 31 December 2017

	Debit	Credit
	£	£
Revenue		66,500
Purchases	20,000	
Fixtures and fittings (at cost)	20,000	
Trade receivables	2,000	
Trade payables		8,400
Cash and cash equivalents	14,500	
Bank interest received		100
Rent	24,000	
Salaries	21,500	
Insurance	2,000	
Lighting and heating	500	
Telephone and Internet	400	
Advertising	100	
Share capital at 1 January 2017		30,000
	105,000	105,000

Additional information at 31 December 2017:

- Inventory was valued at £8,000.
- Estimated current tax payable is £2,000.
- The company classifies expenses by nature.

Required

Use the relevant figures in the above information to prepare a draft statement of profit or loss for Uplights Ltd for the year ended 31 December 2017. Show all your workings.

5 On 1 July 2017 Mark Farmer opened a shop called Miphone Ltd. The trial balance for the first year is shown below.

Miphone Ltd Trial balance at 30 June 2018	Debit £	Credit £
Revenue		75,200
Purchases	12,160	
Plant and equipment at cost	25,000	
Trade receivables	1,200	
Trade payables		1,600
Cash and cash equivalents	3,260	
Other income		1,200
Salaries	24,000	
Rent	18,000	
Insurance	7,200	
Advertising	860	
Lighting and heating	620	
Telephone and Internet	450	
General expenses	250	
Share capital at 1 July 2017		15,000
	93,000	93,000

Additional information at 30 June 2018:

- Inventory is valued at £890.
- Advertising paid in advance is £260.
- Accrued expenses are lighting and heating £540, telephone and Internet £290 and general expenses £160.
- Estimated current tax payable is £1,200.
- No dividends will be paid and there is no other comprehensive income.

Required

(a) Using a spreadsheet, prepare a draft statement of profit or loss for Miphone Ltd for the year ended 30 June 2018, classifying expenses by nature.

(b) After taking advice from his accountant, Mark has decided to depreciate equipment using the straight-line method over five years, with no residual value. He has also decided to make an allowance for doubtful receivables and has decided to base it on 10% of opening trade receivables. Make these adjustments to your spreadsheet and revise the draft statement of profit or loss for Miphone Ltd for the year ending 30 June 2018, classifying expenses by nature.

(c) The accountant's final suggestion is that Mark should reclassify the expenses by function: 50% to distribution costs and 50% to administrative expenses, with the exception of advertising which should be allocated 100% to distribution costs and the allowance for doubtful receivables which should be allocated 100% to administrative expenses. Make these changes to your spreadsheet and generate a statement of profit or loss for Miphone Ltd, classifying the expenses by function.

6 Kavita Patel is the owner of Beauty Box Ltd which started trading on 1 July 2016. At the end of the second year, her accountant generates the following trial balance from the accounting system.

Beauty Box Ltd
Trial balance at 30 June 2018

	Debit £	Credit £
Revenue		104,900
Purchases	39,700	
Inventory at 1 July 2017	10,000	
Equipment at cost	20,000	
Trade receivables	6,000	
Trade payables		8,000
Cash and cash equivalents	15,300	
Interest received		100
Salaries	30,000	
Rent	15,000	
Insurance	3,000	
Lighting and heating	1,500	
Telephone and Internet	2,000	
Advertising	500	
Allowances at 1 July 2017:		
Depreciation on plant and equipment		4,000
Doubtful receivables		1,000
Share capital at 1 July 2017		20,000
Retained profit at 1 July 2017		5,000
	143,000	143,000

Additional information at 30 June 2018:

- Inventory is valued at £12,000.
- Equipment has a useful life of five years and no residual value. It is depreciated using the straight-line method.
- The company makes an allowance for doubtful receivables based on 10% of opening trade receivables.
- The company classifies expenses by nature.
- Estimated income tax expense for the year is £4,500.
- No dividends will be paid and there is no other comprehensive income.

Required

Use the relevant figures in the above information to prepare a statement of profit or loss and other comprehensive income for Beauty Box Ltd for the year ending 30 June 2018. Show all your workings.

7 Yousuf Jumani launched his trading company, Jumani Ltd, on 1 January 2016 after successfully completing an MBA programme. The following data are available at the end of the second year.

Trial balance at 31 December 2017		
	£	£
Revenue		170,000
Purchases	70,000	
Property, plant and equipment at cost	50,000	
Accumulated depreciation on PPE		10,000
Inventories at 1 January 2017	8,000	
Interest on bank loan	250	
Accrued expenses		1,000
Distribution costs	20,000	
Administrative expenses	50,000	
Trade payables		7,000
Trade receivables	15,000	
Cash at bank	22,750	
5% bank loan repayable 2022		5,000
Share capital at 1 January 2017		21,000
Retained earnings at 1 January 2017		22,000
	236,000	236,000

The following additional information is available:

- Inventories at 31 December 2017 cost £28,000. This figure includes inventories that cost £2,480, whose net realizable value is only £1,000.
- There are additional distribution costs of £120 for December 2017.
- Administrative expenses include insurance expenses of £4,500, one-third of which relate to building insurance for 2018.
- The company classifies expenses by function.
- Income tax payable for the year has been calculated as £19,020.
- No dividends will be paid and there is no other comprehensive income.

Required

Use the relevant figures in the above information to prepare a statement of profit or loss and other comprehensive income for the year ended 31 December 2017. Show all your workings.

8 Leilei Zhang started *Oriental Silks Ltd* on 1 April 2017. The trial balance at the end of the second year of trading is shown below.

Trial balance at 31 March 2019		
	£	£
Revenue		104,017
Purchases	18,000	
Property, plant and equipment at cost	25,000	
Accumulated depreciation on PPE		5,000
Inventories at 1 April 2018	8,860	
Interest on bank loan	200	
Accruals		426
Distribution costs	18,985	
Administrative expenses	50,038	
Trade payables		7,000
Trade receivables	6,000	
Cash and cash equivalents	38,317	
8% bank loan repayable 2022		5,000
Share capital at 1 April 2018		20,000
Reserves:		
Share premium		1,000
Retained earnings at 1 April 2018		22,957
	165,400	165,400

The following additional information is available:

- Inventories at 31 March 2019 cost £8,400. This figure includes inventories that cost £480, but the net realizable value is only £80.
- There are additional administration expenses of £120 for March 2019.
- The company classifies expenses by function.
- Interest on the bank loan for the last six months of the period has not been included.
- Income tax payable for the year has been calculated as £1,614.
- No dividends will be paid and there is no other comprehensive income.

Required

Prepare the statement of profit or loss and other comprehensive income for the year ended 31 March 2019. Show all your workings.

 Suggested research questions for dissertation students

Students interested in revenue recognition may wish to investigate one or more of the following research questions:

- Why do the concepts of revenue recognition and profit or loss recognition matter?
- What are the views of stakeholders on IFRS 15, *Revenue from Contracts with Customers* (applicable from 1 January 2018)?

Preliminary reading

Antle, R. and Demski, J.S. (1989) 'Revenue recognition', *Contemporary Accounting Research*, 5(2), pp. 423–451.

Ohlson, J.A., Penman, S.H., Biondi, Y., Bloomfield, R.J., Glover, J.C., Jamal, K. and Tsujiyama, E. (2011) 'Accounting for revenues: A framework for standard setting', *Accounting Horizons*, 25(3), pp. 577–592.

Wagenhofe, A. (2014) 'The role of revenue recognition in performance reporting', *Accounting and Business Research*, 44(4), pp. 349–379. *Special Issue: International Accounting Policy Forum.*

7 The statement of financial position

Learning objectives

When you have studied this chapter, you should be able to:

- Explain the purpose of the statement of financial position
- Differentiate between non-current assets and current assets
- Differentiate between non-current liabilities and current liabilities
- Calculate depreciation using the reducing balance method
- Prepare a statement of financial position

7.1 Introduction

In Chapter 6 we discussed the difference between cash and profit and explained how a statement of profit or loss and other comprehensive income can be prepared from cash accounting information or from a trial balance generated from a double-entry bookkeeping system. We described the main post trial balance adjustments that need to be made and how they are shown in the statement of profit or loss and other comprehensive income. This financial statement is prepared on an accrual basis and summarizes information about the entity's income and expenses. Users of the financial statements are interested in the statement of profit or loss and other comprehensive income because it shows the financial performance of the business over the accounting period, but this is not the only aspect of the company's 'financial health' that is of interest to them.

Under IAS 1, *Presentation of Financial Statements* (IASB, 2014a) and the *IFRS for SMEs* (IASB, 2015b), a full set of financial statements also includes a statement of financial position. This important financial statement is the focus of this chapter.

7.2   Purpose of the statement of financial position

Users of general purpose financial statements have a common interest in information about the effects of transactions and other events that change a reporting entity's economic resources and claims. You know from Chapter 6 that this is shown in the statement of profit or loss and other comprehensive income. However, users also need information about the entity's economic resources and the claims against the reporting entity, and this information is shown in the *statement of financial position*. The *purpose* of the statement of financial position is to summarize the assets, equity and liabilities of the business on the last day of the accounting period for which the statement of profit or loss and other comprehensive income was prepared. Because it looks at what the business owns and owes at one particular point in time, it is sometimes referred to as a 'financial snapshot'. The elements that relate to the measurement of financial position are *assets*, *liabilities* and *equity*.

Key definitions

An asset is a present economic resource controlled by the entity as a result of past events.

An economic resource is a right that has the potential to produce economic benefits.

A liability is a present obligation of the entity to transfer an economic resource as a result of past events.

Equity is the residual interest in the assets of the entity after deducting all its liabilities.

Source: IASB, 2015a [4.4]. Reproduced with permission from the IFRS Foundation.

All businesses need assets such as premises, machinery, vehicles, equipment, inventory and cash. Before the business can acquire any assets, it must have the necessary finance. In a new business the most likely source of finance is the capital invested by the owner(s), which form part of the equity of the business. The business is also likely to have liabilities, such as a bank overdraft or a loan, or it may owe money for goods and services received on credit from suppliers.

The relationship between the assets, equity and liabilities forms what is known as the *accounting equation*:

$$Assets = Equity + Liabilities$$

The accounting equation reflects the dual nature of business transactions by stating that the assets of the entity are always equal to the claims against them: the equity and other liabilities. The point about any equation is that it balances; in other words, the total of the values on each side of the equation are equal. You may remember the following activity from Chapter 3.

Activity

A business has capital of £20,000 and assets of £20,000. It then borrows £10,000 from the bank to finance the purchase of some new office equipment. How does this affect the accounting equation?

In this case the business has assets of £20,000 which will increase by £10,000 (the new equipment), making total assets of £30,000. The equity of £20,000 remains the same, but the business has increased its liabilities by £10,000 (the bank loan), but the accounting equation still balances as shown below.

Assets	=	Equity	+	Liabilities
£		£		£
20,000		20,000		10,000
10,000				
30,000		20,000		10,000

This accounting equation underpins the statement of financial position.

7.3 Preparing a draft statement of financial position

The statement of financial position shows the assets, equity and liabilities on the last day of the accounting period and this financial statement is presented in two parts. Although IAS 1 and the IFRS for SMEs suggest how the statement of financial position should be presented, they do not prescribe the format of the statement or the order in which the items should be shown. The format we are going to illustrate presents the assets in the first part of the statement and the equity and liabilities in the second part, which reflects the accounting equation.

Assets are separated into two groups:

- *Non-current assets* are assets that are intended for continuing use in the business. You may find it helpful to think of them as the long-term assets of the business. Non-current assets are subdivided into *tangible* non-current assets and *intangible* non-current assets. Tangible assets are non-monetary assets with physical substance such as property, plant and equipment, and intangible assets are identifiable non-monetary assets without physical substance, such as brands, patents, copyrights and licences. Other non-current assets include long-term investments.
- *Current assets* are not intended for continuing use in the business. You may find it helpful to think of them as the short-term assets of the business. In a business that trades or manufactures goods, current assets will be constantly changing from cash to inventory to trade receivables, to cash and possibly to short-term investments.

Trade receivables are amounts owed by customers who have received goods or services on credit and have not yet paid.

Equity is separated into three groups:

- *Share capital* is the finance received by the company from its owner(s) in exchange for shares.
- *Retained earnings* are reserves of profits that are retained in the business to help it grow.
- *Other reserves* include the *share premium*, which is the amount of money paid (or promised to be paid) for a share in excess of its nominal (or par) value. The nominal value is an arbitrary amount that is determined when the company is incorporated.

Liabilities are separated into two groups:

- *Non-current liabilities* are amounts that are due to be paid to lenders and creditors more than one year after the date of the statement of financial position. You may find it helpful to think of them as long-term liabilities. Examples include long-term finance lease obligations, borrowings and employee benefit liabilities such as pensions.
- *Current liabilities* are amounts due to be paid to lenders and creditors within one year of the date of the statement of financial position. You may find it helpful to think of them as short-term liabilities. Examples include trade and other payables, dividends payable, current tax liability and short-term provisions, borrowings and finance lease liabilities. Trade payables are amounts due to suppliers who have supplied goods or services on credit and who have not yet been paid.

The accounting equation and the classification of assets, equity and liabilities in the statement of financial position is summarized in Figure 7.1.

Figure 7.1 Classifying assets, equity and liabilities

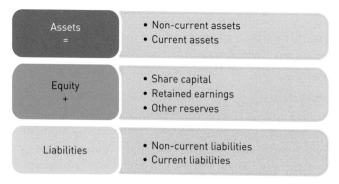

You need to remember that accountants classify expenditure as follows:

- *Revenue expenditure* is the collective term for the costs and expenses that are written off in the statement of profit or loss and other comprehensive income for the accounting period to which they relate.

- *Capital expenditure* is the collective term for the cost of non-current assets that are capitalized in the statement of financial position.

To illustrate the statement of financial position, we will continue to use the example of Candlewick Ltd, the company started by Sarah Wick on 1 January 2018. As you may remember from Chapter 6, on that day she opened a business bank account with her savings of £10,000 and took out a loan of £6,500, which was also put into the business bank account. Using the company credit card, she then bought office and other equipment for £13,000 which would not need to be paid for until February.

Financial accounting and reporting is guided by the *business entity concept* (see Chapter 3). Therefore, Candlewick Ltd is considered to exist separately from its owner, Sarah Wick. This separation is crucial because the statement of financial position shows the financial position of the business and not that of its owner. On 1 January 2018 the draft statement of financial position for Candlewick Ltd looked like this.

Candlewick Ltd

Draft statement of financial position at 1 January 2018

	£
ASSETS	
Non-current assets	
Equipment (at cost)	13,000
Current assets	
Cash and cash equivalents	16,500
Total assets	29,500
EQUITY AND LIABILITIES	
Equity	
Share capital	10,000
Non-current liabilities	
Loan	6,500
Current liabilities	
Trade and other payables	13,000
Total equity and liabilities	(29,500)

As you can see, the name of the business and the date at which the statement of financial position has been prepared is given at the top of the statement. The assets on that date are listed in the first part of the statement and the equity and liabilities in the second part. Moreover, the total assets are equal to the total equity and liabilities. The order in which the assets are shown is based on liquidity, starting with those that would take the longest to turn into cash and ending with the most liquid. The order in which the liabilities are shown is based on immediacy, starting with long-term liabilities and ending with those that must be paid the soonest.

A statement of financial position can be prepared at any moment in time, so we will move forward to 2 January, by which time Sarah has started trading by buying 100 boxes of candles at £15 each, which the business will not need to pay for until February.

Candlewick Ltd

Draft statement of financial position at 2 January 2018

	£
ASSETS	
Non-current assets	
Equipment (at cost)	13,000
Current assets	
Inventory	1,500
Cash and cash equivalents	16,500
	18,000
Total assets	31,000
EQUITY AND LIABILITIES	
Equity	
Share capital	10,000
Non-current liabilities	
Loan	6,500
Current liabilities	
Trade other payables	14,500
Total equity and liabilities	(31,000)

As you can see, although the figures have changed, the statement of financial position still balances. The business has £31,000 in assets, which have been financed by a combination of Sarah's capital and creditors. Current liabilities are £13,000 owing on the company credit card for the equipment and £1,500 owed to the supplier for the boxes of candles bought in January, giving a total of £14,500. Credit cards and credit agreed with suppliers are useful sources of interest-free credit as long as the debt is paid off within the agreed period.

Activity

We will now move on to 7 January, which is the end of the first week of trading. The business has made cash sales of 10 boxes of candles at £20 each and credit sales of 20 boxes of candles at £20 each. Using the following pro forma, prepare a draft statement of financial position at 7 January. Any profit the business has made should be shown beneath the figure for share capital as retained earnings. Like the share capital, profit is a liability because it is owed by the business to the owner. At this stage in trading you can ignore the fact that a proportion of operating expenses should be deducted from the profit, and simply calculate the gross profit.

Candlewick Ltd

Draft statement of financial position at 7 January 2018

£

ASSETS

Non-current assets

Equipment (at cost) _____

Current assets

Inventory

Trade and other receivables _____

Cash and cash equivalents _____

Total assets _____

EQUITY AND LIABILITIES

Equity

Share capital

Retained earnings _____

_____

Non-current liabilities

Loan

Current liabilities

Trade and other payables _____

_____

Total equity and liabilities _____

There are a number of computations you need to make before you can complete the statement of financial position. One of these calculations is to find out what profit the business has made over the period. For this reason, it is usual to prepare the statement of profit or loss and other comprehensive income for the period before drawing up the statement of financial position. We will now review the computations needed to calculate the gross profit. The first working calculates the revenue.

Working 1

	£
Cash sales (£20 x 10)	200
Credit sales (£20 x 20)	400
Revenue	600

Working 2 calculates the quantity of closing inventory. There is no opening inventory because this is a new business, so we only need to subtract the quantity sold from the quantity purchased.

Working 2

	Quantity
Purchases	100
Cash sales	(10)
Credit sales	(20)
Closing inventory	70

This allows us to calculate the cost of sales in Working 3 by subtracting the value of closing inventory from the cost of purchases.

Working 3

	£
Purchases (£15 × 100)	1,500
Closing inventory (£15 × 70)	(1,050)
Cost of sales	450

We can now draft the trading section of the statement of profit or loss which shows that the gross profit made by Candlewick Ltd during the first week was £150.

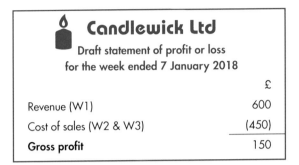

Candlewick Ltd
Draft statement of profit or loss
for the week ended 7 January 2018

	£
Revenue (W1)	600
Cost of sales (W2 & W3)	(450)
Gross profit	150

Strictly speaking, we should deduct a proportion of the expenses for the period and calculate the profit for the period, but since trading has barely commenced we are going to use the gross profit figure.

We can now turn our attention to the draft statement of financial position. On 7 January the company still has non-current assets (the equipment), which cost £13,000, but the current assets have changed since the statement of financial position on 2 January. The trading account for the week ended 7 January shows that value of closing inventory was £1,050, but since Candlewick Ltd has begun trading we need to consider the effect on the other current assets. The company has customers who have not yet paid for 20 boxes of candles sold on credit at £20 each (£400), and cash from the sale of 10 boxes of candles at £20 each (£200). Current liabilities are still £13,000 owing on the business credit card for the equipment and £1,500 owed to the supplier for the boxes of candles bought in January:

Working 4

	£
Trade payables	1,500
Other payables	13,000
Trade and other payables	14,500

Check your figures against the following draft statement of financial position at 7 January.

```
         🕯   Candlewick Ltd
    Draft statement of financial position at 7 January 2018

                                                    £
    ASSETS
    Non-current assets
    Equipment (at cost)                          13,000
    Current assets
    Inventory                                     1,050
    Trade and other receivables                     400
    Cash and cash equivalents                    16,700
                                                 18,150
    Total assets                                 31,150

    EQUITY AND LIABILITIES
    Equity
    Share capital                                10,000
    Retained earnings                               150
                                                 10,150
    Non-current liabilities
    Loan                                          6,500
    Current liabilities
    Trade and other payables (W4)                14,500
    Total equity and liabilities                 31,150
```

We could continue to construct a series of statements of financial position covering Sarah's business on a day-to-day basis, but this would be very tedious. So we will move on to the end of the first six months and prepare a draft statement of financial position at 30 June 2018 based on the following information from Chapter 6:

- On 1 January, Candlewick Ltd bought office and other equipment for £13,000 which was paid for in full in February. The equipment is for long-term use in the business.
- The value of closing inventory at 30 June was £2,250 (150 boxes of candles at £15).
- Since the company allows credit customers two months to pay, customers buying in May and June have not yet paid for their candles. Therefore, trade receivables are £16,700 (total credit sales for the period of £40,700 minus £24,000 cash received from credit sales).
- The company had a cash surplus of £500 at 30 June.

- Sarah has invested £10,000 capital in the business and the company is also financed by a medium-term bank loan of £6,500.
- We know from the draft statement of profit or loss for the six months ended 30 June 2018 (see Chapter 6) that the profit for the period was £4,865.
- Sarah has not taken any of the profit as dividends.
- Trade suppliers give one month's credit, which means that inventory purchased in June has not yet been paid for. Therefore, trade payables are £9,000 (total purchases of £45,900 minus £36,900 cash paid to suppliers).
- The estimated current tax liability is £2,085.

Activity

Using the following pro forma, prepare a draft statement of financial position for Candlewick Ltd at 30 June 2018.

Candlewick Ltd

Draft statement of financial position at 30 June 2018

£

ASSETS

Non-current assets

Equipment (at cost) _____

Current assets

Inventory

Trade and other receivables

Cash and cash equivalents _____

_____

Total assets ===========

EQUITY AND LIABILITIES

Equity

Share capital

Retained earnings _____

_____

Non-current liabilities

Loan

Current liabilities

Trade and other payables

Current tax liability _____

_____

Total equity and liabilities ===========

Your completed statement of financial position should look like this:

Candlewick Ltd

Draft statement of financial position at 30 June 2018

	£
ASSETS	
Non-current assets	
Equipment (at cost)	13,000
Current assets	
Inventory	2,250
Trade and other receivables	16,700
Cash and cash equivalents	500
	19,450
Total assets	32,450
EQUITY AND LIABILITIES	
Equity	
Share capital	10,000
Retained earnings	4,865
	14,865
Non-current liabilities	
Loan	6,500
Current liabilities	
Trade and other payables	9,000
Current tax liability	2,085
	17,585
Total equity and liabilities	32,450

An important point is that if Sarah takes boxes of candles from the business for her own use or to give to her friends and family, she must pay for them. If she takes cash out of the business, this transaction is treated as dividends, which reduces the amount of retained earnings. By keeping Sarah's personal transactions separate from the economic transactions of the business in this way, the statement of financial position demonstrates compliance with the business entity concept. Therefore, it presents the financial position of the business and not that of its owner.

You may have noticed that when you were preparing the draft statement of financial position, you needed some of the figures from the statement of profit or loss. The closing inventory shown in the statement of profit or loss also appeared in the statement of financial position. In addition, you will recall that the difference between the figure for revenue in the cash flow statement (cash received from cash and credit sales during the period) and the figure for revenue in the statement of profit or loss (total revenue for the period irrespective of whether cash has been received) is shown as trade receivables in the statement of financial position. Similarly, the difference between the figure for purchases in the cash flow statement (cash paid for purchases of inventory) and the figure for purchases in the statement of comprehensive income (total purchases for the period irrespective of whether cash has been paid) is shown as trade payables in the statement of financial position. You are now beginning to see the relationship between the two main financial statements.

So far we have only prepared a draft statement of financial position using cash information. We will now explain how the statement of financial position is prepared from a trial balance and other information available at the end of the accounting period. First we will explain how the *post trial balance adjustments* affect the statement of financial position. Here is the trial balance at 31 December 2018, which marks the end of the first year of trading for Candlewick Ltd.

Candlewick Ltd

Trial balance at 31 December 2018

	Debit £	Credit £
Revenue		173,200
Purchases	113,400	
Equipment (at cost)	13,000	
Trade receivables	27,500	
Trade payables		15,000
Cash and cash equivalents	26,150	
Salaries	14,500	
Rent	6,000	
Telephone and Internet	1,960	
Postage and packing	1,100	
Advertising	600	
Interest paid on loan	490	
Loan		6,500
Share capital at 1 January 2018		10,000
	204,700	204,700

As mentioned in the previous chapter, all the post trial balance adjustments would normally be entered in the ledger accounts and a revised trial balance would be generated. However, we will show the post trial balance items of information as notes since this is the way you are likely to encounter them in your assessments.

7.4 Inventory, accruals and prepayments

7.4.1 Inventory

As explained in Chapter 6, the valuation of inventory is guided by IAS 2, *Inventories* (IASB, 2003) and the IFRS for SMEs, both of which require closing inventory to be valued at the lower of cost or net realizable value (NRV). Sarah carried out an inventory counting exercise on 31 December 2018 and found that Candlewick Ltd had 50 boxes of candles in stock which had cost £15 each. Therefore, the value of closing inventory is £15 x 50 = £750. In Chapter 6 you made an adjustment in the statement of profit or loss for the year ended 31 December 2018, by deducting £750 from the cost of purchases. Since inventory is one of the assets of the business that it hopes to sell in the next accounting period, you need to make a corresponding adjustment in the statement of financial position by showing inventory amounting to £750 under current assets.

7.4.2 Accruals

You will remember from Chapter 6 that an *accrual* is an estimate of a liability that is not supported by an invoice or a request for payment at the time when the accounts are prepared. Candlewick Ltd has three accruals:

- The trial balance shows telephone and Internet expenses of £1,960, but these only cover the first 11 months and the accountant Sarah has employed estimates that a further £200 is owed for December. This means that the expense shown in the statement of profit or loss should be £1,960 + £200 = £2,160.
- The accountant knows from the invoices for advertising that the total amount paid was £600, but during December Sarah took out extra advertisements to promote sales over the festive season. The company will not be invoiced for these advertisements until January, but the accountant estimates the amount will be £100. This means that the expense shown in the statement of profit or loss should be £600 + £100 = £700.
- On 1 July 2018 the interest rate on the company's loan increased to 9.23%, which means the interest on the loan is £50 per month. The trial balance shows loan interest of £490 because the company pays one month in arrears and the interest for December 2018 will not be paid until January 2019. Therefore, the finance cost shown in the statement of profit or loss should be £490 + £50 = £540.

You need to make a corresponding adjustment in the statement of financial position by adding together the accruals (£200 + £100 + £50 = £350) and including this aggregated amount in the calculation of trade and other payables. Trade and other payables are shown under current liabilities because they will be paid during the next accounting period.

7.4.3　Prepayments

A *prepayment* is a payment made for goods or services before they are received. The amount that belongs to the next accounting period needs to be deducted from the trial balance figure for that expense. Candlewick Ltd has one prepayment. Sarah has recorded printing, postage and stationery expenses of £1,100 in the accounts, but at the end of December she realizes that she has accumulated a small surplus of these items that the business will not use until January. The cost of these items was £100. Therefore, the expense shown in the statement of profit or loss should be £1,100 – £100 = £1,000.

You now need to make a corresponding adjustment in the statement of financial position. The general rule is to include the aggregated prepaid amounts in the calculation of trade and other receivables which are shown under current assets.

7.5　Depreciation of property, plant and equipment

In Chapter 6 we explained that under IAS 16, *Property, Plant and Equipment* (IASB, 2014b) and the IFRS for SMEs, most items of property, plant and equipment (PPE) with a finite life must be depreciated. *Depreciation* is the systematic allocation of the depreciable amount of an asset over its useful life. This allows the accountant to spread the original cost of the asset over the period in which it brings economic benefits to the business. It does not reflect the fair value of the asset, such as the replacement value or the market value.

Candlewick Ltd has one non-current tangible asset, which is the equipment bought on 1 January at a cost of £13,000. The equipment has a residual value of £1,000 at the end of its useful life of four years. The accountant has advised Sarah to use the *straight-line method* of depreciation which spreads the cost (or revalued amount) evenly over the life of the asset.

Activity

Using the following formula, calculate the allowance for depreciation for the year ended 31 December 2018:

$$\frac{\text{Cost} - \text{Residual value}}{\text{Useful life}}$$

You should have found this exercise easy, since we explained it in the previous chapter. Check your answer against the calculations below:

$$\frac{£13,000 - £1,000}{4 \text{ years}} = \frac{£12,000}{4 \text{ years}} = £3,000$$

The allowance for depreciation on equipment of £3,000 is included in the calculation of administrative expenses in the statement of profit or loss for the year ended 31 December 2018. Since part of the cost of the asset has been apportioned as an expense for the period, you now need to make an adjustment to the value of the asset in the statement of financial position. Instead of showing the asset at cost, as Sarah did when preparing the draft statement of financial position, the accountant tells her that it will be shown at the *carrying amount* (sometimes referred to as the net book value or the written down value of the asset). The carrying amount is the amount at which an asset is recognized after deducting any accumulated depreciation and accumulated impairment losses. The residual value and useful life must be reviewed annually. If an asset is revalued, the valuation is substituted for the carrying amount and this will result in a revaluation gain or loss. An impairment loss is a reduction in the recoverable amount of the asset due to obsolescence, damage or a fall in the market value of such assets.

We now need to calculate the carrying amount of the equipment that will be shown under non-current assets in the statement of financial position. The equipment was bought on 1 January and at the end of the first year the carrying amount is calculated as follows:

$$\text{Cost} - \text{Depreciation} = £13,000 - £3,000 = £10,000$$

The closing carrying amount at the end of one year becomes the opening carrying amount at the start of the next, and each year the opening carrying amount will be reduced by £3,000 until at the end of the fourth year only the residual value of £1,000 remains. The following table illustrates a convenient way of setting out your workings.

Year	Opening carrying amount	Allowance for depreciation	Closing carrying amount
	£	£	£
1	13,000	(3,000)	10,000
2	10,000	(3,000)	7,000
3	7,000	(3,000)	4,000
4	4,000	(3,000)	1,000

Sarah's accountant tells her about a second method that can be used. It is known as the *diminishing balance method* of depreciation because the cost reduces over the life of the asset. The method involves applying a depreciation rate to the opening carrying amount each year. In the first year, the opening carrying amount is the cost of the asset and the formula is:

$$\text{Cost} \times \text{Depreciation rate } (\%)$$

In subsequent years the formula is:

$$\text{Opening carrying amount} \times \text{Depreciation rate (\%)}$$

The following table shows how the diminishing balance method would be applied to the equipment. As a very rough rule of thumb, the depreciation rate is nearly double that required for the straight-line method. Since the annual allowance for depreciation under the straight-line method was 25% (£3,000 ÷ £12,000), we will use a rate of 47.25% in this illustration of the diminishing balance method. The first step is to calculate the allowance for depreciation for the first year:

$$£13,000 \times 47.25\% = £6,143$$

We can now use this to work out the closing carrying amount at the end of Year 1 (£6,858), which becomes the opening carrying amount for Year 2. The depreciation rate of 47.25% is then applied to find the depreciation charge for Year 2 (£6,858 × 47.25% = £3,240). This is then deducted from the opening carrying amount to arrive at the closing carrying amount. This continues until the end of Year 4, when the following table shows that we are left with the residual value of just over £1,000.

Year	Opening carrying amount	Depreciation 47.25%	Closing carrying amount
	£	£	£
1	13,000.00	(6,142.50)	6,857.50
2	6,857.50	(3,240.17)	3,617.33
3	3,617.33	(1,709.19)	1,908.14
4	1,908.14	(901.60)	1,006.55

Sarah's accountant tells her that methods based on usage, such as the units of production method, are also permitted. These would be relevant to businesses in the manufacturing sector. The depreciation method chosen should reflect the pattern in which the asset's economic benefits are consumed by the entity. If the pattern by which the entity expects to consume an asset's future economic benefits has changed significantly since the last annual reporting date, management must review the present depreciation method. If the differences are expected to continue, the method should be changed to reflect the new pattern.

The straight-line method is widely used as it is simple and easy to use and apportions the cost of the asset evenly over its useful life to the business. If the pattern in which the economic benefits are consumed is uncertain, the straight-line method is usually adopted. Although the diminishing balance method is more complex, the lower depreciation charge in later years helps to offset higher maintenance costs that are likely when assets such as plant, machinery and vehicles age. Thus the overall cost of such assets is spread evenly. To aid comparison, the same depreciation method is used for all assets that are classified as belonging to the same group and it is applied consistently from one period to the next.

7.6   Bad debts and doubtful receivables

As discussed in Chapter 6, Candlewick Ltd did not have any bad debts during the first year of trading. A *bad debt* is an amount owed by customers that is considered to be irrecoverable and it must be written off as a charge against profit or against an existing allowance for doubtful receivables in the statement of profit or loss. As mentioned in the previous chapter, Candlewick Ltd did not have any bad debts during the first year of trading. Sarah's accountant has advised her that she should make an *allowance for doubtful receivables* to allow for the estimated non-recovery of receivables. She has decided to base the allowance on 10% of trade receivables: £27,500 x 10% = £2,750. Therefore, this is the amount that was included in the distribution costs in the statement of profit or loss and needs to be deducted from trade receivables in the statement of financial position.

Sarah's accountant tells her about an alternative method based on the age of the debt. The following table shows an age analysis of the company's trade receivables. Most debts are two months old or less because the business gives customers two months to pay. However, some debts are more than three months old, which means some customers are taking much longer than the agreed two months. If Sarah does not improve her credit control, there is a risk that some customers will not pay and this is reflected in the higher percentages the accountant has applied to older debts when calculating the allowance for doubtful receivables.

Age of debt (months)	Trade receivables	Estimated bad receivables	Allowance for doubtful receivables
	£		£
1	12,500	1%	125
2	10,500	10%	1,050
3	3,000	50%	1,500
4 or more	1,500	75%	1,125
Total	27,500		3,800

It is important to remember that methods based on arbitrary percentages are estimates of the proportion of receivables that will not be paid. For financial reporting purposes, the entity should choose the method that gives the most realistic allowance and then use it consistently to aid comparability.

7.7   Finalizing the statement of financial position

We now have all the information we need to prepare the statement of profit or loss and other comprehensive income for Candlewick Ltd for the year ended 31 December 2018 and the statement of financial position at that date. Here are the trial balance and the notes that represent the post trial balance adjustments.

Candlewick Ltd

Trial balance at 31 December 2018

	Debit £	Credit £
Revenue		173,200
Purchases	113,400	
Equipment (at cost)	13,000	
Trade receivables	27,500	
Trade payables		15,000
Cash and cash equivalents	26,150	
Salaries	14,500	
Rent	6,000	
Telephone and Internet	1,960	
Printing, postage and stationery	1,100	
Advertising	600	
Interest paid on loan	490	
Loan		6,500
Share capital at 1 January 2018		10,000
	204,700	204,700

Additional information available at 31 December 2018:

- Closing inventory is valued at £750.
- Rent, printing, postage and stationery, and salaries are allocated 50% to distribution costs and 50% to administrative expenses.
- Advertising is classified as a distribution expense.
- Telephone and Internet are classified as administrative expenses.
- There are accruals of £100 for advertising, £200 for telephone and Internet, and £50 for unpaid loan interest.
- Printing, postage and packaging include a prepayment of £100.
- The equipment is expected to have a useful life of four years, and an estimated residual value of £1,000. Depreciation on equipment will be charged 50% to distribution costs and 50% to administrative expenses.

- An allowance for doubtful receivables will be made based on 10% of trade receivables. This allowance will be charged 100% to administrative expenses.
- The estimated current tax liability is £8,970.
- Sarah has decided to leave all profits in the company to help it grow, rather than take some for herself in the form of a dividend.
- The company has no other comprehensive income.

Activity

Prepare a statement of profit or loss and other comprehensive income for Candlewick Ltd for the year ended 31 December 2018 and a statement of financial position at that date. Use all the items in the trial balance and take account of every item of additional information. Tick each item every time you use it.

When you have finished, all the items in the trial balance will have one tick because they are either shown in the statement of profit or loss and other comprehensive income or in the statement of financial position. On the other hand, there should be two ticks for every item of additional information because these are the post trial balance adjustment: one tick for when you adjust an item in the statement of profit or loss and other comprehensive income and a second tick when you adjust an item in the statement of financial position.

You will find it useful to start by drawing together all the calculations we made in connection with the post trial balance adjustments at 31 December 2018. These can be summarized as follows.

Working 1	£
Purchases	113,400
Closing inventory	(750)
Cost of sales	112,650

Put one tick against the information about closing inventory when you use it to calculate cost of sales in the statement of profit or loss and a second tick when you include it under current assets in the statement of financial position.

Working 2

$$\text{Depreciation on equipment} = \frac{£13,000 - £1,000}{4 \text{ years}} = £3,000$$

Closing carrying amount = £13,000 − £3,000 = £10,000

Put one tick against the information about the allowance for depreciation on equipment when you use it to calculate distribution costs and administrative expenses in the statement of profit or loss and another when you show the carrying amount of equipment under non-current assets in the statement of financial position.

Working 3

Allowance for doubtful receivables = £27,500 × 10% = £2,750

Put one tick against the information about the allowance for doubtful receivables when you use it to calculate distribution costs and administrative expenses in the statement of profit or loss and another when you include it in the calculation of trade and other receivables under current assets in the statement of financial position.

Working 4	Amount	Distribution costs	Administrative expenses	Finance costs
	(£)	(£)	(£)	(£)
Rent	6,000	3,000	3,000	
Advertising (600 + 100)	700	700		
Telephone and Internet (1,960 + 200)	2,160		2,160	
Printing, postage and stationery (1,100 − 100)	1,000	500	500	
Interest on loan (490 + 50)	540			540
Salaries	14,500	7,250	7,250	
Depreciation (W2)	3,000	1,500	1,500	
Doubtful receivables (W3)	2,750		2,750	
Total	30,650	12,950	17,160	540

Working 5	£
Trade receivables in trial balance	27,500
Doubtful receivables (10%)	(2,750)
Trade receivables	24,750
Prepayments	100
Trade and other receivables	24,850

Working 6	£
Trade payables in trial balance	15,000
Accruals	350
Trade and other payables	15,350

Your completed financial statements should look like this.

Candlewick Ltd

Statement of profit or loss and other comprehensive income for the year ended 31 December 2018

	£
Revenue	173,200
Cost of sales (W1)	(112,650)
Gross profit	60,550
Distribution costs (W2, W3, W4)	(12,950)
Administrative expenses (W2, W3, W4)	(17,160)
Operating profit	30,440
Finance costs (W4)	(540)
Profit before tax	29,900
Income tax expense	(8,970)
Profit for the period	20,930
Other comprehensive income	–
Total comprehensive income for the period	20,930

Candlewick Ltd

Statement of financial position at 31 December 2018

	£
ASSETS	
Non-current assets	
Equipment (W2)	10,000
Current assets	
Inventory	750
Trade and other receivables (W5)	24,850
Cash and cash equivalents	26,150
	51,750
Total assets	61,750
EQUITY AND LIABILITIES	
Equity	
Share capital	10,000
Retained earnings	20,930
	30,930

Non-current liabilities	
Loan	6,500
Current liabilities	
Trade and other payables (W6)	15,350
Current tax liability	8,970
	30,820
Total equity and liabilities	61,750

These are fairly simple financial statements and because it is the company's first year of trading, it is not possible to provide comparative figures for the previous year. You will find it useful to learn the following more detailed layout for the statement of financial position, which is consistent with the minimum requirements of IAS 1.

Name of entity

Statement of financial position at (date)

	This year £	Last year £
ASSETS		
Non-current assets		
Property, plant and equipment	X	X
Intangible assets	X	X
Investments	X	X
	X	X
Current assets		
Inventories	X	X
Trade and other receivables	X	X
Investments	X	X
Cash and cash equivalents	X	X
	X	X
Total assets	X	X
EQUITY AND LIABILITIES		
Equity		
Share capital	X	X
Retained earnings	X	X
Other reserves	X	X
	X	X

Non-current liabilities		
Finance lease liabilities	X	X
Borrowings	X	X
	X	X
Current liabilities		
Trade and other payables	X	X
Dividends payable	X	X
Current tax liability	X	X
Provisions	X	X
Borrowings	X	X
Finance lease liabilities	X	X
	X	X
Total equity and liabilities	X	X

The knowledge you gained in Chapter 6 should have been reinforced as you studied this chapter because we have shown you how to reflect the post trial balance adjustments in the statement of profit or loss and other comprehensive income and in the statement of financial position. As you worked through this chapter you may have noticed that financial accounting is not an exact science. In fact, these general purpose financial statements suffer from a number of limitations:

- To a large extent, financial statements are based on estimates, judgements and models rather than exact depictions.
- Figures in financial statements can be misleading if there is high inflation or unscrupulous manipulation. However, if an unusual accounting treatment has been used, the figures for earlier years are adjusted in published trends.
- There is a substantial degree of classification and aggregation in the financial statements and the effect of allocating continuous operations to the reporting period. Financial statements only contain quantitative data.
- They do not focus on any non-financial effects of transactions or events.
- They do not reflect future transactions or events that may enhance or impair the entity's operations.
- They do not anticipate the impact of potential changes in the economic environment.

7.8   Conclusions

In this chapter we have explained that the purpose of the statement of financial position is to measure the financial position of the business on the last day of the accounting period for which the statement of profit or loss and other comprehensive income has been prepared. The statement of financial position gives users important information about the assets, equity and liabilities of the business. We have shown you how a business that uses cash records can prepare these two financial statements after making some adjustments. We have also explained how these financial statements can be prepared from a trial balance generated by a double-entry book-keeping system.

In the exercises in this book, the post trial balance adjustments are shown as additional information below the trial balance. If you adopt a ticking system when using the information to prepare the two financial statements, you should find that you have one tick against every item in the trial balance and two ticks against every adjustment. You tick every adjustment twice because you make one adjustment to an item in the statement of profit or loss and other comprehensive income and a corresponding adjustment in the statement of financial position. After the first year, the previous year's figures must be disclosed in these financial statements to enhance the comparability of the information.

Common problems to avoid

Common mistakes students make when drawing up the statement of financial position are:

- Not showing the name of the business
- Not stating the date at which the statement of financial position is prepared
- Forgetting to include the currency symbol
- Confusing opening inventory with closing inventory
- Not making all the post trial balance adjustments
- Not classifying assets and liabilities correctly
- Forgetting that it is only the two balancing figures that are double underlined (total assets in the first part and total equity and liabilities in the second part)
- Forgetting to show all workings

References

IASB (2003) IAS 2, *Inventories*, London: International Accounting Standards Board.
IASB (2014a) IAS 1, *Presentation of Financial Statements*, London: IFRS Foundation.
IASB (2014b) IAS 16, *Property, Plant and Equipment*, London: IFRS Foundation.
IASB (2015a) *Exposure Draft Conceptual Framework for Financial Reporting*, London: IFRS Foundation.
IASB (2015b) *IFRS for SMEs*, London: IFRS Foundation.

Discussion questions

1 Discuss the general purpose of the statement of financial position and the meaning of the terms *asset, liability* and *equity* as defined by the Conceptual Framework for Financial Reporting (IASB, 2015a).

2 Discuss the going concern basis of accounting and the principles involved, taking the example of the valuation of tangible assets in the statement of financial position.

? Practice questions

3 Insert the missing figures in the following examples, remembering that some items will be added and others will be subtracted.

	(a) £	(b) £	(c) £	(d) £	(e) £
ASSETS					
Non-current assets	12,400	22,800	?	42,200	?
Current assets	?	3,700	4,200	?	11,800
Total assets	15,800	?	36,200	52,800	66,000
EQUITY AND LIABILITIES					
Equity					
Capital	?	6,000	10,000	?	10,000
Retained earnings	4,800	13,300	?	25,800	?
	9,800	?	32,700	40,800	47,700
Liabilities					
Non-current liabilities	?	6,000	2,000	10,000	?
Current liabilities	1,000	1,200	?	2,000	3,300
	6,000	?	3,500	?	18,300
Total equity and liabilities	?	?	?	?	?

4 Salma Ibrahim set up a company called Uplights Ltd and opened a lighting shop on 1 January 2017. Her brother is studying for his accountancy exams and helps her by doing the bookkeeping and managing the inventory. At the end of the first year of trading, he generates the following trial balance from the accounting records.

Uplights Ltd
Trial balance at 31 December 2017

	Debit	Credit
	£	£
Revenue		66,500
Purchases	20,000	
Fixtures and fittings (at cost)	20,000	
Trade receivables	2,000	
Trade payables		8,400
Cash and cash equivalents	14,500	
Bank interest received		100
Rent	24,000	
Salaries	21,500	
Insurance	2,000	
Lighting and heating	500	
Telephone and Internet	400	
Advertising	100	
Share capital at 1 January 2017		30,000
	105,000	105,000

Additional information at 31 December 2017:

- Inventory was valued at £8,000.
- Estimated current tax payable is £2,000.
- The company classifies expenses by nature.

Required

Prepare a draft statement of profit or loss for Uplights Ltd for the year ended 31 December 2017 and a draft statement of financial position at that date. Show all your workings.

5 On 1 July 2017 Mark Farmer opened a shop called Miphone Ltd. The trial balance for the first year is shown below.

Miphone Ltd

Trial balance at 30 June 2018

	Debit £	Credit £
Revenue		75,200
Purchases	12,160	
Plant and equipment at cost	25,000	
Trade receivables	1,200	
Trade payables		1,600
Cash and cash equivalents	3,260	
Other income		1,200
Salaries	24,000	
Rent	18,000	
Insurance	7,200	
Advertising	860	
Lighting and heating	620	
Telephone and Internet	450	
General expenses	250	
Share capital at 1 July 2017		15,000
	93,000	93,000

Additional information at 30 June 2018:

- Inventory is valued at £890.
- Advertising paid in advance is £260.
- Accrued expenses are lighting and heating £540, telephone and Internet £290 and general expenses £160.
- Estimated current tax payable is £1,200.
- No dividends will be paid and there is no other comprehensive income.

Required

(a) Using a spreadsheet, prepare a draft statement of profit or loss for Miphone Ltd for the year ended 30 June 2018, classifying expenses by nature. In addition, prepare a draft statement of financial position at that date.

(b) After taking advice from his accountant, Mark has decided to depreciate equipment using the straight-line method over five years, with no residual value. He has also decided to make an allowance for doubtful receivables and has decided to base it on 10% of opening trade receivables. Make these adjustments to your spreadsheet and prepare a statement of profit or loss for Miphone Ltd for the year ended 30 June 2018, classifying expenses by nature. In addition, revise your draft statement of financial position at that date.

6 Kavita Patel owns a business called Beauty Box Ltd which started trading on 1 July 2016. At the end of the second year, her accountant provides the following trial balance from the accounting system.

Beauty Box Ltd

Trial balance at 30 June 2018

	Debit £	Credit £
Revenue		104,900
Purchases	39,700	
Inventory at 1 July 2017	10,000	
Equipment at cost	20,000	
Trade receivables	6,000	
Trade payables		8,000
Cash and cash equivalents	15,300	
Interest received		100
Salaries	30,000	
Rent	15,000	
Insurance	3,000	
Lighting and heating	1,500	
Telephone and Internet	2,000	
Advertising	500	
Allowances at 1 July 2017:		
Depreciation on plant and equipment		4,000
Doubtful receivables		1,000
Share capital at 1 July 2017		20,000
Retained profit at 1 July 2017		5,000
	143,000	143,000

Additional information at 30 June 2018:

- Inventory is valued at £12,000.
- Equipment has a useful life of five years and no residual value. It is depreciated using the straight-line method.

- The company makes an allowance for doubtful receivables based on 10% of opening trade receivables.
- The company classifies expenses by nature.
- Estimated income tax expense for the year is £4,500.
- No dividends will be paid and there is no other comprehensive income.

Required

Prepare a statement of profit or loss and other comprehensive income for Beauty Box Ltd for the year ended 30 June 2018. In addition, prepare a statement of financial position at that date. Show all your workings.

7 Yousuf Jumani launched his trading company, Jumani Ltd, on 1 January 2016 after successfully completing an MBA programme. The following data are available at the end of the second year.

Trial balance at 31 December 2017		
	£	£
Revenue		170,000
Purchases	70,000	
Property, plant and equipment at cost	50,000	
Accumulated depreciation on PPE		10,000
Inventories at 1 January 2017	8,000	
Interest on bank loan	250	
Accrued expenses		1,000
Distribution costs	20,000	
Administrative expenses	50,000	
Trade payables		7,000
Trade receivables	15,000	
Cash at bank	22,750	
5% bank loan repayable 2022		5,000
Share capital at 1 January 2017		21,000
Retained earnings at 1 January 2017		22,000
	236,000	236,000

The following additional information is available:

- Inventories at 31 December 2017 cost £28,000. This figure includes inventories that cost £2,480, whose net realizable value is only £1,000.
- There are additional distribution costs of £120 for December 2017.

- Administrative expenses include insurance expenses of £4,500, one-third of which relates to building insurance for 2018.
- The company classifies expenses by function.
- Income tax payable for the year has been calculated as £19,020.
- No dividends will be paid and there is no other comprehensive income.

Required

Prepare a statement of profit or loss and other comprehensive income for the year ended 31 December 2017. In addition, prepare a statement of financial position at that date. Show all your workings.

8 Leilei Zhang started *Oriental Silks Ltd* on 1 April 2017. The trial balance at the end of the second year of trading is shown below.

Trial balance at 31 March 2019	£	£
Revenue		104,017
Purchases	18,000	
Property, plant and equipment at cost	25,000	
Accumulated depreciation on PPE		5,000
Inventories at 1 April 2018	8,860	
Interest on bank loan	200	
Accruals		426
Distribution costs	18,985	
Administrative expenses	50,038	
Trade payables		7,000
Trade receivables	6,000	
Cash and cash equivalents	38,317	
8% bank loan repayable 2022		5,000
Share capital at 1 April 2018		20,000
Reserves:		
Share premium		1,000
Retained earnings at 1 April 2018		22,957
	165,400	165,400

The following additional information is available:

- Inventories at 31 March 2019 cost £8,400. This figure includes inventories that cost £480, but the net realizable value is only £80.

- There are additional administration expenses of £120 for March 2019.
- The company classifies expenses by function.
- Interest on the bank loan for the last six months of the period has not been included.
- Income tax payable for the year has been calculated as £1,614.
- No dividends will be paid and there is no other comprehensive income.

Required

Prepare the statement of profit or loss and other comprehensive income for the year ended 31 March 2019. In addition, prepare a statement of financial position at that date. Show all your workings.

 Suggested research questions for dissertation students

Students interested in accounting for leases may wish to investigate one or more of the following research questions:

- What are the historical reasons for differentiating between an operating lease and a finance lease?
- What are the views of stakeholders on IFRS 16, *Leases* (applicable from 1 January 2019)?

Preliminary reading

Beattie, V., Goodacre, A. and Thomson, S.J. (2006) 'International lease-accounting reform and economic consequences: The views of UK users and preparers', *The International Journal of Accounting*, 41(1), pp. 75–103.

Bennett, B. and Bradbury, M. (2003) 'Capitalizing non-cancellable operating leases', *Journal of International Financial Management and Accounting*, 14(2), pp. 101–114.

Durocher, S. (2008) 'Canadian evidence on the constructive capitalization of operating leases', *Accounting Perspectives*, 7(3), pp. 227–256.

Durocher, S. and Fortin, A. (2009) 'Proposed changes in lease accounting and private bankers' credit decisions', *Accounting Perspectives*, 8(1), pp. 9–42.

Frecka, T. (2008) 'Ethical issues in financial reporting: Is international structuring of lease contracts to avoid capitalization unethical?' *Journal of Business Ethics*, 80(1), pp. 45–59.

Hussey, R. and Ong, A. (2010) 'Proposals to change lease accounting: Evidence from Canada and Malaysia', *Journal of Law and Financial Management*, 9(2), pp. 2–15.

Imhoff, E., Lipe, R. and Wright, D. (1991) 'Operating leases: Impact of constructive capitalization', *Accounting Horizons*, 5(1), pp. 51–63.

Students interested in accounting for intangible assets may wish to investigate one or more of the following research questions:

- Should more intangible assets be recognized in the financial statements?
- What are the effects of recognizing intellectual capital in financial statements?

Preliminary reading

Bence, D. and Fry, N. (2004) 'The International Accounting Standards Board's search for a general purpose accounting model', *Journal of Financial Reporting, Regulation and Governance*, 3(1), pp. 1–29.

Booth, B. (2003) 'The Conceptual Framework as a coherent system for the development of Accounting Standards', *ABACUS*, 39(3), pp. 310–324.

Cummins, J. and Bawden, D. (2010) 'Accounting for information: Information and knowledge in the annual reports of FTSE 100 companies', *Journal of Information Science*, 36(3), pp. 283–305.

El-Tawy, N. and Tollington, T. (2012) 'Intellectual capital: Literature review', *International Journal of Learning and Intellectual Capital*, 9(3), pp. 241–257.

El-Tawy, N. and Tollington, T. (2008) 'The recognition and measurement of brand assets: An exploration of the accounting/marketing interface', *Journal of Marketing and Management*, 24(7–8), pp. 711–731.

Wilson, R. and Stenson, J. (2008) 'Valuation of information assets on the balance sheet: The recognition and approaches to the valuation of intangible assets', *Business Information Review*, 25(3), pp. 167–182.

8 The statement of cash flows

Learning objectives

When you have studied this chapter, you should be able to:

- Explain the purpose of the statement of cash flows
- Differentiate between cash and cash equivalents
- Classify cash flows into operating, investing or financing activities
- Prepare a statement of cash flows using the direct method
- Prepare a statement of cash flows using the indirect method

8.1 Introduction

Users of general purpose financial statements (see Chapter 5) have a common interest in information about the effects of transactions and other events that change a reporting entity's economic resources and claims. This is shown in the statement of profit or loss and other comprehensive income (see Chapter 6). Users also need information about the entity's economic resources and the claims against the reporting entity and this information is shown in the statement of financial position (see Chapter 7). However, users are also interested in the entity's ability to generate positive cash flows from its activities.

Under IAS 1, *Presentation of Financial Statements* (IASB, 2014) and the *IFRS for SMEs* (IASB, 2015), a full set of financial statements also includes a statement of cash flow. This important financial statement is the focus of this chapter.

8.2 Purpose of the statement of cash flows

Users of the published financial statements need information that will not only help them evaluate the financial performance and financial position of the entity, but also help them assess prospects for future net cash inflows to the entity. Having sufficient cash is crucial to the long-term survival of any business as cash is needed to pay for inventory, distribution costs, administration and other expenses, finance costs and taxation. Cash is also needed to acquire or replace property, plant and equipment, and to pay dividends to shareholders. The importance of cash has led to the maxim, 'cash is king'.

The accrual basis of accounting means that a business can make a profit over the accounting period and yet it may not have enough cash at the end of the period to continue as a going concern. This leads to the saying, 'revenue is vanity, profit is sanity, but cash is reality'. The figure for revenue in the statement of comprehensive income has limited use because it does not take account of the costs and expenses incurred by the business. The profit figure is more informative because it reflects the financial performance of the business, but it reflects the effects of economic transactions and events in the period in which they occur, which may not coincide with when the related cash is received or paid. Therefore, the profit or loss for the accounting period differs from the cash position at the end of that period.

Activity

Identify three business transactions where the revenue or expense reported in the statement of profit or loss differs from the amount of cash received or paid during the year.

Perhaps you have chosen some of the following examples. A business that sells the majority of its goods on credit may be profitable, but it could be experiencing serious cash flow problems because it has to wait up to 90 days before receiving cash payment from its customers. Alternatively, a business may have used cash to purchase more inventory than it sells during the period, but this is not reflected in the statement of profit or loss because the cost of closing inventory is excluded from cost of sales. Another example is where a business pays a substantial amount of cash to acquire a tangible non-current asset with a finite life, but the statement of profit or loss only includes the annual depreciation on the asset as an operating expense. A business might also have made a prepayment during the period, but that prepaid expense will be excluded from the statement of profit or loss. Because of these differences, the statement of profit or loss rarely tells us anything about an entity's cash flow.

The statement of cash flows is an essential component of a set of general purpose financial statements. When used in conjunction with the other financial statements, it provides users with information that enables them to:

- evaluate changes in an entity's net assets (i.e. changes in total assets less liabilities)
- evaluate an entity's financial structure, liquidity and solvency (i.e. the balance between the assets and liabilities of the business, the nature of its assets and borrowings, and ability of the business to pay its debts when they fall due)

- evaluate an entity's ability to alter the amount and timing of cash flows in order to adapt to changes in the business environment and exploit business opportunities
- model and predict an entity's future cash flows.

IAS 7, *Statement of Cash Flows* (IASB, 2017) requires all entities that comply with IFRS to prepare a statement of cash flows. This should provide information about the historical changes in cash and cash equivalents of an entity by means of a statement of cash flows which classifies cash flows during the period from operating, investing and financing activities. It is important to note that there is no requirement to give estimates of future cash flows. Therefore, the statement of cash flows is very different from the internal cash flow forecast we prepared for Candlewick Ltd in Chapter 2 to help Sarah Wick to plan the capital requirements of her business.

External users need a financial statement that will help them evaluate the cash generating ability of the business and its liquidity. Cash is essential to the survival of the business. It needs cash for the following main reasons:

- to pay employees
- to pay creditors
- to acquire or replace equipment
- to make investments or acquire other companies
- to repay loans
- to distribute dividends to investors.

The *purpose* of the statement of cash flows is to provide historical information about changes in cash and cash equivalents resulting from the inflows and outflows of cash. *Cash inflows* are the cash receipts of the business and *cash outflows* are the cash payments made by the business. The difference between the inflows and outflows of cash is known as the *net cash flow* (a positive figure indicates a cash surplus and a negative figure indicates a cash deficit).

Key definitions

Cash inflows are the cash receipts of a business.

Cash outflows are the cash payments made by a business.

Net cash flow is the difference between the cash inflows and the cash outflows.

The statement of cash flows calculates the change in cash and cash equivalents based on the following equation:

$$\text{Change in cash and cash equivalents} = \text{Cash inflows} - \text{Cash outflows}$$

8.3   Cash and cash equivalents

IAS 7 requires a statement of cash flows to provide information about the historical changes in *cash and cash equivalents*. This term should be familiar because it is one of the items shown under current assets in the statement of financial position. IAS 7 distinguishes between them as follows:

- Cash is defined as cash on hand and demand deposits. Examples of cash on hand are money and cheques held in the business or money at the bank. Examples of demand deposits are money held on short-term deposit at a bank or other financial institution.
- Cash equivalents are defined as short-term, highly liquid investments that are readily convertible into a known amount of cash and are subject to insignificant risk of changes in value. Examples of cash equivalents are treasury bills, short-term government bonds and money market holdings. Cash equivalents are held for the purpose of meeting short-term cash commitments rather than for investment or other purposes.

An investment qualifies as a cash equivalent if it is readily convertible to a known amount of cash and is subject to an insignificant risk of changes in value. Therefore, an investment normally qualifies as a cash equivalent when it has a short maturity of, say, three months or less from the date of acquisition. Equity investments are excluded from cash equivalents unless they are, in substance, cash equivalents (such as preference shares acquired within a short period of their maturity and with a specified redemption date).

Bank overdrafts are generally classified as borrowings, but IAS 7 notes that if a bank overdraft is repayable on demand and forms an integral part of an entity's cash management, it is included as a component of cash and cash equivalents. A characteristic of such a banking arrangement is that the bank balance often fluctuates from being positive to overdrawn.

Key definitions

Cash comprises cash on hand and demand deposits

Cash equivalents are short-term, highly liquid investments that are readily convertible to known amounts of cash and which are subject to an insignificant risk of changes in value

Source: IAS 7, IASB, 2017 [6]. Reproduced with permission from the IFRS Foundation.

8.4   Classification of cash flows

IAS 7 requires the information in the statement of cash flows to be classified into cash flows from three different activities: *operating*, *investing* and *financing activities*. These terms should be familiar as you used them in the statement of profit or loss and other comprehensive income to distinguish between operating expenses, investment costs and finance costs. We will now look at them in more detail.

Operating activities are defined as the principal revenue-producing activities of the entity and other activities that are not investing or financing activities [7.6]. Examples include:

- cash receipts from customers
- cash receipts from other revenue, such as royalties and commissions
- cash payments to suppliers
- cash payments to and on behalf of employees
- cash payments in respect of interest on loans for operating purposes
- cash payments of income tax and receipts from income tax refunds relating to operating activities.

These cash flows relate to transactions and events reported in the statement of comprehensive income. The net cash flow from operating activities is an important measure of an entity's ability to generate sufficient cash to replace assets, pay dividends and make new investments without having to use external sources of finance. This information can also be used to forecast future operating cash flows.

Investing activities are defined as the acquisition and disposal of long-term assets and other investments not included in cash equivalents [7.6]. Examples include:

- cash receipts from the sale of redundant non-current assets and intangible assets
- cash receipts from the sale of equity or debt instruments (such as shares or debentures) of other entities
- cash receipts from the repayment of advances and loans made to other parties
- cash payments to acquire property, plant and equipment and intangible assets
- cash payments to acquire equity and debt instruments (such as shares or debentures) of other entities
- cash payments in respect of advances and loans made to other parties.

Financing activities are defined as activities that result in changes in the size and composition of the contributed equity and borrowings of the entity [7.6]. Examples include:

- cash receipts from issuing shares
- cash receipts from issuing debentures and loans
- cash payments to owners to acquire or redeem the entity's shares
- cash repayments of amounts borrowed or amounts paid to reduce a liability under a finance lease.

Key definitions

Operating activities are the principal revenue generating activities of the entity and other activities that are not investing or financing activities.

Investing activities are the acquisition and disposal of long-term assets and other investments not included in cash equivalents.

Financing activities are activities that result in changes in the size and composition of the contributed equity and borrowings of the entity.

Source: IAS 7, IASB, 2017 [6]. Reproduced with permission from the IFRS Foundation.

It is usually fairly easy to classify the cash flows into one of these three categories. You need to bear in mind that all businesses have operating activities, but some may not have investing and/or financing activities. You may also find that you need to identify the elements within a transaction so that you can classify each element appropriately. For example, if a mortgage repayment also includes interest, the interest element may be classified as an operating or financing activity, while the repayment element must be shown as a financing activity.

While IAS 7 requires that all cash flows from interest and dividends paid and received must be disclosed separately, these items can be classified in a manner appropriate for an entity's specific business. Interest and dividends received may be classified as either operating or investing cash flows, and interest and dividends paid should be presented as either operating or financing cash flows. However, despite this apparent flexibility in presentation, interest and dividend cash flows must be classified consistently from period to period. Cash flows arising from taxes on income are normally classified as operating activities, unless specifically identified with financing or investing activities.

For example, for a financial institution such as a bank, interest paid and interest and dividends received are generally classified as operating cash flows. In contrast, for a manufacturing business, interest and dividends received might be better classified as investing cash flows, as they are cash inflows that do not arise from the normal day-to-day operations for this type of entity. Similarly, dividends paid may be better classified as a financing activity because they are a cost of obtaining financial resources from shareholders. However, there is an argument for including dividends paid within operating cash flows, as this helps to better assess whether a business can pay dividends from its current operating cash flow.

Activity

Decide whether a manufacturer of aircraft engines should classify the following cash flows as operating, investing or financing activities, giving reasons to support your answer.

(a) Interest paid

(b) Interest received

(c) Dividends received

(d) Dividends paid

When discussing the classification of these cash flows you must remember that IAS 7 allows an entity to present them in the most appropriate manner for its business. We also need to consider the qualitative characteristics of useful financial information we discussed in Chapter 5. As our example focuses on an engineering company whose main operating activity is making airline engines, it would be logical to classify interest and dividends received as cash flows from investing rather than operating activities. It could be argued that such a treatment would provide a faithful representation of the company's operating, investing and financing cash flows. It would also provide users with more relevant information, as operating cash flows would not be distorted by the cash flows obtained from non-core activities and investments. In a similar manner, interest and dividends paid are best classified as cash flows from financing rather than operating activities.

Having considered a theoretical example on how to appropriately classify cash flows, we will now examine the statements of cash flows prepared by two UK companies. Our first example is Rolls-Royce plc, which is a manufacturer of power systems such as aerospace engines. The second example is Ted Baker Plc, whose annual report and accounts we discussed in Chapter 5. As Rolls-Royce and Ted Baker are both listed companies, their annual report and accounts are prepared in accordance with EU-adopted IFRS. Therefore, their statements of cash flows should comply with IAS 7. Figure 8.1 shows the consolidated cash flow statement for Rolls-Royce for the year ended 31 December 2015.

Figure 8.1   Consolidated cash flow statement for Rolls-Royce Holdings plc

CONSOLIDATED CASH FLOW STATEMENT
For the year ended 31 December 2015

	Notes	2015 £m	2014 £m
Reconciliation of cash flows from operating activities			
Operating profit from continuing operations		1,499	1,390
Operating loss from discontinued operations		–	(1)
Operating profit		1,499	1,389
Loss/(profit) on disposal of property, plant and equipment		8	(3)
Share of results of joint ventures and associates	11	(100)	(94)
Dividends received from joint ventures and associates	11	63	73
Return of capital from joint ventures	11	–	3
Gain on consolidation of previously non-consolidated subsidiary		–	(3)
Amortisation and impairment of intangible assets	9	432	367
Depreciation and impairment of property, plant and equipment	10	378	375
Impairment of investments	11	2	–
(Decrease)/increase in provisions		(151)	129
Decrease in inventories		63	166
Increase in trade and other receivables		(836)	(878)
Increase in trade and other payables		242	214
Cash flows on other financial assets and liabilities held for operating purposes		(305)	(30)
Net defined benefit post-retirement cost recognised in profit before financing	19	213	170
Cash funding of defined benefit post-retirement schemes		(259)	(322)
Share-based payments	21	5	21
Net cash inflow from operating activities before taxation		1,254	1,577
Taxation paid		(160)	(276)
Net cash inflow from operating activities		1,094	1,301
Cash flows from investing activities			
Additions of unlisted investments		(6)	(11)
Additions of intangible assets		(408)	(477)
Disposals of intangible assets		4	–
Purchases of property, plant and equipment		(487)	(648)
Government grants received		8	11
Disposals of property, plant and equipment		33	65
Acquisitions of businesses		(5)	(3)
Acquisition of non-controlling interest		–	(1,937)
Disposal of discontinued operations		(121)	1,027
Disposals of other businesses		2	24
Investments in joint ventures and associates		(15)	(17)
Net cash outflow from investing activities		(995)	(1,966)
Cash flows from financing activities			
Repayment of loans		(54)	(233)
Proceeds from increase in loans and finance leases		1,150	49
Capital element of finance lease payments		(1)	–
Net cash flow from increase/(decrease) in borrowings and finance leases		1,095	(184)
Interest received		5	18
Interest paid		(58)	(63)
Interest element of finance lease payments		(2)	–
Decrease in short-term investments		5	313
Issue of ordinary shares (net of expenses)		32	1
Purchase of ordinary shares – share buyback		(433)	(69)
Purchase of ordinary shares – other		(2)	(2)
Dividend paid to non-controlling interest		–	(76)
Redemption of C Shares		(421)	(406)
Net cash inflow/(outflow) from financing activities		221	(468)
Change in cash and cash equivalents		320	(1,133)
Cash and cash equivalents at 1 January		2,862	3,987
Exchange (losses)/gains on cash and cash equivalents		(6)	8
Cash and cash equivalents at 31 December		3,176	2,862

(Continued)

Figure 8.1 (Continued)

	2015 £m	2014 £m
Reconciliation of movements in cash and cash equivalents to movements in net funds		
Change in cash and cash equivalents	320	(1,133)
Cash flow from (increase)/decrease in borrowings and finance leases	(1,095)	184
Cash flow from decrease in short-term investments	(5)	(313)
Change in net funds resulting from cash flows	(780)	(1,262)
Net funds (excluding cash and cash equivalents) of businesses acquired	–	(30)
Exchange gains on net funds	3	19
Fair value adjustments	45	(59)
Movement in net funds	(732)	(1,332)
Net funds at 1 January excluding the fair value of swaps	608	1,940
Net funds at 31 December excluding the fair value of swaps	(124)	608
Fair value of swaps hedging fixed rate borrowings	13	58
Net funds at 31 December	(111)	666

The movement in net funds (defined by the Group as including the items shown below) is as follows:

	At 1 January 2015 £m	Funds flow £m	Exchange differences £m	Fair value adjustments £m	Reclassifications £m	At 31 December 2015 £m
Cash at bank and in hand	739	(69)	(8)	–	–	662
Money-market funds	692	92	(1)	–	–	783
Short-term deposits	1,431	297	3	–	–	1,731
Cash and cash equivalents	2,862	320	(6)	–	–	3,176
Short-term investments	7	(5)	–	–	–	2
Other current borrowings	(67)	(64)	–	8	(294)	(417)
Non-current borrowings	(2,149)	(1,027)	12	37	294	(2,833)
Finance leases	(45)	(4)	(3)	–	–	(52)
Net funds excluding fair value of swaps	608	(780)	3	45	–	(124)
Fair value of swaps hedging fixed rate borrowings	58			(45)		13
Net funds	666	(780)	3	–	–	(111)

Rolls-Royce classifies its cash flows from dividends and interest as follows:

- £63m of dividends received from joint ventures and associates are classified as cash flows from operations.
- While no dividends were paid to non-controlling interests in 2015, these are classified as cash flows from financing activities, as are £5m of interest received and £58m of interest paid.

Ted Baker's cash flow statement for the year ended 30 January 2016 is presented in Figure 8.2.

Figure 8.2   Group and company cash flow statements for Ted Baker Plc

GROUP AND COMPANY CASH FLOW STATEMENT

FOR THE 52 WEEKS ENDED 30 JANUARY 2016	GROUP 52 WEEKS ENDED 30 JANUARY 2016	GROUP 53 WEEKS ENDED 31 JANUARY 2015	COMPANY 52 WEEKS ENDED 30 JANUARY 2016	COMPANY 53 WEEKS ENDED 31 JANUARY 2015
	£'000	£'000	£'000	£'000
CASH GENERATED FROM OPERATIONS				
Profit for the period	44,235	35,850	24,016	18,013
Adjusted for:				
Income tax expense	14,429	12,921	–	–
Depreciation and amortisation	14,929	12,536	–	–
Impairment	188	–	–	–
Loss on disposal of property, plant and equipment	58	462	–	–
Share-based payments	2,019	1,390	247	176
Net finance expense	1,400	1,513	–	–
Net change in derivative financial assets and liabilities carried at fair value through profit or loss	840	(1,507)	–	–
Share of profit in joint venture	(695)	(525)		
Decrease in non-current prepayments	52	71	–	–
Increase in inventory	(12,142)	(29,131)	–	–
Increase in trade and other receivables	(10,805)	(1,815)	(5,977)	(2,401)
Increase in trade and other payables	1,566	11,653	–	–
Interest paid	(1,376)	(1,594)	–	–
Income taxes paid	(13,127)	(11,419)	–	–
NET CASH GENERATED FROM OPERATING ACTIVITIES	41,571	30,405	18,286	15,788
CASH FLOW FROM INVESTING ACTIVITIES				
Purchases of property, plant and equipment and intangibles	(89,535)	(25,476)	–	–
Proceeds from sale of property, plant and equipment	–	5	–	–
Investment in subsidiaries	–	–	–	(333)
Dividends received from joint venture	344	259	–	–
Interest received	–	1	–	–
NET CASH FROM INVESTING ACTIVITIES	(89,191)	(25,211)	–	(333)
CASH FLOW FINANCING ACTIVITIES				
Proceeds from term loan	60,000	–	–	–
Dividends paid	(18,543)	(15,506)	(18,543)	(15,506)
Proceeds from issue of shares	289	194	289	194
NET CASH FROM FINANCING ACTIVITIES	41,746	(15,312)	(18,254)	(15,312)
NET (DECREASE)/INCREASE IN CASH AND CASH EQUIVALENTS	(5,874)	(10,118)	32	143
Net cash and cash equivalents at the beginning of the period	(18,824)	(8,761)	583	440
Exchange rate movement	124	55	–	–
NET CASH AND CASH EQUIVALENTS AT THE END OF THE PERIOD	(24,574)	(18,824)	615	583
Cash and cash equivalents at the end of the period	13,295	7,380	615	583
Bank overdraft at the end of the period	(37,869)	(26,204)	–	
NET CASH AND CASH EQUIVALENTS AT THE END OF THE PERIOD	(24,574)	(18,824)	615	583

Source: Ted Baker Plc, 2016, p. 71. Reproduced by permission of Ted Baker Plc.

In terms of presentation, Ted Baker classifies interest cash flows and dividends received differently from Rolls-Royce:

- £1,376,000 of interest paid is classified as an operating activity.
- Interest received is classified as an investing activity, although there was no interest received during 2015/16.
- £344,000 of dividends received from joint ventures is classified as an investing activity.
- £18,543,000 of dividends paid is classified as a financing cash flow, like Rolls-Royce.

How can we assess the changes in cash and cash equivalents at Ted Baker during the year? During the year ended 30 January 2016, the Group generated £41,571,000 net cash from operating activities and invested £89,535,000 in purchasing property, plant and equipment and intangible assets. In addition, the Group used £18,543,000 to pay shareholders a dividend. When all the net cash from operating, investing and financing activities during the year are aggregated, there is a net decrease in cash and cash equivalents of £5,874,000, leaving the Group with negative cash and cash equivalents at 30 January 2016 amounting to £24,574,000. This comprised a £37,869,000 bank overdraft that was partially offset by £13,295,000 in cash and cash equivalents at the end of the period. It is worth noting that Ted Baker classifies the bank overdraft as cash and cash equivalents, rather than a financing activity. This makes sense as it can be argued that a bank overdraft is repayable on demand and forms an integral part of cash management.

The above examples demonstrate that classifying the cash inflows and outflows according to the operating, investing and financing activities of the business provides useful information, but to calculate the change in cash and equivalents, we need to aggregate the net cash flow (NCF) from each category. This is reflected in the following expanded equation that underpins the statement of cash flows:

$$\text{Change in cash and cash equivalents} = \text{NCF from operating activities} + \text{NCF from investing activities} + \text{NCF from financing activities}$$

IAS 7 allows two methods for reporting the cash flows from operating activities: the direct method and the indirect method. Both methods result in the same figure for the net cash flows from operating activities; it is merely the presentation and method of calculation that differs. However, IAS 7 encourages the use of the direct method, as it supplies more relevant information and is more understandable to users. The presentation of the cash flows from investing and financing activities does not differ between the methods.

Regardless of whether the direct or the indirect method is used to report the cash flows from operating activities, the cash flows arising from the following transactions must be disclosed separately in the statement of cash flows:

- interest received
- interest paid
- dividends received
- dividends paid
- income taxes paid or refunded.

8.5   Cash flows from operating activities under the direct method

Under the direct method, each major class of gross cash receipts and gross cash payments from operating activities is shown separately and then aggregated to give the total cash generated from operating activities.

In Chapter 7, we prepared a statement of profit or loss and other comprehensive income, and a statement of financial position for Candlewick Ltd. We will now use this data to prepare a statement of cash flows for the company in accordance with IAS 7. Sarah started the business on 1 January 2018 and was preparing her financial statements for her first year of trading. It would be impossible to calculate the company's statement of cash flows without information from its last statement of profit or loss and other comprehensive income and the entity's opening and closing statements of financial position. It is important that you learn to appreciate the links between the income statement, statement of financial position and the statement of cash flows, as each statement can only be truly understood if read in conjunction with the other two.

The financial statements of Candlewick Ltd from Chapters 6 and 7 are reproduced below. You will see that the statement of financial position includes the comparative position at 1 January 2018 when the company started trading. In future years, the statement of financial position for the previous year will provide the comparative position. There is also a breakdown of the company's expenses for 2018.

Candlewick Ltd

Statement of profit or loss and other comprehensive income for the year ended 31 December 2018

	£
Revenue	173,200
Cost of sales	(112,650)
Gross profit	60,550
Distribution costs	(12,950)
Administrative expenses	(17,160)
Operating profit	30,440
Finance costs	(540)
Profit before tax	29,900
Income tax expense	(8,970)
Profit for the period	20,930

Candlewick Ltd

Statements of financial position at:

	31 Dec 2018	1 Jan 2018	Change
	£	£	£
ASSETS			
Non-current assets			
Property, plant and equipment	10,000	–	10,000
Current assets			
Inventory	750	–	750
Trade and other receivables	24,850	–	24,850
Cash and cash equivalents	26,150	10,000	26,150
	51,750	10,000	
Total assets	61,750	10,000	
EQUITY AND LIABILITIES			
Equity			
Share capital	10,000	10,000	–
Retained earnings	20,930	–	20,930
	30,930	10,000	
Non-current liabilities			
Bank loan	6,500	–	6,500
Current liabilities			
Trade and other payables	15,350	–	15,350
Current tax liability	8,970		8,970
Total equity and liabilities	61,750	10,000	

Expense	Trial balance	Adjustment	Total	Distribution costs	Administration expenses	Finance costs
	£	£	£	£	£	£
Rent	6,000	–	6,000	3,000	3,000	
Advertising	600	100	700	700		
Telephone	1,960	200	2,160		2,160	
Printing and postage	1,100	(100)	1,000	500	500	
Finance costs	490	50	540			540
Salaries	14,500	–	14,500	7,250	7,250	
Depreciation on equipment	3,000	–	3,000	1,500	1,500	
Increase in doubtful receivables	2,750	–	2,750		2,750	
Total	30,400	250	30,650	12,950	17,160	540

The following information is also available at 31 December 2018:

- The company purchased £13,000 of equipment during 2018. The equipment was expected to have a useful life of four years and a residual value of £1,000.
- Distribution costs included salaries of £7,250 and depreciation on equipment of £1,500.
- Administrative expenses included salaries of £7,250, depreciation on equipment of £1,500 and an allowance for doubtful receivables of £2,750.
- Trade receivables were £27,500 less the £2,750 allowance for doubtful receivables, and other receivables included a prepayment of £100.
- Trade payables were £15,000 and other payables were accrued expenses of £350. The accrued expenses included £300 of operating costs, and £50 of accrued finance costs on the company's bank loan.
- There were no non-current asset disposals during the year to 31 December 2018 and no dividends were paid. There was no investment income.

If you look at Candlewick's statement of financial position at 1 January 2018 you will see that it held £10,000 of cash and cash equivalents on its first day of trading. At the end of the year, the company's cash and cash equivalents increased to £26,150, which means that cash increased by £16,150 during the year. What remains unclear is whether this increase in cash is the result of operating, investing or financing activities. To answer this question, we need to prepare a statement of cash flows.

We will now use the information for Candlewick Ltd to illustrate the operating section of the statement of cash flows using the direct method. You will find it useful to learn the following layout:

Cash flows from operating activities	£
Cash receipts from customers	X
Cash paid to suppliers	(X)
Cash paid to employees	(X)
Cash generated from operating activities	X
Interest paid	(X)
Income taxes paid	(X)
Net cash flow from operating activities	X

Step 1. Calculate the cash flows from cash receipts from customers by adjusting revenue for opening and closing trade receivables as shown in Working 1.

Working 1	£
Revenue	173,200
Add opening trade receivables	–
Add opening allowance for doubtful receivables	–
Less closing trade receivables	(24,750)
Less closing allowance for doubtful receivables	(2,750)
Cash receipts from customers	145,700

Under the direct method, you must use the gross amount of trade receivables by adding back any allowance for doubtful receivables to the opening or closing trade receivables shown on the balance sheet. The company's total cash receipts from customers for the year were £145,700 and this is treated as a cash inflow in the statement of cash flows.

Step 2. Calculate the cash paid to suppliers. Cash paid for inventory is calculated by adjusting purchases for opening and closing trade payables. There also needs to be an adjustment for the net increase or decrease in other payables. In this case, the other payables are accrued operating expenses of £300 and prepaid expenses of £100, so the net increase is £200. Cash paid for distribution costs and administrative expenses require adjustments for non-cash expenses (in this case, depreciation and the allowance for doubtful receivables). Finally, cash paid for salaries is excluded because salaries are shown separately. Working 2 shows these calculations.

Working 2	£
Cost of sales	112,650
Less opening inventory	–
Add closing inventory	750
Purchases of inventory	113,400
Add opening trade payables	–
Less closing trade payables	(15,000)
Distribution costs	12,950
Administration costs	17,160
Less increase in accrued expenses	(300)
Add increase in prepaid expenses	100
Less depreciation expense	(3,000)
Less increase in allowance for doubtful receivables	(2,750)
Less salaries	(14,500)
Cash payments to suppliers	108,060

When all of these calculations are aggregated, Candlewick made cash payments to its suppliers of £108,060 during the year ended 31 December 2018.

Step 3. Calculate the cash paid to employees. This is straightforward as Candlewick paid employee salaries of £14,500 in cash and there are no associated accruals or prepayments.

Step 4. Add the figures from the first three steps to provide the subtotal of cash generated from operating activities. Then adjust for any interest or finance costs paid (£490 in this case), interest received and income tax payments made, to arrive at the net cash flow from operating activities. Although Candlewick incurred an income tax expense of £8,970 during 2018, this was unpaid at the year end, so no adjustment is necessary for the purposes of the statement of cash flows.

Remember that IAS 7 allows the amounts for interest paid and received to be included as financing and investing activities, respectively. We have included the interest paid of £490 as an operating cash flow, for ease of presentation.

Activity

Complete step 4 and prepare the operating section of the statement of cash flows under the direct method.

Check your answer against the following:

Cash flows from operating activities	£
Cash receipts from customers	145,700
Cash paid to suppliers	(108,060)
Cash paid to employees	(14,500)
Cash generated from operating activities	23,140
Interest paid	(490)
Income taxes paid	(−)
Net cash flow from operating activities	22,650

During the year ended 31 December 2018, the company generated £22,650 of net cash from operating activities (£23,140 – £490 interest paid). One final point to mention is that we could have decided to classify the interest paid as a financing activity, which would have meant that the net cash flow from operating activities would have been higher at £23,140.

8.6 Cash flows from operating activities under the indirect method

Under the *indirect method*, the starting point is the profit before tax, which is then adjusted for the effects of the following transactions which are part of the operating activities of the business:

- Non-cash expenses, such as depreciation, the impairment of assets and any increase in the allowance for trade receivables. Where an increase in the allowance for doubtful receivables does not involve an actual bad debt write off, we can automatically account for this by calculating the change in trade receivables on a net basis (i.e. calculating the periodic change in trade receivables after deducting any allowance for doubtful receivables).
- Non-cash income, such as gains on the sale of non-current assets.
- Changes in non-cash working capital items, such as inventory, trade receivables, prepaid expenses, trade payables and accrued expenses.
- Items of income or expense included in the calculation of profit before tax which represent cash flows from investing or financing cash activities. In addition, any interest or finance expenses must be added back and investment income must be deducted, as IAS 7 requires the separate disclosure of these items.

We will now use the indirect method to prepare Candlewick's statement of cash flows for the year ended 31 December 2018 using the figures given in the statement of profit or loss and other comprehensive income, the statement of financial position and the additional information provided. You will find it useful to learn the following layout for the operating section of the statement of cash flows under the indirect method:

Cash flows from operating activities	£
Profit before tax	X
Depreciation	X
Impairment of assets	X
Increase in inventory	(X)
Increase in net trade receivables	(X)
Increase in prepaid expenses	(X)
Increase in trade payables	X
Increase in accrued expenses	X
Interest expense	X
Investment income	(X)
Cash generated from operating activities	X
Interest paid	(X)
Interest received	X
Income taxes paid	(X)
Net cash flow from operating activities	X

Step 1. Adjust the profit before tax for expenses that do not involve a flow of cash. The general rule is to add back non-cash expenses, such as depreciation of property, plant and equipment (PPE) and amortization of goodwill (writing off goodwill to the profit or loss account in regular instalments over the period of its economic life). The figures for Candlewick Ltd are shown in Working 1. As this is the first year of trading, there is no adjustment for changes in the allowance for doubtful receivables.

Working 1	£
Profit before tax	29,900
Depreciation	3,000

Step 2. Adjust for income that does not involve a flow of cash. The general rule is to deduct any non-cash income, such as a gain on disposal of a non-current asset. Candlewick has no non-cash income this year, as you can see from Working 2, so we can move on to the next step.

Working 2	£
Profit before tax	29,900
Depreciation	3,000
Non-cash income	(–)

Step 3. Adjust for changes in non-cash working capital items. The general rule is to deduct an increase in inventory, trade receivables or prepaid expenses because they require more cash to be paid to suppliers (inventory and prepaid expenses) or delay the receipt of cash from customers (trade receivables). By the same logic, you add an increase in trade payables or accrued expenses because they mean less cash is being paid to suppliers. You must also add back any interest expense and deduct any investment income. These adjustments are shown in Working 3. By calculating the change in trade receivables on a net basis, we automatically accounted for the non-cash expenses relating to the allowance for doubtful receivables (i.e. the allowance for doubtful receivables increased by £2,750 during the year).

Working 3	£
Profit before tax	29,900
Depreciation	3,000
Increase in inventory	(750)
Increase in trade receivables	(24,750)
Increase in prepaid expenses	(100)
Increase in trade payables	15,000
Increase in accrued expenses	300
Interest expense	540

A useful tip for remembering whether you are going to add the item to the operating profit or deduct it is to consider whether it reflects a cash flow. If it does not, it is a non-cash item and you need to add it back into profit. If it does have an effect on cash, you need to decide whether the increase or decrease in the item results in an increase or decrease in cash. Figure 8.3 summarizes the main adjustments we have covered in the above three steps.

Step 4. Using the figures from the first three steps, provide the subtotal of cash generated from operations. Then adjust for any interest paid in connection with operating activities (£490 in this case) and income tax payments, to arrive at the net cash flow from operating activities. Although Candlewick Ltd incurred an income tax expense of £8,970 during 2018, this was unpaid at the year end, so no adjustment is necessary.

Activity

Complete step 4 and prepare the operating section of the statement of cash flows under the indirect method.

Figure 8.3 Indirect method: main adjustments to operating income and expenses

Adjustment	Reason
Add depreciation	Non-cash item
Add an increase in the allowance for doubtful receivables*	Non-cash item
Deduct a decrease in the allowance for doubtful receivables*	Non-cash item
Add a decrease in trade receivables	Increases cash
Deduct an increase in trade receivables	Reduces cash
Add a decrease in inventory	Increases cash
Deduct an increase in inventory	Reduces cash
Add an increase in trade payables	Increases cash
Deduct a decrease in trade payables	Reduces cash
Add an increase in accrued expenses	Increases cash
Deduct a decrease in accrued expenses	Reduces cash
Add a decrease in prepaid expenses	Increases cash
Deduct an increase in prepaid expenses	Reduces cash

* Under the indirect method, these items are automatically accounted for if you calculate the change in trade receivables on a net basis (i.e. trade receivables less the allowance for doubtful receivables).

You should have found this easy as it is similar to what you did when using the direct method. Check your answer against the following:

Cash flows from operating activities	£
Profit before tax	29,900
Depreciation	3,000
Increase in inventory	(750)
Increase in trade receivables	(24,750)
Increase in prepaid expenses	(100)
Increase in trade payables	15,000
Increase in accrued expenses	300
Interest expense	540
Cash generated from operating activities	23,140
Interest paid	(490)
Income taxes paid	(–)
Net cash flow from operating activities	22,650

Although you have used the indirect method, the figures for cash generated from operating activities and the net cash flow from operating activities are the same as those you calculated under the direct method. As with our calculations for the direct method, we could have decided to classify the interest paid as a financing activity, which would have meant that the net cash flow from operating activities would have been higher at £23,140.

8.7   Finalizing the statement of cash flows

We will now complete the final steps, which apply irrespective of which method you used to calculate the figures for the operating section of the statement of cash flows.

Step 5. Calculate the cash flow from investing activities. Start by identifying any changes in the company's holding of non-current assets, being careful to exclude any investments that are cash equivalents. Candlewick Ltd had no property, plant and equipment (PPE) on 1 January 2018, but at 31 December 2018 the carrying amount was £10,000. The annual charge for depreciation was £3,000 and this must be taken into account in order to calculate cash paid to acquire the assets. In this case, the result represents the net cash flows from investing activities (see Working 5).

Working 5	£
Closing carrying amount for PPE	10,000
Opening carrying amount for PPE	(–)
Depreciation for year	3,000
Carrying amount of PPE disposed during year	–
Cash flow from investing activities	13,000

Step 6. Calculate the cash flows from financing activities. This is straightforward because the opening share capital was the same as the closing share capital, but Candlewick Ltd obtained a £6,500 bank loan during the year. In this example, this figure represents the net cash flows from financing activities.

Step 7. Calculate the net increase or decrease in cash and cash equivalents by adding the results from steps 4, 5 and 6 to your net cash flow from operating activities (see Working 7).

Working 7	£
Net cash flow from operating activities	22,650
Net cash flow from investing activities	(13,000)
Net cash flow from financing activities	6,500
Increase in cash and cash equivalents	16,150

Step 8. Reconcile the net increase or decrease in cash and cash equivalents with the opening and closing figures in the statement of financial position. Candlewick Ltd had £10,000 in cash and cash equivalents on 1 January 2018 and increased it to £26,150 on 31 December 2018. The difference is £16,150 which balances with the calculations in Working 7.

We know from the statement of financial position that on 1 January 2018 Candlewick Ltd had cash and cash equivalents of £10,000 (the capital Sarah Wick invested in the business), but at 31 December 2018 the cash and cash equivalents amounted to £26,150. Therefore, the business generated a net cash flow of £16,150 (£26,150 − £10,000) during the year. We now need to finalize the statement of cash flows to determine whether this increase in cash was the result of operating, investing or financing activities.

Activity

Prepare the statement of cash flows for Candlewick Ltd for the year ended 31 December 2018 using the indirect method, which is the one most widely used because it can be prepared from the statement of profit or loss and the opening and closing statements of financial position.

Check your answer against the following statement of cash flows, which is based on the indirect method.

Candlewick Ltd
Statement of cash flows for the year ended 31 December 2018

	£
Cash flows from operating activities	
Profit before tax	29,900
Depreciation	3,000
Increase in inventory	(750)
Increase in trade receivables	(24,750)
Increase in prepaid expenses	(100)
Increase in trade payables	15,000
Increase in accrued expenses	300
Interest expense	540
Cash generated from operating activities	23,140
Interest paid	(490)
Income taxes paid	(–)
Net cash flow from operations	22,650

Cash flows from investing activities	
Acquisition of property, plant and equipment	(13,000)
Cash flows from financing activities	
Loan	6,500
Net increase in cash and cash equivalents	16,150
Cash and cash equivalents at 1 January 2018	10,000
Cash and cash equivalents at 31 December 2018	26,150

Now you have seen how to calculate the cash flows from investing and financing activities, you are ready to complete the statement of cash flows you started in section 8.5 using the direct method.

Activity

Prepare a complete statement of cash flows for Candlewick Ltd for the year ended 31 December 2018 using the direct method.

Check your answer against the following solution.

Candlewick Ltd

Statement of cash flows for the year ended 31 December 2018

	£
Cash flows from operating activities	
Cash receipts from customers	145,700
Cash paid to suppliers of goods and services	(108,060)
Cash paid to employees	(14,500)
Cash generated from operations	23,140
Interest paid	(490)
Taxation paid	–
Net cash from operations	22,650
Cash flows from investing activities	
Acquisition of property, plant and equipment	(13,000)
Cash flows from financing activities	
Loan	6,500
Net increase in cash and cash equivalents	16,150
Cash and cash equivalents at 1 January 2018	10,000
Cash and cash equivalents at 31 December 2018	26,150

Regardless of which method is used, the statement of cash flows shows that during the year Candlewick Ltd generated net cash inflows of £22,650 from its operating activities and £6,500 from its financing activities and this was more than sufficient to cover the net cash outflows of £13,000 from its investing activities. During the first year of trading, the company had generated a net increase in cash and cash equivalents of £16,150. Although there are cash and cash equivalents of £26,150 at the end of the period, Candlewick must remember that the company will need £8,970 of this to pay the current tax liability.

Activity

Compare the advantages and disadvantages of a statement of cash flows prepared under the direct and indirect methods.

The main points are:

- The information presented by the direct method is more detailed and understandable, as it provides information about the operating cash inflows from customers, cash paid to suppliers and cash payments to employees. However, it is more complex and time-consuming to calculate, and can reveal information about a company's operating cash flows that may prove useful to competitors. As a result, the majority of large public companies use the indirect method.
- The indirect method is easier to calculate and provides a clear link between profit and cash flows. However, the indirect method's reconciliation of profit before tax to cash generated from operations can be difficult to understand, and is subject to distortion if the company reclassifies assets from non-current to current during the period.

A survey of the statements of cash flows published by 20 listed companies in Standard & Poor's Europe 350 dataset found that all of them used the indirect method for reporting their operating cash flows (Company Reporting, 2012). This is also true of Rolls-Royce and Ted Baker, whose statements of cash flows we examined in this chapter.

8.8   Conclusions

The statement of cash flows is the third of four financial statements that are prepared by reporting entities at the end of the accounting period. The purpose of the statement of cash flows is to provide historical information about changes in cash and cash equivalents resulting from the inflows and outflows of cash. Cash is essential to the survival of the business and this financial statement gives external users important information about the entity's cash generating ability and its liquidity.

The preparation of this financial statement is guided by IAS 7, *Statement of Cash Flows* (IASB, 2017), which allows two methods for reporting the cash flows from operating activities: the direct method and the indirect method. Both methods result in the same figure for the net cash flows from operating activities. Although IAS 7 encourages the use of the direct method, because it supplies more relevant information and is more understandable to users, the indirect method is more commonly used. When making a decision, companies need to weight up the advantages and disadvantages of the two methods. It is important to remember that the presentation of the cash flows from investing and financing activities does not differ between the methods.

 ## Common problems to avoid

Common mistakes students make when drawing up the statement of cash flows are:

- Not showing the name of the business
- Not stating the period covered by the financial statement
- Forgetting to include the currency symbol
- Forgetting that the interest expense for the period may not be the same as the interest paid
- Forgetting to add back non-cash expenses (e.g. depreciation) when reconciling profit before tax to net cash flow from operations under the indirect method
- Adding increases in non-cash working capital items to profit before tax when calculating the net cash flow from operations under the indirect method
- Forgetting to add cash proceeds from the disposal of property, plant and equipment as a positive investing cash flow
- Forgetting to show dividends paid as a cash outflow
- Not showing a reconciliation of opening and closing cash and cash equivalents at the very end of the statement of cash flows
- Forgetting to show all workings

References

Company Reporting (2012) *CR Common Practices: Cash Flow Statements under IFRS*, Edinburgh: Company Reporting, 8 May 2012. Available at: www.company reporting.com (Accessed 1 June 2016).[1]
IASB (2014) IAS 1, *Presentation of Financial Statements*, London: IFRS Foundation.
IASB (2015) *IFRS for SMEs*, London: IFRS Foundation.
IASB (2017) IAS 7, *Statement of Cash Flows*, London: IFRS Foundation.
Rolls-Royce Holdings plc (2016) *Rolls-Royce plc Annual Report 2015*. Available at: www.rolls-royce.com/˜/media/Files/R/Rolls-Royce/documents/investors/annual-reports/2015-annual-report-v1.pdf (Accessed 1 June 2016).
Ted Baker Plc (2016) *Ted Baker Plc Annual Report and Accounts 2015/16*. Available at: www.tedbakerplc.com/˜/media/Files/T/Ted-Baker/results-and-reports/report/2016/2016-annual-report.pdf (Accessed 1 June 2016).

---

1. You can access this survey via a free trial access to the website.

Discussion questions

1 Discuss the difference between cash flows from operating activities and cash flows from investing activities.

2 Discuss the reasons why the amount of interest paid during a year might exceed the amount of interest expense reported in the yearly income statement.

3 Debate the pros and cons of the direct method versus the indirect method in the context of companies listed on the London Stock Exchange.

Practice questions

4 IAS 7 requires that the cash flows for interest and dividends paid and received are classified in a manner appropriate for the reporting entity's business. For each of the businesses in the table below, indicate whether the cash flow listed in the first column should be classified as an operating, investing or financing activity.

	Bank	Pension fund	Airline	Supermarket
Interest paid				
Interest received				
Dividends received				
Dividends paid				

5 Explain why IAS 7 allows some flexibility in the classification of cash flows as operating, investing and financing activities. In addition, discuss whether a single approach would hinder or assist investors when comparing potential investments across industrial sectors.

6 The following information has been extracted from the financial statements of Beauty Box Ltd.

Beauty Box Ltd		
Statements of financial position at		
	30 June 2018	30 June 2017
	£	£
ASSETS		
Non-current assets		
Property, plant and equipment	12,000	16,000
Current assets		
Inventory	12,000	10,000
Trade receivables	5,400	9,000
Cash and cash equivalents	15,300	8,000
	32,700	27,000
Total assets	44,700	43,000
EQUITY AND LIABILITIES		
Equity		
Share capital	20,000	20,000
Retained earnings	12,200	5,000
	32,200	25,000
Non-current liabilities		
Bank loan	–	11,000
Current liabilities		
Trade payables	8,000	4,000
Current tax liability	4,500	3,000
Total equity and liabilities	44,700	43,000

Beauty Box Ltd	
Statement of profit or loss for year ended 30 June 2018	
	£
Revenue	104,900
Cost of sales	(37,700)
Gross profit	67,200
Salaries	(30,000)
Rent	(15,000)
Insurance	(3,000)
Lighting and heating	(1,500)
Telephone and Internet	(2,000)

Advertising	(500)
Depreciation on equipment	(4,000)
Allowance for doubtful receivables	400
Operating profit	11,600
Investment income	100
Profit before tax	11,700
Income tax expense	(4,500)
Profit for the period	7,200

The following additional information is available:

- The following disclosure note relates to trade receivables:

	At 30 June 2018	At 30 June 2017
Trade receivables (gross)	6,000	10,000
Allowance for doubtful receivables	(600)	(1,000)
Trade receivables	5,400	9,000

- The company did not purchase or dispose of any property, plant and equipment during the year ended 31 June 2018.

- The investment income of £100 was received in full during the year.

Required

(a) Prepare a statement of cash flows for Beauty Box Ltd for the year ended 30 June 2018 using the indirect method.

(b) Prepare a statement of cash flows for Beauty Box Ltd for the year ended 30 June 2018 using the direct method.

(c) Review the company's cash flow position for the year ended 30 June 2018.

7 The following information has been extracted from the financial statements of Manning Ltd.

Manning Ltd
Statement of profit or loss for year ended 31 December 2017

	£
Revenue	120,000
Cost of sales	(60,000)
Gross profit	60,000
Employee salaries	(20,000)
Rent	(5,600)
Lighting and heating	(4,000)
Profit on disposal of property, plant and equipment	9,000
Depreciation on equipment	(8,000)
Allowance for doubtful receivables	(2,000)
Operating profit	29,400
Finance costs	(1,100)
Profit before tax	28,300
Income tax expense	(4,500)
Profit for the period	23,800

Manning Ltd
Statements of financial position at

	31 December 2017 £	31 December 2016 £
ASSETS		
Non-current assets		
Property, plant and equipment	20,000	16,000
Current assets		
Inventory	12,000	10,000
Trade receivables	27,000	9,000
Cash and cash equivalents	12,300	8,000
	51,300	27,000
Total assets	71,300	43,000

EQUITY AND LIABILITIES		
Equity		
Share capital	20,000	20,000
Retained earnings	22,800	5,000
	42,800	25,000
Non-current liabilities		
Bank loan	16,000	11,000
Current liabilities		
Trade payables	8,000	4,000
Current tax liability	4,500	3,000
Total equity and liabilities	71,300	43,000

The following additional information is available:

■ Trade receivables are analyzed as follows:

	At 30 June 2017	At 30 June 2016
Trade receivables (gross)	30,000	10,000
Allowance for doubtful receivables	(3,000)	(1,000)
Trade receivables	27,000	9,000

■ The company purchased £15,000 of property, plant and equipment during 2017.
■ During 2017 equipment originally purchased for £5,000 was sold for £12,000. The accumulated depreciation on the equipment was £2,000 at the date of sale.
■ Dividends of £6,000 were paid to shareholders on 1 July 2017.
■ The finance costs of £1,100 represent bank interest charges. The interest was paid in full during the year.

Required

(a) Prepare a statement of cash flows for Manning Ltd for the year ended 31 December 2017 using the direct method.

(b) Prepare a statement of cash flows for Manning Ltd for the year ended 31 December 2017 using the indirect method.

(c) Review Manning's cash flow position for the year ended 31 December 2017.

8 The statement of cash flows for Surrey Engines Ltd for the year ended 31 December 2018 is shown below.

Surrey Engines Ltd
Statement of cash flows for year ended 31 December 2018

	£
Cash flows from operating activities	
Profit before tax	5,000
Depreciation	500
Investment income	(5,000)
Finance costs	7,000
Cash generated from operations	7,500
Taxation paid	(2,000)
Interest paid	(5,000)
Interest received	9,000
Dividends paid	(8,500)
Dividends received	20,000
Net cash from operating activities	21,000
Cash flows from investing activities	
Acquisition of property, plant and equipment	(28,000)
Cash flows from financing activities	
Loan from the bank	6,500
Net decrease in cash and cash equivalents during year	(500)
Cash and cash equivalents at 1 January 2018	7,000
Cash and cash equivalents at 31 December 2018	6,500

The following additional information is available:

- Surrey Engines is a manufacturer of car engines.
- The company holds equity investments in national airline companies.
- The company holds long-term investments in interest-bearing government bonds.
- The company makes use of long-term bank financing to finance its business.

Required

(a) Review the statement of cash flows prepared by Surrey Engines Ltd for the year ended 31 December 2018 and determine whether each of the following items is appropriately classified as an operating, investing or financing activity:

- interest paid
- interest received
- dividends paid
- dividends received

(b) Using your answer from part (a), redraft the statement of cash flows for Surrey Engines Ltd to provide more relevant and useful information for investors, lenders and creditors. Ensure that your answer complies with IAS 7.

 ## Suggested research questions for dissertation students

Students interested in the effects of IAS 7 may wish to investigate one or more of the following research questions:

- Is there a difference in the choice of method (direct or indirect) used by FTSE-100 companies and those listed on the Alternative Investment Market (AIM)?

- Do investors, lenders and other creditors prefer the statement of cash flows of public companies to be prepared using the direct method?

- How do FTSE-100 companies classify interest and dividends received in their statements of cash flows?

- What accounting policies do FTSE-350 UK listed companies use to determine the treatment of bank overdrafts within the statement of cash flows?

- Does the classification of interest and dividends received in the statements of cash flow prepared by European public companies differ between industrial sectors?

Preliminary reading

Bahnson, P., Miller, P. and Budge, B. (1996) 'Non-articulation in cash flow statements and implications for education, research and practice', *Accounting Horizons*, 10(4), pp. 1–15.

BDO International (2014) *IFRS in Practice: IAS 7 Statement of Cash Flows*, London: BDO IFR Advisory. Available at: www.bdo.global/getattachment/Services/Audit-Assurance/IFRS/IFRS-in-Practice/IFRS_IAS7_print.pdf.aspx?lang=en-GB (Accessed 6 December 2016).

Mechelli, A. (2009) 'Accounting harmonization and compliance in applying IASB Standards: An empirical survey about the first time adoption of IAS 7 by Italian listed groups', *Accounting in Europe*, 6(2), pp. 231–270.

Ohlson, J. and Aier, J. (2009) 'On the analysis of firms' cash flows', *Contemporary Accounting Research*, 26(4), pp. 1091–1114.

9 Consolidated financial statements

Learning objectives

When you have studied this chapter, you should be able to:

- Explain the purpose of consolidated financial statements
- Prepare a consolidated statement of financial position
- Prepare a consolidated statement of profit or loss and other comprehensive income
- Prepare a consolidated statement of changes in equity
- Account for an investment in an associate or a joint arrangement

9.1 Introduction

So far we have focused on the financial statements published by single entities as these represent the vast majority of reporting entities in the UK. However, many large companies are the result of a business combination. A business combination can be structured in various ways, such as one entity becoming the subsidiary of another entity (the parent), the transfer of net assets from one entity to another entity or to a new entity. Each company in the group prepares its own financial statements, but they are then aggregated to provide users with a single set of consolidated financial statements.

The process of consolidation is the focus of this chapter. We also describe the different accounting treatments used when the investment is not in a subsidiary but in an associate or a joint arrangement.

9.2   Purpose of consolidated financial statements

IFRS 3, *Business Combinations* (IASB, 2013a) explains that a *business combination* is a transaction or other event in which an investor obtains control of one or more businesses (the investees). Mergers of equals are also business combinations. Examples of how a business combination can occur include transferring cash, incurring liabilities, issuing equity instruments or by contract alone. The business combination can be structured in various ways such as one entity becoming a subsidiary of another entity, the transfer of net assets from one entity to another entity or to a new entity.

A business combination involves the acquisition or creation of a business, which generally consists of three elements:

- Inputs – economic resources that create outputs when one or more processes are applied to it (e.g. non-current assets or intangible assets).
- Processes – a system, standard, protocol, convention or rule that when applied to an input or inputs, creates outputs (e.g. strategic management or operational processes).
- Outputs – the result of inputs and processes applied to those inputs.

Key definition

A business combination is a transaction or other event in which an acquirer obtains control of one or more businesses.

Source: IFRS 3, IASB, 2013a, Appendix A. Reproduced with permission from the IFRS Foundation.

A group comprises a parent entity and one or more subsidiaries. IFRS 10, *Consolidated Financial Statements* (IASB, 2014a) describes a parent as an entity that controls one or more entities. An entity that is controlled by a parent is known as a subsidiary. The subsidiary can be a company or an unincorporated entity and can be created or acquired. The parent company is the investor (or acquirer) and the subsidiary is the investee (or the acquiree).

The main advantages of a group structure are:

- The parent can assign accountability and responsibility to the manager of each subsidiary as they control the activities of their respective business.
- Each subsidiary has its own separately audited financial statements, giving them an ability to borrow without the need for parental involvement.
- The assets of the subsidiary can be offered as security against its borrowings without restricting the activities of other group entities.
- It allows for the easier acquisition and disposal of individual businesses.

Key definition

A parent is an entity that controls one or more entities.

Source: IFRS 10, IASB, 2014a, Appendix A. Reproduced with permission from the IFRS Foundation.

The *purpose* of consolidated financial statements is to present the assets, liabilities, equity, income, expenses and cash flows of the parent company and its subsidiaries as those of a single economic entity. IFRS 10 requires a parent to prepare consolidated financial statements for the shareholders of the parent company, who will receive them in addition to the parent's financial statements. As the requirements of IAS 1, *Presentation of Financial Statements* (IASB, 2014b) also apply, a complete set of consolidated financial statements includes:

- a consolidated statement of financial position
- a consolidated statement of comprehensive income
- a consolidated statement of changes in equity
- a consolidated statement of cash flows.

Activity

Why do you think parent companies need to prepare consolidated financial statements?

Without the requirement to consolidate the activities of the parent and its subsidiaries, the shareholders of the parent company would only receive the financial statements of the parent. These would not include the assets, liabilities and profits of the subsidiaries and the parent could exploit its group structure to manipulate the financial and business performance it reports in its own accounts. For example, a parent could disguise the extent of its debt finance by using its subsidiaries to secure off-balance sheet finance. The key principle is that the consolidated financial statements present a faithful representation (see Chapter 5) of the economic activities of the group as a single economic entity.

A parent is not required to present consolidated financial statements if:

- It is a wholly-owned subsidiary or a partially-owned subsidiary of another entity and its other owners do not object to the parent not presenting consolidated financial statements.
- Its debt or equity instruments are not traded in a public market (in other words, it is not a listed company).
- It did not file, nor is it in the process of filing, its financial statements with a securities commission or other regulatory organization for the purpose of issuing any

class of instruments in a public market (in other words, it is not in the process of obtaining a listing).

- Its ultimate or any intermediate parent produces consolidated financial statements available for public use that comply with International Financial Reporting Standards (IFRSs).

IFRS 10 contains special requirements for investment entities. An *investment entity* is an entity that:

- obtains funds from one or more investors for the purpose of providing those investor(s) with investment management services;
- commits to its investor(s) that its business purpose is to invest funds solely for returns from capital appreciation, investment income, or both; and
- measures and evaluates the performance of substantially all of its investments on a fair value basis.

An investment entity is generally not required to consolidate its subsidiaries and must measure these investments at fair value through the income statement in accordance with IFRS 9, *Financial Instruments* (IASB, 2014c).

9.3   The concept of control

The concept of *control* provides the threshold test for determining whether the financial statements of an entity should be included in the consolidated financial statements of the group. Under IFRS 10, an investor determines whether it is a parent by assessing whether it controls one or more investees, and the investor must consider all the relevant facts and circumstances when making this assessment. An investor controls an investee when the investor possesses all the following elements of control:

- Power over the investee – The investor has existing rights that give it the ability to direct the relevant activities of the investee (the activities that significantly affect the investee's returns). Power arises from rights such as voting rights or rights resulting from contractual arrangements.
- Exposure to or rights to variable returns from its involvement with the investee – To exercise control over an investee, the investor must be exposed to or have rights to variable returns from its involvement with the investee. Variable returns are those that vary with the investee's performance. Therefore, they can be positive, negative, or both. Examples include changes in the value of the investor's investment, dividends and returns that are unavailable to other interest holders (such as cost savings or synergies obtained from interactions between the investor and investee).
- The ability to use its power over the investee to affect the amount of the investor's returns – A parent must also be able to use its power over the investee to influence its returns from its involvement with the investee.

The concept of control focuses on power and returns, rather than on voting rights. Power rests with the party that has the ability to direct decisions about the *relevant activities* that significantly affect the investee's returns. Relevant activities are activities of the investee that significantly affect the investee's returns. Examples include:

- product development
- purchases and sales of goods or services
- acquiring and disposing of assets
- obtaining finance.

Key decisions about relevant activities may include:

- devising and establishing operating policies
- controlling capital expenditure decisions
- appointing key management personnel.

Key definitions

Control of an investee is achieved when the investor is exposed, or has rights, to variable returns from its involvement with the investee and has the ability to affect those returns through its power over the investee.

Power refers to existing rights [of the investor] that give the current ability to direct the relevant activities [of the investee].

Protective rights are rights designed to protect the interest of the party holding those rights without giving that party power over the entity to which those rights relate.

Relevant activities are the activities of the investee that significantly affect the investee's returns.

Source: IFRS 10, IASB, 2014a, Appendix A. Reproduced with permission from the IFRS Foundation.

When assessing whether an investor has *power* over an investee, the following sources of power must be considered:

- Voting rights.
- Potential voting rights that the holder could exercise (e.g. those obtained from a share option or convertible financial instrument).
- An investor's contractual and non-contractual rights (e.g. the ability to appoint an investee's key personnel or veto significant transactions).
- Special relationships between an investor and investee (e.g. the investee's operations may be dependent on the investor or its key personnel may also be employed by the investor).

Only substantive rights are capable of providing power. A right is substantive if it grants the holder the practical ability to exercise the right when decisions about the relevant activities of the investee need to be made. For example, the right of a lender to seize assets in the event of an investee defaulting on its debt is not substantive, as it does not give the lender power over the investee's relevant activities. In other cases, an investor might have power and secure *de facto* control over an investee due to:

- the size of its voting rights relative to the size and dispersion of other vote holders
- voting patterns and lack of attendance at the investee's previous shareholders' meetings.

An investor must be able to influence returns through its power over the investee's decision making. This relationship between power and returns is an essential component of control under IFRS 10. In the following examples, the investor does *not* control the investee:

- Investor A has the power to direct the relevant activities of an investee, but has no right to a variable return from its involvement with the investee.
- Investor B receives a return from an investee, but cannot use its power to direct the relevant activities of the investee.

While power to direct decision making over relevant activities is an important determinate of control, it also requires that an investor benefit from this power in the form of a variable return from its involvement with the investee. The returns must vary as a result of the investee's performance and can be positive, negative or both. Examples of investor returns include:

- changes in the value of the investor's investment
- dividends
- returns that are unavailable to other interest holders (e.g. cost savings or synergies obtained from interactions between the investor and investee).

Establishing an appropriate definition of control is more difficult than it first appears. For example, control can often be achieved without an investor possessing direct legal ownership of the investee. When an investor acquires an ownership interest in the ordinary share capital of another entity it normally grants ownership of an equal proportion of the investee's voting rights. Control is achieved when an investor acquires more than 50% of the investee's voting rights. However, an investor may exercise indirect control over an investee through intermediate companies that are controlled by the investor. Control does not always require possession of the majority of an investee's voting rights due to the size of the investor's voting rights relative to the size and dispersion of other vote holders. For example, a parent company could hold 40% of the voting rights in a subsidiary with the remaining shares held by thousands of individual shareholders who have not participated in voting in the past. In such circumstances, the 40% shareholder is deemed to have *de facto* control.

Activity

Supermarket PLC acquires 48% of the voting rights of Grocer Ltd by purchasing 48% of Grocer's ordinary share capital. The remaining voting rights are held by 50,000 individual shareholders, none of whom hold more than 1% of the voting rights or make collective decisions. Indeed, none of them have voted at Grocer's previous shareholders' meetings.

Assess whether Supermarket PLC has control over Grocer Ltd, using the definition of control in IFRS 10 and the above information.

You need to remember that all three elements of control must be present:

- Although Supermarket does not control the majority of the voting rights in Grocer, it has power over Grocer's relevant activities. This power is obtained from the size of Supermarket's voting rights relative to the size and dispersion of the other vote holders. Supermarket's power is reinforced by the fact that the 50,000 other shareholders have never voted at a shareholders' meeting.
- Supermarket obtains variable returns from its investment, as its ownership of Grocer's ordinary shares provides dividends and a 48% share of any change in the value of Grocer.
- Supermarket has the power to influence its returns from Grocer by directing Grocer's relevant activities.

As all the elements of control exist, we can conclude that Supermarket PLC has control over Grocer Ltd, even though it has only 48% of Grocer's ordinary share capital. Note that the remaining 52% of Grocer's equity is referred to as the *non-controlling interest* (NCI), and is held by outside investors. Having control over Grocer means that Supermarket is the parent and must include this investee in the consolidated financial statements. The concept of control is the critical threshold for determining how each investee is consolidated in the group financial statements. Figure 9.1 illustrates how Supermarket's control over Grocer requires the investee to be included within the group consolidated financial statements prepared for Supermarket's shareholders.

Key definition

A non-controlling interest (NCI) is the equity in a subsidiary not attributable, directly or indirectly, to a parent.

Source: IFRS 3, IASB, 2013a, Appendix A. Reproduced with permission from the IFRS Foundation.

Figure 9.1   Supermarket PLC's control over Grocer Ltd

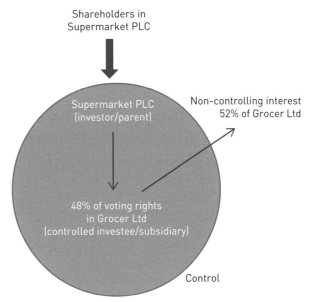

9.4   Consolidated statement of financial position at acquisition

Under IFRS 3, a business combination is accounted for at acquisition by preparing consolidated financial statements using the *acquisition method*. The main stages are:

- Identify the acquirer (the entity that obtains control of the acquiree).
- Determine the acquisition date (the date on which the acquirer obtains control of the acquiree).
- Recognize all identifiable assets acquired and liabilities assumed and measure them at acquisition-date *fair value* (there are exceptions for certain assets and liabilities). Measure any NCI at acquisition-date fair value or at the proportionate share of the acquiree's identifiable net assets (the difference between total assets and total liabilities).
- Recognize and measure *goodwill* or a gain from a bargain purchase. The consideration transferred consists of assets transferred, liabilities incurred, equity interests issued and contingent consideration. These are measured at acquisition-date fair value. Goodwill is calculated as follows:

$$\text{Goodwill} = \frac{\text{Consideration}}{\text{transferred}} + \text{Amount of NCI} + \frac{\text{Fair value of previous}}{\text{equity interests}} - \frac{\text{Net assets}}{\text{recognized}}$$

If the difference is negative, the acquirer recognizes a gain from a bargain purchase.

> **Key definitions**
>
> Fair value is the price that would be received to sell an asset or paid to transfer a liability in an orderly transaction between market participants at the measurement date.
>
> Source: IFRS 13, IASB, 2013c, Appendix A. Reproduced with permission from the IFRS Foundation.
>
> Goodwill is an asset representing the future economic benefits arising from other assets acquired in a business combination that are not individually identified and separately recognised.
>
> Source: IFRS 3, IASB, 2013a, Appendix A. Reproduced with permission from the IFRS Foundation.

9.4.1 Acquisition of a wholly-owned subsidiary

To illustrate the main stages in the consolidation process, we will look at an example. On 31 January 2017 Global PLC paid £3.50 per share in order to acquire 100% of the £1 ordinary shares of Local Ltd, and control over the investee. This means that Local Ltd will become a wholly-owned subsidiary of the parent company, Global PLC. At this date all of Local Ltd's assets and liabilities were valued at fair value. We will assume that the acquirer's share of the acquiree is the same as the percentage of ordinary shares acquired. The statements of financial position of the two companies at the date of acquisition were as follows.

Statements of financial position at 31 January 2017	Global PLC £'000	Local Ltd £'000
ASSETS		
Non-current assets		
Property, plant and equipment	1,500	3,000
Investment in Local Ltd	3,500	–
	5,000	3,000
Current assets	1,000	1,000
Total assets	6,000	4,000
EQUITY AND LIABILITIES		
Equity		
Ordinary share capital	2,000	1,000
Retained earnings	2,000	2,000
	4,000	3,000
Current liabilities	2,000	1,000
Total equity and liabilities	6,000	4,000

There are five main stages in the consolidation process:

Step 1. Calculate whether control exists and establish the parent's proportional share of the subsidiary at the date of acquisition. Global PLC has taken control of Local Ltd by purchasing 100% of its ordinary share capital for £3.50 per share, so Local Ltd becomes a wholly-owned subsidiary of Global PLC.

Step 2. Calculate the fair value of the consideration transferred by the parent. An investor does not always use cash to invest in a subsidiary, so the consideration includes the fair value of any assets given, liabilities incurred or assumed, and the shares issued by the parent. The ordinary share capital of Local has a nominal value of £1 per share, so it has 1m ordinary shares (£1m ordinary share capital ÷ £1 per share). At a purchase price of £3.50 per share, the fair value of the consideration transferred by Global PLC was £3.5m (1m shares x £3.50 per share).

Step 3. Calculate the fair value of the subsidiary's assets and liabilities recognized at the date of acquisition. The assets and liabilities of Local were already valued at acquisition-date fair value. In exchange for the consideration transferred, Global obtains control over Local's identifiable net assets which had a fair value of £3m at the date of acquisition (£4m assets – £1m current liabilities). IFRS 3 requires measurement of a subsidiary's assets and liabilities at fair value as it provides a *faithful representation* of their economic value at the date of acquisition. To qualify for recognition, the assets and liabilities of the subsidiary must be part of the business acquired and meet the definitions of an asset and liability in the Conceptual Framework for Financial Reporting (IASB, 2015). The term *net assets* refers to the difference between total assets and total liabilities and is equal to equity in the accounting equation.

Step 4. Calculate the NCI's proportionate share of the subsidiary's identifiable net assets at the date of acquisition. As Global PLC has acquired 100% of Local Ltd's ordinary share capital there is no NCI. A parent does not need to acquire 100% of a subsidiary's ordinary shares to obtain control. The holders of any remaining shares are referred to as the NCI and represent the subsidiary's equity that is not attributable to the parent. As the purpose of consolidated accounts is to show the effectiveness of the parent's control, all the assets and liabilities of the subsidiary are included within the consolidated statement of financial position and a NCI should be shown as partly financing those net assets. Under IFRS 3, the NCI is typically measured at the NCI's proportionate share of the subsidiary's identifiable net assets. This is the method used to compute NCI throughout this chapter, but IFRS 3 does provide an alternative option for measuring NCI at fair value.

Step 5. Calculate the goodwill at the date of acquisition. The consideration transferred by Global was £0.5m more than the fair value of Local's identifiable net assets at the acquisition date (£3.5m consideration – £3m Local's net assets). As there is no NCI, this excess represents the goodwill:

Goodwill on acquisition of Local	£'000
Fair value of the consideration transferred	3,500
Non-controlling interest at acquisition	–
Fair value of subsidiary's net assets at acquisition	(3,000)
Goodwill	500

Goodwill is an intangible non-current asset that represents the future economic benefits arising from assets acquired in a business combination that cannot be individually separately identified and recognized. Examples include the entity's brand reputation and the loyalty of its customers. Positive goodwill that arises from a business combination is recognized in the consolidated statement of financial position at cost, and should be tested annually for impairment in accordance with IAS 36, *Impairment of Assets* (IASB, 2013b). Although goodwill is normally a positive amount, negative goodwill can occur when a subsidiary is purchased at a bargain price.

Under the acquisition method, the subsidiary's assets, equity and liabilities are incorporated line by line into the consolidated statement of financial position through a process of elimination based on off-setting, leaving only the group's assets, equity and liabilities.

- The carrying amount of the parent's investment (the consideration transferred) is eliminated against the parent's share of the subsidiary's equity at the date of acquisition. Any excess is shown as goodwill. As a result, the investment in the subsidiary is replaced by the net assets that the parent has acquired.
- Any intra-group debts resulting from trading between entities in the group are eliminated by off-setting the amount payable by one entity against the amount receivable in the other. There are no intra-group items in this example.

Because consolidated financial statements are prepared for the shareholders of the parent company, only the parent's share capital must be included.

Working 1 (W1) in the following consolidated statement of financial position for Global PLC shows the elimination process. The £3.5m investment in Local Ltd is eliminated against Global's 100% share of Local's £3m equity at the acquisition date (£1m ordinary share capital + £2m retained earnings). After these amounts are eliminated, £0.5m of the investment remains. This is shown as goodwill under intangible non-current assets. The remaining assets and liabilities of Global PLC and Local Ltd (property, plant and equipment, current assets and current liabilities) are aggregated item by item to provide the figures for the consolidated statement of financial position.

You need to remember that we are using this layout to illustrate the consolidation process and the eliminations and other workings are not published.

Global PLC

Consolidated statement of financial position at 31 January 2017

	Global PLC £'000	Local Ltd £'000	W1 £'000	Group £'000
ASSETS				
Non-current assets				
Property, plant and equipment	1,500	3,000	–	4,500
Investment in Local Ltd	3,500	–	(3,500)	
Intangible assets (goodwill)	–	–	500	500
	5,000	3,000	(3,000)	5,000
Current assets	1,000	1,000	–	2,000
Total assets	6,000	4,000	(3,000)	7,000
EQUITY AND LIABILITIES				
Equity				
Ordinary share capital	2,000	1,000	(1,000)	2,000
Retained earnings	2,000	2,000	(2,000)	2,000
	4,000	3,000	(3,000)	4,000
Current liabilities	2,000	1,000	–	3,000
Total equity and liabilities	6,000	4,000	(3,000)	7,000

9.4.2 Acquisition of a partially-owned subsidiary

In many business combinations, the parent acquires less than 100% of a subsidiary, as in the next example. On 30 April 2017, Giga PLC paid £7.50 per share in order to acquire 90% of the 25p ordinary shares of Mega Ltd. This investment gives Giga control over Mega Ltd. The statements of financial position for each company at the date of acquisition are shown below.

The following information about Mega Ltd's net assets at the date of acquisition is available:

- Freehold property with a carrying value of £1.8m had a market value of £2.9m.
- Current assets include £0.5m inventory with a net realizable value of only £250,000.

Activity

Work through the five steps and calculate the figures you need for the consolidated statement of financial position for Giga PLC.

Statements of financial position at 30 April 2017

	Giga PLC £'000	Mega Ltd £'000
ASSETS		
Non-current assets		
Property, plant and equipment	2,600	3,000
Investment in Mega Ltd	5,400	–
	8,000	3,000
Current assets	1,500	1,200
Total assets	9,500	4,200
EQUITY AND LIABILITIES		
Ordinary share capital	2,500	200
Retained earnings	2,000	3,300
	4,500	3,500
Current liabilities	5,000	700
Total equity and liabilities	9,500	4,200

Check your answer against the following solution.

1. Giga PLC acquired 90% of Mega Ltd. As Mega's £200,000 of ordinary share capital has a nominal value of 25p per share, the subsidiary has a total of 800,000 shares available for purchase. Giga Ltd purchased 720,000 of these shares.

2. Giga PLC purchased 90% of Mega Ltd's ordinary shares for £7.50 per share. The consideration transferred was £5.4m (720,000 shares x £7.50 per share).

3. Mega Ltd's identifiable net assets must be restated to their fair value at the date of acquisition. Before these adjustments, Mega's net assets had a carrying value of £3.5m (total assets £4.2m – current liabilities £0.7m). At this date, its net assets could also be measured using the £3.5m of total equity. The fair value adjustments to Mega's assets require the value of freehold property to be increased by £1m and a balancing revaluation reserve created in Mega's statement of financial position. In addition, current assets must be reduced by £250,000 to reflect the lower value of the inventory. This reduces Mega's retained earnings by £250,000. These fair value adjustments for Mega are shown below.

	Original £'000	Adjustment £'000	Fair value £'000
ASSETS			
Non-current assets			
Property, plant and equipment	3,000	1,100	4,100
Current assets	1,200	(250)	950
Total assets	4,200	850	5,050
EQUITY AND LIABILITIES			
Equity			
Ordinary share capital	200	–	200
Retained earnings	3,300	(250)	3,050
Revaluation reserve	–	1,100	1,100
	3,500	850	4,350
Current liabilities	700	–	700
Total equity and liabilities	4,200	850	5,050

4. In this case there is a 10% NCI in Mega Ltd, which is measured as the proportionate share of the identifiable net assets (£4,350,000 x 10% = £435,000). This amount must be included in the group statement of financial position under equity.

5. Goodwill on the acquisition of Mega Ltd is calculated as follows.

Goodwill on the acquisition of Mega	£'000
Fair value of the consideration transferred	5,400
NCI at the acquisition date	435
Fair value of Mega's net assets at the acquisition date	(4,350)
Goodwill	1,485

Activity

Use your five workings to prepare a consolidated statement of financial position for Giga PLC at 30 April 2017.

Remember to use the fair values you have calculated for Mega Ltd when preparing the consolidated statement of financial position. Start by eliminating Giga PLC's investment of £5.4m against the 90% share (£3.915m) of the equity of Mega Ltd at the date of acquisition. The balancing figure (£1.485m) represents goodwill, which is recognized as an intangible non-current asset in the group accounts. The elimination process is shown in the column headed 'W1', where the total amount eliminated is £3.915m, which represents Giga's 90% share of Mega's equity at the date of acquisition.

Giga's share of Mega's equity at acquisition		£'000
Ordinary share capital	(£200,000 x 90%)	180
Retained earnings	(£3,050,000 x 90%)	2,745
Revaluation reserve	(£1,100,000 x 90%)	990
Total equity (net assets acquired)		3,915

After the elimination process, the remaining 10% of Mega's equity and reserves represent the NCI in Mega. This is eliminated and shown in the group accounts as a NCI of £435,000. This adjustment is shown in column W2 of the solution. The underlying calculations are as follows.

10% NCI share of Mega's equity at acquisition		£'000
Ordinary share capital	(£200,000 x 10%)	20
Retained earnings	(£3,050,000 x 10%)	305
Revaluation reserve	(£1,100,000 x 10%)	110
Total equity (net assets acquired)		435

The next step is to combine the individual figures for property, plant and equipment, current assets and current liabilities for each entity. Remember that you should only include the equity of the parent and the NCI in the consolidated statement of financial position. Check your answer against the following solution.

Giga PLC

Consolidated statement of financial position at 30 April 2017

	Giga PLC	Mega Ltd at fair value	W1	W2	Group
	£'000	£'000	£'000	£'000	£'000
ASSETS					
Non-current assets					
Property, plant and equipment	2,600	4,100	–	–	6,700
Investment in Mega Ltd	5,400	–	(5,400)	–	
Intangible assets (goodwill)	–	–	1,485	–	1,485
	8,000	4,100	(3,915)	–	8,185
Current assets	1,500	950	–	–	2,450
Total assets	9,500	5,050	(3,915)	–	10,635
EQUITY AND LIABILITIES					
Equity					
Ordinary share capital	2,500	200	(180)	(20)	2,500
Retained earnings	2,000	3,050	(2,745)	(305)	2,000
Revaluation reserve		1,100	(990)	(110)	–
Non-controlling interest				435	435
	4,500	4,350	(3,915)	–	4,935
Current liabilities	5,000	700			5,700
Total equity and liabilities	9,500	5,050	(3,915)	–	10,635

9.5 Consolidated statement of financial position after acquisition

We will now examine what happens after acquisition when the subsidiary continues to trade. The profit made by a subsidiary after acquisition represents the return the parent receives on the investment. Therefore, the parent's share of the post-acquisition profit is added to the group's retained earnings in the consolidated statement of financial position and the share of any NCI is added to the carrying amount of the NCI in the group accounts. If a subsidiary makes a post-acquisition loss, the same process applies in reverse. While a subsidiary's retained earnings are the most likely of its reserves to have changed since it was first acquired by its parent, it is possible that other reserves, such as the revaluation reserve, have changed. If so, these changes should be accounted for in the same way as movements in a subsidiary's post-acquisition retained earnings.

Another issue to consider is whether the goodwill recognized in the group accounts has suffered an impairment loss since the date of acquisition. Goodwill must be tested for any impairment loss at least annually. An impairment loss arises if the *recoverable amount* of the asset falls below its carrying amount. IAS 36, *Impairment of Assets* (IASB, 2013b) defines the recoverable amount as the higher of its fair value less costs of disposal, and its value in use. After acquisition, goodwill is shown in the group statement of financial position at cost less any accumulated impairment losses. Any impairment is recognized in the consolidated income statement and reduces the retained earnings of the group.

One year has passed since Giga PLC acquired 90% of Mega Ltd and the statements of financial position for the two companies are shown below. The statement of financial position for Mega Ltd at 30 April 2018 incorporates the fair value adjustments made on 30 April 2017.

Statements of financial position at 30 April 2018	Giga PLC £'000	Mega Ltd £'000
ASSETS		
Non-current assets		
Property, plant and equipment	2,900	4,400
Investment in Mega Ltd	5,400	–
	8,300	4,400
Current assets	1,500	1,050
Total assets	9,800	5,450
EQUITY AND LIABILITIES		
Equity		
Ordinary share capital	2,500	200
Retained earnings	2,500	3,550
Revaluation reserve	–	1,100
	5,000	4,850
Current liabilities	4,800	600
Total assets and liabilities	9,800	5,450

The following post-acquisition transactions and events took place during the year ending 30 April 2018:

- Giga PLC and Mega Ltd each generated a profit of £500,000.
- Following an impairment review, it was found that the £1.485m goodwill arising on consolidation had suffered an impairment loss of 40% due to increased market competition.

Activity

Prepare a consolidated statement of financial position for Giga PLC at 30 April 2018 that reflects the post-acquisition transactions and events.

Check your answer against the following solution, which shows the workings in columns W1–W4.

- W1 and W2 are identical to the calculations for the consolidated statement of financial position at 30 April 2017.
- W3 shows the adjustments needed to apportion Mega's post-acquisition profit (£500,000) between the group and the NCI. Mega's total equity has increased by £500,000 since being acquired by Giga on 30 April 2017: 90% (£450,000) is allocated to the retained earnings of the group and 10% (£50,000) is added to the carrying value of the NCI. As a result, the carrying value of the NCI in the group increases to £485,000 (£435,000 at acquisition + £50,000 share of Mega's post-acquisition profit).
- W4 accounts for the 40% impairment of goodwill. The carrying value of goodwill is reduced by £594,000 (£1,485,000 x 40%). This amount is written off against the retained earnings of the group.

Giga PLC

Consolidated statement of financial position at 30 April 2018

	Giga PLC £'000	Mega Ltd £'000	W1 £'000	W2 £'000	W3 £'000	W4 £'000	Group £'000
ASSETS							
Non-current assets							
Property, plant and equipment	2,900	4,400	–	–	–	–	7,300
Investment in Mega Ltd	5,400	–	(5,400)	–	–	–	–
Intangible assets (goodwill)	–	–	1,485	–	–	(594)	891
	8,300	–	–	–	–	(594)	8,191
Current assets	1,500	1,050	–	–	–		2,550
Total assets	9,800	5,450	(3,915)	–	–	(594)	10,741
EQUITY AND LIABILITIES							
Equity							
Ordinary share capital	2,500	200	(180)	(20)	–	–	2,500
Retained earnings:							
Mega Ltd pre-acquisition	–	3,050	(2,745)	(305)	–	–	–
Giga PLC's earnings and Mega Ltd's post-acquisition earnings	2,500	500	–	–	(50)	(594)	2,356
Revaluation reserve	–	1,100	(990)	(110)			–
Non-controlling interest	–	–	–	435	50		485
	5,000	4,850	(3,915)	–	–	(594)	5,341
Current liabilities	4,800	600	–	–	–		5,400
Total equity and liabilities	9,800	5,450	(3,915)	–	–	(594)	10,741

The group statement of financial position for Giga PLC at 30 April 2018 reflects the impact of the combined business transactions for the post-acquisition period.

9.6 Consolidated statement of profit or loss and consolidated statement of changes in equity

We will start by looking at the *consolidated statement of profit or loss and other comprehensive income*, which presents a calculation of the profit or loss of the combined group as if it were a single economic entity. It is usually provided in the annual report and accounts instead of the parent's statement of comprehensive income. Under the *acquisition method*, all the subsidiary's revenue and expenses are incorporated line by line into the consolidated statement of comprehensive income and intra-group items are eliminated. The main stages are:

Step 1. Eliminate intra-group sales by deducting from group revenue and deducting from group cost of sales. Deduct any unrealized profit on intra-group sales from closing inventory and add to group cost of sales.

Step 2. Cancel out other intra-group items, such as interest payable or management expenses.

Step 3. Show any impairment loss on goodwill as an expense.

Step 4. Deduct any profit after tax attributable to an NCI, leaving only the profit attributable to the group.

Step 5. Cancel out dividends paid by a subsidiary to its parent against dividends received by the parent.

We will now illustrate this with an example. The statements of profit or loss and other comprehensive income for Giga PLC and Mega Ltd for the year ended 30 April 2018 are shown below.

Statements of profit or loss and other comprehensive income for year ended 30 April 2018	Giga PLC £'000	Mega Ltd £'000
Revenue	2,200	2,000
Cost of sales	(700)	(800)
Gross profit	1,500	1,200
Administrative expenses	(400)	(300)
Distribution costs	(350)	(150)
Operating profit	750	750
Income tax expense	(250)	(250)
Profit for the period	500	500

The following transactions and events took place during the year ending 30 April 2018:

- Giga PLC sold inventory to Mega Ltd for £200,000 plus a mark-up of 50%. By the end of the year, Mega had sold this inventory.
- The group's goodwill of £1,485,000 suffered an impairment loss of 40%.

Activity

Prepare the consolidated statement of comprehensive income for the year ended 30 April 2018 for Giga PLC.

Check your answer against the following solution.

Giga PLC

Consolidated statement of profit or loss and other comprehensive income
for the year ended 30 April 2018

	Giga PLC £'000	Mega Ltd £'000	W1 £'000	Group £'000
Revenue	2,200	2,000	(300)	3,900
Cost of sales	(700)	(800)	300	(1,200)
Gross profit	1,500	1,200	–	2,700
Administrative expenses	(400)	(300)	–	(700)
Distribution costs	(350)	(150)	–	(500)
Impairment of goodwill (W2)			–	(594)
Operating profit	750	750	–	906
Income tax expense	(250)	(250)	–	(500)
Profit for the period	500	500	–	406
Profit attributable to:				
Non-controlling interest (W3)				50
Giga PLC's shareholders (balancing figure)				356
Profit for the period				406

Many items in the individual statements of comprehensive income statement for the parent and subsidiary can be aggregated to provide the figures for the consolidated financial statement. However, you need to make three adjustments:

- W1 eliminates intra-group sales. The cost to Giga of the inventory was £200,000 but Giga added a 50% mark-up (£100,000) before selling it to Mega. Therefore, revenue is reduced by £300,000 (£200,000 + £100,000) to remove the intra-group revenue. An offsetting amount of £300,000 is deducted from the group's cost of sales.
- W2 accounts for the 40% impairment to the £1,485,000 of goodwill on the acquisition of Mega Ltd. The impairment loss (£1,485,000 x 40% = £594,000) is included as an expense in the group statement of comprehensive income.
- W3 shows the division of the group's £406,000 profit for the period between the parent and the NCI. The shareholders owning the 10% NCI are entitled to 10% of Mega's profit (£500,000 x 10% = £50,000) and the balance of the group's profit is attributable to Giga's shareholders (£406,000 – £50,000 = £356,000).

Although the parent, Giga PLC, and the subsidiary, Mega Ltd, both achieved profits of £500,000 in the year after acquisition, the group profit was only £406,000 due to the impairment of goodwill. We can check whether the calculation of group profit is correct by preparing a *consolidated statement of changes in equity*. This shows the changes in equity and reserves during the period and provides a link between the consolidated statement of comprehensive income and the amount of equity shown in the consolidated statement of financial position.

In the following consolidated statement of changes in equity for the year ended 30 April 2018, the columns for share capital and retained earnings show the separate amounts attributable to shareholders of Giga and the NCI. The balances at 30 April 2017 and 30 April 2018 are taken from the two consolidated statements of financial position you prepared in previous activities in this chapter. The figure of £406,000 for the consolidated comprehensive income for the year is correct because it matches the change in the group's total equity for the period (£5.341m at 30 April 2018 – £4.935m at 30 April 2017).

Giga PLC

Consolidated statement of changes in equity for year ended 30 April 2018

	Share capital	Retained earnings	Total	NCI	Group
	£'000	£'000	£'000	£'000	£'000
Balance at 30 April 2017	2,500	2,000	4,500	435	4,935
Comprehensive income for the period		356	356	50	406
Balance at 30 April 2018	2,500	2,356	4,856	485	5,341

9.7   Associates

Where an investment does not result in an investor having control over an investee, the investment must be accounted for differently within the consolidated financial statements. An *associate* is an entity over which an investor has *significant influence* rather than control. Significant influence only provides the power to participate in rather than control the financial and operating policy decisions of the investee.

IAS 28, *Investments in Associates and Joint Ventures* (IASB, 2014d) explains that an investment that grants significant influence is presumed to exist where an investor holds 20% or more of the voting power (directly or indirectly) of an investee and can also be shown when one or more of the following exists:

- an investor has representation on the investee's board of directors
- an investor participates in policy-making decisions at the investee
- there are material transactions between the investor and investee
- there is an interchange of managerial personnel between the entities
- there is provision of essential technical information between the entities.

Key definitions

An associate is an entity over which the investor has significant influence.

Significant influence is the power to participate in the financial and operating policy decisions of the investee but is not control or joint control of those policies.

Source: IAS 28, IASB, 2014d [3]. Reproduced with permission from the IFRS Foundation.

IAS 28 requires the use of the *equity method* to account for an investment in an associate. The equity method is very different from the acquisition method of accounting we used earlier in this chapter, as an investment in an associate is included as a single non-current asset in the consolidated statement of financial position. The main stages in the equity methods are:

Step 1. Calculate whether the investor has significant influence over the investee and establish the investor's proportional share of the associate at the date of acquisition.

Step 2. Calculate the fair value transferred by the investor. An investor does not always use cash to invest in an associate, so the cost of the investment includes the fair value of any assets given, liabilities incurred or assumed, and any shares issued by the investor.

Step 3. Calculate the value of the associate's assets and liabilities recognized at the date of acquisition.

Step 4. Calculate the goodwill at the date of acquisition. Although goodwill is not recognized separately under the equity method, this calculation is necessary to determine whether there is any negative goodwill. If negative goodwill exists, it must be added to the carrying value of the investment in the consolidated statement of financial position, and recognized as income within the investor's consolidated statement of financial position.

Step 5. Determine the cost of the investor's initial investment in the associate at the date of acquisition.

Step 6. Calculate the investor's share of the associate's profit after eliminating any transactions between the investor and the associate.

We will illustrate this with another example. Tiroli PLC is the parent of several wholly-owned subsidiaries. On 1 April 2017, Tiroli PLC acquired 20% of the £1 ordinary shares of Astio Ltd for £20,000, which gave it significant influence rather than control over the investee. As illustrated in Figure 9.2, Astio Ltd becomes an associate of Tiroli PLC.

Figure 9.2   Tiroli PLC's significant influence over Astio Ltd

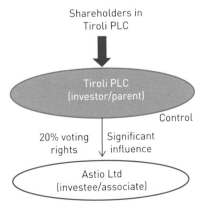

Astio's retained earnings on 1 April 2017 were £40,000, and its assets and liabilities were carried at fair value. The consolidated financial statements for Tiroli PLC for the year ended 31 March 2018 and the financial statements of Astio Ltd for the same period are shown below.

Statements of financial position at 31 March 2018

	Tiroli PLC and subsidiaries £'000	Astio Ltd £'000
ASSETS		
Non-current assets		
Property, plant and equipment	550	130
Investment in Astio Ltd	20	–
	570	130
Current assets	230	30
Total assets	800	160
EQUITY AND LIABILITIES		
Equity		
Ordinary share capital	200	60
Retained earnings	500	60
	700	120
Current liabilities	100	40
Total assets and liabilities	800	160

Statements of profit or loss and other comprehensive income for year ended 31 March 2018

	Tiroli PLC and subsidiaries £'000	Astio Ltd £'000
Revenue	900	300
Cost of sales	(300)	(150)
Gross profit	600	150
Administrative expenses	(125)	(55)
Distribution costs	(100)	(50)
Operating profit	375	45
Income tax expense	(75)	(25)
Profit for the period	300	20

Activity

Use the equity method to integrate Astio Ltd in the consolidated statements of comprehensive income and financial position of Tiroli PLC for the year ended 31 March 2018.

Check your calculations against the following solution.

Tiroli PLC

Consolidated statement of profit or loss and other comprehensive income for the year ended 31 March 2018

	£'000
Revenue	900
Cost of sales	(300)
Gross profit	600
Administrative expenses	(125)
Distribution costs	(100)
Operating profit	375
Share of profit of associate	4
Profit before tax	379
Income tax expense	(75)
Profit for the period	304

1. Tiroli's purchase of 20% of Astio's ordinary share capital has given Tiroli significant influence over Astio, so Astio Ltd becomes an associate of Tiroli PLC and we must use the equity method to account for this investment in the consolidated financial statements.
2. The ordinary share capital of Astio has a nominal value of £1 per share, so it has 60,000 shares (£60,000 ordinary share capital ÷ £1 per share). At a purchase price of £1.00 per share, the fair value of the consideration transferred by Tiroli PLC was £20,000 (20,000 shares x £1.00 per share).
3. The assets and liabilities of Astio were already valued at acquisition-date fair value. In exchange for its investment of £20,000, Tiroli obtained 20% of Astio's identifiable net assets which had a fair value of £100,000 at the date of acquisition. The total net assets acquired were £20,000. The underlying calculations are as follows.

	Fair value of Astio's equity at acquisition £'000	Tiroli PLC's 20% share of associate £'000
Ordinary share capital	60	12
Retained earnings	40	8
Total	100	20

4. As Tiroli paid £20,000 to acquire net assets with a fair value of £20,000, there was no goodwill.

Goodwill	£'000
Fair value of the consideration transferred	20
Fair value of associate's net assets acquired	(20)
Goodwill	–

5. The cost of the investor's initial investment in the associate at the date of acquisition is calculated as follows.

	£'000
Fair value of the consideration transferred	20
Negative goodwill	–
Tiroli PLC's initial investment in Astio Ltd	20

There were no transactions between Tiroli and Astio during the year. As Astio's profit for the year ended 31 March 2018 was £20,000, Tiroli is entitled to receive a £4,000 share of this total amount (£20,000 x 20% = £4,000). This amount must be added to the investor's consolidated statement of profit or loss and other comprehensive income, and increases the carrying value of the associate's investment in the consolidated statement of financial position. The total profit in Tiroli's consolidated statement of profit or loss and other comprehensive income for the year ended 31 March 2018 is now £304,000 (£300,000 + £4,000 = £304,000). As group profit for the year increases by £4,000, the carrying value of the associate investment in the consolidated statement of financial position also increases by £4,000, and will now be recognized at £24,000. The retained earnings of the group also increase by £4,000 to give a total of £504,000 at 31 March 2018.

Tiroli PLC

Consolidated statement of financial position at 31 March 2018

	£'000
ASSETS	
Non-current assets	
Property, plant and equipment	550
Investment in associate	24
	574
Current assets	230
Total assets	804
EQUITY AND LIABILITIES	
Equity	
Ordinary share capital	200
Retained earnings	504
	704
Current liabilities	100
Total equity and liabilities	804

If we were required to account for Tiroli's investment in Astio at the end of the next accounting period, we would simply start from step 6 and continue as follows:

- Eliminate any unrealized profits resulting from intra-group transactions according to Tiroli's interest in Astio.
- Recognize Tiroli's share of Astio's comprehensive income in the consolidated statement of comprehensive income, and add this amount to the existing £24 value of the associate investment within the consolidated statement of financial position.

One of the limitations of the equity method is that as a form of simplified consolidation it does not meet the criterion of control. In addition, it can be argued that it does not provide a good guide to forecasting the cash flows of the parent company.

9.8   Joint arrangements

IAS 28, *Investments in Associates and Joint Ventures* (IASB, 2014d) explains that a *joint arrangement* is an investment that results in the investor entity having *joint control* with one or more other parties over an economic activity or entity. There are two types of joint arrangement:

- A *joint operation* is where the parties that have joint control of the arrangement have rights to the assets, and obligations for the liabilities, relating to the arrangement. In a joint operation the parties usually share revenues, purchase jointly controlled assets, incur their own expenses and are responsible for raising their own finance. A joint agreement that is not structured through a separate legal entity (such as a corporation) is always classified as a joint operation.
- A *joint venture* is where the parties that have joint control of the arrangement have rights to the net assets of the arrangement. In a joint venture, the parties do not have individual rights to assets and obligations for the liabilities of the joint venture.

You may have noticed that joint control is mentioned as a characteristic of both types of joint arrangement. An investment that offers joint control provides a contractually agreed sharing of control where strategic decisions about the relevant activities, such as capital expenditure and approving a business plan, require the unanimous consent of the parties sharing control. The key aspects of joint control are:

- Collective control – the parties must collectively control the arrangement in accordance with the definition of control in IFRS 10 (see above).
- Contractually agreed – written contractual agreements are usually established that provide the terms of the arrangement.
- Unanimous consent – any party can prevent any of the other parties from making unilateral decisions (about the relevant activities) without its consent.

> **Key definition**
>
> A joint operation is a joint arrangement whereby the parties that have joint control of the arrangement have rights to the assets, and obligations for the liabilities, relating to the arrangement.
>
> A joint venture is a joint arrangement whereby the parties that have joint control of the arrangement have rights to the net assets of the arrangement.
>
> Joint control is the contractually agreed sharing of control of an arrangement, which exists only when decisions about the relevant activities over an economic activity require the unanimous consent of the parties sharing control.
>
> Source: IFRS 11, IASB, 2014e, Appendix A. Reproduced with permission from the IFRS Foundation.

You already know that accounting for subsidiaries is guided by IFRS 3, *Business Combinations* and IFRS 10, *Consolidated Financial Statements*, which require the investor (the parent company) to use the acquisition method. However, accounting for joint operations is guided by IFRS 11, *Joint Arrangements* (IASB, 2014e) and IAS 28, *Investments in Associates and Joint Ventures* (IASB, 2014d), which require the equity method to be used. Determining whether an investee is a subsidiary, associate or joint arrangement is a matter of judgement. Therefore, IFRS 12, *Disclosure of Interests in Other Entities* (IASB, 2014f) requires disclosure of the significant assumptions made in determining whether the investor has control, significant influence or joint control over each investee in the consolidated financial statements. Table 9.1 summarizes this information.

Table 9.1   Accounting methods for different types of investee

Level of control/influence	Classification	Accounting method
Control	Subsidiary	Consolidation under IFRS 3 and IFRS 10
Significant influence	Associate	Equity method under IAS 28
Joint control	Joint venture	Equity method under IAS 28
Joint control	Joint operation	Each party to recognize the assets, liabilities, income and expenses from their involvement in the operation under IFRS 11

As each type of joint arrangement provides joint control, rather than outright control or significant influence over an investee, they result in different forms of group accounting which are illustrated in Figure 9.3.

Figure 9.3 Joint arrangements

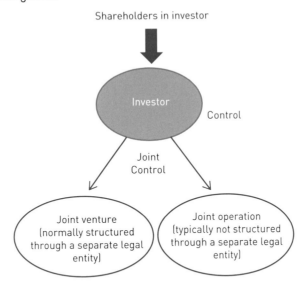

As we have described the equity method in the previous section on associates, we will focus on accounting for joint operations. Each party in the joint operation must recognize the following in relation to its interest in the joint operation:

- its assets and liabilities, including its share of any jointly held assets or liabilities
- its share of the income and expenses from the joint operation.

The required accounting entries are shown in the investor's own individual financial statements, and are included within the consolidated financial statements if the investor is part of a group.

To illustrate this, we will look at an example. On 1 January 2018, Air PLC and Jet PLC each agreed to contribute £2.5m towards the purchase and installation of baggage handling equipment. The equipment cost £5m to purchase and install, and had an estimated useful life of ten years with no residual value. A separate legal entity was not created for the arrangement, but the directors of the companies signed an agreement which stated that all operational decisions would require the unanimous consent of both parties. The agreement specified that annual income and expenses would be shared equally. Air PLC employs the baggage handling operatives. The following cash flow information is available about the joint operation:

Cash flows for the year ended 31 December 2018

	Air PLC £'000	Jet PLC £'000
Cash inflows		
Revenue	850	–
Cash outflows		
Equipment costs	(2,000)	(2,000)
Installation costs	(1,000)	–
Operatives' salaries	(200)	–
Net cash flow	(2,350)	(2,000)

Air PLC financed its involvement in the joint operation with a £2.5m interest-free loan from a government agency.

Activity

Decide whether the joint arrangement should be accounted for as a joint venture or a joint operation.

You would be right in thinking that joint control exists for this arrangement because:

- The parties have collective control over the arrangement.
- A contractual agreement exists.
- Decisions regarding the relevant activities of the baggage operation require the unanimous consent of both airlines.

This joint arrangement should be accounted for as a joint operation because it is not structured as a separate legal entity, and each party jointly owns the baggage equipment. The main stages in accounting for a joint operation are:

Step 1. Calculate the total annual income and expenditure from the joint operation.

Step 2. Calculate the transfers that each party must make to recognize the contractually agreed amounts of revenues, expenses, liabilities and assets at the balance sheet date.

The financial accountant at Air PLC has prepared the following draft financial statements that identify the revenue, expenses, assets and liabilities from the company's activities on the joint operation during 2018.

Air PLC

Draft statement of profit or loss for the joint
operation for the year ended 31 December 2018

	£'000
Revenue	850
Depreciation	(250)
Operatives' salaries	(200)
Profit for the period	400

Air PLC

Draft statement of financial position for the joint
operation at 31 December 2018

	£'000
ASSETS	
Non-current assets	
Property, plant and equipment	2,500
Accumulated depreciation	(250)
	2,250
Current assets	
Recoverable from Jet PLC	500
Cash	150
Total assets	2,900
EQUITY AND LIABILITIES	
Equity	
Retained earnings (operating profit from joint operation)	400
Non-current liabilities	
Loan	2,500
Total equity and liabilities	2,900

Although these draft financial statements record Air's transactions related to the joint operation for 2018, they need to be adjusted to account for the specific terms of the agreement, which include the following provisions:

- Annual expenses and revenues must be shared equally.
- Each company agreed to contribute £2.5m towards the cost of the baggage equipment.

As a result, the draft financial statements must be adjusted to account for the following issues:

- The income statement includes £850,000 of revenue collected by Air PLC, although £425,000 of this (50%) belongs to Jet PLC.
- Air PLC paid operatives' salaries of £200,000, although Jet PLC should pay 50% of this expense.

1. The first step is to calculate the total income and expenditure of the joint operation for the year ended 31 December 2018 so that 50% can be shared between the parties. Total revenue of £850,000 was received by Air PLC from other airlines. The baggage equipment had a total cost of £5m (£2m x 2 = £4m + £1m installation cost) and has a useful economic life of 10 years. Therefore, the annual straight-line depreciation was £500,000 (£5m ÷ 10 years). Air PLC paid £200,000 in operatives' salaries during the year. Combining these revenues and expenses, the annual profit from the joint operation was £150,000. Air's statement of profit or loss and other comprehensive income should reflect 50% of this amount, and both parties should report a profit for the period of £75,000. As Air's draft statement of comprehensive income reported a profit for the year of £400,000, this amount must be restated by transferring the contractually agreed shares of revenues and expenses. The underlying calculations are as follows.

	100% of joint operation	50% of joint operation
	£'000	£'000
Revenue	850	425
Depreciation	(500)	(250)
Operatives' salaries	(200)	(100)
Profit for the period	150	75

2. Air PLC's draft statement of financial position includes a current asset for the £500,000 receivable from Jet PLC for the unpaid share of the £1m installation costs (£1m x 50% = £500,000). However, the amount recoverable must be adjusted to account for the revenue that Air owes to Jet (£850,000 x 50% = £425,000) and Jet's share of the operatives' salaries (£200,000 x 50% = £100,000). Once the transfers are made for all the contractual obligations, Air should receive £175,000 from Jet PLC at 31 December 2018 to cover the unpaid share of the joint costs of the arrangement as shown below, and this must be shown as a current asset in Air's individual financial statements.

	Air PLC	Jet PLC's 50% share	Due to/from Jet PLC
	£'000	£'000	£'000
Installation costs paid	(1,000)	(500)	500
Operatives' salaries paid	(200)	(100)	100
Revenue received	850	425	(425)
Net amount receivable by Air PLC			175

Activity

Using the above information, re-draft the financial statements of Air PLC to show its share of the income, expenses, assets and liabilities from the joint operation for the year ended 31 January 2018.

If you have worked through all the activities in this chapter, you should not have had too much difficulty with this. Check your answer against the following solutions.

Air PLC

Statement of profit or loss for the joint operation
for the year ended 31 December 2018

	Draft £'000	50% share £'000	W1 £'000	Adjusted £'000
Revenue	850	425	(425)	425
Depreciation	(250)	(250)	–	(250)
Operatives' wages	(200)	(100)	(100)	(100)
Profit for the period	400	75	(325)	75

Air PLC

Statement of financial position for the joint operation at 31 December 2018

	Draft £'000	W2 £'000	Adjusted £'000
ASSETS			
Non-current assets			
Property, plant and equipment	2,500	–	2,500
Depreciation	(250)	–	(250)
	2,250	–	2,250
Current assets			
Accounts receivable	500	(325)	175
Cash [W3]	150	–	150
Total assets	2,900	(325)	2,575
EQUITY AND LIABILITIES			
Equity			
Retained earnings	400	(325)	75
Non-current liabilities			
Loan	2,500	–	2,500
Total equity and liabilities	2,900	(325)	2,575

- W1 shows the changes that need to be made to Air's draft income statement to only report its share of the income and expenses from the joint operation. Air must transfer 50% of the revenue (£850,000 x 50% = £425,000) to Jet and receive 50% of the operatives' salaries from Jet (£200,000 x 50% = £100,000). These adjustments reduce Air's profit from its involvement in the joint operation to £75,000, which equals 50% of the total profit for the year of £150,000. In total, these transfers result in £325,000 of transfers to Jet from Air.
- W2 shows how an adjustment of £325,000 is needed to correctly calculate the ending amount Air is due to receive from Jet PLC. The £500,000 of accounts receivable shown in Air's draft statement of financial position was based on the share of the installation costs that Jet owed Air (£1m x 50% = £500,000). This amount is reduced to £175,000 (£500,000 – £325,000 = £175,000) to reflect the income and expenses Air PLC has transferred to Jet PLC in W1.
- W3 refers to the calculation of the closing cash position for Air PLC. Air spent £3.2m cash (£2m for equipment, £1m for installation costs and £200,000 for operatives' salaries) and received £3.35m cash during the period (£850,000 revenue from the joint operation and £2,500,000 from the government loan), leaving a positive cash balance of £150,000.

We have presented the workings for Air PLC's joint operation in the form of a draft income statement and statement of financial position to help you understand the process. IFRS 11 does not require entities to prepare separate financial statements for a joint operation, but merely that the investor recognizes the assets, liabilities, income and expenses from the joint operation in its financial statements. As Air PLC controls other subsidiaries, the assets, liabilities, income and expenses from the joint operation shown in the adjusted column of the solution will be combined with those of the group in the consolidated financial statements.

9.9   Conclusions

A business combination is a transaction or event in which an investor (the parent company) obtains control of another entity (the subsidiary). Mergers of equals are also business combinations. Control is achieved when the investor is exposed to or has rights to variable returns from its involvement with the investee and has the ability to affect those returns through its power over the investee. A non-controlling interest (NCI) is the equity in a subsidiary not attributable, directly or indirectly, to the parent. A parent company is required to prepare consolidated financial statements for its shareholders.

The purpose of consolidated financial statements is to present the assets, liabilities, equity, income, expenses and cash flows of the parent and its subsidiaries as if they were a single economic entity. The consolidated statement of changes in equity shows the changes in equity and reserves during the period, thus providing a link between the consolidated statement of financial position and the consolidated statement of profit and loss and other comprehensive income.

The classification of an investee is determined by the level of control or influence of the investor. We have discussed the consolidation method for subsidiaries under FRS 3 and IFRS 10, the equity method for associates and joint ventures under IAS 28, and the accounting method for joint operations under IFRS 11. The underlying principle of all these methods is that the consolidated financial statements of the investor show a faithful representation of the investment and the level of control or influence over the investee.

 ## Common problems to avoid

Common mistakes students make when preparing consolidated financial statements are:

- Not showing the name of each business
- Not stating the period covered by the consolidated statement of profit or loss, or the date at which the consolidated statement of financial position is prepared
- Forgetting to include the currency symbol
- Forgetting to revalue the subsidiary's net assets at the acquisition date to their fair value
- Valuing a subsidiary at the date of acquisition using its total assets rather than its net assets
- Forgetting that the calculation of goodwill requires the calculation of NCI
- Forgetting that a subsidiary's ordinary share capital is never shown in the consolidated statement of financial position
- Including goodwill in the parent's financial statements
- Forgetting to account for the NCI's share of a subsidiary's post-acquisition profits
- Forgetting to show all workings

References

IASB (2013a) IFRS 3, *Business Combinations*, London: IFRS Foundation.

IASB (2013b) IAS 36, *Impairment of Assets*, London: IFRS Foundation.

IASB (2013c) IFRS 13, *Fair Value Measurement*, London: IFRS Foundation.

IASB (2014a) IFRS 10, *Consolidated Financial Statements*, London: IFRS Foundation.

IASB (2014b) IAS 1, *Presentation of Financial Statements*, London: IFRS Foundation.

IASB (2014c) IFRS 9 *Financial Instruments*, London: IFRS Foundation.

IASB (2014d) IAS 28, *Investments in Associates and Joint Ventures*, London: IFRS Foundation.

IASB (2014e) IFRS 11, *Joint Arrangements*, London: IFRS Foundation.

IASB (2014f) IFRS 12, *Disclosure of Interests in Other Entities*, London: IFRS Foundation.

IASB (2015) *Exposure Draft Conceptual Framework for Financial Reporting*, London: IFRS Foundation.

Discussion questions

1 Discuss the reasons why the net assets of a subsidiary should be adjusted to their fair value at the date of acquisition.

2 Discuss the reasons why goodwill is only shown in a group's consolidated financial statements.

Practice questions

3 Briefly explain the difference between

(a) control and joint control
(b) joint venture and joint operation.

4 Agro Ltd acquired 80% of Seeds Ltd for £500,000 on 1 July 2017 to obtain control over the investee. Seed Ltd's net assets include property, plant and equipment, inventory and trade receivables with a total book value of £200,000 at the date of acquisition. Following independent appraisal of the property, plant and equipment at the acquisition date, it was discovered that these assets had a fair value £100,000 greater than their book value.

Required

Calculate the following figures that will be shown in the consolidated statement of financial position at the acquisition date:

(a) goodwill
(b) the non-controlling interest.

5 Maxi PLC is a parent company with a number of subsidiaries. On 1 January 2017 Maxi PLC purchased 20% of the 500,000 £1 ordinary shares of Mini Ltd for £100,000. This investment gave Maxi significant influence over the investee. The fair value of Mini's identifiable net assets was £400,000 at the acquisition date. During the year ended 31 December 2017, Mini generated a profit for the year of £40,000.

Required

Explain how these transactions would be shown in the consolidated financial statements for Maxi PLC for the year ended 31 December 2017.

6 On 1 January 2018, Senior PLC acquired 70% of the ordinary share capital of Junior Ltd. This investment gave Senior PLC control over the investee. The statements of profit or loss and other comprehensive income for the two companies for the year ended 31 December 2018 are shown below.

Statements of profit or loss and other comprehensive income for year ended 31 December 2018		
	Senior PLC	Junior Ltd
	£'000	£'000
Revenue	2,000	800
Cost of sales	(700)	(200)
Gross profit	1,300	600
Administrative expenses	(200)	(80)
Distribution costs	(100)	(20)
Operating profit	1,000	500
Income tax expense	(300)	(150)
Profit for the period	700	350

The following information is available:

- During the year, Senior PLC sold £20,000 of inventory to Junior Ltd. This inventory cost Senior £10,000. At 31 December 2018, 50% of this inventory had been sold by Junior Ltd.

Required

Prepare the consolidated statement of profit or loss and other comprehensive income for Senior PLC for the year ended 31 December 2018.

7 On 31 January 2018, Ocean PLC paid £4.00 per share to acquire 600,000 of the £1 ordinary shares of Lake Ltd and control over the investee. At this date all of Lake's assets and liabilities were valued at fair value. The statements of financial position for the two companies at the date of acquisition are shown below.

Statements of financial position at 31 January 2018		
	Ocean PLC	Lake Ltd
	£'000	£'000
ASSETS		
Non-current assets		
Property, plant and equipment	1,500	3,000
Investment in Lake Ltd	2,400	–
	3,900	3,000
Current assets	1,000	1,000
Total assets	4,900	4,000
EQUITY AND LIABILITIES		
Equity		
Ordinary share capital	2,000	1,000
Retained earnings	2,000	2,000
	4,000	3,000
Current liabilities	900	1,000
Total equity and liabilities	4,900	4,000

Required

(a) Calculate the goodwill that was paid by Ocean PLC on the acquisition of Lake Ltd.
(b) Prepare the consolidated statement of financial position for Ocean PLC at 31 January 2018.

8   On 1 August 2017, Major Ltd paid £1.50 per share to acquire 40,000 of the £1 ordinary shares of Minor Ltd and control over the investee. At this date, the share capital and reserves of Minor Ltd were:

	£
£1 ordinary share capital	50,000
Retained earnings	16,250
Total	66,250

The statements of financial position for the two companies at 31 July 2018 were as follows.

Statements of financial position at 31 July 2018		
	Major Ltd	Minor Ltd
	£	£
ASSETS		
Non-current assets		
Property, plant and equipment	150,000	82,000
Investment in Minor Ltd	60,000	
	210,000	
Current assets	195,000	92,250
Total assets	405,000	174,250
EQUITY AND LIABILITIES		
Equity		
Ordinary share capital	250,000	50,000
Retained earnings	32,000	36,250
Revaluation reserve		10,000
	282,000	96,250
Current liabilities	123,000	78,000
Total equity and liabilities	405,000	174,250

Following an impairment review on 31 July 2018, it was found that goodwill had suffered an impairment loss of 50% since the acquisition of Minor Ltd.

Required

(c) Calculate the goodwill that was paid by Major Ltd on the acquisition of Minor Ltd.
(d) Prepare the consolidated statement of financial position for Major Ltd at 31 July 2018.

Suggested research questions for dissertation students

Students interested in the effects of IFRS 10 may wish to investigate one or more of the following research questions:

- Why does the accounting treatment of purchased goodwill matter?

- Why is there stakeholder disagreement about the appropriate treatment of purchased goodwill?

- What effect has the revised concept of control in IFRS 10, *Consolidated Financial Statements* (IASB, 2014a) had on the accounting policies relating to the classification of investees in consolidated financial statements of FTSE 100 companies?

- Should the definition of control be based on a principle or a rule?

- Do FTSE 100 companies have a preference for investments structured as joint ventures or joint operations?

- Does the market react negatively to goodwill impairments under IFRS?

Preliminary reading

Grant Thornton (2012) *Under Control? A Practical Guide to IFRS 10 Consolidated Financial Statements*. Available at: www.grantthornton.ca/resources/insights/adviser_alerts/Under_control_a_practical_guide_to_IFRS10_final_August2012.pdf (Accessed 1 June 2016).

Kimbro, M. and Xu, D. (2016) 'The accounting treatment of goodwill, idiosyncratic risk, and market pricing', *Journal of Accounting, Auditing and Finance*, 31(3), pp. 365–387.

Knauer, T. and Wöhrmann, A. (2015) 'Market reaction to goodwill impairments', *European Accounting Review*, 25(3), pp. 421–449.

Mattias, H. and Leif-Atle, B. (2014) 'Changes in the value relevance of goodwill accounting following the adoption of IFRS 3', *Journal of Accounting, Auditing and Taxation*, 23(2), pp. 59–73.

Wines, G., Dagwell, R. and Windsor, C. (2007) 'Implications of the IFRS goodwill accounting treatment', *Managerial Auditing Journal*, 22(9), pp. 862–880.

10 Financial statement analysis

Learning objectives

When you have studied this chapter, you should be able to:

- Explain the purpose of ratio analysis
- Calculate the main investment and profitability ratios
- Calculate the main liquidity, efficiency and solvency ratios
- Interpret the meaning of these ratios and recognize their limitations

10.1 Introduction

In the last four chapters we have focused on how to prepare corporate financial statements in order to build up your knowledge of financial accounting. In this chapter we are going to take a user perspective and introduce you to financial statement analysis, with a particular focus on ratio analysis. This is the traditional technique used to analyze financial statements by existing and potential investors, lenders, creditors and other stakeholders, such as major customers and suppliers, management and financial analysts. Financial statement analysis helps you identify the financial strengths and weaknesses of the business, and compare your results with previous periods, similar businesses or industry benchmarks.

We will start by showing you how different types of ratio can be calculated and then used to assess the operating performance, liquidity and efficiency in the management of the working capital of a business. We then look at the ratios used to examine the financial structure of the business, assess financial risk and evaluate the shareholders' return. Although we will be illustrating the analysis by applying ratios to the annual financial statements of a public limited company, you should bear in mind that ratio analysis can be conducted on the financial statements of smaller entities and also on financial statements prepared for interim reporting or for management purposes.

10.2 Ratio analysis

Financial statement analysis evaluates the relationship between key components of the financial statements through the use of accounting ratios. *The purpose* of *ratio analysis* is to help internal and external users gain a better understanding of the financial performance and stability of an entity by examining accounting ratios that describe the quantitative relationship between two data items. The relationship can be expressed in a variety of ways, such as:

- a ratio (x:1)
- a percentage (x%)
- the monetary value (x pence)
- the average number of times over the period (x times)
- the average length of time over the period (x days or x months)

Once a ratio has been calculated, it is compared with:

- the predetermined budget or target (internal users only)
- previous periods for the same business
- other businesses in the same sector (inter-firm comparison)
- industry benchmarks (published averages for the sector).

Key definition

Ratio analysis is a technique for evaluating the financial performance and financial stability of an entity through the use of accounting ratios. Comparisons are made with previous periods, other companies and industry averages.

It is important to note that there are no standard definitions of the terms used in accounting ratios. Therefore, if you are using ratios published in the annual report and accounts, the financial press or those provided in financial databases, you would need to know what formulae were used and how the accounting terms in the formulae were defined before you could fully understand what is being referred to and whether comparisons are appropriate. Obviously, you cannot compare ratios from different sources if they have not been calculated on the same basis. When calculating ratios, you need to state the formulae and define the terms you are using. You will see from the examples in this chapter that we have rounded the final figure in our calculations to two decimal places.

There are four main types of ratio and each has a different purpose:

- *Investment ratios* are used to evaluate the shareholders' return.
- *Profitability ratios* are used to assess the operating performance of the business.
- *Liquidity and efficiency ratios* are used to evaluate the solvency, financial stability and management of working capital of the business.
- *Gearing ratios* are used to examine the financial structure of the business and assess financial risk.

We will examine a selection of the main ratios in each of the above categories, but in any financial analysis, the choice of ratios depends on the needs of the user and the availability of relevant data. Figure 10.1 summarizes the main types of ratios and those we will describe in this chapter.

Figure 10.1 Examples of main types of ratio

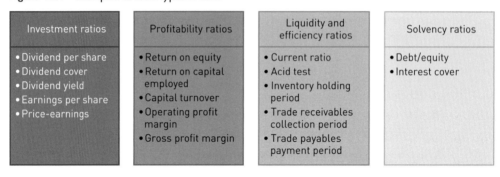

Ratios can be applied to the financial statements of any size and type of business. We are going to apply them to the financial statements of Ted Baker Plc, whose annual report and accounts we discussed in Chapter 4. Extracts from the Group Income statement and Other Comprehensive Income (also known as the statement of profit or loss and other comprehensive income) and the Group Balance Sheet (also known as the statement of financial position) are reproduced in Figure 10.2.

Figure 10.2 Ted Baker Plc Annual Report and Accounts 2015/16 (abridged extracts)

GROUP INCOME STATEMENT	NOTE	52 WEEKS ENDED	52 WEEKS ENDED
FOR THE 52 WEEKS ENDED 30 JANUARY 2016		30 JANUARY 2016	31 JANUARY 2015
		£'000	£'000
Revenue	2	456,169	387,564
Cost of sales		(183,147)	(152,359)
GROSS PROFIT		273,022	235,205
Distribution costs		(169,762)	(144,584)
Administrative expenses		(57,435)	(51,034)
Exceptional costs	3	–	(5,339)
Licence income		14,384	11,665
Other operating (expense)/income		(840)	(812)
Exceptional income	3	–	4,658
OPERATING PROFIT		59,369	49,759
Finance income	4	531	108
Finance expenses	4	(1,931)	(1,621)
Share of profit of jointly controlled entity, net of tax	12	695	525
PROFIT BEFORE TAX	3	58,664	48,771
Income tax expense	6	(14,429)	(12,921)
PROFIT FOR THE PERIOD		44,235	35,850

GROUP STATEMENT OF COMPREHENSIVE INCOME

FOR THE 52 WEEKS ENDED 30 JANUARY 2016

	52 WEEKS ENDED 30 JANUARY 2016	52 WEEKS ENDED 31 JANUARY 2015
	£'000	£'000
PROFIT FOR THE PERIOD	**44,235**	**35,850**
OTHER COMPREHENSIVE INCOME		
Net effective portion of changes in fair value of cash flow hedges	951	1,328
Net change in fair value of cash flow hedges transferred to profit or loss	(669)	1,890
Exchange differences on foreign operations net of tax	2,599	2,692
OTHER COMPREHENSIVE INCOME FOR THE PERIOD	**2,881**	**5,910**
TOTAL COMPREHENSIVE INCOME FOR THE PERIOD	**47,116**	**41,760**

GROUP BALANCE SHEET

AT 30 JANUARY 2016

	NOTE	30 JANUARY 2016	31 JANUARY 2015
		£'000	£'000
Intangible assets	10	17,247	12,855
Property, plant and equipment	11	123,397	51,804
Investment in equity accounted investee	12	1,641	1,290
Deferred tax assets	13	6,313	5,659
Prepayments		414	461
NON-CURRENT ASSETS		**149,012**	**72,069**
Inventories	14	125,323	111,114
Trade and other receivables	15	49,303	36,873
Amount due from equity accounted investee	12	563	679
Derivative financial assets	16	2,850	3,547
Cash and cash equivalents	17	13,295	7,380
CURRENT ASSETS		**191,334**	**159,593**
Trade and other payables	18	(61,088)	(57,046)
Bank overdraft	17	(37,869)	(26,204)
Term loan	22	(1,500)	—
Income tax payable		(8,382)	(7,202)
Derivative financial liabilities	16	(352)	(636)
CURRENT LIABILITIES		**(109,191)**	**(91,088)**
Deferred tax liability	13	(56)	—
Term loan	22	(58,500)	—
NON-CURRENT LIABILITIES		**(58,556)**	**0**
NET ASSETS		**172,599**	**140,574**
EQUITY			
Share capital	19	2,199	2,196
Share premium account	19	9,617	9,331
Other reserves	19	1,650	1,368
Translation reserve	19	2,311	(288)
Retained earnings	19	156,822	127,967
TOTAL EQUITY ATTRIBUTABLE TO EQUITY SHAREHOLDERS OF THE PARENT COMPANY		172,599	140,574
Non-controlling interest		—	—
TOTAL EQUITY		**172,599**	**140,574**

(Continued)

Figure 10.2   (Continued)

EXTRACTS OF SELECTED NOTES TO THE FINANCIAL STATEMENTS	30 JANUARY 2016	31 JANUARY 2015
4 Of which, interest payable (£'000)	(1,430)	(1,184)
8 Total dividends for the period (£'000)	21,018	17,679
9 Weighted number of ordinary shares ('000)	43,950	43,703
15 Of which, trade receivables (£'000)	30,136	25,823
18 Of which, trade payables (£'000)	(31,657)	(32,241)
20 Maximum risk free interest rate (%)	0.84	2.77
Market share price at year end from company website (pence)	3,009.0	2,141.0

Below the financial statements, you will see extracts of selected notes to the financial statements. This may be the way in which the information is provided in some exams. However, you will find it very useful to download a pdf copy of Ted Baker's Annual Report and Accounts from www.tedbakerplc.com/investor-relations/results-and-reports/2016. This will allow you to become familiar with the different sections in the document and search the notes to the financial statements for the information you need. This experience will be useful if your exam or coursework is based on a more independent case study approach.

10.3 Investment ratios

We are starting our analysis from an investor perspective, since existing and potential investors are the first of the three primary user groups. We are going to look at five *investment ratios* that are widely used by personal and institutional investors, investment analysts and financial journalists to evaluate shareholders' return and aid investment decisions:

- Dividend per share
- Dividend yield
- Dividend cover
- Earnings per share
- Price-earnings.

10.3.1 Dividend per share

The first investment ratio we are going to calculate is the *dividend per share*. The dividend per share measures the amount of dividend paid on one ordinary share during the year. You will remember that dividends are a distribution of part of the earnings of the entity to its ordinary shareholders. Therefore, dividends represent a portion of the return to shareholders on their investment that is paid in cash. At the end of the year, the directors make a decision about how much of the current year's earnings will be kept in the business to help it grow and how much will be distributed as dividends. The directors will want to increase the dividend or at least keep it stable in order to satisfy existing shareholders and attract new investors. Therefore, during times of economic recession when profits may be relatively low, the directors may decide to use some of the retained profits to maintain dividend levels. Dividend per share is expressed in pence and is calculated using the following formula:

$$\text{Dividend per share} = \frac{\text{Total dividends}}{\text{Number of ordinary shares}} \quad [\times 100 \text{ for pence}]$$

Activity

Calculate Ted Baker's dividend per share for ordinary shareholders for 2016 and 2015.

The data for this ratio are given in Notes 8 and 9 on pages 83 and 84 in the Annual Report and Accounts 2015/16. The first step is to calculate the total dividends for the period. You need to read the information carefully and decide whether the dividend relates to the year in question or the prior year. Check your answer against the following solution. Note that the letter 'k' in the calculations of the ratios denotes thousands.

Working 1

	2015/16 £'000	2014/15 £'000
Interim dividend	5,804	4,940
Final dividend	15,214	12,739
Total dividends	21,018	17,679

2015/16	**2014/15**

$$\text{Dividend per share} = \frac{£21,018k}{43,950k} \times 100 = 47.82p \qquad \frac{£17,679k}{43,703k} \times 100 = 40.45p$$

The good news for investors is that the dividend per share increased by just over 7p in 2015/16 compared to the previous year. This reflects the increased proportion of total dividends to the number of ordinary shares.

10.3.2 Dividend yield

Dividend yield builds on the above ratio and measures the dividend yielded on one ordinary share in relation to the market share price. The ratio is shown as a percentage and is calculated using the following formula:

$$\text{Dividend yield} = \frac{\text{Dividend per share}}{\text{Market share price}} \quad [\times 100 \text{ for } \%]$$

Activity

Calculate Ted Baker's dividend yield for 2015/16 and 2014/15.

You have just calculated the dividend per share, but you may have wondered where to find the market share price. You could look up the current share price in the *Financial Times* or on Ted Baker's website. However, for the sake of this comparison, we are illustrating this ratio using the market share price on the last day of the accounting period for 2015/16 and 2014/15. We provided these figures as a final note below the financial statements. Check your answer against the following solution.

	2015/16	2014/15
Dividend yield =	$\frac{47.82p}{3,009p} \times 100 = 1.59\%$	$\frac{40.45p}{2,141p} \times 100 = 1.89\%$

The dividend yield can range from 0% to around 5% and, of course, it depends on the amount of dividends the directors have decided to distribute to shareholders and the share price at any one time. The directors of young, high growth companies may prefer to retain most of the profits to finance further growth and this would result in a low dividend yield. The results for Ted Baker show that the proportionately high increase in the share price compared with the dividend per share in 2015/16 produced a small decrease in the dividend yield.

10.3.3 Dividend cover

Dividend cover assesses the relative safety of dividend payments by measuring the number of times dividends can be paid out of the available profits. The ratio is calculated using the following formula:

$$\text{Dividend cover} = \frac{\text{Profit for ordinary shareholders}}{\text{Total dividends}}$$

Activity

Calculate Ted Baker's dividend cover for 2015/16 and 2014/15.

You may have wondered which figure of profit to use. If you are analyzing a group that has one or more subsidiaries, you will see that the statement of profit or loss gives a breakdown of profit attributable to the shareholders of the parent company and the company in which it has a non-controlling interest. However, you must not be distracted by this. In all cases, you need to use the profit for the period, which is the profit after interest and tax.

	2015/16	2014/15
Dividend per share =	$\frac{£44,235k}{£21,018k} = 2.10$ times	$\frac{£35,850k}{£17,679k} = 2.03$ times

A high dividend cover may suggest that a substantial proportion of earnings were retained, whereas a low dividend cover could suggest that the business had difficulty in maintaining an acceptable level of dividends. In this case, there is no significant change since last year and the results for Ted Baker show that profits are more than adequate to fund the dividends paid. Therefore, the shareholders should have no cause for concern.

10.3.4 Earnings per share

The next ratio we are going to illustrate is the *earnings per share (EPS)*. So far we have only looked at ratios that focus on profit distributed to shareholders as dividends. However, the directors need to retain some of the profit earned during the year to invest in new assets to help the business earn more profits in the future. Nevertheless, the profit retained still belongs to the shareholders. By focusing on total profit, EPS measures the shareholders' total return and calculates the amount of profit earned by one ordinary share. It is shown in pence and is calculated using the following formula:

$$\text{Earnings per share} = \frac{\text{Profit for ordinary shareholders}}{\text{Number of ordinary shares}} \quad [\times 100 \text{ for pence}]$$

Activity

Calculate Ted Baker's earnings per share for ordinary shareholders for 2015/16 and 2014/15.

This should be straightforward as you have used both the figures you need in ratios you calculated earlier, so all you have to do is insert them into the formula. Check your answer against the following solution.

	2015/16	2014/15
EPS =	$\dfrac{£44,235k}{43,950k} \times 100 = 100.65p$	$\dfrac{£35,850k}{43,703k} \times 100 = 82.03p$

EPS is a measure on which many shareholders place considerable weight. In the case of Ted Baker, there was an increase of nearly 19p in 2015/16, which reflects the higher profit performance for shareholders in that year. It is important to remember that EPS is a measure of the entity's performance and not an amount of money distributed to shareholders. You will remember that the ratio that shows the amount of money paid on one share is the dividend per share. That figure is always lower than EPS because it is based on the dividends, which are only part of the profit for the year. EPS is based on the total profit for the year: dividends plus retained profit.

In order to improve performance comparisons between different entities in the same reporting period and between periods for the same entity, IAS 33, *Earnings per share* (IASB, 2003) sets out the principles for determining and presenting EPS. If you look at page 66 in Ted Baker's Annual Report and Accounts 2015/16, you will see that there are figures for the basic and diluted EPS. Basic EPS is calculated by dividing profit or loss attributable to ordinary shareholders by the weighted average number of ordinary shares during the period as we have done. Diluted EPS is based on adjusting the earnings and number of shares for the effects of dilutive options and events after the balance sheet date that may affect the EPS.

10.3.5 Price-earnings ratio

The final investment ratio we are going to examine is the *price-earnings (P/E)* ratio, which is based on EPS. This compares the amount invested in one share with the EPS and reflects the stock market's view on how long the current level of earnings per share will be sustained. It is measured in years and is calculated using the following formula:

$$\text{Price/Earnings} = \frac{\text{Market share price}}{\text{Earnings per share}}$$

Activity

Calculate Ted Baker's P/E ratio for 2015/16 and 2014/15.

Calculating this ratio should be straightforward. Check your answer against the following solution.

2015/16	2014/15
$\text{P/E} = \dfrac{3{,}009\text{p}}{100.65\text{p}} = 29.90 \text{ years}$	$\dfrac{2{,}141\text{p}}{82.03\text{p}} = 26.10 \text{ years}$

A high P/E ratio suggests that investors expect that earnings will grow rapidly. Therefore, Ted Baker's higher P/E ratio in 2015/16 indicates that investors were more confident than in 2014/15 about how long the current level of EPS will be sustained. As you can see, the length of time has increased by more than three-and-a-half years. This optimism about Ted Baker's future prospects may mean that investors will be willing to pay more for the shares than is justified by the current level of earnings.

If we had the data, it would be useful to analyze all the investment ratios for Ted Baker over a longer period of time to identify the trend. We could also compare them with similar businesses and industry benchmarks.

10.4 Profitability ratios

Profitability ratios are used by internal and external users to assess how effectively the directors have been in managing the business in terms of generating income and controlling costs. Potential and existing investors, lenders and creditors are interested in the profitability of the business, but so are employees, major suppliers and customers. We are going to look at the following widely used ratios in this category:

- Return on equity
- Return on capital employed
- Capital turnover
- Operating profit margin
- Gross profit margin.

10.4.1 Return on equity

The first profitability ratio we are going to look at is the *return on equity (ROE)*. This is of particular interest to investors because it focuses on the profit generated on the investment of shareholders' funds. This helps them assess the stewardship of management. The ratio focuses solely on shareholders' equity and ignores any long-term finance shown under non-current liabilities. For this ratio we will define *return* as profit for ordinary shareholders. It is calculated using the following formula:

$$\text{Return on equity} = \frac{\text{Profit for ordinary shareholders}}{\text{Equity}} \quad [\times 100 \text{ for } \%]$$

Activity
Calculate Ted Baker's ROE for 2015/16 and 2014/15.

The figure of profit you need is the profit for the period, which is the profit after interest and tax. If you are analyzing a statement of financial position (balance sheet) for a group that has one or more subsidiaries, it will show the breakdown of equity attributable to the shareholders of the parent company and the company in which it has a non-controlling interest. However, do not be distracted by this. In all cases, you need to use the figure for total equity. Check your answer against the following solution.

	2015/16	**2014/15**
ROE =	$\dfrac{£44,235k}{£172,599k} \times 100 = 25.63\%$	$\dfrac{£35,850k}{£140,574k} \times 100 = 25.50\%$

The results show no significant change. In both years, Ted Baker earned just over £25 for every £100 of equity and this is considerably higher than the maximum risk free interest rate of 0.84% and 2.77% respectively.

10.4.2 Return on capital employed

The *return on capital employed (ROCE)* measures the percentage return on the total funds used to finance the business. This provides useful information about management's effectiveness in generating income from all the resources and controlling costs. For this ratio we will define *return* as the operating profit, which is the profit before interest and tax, and *capital employed* as equity plus non-current liabilities. This means we will include the shareholders' funds and all sources of long-term finance. The ratio is calculated using the following formula:

$$\text{Return on capital employed} = \frac{\text{Operating profit}}{\text{Equity} + \text{Non-current liabilities}} \quad [\times 100 \text{ for } \%]$$

Activity

Calculate Ted Baker's ROCE for 2015/16 and 2014/15.

Finding the operating profit should be straightforward, but you need to calculate the capital employed by adding total equity to the total for non-current liabilities (ignore the negative sign on the total non-current liabilities). Check your answer against the following solution.

Working 1

	2015/16 £'000	2014/15 £'000
Equity	172,599	140,574
Non-current liabilities	58,556	–
Capital employed	231,155	140,574

	2015/16	2014/15
ROCE =	$\dfrac{£59,369k}{£231,155k} \times 100 = 25.68\%$	$\dfrac{£49,759k}{£140,574k} \times 100 = 35.40\%$

Ted Baker's increased capital employed in 2015/16 did not result in proportionately higher operating profits and the results show a decrease of nearly 10% in ROCE compared with the previous year. This may suggest that the investment facilitated by the new term loan is taking time to generate additional earnings. ROCE should reflect the element of risk in the investment and can be compared with interest rates for other investments where there is barely any risk, such as bank deposit rates. In this case, the return in both years is well above the maximum risk free interest rate of 0.84% and 2.77% respectively.

If you compare the ratios you calculated for ROCE with those you calculated for ROE, you will see that ROE shows a more modest return. This is because ROCE does not take account of the obligation the business has to service and repay long-term debt. The definition of capital employed was equity plus non-current assets, which is the same as total assets minus current liabilities. If we compare the two ratios:

$$\text{ROCE} = \frac{\text{Operating profit}}{\text{Equity + Non-current liabilities}} \quad \frac{\text{(Profit before finance expenses)}}{\text{(Total assets – Current liabilities)}}$$

$$\text{ROE} = \frac{\text{Profit for ordinary shareholders}}{\text{Equity}} \quad \frac{\text{(Profit after finance expenses)}}{\text{(Total assets – Total liabilities)}}$$

ROCE is referred to as the prime ratio because it is related to two subsidiary ratios: capital turnover and operating profit margin, which show how this profitability has been achieved and how it can be improved. We will look at capital turnover next.

10.4.3 Capital turnover

Capital turnover measures the number of times capital employed was used during the year to achieve the revenue. The formula is:

$$\text{Capital turnover} = \frac{\text{Revenue}}{\text{Equity + Non-current liabilities}}$$

Activity

Calculate Ted Baker's capital turnover for 2015/16 and 2014/15.

Finding the figure for revenue should be straightforward and you have already calculated the figure for capital employed, so all you need to do is insert them in the formula. Check your answer against the following solution.

	2015/16	2014/15
Capital turnover =	$\dfrac{£456,169k}{£231,155k} = 1.97$ times	$\dfrac{£387,564k}{£140,574k} = 2.76$ times

The level of activity should be as high as possible for the lowest level of investment. In this case, Ted Baker's capital employed was higher in 2015/16 and was turned over nearly twice to achieve the revenue. Although the capital employed was lower in 2014/15, it was turned over more than two and three-quarter times. This may suggest that the investment facilitated by the new term loan in 2015/16 is taking time to generate additional revenue.

10.4.4 Operating profit margin

The *operating profit margin* measures the percentage return on revenue based on the operating profit. The ratio is calculated using the following formula:

$$\text{Operating profit margin} = \frac{\text{Operating profit}}{\text{Revenue}} \quad [\times 100 \text{ for } \%]$$

Activity

Calculate Ted Baker's operating profit margin for 2015/16 and 2014/15.

All you need to do is to identify the figures in the income statement. Check your answer against the following solution.

	2015/16	2014/15
Operating profit margin =	$\frac{£59,369k}{£456,169k} \times 100 = 13.01\%$	$\frac{£49,759k}{£387,564k} \times 100 = 12.84\%$

The results show that Ted Baker's operating profit margin was similar in both years, with the business making an operating profit of £13.01 on every £100 of revenue in 2015/16. The operating profit margin can be improved by increasing selling prices to increase revenue (if the market permits) or to find ways to cut operating costs. However, you need to remember that the operating profit margin does not take into account the investment needed to generate the profit, whereas the two return on investment ratios (ROE and ROCE) do take account of this.

The last three ratios we have looked at are interrelated:

$$\text{Capital turnover} \times \text{Operating profit margin} = \text{ROCE}$$

We can test this by inserting the ratios we have calculated for Ted Baker. The slight difference in the decimal places in the calculation of ROCE in the solution below is due to rounding the other two ratios to two decimal places.

2015/16   **2014/15**

1.97 × 13.01 = 25.63%   2.76 × 12.84 × = 35.44%

A business can improve ROCE (the prime ratio) by reducing costs and/or raising selling prices if that is feasible, and this will improve its operating profit margin. Alternatively, it can increase its sales volume and/or reduce its capital employed, which will improve its capital turnover.

Activity

Which of the following methods would you suggest Ted Baker's directors should use to try to improve the capital turnover?

(a) Decrease the sales volume

(b) Increase the sales volume

(c) Reduce the capital invested in the business

(d) Keep the capital invested in the business at the same level.

What the directors need to do is increase the sales volume and at the same time keep the capital invested at the same level or lower if that is possible. Therefore, all the answers are correct except (a).

Publicly accountable companies must provide a single statement of profit or loss and other comprehensive income or the same information presented as two separate, but consecutive, statements (as Ted Baker has done) that discloses the gross profit. For businesses in the retail sector in particular, the gross profit is considered to be an essential feature of management control and a guide to pricing and purchasing policies. Therefore, we will look at a ratio based on the gross profit next.

10.4.5 Gross profit margin

The *gross profit margin* measures the percentage return on revenue based on the gross profit. The ratio is calculated using the following formula:

$$\text{Gross profit margin} = \frac{\text{Gross profit}}{\text{Revenue}} \quad [\times 100 \text{ for } \%]$$

Activity

Calculate Ted Baker's gross profit margin for 2015/16 and 2014/15.

Both these figures are given in Ted Baker's income statement, so you just need to insert them into the formula. Check your answer against the following solution.

2015/16	2014/15

$$\text{Gross profit margin} = \frac{£273,022k}{£456,169k} \times 100 = 59.85\% \qquad \frac{£235,205k}{£387,564k} \times 100 = 60.69\%$$

As you can see, the gross profit margin was similar in both years, with the business making a gross profit of £59.85 on every £100 of revenue in 2015/16. An increase in gross profit margin would suggest higher selling prices and/or lower cost of sales. The gross profit margin is much higher than the operating profit margin because the gross profit only takes account of the cost of sales, whereas the operating profit margin takes account of the cost of sales plus all the other operating costs.

Further interpretation of the profitability ratios we have calculated in this section would be possible if we analyzed them over a longer period of time and identified the trend. We could also extend our understanding by conducting a competitor analysis to compare the ratios for Ted Baker with those of similar businesses and with industry benchmarks.

10.5 Liquidity and efficiency ratios

Liquidity ratios are used to evaluate the ability of the business to generate cash to meet its short-term liabilities. They are relevant to all stakeholders with an interest in whether the business is a going concern. Liquidity is of particular importance to existing and potential lenders and creditors, who need to assess whether the business is able to service loans and pay for goods and services bought on credit. *Efficiency ratios* (or *funds management ratios*) are used to assess how effectively the directors have managed the *working capital* of the business (the current assets and current liabilities). These ratios are likely to be of interest to existing investors, lenders and creditors. We will examine the following widely used ratios in these categories:

- Current ratio
- Acid test
- Inventory holding period
- Trade receivables collection period
- Trade payables payment period.

10.5.1 Current ratio and the acid test ratio

We will start by looking at the *current ratio*. This is a liquidity ratio that measures the relationship between current assets and short-term liabilities and is expressed as x:1. The formula is:

$$\text{Current ratio} = \frac{\text{Current assets}}{\text{Current liabilities}}$$

The *acid test ratio* (or *quick ratio*) is more stringent and measures the relationship between the liquid assets and short-term liabilities. We will define liquid assets as current assets minus inventories, which cannot be converted into cash at short notice. The formula is:

$$\text{Acid test ratio} = \frac{\text{Current assets} - \text{Inventories}}{\text{Current liabilities}}$$

Activity

Calculate Ted Baker's current ratio and acid test ratio for 2015/16 and 2014/15.

The figures you need are disclosed in Ted Baker's balance sheet (statement of financial position), so all you need to do is insert them into each formula. Check your answer against the following solution.

	2015/16		2014/15	

$$\text{Current ratio} = \frac{£191,334k}{£109,191k} = 1.75{:}1 \qquad \frac{£159,593k}{£91,088k} = 1.75{:}1$$

$$\text{Acid test ratio} = \frac{£191,334k - £125,323k}{£109,191k} = 0.60{:}1 \qquad \frac{£159,593k - £111,114k}{£91,088k} = 0.53{:}1$$

The results demonstrate that these liquidity ratios are stable. In 2015/16 there was £1.75 of current assets for every £1 of current liabilities and £0.60 of liquid assets for every £1 of current liabilities. You may think that because the acid test ratio is less than 1:1 Ted Baker would have difficulty in paying current creditors. However, trade payables at the end of the year will be due at different times in the next financial year and it is unlikely that all suppliers would demand immediate payment. It is important to recognize that companies in different business sectors operate effectively on different ratios. For example, Ted Baker is in the retail sector where most customers pay for goods with cash or on their credit cards. Therefore, trade receivables (which are part of current assets) are relatively low compared to trade payables (which are part of current liabilities).

Another reason why a ratio of less than 1:1 is not always cause for concern is that the accounts are prepared on a prudent basis. This means that all possible costs and losses are accrued even if the amounts are based on estimates. It is also good funds management to give a shorter credit period to customers than agreed with suppliers. For example, some businesses give their customers 30 days' credit, but negotiate 90 days' credit from their suppliers. Such a trading policy would result in lower trade receivables than trade payables. It is difficult to generalize about ideal levels of liquidity, but in many industries there are benchmarks of what is considered to be a good acid test ratio.

10.5.2 Inventory holding period

The *inventory holding period* is an efficiency ratio that measures the average period between purchase and sale (or use) of inventory over the year. We will use a formula that calculates the ratio in months:

$$\text{Inventory holding period} = \frac{\text{Inventory}}{\text{Cost of sales}} \quad [\times \text{ 12 for months}]$$

Ideally we should use the average inventory:

$$\frac{\text{Opening inventory} + \text{Closing inventory}}{2}$$

Since closing inventory for one year is opening inventory for the next, we would be able to calculate Ted Baker's average inventory for 2015/16. However, because companies do not have to disclose their opening inventory for the previous year, we have a problem using this formula. Therefore, we will define inventory as closing inventory to allow us to compare the ratios for the two years.

Activity

Calculate Ted Baker's inventory holding period for 2015/16 and 2014/15.

You need to identify the figures for inventories in Ted Baker's Group Balance Sheet (otherwise known as the statement of financial position) and the cost of sales figures from the Group Income Statement (otherwise known as the statement of profit or loss). Check your answer against the following solution.

	2015/16	2014/15
Inventory holding period	$= \dfrac{£125,323k}{£183,147k} \times 12 = 8.21$ months	$\dfrac{£111,114k}{£152,359k} \times 12 = 8.75$ months

In general, the shorter the period inventories are held the better as this reduces storage costs and the risk of damage, wastage and obsolescence. This must be balanced against the risk of running out of inventory. The results show a slight improvement in 2015/16 because management has moved inventory a little faster than the previous year. In both years, you can see that on average it took around 8 months to sell (or use) the inventories. To some extent, this is likely to reflect the length of the Spring/Summer and Autumn/Winter fashion seasons, although some of Ted Baker's product ranges may be unaffected by seasonal changes.

10.5.3 Trade receivables collection period

The *trade receivables collection period* is an efficiency ratio that measures the average time customers took to pay for goods and services bought on credit over the year. Ideally we should use the average of opening and closing trade receivables, but because we do not have the opening receivables for the previous year, we will use closing receivables to allow us to compare the ratios for the two years. We will use a formula that calculates the ratio in months:

$$\text{Trade receivables collection period} = \frac{\text{Trade receivables}}{\text{Revenue}} \times 12$$

Activity

Calculate Ted Baker's trade receivables collection period for 2015/16 and 2014/15.

You will find the data you need for trade receivables in Note 15 on page 91 of Ted Baker's Annual Report and Accounts 2015/16 and you have already identified the figure for revenue in an earlier activity. Check your answer against the following solution.

	2015/16	**2014/15**

$$\text{Trade receivables collection period} = \frac{£30,136\text{k}}{£456,169\text{k}} \times 12 = 0.79 \text{ months} \qquad \frac{£25,823\text{k}}{£387,564\text{k}} \times 12 = 0.80 \text{ months}$$

In any business that gives customers credit, the credit controller should collect the money owed as quickly as possible so that it does not have an adverse effect on cash flow. The results for Ted Baker show no significant change and the average period customers took to settle their debts was less than one month in both years. If the Group's policy is to give customers one month's credit, then this suggests management has an efficient system of credit control. However, we would want to confirm this assumption before drawing firm conclusions.

10.5.4 Trade payables payment period

The *trade payables payment period* is an efficiency ratio that measures the average time the business took to pay for goods and services purchased on credit from trade suppliers over the year. If all the figures were available, we would use the average of opening and closing trade payables, but we will use closing payables instead as this will allow us to compare the ratios for the two years. Ideally we should divide it by purchases, but as this figure is not disclosed we will use cost of sales. This is an inferior proxy because it is affected by fluctuations in inventory levels, but as long as we are consistent, it is possible to draw conclusions from it. We use a formula that calculates the ratio in months:

$$\text{Trade payables payment period} = \frac{\text{Trade payables}}{\text{Cost of sales}} \times 12$$

Activity

Calculate Ted Baker's trade payables payment period for 2015/16 and 2014/15.

You will find the data you need for trade payables in Note 18 on page 92 in Ted Baker's Annual Report and Accounts 2015/16 and you have already identified the figure for cost of sales in an earlier activity. Check your answer against the following solution.

	2015/16	**2014/15**

$$\text{Trade payables payment period} = \frac{£31,657\text{k}}{£183,147\text{k}} \times 12 = 2.07 \text{ months} \qquad \frac{£32,241\text{k}}{£152,359\text{k}} \times 12 = 2.54 \text{ months}$$

The interpretation of the results depends on the length of credit period agreed with trade suppliers. If Ted Baker had a credit period of two months in 2015/16, then the result for that year shows good funds management because the Group is making maximum use of the credit period. However, we would want to confirm this assumption before drawing firm conclusions. Exceeding the credit period can be interpreted as bad financial management because suppliers are likely to charge interest on late payment and/or reduce the period granted. The higher average trade payables payment period in 2014/15 may indicate that Ted Baker had negotiated a longer credit period with suppliers at that time. As you can see, it is difficult to interpret the results without knowing the average credit period granted by suppliers.

Some people do not like getting into debt and prefer to pay invoices straight away, rather than wait until they are due. However, this is not a good way to manage cash because receiving goods and services on credit is equivalent to being given an interest-free loan. In a business context, if suppliers do not give credit, the business may have to go into overdraft to pay cash for the goods and services. This does not mean that a business should wait until it receives a solicitor's letter or risks supplies being cut off, but management should take the maximum time allowed to pay suppliers.

If we had the data, it would be useful to analyze all the liquidity and efficiency ratios for Ted Baker over a longer period of time to identify the trend. We could also extend our understanding by conducting a competitor analysis and compare the ratios for Ted Baker with those of similar businesses and with industry benchmarks.

10.6 Solvency ratios

Solvency ratios are used to evaluate the long-term ability of a business to generate cash internally or externally to meet its long-term liabilities. The financial structure of a business can have an impact on its financial performance and solvency ratios are used by investors and lenders to assess financial risk when a business has an obligation to service and repay long-term debt. The following are the two main ratios used:

- Debt/equity
- Interest cover.

10.6.1 Debt/equity ratio (gearing)

The *debt/equity ratio* (or *gearing*) reflects the relationship between equity finance and long-term debt finance in the business. The *debt/equity ratio* focuses on the statement of financial position and describes the financial structure of the business in terms of the proportion of long-term debt to shareholders' funds. There are a number of ways in which *debt* can be defined, but we will define it as non-current liabilities. The ratio is shown as a percentage and can be calculated using the following formula:

$$\text{Debt/equity ratio} = \frac{\text{Non-current liabilities}}{\text{Equity}} \quad [\times\ 100\ \text{for}\ \%]$$

Activity

Calculate Ted Baker's debt/equity ratio for 2015/16 and 2014/15.

You should have had little difficulty with this, as both figures are shown in Ted Baker's Group Balance Sheet. Check your answer against the following solution.

	2015/16	**2014/15**
Debt/equity ratio =	$\dfrac{£58,556\text{k}}{£172,599\text{k}} \times 100 = 33.93\%$	$\dfrac{£0\text{k}}{£140,547\text{k}} \times 100 = 0\%$

The general interpretation of this ratio is that the higher the gearing, the higher the risk that the business will be unable to pay the interest on its loans or make repayments when profits are low. On the other hand, the higher the gearing, the higher the returns will be to shareholders in strong economic conditions. The results for Ted Baker show that in 2015/16 the Group had £33.93 of long-term debt for every £100 of equity compared with none in the previous year. To analyze the potential risk to lenders and investors, we need to calculate the interest cover.

10.6.2 Interest cover

Interest cover is a gearing ratio that assesses the relative safety of interest payments by measuring the number of times interest payable on long-term debt is covered by the available profits. This avoids problems relating to the different ways in which debt can be defined. The ratio can be calculated using the following formula:

$$\text{Interest cover} = \frac{\text{Operating profit}}{\text{Interest payable}}$$

Activity

Calculate Ted Baker's interest cover for 2015/16 and 2014/15.

Interest payable is one of the finance expenses and you will find the data you need in Note 4 on page 56 in Ted Baker's Annual Report and Accounts 2015/16. You have already identified the operating profit in an earlier activity so this should be straight-forward. Check your answer against the following solution.

2015/16	2014/15

$$\text{Interest cover} = \frac{£59,369\text{k}}{£1,430\text{k}} = 41.52 \text{ times} \qquad \frac{£49,759\text{k}}{£1,184\text{k}} = 42.03 \text{ times}$$

There is no significant change because the increased finance costs in 2015/16 were offset by the increased operating profit. In both years, the interest payable was covered by operating profit more than 40 times, which seems very safe. Therefore, the risk to lenders and other creditors that Ted Baker is unable to service its debts is low.

   If we had the data, it would be useful to analyze the gearing ratios we have cal-culated for Ted Baker over a longer period of time to identify the trend. We could also extend our understanding by conducting a competitor analysis and compare the ratios for Ted Baker with those of similar businesses and with industry benchmarks.

10.7 Trend analysis

We have mentioned several times how useful it would be if we had the data to calcu-late the ratios for more than two years. Most companies provide five-year summaries of key figures in the notes to the financial statements in their annual reports and accounts. This makes it possible to conduct a *trend analysis* (or *horizontal analysis*). A simple approach is to calculate the percentage change in a key figure year on year. The general formula is:

$$\frac{\text{This year's figure} - \text{Last year's figure}}{\text{Last year's figure}} \times 100$$

We will illustrate this using data relating to Ted Baker's operating profit which we have taken from the Group's annual reports and accounts over the past 11 years.

Operating profit (£'000)

2006	2007	2008	2009	2010	2011	2012	2013	2014	2015	2016
18,334	20,049	22,142	17,161	19,782	24,132	24,269	29,514	39,588	49,759	59,369

Activity

Calculate the change in Ted Baker's operating profit for the years 2007 and 2008.

All you need to do is insert the appropriate figures into the formula. Start by calculating the change in operating profit in 2007 since 2006, then the change between 2008 and 2007. Check your answer against the following solution.

$$\text{Change in 2007} = \frac{£20,049k - £18,334k}{£18,334k} \times 100 = 9\%$$

$$\text{Change in 2008} = \frac{£22,142k - £20,049k}{£20,049k} \times 100 = 10\%$$

As you can see, there has been an improvement of 1%, but this is not sufficient to show the trend. This horizontal analysis is much more useful if we examine the change over five to ten years. Figure 10.3 shows the percentage change in operating profit for Ted Baker over the ten-year period 2007 to 2016.

Figure 10.3 Ted Baker percentage change in operating profit: 2007–2016

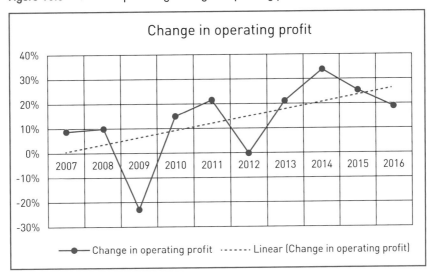

While the drop in net profit margin in 2009 was due to the downturn in the economy, the decrease in 2012 was due to reinvesting in the company's future. As you can see, since 2012 there has been a steady improvement. The dotted line shows the linear change and confirms an upward trajectory.

10.8 Limitations of ratio analysis

The choice of ratios calculated for a financial statement analysis depends on the needs of the user and the availability of the data. It is very easy to focus most of your attention on calculating the ratios, but you need to remember that the interpretation of the results needs to be made in the context of all the available information. As a student, this will be limited to the data you are given in an exam question or the information you can gather from the company's website and other sources on the Internet if your analysis is part of an assignment. The main *limitations* of ratio analysis are as follows:

- There are no agreed definitions of the terms used, so ratios based on different definitions will not be comparable.
- Data needed to calculate the ratios may not be disclosed and less precise alternatives may have to be used.
- Comparative data may not be available for previous periods (e.g. trend analysis is not possible for a new business).
- Care must be taken when comparing ratios with those of competitors as they may have adopted different accounting policies in respect of depreciation or valuation of inventory for example.
- Comparative data may not be available for competitors (e.g. the business may occupy a niche market or industry benchmarks may not be available).
- Ratios can be misinterpreted if all the evidence is not available. For example, a decrease in the gross profit margin may be interpreted as poor management, but it may have been due to a deliberate policy to reduce selling prices to increase revenue or a downturn in the economy having an adverse effect on sales.
- Ratio analysis does not take account of non-financial factors, such as whether the business has sound plans for the future, a good reputation, a strong customer base, reliable suppliers, loyal employees, obsolete assets, strong competitors, poor industrial relations, activities in a high risk industry or the business environment. As a result, financial analysts and investors are unlikely to focus solely on financial statement analysis, but will take account of information about the general economic conditions and expectations, political events and political climate, and industry and company outlooks.

If you are required to comment on the limitations of your analysis, be sure to focus on the specific constraints you faced, which may not include all of the above. Any discussion of the limitations of ratio analysis would be incomplete without linking them to the limitations of financial statements. The main limitations of general purpose financial statements are as follows:

- To a large extent, financial statements are based on estimates, judgements and models rather than exact depictions.
- Figures in financial statements can be misleading if there is high inflation or unscrupulous manipulation. However, if an unusual accounting treatment has been used, the figures for earlier years are adjusted in published trends.
- There is a substantial degree of classification and aggregation in the financial statements and the effect of allocating continuous operations to the reporting period.
- Financial statements only contain quantitative data.
- They do not focus on any non-financial effects of transactions or events.
- They do not reflect future transactions or events that may enhance or impair the entity's operations.
- They do not anticipate the impact of potential changes in the economic environment.

Despite these drawbacks, ratio analysis is a valuable tool for appraising general purpose financial statements. Nevertheless, users should not treat ratios as absolute answers, but as an indication of where further investigation might be directed to better understand the present and future financial performance and position.

10.9 Conclusions

In this chapter we have examined a technique for analyzing the financial statements of a business known as ratio analysis. This type of analysis is widely used by management, investors, lenders and creditors, as well as major customers, investment analysts and financial journalists. We have described a number of the main investment, profitability, liquidity, efficiency and gearing ratios.

In order to interpret ratios effectively, there needs to be some basis of comparison. This can be between businesses in the same industrial sector or a particular business and the industry benchmark. Comparison of ratios relating to the current period and the preceding period for a particular business are useful. However, a horizontal analysis that examines the percentage change in key financial figures over five to ten years is more reliable because it can indicate the trend. Ultimately the choice of analysis depends on the needs of the user and the availability of the data. In this chapter we have considered the main limitations of ratio analysis, but despite some drawbacks, you need to remember that this method of interpreting financial statements is one of the most useful and commonly used techniques in the financial world.

References

IASB (2003) IAS 33, *Earnings Per Share*, London: International Accounting Standards Board.

Ted Baker (2016) *Ted Baker Plc Annual Report and Accounts 2015–16*. Available at: www.tedbakerplc.com/investor-relations/results-and-reports/2016 (Accessed 11 May 2016).

Discussion questions

1 Discuss the purpose of ratio analysis and its limitations as a tool for evaluating the financial statements of a business.

Practice questions

2 The following figures are taken from the statement of financial position at 30 June 2016 and the notes to the accounts of Vita Ltd.

	£
Inventories	217,540
Trade receivables	188,600
Cash and cash equivalents	3,200
Trade payables	221,300

The company belongs to a trade association which conducts an annual survey of its members and publishes industry averages for the sector. The liquidity ratio benchmarks for 2017 were:

Current ratio	1.62:1
Acid test ratio	0.93:1

Required

(a) Calculate the current ratio and the acid test ratio for Vita Ltd, showing the formulae and all your workings.

(b) In addition, decide which of the following statements is correct:
  (i) Vita Ltd's current ratio and acid test ratio are lower than the industry benchmark.
  (ii) Vita Ltd's current ratio is lower than the industry benchmark, but the acid test ratio is higher.
  (iii) Vita Ltd's current ratio and acid test ratio are higher than the industry benchmark.
  (iv) Vita Ltd's current ratio is higher than the industry benchmark, but the acid test ratio is lower.

3 The following information has been extracted from the financial statements of Adams Ltd and Evelyn Ltd.

	Adams Ltd	Evelyn Ltd
	£	£
Revenue	354,900	706,260
Gross profit	71,400	156,200
Operating profit	29,500	41,500
Capital employed	281,000	596,000

Required

(a) Calculate the main profitability ratios for both companies.
(b) Suggest reasons for any differences you find.

4 The following information is taken from Ted Baker's Report and Accounts 2012/13.

Group Income Statement For the 52 weeks ended 26 January 2013	Note	52 weeks ended 26 January 2013 £'000	52 weeks ended 26 January 2012 £'000
Revenue	2	254,466	215,625
Cost of sales		(95,740)	(83,419)
Gross profit		**158,726**	**132,206**
Distribution costs		(101,357)	(82,358)
Administrative expenses		(32,984)	(29,640)
Exceptional costs		(2,614)	(2,814)
Licence income		7,509	6,733
Other operating income		234	142
Operating profit		**29,514**	**24,269**
Finance income	4	34	45
Finance expenses	4	(824)	(208)
Share of profit of jointly controlled entity, net of tax	12	198	149
Profit before tax	3,6	**28,922**	**24,255**
Income tax expense	6	(7,325)	(6,698)
Profit for the period			**17,557**

Group Statement of Comprehensive Income For the 52 weeks ended 26 January 2013	Note	52 weeks ended 26 January 2013 £'000	52 weeks ended 26 January 2012 £'000
Profit for the period		**21,597**	**17,557**
Other comprehensive income			
Net effective portion of changes in fair value of cash flow hedges		(320)	(190)
Net change in fair value of cash flow hedges transferred to profit or loss		723	26
Exchange differences on foreign operations net of tax		152	(92)
Other comprehensive income for the period		**555**	**(256)**
Total comprehensive income for the period			**17,301**

Group Balance Sheet At 26 January 2013	Note	26 January 2013 £'000	26 January 2012 £'000
Non-current assets			
Intangible assets	10	983	968
Property, plant and equipment	11	45,412	35,680
Investment in equity accounted investee	12	693	494
Deferred tax assets	13	4,523	3,418
Prepayments		674	695
		52,285	41,255

(Continued)

Current assets			
Inventories	14	67,673	51,872
Trade and other receivables	15	34,124	30,587
Amount due from equity accounted investee	12	225	407
Derivative financial assets	16	544	411
Cash and cash equivalents	17	9,823	8,560
		112,389	**91,837**
Current liabilities			
Trade and other payables	18	(40,793)	(35,281)
Bank overdraft	17	(19,862)	(6,790)
Income tax payable		(4,360)	(3,353)
Derivative financial liabilities	16	(269)	(1,063)
			(46,487)
Non-current liabilities			
Deferred tax liabilities	13	(497)	(1,420)
			(1,420)
Net assets			**85,185**
Equity			
Share capital	19	2,160	2,160
Share premium account	19	9,137	9,137
Other reserves	19	91	(312)
Translation reserve	19	296	144
Retained earnings	19	87,209	74,056
Total equity attributable to equity shareholders of the parent company		98,893	85,185
Non-controlling interest			
Total equity		—	—
			85,185

Selected notes to the financial statements	26 January 2013	26 January 2012
4 Of which, interest payable (£'000)	646	(208)
8 Total dividends for the period (£'000)	11,328	9,744
9 Weighted number of ordinary shares ('000)	43,282	41,637
15 Of which, trade receivables (£'000)	19,529	19,744
18 Of which, trade payables (£'000)	(22,097)	15,910
20 Maximum risk free interest rate (%)	4.60	4.70
Market share price at year end from company website (pence)	1,185	745

Required

Calculate the following ratios for 2012/13 and 2011/12. In each case, include the formula in words, your workings and append brief comments that explain the purpose of the ratio and an interpretation of the results.

(a) Dividend per share

(b) Dividend yield

(c) Earnings per share
(d) Price-earnings
(e) Return on equity
(f) Return on capital employed
(g) Operating profit margin
(h) Capital turnover

5 This question also refers to the information from Ted Baker's Report and Accounts 2012/13 given in Question 4.

Required

Calculate the following ratios for 2012/13 and 2011/12. In each case, include the formula in words, your workings and append brief comments that explain the purpose of the ratio and an interpretation of the results.

(a) Current ratio
(b) Acid test
(c) Inventory holding period
(d) Trade receivables collection period
(e) Trade payables payment period.
(f) Debt/equity
(g) Interest cover

6 The following information is taken from Ted Baker's Report and Accounts 2014/15.

GROUP INCOME STATEMENT FOR THE 52 WEEKS ENDED 31 JANUARY 2015	NOTE	52 WEEKS ENDED 31 JANUARY 2015	52 WEEKS ENDED 25 JANUARY 2014
		£'000	£'000
Revenue	2	387,564	321,921
Cost of sales		(152,359)	(123,451)
GROSS PROFIT		**235,205**	**198,470**
Distribution costs		(144,584)	(123,211)
Administrative expenses		(51,034)	(43,381)
Exceptional costs	3	(5,339)	(1,046)
Licence income		11,665	8,888
Other operating (expense)/income		(812)	(132)
Exceptional income	3	4,658	–
OPERATING PROFIT		**49,759**	**39,588**
Finance income	4	108	316
Finance expenses	4	(1,621)	(1,312)
Share of profit of jointly controlled entity, net of tax	12	525	331
PROFIT BEFORE TAX	3	**48,771**	**38,923**
Income tax expense	6	(12,921)	(10,071)
PROFIT FOR THE PERIOD		**35,850**	**28,852**

(Continued)

GROUP STATEMENT OF COMPREHENSIVE INCOME

FOR THE 52 WEEKS ENDED 30 JANUARY 2015	52 WEEKS ENDED 31 JANUARY 2015	52 WEEKS ENDED 25 JANUARY 2014
	£'000	£'000
PROFIT FOR THE PERIOD	35,850	28,852
OTHER COMPREHENSIVE INCOME		
Net effective portion of changes in fair value of cash flow hedges	1,328	(2,486)
Net change in fair value of cash flow hedges transferred to profit or loss	1,890	545
Exchange differences on foreign operations net of tax	2,692	(3,276)
OTHER COMPREHENSIVE INCOME FOR THE PERIOD	5,910	(5,217)
TOTAL COMPREHENSIVE INCOME FOR THE PERIOD	41,760	23,635

GROUP BALANCE SHEET
AT 30 JANUARY 2015

	NOTE	31 JANUARY 2015	25 JANUARY 2014
		£'000	£'000
Intangible assets	10	12,855	6,080
Property, plant and equipment	11	51,804	45,083
Investment in equity accounted investee	12	1,290	1,024
Deferred tax assets	13	5,659	4,450
Prepayments		461	564
NON-CURRENT ASSETS		72,069	57,201
Inventories	14	111,114	80,432
Trade and other receivables	15	36,873	34,793
Amount due from equity accounted investee	12	679	164
Derivative financial assets	16	3,547	499
Cash and cash equivalents	17	7,380	28,521
CURRENT ASSETS		159,593	144,409
Trade and other payables	18	(57,046)	(45,289)
Bank overdraft	17	(26,204)	(37,282)
Income tax payable		(7,202)	(3,857)
Derivative financial liabilities	16	(636)	(3,118)
CURRENT LIABILITIES		(91,088)	(89,546)
NON-CURRENT LIABILITIES		0	0
NET ASSETS		140,574	112,064
EQUITY			
Share capital	19	2,196	2,194
Share premium account	19	9,331	9,139
Other reserves	19	1,368	(1,850)
Translation reserve	19	(288)	(2,980)
Retained earnings	19	127,967	105,561
TOTAL EQUITY ATTRIBUTABLE TO EQUITY SHAREHOLDERS OF THE PARENT COMPANY		140,574	112,064
TOTAL EQUITY		140,574	112,064

SELECTED NOTES TO THE FINANCIAL STATEMENTS	31 JANUARY 2015	25 JANUARY 2014
4 Of which, interest payable (£'000)	(1,184)	(1,279)
8 Total dividends for the period (£'000)	17,679	14,711
9 Weighted number of ordinary shares ('000)	43,703	42,960
15 Of which, trade receivables (£'000)	25,823	23,105
18 Of which, trade payables (£'000)	(32,241)	(22,049)
20 Maximum risk free interest rate (%)	2.77	2.77
Market share price at year end from company website (pence)	2,141.0	2,111.0

Required

You work for a firm of investment analysts and your manager asks you to conduct a financial analysis to help clients monitor their investments in Ted Baker Plc. Calculate appropriate ratios for 2014/15 and 2013/14 showing the formulae and all your workings. In each case, explain the purpose of the ratio and interpret your results. Include brief comments on any change in the risks and rewards to investors over the period.

7 Now imagine that you work for the bank that provides finance to Ted Baker Plc. Your manager asks you to conduct a financial analysis to help the bank monitor the lending risks and returns.

Required

Calculate appropriate ratios for 2014/15 and 2013/14 showing the formulae and all your workings. In each case, explain the purpose of the ratio and interpret your results. Include brief comments on any change in the lending risk over the period. In addition, describe the limitations of the analysis you have conducted.

8 Imagine that you work for a competitor of Ted Baker. Your manager gives you the following summary of key statistics for Ted Baker for the five years 2011/12 to 2015/16.

KEY STATISTICS	2011/12	2012/13	2013/14	2014/15	2015/16
Investment ratios					
Dividend per share (pence)	23.40	26.17	34.24	40.45	47.82
Dividend yield	3.14%	2.21%	1.62%	1.89%	1.59%
Dividend cover (times)	1.80	1.91	1.96	2.03	2.10
Basic EPS (pence)	42.17	49.90	67.16	82.03	100.65
Price/earnings (years)	17.67	23.75	31.43	26.10	29.90
Profitability ratios					
Return on equity	20.61%	21.84%	25.75%	25.50%	25.63%
Return on capital employed	28.02%	29.70%	35.33%	35.40%	25.68%
Capital turnover (times)	2.49	2.56	2.87	2.76	1.97
Operating profit margin	11.26%	11.60%	12.30%	12.84%	13.01%
Gross profit margin	61.31%	62.38%	61.65%	60.69%	59.85%
Liquidity ratios					
Current ratio (:1)	1.98	1.72	1.61	1.75	1.75
Acid test ratio (:1)	0.86	0.68	0.71	0.53	0.60
Efficiency ratios					
Inventory holding period (months)	7.46	8.48	7.82	8.75	8.21
Trade receivables collection period (months)	1.10	0.92	0.86	0.80	0.79
Trade payables payment period (months)	2.29	2.77	2.14	2.54	2.07
Solvency ratios					
Debt/equity (gearing)	1.67%	0.50%	0.00%	0.00%	33.93%
Interest cover (times)	116.68	45.69	30.95	42.03	41.52

Required

Write a short report that identifies the strengths and weaknesses of the company as revealed by this five-year summary. Conclude with a discussion of the benefits and limitations of ratio analysis.

 Suggested research questions for dissertation students

Components of earnings that are used in ratio analysis can be manipulated. For example, depreciation is more easily 'managed' than revenue. Students interested in earnings management may wish to investigate one or more of the following research questions:

- What is the propensity for companies to manage earnings in [country]?

- Do corporate governance mechanisms increase financial reporting quality?

Preliminary reading

Burgstahler, D. and Dichev, I. (1997) 'Earnings management to avoid earnings decreases and losses', *Journal of Accounting and Economics*, 24, pp. 99–129.

Cornett, M., Marcus, A. and Tehranian, H. (2008) 'Corporate governance and pay-for-performance: The impact of earnings management', *Journal of Financial Economics*, 87, pp. 357–373.

Dechow, P., Ge, W. and Schrand, C. (2010) 'Understanding earnings quality: A review of the proxies, their determinants and their consequences', *Journal of Accounting & Economics*, 50(2/3), pp. 344–401.

Dechow, P., Sloan, R. and Sweeney, A. (1995) 'Detecting earnings management', *The Accounting Review*, 70, pp. 3–42.

Healy, P. and Wahlen, J. M. (1999) 'A review of the earnings management literature and its implications for standard setting', *Accounting Horizons*, 13(4), pp. 365–383.

Klein, A. (2002) 'Audit Committee, board of director characteristics and earnings management', *Journal of Accounting and Economics*, 33, pp. 375–400.

Rohen, J. and Yaari, V. (2015) 'Earnings management: Implications and controversies', in Jones, S. (ed.), *The Routledge Companion to Financial Accounting Theory*, pp. 254–340.

11 Corporate governance, stewardship, social responsibility and integrated reporting

Learning objectives

When you have studied this chapter, you should be able to:

- Explain the purpose of corporate governance
- Describe the requirements of the UK Corporate Governance Code
- Discuss the principles of the UK Stewardship Code
- Explain the role of corporate social responsibility reporting
- Discuss the need for integrated reporting

11.1 Introduction

In previous chapters we explained that financial reporting refers to the statutory disclosure of general purpose financial information by limited liability entities via the annual report and accounts. We also discussed the need for a regulatory framework to guide this important activity. The regulatory framework for financial reporting in the UK has three main elements: company law, accounting standards and, for listed companies, stock exchange rules. While high quality financial reporting is vitally important, many users are also interested in receiving information about whether a reporting entity has followed governance standards, whether its board of directors has adequately overseen the actions of management, how the entity has approached its environmental and social responsibilities.

This chapter focuses on a number of mechanisms that have been developed to meet these information needs. Corporate governance and stewardship are primarily concerned with the way in which the directors are managing the resources for the benefit of the investors, whereas corporate social responsibility focuses on the expectations that investors, consumers and other stakeholders have that the company is being managed in a sustainable and socially responsible manner. Corporate governance, stewardship and corporate social reporting are often considered together because they relate to how well the entity is managed and how successful management is in communicating this. However, separate reports on these matters within the annual report and accounts can only provide a partial picture of how the entity adds economic, social and environmental value. This has led to calls for an integrated report that provides a concise communication about value creation over time and covers the entity's strategy, governance, performance and prospects.

11.2 Corporate governance

In Chapter 4 we explained that the annual report and accounts allows investors to assess how effectively and efficiently the directors have discharged their responsibilities; in other words, it provides information that helps investors assess the stewardship of the directors who manage the business on their behalf. In this stewardship role, the board of directors establishes the culture, values and ethics of the company and creates a system by which the entity is directed and controlled. *Corporate governance* refers to 'the system by which companies are directed and controlled. Boards of directors are responsible for the governance of their companies. The shareholders' role in governance is to appoint the directors and the auditors and to satisfy themselves that an appropriate governance structure is in place. The responsibilities of the board include setting the company's strategic aims, providing the leadership to put them into effect, supervising the management of the business and reporting to shareholders on their stewardship. The board's actions are subject to laws, regulations and the shareholders in general meeting' (Cadbury, 1992, p. 15). The *purpose* of corporate governance is to facilitate effective management that can deliver the long-term success of the company.

The key relationship in corporate governance is between the company and its shareholders, not between the company and regulatory agencies. As a result, a company's board and its shareholders should theoretically engage in a positive and transparent dialogue about corporate governance issues, and not merely seek to provide the minimum disclosures allowed under the regulations. While the regulatory framework gives investors the right to receive corporate governance information, the way this information is communicated is often influenced by the relationship that the Board has with its shareholders. In the 1990s, many UK public companies used generic or 'boilerplate' disclosures where the corporate governance information provided was almost meaningless. More recently, disclosures have generally become more transparent and informative due to shareholder demand (Grant Thornton, 2013).

> **Key definition**
>
> Corporate governance is the system by which companies are directed and controlled by the directors, and the nature of their accountability to the investors.

The UK's long tradition in developing guidelines for corporate governance started with the publication of the *Cadbury Report* in 1992, which established a voluntary code of practice for UK public companies. Over the next 25 years, this code was developed and expanded into the current *UK Corporate Governance Code* (FRC, 2016). The UK Corporate Governance Code (UK CG Code) is issued by the *Financial Reporting Council (FRC)*. You will remember from Chapter 4 that the FRC is the independent regulator responsible for promoting confidence in financial reporting and corporate governance. The UK CG Code sets out principles of best practice for board leadership and effectiveness, remuneration, accountability and relations with shareholders.

In the UK, the regulation of corporate governance adopts the principle of code not law. It sets out a non-prescriptive set of best practice principles and provisions, but recognizes that companies are different and allows them to adapt provisions according to specific company needs. Rather than being a rigid set of rules, the UK CG Code provides a set of general principles that allows companies a flexible 'comply or explain' approach on how to apply them. Companies are required to apply the main principles and report to shareholders on how they have done so. A company is permitted to depart from following a provision if good governance can be achieved by other means. However, the company's reasons for each departure must be clearly explained to shareholders and must illustrate how the alternate practices are consistent with the principle to which the provision relates, contribute to good governance and fulfil business objectives.

The main elements of the UK regulatory framework for corporate governance are:

- legislation, particularly CA 2006
- the Listing Rules, the Disclosure and Transparency Rules, and the Prospectus Rules, all of which are issued and enforced by the *Financial Conduct Authority* (FCA) as the UK Listing Authority
- the UK Corporate Governance Code and the UK Stewardship Code for institutional shareholders, which are issued by the FRC
- the Takeover Code, which is issued and administered by the Takeover Panel.

The UK CG Code requires companies to disclose certain information, and provide an explanation where they choose not to comply with a specific disclosure. Certain types of company that are listed on the *London Stock Exchange* (LSE) are required by the FCA to report on how they have applied the main principles of the UK CG Code in their annual report and accounts. If they have not complied with the CG Code, they must explain their reasons.

While the Disclosure and Transparency Rules apply to all entities whose securities are traded on a regulated market, the specific requirements of the Listing Rules and UK CG Code only apply to issuers that have premium listed equity shares. A *premium listing* is only available for the equity shares of trading companies and certain investment entities. To obtain such a listing an entity is expected to comply with all UK regulations and as a direct consequence may enjoy a lower cost of capital through enhanced investor confidence. Private limited companies, and those public companies without a premium listing, may comply with certain aspects of the UK CG Code on a voluntary basis.

Under Listing Rule 9.8.6 R, any domestic or overseas company with a premium listing of equity shares, must include a corporate governance statement within the annual report and accounts that provides:

- A statement of how the listed company has applied the main principles set out in the UK Corporate Governance Code, in a manner that would enable shareholders to evaluate how the principles have been applied.
- A statement as to whether the listed company has complied with all relevant provisions set out in the UK CG Code or not complied with all relevant provisions set out in the UK CG Code.
- If the latter, a statement describing the provisions it has not complied with and the company's reasons for non-compliance.

Where a public company does not have a premium listing of equity shares, the Disclosure and Transparency Rules require the entity to produce a corporate governance statement. This must be either included in the directors' report, in a separate report published together with the annual report, or on the issuer's website. The company must reference the corporate governance codes to which the company is subject and, where it deviates from that code, it must explain the departures, giving reasons.

Public companies without a premium listing on the LSE (the main market) can adopt the *Corporate Governance Code for Small and Mid-Size Quoted Companies* issued by the Quoted Companies Alliance (QCA, 2013). The QCA Code is endorsed by the FRC and adopts key elements of the UK CG Code and other relevant guidance to derive a corporate governance code suitable for the needs of small and mid-size quoted companies on a public market, including standard listed companies and those on the Alternative Investment Market (AIM). The QCA Code is based on 12 principles, and recommends that companies include a corporate governance statement in their financial statements and/or their website. As with the main UK CG Code, the QCA Code uses a 'comply or explain' approach, which encourages companies to consider how they should apply its principles to achieve good governance, and provide quality explanations about what they have done.

While all UK public listed companies must produce a corporate governance statement, private companies have no such requirement, even though they represent the majority of the UK's registered companies. Despite this, the owners and managers of private companies should still adhere to high standards of corporate governance to ensure the growth and long-term success of their businesses. In order to help UK private companies to construct an effective corporate governance framework, the Institute of Directors (IoD, 2010) published *Corporate Governance Guidance and Principles for Unlisted Companies in the UK*, which sets out 14 voluntary principles for good governance for unlisted companies. These take into account the size, complexity and level of maturity of individual entities, and provide a framework through which unlisted companies can bring external parties to their boards, attract funds, and solve issues between shareholders and other stakeholders.

In terms of the corporate governance requirements for public companies, there is considerable overlap between the mandatory disclosures required by the Disclosure and Transparency Rules and those expected under the UK CG Code. As a result, the remainder of this chapter will concentrate on explaining the requirements and disclosures for public companies under the UK CG Code.

Activity

What are the advantages of allowing a premium listed company to select which parts of the UK CG Code it will comply with?

You may not have thought that the flexibility this offers is an advantage because you may feel that a premium listed company should not be allowed to decide which of the UK CG Code's requirements to follow. However, consider the following case. At present the FRC only requires companies in the FTSE 350 to comply with the annual director re-election provision, but management may consider this is not appropriate if they are engaged in a takeover. Therefore, it would be acceptable for the company to explain rather than comply. Enforcement can be made by the FCA, but the UK CG Code will continue to be enforced primarily by the shareholders, through engagement and the use of legal rights, such as their voting rights. To this end, the FRC published *The UK Stewardship Code* (FRC, 2012b) with the aim of enhancing the quality of engagement between companies and their institutional investors. The UK Stewardship Code is complementary to the UK CG Code and provides additional emphasis to the concept of 'comply or explain' by providing a stronger link between governance and the investment process. We will discuss the Stewardship Code in more detail later on in this chapter.

In addition to the specific corporate governance disclosures required by the Listing Rules, Disclosure and Transparency Rules and the UK CG Code, CA 2006 requires that the board publish a directors' report and strategic report that provide additional governance information depending on the size of the entity. We discussed some of these requirements within Chapter 4, and will explain the disclosures related to environmental and social issues later in the chapter.

While the 'comply or explain' approach to regulating corporate governance is now the predominant approach in most worldwide jurisdictions, it is very different from the legalistic 'comply or else' approach used in certain jurisdictions. In the USA, for example, all domestic and overseas public companies that have securities (debt or equity) registered with the Securities and Exchange Commission (SEC) must comply with the mandatory corporate governance rules and requirements of the Sarbanes Oxley Act 2002, regardless of company size or circumstances.

Despite the non-prescriptive 'comply or explain' nature of the UK CG Code, levels of compliance with each of its provisions is high and steadily increasing over time. In a 2015 survey of the annual reports of 312 FTSE 350 companies, 57% complied in full with the UK CG Code, and 90% of companies complied with all but one or two of the Code's provisions (Grant Thornton, 2015, p.2).

Activity

Do you think compliance with the UK CG Code should be mandatory for all types of company?

It may occur to you that the main problem lies with the difference between principles and rules, a debate we have discussed in connection with international differences in the development of accounting standards. Ensuring that companies comply with the accounting regulatory framework is a key part of corporate governance and it is clear that the internal rules, systems and processes by which authority is exercised and controlled are also the mechanisms by which management is held to account. However, it should not be forgotten that corporate governance in non-publicly accountable smaller entities is equally important. Although the operations of such entities may be less complex, the business environment is not. Therefore, good corporate governance is still useful to ensure that they comply with the operational and financial reporting regulations. If the business is expanding its activities into unfamiliar operations or geographical sectors, it needs to have appropriate procedures in place to ensure that it is not penalized for non-compliance.

Before we discuss the development of the UK regulatory approach to corporate governance in more detail, we will examine how the UK CG Code has been influential in shaping and influencing international approaches to corporate governance.

11.3 International corporate governance codes

At an international level, the *Organisation for Economic Co-operation and Development* (OECD) developed a set of principles for best practice in corporate governance in 1999, which was revised in 2015. The *Principles of Corporate Governance* (OECD, 2015) focus on board responsibilities, disclosure and transparency requirements and the rights of shareholders in large PLCs. They help policymakers evaluate and improve the legal, regulatory and institutional framework for corporate governance, with the objective of supporting economic efficiency, sustainable growth and financial stability. They have become an international benchmark for policy makers, investors, corporations and other stakeholders, and have contributed to legislative and regulatory initiatives in a number of countries, including the UK.

The regulation of corporate governance in the EU comes from a range of principles and rules, including recommendations about the independence of non-executive directors, the structure of board committees and remuneration policy. In addition, EU Directives on takeover bids (2004/25/EC), transparency of listed companies (2013/50/EC), shareholders' rights (2007/36/EC), market abuse (2003/6/EC) and audit (2014/56/EC) have helped shape corporate governance in EU Member States. Article 20 of the Accounting Directive (Directive 2013/34/EU) requires public-interest entities to include a corporate governance statement in a separate section of the management report. This statement must include:

- details about the corporate governance code(s) that the entity has complied with;
- essential information about an entity's corporate governance arrangements, such as its:
  - internal control and risk management systems;
  - the shareholder meeting and its powers;
  - shareholders' rights; and
  - administrative, management and supervisory bodies and their committees;
- explanations of the reasons for any departure from a corporate governance code.

While the UK requires public companies to present their corporate governance statement within the annual report and accounts, other Member States allow the required information to be provided on a company's website. In terms of enforcement, the company's auditor must check that the required corporate governance information has been provided, and must also express an opinion as to whether the company has complied with applicable corporate governance requirements, especially with regard to the principle of 'comply or explain'.

From its original origins with the UK CG Code, the 'comply or explain' principle has now become a key feature of European corporate governance. According to this principle, companies that depart from a corporate governance code must explain in their corporate governance statement which parts of the code they depart from and the reasons for doing so. While the 'comply or explain' principle is widely supported by companies, investors and regulators throughout the EU, a 2011 Green Paper on EU corporate governance framework identified shortcomings in the way that the principle was being applied in practice, in particular as regards the quality of the explanations being provided by companies departing from corporate governance codes (EC, 2011a, b). Because of this, the EC initiated a 2012 Action Plan on corporate governance and company law, aimed at improving the quality of corporate governance reports and the quality of explanations in particular. This resulted in EC Recommendation 2014/208/EU which provides guidance to Member States for improving the overall quality of corporate governance reporting, and specifically, the quality of explanation provided by companies in cases of departure from a relevant corporate governance code (EC, 2014a).

Since its original publication in 1992, the UK CG Code has been copied or adapted for use in every Member State of the European Union and in more than 60 other countries worldwide (FRC, 2012a). The *European Corporate Governance Institute* (ECGI) maintains a database of worldwide corporate governance codes, and this lists over 400 national codes, code revisions or code-like publications, which illustrates the impact of corporate governance codes and the 'comply or explain' principle throughout the world.

Activity

Why do you think there is no EU code on corporate governance?

Despite the requirements of Accounting Directive (2013/34/EU), there is no standard format for corporate governance reporting throughout the EU. This may be explained by the presence of national differences in how companies are managed, financed and regulated. In Chapter 4, we discussed reasons for international differences in GAAP, and many of these reasons can be used to explain the lack of a single EU code on corporate governance. In addition, there is no single model of good corporate governance. For example, most UK companies are governed by a single management board or 'board of directors'. In contrast, German public companies commonly adopt a dual-board structure, which includes both a management and a supervisory board. As a result, the German Corporate Governance Code (the Kodex) includes specific requirements and provisions for the supervisory board that are not needed in the UK CG Code (Regierungskommission, 2015).

11.4 The UK Corporate Governance Code

The development of corporate governance guidance in the UK was a response to the financial scandals of the late 1980s and early 1990s, and a general lack of confidence in financial reporting. As a result, the FRC, LSE and the accountancy profession established the *Committee on the Financial Aspects of Corporate Governance*. In 1992 the Committee published the Cadbury Report, which established a set of principles which formed a code for good practice in corporate governance. The principles were enshrined into the Listing Rules of the LSE and formed a code of best practice for corporate governance for all listed companies. The Cadbury Report introduced the principle of 'comply or explain', whereby listed companies had to produce a narrative statement detailing the extent of their compliance with the code and an explanation if they had not complied with any of its principles.

Since the creation of the UK CG Code in 1992, a number of reports have been issued that have further developed and extended its original guidance. Many of these investigations were prompted by high profile financial scandals, such as the failure of the Enron Corporation in 2001 and the associated demise of Arthur Andersen, which had been one of the Big Five accountancy firms. In the US, this accounting scandal resulted in the Sarbanes-Oxley Act 2002. The Act requires all US public companies to submit an annual assessment of the effectiveness of their internal control systems to the SEC. It also requires the company's auditors to audit and report on the internal control reports produced by management, in the same way as they audit financial statements (Solomon, 2007). The UK government's response to Enron was to commission a 2003 review of the role and effectiveness of non-executive directors, with the aim of improving the existing Code. The same year, the FRC published its own report about audit committees. The recommendations from both reviews led to the revised 2003 version of the UK CG Code. Since then, the FRC has kept the Code under review, with regular revisions.

Following the 2007 global financial crisis, the FRC published a further major revision of the UK CG Code in 2010 that:

- reiterated the leadership role of the chairman and the key role of non-executive directors
- required boards to be externally evaluated at least once every three years
- made boards responsible for establishing the company's risk profile and required them to describe its business model in the annual report
- improved board accountability by requiring the directors of FTSE 350 listed companies to face annual re-election.

Of these changes, the requirement for directors to face annual re-election proved to be the most controversial, with certain companies explaining that this requirement was potentially disruptive to the effective functioning of the board.

Activity

Do you think directors of large public companies should face annual re-election by shareholders?

When this requirement was first announced, a number of the UK's largest institutional investors and pension funds announced that the annual re-election of directors was unnecessary and could damage the interests of their investee companies. Critics believed that the annual re-election of directors tempts directors to focus on short-term corporate performance in order to safeguard their position on the board. Furthermore, annual re-election may create boardroom instability, and make companies more vulnerable to shareholder activists wishing to influence company policies. The FRC's view was that the annual re-election of directors provided investors with more practical control over the composition of the board, reinforced discipline in boardrooms and encouraged long-term shareholders to exercise their additional voting rights responsibly to preserve the long-term value of their investments (Lovells, 2010).

Following the FRC's dissatisfaction with the poor quality of explanations by companies for non-compliance, further amendments were made to the UK CG Code in 2012, including:

- Companies should provide more detailed explanations to shareholders as to why they chose not to follow a provision.
- Audit committees must provide shareholders with information on how they have carried out their responsibilities, including how they assessed the effectiveness of the external audit process.
- Companies should explain their board's policy on diversity.

The UK CG Code's diversity requirement resulted from the *Davies Report*, which examined gender diversity on the boards of directors of UK's FTSE 100 companies (BIS, 2011). The results showed that women represented only 12.5% of board membership in 2010 and consequently companies were failing to draw from the widest possible range of managerial talent. The Davies Report recommended that all FTSE 100 companies aim for a minimum of 25% female representation by 2015. Accordingly, the FRC amended the UK CG Code to require listed companies to establish a policy concerning boardroom diversity. While no specific quota for women on boards is imposed, the UK CG Code requires boards to report on boardroom diversity. By October 2015, there were no longer any all-male boards among FTSE 100 companies, and they had all met the voluntary target of at least 25% of board members being women (BIS, 2015, p.2).

In 2014 the FRC addressed the information that investors receive about the long-term health and strategy of companies by requiring boards to produce a viability statement. The viability statement assesses the company's long-term solvency, liquidity and principal risks, and should cover the following issues:

- The directors should state whether it is appropriate to adopt the going concern basis of accounting and identify any material uncertainties to the company's ability to continue to do so.
- The directors should assess the company's principal risks and explain how they are being managed and mitigated.
- Companies should state whether they believe they will be able to continue in operation and meet their liabilities taking account of their current position and principal risks, and specify the period covered by this statement and why they consider it appropriate. It is expected that the period assessed will be significantly longer than 12 months.
- The board should monitor the company's risk management and internal control system and, at least annually, carry out a review of their effectiveness, and annually report on that review.

While the viability statement is expected to look forward significantly beyond the next year of trading, critics suggest that this is not always possible due to the ever-changing nature of the business environment.

In 2016 the FRC published a revised version of the UK CG Code, which applies to accounting periods beginning on or after 17 June 2016. The 2016 update incorporates the requirements of the Audit Directive (2014/56/EU) ('the Directive') and Audit Regulation (537/2014) ('the Regulation'), and now includes a requirement that the audit committee has competence relevant to the sector in which the company operates.

As we described earlier, premium listed companies are required to report on how they have applied the main principles of the UK CG Code, and either confirm that they have complied with its provisions or, where they have not, provide an explanation. The increased importance placed on corporate governance is evident in the ever-increasing number of pages devoted to this topic in the annual report and accounts.

In total, the 2016 UK CG Code includes 18 main principles and 55 provisions. While the principles apply to all premium listed companies, some of its provisions do not apply to smaller listed companies. As a result, companies outside the FTSE 350 do not have to comply with certain provisions, although many do so on a voluntary basis. In addition to its 'comply or explain' requirement, the UK CG Code requires a listed entity to provide the following 20 disclosures in its annual report and accounts:

1. A statement of how the board of directors operates, including a high level statement of which types of decisions are to be taken by the board and which are to be delegated to management.
2. The names of the chairman, the deputy chairman, the chief executive, the senior independent director, the chairmen and members of the board committees.
3. The individual attendance record for directors at board and committee meetings.
4. Where a chief executive is appointed chairman, the reasons for their appointment (this only needs to be done in the annual report following the appointment).
5. The names of the independent non-executive directors, with reasons where necessary to justify independence.
6. A separate section describing the work of the nomination committee, including the process it has used in relation to board appointments; a description of the board's policy on diversity, including gender; any measurable objectives that it has set for implementing the policy, and progress on achieving the objectives.
7. Any significant external commitments of the chairman and any changes during the year.
8. An explanation of how performance evaluation of the board has been conducted.
9. An explanation from the directors of their responsibility for preparing the accounts and a statement that they consider them to be fair, balanced and understandable. There should also be a statement by the auditors about their reporting responsibilities.
10. An explanation from the directors of the basis on which the company generates or preserves value over the longer term (the business model) and the strategy for delivering the objectives of the company.

11. A statement from the directors as to whether they consider it appropriate to adopt the going concern basis of accounting, with supporting assumptions or qualifications as necessary.
12. Confirmation by the directors that they have carried out an assessment of the principal risks facing the company. The directors should also describe these risks and explain how they are being managed or mitigated.
13. A statement from the directors explaining how they have assessed the prospects of the company, over what period they have done so and why they consider that period to be appropriate. The directors should state whether they have a reasonable expectation that the company will be able to continue in operation and meet its liabilities as they fall due over the period of their assessment.
14. A report on the board's review of the effectiveness of the company's risk management and internal controls systems.
15. Where there is no internal audit function, explain the reasons for its absence.
16. Where the board does not accept the audit committee's recommendation on the appointment, reappointment or removal of an external auditor, a statement from the audit committee explaining the recommendation and the reasons why the board has taken a different position.
17. A statement describing the work of the audit committee in discharging its responsibilities, including: the significant issues that it considered in relation to the financial statements, and how these issues were addressed; an explanation of how it assessed the effectiveness of the external audit process and the approach taken to the appointment or reappointment of the external auditor, including the length of tenure of the current audit firm, when a tender was last conducted and advance notice of any tendering plans; and if the auditor provides non-audit services, an explanation of how auditor objectivity and independence is safeguarded.
18. A description of the work of the remuneration committee including where an executive director serves as a non-executive director elsewhere, whether or not the director will retain such earnings and what the remuneration is.
19. Where remuneration consultants are appointed they should be identified and a statement made as to whether they have any other connection with the company.
20. The steps taken to ensure that members of the board, in particular the non-executive directors, develop an understanding of the views of major shareholders about their company.

The corporate governance disclosures required by the UK CG code can be clearly seen in the governance section of the annual report and accounts of Ted Baker Plc for 2015/16 (Ted Baker, 2016a). As the company has a premium listing on the London Stock Exchange, it must report on how it has applied the main principles of the UK CG Code, and selected corporate governance extracts from its latest annual report are shown in Figures 11.1a, 11.2, 11.4, 11.5 and 11.6a. As Ted Baker's latest annual report and accounts covers a financial year that commenced before 17 June 2016, the company only needed to comply with the disclosure requirements of the earlier 2014

UK CG rather than the new 2016 Code. In order to illustrate the differing approaches used to comply with the UK CG Code, we will also discuss the corporate governance disclosures from the 2015 report and accounts of Derwent London Plc, a London-focused property company (Derwent London, 2016).

Figure 11.1   Examples of statements of compliance with the 2014 UK CG Code

(a) Ted Baker Plc

STATEMENT OF COMPLIANCE WITH THE CODE

During the period the Company was subject to the UK Corporate Governance Code dated September 2014 (the "Code"). The Code was issued by the Financial Reporting Council and is available for review on the Financial Reporting Council's website, https://www.frc.org.uk/. The Board confirms that the Company has complied with the provisions set out in the Code throughout the year, except in respect of Code Provision C.3.1 (Audit Committee to have at least three independent Non-Executive Directors). An explanation of the reason for this departure from the Code is set out on page 22.

An explanation of how the Main Principles have been applied is set out on pages 56 to 58 and, in connection with Directors' remuneration, in the Directors' Remuneration Report on pages 39 to 55.

Source: Ted Baker, 2016a, p. 19. Reproduced with permission from Ted Baker Plc.

(b) Derwent London Plc

Dear Shareholder,

On behalf of the Board I am again pleased to introduce the Group's Corporate Governance report.

In terms of regulation, the Company is subject to the provisions of the UK Corporate Governance Code (the 'Code'), which was last updated in September 2014, and I am pleased to report that the Company has applied the main and supporting principles of the Code, and has complied with all provisions. The Company's position regarding the independence of Stuart Corbyn, is discussed on page 86.

However, in addition to the regulations represented by the Code, it is increasingly being questioned whether compliance with the Code is sufficient to ensure a viable and sustainable business. This revised perspective, nearly 25 years after the introduction of the original Cadbury Report, is demonstrated by the Culture Project launched by the Financial Reporting Council (FRC) last October, and signifies a greater emphasis being placed on the culture of a company. This is referred to in the preface to the Code but recent studies have emphasised its importance in underpinning a company's behaviour and also stressed that, to be truly embedded, it must be set by the Board.

Source: Derwent London, 2016, p. 85. Reproduced with permission from Derwent London Plc.

As each of these companies has a premium listing on the London Stock Exchange, they must make a statement about how they have applied the main provisions of the UK CG Code, and clearly explain any non-compliance. Neither company complied with all of the provisions of the 2014 UK CG Code. Ted Baker failed to comply with provision C.3.1, which requires that the board should establish an audit committee of at least three independent non-executive directors. Derwent London did not comply with provision B.1.1, which deals with the independence of the company's non-executive directors. In addition, Derwent London also highlighted whether compliance with the UK CG Code is sufficient to ensure a viable and sustainable business, and stresses that having the appropriate corporate culture is as important to ensuring good corporate governance.

Ted Baker's explanation for its non-compliance with the 2014 UK CG Code is shown in Figure 11.2. Ted Baker should have at least three independent non-executive directors, excluding the chairman, on its audit committee. Furthermore, in larger companies included within the FTSE 350, the Chairman should not normally be a member of this committee. During the year ended 30 January 2016, Ted Baker failed to have three independent non-executive directors on its audit committee, and its Chairman was also a member of this committee. The company explains that the inclusion of the Chairman on the audit committee was due to his recent and extensive relevant financial experience.

Figure 11.2 Example of Ted Baker's explanation for non-compliance with the UK CG Code

AUDIT COMMITTEE MEMBERSHIP

During the period, Ronald Stewart was Chairman of the Audit Committee. The other members were David Bernstein and Andrew Jennings.

Provision C.3.1 of the Code provides that the Audit Committee should comprise of at least three independent Non-Executive Directors, and that the Chairman should not be a member of the Audit Committee. The Board recognises that the Company has not been compliant with Provision C.3.1 of the Code during the period but considers David Bernstein, notwithstanding his appointment as Chairman, to be a valuable member of the Audit Committee because of his recent and extensive relevant financial experience.

The terms of reference for the Audit Committee are available on the Company's website www.tedbakerplc.com.

Source: Ted Baker, 2016a, p. 22. Reproduced with permission from Ted Baker Plc.

In contrast, Derwent London complied with provision C.3.1 of the UK CG Code, as its chairman was not a member of either the audit or remuneration committee, and it had at least three independent non-executive directors on each committee.

Derwent London's explanation for its non-compliance with provision B.1.1 of the 2014 UK CG Code is shown in Figure 11.3. The UK CG Code requires that the board identify in the annual report each non-executive director it considers to be independent. According to the provision B.1.2 of UK CG Code (FRC, 2016, p. 11), except for smaller companies outside the FTSE 350, at least half the board, excluding the chairman should be independent non-executive directors. A non-executive director is someone who participates in policy making and planning, but does not engage in the everyday management of the company. As a result, non-executive directors monitor the executive directors for shareholders, and are not directly employed by the company. The factors that may be relevant in determining independence include if the director:

- has been an employee of the company or group within the last five years;
- has, or has had within the last three years, a material business relationship with the company either directly, or as a partner, shareholder director or senior employee of a body that has such a relationship with the company;
- has received or receives additional remuneration from the company apart from a director's fee, participates in the company's share option or a performance-related pay scheme, or is a member of the company's pension scheme;

- has close family ties with any of the company's advisers, directors or senior employees;
- holds cross-directorships or has significant links with other directors through involvement in other companies or bodies;
- represents a significant shareholder; or
- has served on the board for more than nine years from the date of their first election.

From Derwent London's perspective, while the length of service on the board does not prevent a director from being deemed as independent, any director serving nine years on the board would not seek re-election.

Figure 11.3 Derwent London's explanation for non-compliance with the 2014 UK CG Code

As noted in the Chairman's letter on Corporate Governance above, Stuart Corbyn is not deemed independent under the criteria set out in provision B.1.1. of the Code having served on the Board for more than nine years.

Whilst the Board, together with a number of institutional investors, does not consider length of service alone to be an accurate guide to a Director's independence, in view of Stuart's tenure it has specifically considered his independence.

As part of its review, the Board noted that Stuart had no relationships with management that might compromise his independence and that he had demonstrated commitment and diligence in carrying out his duties during the year. Given these factors, together with the robust challenge that he consistently presented to the executives and the manner with which he exercised his judgement, the Board was satisfied that Stuart maintained an independent state of mind.

However, despite this conclusion, in the interest of good governance, Stuart has stepped down from his positions as the Group's Senior Independent Director and Chairman of the Nomination Committee on 31 December 2015. In both of these roles he has been replaced by Simon Fraser.

Source: Derwent London, 2016, p. 86. Reproduced with permission from Derwent London Plc.

The disclosure by Ted Baker about its non-executive directors and their independence is shown in Figure 11.4, and illustrates that the company views them all as independent for the purposes of the Code.

Figure 11.4   Example of disclosures about non-executive directors and their independence

> **BOARD COMPOSITION**
>
> The Board currently comprises the Non-Executive Chairman, the Chief Executive, the Chief Operating Officer & Group Finance Director and three independent Non-Executive Directors. Biographies of these Directors appear on page 38. The Board is of the view that its current membership provides an appropriate balance of skills, experience, independence and knowledge, which enables it to discharge its responsibilities effectively. This is reinforced by the findings of the external Board evaluation (see page 20).
>
> **BOARD INDEPENDENCE**
>
> The Board considers Non-Executive Directors Ronald Stewart, Anne Sheinfield and Andrew Jennings to be independent for the purposes of the Code.

Source: Ted Baker, 2016a, p. 19. Reproduced with permission from Ted Baker Plc.

As Figure 11.5 illustrates, Ted Baker takes its responsibility to communicate with its shareholders very seriously. The company provides shareholders with a copy of the annual report and accounts and welcomes their attendance at the AGM. Institutional investors are given half-yearly presentations and the chance to discuss issues with the directors. The company's disclosure about these issues is outlined below.

Figure 11.5   Example of disclosure on communications with shareholders

> **COMMUNICATION WITH SHAREHOLDERS**
>
> The Group attaches considerable importance to the effectiveness of its communication with its shareholders. The full report and accounts are sent to all shareholders and further copies are distributed to others with potential interest in the Group's performance.
>
> Led by the Chief Executive, the Chief Operating Officer and the Finance Director, the Group seeks to build on a mutual understanding of objectives between the Company and its institutional shareholders by making general presentations after the interim and preliminary results; meeting shareholders to discuss long-term issues and gather feedback; and communicating regularly throughout the year via its investor relations programme. All shareholders have access to these presentations, as well as to the Annual Report and Accounts and to other information about the Company, through the website at www.tedbakerplc.com. Shareholders may also attend the Company's Annual General Meeting at which they have the opportunity to ask questions.
>
> Non-Executive Directors are kept informed of the views of shareholders by the Executive Directors and are provided with independent feedback from investor meetings.

Source: Ted Baker, 2016a, p. 21. Reproduced with permission from Ted Baker Plc.

The UK CG Code requires companies to disclose details about the board's policy on boardroom diversity. The diversity statements for both Ted Baker and Derwent London are shown in Figure 11.6. Ted Baker's board has a membership of six, one of whom is female. While the company does not set a target for boardroom diversity, it is seen as an important consideration when developing a 'balanced Board'.

Figure 11.6   Examples of disclosure about boardroom diversity

(a) Ted Baker

DIVERSITY

We strongly support the principle of boardroom diversity, of which gender is one element. Anne Sheinfield has been on the Board since June 2010 and the Board is very pleased to benefit from her valuable contribution.

Boardroom diversity, including gender, is an important consideration when assessing a candidate's ability to contribute to, and complement the abilities of, a balanced Board.

Our Board appointments will always be made on merit against objective criteria, and this will continue to be the priority rather than aiming to achieve an externally prescribed diversity target.

As noted in the People Report on page 34 to 35, the continued expansion of the Company means that Ted Baker's workforce is becoming increasingly diverse. The Company will continue to support the development and progression of all employees, with the aim of maintaining and achieving diversity throughout all levels of the organisation.

Source: Ted Baker, 2016a, p. 29. Reproduced with permission from Ted Baker Plc.

(b) Derwent London

The Group's Nominations Committee continues to monitor the composition, independence and balance of the Board to ensure that the non-executive Directors are able to constructively test the views of the executive Directors.

A key element of this monitoring process relates to the diversity of the Board having due regard to the requirements of the UK Corporate Governance Code and the requests made by Lord Davies of Abersoch through the Department for Business, Innovation & Skills. Whilst the Board does not consider quotas to be an appropriate determinant of its composition, it notes Lord Davies' original 25% target for women's representation on boards and the progress made towards this as set out in the 'Women on Boards – Five year summary' paper published in October 2015. The Board's policy in this regard is to avoid positive discrimination and continue to make appointments based purely on merit with the aim of ensuring that the Board has the correct balance of skills, experience, length of service and knowledge of the Group to meet the requirements of the business.

The appointments of Claudia Arney and Cilla Snowball during 2015 met last year's aim of the Nomination Committee to recruit an additional female director but, more importantly, the skills and experience that they bring to the Board enhance its diversity on a much broader basis.

The Board currently includes two females (15%) and the gender mix throughout the Group is illustrated in the diagrams on page 70.

Taking all factors into account the Directors believe that the Board has an appropriate balance of skills, experience, knowledge and independence to deliver the Group's strategy and to satisfy the requirements of good corporate governance.

Source: Derwent London, 2016, p. 86. Reproduced with permission from Derwent London Plc.

Derwent London's board has a membership of eleven, including two female directors. Like Ted Baker, the company does not consider gender quotas to be an appropriate determinant for board composition, and wishes to avoid positive discrimination when making future board appointments. Both Derwent London and Ted Baker have not yet achieved the 25% target for women's representation on boards outlined in the Davies Report, but both companies have established a clear policy on this issue that must be reported on annually.

The 2014 UK CG Code introduced a requirement that listed companies must provide a viability statement about the principal risks of the company. The viability statement for Derwent London is shown in Figure 11.7. The company's statement assesses the viability of the business over the next five years, and the reasons for choosing this period are explained by reference to the company's business model and strategy. Derwent London owns and manages an investment portfolio of 5.8 million square feet of property, and its primary operations involve redeveloping properties and finding suitable tenants. Both these activities involve a degree of risk, due to the need to secure planning permission and the uncertainty of future rental payments from tenants. As planning permission normally takes a maximum of five years, and rental payments are normally reviewed every five years, it appears appropriate to ascertain the company's long-term viability over a five-year period. Based upon its analysis, the Board of Derwent London are confident that the company will be able to continue in operation over the same time frame.

Figure 11.7 Derwent London's viability statement

Viability statement
In accordance with provision C.2.2 of the 2014 Code, the Directors have assessed the prospect of the Company over a longer period than the 12 months required by the 'Going Concern' provision (see page 92). The Board conducted this review for a period of five years, which was selected for the following reasons:

i) The Group's strategic review covers a five year period.

ii) For a major scheme five years is a reasonable approximation of the maximum time taken from obtaining planning permission to letting the property.

iii) Most leases contain a five year rent review pattern and therefore five years allows for the forecasts to include the reversion arising from those reviews.

The five year strategic review considers the Group's cash flows, dividend cover, REIT compliance and other key financial ratios over the period. These metrics are subject to sensitivity analysis which involves flexing a number of the main assumptions underlying the forecast both individually and in unison. Where appropriate, this analysis is carried out to evaluate the potential impact if those of the Group's principal risks that most directly affect its solvency or liquidity actually occurred. The Board also reviewed certain assumptions in the five year review concerning the normal level of capital recycling likely to occur and, in the light of recent refinancing activity which extended the duration and quantum of the Group's loans, considered whether additional financing facilities could be required.

Based on the results of this analysis, the Directors have a reasonable expectation that the Company will be able to continue in operation and meet its liabilities as they fall due over the five year period of their review.

Source: Derwent London, 2016, p. 77. Reproduced with permission from Derwent London Plc.

Our analysis of the corporate governance disclosures for Ted Baker and Derwent London has only reviewed a small part of the companies' total disclosures on governance mechanisms and structures. You can read the whole of their governance statements by downloading their annual reports and accounts from their websites. What is apparent is that the design and organization of corporate governance disclosures varies from one company to another, as the UK CG Code does not prescribe a specific format for the required disclosures.

11.5 The UK Stewardship Code

In Chapter 4 we explained that *stewardship* is the obligation that directors have to provide relevant and reliable financial information relating to the resources which they have control but are owned by the shareholders. While the primary responsibility for stewardship lies with the board of the company, which oversees the actions of its management, investors in the company also play an important role in holding the board to account for the fulfilment of its responsibilities (FRC, 2012b).

As a result, although the board of directors is ultimately responsible for corporate governance and stewardship, investors have a shared responsibility for these issues since they appoint the directors and hold the board to account. For investors, stewardship is more than just voting at a company's annual general meeting. Steward-ship activities may include monitoring and engaging with companies on matters such as strategy, performance, risk, capital structure, and corporate governance, including culture and remuneration. As a result, investor engagement should involve a dialogue with companies on these matters as well as on issues that are the immediate subject of votes at general meetings. While the UK CG Code identifies the principles that underlie an effective board, the principles of effective stewardship by investors are set out in *The UK Stewardship Code* issued by the FRC (FRC, 2012b).

Activity

What role do institutional investors play in the stewardship of public listed companies?

According to survey of UK companies conducted by the Institute of Chartered Secretaries and Administrators (ICSA, 2015), the main *purposes* of stewardship by investors are:

- building mutual trust between the company and its institutional investors
- shareholders holding boards accountable for company performance
- shareholders raising environmental, social and governance issues
- an essential part of the legal structure through which companies are managed
- a shareholder's 'public duty'.

Stewardship is about investors demonstrating effective control of companies, which involves an active dialogue with, and questioning of, company boards. Before we discuss the *UK Stewardship Code*, it is important to note that the UK CG Code out-lines best practice for companies' relations with shareholders in Main Principle E.1: 'There should be a dialogue with shareholders based on the mutual understanding of objectives. The board as a whole has responsibility for ensuring that a satisfac-tory dialogue with shareholders takes place' (FRC, 2016, p. 22). Other provisions within the UK CG Code are also relevant to shareholder relations as they state that companies should consult with major shareholders in certain circumstances, such as if the board decided that a chief executive should be appointed chairman (Code provision A.3.1). The Listing Rules and the Disclosure and Transparency Rules also cover relations between companies and their investors as listed companies must make announcements to the market in certain situations, such as needing to secure share-holder approval before making a rights issue of new shares.

    Large providers of capital, such as pension funds, insurance companies and invest-ment trusts, set the tone for stewardship and may influence behavioural changes that lead to better stewardship by asset managers and companies (FRC, 2012b). As a result, the UK Stewardship Code is directed at institutional investors, by which is meant asset owners and asset managers with equity holdings in UK listed companies. The UK Stewardship Code requires institutional investors to:

- publicly disclose their policy on how they will discharge their stewardship responsibilities
- have a robust policy on managing conflicts of interest in relation to stewardship which should be publicly disclosed
- monitor their investee companies
- establish clear guidelines on when and how they will escalate their stewardship activities
- be willing to act collectively with other investors where appropriate
- have a clear policy on voting and disclosure of voting activity
- report periodically on their stewardship and voting activities.

The aim of these principles is to protect and enhance the value that accrues to the ultimate beneficiary of the investments. While some people directly own shares in listed companies, many others hold such investments indirectly by investing in pension or investment funds. As a result, large institutional investors must act as stewards for their own investors, and ensure that all investee companies are appropriately governed and managed. Unlike the UK CG Code, adoption of the UK Stewardship Code is optional for most institutional investors. However, since December 2010 all UK-authorized asset managers are required under the FCA's Conduct of Business Rules to produce a statement of commitment to the Stewardship Code or explain why it is not appropriate to their business model. As of June 2016, 298 organizations had publicly registered as signatories of the Stewardship Code, including 196 asset managers, 88 asset owners and 14 service providers.

Like the UK CG Code, the UK Stewardship Code includes a 'comply or explain' requirement. The FRC expects signatories of the Code to publish on their website a statement that:

- describes how they have applied each of the Code's principles and discloses the specific information the Code requires; or
- explains why they have not complied if any of the principles have not been applied or the specific information requested has not been disclosed.

In summary, the UK Stewardship Code supplements the UK CG Code by helping to improve the quality of the engagement between investors and the companies in which they invest. It also increases the accountability of institutional investors to their clients and investment beneficiaries.

11.6 Corporate social responsibility

While corporate governance is primarily concerned with the way in which the directors are managing the resources for the benefit of the investors, *corporate social responsibility (CSR)* focuses on the concerns of investors, consumers and other stakeholders about whether the company is being managed in a sustainable and socially responsible manner. The term *stakeholder* refers to investors and all other parties with interests in the company who could be affected by the environmental or social consequences of the company's activities. Although there are many definitions of CSR, there is general agreement that a socially responsible entity adopts an approach to business that 'embodies transparency and ethical behaviour, respect for stakeholder groups and a commitment to add economic, social and environmental value' (Sustainability, 2004, p. 4).

Many UK companies now take their CSR responsibilities very seriously, and even publish substantial voluntary information about their social and environmental impacts on their websites and as additional reports. By way of contrast, other UK companies choose to discharge their obligations by producing a few brief paragraphs about CSR within their annual report and accounts. Whatever approach is adopted, it must be noted that enhanced CSR disclosure does not necessarily imply that a company is acting is a socially and environmentally responsible manner.

We will now look at the legal requirements for UK companies to provide CSR information. As mentioned in Chapter 4, the UK legal requirements for CSR disclosures are set out in Section 414C of CA 2006, which covers the contents of the strategic report. Large or medium-sized quoted companies must prepare a strategic report that includes information about the development and performance of the business, including a description of the principal risks and uncertainties facing the company. In addition, the strategic report must, to the extent necessary for giving an understanding of the development and performance of the company, provide CSR information about:

- environmental matters, including the impact that the business has on the environment
- the entity's employees, including quantitative information about gender diversity
- social, community and human rights issues.

In addition to the CSR information required in the strategic report, the directors' report of a large or medium-sized listed company must also disclose the following information about *greenhouse gas (GHG)* emissions:

- The annual quantity of carbon dioxide emissions from activities for which the company is responsible including:
  - the combustion of fuel
  - the operation of any facility.
- The annual quantity of carbon dioxide emissions resulting from the purchase of electricity, heat, steam or cooling by the company for its own use.
- The methodologies used to calculate the information about carbon dioxide emissions.

If the CSR information required by CA 2006 is not disclosed, the annual report must state what information is excluded and explain why.

Activity

Download Ted Baker's annual report and accounts for 2015/16 and review its CSR disclosures on pages 30–35. What type of information does the company disclose about these issues? Acting as a potential stakeholder, would you be satisfied with the level of detail and content provided?

Ted Baker has chosen to disclose all of its statutory CSR information in the Directors' Report, rather than the Strategic Report. The information reveals what this company views as important to show in terms of its statutory obligation to report on CSR issues, which includes sections about:

- Sustainability
- The company's environmental impacts
- Ethical and sustainable sourcing
- Community
- Greenhouse gas emissions
- The Bribery Act 2010 and the Modern Slavery Act 2015
- People, including details about employee remuneration, learning and development, diversity, health and safety and welfare, employees with disabilities, culture and employee engagement.

Ted Baker's 2015/16 CSR report provides detailed information about sustainability and the environment, ethical sourcing of products, community involvement, diversity in the workplace, health and safety and the corporate policy on the recruitment of disabled employees. When reviewing these disclosures, it is clear that the company is attempting to provide detailed information about its CSR policies together with numeric information about certain aspects of its current CSR performance. Figure 11.8 reproduces Ted Baker's disclosures for GHG emissions and employee diversity information in accordance with the UK regulatory framework.

Ted Baker's disclosures for GHG emissions and diversity are mandatory under UK law, and would not be typically found in the annual report and account of companies from other countries. For example, public companies in the USA are not required to disclose information about diversity or environmental impacts within the financial statements.

The volume and detail of the CSR information disclosed by Ted Baker in 2015/16 is considerably greater than that provided in 2010/11, which may be an ongoing response to criticisms about the company's employment and manufacturing practices in developing countries. For example, in 2007, the employment rights groups, Labour behind the Label and War on Want, identified Ted Baker as one of the clothing brands that failed to disclose transparent information about the employment and ethical treatment of overseas workers: 'These brands make no meaningful information available to suggest that they have engaged with the living wage or other labour rights

Figure 11.8 Examples of CSR disclosures on (a) greenhouse gas emissions and (b) diversity

GREENHOUSE GAS EMISSIONS

The Group has, for a number of years, participated in the Carbon Disclosure Project and is now required, in accordance with The Companies Act 2006 (Strategic Report and Directors' Report) Regulations 2013 (the 'Regulations'), to report its greenhouse gas emissions ('GHG').

The Group has adopted a greenhouse gas reporting policy and a management system based on the ISO 14064-1:2006 methodology, which has been used to calculate the Group's Scope 1 and 2 emissions in the period for activities within the financial control of the Group.

In measuring the Group's greenhouse gas emissions, all the Group's stores, warehouses and head offices around the world were taken into account. The space occupied by the Group within concession stores is excluded from Scope 1 and 2 calculations because the Group has neither financial nor operational control over a concession area. Such emissions are included in the Group's Scope 3 figures which are published in our annual Carbon Disclosure Project Report.

The Group's GHG emissions during the period are disclosed in the table below.

	2016	2015
Scope 1 – Direct CO_2 emissions (tonnes CO_2e)	138	220
Scope 2 – Indirect CO_2 emissions (tonnes CO_2e)	4,062	4,538
Total tonnes CO_2e emissions	4,200	4,758
tCO_2e per sq ft	0.012	0.014
tCO_2e per £'000 sales	0.009	0.012

GHG emissions for the year ended 30 January 2016 have been calculated using the appropriate 2015 UK Government Conversions Factors for Company Reporting.

DIVERSITY

The Group believes in respecting individuals and their rights in the workplace, and that diversity supports the dynamic of our teams to deliver success. With this in mind, specific policies are in place setting out our stance and commitment to managing harassment and bullying, whistle blowing and equality and diversity. Our team represents a wide and diverse workforce from all backgrounds, sexual orientation, nationality, ethnic and religious groups. We support sponsorship of visa applications, where appropriate, to retain specific talent within the business. With continued overseas expansion our workforce is becoming more diverse and we respect cultural difference and actively seek to learn about each territory we operate within.

Our commitment to diversity across the Group continues and consideration to diversity and gender is given with a view to appointing the best placed individual for each new role. The charts below demonstrate the gender split across the Board of Directors, the Group's leadership and senior management teams and global employees as at 30 January 2016.

	2016			2015		
	MALE	FEMALE	TOTAL	MALE	FEMALE	TOTAL
Ted Baker Plc Board of Directors	5	1	6	5	1	6
Executive Committee and other senior managers	34	54	88	27	39	66
Global employees	1,108	2,168	3,276	995	1,842	2,837

	UK		North America		Europe		Asia		
	MALE	FEMALE	MALE	FEMALE	MALE	FEMALE	MALE	FEMALE	TOTAL
Ted Baker Plc Board of Directors	5	1	-	-	-	-	-	-	6
Executive Committee and other senior managers	21	31	9	14	1	4	3	5	88
Global employees	695	1,226	244	456	111	358	58	128	3,276

Source: Ted Baker, 2016a, p. 32 and p. 35. Reproduced with permission from Ted Baker Plc.

issues, and continue not to respond to our inquiries about their policies and practices' (Hearson and Morser, 2007, p. 14). Therefore, from the perspective of certain pressure groups, Ted Baker, like many other UK clothing retailers, fails to provide the detailed CSR disclosures that stakeholders demand: 'Retailers cannot continue to pay lip service to corporate social responsibility while engaging in buying practices that systematically undermine the principles of decent work' (War on Want, 2008, p. 1).

Activity

What additional voluntary CSR information do *you* think Ted Baker might disclose? Go to the 'Ted's Responsibilities' section of Ted Baker's website and discuss the CSR content that it provides about the company (www.tedbakerplc. com/teds-responsibilities/sustainability-and-the-environment). Does this website provide stakeholders with any useful additional information?

Ted Baker supplements the statutory CSR disclosures contained within its annual report with a section on its website called 'Ted's Responsibilities' which contains detailed information about the way the company conducts business and fulfils its responsibilities to stakeholders. While some of this merely restates information contained within the company's latest annual report and accounts, it also includes documents entitled *Ted's Ethical Statement* (Ted Baker, 2016b) and *Ted's Ethical Code of Conduct* (Ted Baker, 2016c) which together describe the company's ethical position and approach. The main document is the Ethical Statement, which formally defines the values, standards and policy that the company has on the ethical treatment of its employees, environmental and sustainability issues, animal testing and charitable donations. The main part of Ted's Ethical Statement is reproduced in Figure 11.9, but there are additional sections on the website that provide further details about the company's policies toward the environment, ethical conduct, sustainability, animal welfare, beauty and charity.

Ted Baker's *Ethical Code of Conduct* (Ted Baker, 2016c) is not reproduced here but contains additional information about the company's ethical employment practices, including details of its policies to supply a safe and healthy working environment, to pay a living wage to workers and to outlaw the use of child labour. These additional web-based CSR disclosures are voluntary and supply much extra information about Ted Baker's CSR responsibilities. However, Ted Baker's disclosures must not be seen as an exemplar of CSR practice, as many worldwide companies, including Royal Dutch Shell, McDonalds, Nokia, Bayer and Puma, produce far greater levels of detailed voluntary CSR information. Royal Dutch Shell, for example, produces a voluntary sustainability report that includes annual environmental and social performance data about its generation of GHG emissions, worker injury-levels and total expenditure on community development projects (Royal Dutch Shell, 2016).

Figure 11.9   Example of website CSR disclosures

Ted's Ethical Statement

At our head office, stores and warehouses we are working tirelessly to reduce the amount of waste we send to landfill, and we would love you to help us by thinking about your waste too. After all, one man's trash is another man's treasure.

We especially want to make sure that all electrical products are taken care of properly; things like batteries can be extremely harmful to the environment if not disposed of correctly. Within the UK, we have grouped together with other retailers and joined the 'Distributor Take Back Scheme', helping the UK's local councils with the provision of improved recycling facilities for you as part of our commitment to the UK and European WEEE Directive (Waste Electrical and Electronic Equipment).

This is why on these products we display the crossed-out wheelie bin symbol. Please do not dispose of these with your household waste. For our UK customers, please take them to your local recycling centre run by your local council. You can find your closest centre at www.recycle-more.co.uk. Here you can also find out where to recycle things as diverse as fridges, milk cartons and even your old Ted clothes.

We also believe in playing fair. It's not just about being honest and open in the way we do business. We encourage our suppliers to do the same. Important as those points are, it's bigger than that, global in fact.

You see we also have a responsibility to do right by the environment in terms of reducing our waste and consumption of resources. In other words, keeping our carbon footprint as dainty as possible.

We have joined forces with MADE-BY, a not for profit association who are helping Ted to look at our garments a bit more closely, from the fibres we use to make the products to the conditions for the people who work within our factories. They have helped us to set targets to continuously improve the overall sustainability of our collections, and you will soon be able see our progress measured against MADE-BY's internationally accredited and recognised benchmarks on their website www.made-by.org.

Source: Ted Baker, 2016b. Reproduced with permission from Ted Baker Plc.

11.7 Integrated reporting

It can be argued that separate financial, environmental and corporate responsibility reports within the annual report and accounts only provide a partial picture of how the entity adds economic, social and environmental value. This has led to calls for an *integrated report* that provides a concise communication about value creation over time and covers the entity's strategy, governance, performance and prospects. To aid the preparation of such a report, the International Integrated Reporting Council (IIRC) published the *International Integrated Reporting <IR> Framework* in December 2013 (IIRC, 2013).

Key definition

An integrated report is a concise communication about how an organisation's strategy, governance, performance and prospects, in the context of its external environment, lead to the creation of value over the short, medium and long term.

Source: IIRC, 2013, p. 7. Copyright © December 2013 by the International Integrated Reporting Council ('the IIRC'). Used with permission of the IIRC.

The IIRC's vision is to align capital allocation and corporate behaviour to wider goals of financial stability and sustainable development through the cycle of integrated reporting and thinking. According to the IIRC, the objectives for integrated reporting include:

- Improving the quality of information made available to the providers of financial capital to enable a more efficient and productive allocation of capital.
- Providing a more cohesive and efficient approach to corporate reporting that utilizes different reporting strands and communicates the full range of factors that materially affect the ability of an organisation to create value over time.
- Enhancing accountability and stewardship for the full range of capitals (financial, manufactured, intellectual, human, social and natural) and promoting understanding of their interdependencies within an organization's value creation.
- Promoting integrated thinking, decision making and actions that focus on the creation of value over the short, medium and long term.

Integrated reporting provides a more complete report of the value created by a business, as it considers the importance of non-financial resources such as intellectual, human, social and natural capitals as well as financial and manufactured capital. All organizations depend on various forms of capital for their success. The IIRC has defined six different types of capital that represent stocks of value that are increased, decreased, or transformed by the business activities and outputs of the organization. Figure 11.10 illustrates how the six capitals are transformed by the value creation process.

Figure 11.10 The value creation process within integrated reporting

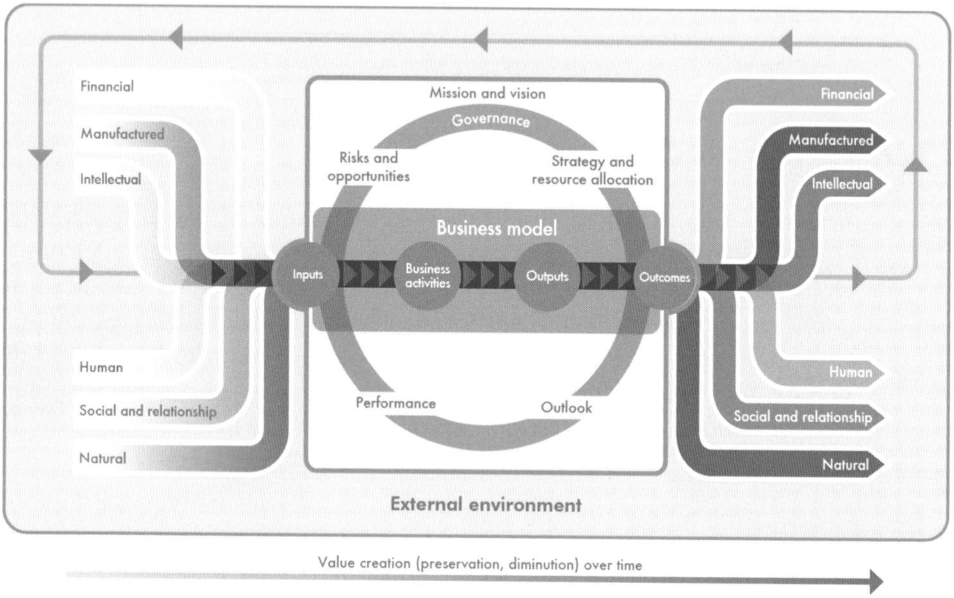

In order to create value, an organization's business activities and outputs must generate positive internal or external outcomes for the capitals. To facilitate this process, an entity must create an appropriate governance framework, adopt a viable business model, and adapt to changes within the external environment, such as technological change or environmental challenges.

Financial and manufactured capitals are those reported on most frequently by companies. Intellectual, social and relationship, and human capitals are linked to the activities of humans. Natural capital represents the natural resources and environment. Not all capitals are equally relevant to all organizations, and only where interactions are material must they be reported on within an integrated report. For example, natural capital is critical to the business models of mining companies, which draw directly on natural resources, but is also relevant to other organizations that rely on renewable and non-renewable resources and processes to provide goods or services.

Assessing how these six types of capital affect the value created or destroyed for investors and other shareholders requires 'integrated thinking' by management, as it requires consideration about how each type of capital affects both the business and society, now and in the future. As a result, the long-term success of an organization requires consideration of the interests and expectations of a wide range of stakeholders, and responding to changing expectations, opportunities, and threats that influence the future of an organization. As information about these uncertainties is not typically provided by mainstream financial reporting, corporate boards need to consider how information about value creation can be communicated in a manner that supports internal processes and decision making. The primary *purpose* of an integrated report is to explain to providers of financial capital how an organization creates value over time. However, its information should benefit all stakeholders interested in an organization's ability to create value over time, including employees, customers, suppliers, business partners, local communities, legislators, regulators and policy makers.

According to the <IR> Framework, an integrated report should provide insight about an organization's strategy and stakeholders' relationships. It does this by providing eight content elements that are fundamentally linked to each other and are not mutually exclusive (IIRC, 2013, p. 5):

- Organizational overview and external environment: What does the organization do and what are the circumstances under which it operates?
- Governance: How does the organization's governance structure support its ability to create value in the short, medium and long term?
- Business model: What is the organization's business model?
- Risks and opportunities: What are the specific risks and opportunities that affect the organization's ability to create value over the short, medium and long term, and how is the organization dealing with them?
- Strategy and resource allocation: Where does the organization want to go and how does it intend to get there?

- Performance: To what extent has the organization achieved its strategic objectives for the period and what are its outcomes in terms of effects on the capitals?
- Outlook: What challenges and uncertainties is the organization likely to encounter in pursuing its strategy, and what are the potential implications for its business model and future performance?
- Basis of presentation: How does the organization determine what matters to include in the integrated report and how are such matters quantified or evaluated?

The *Companies Act 2006 (Strategic Report and Directors' Reports) Regulations 2013* requires UK listed companies to prepare a strategic report that provides information about their environmental impacts, the company's employees, and other social issues. As its name suggests, the strategic report focuses on the company's strategy and provides a narrative about how its business model, risks and key performance indicators are linked to its current strategic position. Certain information within the strategic report is clearly relevant for integrated reporting. However, integrated reporting focuses on the key resources, relationships and capital dependencies within a company's business model, and provides a more long-term and future-orientated narrative about its entire value creation process. As a result, the information provided by an integrated report as proposed by the IIRC, differs from that provided by the UK's strategic report.

The UK requirement for quoted companies to produce a strategic report and report on GHG emissions in their directors' report has led to a growing interest in integrated reporting among companies, investors and other stakeholders. As a result, an increasing number of companies are now providing some type of integrated report. A global study by PricewaterhouseCoopers (PwC, 2013) assessed the external reports of 400 larger listed companies against the IIRC's Integrated Reporting Framework and found that many companies were reporting information about strategic priorities, key risks and key performance indicators within their strategic reports. The key findings were as follows (PwC, 2013, p. 2):

- Many companies already report key content elements of the <IR> framework, such as strategic priorities, key risks and key performance indicators. However, many guiding principles in the framework, such as connectivity and future orientation, are less well-addressed. This makes it hard for stakeholders to understand the company's value now or in the future. For example, reports failed to explain each organization's dependency on key relationships and external resources to create value. Moreover, current reporting remains largely focused on financial performance, with little attention paid to measuring the impact an organization has on other types of capital.
- South Africa, the UK and Germany are leading the adoption of many <IR> principles, perhaps because of regulatory changes to improve the quality and integration of reporting.

- A number of industries are slightly ahead of their peers, particularly mining, chemicals and real estate, reflecting more advanced stakeholder demand for broader information sets.

However, the research also identified a number of challenges that more integrated thinking is trying to overcome (PwC, 2013, p. 2):

- Current reporting often shows a lack of connectivity, perhaps reflecting the reality of organizational behaviours and diverse information sets. Better connection between different internal departments is seen as a key benefit of integrated thinking and reporting.
- Many reports focus on the last year's performance. An integrated report should have forward-looking elements, using current information to shape strategic insight over the long term.
- Many reports lack insight into how dependent the company is on key relationships and resources outside the organization to create value. It is rare to get a clear sense of how the dynamics of their risks and opportunities are evolving. Integrated thinking and reporting encourage a broader perspective, better understanding of the wider impacts and how these factors feed into the business model and drive sustainable value creation.
- Current reporting remains largely focused on financial performance. Measuring the impact an organization has beyond traditional reporting boundaries and across multiple 'capitals' is at the heart of the value of integrated thinking and reporting.

A follow-up survey of 270 annual reports from larger public companies in 16 countries found that 44% of reports did not look beyond short-term initiatives (KPMG, 2016). Only 14% mentioned business strategy, 11% showed how a company's risk profile has been managed over time and a meagre 9% provided a track record of operational performance. Consequently, the gap in information provided to investors remains.

As Ted Baker does not provide an integrated report, we will consider two examples of integrated reporting by two other public listed companies. As well as preparing a separate annual sustainable development report, Anglo American Plc, a UK listed mining company provides integrated reporting information within its annual report and accounts (Anglo American, 2016). Aegon, a Dutch listed financial services company, prepares a stand-alone integrated review (Aegon, 2016) that provides a complete overview of the company, from both a financial and non-financial performance perspective. While we cannot reproduce all of the integrated reporting information that each company provides, it is important to show some of the key features of this type of information. Figure 11.11 shows how Anglo American describes the connectivity within its business model by explaining how different types of capital are used to create corporate value and societal outputs. The company utilizes six types of capital within its activities, and its integrated reporting information shows how these capitals are used to provide six types of business outcome.

Figure 11.11   Example of integrated reporting by Anglo American

TOGETHER, WE CREATE SUSTAINABLE VALUE THAT MAKES A REAL DIFFERENCE

BUSINESS INPUT CAPITALS

These capitals are the key stocks of value that are increased, decreased or transformed through the activities of our organisation, over the short, medium and long term.

FINANCIAL

Our shareholders own the business. They expect attractive, sustainable returns, reflecting the risk they take in funding the business.

HUMAN

Our people are the business. We aim to resource the organisation with a capable, engaged and productive workforce. We are committed to ensuring no harm comes to any of our workforce.

INTELLECTUAL

We aim to drive aggressive innovation to support consistent over-delivery on commitments. We link our technical and marketing knowledge to ensure we invest our efforts in the key leverage points in the 'mine to market' value chain.

NATURAL

In order for us to mine, we first need to find locations rich in the minerals our customers need. Once operational, we require water, electricity and fuel in order to run our mines, process our products and move them to our customers.

MANUFACTURED

Throughout our value chain, we require a host of specialised equipment. The products we purchase, through our optimised supply chain, must deliver optimum value.

SOCIAL AND RELATIONSHIPS

Open and honest engagement with our stakeholders is critical in gaining and maintaining our social and legal licence to operate and, therefore, the sustainability of our business.

CREATING VALUE THROUGH MINING THE RAW MATERIALS REQUIRED TO MEET GROWING CONSUMER-DRIVEN DEMAND

The transition to a more streamlined business delivers a portfolio uniquely positioned for the expanding consumer-driven markets through:

- Focusing on those commodities positioned to meet the shift away from infrastructure investment towards consumer-driven demand, i.e. diamonds, PGMs and copper.
- Retaining and developing our highest quality world class ore bodies with competitive industry cost positions, driving sustainable profitability throughout the cycle.
- Streamlining the portfolio, though preserving balance to ensure there is not over-reliance on any one product group or geography, while retaining established technical and marketing capabilities and the critical mass to compete effectively for, and deliver, future opportunities.

OUR DIVERSE VALUE CHAIN...

As a company, we operate across the entire mining value chain – from exploration through to marketing. Although we are focused on resource development, mining and operations, we are developing other areas of the value chain, e.g. our marketing capabilities, when we can see opportunities to deliver increased value.

 Find: our exploration teams discover mineral deposits in a safe and responsible way to replenish the Mineral Resources that underpin our future success.

 Plan and build: working with all our stakeholders, we plan and build some of the most effective, efficient and environmentally sound mines in the world.

 Mine: we operate open pit and underground mines, although we will move to predominantly open pit mining as we transition the portfolio.

 Process: we generate additional value by processing and refining many of our products.

 Move and market: we provide products to our customers around the world, meeting their specific technical and logistical requirements.

 Close or divest: In whatever way we exit an operation, we do so in accordance with our Good Citizenship Business Principles, with a focus on the social and environmental impact.

STRATEGY

The Group Management Committee (GMC) is responsible for developing Anglo American's strategy and policies, as discussed and approved by the Board. Implementation of the strategy is monitored by the GMC, and measured through our KPIs, against our pillars of value.

 For more information **See page 14**

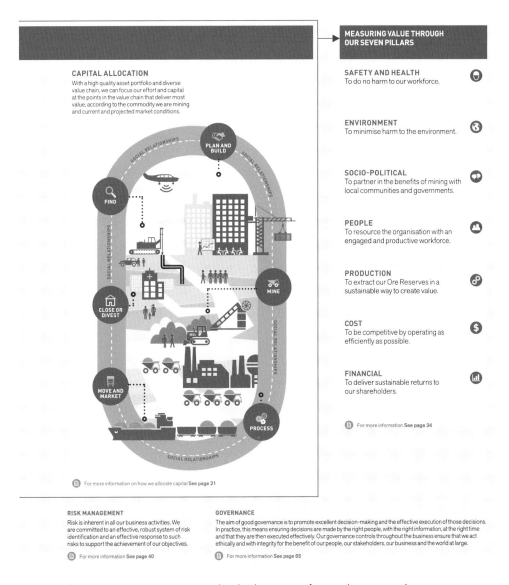

MEASURING VALUE THROUGH OUR SEVEN PILLARS

CAPITAL ALLOCATION
With a high quality asset portfolio and diverse value chain, we can focus our effort and capital at the points in the value chain that deliver most value, according to the commodity we are mining and current and projected market conditions.

SAFETY AND HEALTH
To do no harm to our workforce.

ENVIRONMENT
To minimise harm to the environment.

SOCIO-POLITICAL
To partner in the benefits of mining with local communities and governments.

PEOPLE
To resource the organisation with an engaged and productive workforce.

PRODUCTION
To extract our Ore Reserves in a sustainable way to create value.

COST
To be competitive by operating as efficiently as possible.

FINANCIAL
To deliver sustainable returns to our shareholders.

For more information See page 34

For more information on how we allocate capital See page 21

RISK MANAGEMENT
Risk is inherent in all our business activities. We are committed to an effective, robust system of risk identification and an effective response to such risks to support the achievement of our objectives.

For more information See page 40

GOVERNANCE
The aim of good governance is to promote excellent decision-making and the effective execution of those decisions. In practice, this means ensuring decisions are made by the right people, with the right information, at the right time and that they are then executed effectively. Our governance controls throughout the business ensure that we act ethically and with integrity for the benefit of our people, our stakeholders, our business and the world at large.

For more information See page 65

Source: Anglo American, 2016, pp. 6–7. Reproduced with permission from Anglo American Plc.

Figure 11.12 shows how Aegon's value chain creates and shares value for its customers and stakeholders. Aegon's value chain maps the company's relationships with a wide range of key stakeholder groups, capturing the inputs (capitals/resources) and outputs of the value creation process. Within the company's annual review for 2015, this diagram is accompanied by a detailed narrative of the value creation at Aegon on a stakeholder-by-stakeholder basis, which illustrates the connectivity within integrated reporting information (see Aegon, 2016).

Figure 11.12 Example of integrated reporting by Aegon

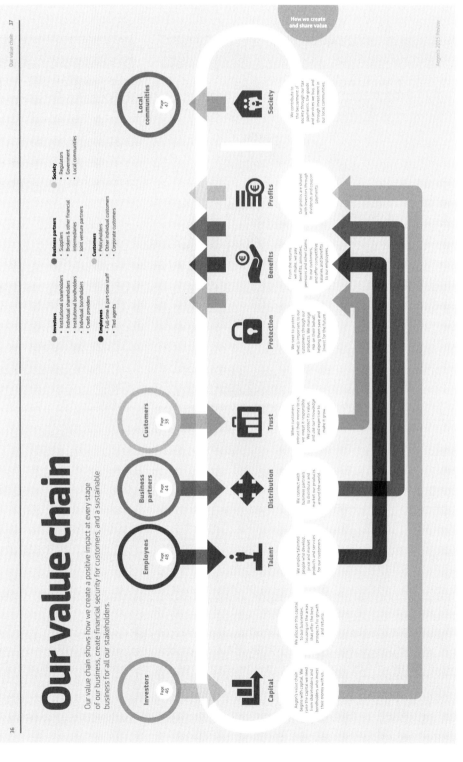

Source: Aegon, 2016, pp. 36–37. Reproduced with permission from Aegon NV.

While we have examined the CSR and integrated reporting practices for a small number of public entities, what is the overall state of CSR and integrated reporting by European companies? Although the EU Accounting Directive 2013/34/EU does address the disclosure of non-financial CSR information by companies, its requirements have been applied in different ways in different Member States. As a result, fewer than 10% of the largest EU companies regularly disclose such information (EC, 2014b). While certain Member States, including the UK, Sweden, Denmark, Spain and France, have introduced CSR disclosure requirements that go beyond the Accounting Directive, others have not. As a result, the EU issued Directive 2014/95/EU (EC, 2014c) in order to increase EU companies' transparency and performance on environmental and social matters and, therefore, to contribute effectively to long-term economic growth and employment. This amends Directive 2013/34/EU by requiring large public-interest entities with more than 500 employees to disclose in their management report relevant and useful information on their policies, main risks and outcomes relating to:

- environmental matters
- social and employee aspects
- respect for human rights
- anti-corruption and bribery issues
- diversity in their board of directors.

The Directive gives companies significant flexibility in how they disclose this information (including reporting in a separate report), and which international, European or national guidelines they use to prepare the data (for instance, the UN Global Compact, ISO 26000 Social Responsibility or the OECD Guidelines for Multinational Enterprises).

While the Directive focuses on environmental and social disclosures, it does not require companies to comply with integrated reporting. The EU press release for the Directive stated that integrated reporting is a step ahead and that the European Commission is monitoring the evolution of the integrated reporting concept, and, in particular, the work of the IIRC (EU, 2014b). The new Directive is effective for financial years starting on 1 January 2017. As the non-financial and diversity disclosures required by the EU Directive are already required by the UK CG Code and CA 2006, it will have little impact on UK companies. However, it will improve the CSR information provided by companies in many other Member States.

Overall, the importance of CSR is growing and stakeholder groups within society are increasingly demanding disclosure of information about the social and environmental impact of business operations. As a result, an increasing number of companies are producing sustainability reports or providing integrated reporting information. While legal changes have underlined the importance of CSR disclosure, there is still room for improvement, as can be seen from the growing interest in integrated reporting.

11.8 Conclusions

The regulatory framework provided by UK GAAP ensures that the statutory annual report and accounts communicate high quality, reliable information and allow users to assess the stewardship of management. The additional guidance provided by the UK CG Code and those relating to CSR aid this objective. In this chapter we have reviewed the development of the UK CG Code and Stewardship Code, and reviewed international approaches to providing good corporate governance. We have also examined how these codes and notions of corporate social responsibility (CSR) are integrated into UK financial reporting practice and looked at examples. We then discussed the growing importance of integrated reporting and illustrated how companies are currently reporting such information to provide investors with a complete account of the entire value creation process.

Corporate governance is an important aspect of management and the aim of the UK CG Code is to promote best practice. Companies should comply with the spirit of the UK CG Code rather than devise mechanisms that create the illusion of compliance. The same is true for CSR and <IR>. A business must accept that it has a responsibility to all stakeholders and disclose meaningful information about the social and environmental impact of its operations. There is growing interest in <IR> among companies and investors, and you should keep up to date with developments in this area by looking at the IIRC and FRC websites.

References

Aegon (2016) *Aegon's 2015 Review*. Available from: www.aegon.com/Documents/aegon-com/Sitewide/Reports-and-Other-Publications/Annual-reports/2015/Aegon-Annual-Review-2015.pdf (Accessed 1 June 2016).

Anglo American (2016) *Annual Report 2015*. Available at: www.angloamerican.com/~/media/Files/A/Anglo-American-PLC-V2/documents/aa-ar-15.pdf (Accessed 1 June 2016).

BIS (2011) *Women on Boards*, London: Department for Business, Innovation & Skills (BIS), BIS/11/745. Available from: www.gov.uk/government/uploads/system/uploads/attachment_data/file/31480/11-745-women-on-boards.pdf (Accessed 1 June 2015).

BIS (2015) *Improving the Gender Balance on British Boards*, London: Department for Business, Innovation & Skills (BIS), BIS/15/585. Available from: www.gov.uk/government/uploads/system/uploads/attachment_data/file/482059/BIS-15-585-women-on-boards-davies-review-5-year-summary-october-2015.pdf (Accessed 10 June 2016).

Cadbury (1992) *The Report of the Committee on the Financial Aspects of Corporate Governance*, December, London: Gee Professional Publishing.

Derwent London (2016) *Derwent London plc Annual Report 2015*. Available from: www.derwentlondon.com/investors/results-and-reports (Accessed 10 December 2016).

EC (2011a) European Corporate Governance Forum page. Available from: http://ec.europa.eu/internal_market/company/ecgforum/studies_en.htm (Accessed 6 December 2015).

EC (2011b) *Green Paper: The EU Corporate Governance Framework*. Available from: http://ec.europa.eu/internal_market/company/docs/modern/com2011-164_en.pdf (Accessed 6 June 2016).

EC (2014a) *Commission Recommendation of 9 April 2014 on the Quality of Corporate Governance Reporting ('Comply or Explain')*, 2014/208/EU, OJ L109/43. Available at: http://eur-lex.europa.eu/legal-content/EN/TXT/PDF/?uri=CELEX:32014H0208&from=EN (Accessed 6 December 2015).

EC (2014b) *Disclosure of Non-financial and Diversity Information by Large Companies and Groups – Frequently Asked Questions*. Available at: http://europa.eu/rapid/press-release_MEMO-14-301_de.htm (Accessed 6 December 2015).

EC (2014c) *Amending Directive 2013/34/EU as Regards Disclosure of Non-financial and Diversity Information by Certain Large Undertakings and Groups*, 2014/95/EU, OJ L330/1. Available at: http://eur-lex.europa.eu/legal-content/EN/TXT/PDF/?uri=CELEX:32014L0095&from=EN (Accessed 6 December 2015).

FRC (2012a) *Comply or Explain 20th Anniversary of the UK Corporate Governance Code*, London: Financial Reporting Council. Available from: www.frc.org.uk/Our-Work/Publications/Corporate-Governance/Comply-or-Explain-20th-Anniversary-of-the-UK-Corpo.pdf (Accessed 6 November 2015).

FRC (2012b) *The UK Stewardship Code*, London: Financial Reporting Council. Available from: www.frc.org.uk/Our-Work/Publications/Corporate-Governance/UK-Stewardship-Code-September-2012.pdf (Accessed 1 June 2016).

FRC (2016) *The UK Corporate Governance Code*, London: Financial Reporting Council. Available from: www.frc.org.uk/Our-Work/Publications/Corporate-Governance/UK-Corporate-Governance-Code-April-2016.pdf (Accessed 10 June 2016).

Grant Thornton (2013) *Corporate Governance Review 2013: Governance Steps Up a Gear*, London: Grant Thornton UK LLP. Available from: www.grant-thornton.co.uk/Documents/FTSE-350-Corporate-Governance-Review-2013.pdf (Accessed 6 November 2015).

Grant Thornton (2015) *Corporate Governance Review 2015: Trust and integrity – loud and clear?* London: Grant Thornton UK LLP. Available from: www.grantthornton.co.uk/globalassets/1.-member-firms/united-kingdom/pdf/publication/2015/uk-corporate-governance-review-and-trends-2015.pdf (Accessed 6 June 2016).

Hearson, M. and Morser, A. (2007) *Let's Clean up Fashion: 2007 Update*. Available from: http://media.waronwant.org/sites/default/files/Lets%20Clean%20up%20Fashion%20-%20Update%202007.pdf?_ga=1.92483869.1211096167.1466554124 (Accessed 10 June 2016).

ICSA (2015) *Effective Stewardship*, London: ICSA. Available from: www.icsa.org.uk/knowledge/governance-and-compliance/features/august-2015-add-value-by-increasing-freedom (Accessed 10 December 2016).

IIRC (2013) *The International <IR> Framework*, London: IIRC. Available from: http://integratedreporting.org/wp-content/uploads/2015/03/13-12-08-THE-INTERNATIONAL-IR-FRAMEWORK-2-1.pdf (Accessed 1 June 2016).

IoD (2010) *Corporate Governance Guidance and Principles for Unlisted Companies in the UK*. Available from: www.ecgi.org/codes/documents/cg_principles_unlisted_companies_iod_uk_nov2010_en.pdf (Accessed 12 December 2016).

KPMG (2016) *Room for Improvement – The KPMG Survey of Business Reporting, Second Edition*. Available from: https://home.kpmg.com/xx/en/home/insights/2016/04/kpmg-survey-business-reporting-second-edition.html (Accessed 8 August 2016).

Lovells, H. (2010) *Annual Re-election of Directors*. Available from: www.lexology.com/library/detail.aspx?g=22f99414-649e-4d5a-9816-fa60e802ce37 (Accessed 6 December 2015).

OECD (2015) *Principles of Corporate Governance*. Available from: www.oecd-ilibrary.org/docserver/download/2615021e.pdf?expires=1450403477&id=id&accname=guest&checksum=28A01B11B004891E528FE40DA4A908DB (Accessed 6 December 2015).

PwC (2013) *Seizing Opportunities with Integrated Thinking*. Available at: www.pwc.co.uk/assets/pdf/integrated-thinking-flyer-dec-2013.pdf (Accessed 6 December 2015).

QCA (2013) *Corporate Governance Code for Small and Mid-Size Quoted Companies 2013*. Available from: www.theqca.com/shop/guides/70707/corporate-governance-code-for-small-and-midsize-quoted-companies-2013.thtml (Accessed 6 December 2015).

Regierungskommission (2015) *Deutscher Corporate Governance Kodex*. Available from: www.dcgk.de//files/dcgk/usercontent/en/download/code/2015-05-05_Corporate_Governance_Code_EN.pdf (Accessed 6 June 2016).

Royal Dutch Shell (2016) *Sustainability Report 2015*. Available from: http://reports.shell.com/sustainability-report/2015/servicepages/downloads/files/entire_shell_sr15.pdf (Accessed 10 June 2016).

Solomon, J. (2007) *Corporate Governance and Accountability*, 2nd edn, Chichester: John Wiley & Sons Ltd.

Sustainability (2004) *Gearing Up: From Corporate Responsibility to Good Governance and Scaleable Solutions*, London: Sustainability.

Ted Baker (2016a) *Ted Baker Plc Annual Report and Accounts 2015–16*. Available at: www.tedbakerplc.com/~/media/Files/T/Ted-Baker/results-and-reports/report/2016/2016-annual-report.pdf (Accessed 11 May 2016).

Ted Baker (2016b) *Ted's Ethical Statement*. Available from: www.tedbaker.com/uk/about-ted/ethical-statement (Accessed 1 June 2016).

Ted Baker (2016c) *Ted's Ethical Code of Conduct*. Available from: www.tedbakerplc.com/~/media/Files/T/Ted-Baker/documents/ted-ethical-code-of-conduct-2016.pdf (Accessed 1 June 2016).

War on Want (2008) *Fashion Victims II: How UK Clothing Retailers are Keeping Workers in Poverty*. Available from: http://media.waronwant.org/sites/default/files/Fashion%20Victims%20II.pdf?_ga=1.166468926.1211096167.1466554124 (Accessed 12 December 2016).

Discussion questions

1 Discuss the meaning of the term 'corporate governance' and its importance to investors.

2 Debate the advantages and disadvantages of using a code-based approach to corporate governance.

3 Discuss the meaning of the term 'corporate social responsibility' and why a company has a responsibility to society.

Practice questions

4 Explain how the 'comply or explain' concept in corporate governance affects public companies with a premium listing of equity shares.

5 Obtain a copy of the 2016 UK CG Code from the FRC's website and search it to find answers to the following questions. Your answer should include a reference to the provision or page where you found the answer.

Question	Answer
(i) How many provisions does the UK CG Code include? Do they all apply to smaller companies?	
(ii) Should a former or current chief executive officer be appointed as chairman?	
(iii) What criteria does the UK CG Code use for determining whether a director is independent?	
(iv) What proportion of the board should be represented by independent non-executive directors?	
(v) How often should directors be subject to re-election by shareholders?	

6 Explain why the UK CG Code does not apply to private companies. In addition, discuss the reasons why private companies would comply with the UK CG Code on a voluntary basis.

7 Obtain the latest annual report and accounts for two UK public companies included within the FTSE 350 share index and compare their corporate governance statements. Write a summary analyzing the differences in the wording used and noting any non-compliance with the UK Code of Corporate Governance.

8 Analyze the data provided on corporate governance and on corporate social responsibility by Ted Baker Plc. Interpret your findings from the perspective of:

(a) a present or potential investor

(b) a supplier

(c) a customer

(d) a member of the general public.

 Suggested research questions for dissertation students

Students interested in corporate governance and stewardship may wish to investigate one or more of the following research questions:

- Why do the majority of jurisdictions use a code-based approach to regulating corporate governance in publicly accountable companies?

- Do corporate governance mechanisms increase financial reporting quality?

- What are the benefits of voluntary compliance with the UK CG Code to small companies listed on the AIM?

- Do smaller companies have higher levels of boardroom diversity than larger companies?

- How suitable is the UK Code of Governance for non-publicly accountable small companies?

- How suitable is the UK's Stewardship Code to non-publicly accountable small companies?

Preliminary reading

Burgstahler, D. and Dichev, I. (1997) 'Earnings management to avoid earnings decreases and losses', *Journal of Accounting and Economics*, 24, pp. 99–129.

Cornett, M., Marcus, A. and Tehranian, H. (2008) 'Corporate governance and pay-for-performance: The impact of earnings management', *Journal of Financial Economics*, 87, pp. 357–373.

Dechow, P., Ge, W. and Schrand, C. (2010) 'Understanding earnings quality: A review of the proxies, their determinants and their consequences', *Journal of Accounting & Economics*, 50(2/3), pp. 344–401.

Dechow, P., Sloan, R. and Sweeney, A. (1995) 'Detecting earnings management', *The Accounting Review*, 70, pp. 3–42.

FRC (2012) *The UK Stewardship Code*, London: Financial Reporting Council. Available from: www.frc.org.uk/Our-Work/Publications/Corporate-Governance/UK-Stewardship-Code-September-2012.pdf (Accessed 1 June 2016).

FRC (2016) *The UK Corporate Governance Code*, London: Financial Reporting Council. Available from: www.frc.org.uk/Our-Work/Publications/Corporate-Governance/UK-Corporate-Governance-Code-April-2016.pdf (Accessed 10 June 2016).

Healy, P. M. and Wahlen, J. M. (1999) 'A review of the earnings management literature and its implications for standard setting', *Accounting Horizons*, 13(4), pp. 365–383.

Klein, A. (2002) 'Audit Committee, board of director characteristics and earnings management', *Journal of Accounting and Economics*, 33, pp. 375–400.

QCA (2013) *Corporate Governance Code for Small and Mid-Size Quoted Companies 2013*. Available from: www.theqca.com/shop/guides/70707/corporate-governance-code-for-small-and-midsize-quoted-companies-2013.thtml (Accessed 6 December 2015).

Rohen, J. and Yaari, V. (2015) 'Earnings management: Implications and controversies', in Jones, S. (ed.), *The Routledge Companion to Financial Accounting Theory*, pp. 254–340.

Students interested in environmental and/or corporate social reporting may wish to investigate one or more of the following research questions:

- Are there national differences in environmental reporting?

- What type of information do UK public companies currently disclose about greenhouse gas emissions in their financial statements?

- Are there standards for reporting the environmental consequences of conducting business?

- Is there a relationship between environmental and/or corporate social reporting and financial performance?

- Do non-publicly accountable small companies systematically record and report environmental information?

- How is environmental and/or corporate social reporting information audited?

Preliminary reading

Aguinis, H. and Glavas, A. (2012) 'What we know and don't know about corporate social responsibility: A review and research agenda', *Journal of Management*, 38(4), pp. 932–968.

Brammer, S. and Millington, A. (2008) 'Does it pay to be different? An analysis of the relationship between corporate social and financial performance', *Strategic Management Journal*, 29, pp. 1325–1343.

Gray, R. and Bebbington, J. (2000) 'Environmental accounting, managerialism and sustainability: Is the planet safe in the hands of business?' *Advances in Environmental Accounting & Management*, 1, pp. 1–44.

Jamil, C.Z.M., Mohamed, R., Muhammad, F. and Alid, A. (2015) 'Environmental management accounting practices in small medium manufacturing firms', *Procedia – Social and Behavioral Sciences*, 172, pp. 619–626.

O'Dwyer, B., Owen, D. and Unerman, J. (2011) 'Seeking legitimacy for new assurance forms: The case of assurance on sustainability reporting', *Accounting, Organizations and Society*, 36, pp. 31–52.

Schneider, A. (2015) 'Reflexivity in sustainability accounting and management: Transcending the economic focus of corporate sustainability', *Journal of Business Ethics*, 127, pp. 525–536.

Spence, L.J., Agyemang, G. and Rinaldi, L. (2012) 'Environmental aspects of sustainability: SMEs and the role of the accountant', *ACCA Research Report 128*.

Students interested in strategic or integrated reporting may wish to investigate one or more of the following research questions:

- What are the pros and cons of making integrated reporting mandatory for public companies in [country]?

- What are the challenges in improving the quality and credibility of integrated reports?

- How is integrated reporting information used by investors?

- How is strategic or integrated reporting information audited?

Preliminary reading

Flower, J. (2015) 'The International Integrated Reporting Council: A story of failure', *Critical Perspectives on Accounting*, 27, pp. 1–17.

Grant Thornton (2015) *Corporate Governance – The Tone from the Top: Grant Thornton Global Governance Report 2015*, London: Grant Thornton UK LLP. Available from: www.grantthornton.global/globalassets/1.-member-firms/global/insights/article-pdfs/2015/corporate-governance-final-a4-lr.pdf (Accessed 6 June 2016).

Reuter, M. and Messner, M. (2015) 'Lobbying on the integrated reporting framework', *Accounting, Auditing & Accountability Journal*, 28(3), pp. 365–402.

Solomon, J., Solomon, A., Joseph, N. and Norton, S. (2013) 'Impression management, myth creation and fabrication in private social and environmental reporting: Insights from Erving Goffman', Accounting, Organizations and Society, 38(3), pp. 195–213.

PART III

Management accounting

12 The importance of cost information

Learning objectives

When you have studied this chapter, you should be able to:

- Explain why it is important to know the cost of making a product or providing a service
- Distinguish between direct costs and indirect costs
- Construct a simple total cost statement
- Calculate the total cost per unit and the selling price

12.1 Introduction

If you have studied financial accounting, you will know that it is concerned with communicating a true and fair view of the financial performance and financial position of an entity at the end of an accounting period to external users. Financial accounting is guided by established principles, legal requirements and accounting standards, which are known as the regulatory framework for financial reporting. In this part of the book we focus on management accounting, which has evolved from financial accounting and is concerned with techniques that provide information to internal users.

Originally, the main focus of management accounting was on cost accounting in order to determine and control costs. This is the subject of Chapters 13–14. Subsequently the focus moved to information for planning and control, such as cost-volume-profit analysis for major products and budgeting, which we explain in Chapters 16–18. Then attention moved to the reduction of waste of resources, such as activity-based costing and sensitivity analysis in capital investment appraisal, which we cover in Chapters 15 and 22. More recently, the focus has been on the creation of value through more effective use of resources, such as strategic management accounting (see Chapter 19) and environmental management accounting (see Chapter 20).

In this chapter we are going to introduce the topic of cost accounting and discuss the importance of cost information. Cost accounting is concerned with providing timely and detailed information to management about the cost of manufacturing goods or providing services. We start by explaining why management needs a system that will supply detailed information about costs. We also explain what is meant by a cost unit and a cost centre and the various ways in which costs can be classified. We then demonstrate how the elements of cost are built up to calculate the total cost per unit and how this cost information can be used to establish the selling price per unit. Cost accounting is usually based on budgeted (predicted) figures.

12.2 Need for cost accounting information

You will remember from Chapter 1 that the *purpose* of *management accounting* is to provide managers with financial and other quantitative information to help them carry out their responsibilities, which focus on planning, controlling and decision making. Unlike financial accounting, management accounting focuses on meeting the needs of internal users and is not governed by the regulatory framework. Instead, the emphasis is on providing information that will help the business achieve its financial objectives.

Key definition

Management accounting is the branch of accounting concerned with collecting and analyzing financial and other quantitative information. It is primarily concerned with communicating information to management to help effective performance measurement, planning, controlling and decision making.

Performance measurement involves developing financial and non-financial indicators of progress towards the organization's goals and regularly reviewing progress. Non-financial measures might include delivery time, customer retention and staff turnover. *Planning* includes developing budgets for future activities and operations. *Controlling* involves using techniques for highlighting variances once the actual figures are known, as well as ensuring that costs fall within acceptable levels and revenue targets are achieved. Costing techniques provide information that will help management set the selling prices of products and services.

Research suggests that accounting systems and the information they provide develop according to management's needs; in other words, on a contingency basis (Chapman, 1997). During the early stages of the development of the business the owner-manager obtains information using informal methods and relies on tacit knowledge. As the number of business transactions increases, this informal personal control by the owner-manager becomes stretched and is replaced by formal delegated methods. This does not mean that formerly information and control had been poor, but that they are no longer appropriate to the size and complexity of the business (Perren et al., 1999).

Figure 12.1 summarizes the key characteristics of small firms and compares them with those of their larger counterparts, where it is likely that the need for more detailed and timely information will have led to the development of formal systems of control.

Figure 12.1 Typical characteristics of small and large firms

Small firms	Large firms
Typically, 1–2 owners	Many owners
Likely to be owner-managed	Managed by managers/directors
Little delegation of control	Control is delegated
Operations are relatively simple	Operations are complex and divided into functional areas
Multitasking is common	Need for functional specialists
Systems tend to be informal	Systems tend to be formal
Reliance on tacit knowledge	Reliance on explicit information

In order to run a business successfully, those responsible for management need to know the *cost* of running the business. Costs include:

- the cost of sales, such as the cost of goods sold in a trading business, the cost of goods manufactured in a manufacturing business or the cost of services sold in a business in the service sector
- the overhead expenses and other expenditure.

There are a number of different ways of defining cost in a business context, but we will start with a general definition.

Key definition

Cost is the amount of expenditure on goods and services that are needed to carry out the economic activities of the entity.

The calculation of the cost of sales for a trading business is:

Opening inventory + Purchases – Closing inventory

The accounting principles guide the accountant to value opening inventory and purchases at the *historical cost*, and to value closing inventory prudently at the lower of cost or *net realizable value*. Therefore, calculating the cost of goods sold for a trading business is relatively straightforward. However, calculating the cost of goods manufactured (for an entity in the manufacturing sector) or calculating the cost of services (for an entity in the service sector) is more complex. This is made even more difficult if more than one type of product or service is produced, because the cost of each one must be built up from the individual elements of cost that can be identified.

Activity

To understand the importance of cost information it is useful to consider why managers need such information. Why do you think managers of a business in the manufacturing sector need to know the cost of making a product or supplying a service?

Business is about making money and those managing the business are responsible for ensuring that it makes a profit. Therefore, the main reasons why managers need to have cost information are:

- To value inventory – In a manufacturing business, managers need cost information to help them value inventories of raw materials, work-in-progress and unsold finished goods.
- To plan production – It would be very difficult to determine the best way to plan production without knowing the relevant costs. It is necessary to know the cost of all the elements making up the production process and the funds required to support them. Such costs are not confined to materials and labour, but also include machinery, buildings, transport, administration, maintenance and many other items.
- To maintain control – Managers have no control if they do not know the costs incurred and are unable to compare them with the original plan. This would lead to the organization's resources being employed inefficiently, resulting in waste and, in the worst circumstances, the complete failure of the organization.
- To aid decision making – It is imperative that managers have knowledge of costs for the correct decisions to be taken. For example, managers need information about costs to decide whether it would be worthwhile investing in new manufacturing machinery, to evaluate alternative ways of carrying out activities and to determine the selling prices of products and services.

Although we have used an example of a manufacturing business, many of the above reasons apply to firms in other industrial sectors.

Activity

Having stressed the importance of knowing the costs involved in making a product or providing a service, they are not always easy to identify. Imagine that you buy a box of five packs of printer paper for £30 on Friday. On Sunday a friend asks you to sell him one pack for some urgent work he needs to print by Monday. You know that if you were to replace that single pack of paper on Monday it would cost you £7.00. What is the cost of the paper you sell to your friend?

(a) £6.00
(b) £7.00
(c) Both these figures
(d) Neither of these figures

You may have answered this by taking the original cost of the box of paper (£30) and dividing it by the number of packs to reach the answer of £6.00, or you may have decided that the cost is Monday's price of £7.00. You may be surprised to know that in some senses all the answers are correct. However, to decide the most appropriate answer, we need to define *cost* more precisely and put it in a context. From this example, you can see that one difficulty is that our view of cost is determined by:

- whether we are buyers or sellers
- the context in which we are making our calculations
- our reasons for wanting the information.

12.3 Cost accounting

Cost accounting is a branch of management accounting that has developed to meet managers' need for precise information about costs. It is concerned with providing timely and detailed information to management about the cost of manufacturing goods or providing services and is based on analyzing the costs relating to *cost units* and *cost centres*.

Key definition

Cost accounting is the process of collecting, analyzing and presenting financial and quantitative data to ascertain the cost of designated cost centres and cost units within the entity.

All organizations provide an identifiable output which may be in the form of a service, a product or both. The output of a business can be measured by devising some form of cost unit. A cost unit is a quantitative unit of the product or service to which costs are allocated. A cost unit can be:

- the final product (for example, a chair or a table in a furniture factory)

- a sub-assembly of a more complex product (for example, a car chassis in the motor industry)
- a batch of products where the unit cost of an individual product is very small (for example, a batch of 120 light bulbs in a light bulb factory, or a pallet of 1,000 bricks in a brick manufacturing business).

Key definition

A cost unit is a designated unit of production for which costs are collected.

In a manufacturing business it should be fairly easy to identify the cost units. In a service organization there may not be any easily-identifiable cost units. In a hotel an appropriate cost unit to use might be the room occupancy; in a distribution company a cost unit might be a tonne/mile (the cost involved in moving 1 tonne of goods 1 mile); in a dating agency it may be the cost of matching one couple.

 Activity

Suggest appropriate cost units for the following businesses:

(a) A car manufacturer
(b) A carrier bag manufacturer
(c) A transport business
(d) A plumber
(e) A sports and leisure centre
(f) A hairdresser

Some of these businesses may have been more difficult than others to find suitable cost units for, particularly if you are not familiar with the industries. However, you may have identified some of the following types of cost unit:

- A car manufacturer producing a range of different models could use each model as a cost unit. If the same organization manufactures the engine, gearbox, body and electrical system, these could also be treated as separate cost units.
- A carrier bag manufacturer has the same problems as a brick manufacturer: the costs identified with manufacturing one carrier bag are so small that they cannot be measured. Therefore, a suitable cost unit might be 1,000 bags of each type produced.
- A logistics or transport business is a bit more difficult. You need to consider what information management would find useful. This might be the costs

associated with moving 1 tonne of goods over 1 mile. Therefore, the cost unit will be 1 tonne/mile.

- Plumbers often work on a number of small jobs, which may vary from fitting a bathroom suite to replacing a tap washer. The plumber needs to know the cost of each job and so a suitable cost unit would be each job.

- In the case of a sports and leisure centre the management needs to know the separate cost of supplying badminton, squash, swimming, table tennis, keep fit, etc. for a period of time. Therefore, a suitable cost unit would be each activity for an hour.

- A hairdresser is likely to offer a number of standard services, such as cut and blow dry, restyling, colouring, etc. Therefore, a suitable cost unit would be each standard service.

As you can see from these examples, many businesses offer a range of different products and/or services. Before the cost of each product or service can be calculated, a quantitative unit must be identified to which costs can be allocated.

As well as calculating the costs for each cost unit, management will also probably need to know the costs for particular *cost centres*. A cost centre is an identifiable part of the organization for which costs can be collected such as a location, function, activity or item of equipment.

Activity

Indicate which of the following could be cost centres in the following two businesses:

Toy manufacturer	**Hotel**
Assembly department	Kitchen
Stores department	Cost of drinks sold
Sales team	Reception area
Specialized moulding machine	Laundry
Clerical salaries	Restaurant

You may know nothing about the manufacture of toys, but the definition of a cost centre given above should have helped you to identify the first four of these as possible cost centres. Clerical salaries are usually an expense, not a cost centre. The specialized moulding machine may be a cost centre if it is sufficiently important and complex to allow a number of costs to be identified with that particular activity. Of course, not all toy manufacturers would use the above cost centres, but they are all areas of activity where managers may need to know the costs. As far as the hotel is concerned, the cost of drinks sold is an item of expense, but all the others are potential cost centres.

> **Key definition**
>
> A cost centre is a designated area, function or activity for which costs are collected within the entity.

Cost centres are of two main types:

- *production cost centres* are those concerned with making a product
- *service cost centres* provide a service to other parts of the organization.

Identifying cost centres is relatively easy as they are usually clearly defined. One example is that of a factory canteen or a college refectory. In a manufacturing business, departments may be referred to as shops (for example, the machine shop). The sort of financial information that would be available for a canteen includes employees' wages, the cost of electricity used for cooking, lighting and heating, the cost of food and beverages, etc., and the meals may be used as the cost units.

Figure 12.2 shows typical cost centres in a light bulb factory where costs are collected for a cost unit consisting of a batch of 120 light bulbs.

Figure 12.2 Typical cost centres in a factory

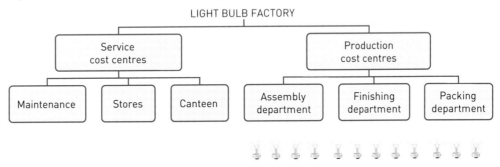

Some businesses do not formally identify their cost centres or cost units, but answering the following questions should help you to identify them:

- What can be regarded as the cost centres and cost units in the organization?
- What financial information is generated in respect of potential cost centres and cost units?
- Is someone directly responsible for any of them or able to influence them?

12.4 Classifying costs

Expenditure can be divided into revenue and capital expenditure:

- *Revenue expenditure* is the collective term for the costs and expenses that are written off in the statement of profit or loss for the accounting period to which they relate.
- *Capital expenditure* is the collective term for the cost of non-current assets that are capitalized in the statement of financial position.

Although it is useful to know the total revenue expenditure for an accounting period, it is even more useful if revenue expenditure is broken down into individual costs and expenses. By classifying costs, we can obtain more detailed information and use it in a variety of ways for planning, controlling and decision making. In addition, classifying costs helps us to understand better what is meant by the term 'cost'.

Costs can be classified by:

- Their *nature,* such as the cost of materials, labour and expenses, and the cost of materials can be divided into raw materials, maintenance materials, cleaning materials, etc.
- Their *function,* such as production costs, distribution costs, administrative expenses, and research and development costs.
- Whether they are *product costs,* which can be identified with the cost unit and are part of the value of inventory, or *period costs,* such as selling costs and administrative expenses, which are deducted as expenses in the current period.
- Whether they are *direct costs,* which can be identified with a specific cost unit, or *indirect costs,* which cannot be identified with a specific cost unit, although they may be traced directly to a particular cost centre. Indirect costs must be shared by the cost units. Examples of direct costs are the cost of materials used to make a product; the cost of labour if employees are paid according to the number of products made or services provided; the cost of expenses, such as subcontract work. Examples of indirect costs are expenses such as rent and managers' salaries.

A further method is to classify costs according to their *behaviour* when the level of production or sales increases or decreases. This is useful for businesses in the manufacturing sector where activity levels fluctuate. Costs are divided into *variable costs,* which in total change in proportion with the level of production or sales activity, and *fixed costs,* which are not affected by fluctuations in activity levels. Direct costs are usually variable costs, and indirect costs are usually fixed costs. Examples of direct costs that are fixed are patents, licences and copyright relating to a particular product and some direct expenses such as the hire of a particular piece of equipment to produce a specific order.

It is important to note that the definitions of variable and fixed costs use the phrase 'in total'. The variable cost per unit (e.g. the direct materials used to make a product) remains constant, but the total variable costs will vary with the number of units produced. Figure 12.3 summarizes the cost behaviour of variable and fixed costs when activity levels change.

Figure 12.3   Behaviour of variable and fixed costs

	Increased activity	Decreased activity
Variable costs:		
In total	Increased	Decreased
Per unit	Unchanged	Unchanged
Fixed costs:		
In total	Unchanged	Unchanged
Per unit	Decreased	Increased

Activity

Classify the following costs into direct costs, indirect costs, variable costs and fixed costs:

(a) Materials used in the product
(b) Factory rent
(c) Insurance of the factory
(d) Depreciation on machinery
(e) Maintenance of machinery
(f) Factory canteen costs
(g) Supervisors' salaries
(h) Wages paid to production workers
(i) Accountants' salaries

Even if you have no experience of working in a manufacturing environment, you should have been able to work out the answers from the definitions of direct and indirect costs. Materials can be identified with the product and are therefore direct costs; so too are the production workers' wages if they are paid according to the number of units produced rather than a flat rate irrespective of the level of production. Rent, insurance, maintenance of machinery, canteen and the salaries cannot be identified with a single product, but must be shared over a number of products; therefore these are indirect costs. In a service industry, the same principles apply.

You may have had more difficulty in distinguishing between fixed and variable costs. One thing you may have noticed is that direct costs in our example are also variable costs and the indirect costs are also fixed costs. For example, the materials used in the product can be identified directly with the product, and the more items produced, the higher the total cost of materials used. Therefore, these *product direct costs* are variable costs. On the other hand, rent and insurance for the period remain the same, regardless of the quantity of products produced, and therefore these are classified as fixed costs.

We will now look more closely at the difference between fixed and variable costs using an example. Sam Reeves has a taxi business. The average mileage by a taxi for three months is 15,000 miles and the following table shows the quarterly costs, analyzed by nature:

Expense	Cost per quarter
	£
Driver's salary	2,670
Petrol and oil	1,050
Annual service	450
Tax and insurance	1,110
Depreciation	870

We can use the details of Sam's business expenses as the basis for calculating further cost information. For example, we can add up the costs so that Sam can find out that the total costs per quarter for 1 taxi are £6,150. From this we can calculate the total cost per mile:

$$\frac{\text{Total costs}}{\text{Total mileage}} = \frac{£6,150}{15,000 \text{ miles}} = 41\text{p per mile}$$

We can now calculate the cost per mile for each of the expenses:

Expense	Cost per quarter	Cost per mile
	£	Pence
Driver's salary	2,670	17.8
Petrol	1,050	7.0
Maintenance and repairs	450	3.0
Tax and insurance	1,110	7.4
Depreciation	870	5.8
Total	6,150	41.0

Sam now has a considerable amount of information, including the total cost per mile, which is further analyzed by the nature of the expense. However, there are some problems if Sam tries to use this cost information without understanding the difference between fixed and variable costs. For example, he may want to know what the cost is per mile if the taxi travelled 30,000 miles in 1 quarter. Your immediate response may be to say that the cost per mile would remain at 41p.

However, on consideration, you may have seen that the cost per mile is likely to be lower. This is because the total fixed costs (the cost of the driver's salary, taxation, insurance and depreciation) will remain the same, even though the mileage has doubled. On the other hand, the total variable costs (the cost of petrol and oil) will change in direct proportion to the change in the level of activity. This means that if activity doubles (in our example, if mileage doubles), the variable costs will double. We shall be looking at the importance of fixed and variable costs again in Chapter 16, but for the moment you need to remember that calculating the average total cost per unit can be misleading if there are significant changes in the activity level of the business.

Figure 12.4 summarizes the classification of costs we have discussed.

Figure 12.4 Classifying revenue expenditure

Product direct costs	Indirect costs
(always variable costs)	(usually fixed costs)
• Direct materials (e.g. components) • Direct labour (e.g. piecework wages) • Direct expenses (e.g. subcontractor)	• Production overheads • Non-production overheads (e.g. administrative expenses, distribution costs, research & development costs)

12.5 Elements of total cost

Having introduced you to the different ways in which costs can be classified, we are now able to explain how the *total cost* of a product or cost unit is built up from a number of different *elements*. In order to identify these elements, costs are classified according to their nature, function, whether they are product or period costs and whether they are direct costs or indirect costs, as we described in the previous section. The following *total cost statement* shows the elements of total cost in a typical manufacturing business.

Total cost statement	
	£
Direct costs	
Direct materials	X
Direct labour	X
Direct expenses	X
Prime cost	X
Production overheads	X
Production cost	X
Distribution costs	X
Administrative expenses	X
Research and development costs	X
Total cost	X

The direct costs, which are costs that can be traced directly to the product or cost unit are added together to give what is known as the *prime cost*. Then the production overheads are added to give the *production cost*. Production overheads are the indirect production costs that cannot be traced directly to the product or cost unit. Finally, the non-production overheads are added to arrive at the total cost.

Direct costs can be classified as:

- direct materials, which are the cost of materials and components used to make the product
- direct labour, which are the costs of employing the workforce that converts the direct materials into the finished product
- direct expenses, which are not always incurred but include such costs as subcontract work or special tools and equipment bought for a particular order.

Indirect costs can be classified as:

- distribution costs, which are the costs of promoting, selling and delivering the products (and any after-sales services)
- administrative expenses, which are the non-production costs of operating the business
- research and development costs, which are not always present but are the costs associated with developing or improving products and production processes.

Key definitions

Direct costs are product costs that can be identified with and traced directly to a product or cost unit.

Indirect costs are costs that cannot be identified with or traced directly to a product or cost unit. Therefore, they are classified as overheads.

Activity

Jon Hazel is the owner-manager of Hazelwood Products Ltd that makes 10 traditionally hand-made bookcases per week. The costs for week ending 7 January
are as follows:

Direct materials	£440
Direct labour	£660
Production overheads	£200
Distribution costs	£60
Administrative expenses	£80

The business has no direct expenses or research and development costs. Using
the following pro forma, calculate the total cost for the week.

Hazelwood Products Ltd
Total cost w/e 7 January (10 bookcases)

	£
Direct costs	
Direct materials	
Direct labour	_____
Prime cost	
Production overheads	_____
Production cost	
Distribution costs	
Administrative expenses	
Total cost	_____

Check your answer against the following solution:

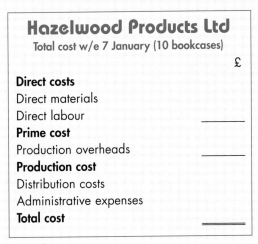

Hazelwood Products Ltd
Total cost w/e 7 January (10 bookcases)

	£
Direct costs	
Direct materials	440
Direct labour	660
Prime cost	1,100
Production overheads	200
Production cost	1,300
Distribution costs	60
Administrative expenses	80
Total cost	1,440

Now he knows the total cost per week, Jon can ensure that the business has sufficient funds to support these costs. The most important source of funds will be the sales revenue generated from selling the bookcases, and further analysis of the above cost information will help Jon decide on an appropriate selling price for the bookcases.

Activity

Using the same layout as before, construct a statement showing the total cost per unit (in this case, 1 bookcase). As this is a very simple business, you can apportion the overheads by dividing them by the number of units produced. In addition, calculate the selling price if Hazelwood Products Ltd wants to make a profit that represents a mark-up of 50% on the production cost.

You should have found this fairly straightforward and the answer is given below.

Hazelwood Products Ltd
Total cost (1 unit)

	£
Direct costs	
Direct materials	44
Direct labour	66
Prime cost	110
Production overheads	20
Production cost	130
Distribution costs	6
Administrative expenses	8
Total cost	144
Profit (£130 × 50%)	65
Selling price	209

The total cost per unit is £144 and all you need to do is add the profit element based on 40% of the production cost (£130 × 50% = £65) to arrive at a selling price of £209. In other words, if each bookcase is sold for £209, the total cost per unit of £144 will be covered and the business will make a profit of £65.

12.6 Conclusions

In this chapter we have looked the importance of cost information to those responsible for the management of a business, particularly those in the manufacturing and service sectors. Cost accounting techniques require costs to be classified so that the cost of all the designated cost centres and cost units can be ascertained. Production cost centres are those concerned with making a product, while service cost centres provide a service to other parts of the organization. A cost unit can be the final product, a sub-assembly or a batch of products.

The classification of costs involves an analysis of the cost by nature and by function, and distinguishing between direct and indirect costs. In a manufacturing business where production levels fluctuate, it is useful to analyze costs into variable and fixed costs according to their behaviour when the level of activity changes. The cost per unit is calculated by identifying the different elements of cost: the direct costs plus a fair share of the indirect costs. A percentage mark-up representing profit can be added to the cost per unit to establish the selling price per unit.

References

Chapman, C.S. (1997) 'Reflections on a contingent view of accounting', *Accounting Organizations and Society*, pp. 189–205.

Perren, L., Berry, A. and Partridge, M. (1999) 'The evolution of management information, control and decision-making processes in small growth-orientated service sector businesses: Exploratory lessons from four cases of success', *Journal of Small Business and Enterprise Development*, 5(4), pp. 351–361.

Discussion questions

1 Discuss the purpose of cost accounting and why it is important for managers to have cost information.

2 Discuss the classifications of cost examined in this chapter.

Practice questions

3 Give three examples of direct materials used in the following products:

(a) A book
(b) A pair of shoes
(c) A winter coat
(d) A jar of coffee
(e) A carton of milk

(f) A loaf of bread

(g) A tin of baked beans

(h) A book

(i) A desk

(j) A chair

(k) A laptop computer

(l) A car

4 Classify the following items of expenditure into capital expenditure and revenue expenditure:

(a) Purchase of a factory

(b) Purchase of plant and equipment

(c) Buildings and contents insurance

(d) Maintenance of plant and equipment

(e) Power for machinery

(f) Electricity for factory lighting and heating

(g) Purchase of delivery vehicles

(h) Tax and insurance of delivery vehicles

(i) Maintenance of delivery vehicles

(j) Depreciation of property, plant and equipment

(k) Salaries paid to factory operatives

(l) Training programme for accounts office staff

5 Classify the following costs incurred in a manufacturing business into production overheads, distribution costs, administrative expenses, and research and development costs:

(a) Factory rent

(b) Maintenance of plant and equipment

(c) Power for machinery

(d) Electricity for office lighting and heating

(e) Tax and insurance of delivery vehicles

(f) Maintenance of delivery vehicles

(g) Salary paid to managing director

(h) Salary paid to new product development manager

(i) Salaries and commission paid to sales team

(j) Salaries paid to accounts office staff

(k) Salaries paid to factory canteen staff

(l) Fees paid to advertising agency

6 Petra Pots Ltd plans to produce 2,000 standard plant pots next month. Each
   pot requires the same amount of clay and takes the same time to produce. The
   expected costs for next month are as follows:

	£
Rent:	
Factory	1,000
Office	400
Lighting and heating:	
Factory	2,000
Office	800
Power	700
Factory wages:	
Operators (piecework)	10,000
Maintenance staff (fixed)	1,500
Canteen staff (fixed)	2,500
Clay	6,000
Depreciation:	
Moulds	2,200
Factory fixtures and fittings	800
Equipment	200
Office salaries	1,800
Sales team's salaries and commission	2,200
Sales team's car expenses	1,600
Delivery expenses	500
Maintenance of equipment	900
Paint and glaze	200
Packaging materials	800

Required

(a) Prepare a costing statement for Petra Pots Ltd that shows the elements of cost
    and calculates the total cost of producing 2,000 pots.
(b) Interpret your statement by explaining the following terms:
    (i)   Direct costs
    (ii) Prime cost
    (iii) Production cost
    (iv) Indirect costs
    (v)   Total cost

7 Using the information for Petra Pots Ltd in the previous question, construct a
   statement that shows the elements of total cost for 1 unit. As this is a very simple

business, you can apportion the overheads by dividing them by the number of units produced. In addition, calculate the selling price of 1 unit if the business requires a profit margin based on 50% of the production cost.

8 Atana Ltd manufactures smart watches. The company's costs are as follows:

Rent and business rates	£50,000 pa
Salaries for administrative staff	£360,000 pa
Salaries for sales and marketing staff	£240,000 pa
Sales commission	5% of revenue
Components	£2 per unit
Piecework wages for production operatives	£5 per unit
Royalties to the designer	3% of revenue
Depreciation of plant and equipment	£5,000 pa
Selling price	£75 per unit

Required

Using the following table, classify the costs into direct and indirect costs and calculate the total cost assuming that:

(a) 50,000 watches are produced and sold
(b) 75,000 watches are produced and sold.

Cost	(a) 50,000 units		(b) 100,000 units	
	Direct £	Indirect £	Direct £	Indirect £
Factory rent				
Office rent				
Business rates				
Salaries for administrative staff				
Salaries for sales and marketing staff				
Sales commission				
Components				
Piecework wages for factory operatives				
Royalties to the inventor				
Depreciation of office equipment				
Depreciation of manufacturing equipment				
Subtotals				
Total cost				

 Suggested research questions for dissertation students

Students interested in cost and management accounting may wish to investigate one or more of the following research questions:

- How do SMEs meet their needs for quantitative and financial information to manage the business?

- What are the factors that determine whether an SME uses management accounting information?

- What are the main sources of advice on cost and management accounting techniques used by SMEs at the start-up stage and beyond?

- Do business relationships influence the firm's management accounting practices?

- Do the management accounting practices of a firm support or constrain the development of business relationships?

Preliminary reading

Becker, W., Ulrich, P. and Staffel, M. (2011) 'Management accounting and controlling in German SMEs: Do company size and family influence matter?' *International Journal of Entrepreneurial Venturing*, 3(3), pp. 281–300.

Chiarini, A. (2012) 'Lean production: Mistakes and limitations of accounting systems inside the SME sector', *Journal of Manufacturing Technology Management*, 23(5), pp. 681–700.

CIMA (2009) *Management Accounting Tools for Today and Tomorrow*, London: Chartered Institute of Management Accountants. Available from: www.cima-global.com/Documents/Thought_leadership_docs/CIMA%20Tools%20and%20 Techniques%2030-11-09%20PDF.pdf (Accessed 11 June 2016).

Collis, J. and Jarvis, R. (2000) 'How owner-managers use accounts', *ICAEW Research Report*, London: The Centre for Business Performance Research. ISBN 1841520500. Available from: www.icaew.com/-/media/corporate/files/technical/ research-and-academics/publications-and-projects/financial-reporting-publications/how-owner-managers-use-accounts.ashx (Accessed 10 December 2016).

Collis, J. and Jarvis, R. (2002) 'Financial information and the management of small private companies', *Journal of Small Business and Enterprise Development*, 9(2), pp. 100–110, 1SSN 1462-6004.

Hakansson, H. and Lind, J. (2004) 'Accounting and network coordination', *Accounting, Organizations and Society*, 29, pp. 51–72.

Johnson, H.T. and Kaplan, R.S. (1987) *Relevance Lost: The Rise and Fall of Management Accounting*, Boston: Harvard Business School Press.

Lavia López, O. and Hiebl, M.R.W. (2014) 'Management accounting in small and medium-sized enterprises: Current knowledge and avenues for further research', *Journal of Management Accounting Research*, 27(1), pp. 81–119.

Lucas, M., Prowle, M. and Lowth, G. (2013) 'Management accounting practices of (UK) small-medium-sized enterprises (SMEs)', *Improving SME Performance through Management Accounting Education*, 9(4). Available from: www.cima-global.com/Documents/Thought_leadership_docs/Management%20and%20

financial%20accounting/ManagementAccountingPracticesOfSmall-Medium-SizedEnterprises.pdf (Accessed 10 December 2016).

Mitchell, F. and Reid, G. (2000) 'Problems, challenges and opportunities: Small business as a setting for management accounting research', *Management Accounting Research*, 11(4), pp. 385–390.

Nandan, R. (2010) 'Management accounting needs of SMEs and the role of professional accountants: A renewed research agenda', *Journal of Management Accounting Research*, 8(1), pp. 65–78.

Perren, L. and Grant, P. (2000) 'The evolution of management accounting routines in small businesses: A social construction perspective', *Management Accounting Research*, 11(4), pp. 391–411.

13 Costing for product direct costs

Learning objectives

When you have studied this chapter, you should be able to:

- Describe the main stages in controlling direct materials
- Calculate the cost of direct materials and closing inventory using different costing methods
- Describe the advantages and disadvantages of different costing methods
- Describe and apply methods for costing direct labour and direct expenses

13.1 Introduction

In the previous chapter we identified the prime cost as one of the key components of the total cost of a cost unit. In this chapter we examine the individual elements of the prime cost, which are the costs relating to direct materials, direct labour and direct expenses. Even in the smallest business, the minimum information required is the total for each of these different cost elements that have been incurred in producing the cost units. However, management usually needs more detailed information and a breakdown of the cost of each product or service helps them in their responsibility for planning, controlling and decision making. Managers need to know the cost of all the different materials used to make a product, the cost of the different types of labour in the factory, the stores, the maintenance department and the factory canteen, and any direct expenses. Once systems have been established to collect this detailed information, the total cost of direct materials, the total cost of direct labour and the total cost of any direct expenses can be calculated for each cost unit. In the manufacturing sector, this information can be used to determine the prime cost of making a particular product; in the civil engineering sector, it can be used to establish the prime cost of constructing a particular building; in the service sector, a plumber can use it to calculate the prime cost for a particular job, and so on.

We start by describing the control system for the purchase and receipt of materials and two methods used to price issues of direct materials from stores and value the remaining inventory. We then describe the procedures and documents used to record the direct labour costs associated with each cost unit before discussing the difficulty of identifying direct expenses.

13.2 Importance of material control

In a manufacturing business, *materials* are the raw materials, components or sub-assemblies used to make a product. The control of materials used in the production process is essential. *Material control* is necessary to ensure that production is not delayed due to shortages of materials and the business does not tie up capital by storing excess quantities of inventory. In a well-managed business, materials are available in the right place, at the right time and in the right quantities, and all materials are properly accounted for.

Key definition

Materials are the raw materials, components or sub-assemblies purchased from a supplier for use in the manufacture of a product.

The cost of materials purchased from a supplier is classified as *revenue expenditure,* which is the collective term for the costs and expenses that are written off in the statement of profit or loss for the accounting period to which they relate. Materials can be divided into direct materials, which feature in the final product produced (such as wood and metal in furniture), or indirect materials, which are necessary to carry out production but do not feature in the final product (such as maintenance and cleaning materials). Initially, deliveries of materials are taken to the place where they will be stored (the stores) and records are kept of quantities received and prices paid. Depending on the amount of space needed to house the materials, the stores may consist of anything from a small store room to a large warehouse or secure yard from which they can be issued conveniently to production when they are required.

Some businesses have just-in-time (JIT) manufacturing systems in which products are produced in time to meet demand, rather than producing products in case they are needed. This greatly reduces or eliminates the need for large inventories of materials. In some cases, the value of materials in stores is very high (for example, precious metals or other scarce resources used in the production process). Records should be maintained of the quantity of goods in store and it is essential that a physical count is made because of the possibility of errors and theft. This is known as an *inventory count* and should be done at least annually. It requires a substantial amount of work and can be very disruptive. Some organizations use continuous inventory counting, where employees check a few items every day so that all inventories are checked at least once a year.

The stores often carry many hundreds of different types of materials. Therefore, the business requires an efficient and accurate system for recording and controlling the cost of materials. This can be either a manual or a computerized system. Although managers devise material control systems and procedures to suit their particular needs, there are a number of different prime documents used at each stage and each of these forms must be properly completed and authorized. The main stages in material control are as follows:

- The stores or production department sends a *purchase requisition* to the purchasing department, giving details of the quantity and type of materials required.
- The buyer in the purchasing department sends a *purchase order* to the supplier.
- The supplier sends the materials with a *goods received note*, which is checked against the materials received and the purchase order.
- The materials are added to the existing inventory in the stores and the quantity is added to the inventory level shown on the *bin card*.
- When materials are required, the production department sends a *materials requisition* to the stores and the stores issues the materials and deducts the quantity from the inventory level shown on the *bin card*. Periodic inventory counting ensures that a physical count of all inventories is made to confirm that the actual quantities support the levels shown on the bin cards.

Copies of all prime documents are sent to the accountant so that he or she can check that materials have been properly ordered and received before paying the supplier's invoice. The accountant also records all inventory movements (the quantity and value of receipts and issues of materials) and the quantity and value of inventory balances for each type of material are recorded in an *inventory account*. This allows the cost of materials used in each cost unit to be calculated.

Activity

Draw a diagram showing the flow of documents used to control the movement of materials.

The design of your diagram will depend on your creative abilities and the assumptions you have made, but you should have shown a logical flow of information that relates to the main stages in material control we have outlined in this section (see Figure 13.1).

Figure 13.1   Main stages in material control

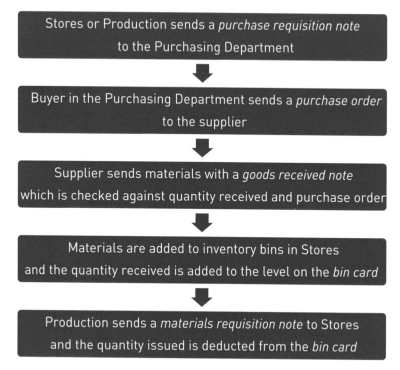

Stores or Production sends a *purchase requisition note*
to the Purchasing Department

⬇

Buyer in the Purchasing Department sends a *purchase order*
to the supplier

⬇

Supplier sends materials with a *goods received note*
which is checked against quantity received and purchase order

⬇

Materials are added to inventory bins in Stores
and the quantity received is added to the level on the *bin card*

⬇

Production sends a *materials requisition note* to Stores
and the quantity issued is deducted from the *bin card*

13.3 Costing direct materials

The purchase of direct materials used in the production process represents a substantial cost and managers require information to establish what these costs are. Having looked at the procedures for purchasing, storing and issuing materials, we now need to consider the methods used for costing direct materials issued to production. These focus on the price at which materials are issued from stores to production and an effective system ensures that:

* the correct materials are delivered
* materials are stored and issued only with proper authorization
* production is charged with the cost of materials used
* the inventory of materials in the stores is correctly valued.

Calculating the cost of direct materials can be a problem. For example, it may not be possible to identify each issue of materials with the corresponding receipt into stores or it may be complicated by the fact that materials have been received on different dates and at a number of different purchase prices. Fluctuating prices may be due to a number of reasons, such as the following:

* a general rise in the price of goods or services due to inflation or a general lowering of prices due to deflation

- variations in exchange rates if materials are purchased overseas
- shortages in the supply of materials
- temporary discounts, such as special offers.

There are a number of methods for costing materials issued to production. The method chosen not only has implications for the cost of the units produced, but also for the value of closing inventory remaining in the stores. Although some valuation methods might be satisfactory for management purposes, they are not suitable for valuing inventory for financial reporting purposes. You will remember from earlier chapters that IAS 2, *Inventories*, requires that inventory is valued at the lower of cost or net realizable value. In a manufacturing business, cost refers to the total cost incurred in bringing the product to its present location and condition, including an appropriate proportion of production overhead costs. Therefore, to avoid having to use one method for management accounting purposes and another for financial accounting purposes, most businesses choose the method that is suitable for both. In this book, we examine three main methods:

- The *standard cost* method uses predetermined costs known as standard costs. The standard cost is derived from a standard quantity of materials allowed for the production of a specific cost unit at standard direct materials price. This method of standard costing is closely associated with a system of budgetary control and we will be looking at these topics in subsequent chapters.
- The *first in, first out (FIFO)* method uses the price of the earliest consignment of materials for all issues to production until the quantity received at that price has been issued, then the price of the next consignment.
- The *weighted-average cost (WAC)* method uses the weighted-average price of materials received which is recalculated every time a new consignment of that item is received. The weighted-average price is calculated as the total value of inventory divided by the total quantity of inventory.

We will now look at the last two methods in some detail.

Key definitions

First in, first out cost (FIFO) is a method of valuing units of direct materials that uses the price of the earliest consignment received for all issues to production until all inventory received at that price has been used up. Then the next latest price is used, and so on. The valuation of closing inventory is based on the same FIFO basis.

Weighted-average cost (WAC) is a method of valuing units of direct materials based on the weighted-average price, which is recalculated after each new consignment is received. The valuation of closing inventory is based on the same WAC basis.

Activity

Hazelwood Products Ltd started making bookshelves on 1 January. The goods received notes and the materials requisitions show the following receipts and issues of materials during the first three days.

1 January	Received 50 units at £3.00 per unit
2 January	Received a further 50 units at £4.00 per unit
3 January	Issued 50 units to production

Complete the following record in the inventory account and calculate the cost of the 50 units issued to production on 3 January and 50 units remaining in inventory using FIFO and WAC. The formula for the weighted average price is:

$$\frac{\text{Total value of inventory}}{\text{Total quantity of inventory}}$$

FIFO	Receipts			Issues			Inventory balance	
January	Quantity	Price	Value	Quantity	Price	Value	Quantity	Value
	Unit	£	£	Unit	£	£	Unit	£
1								
2								
3								
Total								

WAC	Receipts			Issues			Inventory balance	
January	Quantity	Price	Value	Quantity	Price	Value	Quantity	Value
	Unit	£	£	Unit	£	£	Unit	£
1								
2								
3								
Total								

Check your answer against the following solutions.

FIFO	Receipts			Issues			Inventory balance	
January	Quantity	Price	Value	Quantity	Price	Value	Quantity	Value
	Unit	£	£	Unit	£	£	Unit	£
1	50	3.00	150.00				50	150.00
2	50	4.00	200.00				100	350.00
3				50	3.00	150.00	50	200.00
Total	100		350.00	50		150.00		

WAC	Receipts			Issues			Inventory balance	
January	Quantity	Price	Value	Quantity	Price	Value	Quantity	Value
	Unit	£	£	Unit	£	£	Unit	£
1	50	3.00	150.00				50	150.00
2	50	4.00	200.00				100	350.00
3				50	3.50	175.00	50	175.00
Total	100		350.00	50		175.00		

We are now going to extend our example by adding information for the rest of the week. As the number of receipts and issues increase, Jon Hazel may find it is more efficient to use a spreadsheet to record the movement of inventory and calculate a continuous inventory balance, and you may wish to do so for the next activity.

Activity

Using the following information, calculate the quantity and value of materials issued to production during the first week and the quantity and value of closing inventory at 7 January using FIFO and WAC.

1 January	Received 50 units at £3.00 per unit
2 January	Received 50 units at £4.00 per unit
3 January	Issued 50 units to production
4 January	Received 10 units at £5.00 per unit
5 January	Issued 40 units to production
6 January	Received 40 units at £4.00 per unit
7 January	Issued 30 units to production

Check your answer against the following solutions.

FIFO	Receipts			Issues			Inventory balance	
January	Quantity	Price	Value	Quantity	Price	Value	Quantity	Value
	Unit	£	£	Unit	£	£	Unit	£
1	50	3.00	150.00				50	150.00
2	50	4.00	200.00				100	350.00
3				50	3.00	150.00	50	200.00
4	10	5.00	50.00				60	250.00
5				40	4.00	160.00	20	90.00
6	40	4.00	160.00				60	250.00
7				10	4.00	40.00	50	210.00
7				10	5.00	50.00	40	160.00
7				10	4.00	40.00	30	120.00
Total	150		560.00	120		440.00		

WAC	Receipts			Issues			Inventory balance	
January	Quantity	Price	Value	Quantity	Price	Value	Quantity	Value
	Unit	£	£	Unit	£	£	Unit	£
1	50	3.00	150.00				50	150.00
2	50	4.00	200.00				100	350.00
3				50	3.50	175.00	50	175.00
4	10	5.00	50.00				60	225.00
5				40	3.75	150.00	20	75.00
6	40	4.00	160.00				60	235.00
7				30	3.92	117.50	30	117.50
Total	150		560.00	120		442.50		

The main thing to remember about using WAC is that you need to recalculate the average price at which inventory will be issued if a new consignment of that particular item has been received. This means calculating the new total value of inventory and dividing it by the new total quantity of inventory at that date. To find the cost of materials issued on 3 January you should have divided the inventory value of £350 by the quantity of inventory (100 units) to arrive at £3.50 per unit. Another consignment is received on 4 January, so the cost of materials issued on 5 January is the new inventory value of £225 divided by the new quantity of inventory (60 units), which is £3.75 per unit. Since further inventory is delivered on 6 January, you need to divide the new inventory value of £235 by the new quantity of inventory (60 units), which is £3.92 per unit (rounded to the nearest 1p). This is the new weighted average price used for the materials issued on 7 January.

We used Microsoft® Excel to prepare the inventory account for Hazelwood Products Ltd and Figure 13.2 shows you the formulae we used. To reveal the formulae in an Excel Workbook (a file with the suffix .xlsx), click on Formulas in the main menu, then select Show Formulas in the Formula Auditing tab. Deselect Show Formulas when you want to return to data view.

13.4 Comparing methods when prices are rising

In the previous chapter we looked at the total costs for Hazelwood Products Ltd for week ending 7 January, when 10 bookcases were produced, in the context of describing the different elements of cost. In the above activity we have been focusing on how the cost of direct materials is calculated. You can see from the total cost statement, which we have reproduced below, that Jon used a figure of £440 as the cost of the direct materials issued to production during the week ending 7 January.

Hazelwood Products Ltd

Total cost w/e 7 January (10 bookcases)

	£
Direct costs	
Direct materials	440
Direct labour	660
Prime cost	1,100
Production overheads	200
Production cost	1,300
Distribution costs	60
Administrative expenses	80
Total cost	1,440

If you look at the total cost of materials issued to production in the two sets of inventory accounts you prepared for the previous activity, you will see that Jon must have been using the FIFO method, as the WAC method results in the higher figure of £442.50. Both figures are correct and this is another example of why business owners and managers need to have some understanding of the techniques used by accountants in order to make informed decisions about their accounting policies.

Figure 13.2 Inventory account formulae

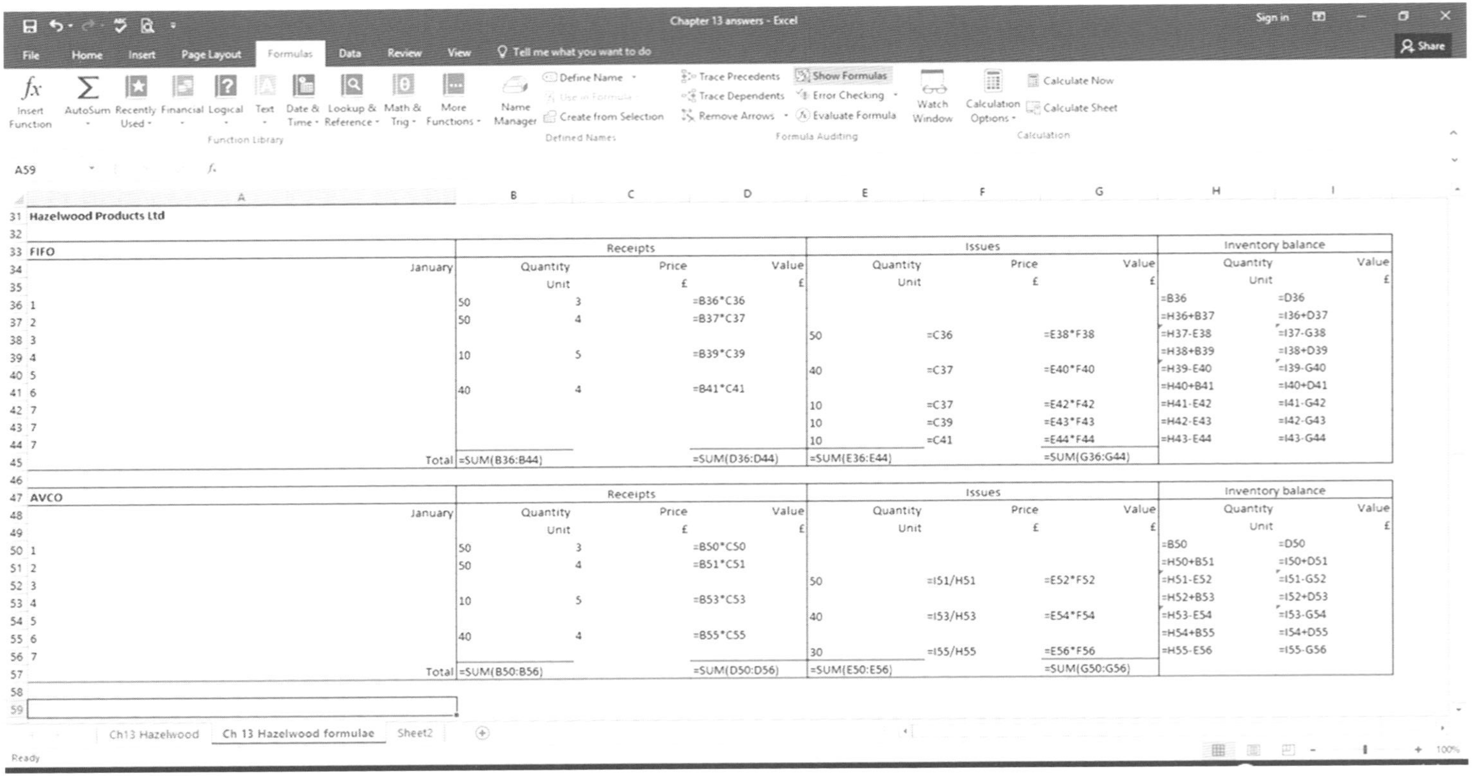

Chapter 13 answers – Excel

Cell: A59

Hazelwood Products Ltd

FIFO

Row	January	Receipts Quantity/Unit	Receipts Price £	Receipts Value £	Issues Quantity/Unit	Issues Price £	Issues Value £	Inventory balance Quantity/Unit	Inventory balance Value £
36 (1)		50	3	=B36*C36				=B36	=D36
37 (2)		50	4	=B37*C37				=B36+B37	=I36+D37
38 (3)					50	=C36	=E38*F38	=B37-E38	=I37-G38
39 (4)		10	5	=B39*C39				=B38+B39	=I38+D39
40 (5)					40	=C37	=E40*F40	=B39-E40	=I39-G40
41 (6)		40	4	=B41*C41				=B40+B41	=I40+D41
42 (7)					10	=C37	=E42*F42	=B41-E42	=I41-G42
43					10	=C39	=E43*F43	=B42-E43	=I42-G43
44					10	=C41	=E44*F44	=B43-E44	=I43-G44
45 Total		=SUM(B36:B44)		=SUM(D36:D44)	=SUM(E36:E44)		=SUM(G36:G44)		=SUM(G36:G44)

AVCO

Row	January	Receipts Quantity/Unit	Receipts Price £	Receipts Value £	Issues Quantity/Unit	Issues Price £	Issues Value £	Inventory balance Quantity/Unit	Inventory balance Value £
50 (1)		50	3	=B50*C50				=B50	=D50
51 (2)		50	4	=B51*C51				=B50+B51	=I50+D51
52 (3)					50	=I51/H51	=E52*F52	=H51-E52	=I51-G52
53 (4)		10	5	=B53*C53				=H52+B53	=I52+D53
54 (5)					40	=I53/H53	=E54*F54	=H53-E54	=I53-G54
55 (6)		40	4	=B55*C55				=H54+B55	=I54+D55
56 (7)					30	=I55/H55	=E56*F56	=H55-E56	=I55-G56
57 Total		=SUM(B50:B56)		=SUM(D50:D56)	=SUM(E50:E56)		=SUM(G50:G56)		=SUM(G50:G56)

Sheet tabs: Ch13 Hazelwood | Ch 13 Hazelwood formulae | Sheet2

We can conclude that the total cost of materials issued to production (and hence the cost of direct materials used in the product) and the value of the inventory remaining in stores vary according to the method used. We are now going to examine the key figures at the end of January under the two methods a little more closely.

Method	Cost of purchases	Cost of materials used	Closing inventory
	£	£	£
FIFO	560.00	440.00	120.00
WAC	560.00	442.50	117.50

When prices are rising, as in our example, the cost of materials issued to production is lower and the value of closing inventory is higher under FIFO than under the WAC method. This means that when prices are rising, FIFO maximizes gross profit. If you have studied financial accounting, you will remember that gross profit is the difference between the sales revenue and the cost of sales (the cost of the goods sold). The key calculations are:

$$Gross\ profit = Revenue - Cost\ of\ sales$$

$$Cost\ of\ sales = Opening\ inventory + Purchases - Closing\ inventory$$

Therefore, FIFO maximizes gross profit when prices are rising for two reasons:

- the cost of sales is lower since the cost of the product is based on earlier, lower prices for materials
- closing inventory is based on later, higher prices paid for materials.

13.5 Advantages and disadvantages of FIFO and WAC

Management needs to weigh up the pros and cons of the costing methods, choose an appropriate method and use it consistently, unless there is a good reason for changing it. This helps achieve comparability, which is a quality that enhances the usefulness of financial information in financial statements. The accounting principle that guides this is known as the *consistency concept*, which states that there should be consistency in the accounting treatment of items of a similar nature within each accounting period and from one period to the next.

Activity

Compare the FIFO and WAC costing methods by drawing up lists of the advantages and disadvantages of each.

Your list may include some of the following:

Advantages of the FIFO method

- It is acceptable to financial accountants in the UK and to HM Revenue and Customs. Therefore, in addition to being used for management accounting purposes, it can be used for financial reporting and computing profits for taxation purposes.
- It is a logical choice if it coincides with the order in which inventory is physically issued to production. For example, if the inventory consists of perishable materials or materials that have a finite life for some other reason, it makes sense to issue those that have been stored the longest first. This avoids the possibility of deterioration, obsolescence and waste.
- It charges the cost of direct materials against profits in the same order as costs are incurred.
- The value of closing inventory is close to current prices.

Disadvantage of the FIFO method

- The cost of direct materials issued to production is based on historical prices.
- When prices are rising, the value of inventory at the end of a period is close to current prices, but still lags behind.

Advantages of the WAC method

- Like FIFO, it is acceptable to financial accountants in the UK and to HM Revenue and Customs. This means that in addition to being used for management accounting purposes, it can be used for financial reporting and for computing profits for taxation purposes.
- It is a logical choice if it coincides with the way in which inventory is physically issued to production. For example, if inventory consists of volume and liquid materials that are stockpiled or intermingled, an averaging method makes sense as it may not be possible to differentiate between old and new inventory held in bulk storage containers.
- It smooths out the impact of price changes in the statement of profit or loss.
- It takes account of quantities purchased and changing prices in the current period as well as prices relating to previous periods.

Disadvantages of the WAC method

- Prices of materials issued to production must be recalculated every time a new consignment is received.
- Prices of materials issued may not match any of the prices actually paid.
- When prices are rising, the cost of direct materials issued to production is closer to current prices than FIFO, but still lags behind.

One of the advantages of the WAC method we listed above is that it is a logical choice if it coincides with the way in which inventory is physically issued to production.

Manufacturers of all types use weighted-average costing methods where it is hard to differentiate between older and newer inventories. For example:

- In chemical manufacturing, one batch of a chemical may be mixed with another batch of the same chemical.
- In the agricultural sector, grain, peas, beans and other vegetables are mass harvested and cannot be accounted for individually.
- In the oil and gas industry, it is not possible to differentiate one batch of fuel from another when they are stored together in bulk.

13.6 Costing direct labour

Apart from materials, a second element of direct costs is expenditure on the wages paid to the workforce who are directly employed in producing the products or cost units. The methods for *costing direct labour* are closely related to the different methods of remuneration. The main types of pay schemes are:

- *piecework schemes*, which are used when workers are paid an agreed amount for each unit produced or piecework time is paid for each unit produced
- *time-based schemes*, which are used when workers are paid a basic rate per time period
- *incentive schemes*, which are used when a time allowance is given for each job and a bonus is paid for any time saved.

The documents used in labour costing depend largely on the method of payment used. The main documents used in a manual system are as follows, but many businesses now use computerized *direct data entry* from individual department terminals:

- *piecework tickets*, which refer to each stage of manufacture
- *clock cards*, which record attendance time
- daily or weekly *time sheets*, which record how workers have spent their time, and are usually required to be countersigned by a supervisor or manager
- *job cards*, which refer to a single job or a batch of small jobs, and record how long each activity takes to pass through the production process.

You should not be misled into thinking that costing for labour is used only in manufacturing businesses. For example, professionals such as solicitors and accountants usually complete *time sheets* so that individual clients can be properly billed for the services they receive. In all organizations it is necessary to have a system to ensure that employees are properly remunerated for their contribution. In many service organizations, some form of bonus or profit-sharing scheme is likely to exist and this requires more detailed information to be kept.

In *piecework schemes* wages can be calculated using the following formula:

$$\text{Units produced} \times \text{Rate of pay per cost unit}$$

For example, if an employee is paid £1.50 per cost unit and produces 240 units in a week, his or her weekly pay will be £360. This method works only where all units are identical. If the employee produces a number of different types of cost unit, a conversion factor must be applied. As a piecework system is based on time spent on production, a standard time allowance is given for each unit to arrive at a total of piecework hours. For example, perhaps the same employee is allowed 15 minutes to produce 1 unit of product A (a simple electronic circuit board) and 30 minutes to produce 1 unit of product B (a more complex electronic circuit board). If the employee produces 40 units of product A and 60 units of product B and is paid £10 per hour, his or her pay can be calculated as follows:

Product	Number of units	Time allowance per unit	Total hours
A	40	0.25 hours	10
B	60	0.50 hours	30
			40
	Pay (40 hours × £10)		£400

Calculating pay for *time-based schemes* is straightforward. A system is required to ensure that the employee is properly appointed and, if necessary, a procedure is in place to record the employee's attendance at the workplace. In many jobs it is assumed that the employee is present unless absence is specifically reported. The records from the clock cards and/or time sheets are then used as the basis for calculating pay.

Incentive schemes are usually introduced where workers are paid under a time-based scheme. There are various types of scheme in operation, but most are based on setting a target for output and actual performance is compared with the target. If actual performance exceeds the target, employees receive a payment for their efficiency. This payment is a proportion of the savings made by the business because of the increased efficiency and therefore the labour cost per unit should be lower. It is important to remember that a performance-based scheme cannot be used if the output cannot be measured reliably. Even though output might be easy to measure, it would be preferable to adopt a time-based method of remuneration where the quality of output is important. This would avoid the danger of quality deteriorating as workers strive to achieve higher levels of output that bring them increased monetary rewards.

Activity

Jon Hazel employs Chris, Mike and Adam in the workshop of Hazelwood Products Ltd. As Chris and Mike are apprentices, they are paid £10 per hour, but Adam has qualifications and experience so is paid £20 per hour. Their time sheets for week ending 7 January show that Chris spent 25 hours, Mike spent 15 hours and Adam spent 10 hours on the bookcases made that week. Jon's accountant, who manages the payroll, estimates that the additional costs incurred for pension contributions, holiday pay, etc., amount to an additional 10% of the wages they are paid. Calculate the direct labour cost for the 10 bookcases produced.

Check your answer against the following workings:

	Hours	Rate per hour	Total
		£	£
Chris	25	10.00	250
Mike	15	10.00	150
Adam	10	20.00	200
			600
Employer's costs (£600 × 10%)			60
Total direct labour costs			660

If you look at the total cost statement for Hazelwood Products Ltd, which is reproduced below, the direct labour costs are the most significant element of the direct costs for this business and therefore a key part of the prime costs for the week. One way in which Jon Hazel controls the direct labour costs in his business is by ensuring that employees complete their time sheets accurately and differentiate between time spent on making bookshelves and time spent on general tasks, such as clearing up and maintenance. Indeed, both Chris and Mike spent an additional half an hour each day on general tasks (£10 per day) and Adam spent one-and-a-half hours each day supervising the apprentices and helping Jon plan the production process (£30 per day). Since this time cannot be identified directly with the products, the week's wages bill for this part of their jobs (£40 x 5 days = £200) is shown as production overheads in the costing statement.

Hazelwood Products Ltd
Total cost w/e 7 January (10 bookcases)

	£
Direct costs	
Direct materials	440
Direct labour	660
Prime cost	1,100
Production overheads	200
Production cost	1,300
Distribution costs	60
Administrative expenses	80
Total cost	1,440

Sometimes students find it difficult to decide which costs are direct labour costs and which are indirect costs when classifying the elements of cost. The guide to remember is that direct labour costs are those which can conveniently be identified with a cost unit. To do this, a documentation system, as described in this chapter, is needed. Indirect labour costs are the wages of indirect workers, such as supervisors and maintenance staff, plus the wages of direct workers when working on indirect tasks, such as cleaning machinery and setting up production lines.

13.7 Costing direct expenses

Apart from direct materials and direct labour, a business may have some *direct expenses*. Examples of direct expenses include subcontract work or hiring special equipment for a particular job. For instance, Jon Hazel might decide to continue to produce bookcases with a simple wax finish, but also make some with a paint finish as chosen by the customer. He may decide to subcontract the finishing of the painted bookcases ordered by customers to an expert. The cost of this extra work is not a direct material, as the paint is never owned by Hazelwood Products Ltd, nor is it direct labour, as the painter is not on the payroll, but the cost can be directly traced to a product. Therefore, it is classified as a direct expense.

The main method for *costing direct expenses* to a product or cost unit is very simple and the accountant bases the cost on the amount shown in the relevant invoice. If it is not possible to do this because it is too difficult to trace the expense to a particular cost unit, the amount is simply added to the production overheads. We will be looking at these in more detail in the next chapter.

13.8 Conclusions

In this chapter we have described the key documents and procedures involved in costing for product direct costs. These are the costs that can be directly traced to a cost unit: direct materials, direct labour and direct expenses. When aggregated, these make up the prime cost.

Goods received notes give details of the direct materials received into the stores and materials requisitions give details of the inventory issued for use in the production process. If the materials are stored for a period of time before they are used, records are kept and monitored to maintain an adequate level of inventory, and periodic inventory counting ensures proper inventory control. In the accounts department, the inventory account records the quantities and prices of materials received and we have examined two methods for pricing direct materials and valuing closing inventory. Direct labour converts the direct materials into the finished goods. Records need to be kept of the time employees spend on cost units. The method used for costing direct labour is related to the method of remuneration. Direct expenses are not always identifiable, but should be included if they can be traced directly to the appropriate cost unit.

In many businesses the systems for recording and controlling direct costs are computerized and part of a management information system that is capable of providing a wide range of information for different purposes. Typically, this includes accounting information that is used for both financial and management accounting purposes.

 # Common problems to avoid

Common mistakes students make when constructing an inventory account are:

- Forgetting to include the unit of measurement or the currency symbol in the column headings
- Forgetting to show the date of each receipt or issue of materials
- Failing to show the opening balance of inventory (if applicable)
- Treating opening inventory as a receipt of materials
- Forgetting the formula for calculating the weighted-average cost

 ## Discussion questions

1 Discuss the main stages in controlling direct materials.

2 Compare and contrast the advantages and disadvantages of the FIFO and WAC methods.

 ## Practice questions

3 Janet's wages are based on piecework and she is paid £10 per piecework hour. Calculate her pay for a 36-hour week in which she produces the following units:

	Number of units	Time allowance per unit
Product A	12	0.8 hours
Product B	30	0.6 hours
Product C	24	0.5 hours

4 Using the following cost codes, classify the costs incurred by Hazelwood Products Ltd.

	Cost code
Direct materials	1
Direct labour	2
Direct expenses	3
Production overheads	4
Distribution costs	5
Administrative expenses	6

(a) Consignment of wood

(b) Factory rent

(c) Factory power, lighting and heating

(d) Wages paid to factory cleaner

(e) Depreciation of office equipment

(f) Maintenance of factory machines and tools

(g) Fuel for delivery vehicles

(h) Salary paid to Jon Hazel

(i) Fees paid to the accountant

(j) Wages paid to Chris, Mike and Adam

(k) Fees paid to French polisher

(l) Consignment of nails, shelf cleats and glue

5 On 1 May, Papa's Pizza Ltd had an opening inventory of 100 kg of flour at £5.00 per kg. The following information is available about the receipts of flour into store and issues to production during the first week of May.

Receipts:

2 May	500 kg at £5.00 per kg
4 May	500 kg at £5.50 per kg
5 May	800 kg at £6.00 per kg

Issues:

| 6 May | 600 kg |
| 7 May | 900 kg |

Required

Prepare the flour inventory account for the first week of May using:

(a) FIFO costing method

(b) WAC method.

6 Perfect Pans Ltd manufactures cooking pans. On 1 December the inventory records show 500 kg of metal alloy, which is valued at £2.00 per kg. The goods received notes and materials requisitions show the following receipts and issues during the month:

2 December	Issued 450 kg to production
7 December	Received 550 kg at £2.10 per kg
8 December	Issued 500 kg to production
14 December	Received 600 kg at £2.20 per kg
15 December	Issued 600 kg to production
30 December	Received 500 kg at £2.30 per kg
31 December	Issued 100 kg to production

Required

(a) Prepare the inventory account for Perfect Pans Ltd and calculate the cost of metal alloy used in the production process during December and the inventory balance in terms of quantity and value at the end of the month using:

(i) FIFO costing method

(ii) WAC method

(b) Assuming that the business needs to choose between the two methods, recommend which method management should adopt, giving your reasons.

7 The following records show the movement of inventory for beans, the main ingredient used by Baked Bean PLC in its products, for the month of September.

| September | Receipts | | Issues |
| | Quantity | Price per tonne | Quantity |
	tonnes	£	tonnes
1	1,000	5.00	
2	1,000	5.50	
3			750
14			750
15	1,000	6.00	
16			750
29	1,000	6.50	
30			750

Required

(a) Prepare the inventory account for Baked Bean PLC and calculate the cost of beans used in the product during September and the inventory balance in terms of quantity and value at the end of the month using:

(i) FIFO costing method

(ii) WAC method

(b) Identify which of the two methods would give the higher profit for the month in this particular case, giving your reasons.

8 On 1 April, Manuka Cakes Ltd had an opening inventory of 40 litres of honey which had cost £2.00 per litre. However, the price of one of the key ingredients in the cakes, Manuka honey, was increasing due to shortages resulting from a drastic reduction in the global population of bees. This was reflected in the prices paid for honey during the first two weeks of April.

On 5 April, the company's usual supplier delivered 50 litres of honey at £3.00 per litre and this was taken into the store. A second consignment of 40 litres of honey at £3.50 per litre was received on 8 April. The company then found another supplier who was able to deliver 60 litres of honey at a cost of £4.00 per litre. This was sufficient for the store manager to issue 120 litres of honey to production on 12 April for the next batch of honey cakes.

Required

(a) Record the entries in the honey inventory account using the FIFO costing method.

(b) Record the entries in the honey inventory account using the WAC method.

(c) Discuss the advantages and disadvantages of the two methods. Conclude by recommending which method the company should adopt, giving your reasons.

 Suggested research questions for dissertation students

Students interested in costing for product direct costs may wish to investigate one or more of the following research questions:

- What are the factors that affect the choice of costing systems in [industry or country]?
- Are the cost accounting tools based on a large company template, appropriate for SMEs?
- Is underperformance in SMEs due to their failure to utilize appropriate product costing tools?

Preliminary reading

Al-Omiri, M. and Drury, M. (2007) 'A survey of factors influencing the choice of product costing systems in UK organizations', *Management Accounting Research*, 18, pp. 300–424.

CIMA (2009) *Management Accounting Tools for Today and Tomorrow*, London: Chartered Institute of Management Accountants. Available from: www.cima-global.com/Documents/Thought_leadership_docs/CIMA%20Tools%20and%20Techniques%2030-11-09%20PDF.pdf (Accessed 11 June 2016).

Johnson, H.T. and Kaplan, R.S. (1987) *Relevance Lost: The Rise and Fall of Management Accounting*, Boston: Harvard Business School Press.

Lucas, M., Prowle, M. and Lowth, G. (2013) 'Management accounting practices of (UK) small-medium-sized enterprises (SMEs)', *Improving SME Performance through Management Accounting Education*, 9(4). Available from: www.cima-global.com/Documents/Thought_leadership_docs/Management%20and%20financial%20accounting/ManagementAccountingPracticesOfSmall-Medium-SizedEnterprises.pdf (Accessed 10 December 2016).

Mitchell, F. and Reid, G. (2000) 'Problems, challenges and opportunities: Small business as a setting for management accounting research', *Management Accounting Research*, 11(4), pp. 385–390.

Nandan, R. (2010) 'Management accounting needs of SMEs and the role of professional accountants: A renewed research agenda', *Journal of Management Accounting Research*, 8(1), pp. 65–78.

Perren, L. and Grant, P. (2000) 'The evolution of management accounting routines in small businesses: A social construction perspective', *Management Accounting Research*, 11(4), pp. 391–411.

14 Costing for indirect costs

Learning objectives

When you have studied this chapter, you should be able to:

- Describe the main purposes of absorption costing
- Explain the main stages in costing indirect costs
- Construct a production overhead analysis
- Calculate the total cost of a cost unit using absorption costing methods
- Describe the problems associated with apportioning and absorbing indirect costs

14.1 Introduction

In Chapter 13 we looked at the methods that allow us to calculate the product direct costs (direct materials, direct labour and direct expenses) for each cost unit. However, the direct costs are only part of the total cost of producing a product or service; there are also the indirect costs of the business that need to be considered when making management decisions. The indirect costs are the overheads incurred by the business, which can be classified as production overheads, administration overheads, distribution overheads or research and development overheads.

In many businesses these indirect costs are very high and it is essential to find a suitable method for charging them to the cost units. Absorption costing is the traditional method used in the manufacturing industry to meet this need and the subject of this chapter. We are going to examine the methods for allocating and apportioning the indirect costs to the cost centres and cost units so that the total costs are absorbed into the cost of each unit. To do this, we will be calculating the total costs of the business.

This information will be similar to that found in the financial accounts, but there are differences. In management accounting, the total costs are required on a monthly basis and at the planning stage they are based on budgeted (predicted) figures. Therefore, the figures may be less accurate than those prepared for financial accounting purposes, but because they are calculated more frequently than once a year, they are more timely. In addition, more detailed information is required in a management accounting system than is needed for financial accounting. However, at the end of the financial year, we would expect the total costs for the business shown in the annual financial statements to be very similar to the aggregated costs in the management accounts.

14.2 Absorption costing

The *purpose* of *absorption costing* is to analyze *revenue expenditure* in order to arrive at a total cost for each cost unit. You will remember from the last two chapters that revenue expenditure refers to the costs and expenses that are written off in the statement of profit or loss for the period in which the expenditure was incurred. Since the focus of absorption costing is on calculating the total cost per unit, it is also known as *total costing*. The production cost of a product or other cost unit is primarily needed for valuing inventory and for planning and controlling production costs, whereas the total cost is needed to determine the selling price.

Key definitions

Absorption costing is a costing method that, in addition to direct costs, assigns production overheads to cost units through the process of absorption. Costs are first allocated or apportioned to the cost centres, where they are absorbed into the cost unit using absorption rates.

An overhead absorption rate (OAR) is a predetermined rate that is used in absorption costing to charge the production overheads to the cost units.

In Chapter 12 we looked at the ways in which costs can be classified and one way is to divide them into *direct costs* and *indirect costs*. The total of the product direct costs is the *prime cost* and if we then add the indirect costs of production (the production overheads) we arrive at the *production cost*. The following activity allows us to examine this in more detail.

Activity

Hazelwood Products Ltd, the business we looked at in previous chapters, is thriving. During the first year, the workshop made 1,000 bookcases with the same design and size specifications. Production overheads for the year were £20,000; direct materials for each bookcase were £50 and direct labour costs for each bookcase were £80. What is the production cost of one bookcase?

You should have had no problem in deciding that the total direct costs are £130, made up of £50 for materials and £80 for labour. However, the total cost must include a fair share of the production overheads, but what is a 'fair share'? As the business is making only one product and they are all the same, a fair method would be to divide the production overheads by the total number of units produced:

$$\frac{£20,000}{1,000} = £20$$

The following production cost statement draws these calculations together.

Hazelwood Products Ltd

Production cost

	1 unit
	£
Direct costs	
Direct materials	50
Direct labour	80
Prime cost	130
Production overheads	20
Production cost	150

As a business grows, it is likely to become more complex than Hazelwood Products Ltd was in its first year. When this happens, a business may decide to organize itself into a number of functional departments. In a manufacturing business, some of these will be production departments; others will be service departments providing services, such as maintenance, storage or canteen facilities, administration, selling and distribution functions, etc. In addition, the business may have a range of different products or other cost units, with each spending a different amount of time in the production department and therefore making different demands on resources. In such cases, the method we have used for Hazelwood Products Ltd is not a fair way of sharing the production overheads over the cost units. However, absorption costing helps overcome this difficulty, by apportioning these indirect (overhead) costs to the cost units using rates that are calculated for each cost centre, as shown in Figure 14.1.

Figure 14.1   Main stages in absorption costing

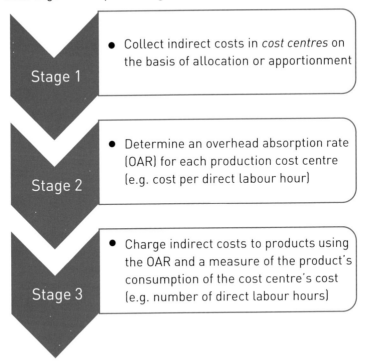

14.3 Allocating and apportioning production overheads

Absorption costing seeks to provide answers to two practical problems:

- How to share the total overheads of the organization over the various production cost centres.
- How to share the overheads for a particular production cost centre over the various products passing through it.

Activity

In the previous example of Hazelwood Products Ltd, was the method used a solution to the first or the second of these problems?

The method used was a solution to the second problem because we were looking at a small organization with only one production department or workshop. By dividing the total overheads by the number of bookcases produced, we shared the production overheads over the products passing through the production department. Usually we have to solve the first problem before we can tackle the second.

One of the ways in which accountants classify overheads is by *nature*, such as rent, wages and depreciation. When overheads are classified in this way, they fall into two main groups. The first group is those that can be wholly identified with one particular cost centre, for example all the depreciation charge on machinery may be due to only one particular production department. This process of charging to one particular cost centre is called *cost allocation*. The second group of overheads is those which cannot be identified with a single cost centre, but must be shared or apportioned over all the cost centres benefiting from them. This process is known as *cost apportionment*; for example, factory rent might be apportioned over the production cost centres on the basis of the proportion of space each department occupies in the factory. To charge the production overheads to cost centres by allocation and apportionment a *production overhead analysis* is prepared. This classifies the total overheads by nature and then shows how they are apportioned across the production cost centres. We will use an activity to illustrate this.

Activity

Jarvis Jackets Ltd makes leather jackets. It has two cost centres: the cutting department where the jackets are cut out by machine, and the stitching department where they are sewn and finished. Some of the production overheads have been allocated to the two cost centres from information available within the business, but the remainder must be apportioned in some way. The following information should help you decide a fair way of sharing them between the two departments.

	Total	Cutting department	Stitching department
Production area	400 sq metres	250 sq metres	150 sq metres
Number of employees	20	5	15
Value of machinery	£120,000	£100,000	£20,0000
Value of inventory	£120,000	£40,000	£80,0000

Before you can complete the following pro forma, you need to decide on the basis on which the production overheads will be apportioned and then calculate the portion that will be borne by each cost centre. The indirect materials and indirect labour used in production have already been allocated and entered in the analysis. The rent has also been apportioned to show you the method. Rent is best apportioned on the basis of the area occupied. The total area is 250 + 150 = 400 sq metres and the rent is £12,000. Therefore, the rent can be apportioned as follows:

$$\text{Cutting department:} \quad \frac{250}{400} \text{ sq metres} \times £12,000 = £7,500$$

$$\text{Stitching department:} \quad \frac{150}{400} \text{ sq metres} \times £12,000 = £4,500$$

Production overhead analysis

Overhead	Total	Basis of Apportionment	Cutting department	Stitching department
	£		£	£
Indirect materials	40,000	Allocated	17,500	22,500
Indirect labour	17,100	Allocated	4,200	12,900
Rent and rates	12,000	Area	7,500	4,500
Lighting and heating	4,000			
Depreciation on machinery	9,000			
Supervisors' salaries	22,000			
Insurance	900			
Total	105,000			

After deciding a fair way of apportioning the production overheads, the calculations should not have presented any great problems. Check your completed analysis against the following solution.

Production overhead analysis

Overhead	Total	Basis of apportionment	Cutting department	Stitching Department
	£		£	£
Indirect materials	40,000	Allocated	17,500	22,500
Indirect labour	17,100	Allocated	4,200	12,900
Rent and rates	12,000	Area	7,500	4,500
Lighting and heating	4,000	Area	2,500	1,500
Depreciation of machinery	9,000	Value of machinery	7,500	1,500
Supervisors' salaries	22,000	No. of employees	5,500	16,500
Insurance	900	Value of inventory	300	600
Total	105,000		45,000	60,000

If your answer differs from the above, it may be because you decided to use different bases of apportionment, so we will look at the reasons for the choices we made. Both rent and electricity would seem to be best shared on the basis of the area occupied by each cost centre. Depreciation is clearly related to the value of the machinery used in each cost centre. Deciding on the best way to apportion the supervisors' salaries is more difficult. In the absence of any other information, we have assumed that their salaries are related to the number of employees. You might argue that they could be related to floor space and in some circumstances you would be right. Finally, the insurance of inventory is based on its value and therefore has been allocated accordingly.

Agreeing on a fair way to apportion overheads is a major problem in many organizations and it is important to remember that the methods of apportionment are arbitrary. Nevertheless, the method chosen should be reasonable. The overheads should be relatively easy to obtain from the records of the business and relate to the manner in which the cost is incurred by the cost centre benefiting from its use. They should reflect the use by the cost centre of the resources represented by the overhead. Later in this chapter we will be looking at the problem of service cost centres, but at this stage we will concentrate on how to allocate or apportion production overheads to our two production departments. Table 14.1 shows some commonly used bases of apportionment.

Table 14.1 **Main bases for apportioning production overheads**

Production overhead	Basis of apportionment
Rent and rates	Area or volume
Lighting and heating	Area or volume
Buildings insurance	Area
Insurance of inventory	Value of inventory
Insurance of machinery	Value of machinery
Depreciation of machinery	Value of machinery
Power for machinery	Machine hours, horsepower or horsepower per hour
Supervisors' salaries	Number of employees
Canteen	Number of employees

14.4 Calculating the production overhead absorption rate

We now know that the total production overheads are £45,000 for the cutting department and £60,000 for the finishing department. Next we must decide on an appropriate *overhead absorption rate* to share the production overheads between all the jackets passing through the two production cost centres. The choice of absorption rate depends on the basis of apportionment and the resources used. We will examine the following methods:

- the cost unit overhead absorption rate
- the direct labour hour overhead absorption rate
- the machine hour overhead absorption rate.

The *cost unit overhead absorption rate* is the simplest method and involves dividing the production overheads for each production cost centre by the number of cost units passing through them. We applied this in the Hazelwood Products Ltd example. In a more complex business there may be more than one production cost centre and a different overhead absorption rate will be needed for each. For example, Jarvis Jackets Ltd makes two styles of jacket: the classic jacket and the designer jacket. In one year, 4,000 classic jackets and 1,000 designer jackets are made, making a total of 5,000 cost units. Using the cost unit overhead absorption rate, we will now calculate the amount of the overheads that will be borne by each jacket. This requires some care, as we need to remember that each jacket must pass through both the cutting department and the stitching department. Therefore, a separate overhead absorption rate per jacket must be calculated for each cost centre and then aggregated.

	Cutting department	Stitching department
Cost unit overhead absorption rate:		

$$\text{Cost unit overhead absorption rate:} \quad \frac{\text{Cost centre overheads}}{\text{Total cost units}} \qquad \frac{£45,000}{5,000} = £9.00 \qquad \frac{£60,000}{5,000} = £12.00$$

The absorption rate will be £21.00 (£9.00 + £12.00). This means that every jacket will absorb £21.00 of the production overheads incurred in running these two production cost centres.

Although using cost unit overhead absorption rate is the easiest method, it would be unfair to charge the same overhead to the different styles of jackets, since the more expensive designer jackets use up more of the resources. It would be fairer if the product that uses up more of the resources bears more of the overhead. For example, if you took your car to the garage merely to have the brakes adjusted and you were charged the same overhead charge as someone who had had a full service, you would be very upset. It would not help if the garage owner told you that he had worked out his overhead charge by dividing his total overheads by the number of cars repaired. So what other basis might he use for charging overheads on the work done?

You may consider that the overheads should be charged on a time basis. Garages usually charge an hourly rate for repairs, as do many other businesses, such as plumbers and electricians. The hourly rate can be calculated on the basis of the time an employee spends working on the product, the direct labour hour rate, or on how long the product is on a machine, the machine hour rate.

Activity

Returning to our example of Jarvis Jackets Ltd, calculate the hourly overhead absorption rate for each department. You can choose to base the rate on direct labour hours or on machine hours. The following table gives details of the direct labour hours and machine hours required in each department to make 5,000 jackets.

	Cutting department	Stitching department
Direct labour hours	10,000	30,000
Machine hours	40,000	5,000

You may have found this difficult. To calculate the direct labour hours overhead absorption rate for each cost centre, you need to divide the overhead by the total direct labour hours and add them together. If you decided to calculate the machine hours overhead absorption rate, for each cost centre, you should have divided the overhead by the total number of machine hours and added them together. Check your answer against the following workings.

	Cutting department		Stitching department	
Direct labour hour overhead absorption rate:				
$\dfrac{\text{Cost centre overheads}}{\text{Total direct labour hours}}$	$\dfrac{£45,000}{10,000}$	$= £4.50$	$\dfrac{£60,000}{30,000}$	$= £2.00$
Machine hour overhead absorption rate:				
$\dfrac{\text{Cost centre overheads}}{\text{Total machine hours}}$	$\dfrac{£45,000}{40,000}$	$= £1.13$	$\dfrac{£60,000}{5,000}$	$= £12.00$

Other types of overhead absorption rates in use are often based on a percentage calculation, but we will concentrate on these three widely used methods as they illustrate the main principles. The following table summarizes the information we have so far.

	Cutting department	Stitching department
Total overheads	£45,000	£60,000
Number of cost units	5,000	5,000
Direct labour hours	10,000	30,000
Machine hours	40,000	5,000
Cost units overhead absorption rate	£9.00	£12.00
Direct labour hour overhead absorption rate	£4.50	£2.00
Machine hour overhead absorption rate	£1.13	£12.00

Although we have calculated three different types of overhead rate for Jarvis Jackets Ltd, only one rate will be used in each department, but you can see that since each produces a different absorption rate, it is important that the management accountant uses the fairest rate for each cost centre, bearing in mind that the same rate need not be used in both departments. We have already pointed out that it would be unfair to use the cost unit absorption rate because the two types of jacket use unequal amounts of resources. With the other two rates, we need to consider the main sources of expenditure in each department by examining the overhead costs. In the cutting department, you can see that the overheads have been incurred mainly in terms of machine hours. Therefore, this is the most appropriate basis for calculating the overhead absorption rate for that cost centre. However, in the finishing department, the work is mainly manual; therefore, the direct labour hour rate is the most appropriate overhead absorption rate to use for this cost centre.

14.5 Calculating the production cost per unit

We have now reached the final and most important stage of our calculations. Although we have spent some time learning how the overheads are calculated, we must not forget to charge for the product direct costs (the direct materials and direct labour used in making the jackets). The following information is available:

	Classic jacket	Designer jacket
Direct materials	£50	£80
Direct labour	£20	£40
Cutting department machine hours	7	12
Stitching department direct labour hours	5	10

We can now calculate the production cost incurred in making each type of jacket.

Jarvis Jackets Ltd

Production cost

	Classic jacket 1 unit £	Designer jacket 1 unit £
Direct costs		
Direct materials	50.00	80.00
Direct labour	20.00	40.00
Prime cost	70.00	120.00
Production overheads		
Cutting department (No. of machine hours x £1.13 per machine hour)	7.91	13.56
Stitching department (No. of direct labour hours x £2.00 per direct labour hour)	10.00	20.00
Production cost	87.91	153.56

You may consider that calculating a different overhead absorption rate for each production department is a complex activity: it would be far simpler to calculate a factory-wide absorption rate. Thus, if a factory had total overheads of £1m and there were 250,000 direct labour hours worked during the period, the overhead absorption rate would be £4.00 per labour hour in all the separate departments. Although this method is simple and inexpensive to apply, it is likely to generate incorrect data, except in the most straightforward production systems. If there are a number of departments and products do not spend an equal time in each department, separate departmental overhead absorption rates must be calculated. If this is not done, some products will receive a higher overhead charge than they should fairly bear and others a lower charge. This will make it difficult for management to control costs and make decisions on pricing and alternative production systems.

14.6 Apportioning service cost centre overheads

So far, we have considered only production cost centres. However, most businesses also have cost centres that provide services to other cost centres. Examples of *service cost centres* include departments associated with the production areas, such as maintenance, stores and canteen, and others which are not, such as administration and distribution. The first stage is to calculate the total production cost as before, but this time we will include the service cost centres associated with the production area. We will deal with other overheads later. The same procedure is used: the different types of production overheads are allocated and apportioned, and subtotalled. Then the subtotal of the service cost centres is apportioned to the production cost centres on a fair basis.

Activity

Jon Hazel's business, Hazelwood Products Ltd, has expanded and now makes bookcases of different sizes. Instead of a single production department, Jon has found it more efficient to divide the work into separate stages and there are now three workshops, each of which is a separate cost centre. The following information is available.

	Joinery workshop	Finishing workshop	Maintenance workshop
Area	200 sq metres	200 sq metres	100 sq metres
Number of employees	12	16	4
Value of machinery	£250,000	£100,000	£50,000

Complete the following production overhead analysis by showing the basis of apportionment and the overhead to be borne by each cost centre. The allocated overheads have been entered for you. Once you have calculated the subtotal for all three cost centres, you must apportion the service costs for the maintenance workshop over the two production cost centres on whatever basis you consider appropriate.

Production overhead analysis

Overhead	Total £	Basis of apportionment	Joinery workshop £	Finishing workshop £	Maintenance workshop £
Indirect materials	10,000	Allocated	6,000	3,000	1,000
Indirect labour	31,500	Allocated	4,000	8,000	19,500
Rent and rates	20,000				
Electricity	5,000				
Depreciation on machinery	40,000				
Supervisors' salaries	36,000				
	142,500				
Apportioned service costs	–				
Total	142,500				-

Your completed production overhead analysis should look like this:

Production overhead analysis

Overhead	Total £	Basis of apportionment	Joinery workshop £	Finishing workshop £	Maintenance workshop £
Indirect materials	10,000	Allocated	6,000	3,000	1,000
Indirect labour	31,500	Allocated	4,000	8,000	19,500
Rent and rates	20,000	Area	8,000	8,000	4,000
Electricity	5,000	Area	2,000	2,000	1,000
Depreciation on machinery	40,000	Value of machinery	25,000	10,000	5,000
Supervisors' salaries	36,000	No. of employees	13,500	18,000	4,500
	142,500		58,500	49,000	35,000
Apportioned service costs	–	Value of machinery	25,000	10,000	(35,000)
Total	142,500		83,500	59,000	–

The overhead costs of £35,000 for the services supplied by the maintenance work-shop have been apportioned to the two production cost centres on the basis of the value of the machinery in these two departments (the value of the machinery in the maintenance department itself is excluded from the calculations). The total cost of machinery is £250,000 + £100,000 = £350,000. Therefore, the maintenance department overheads can be apportioned as follows:

$$\text{Joinery workshop:} \quad \frac{£250,000}{£350,000} \times £35,000 = £25,000$$

$$\text{Finishing workshop:} \quad \frac{£100,000}{£350,000} \times £35,000 = £10,000$$

Continuing this example, the overhead absorption rate in the joinery workshop is based on 10,000 machine hours and in the finishing workshop it is based on 30,000 direct labour hours. We can now calculate the two overhead absorption rates in these two production cost centres. This is done by dividing the total cost centre overhead for the period by the number of units of the basis of absorption. In this case, it is the machine hours in the joinery workshop and the direct labour hours in the finishing workshop.

$$\text{Joinery workshop:} \quad \frac{£83,500}{10,000} = £8.35 \text{ per machine hour}$$

$$\text{Finishing workshop:} \quad \frac{£59,000}{30,000} = £1.97 \text{ per direct labour hour}$$

We will now imagine that a customer has placed an order for a bespoke bookcase for which the direct costs are direct materials £80.00 and direct labour £50.00. It is estimated that the bookcase will require 8 machine hours in the joinery workshop and 10 labour hours in the finishing workshop. The total production cost is calculated as follows.

Hazelwood Products Ltd

Production cost

	1 unit £
Direct costs	
Direct materials	80.00
Direct labour	50.00
Prime cost	130.00
Production overheads	
Joinery department (8 hours x £8.35)	66.80
Finishing department (10 hours x £1.97)	19.70
Production cost	216.50

What we have just calculated is the production cost for the bookcase, but you will remember from Chapter 12 that in order to find out the total cost per unit, we need to add a proportion of the non-production overheads. In this example, these consist of the distribution costs and the administrative expenses. The data for the period is as follows.

	£		£
Direct costs	87,500	Distribution costs	27,750
Production overheads	142,500	Administrative expenses	18,250
Total production cost	230,000	Total non-production overheads	46,000

A simple method for apportioning non-production overheads to a cost unit is to add a percentage representing the proportion of non-production costs to production costs. This is an arbitrary measure, as there is no theoretical justification for a relationship between these two costs. The formula is:

$$\frac{\text{Non-production overheads}}{\text{Production cost}} \times 100$$

Substituting the figures in the formula:

$$\frac{£46,000}{£230,000} \times 100 = 20\% \text{ of the production cost } (£216.50 \times 20\%) = £43.30$$

Now we have all the figures we need to calculate the total cost of the bookcase. This is primarily of use to management for determining the selling price, since inventory valuation and controlling production costs do not require the inclusion of the non-production costs.

Hazelwood Products Ltd

Production cost

	1 unit £
Direct costs	
Direct materials	80.00
Direct labour	50.00
Prime cost	130.00
Production overheads	
Joinery workshop (8 hours × £8.35)	66.80
Finishing workshop (10 hours × £1.97)	19.70
Production cost	216.50
Non-production overheads (Production cost × 20%)	43.30
Total cost	259.80

14.7 Budgeted overhead absorption rates

So far, we have implied that the absorption rates are based on actual costs, but in practice they are usually based on budgeted (predicted) figures. The actual costs are rarely used because the collection, analysis and absorption of overheads to cost units takes a considerable time, and the actual figures may not be available until the end of the financial period. Naturally it would be impossible to wait until then to invoice customers, submit estimates, make decisions on production methods or carry out any other management task.

Before the start of a financial period, which may be as short as a month or as long as a year, decisions will be made on the likely level of activity and the estimated costs that will be incurred during the period. In Chapter 18 we will be looking at budgetary control, which is the process of establishing detailed financial plans for a forthcoming period, comparing them with the actual figures during the period and taking action to remedy any adverse variances. As far as absorption costing is concerned, the budgeted (planned) level of activity will need to be decided, the number of machine hours and labour hours estimated and forecasts made of the likely overhead costs. This will allow a budgeted *overhead absorption rate* to be calculated at the beginning of the financial period and applied throughout the period.

Activity

What problems do you think might arise from using an overhead absorption rate based on budgeted figures instead of actual figures?

You may have thought of the following main problems:

- Actual overheads are likely to differ from those budgeted.
- The actual absorption rate may differ from that used in the budget.
- A combination of the above factors.

When the overheads charged to production are higher than the actual overheads for the period, the variance is known as *over absorption*. In other words, too much overhead has been charged to production. When the overheads charged to production are lower than the actual overheads, the variance is known as *under absorption*. The over or under absorption of overheads is treated as a deduction or addition to expenses in the statement of profit or loss for the period. Therefore, invoicing customers based on a budgeted overhead absorption rate that is too low can have a significantly adverse effect on profit.

14.8 Conclusions

Revenue expenditure can be classified into product direct costs, which can be traced directly to a cost unit, and indirect costs, which cannot. In this chapter, we have focused on absorption costing, which is a cost accounting system that charges each cost unit with a fair share of the indirect costs (or overheads). This enables the total cost (the direct and the indirect costs) of a cost unit to be calculated. The main steps in absorption costing are:

1. Using a production overhead analysis, allocate production overheads to a production cost centre if they relate solely to that cost centre. Where production overheads are shared by cost centres, they need to be apportioned using a fair basis of apportionment that reflects the use of the resources represented by the overhead.
2. Allocate or apportion indirect costs from service cost centres to the production cost centres.
3. Then absorb the resulting overheads from each production cost centre into the cost unit using a suitable overhead absorption rate.
4. Construct a costing statement showing the different elements of direct and indirect costs for the cost unit.

Absorption costing can be based on budgeted or actual costs. The information thus provided can be used to aid the planning and control of costs and for establishing the selling price of products. Although we have used the manufacture of furniture and jackets in this chapter as examples, the same principles of allocating, apportioning and absorbing overheads apply in all organizations where management wants to know the total cost of a cost unit. However, it is important to remember that absorption costing has some limitations. It relies on a series of simple assumptions and rudimentary arithmetical apportioning. For example, it is based on arbitrary decisions about the basis for apportioning and absorbing the overheads and different bases of apportionment will result in a different total overhead cost for each cost centre. We will explain an alternative technique for charging overheads in the next chapter, which examines activity-based costing.

 ## Common problems to avoid

Common mistakes students make in absorption costing are:

- Confusing cost allocation, cost apportionment and cost absorption
- Forgetting the layout for a production overhead analysis
- Using an inappropriate basis for apportioning overheads to the production cost centres
- Forgetting that overhead absorption rates are based on predetermined figures and calculated in advance of the accounting period
- Forgetting to include the currency symbol or the unit of measurement when calculating an overhead absorption rate
- Forgetting to show all workings

Discussion questions

1 Discuss what it means to allocate, apportion and absorb indirect costs.
2 Discuss the main stages for calculating the total cost per unit under absorption costing.
3 Discuss the advantages and disadvantages of using an absorption costing system for calculating the total cost of a product or service.

Practice questions

4 Tom Murphy is planning to open a small business that maintains and repairs computers. He estimates that his total overheads will be £84,000 pa and he intends to charge them on the basis of the predicted number of jobs he expects to do in the first year. You work for the firm of accountants that is advising Tom. Explain the problem with this policy and suggest an alternative.

5 You have an internship in a small manufacturing company. The assistant production manager tells you that they allocate the factory rent on the basis of the number of employees in each production cost centre. Explain the limitations of this policy and suggest alternatives.

6 The monthly production overheads for Toycraft Ltd are as follows:

	£
Indirect materials	24,500
Indirect labour	54,500
Rent and rates	26,000
Electricity	4,000
Depreciation on machinery	36,000
Supervisors' salaries	42,000

The business has two production cost centres and one service cost centre, details of which are given below.

	Machine department	Assembly department	Maintenance department
Allocation of indirect materials	12,000	10,000	2,500
Allocation of indirect labour costs	14,000	18,000	22,500
Area (sq metres)	500	400	100
Value of machinery (£)	300,000	100,000	50,000
Number of employees	7	21	2
Number of machine hours	42,500	–	–
Number of direct labour hours	–	15,000	–

Required

(a) Decide on a suitable basis of apportionment for each of the indirect costs that are not going to be allocated and construct a production overhead analysis for Toy Craft Ltd.

(b) Calculate the machine hour overhead absorption rate for the machine department.

(c) Calculate the direct labour hour overhead absorption rate for the assembly department.

7 West Wales Windsurfers Ltd makes two models of windsurfer: Fun Wave and Hot Racer. The company has two production departments. It also has a canteen, which serves all employees. The predicted sales and costs for next year are as follows:

	Fun Wave	Hot Racer
Production/sales volume	2,000 units	2,500 units
Selling price	£600	£700
Material costs per unit	£80	£50
Direct labour:		
Body workshop (£3 per hour)	50 hours per unit	60 hours per unit
Finishing workshop (£2 per hour)	40 hours per unit	40 hours per unit
Machine hours:		
Body workshop	30 hours per unit	80 hours per unit
Finishing workshop	10 hours per unit	

A breakdown of the production overheads for each cost centre is shown below, together with other data that could be used to apportion them.

	Total	Body workshop	Finishing workshop	Canteen
	£	£	£	£
Variable overheads	350,000	260,000	90,000	0
Fixed overheads	880,000	420,000	300,000	160,000
Total	1,230,000	680,000	390,000	160,000
Number of employees	240	150	90	
Floor area (sq metres)	50,000	40,000	10,000	

Required

(a) Advise West Wales Windsurfers Ltd on the method of overhead absorption that should be used for each cost centre, giving reasons for your choice.

(b) Calculate an appropriate overhead absorption rate for each production department.

(c) Calculate the predicted production cost per unit for each model.

8 The management accountant at Burton's Beds Ltd has calculated the budgeted overhead absorption rates for the two production cost centres from the following budgeted figures for the three months ending 31 March.

	Machine workshop £	Assembly workshop £
Indirect materials	9,000	15,000
Indirect labour	50,000	4,000
Supervisors' salaries	15,000	3,000
Depreciation of factory buildings	4,000	12,000
Depreciation of factory machinery	3,000	33,000
Maintenance of machinery	2,000	10,000
Factory maintenance and cleaning	1,000	4,000
Power, light and heating	1,000	3,000
Canteen costs	5,000	1,000
	90,000	85,000

The budgets for direct labour hours and machine hours for the two workshops are shown below.

	Machine workshop	Assembly workshop
Direct labour hours	3,000	42,500
Machine hours	15,000	2,125

During February, the company completed three orders and the following information is available.

	Order 1	Order 2	Order 3
Direct costs:			
Direct materials	£550	£750	£950
Direct labour:			
Machine workshop	£100	£120	£200
Assembly workshop	£350	£600	£950
Direct labour hours:			
Machine workshop	24	26	55
Assembly workshop	120	200	300
Machine hours:			
Machine workshop	400	500	1,000
Assembly workshop	25	45	55

Required

(a) Calculate an appropriate overhead absorption rate for each production cost centre, giving a rationale for your choice.

(b) Calculate the total production costs for each order using your chosen overhead absorption rates.

 ## Suggested research questions for dissertation students

Students interested in absorption costing may wish to investigate one or more of the following research questions:

- Does absorption costing enhance profitability?
- What are the factors that affect the choice of costing systems in [industry or country]?
- Is absorption costing appropriate for SMEs?

Preliminary reading

Al-Omiri, M. and Drury, M. (2007) 'A survey of factors influencing the choice of product costing systems in UK organizations', *Management Accounting Research*, 18, pp. 300–424.

CIMA (2009) *Management Accounting Tools for Today and Tomorrow*, London: Chartered Institute of Management Accountants. Available from: www.cima-global.com/Documents/Thought_leadership_docs/CIMA%20Tools%20and%20 Techniques%2030-11-09%20PDF.pdf (Accessed 11 June 2016).

Johnson, H.T. and Kaplan, R.S. (1987) *Relevance Lost: The Rise and Fall of Management Accounting*, Boston: Harvard Business School Press.

Lucas, M., Prowle, M. and Lowth, G. (2013) 'Management accounting practices of (UK) small-medium-sized enterprises (SMEs)', *Improving SME Performance through Management Accounting Education*, 9(4). Available from: www.cima-global.com/Documents/Thought_leadership_docs/Management%20and%20 financial%20accounting/ManagementAccountingPracticesOfSmall-Medium-SizedEnterprises.pdf (Accessed 10 December 2016).

Mitchell, F. and Reid, G. (2000) 'Problems, challenges and opportunities: Small business as a setting for management accounting research', *Management Accounting Research*, 11(4), pp. 385–390.

Nandan, R. (2010) 'Management accounting needs of SMEs and the role of professional accountants: A renewed research agenda', *Journal of Management Accounting Research*, 8(1), pp. 65–78.

Perren, L. and Grant, P. (2000) 'The evolution of management accounting routines in small businesses: A social construction perspective', *Management Accounting Research*, 11(4), pp. 391–411.

15 Activity-based costing

Learning objectives

When you have studied this chapter, you should be able to:

- Explain how activity-based costing can add value to the business
- Calculate product costs using activity-based costing
- Apply activity-based costing to marketing and administration functions
- Describe the advantages and disadvantages of activity-based costing

15.1 Introduction

You will remember from previous chapters that revenue expenditure can be classified into product direct costs, which can be traced directly to a cost unit, and indirect costs, which cannot. We looked at the methods for costing product direct costs (direct materials, direct labour and direct expenses) in Chapter 13 and then examined absorption costing in Chapter 14. Absorption costing is based on the allocation and apportionment of indirect costs or overheads to production cost centres and their absorption into the cost of products using overhead absorption rates. Activity-based costing (ABC) has emerged as an alternative to absorption costing because of changes in manufacturing operations. Its name is derived from the fact that costs are assigned first to activities and then to the cost units on the basis of the use they make of these activities.

In this chapter we start by examining why an alternative approach is needed and explain how ABC developed as a reaction to perceived deficiencies in absorption costing, which was the traditional approach. We describe the main stages in ABC and define the terms used. We then go on to provide a worked example in order to demonstrate how the product costs are calculated before considering the advantages and disadvantages of this alternative method. Like other cost accounting techniques, activity-based costing is usually based on budgeted (predicted) figures.

15.2 Need for an alternative to absorption costing

In *absorption costing* (see Chapter 14), each product or cost unit is charged with a fair share of the indirect costs or overheads, thus enabling the total cost (the direct costs plus the indirect costs) of the firm's products to be calculated. Under this system, any overheads that cannot be allocated to a particular production cost centre must be apportioned on whatever is judged to be a fair basis. The resulting total production cost centre overhead is then absorbed into the cost of the product using a budgeted overhead absorption rate. In a simple business with only one product, this rate can be based on the number of cost units passing through the production cost centre. In a more complex business, it is commonly based on time, such as direct labour hours or machine hours.

Although accountants try to be as rigorous as possible in the application of absorption costing, this costing system is based on arbitrary decisions about the basis for apportionment and absorption of overheads. In addition, general overheads are spread across the product range with little regard for how the costs are actually generated. Therefore, there is always some concern that the total cost of each product is not being calculated in the most precise manner. If the business is miscalculating the cost of its products and basing its selling prices on this inaccurate information, it could have a dramatic impact on financial performance. For example, if the inaccuracies result in selling prices that are too high, the business could lose market share to competitors; if they result in selling prices that are too low, the business will not achieve its planned profit. To overcome these potential problems, some firms now use *activity-based costing (ABC)*.

ABC was proposed by Johnson and Kaplan (1987), who questioned the relevance of traditional management accounting practices to modern business. Management accounting has its roots in the Industrial Revolution of the nineteenth century, when manufacturing became the dominant industry. However, as the century progressed, a need for financial accounting began to evolve, and Johnson and Kaplan suggest that the separation of accounting into financial and management accounting was one of the main causes for what they describe as the fall in the relevance of management accounting. A second reason they give is that modern industry is no longer dominated by manufacturing firms and therefore management accounting techniques based on the needs of manufacturers are not relevant to businesses in non-manufacturing sectors.

Activity

Due to the increased complexity of production operations, many manufacturing businesses now use computer-controlled operations and robotic methods of production (car manufacturers, for example). Why do you think this might encourage firms to consider activity-based costing as an alternative to absorption costing?

You may have thought of several reasons, but one key reason is that advances in technology have increased overhead costs, such as power, maintenance and depreciation of machinery. Therefore, it is critical that these costs are charged to the products as accurately as possible. The increased use of technology has also been associated with a decline in the importance of direct labour and a change in its characteristics. Employees who provide direct labour are often paid on a monthly basis rather than an hourly basis as in the past. In addition, their remuneration is less closely related to the level of production and they are likely to receive additional benefits, such as pensions and sick pay, which were formerly only given to managers and administrators.

A further factor that is important in some firms is the amount of inventory they hold. You will recall from previous chapters that the correct value placed on *closing inventory* is critical for calculating the cost of goods sold, which is a deduction from the gross profit for the financial period. In a manufacturing business, the value of the inventory of finished goods normally includes a share of indirect overheads. However, many companies now use just-in-time (JIT) manufacturing systems in which products are produced in time to meet demand, rather than producing product in case they are needed. As we mentioned in Chapter 13, this greatly reduces or eliminates the need for large inventories of materials. Instead, receipts of raw materials and the delivery of finished goods to customers are phased with the production process. As a consequence of low inventories of materials and finished goods, the value of closing inventory has declined in importance.

In addition to these internal developments, competition has been increasing and firms are using a variety of techniques to improve the efficiency of their manufacturing operations. These include *value-added analysis*, where operations that do not add value in converting the raw materials into the final product are examined and eliminated if possible. One of the claims made for ABC is that it enhances the value added to production for a business that has complex manufacturing processes and several different products, because it recognizes that costs are incurred by every activity in the organization and is based on the principle that the cost units should bear costs according to the activities they use. The *purpose* of ABC is to assign costs to activities and then use a cost driver to attach them to the products based on the product's consumption of each activity.

Key definitions

Activity-based costing (ABC) is a method of costing in which overheads are assigned to the activities that take place within the entity and cost drivers are used to attach the activity cost pools to the cost units.

An activity cost pool is a collection of all the indirect costs associated with a particular activity.

A cost driver is any factor that drives the cost of a particular activity. An activity may have multiple cost drivers, such as the number of transactions and the duration of the transactions.

15.3 Main stages in activity-based costing

The two main stages in ABC are shown in Figure 15.1. First, the indirect costs are assigned to the different activities in the business and then cost drivers are used to attach activity costs to the cost units.

Figure 15.1   Main stages in ABC

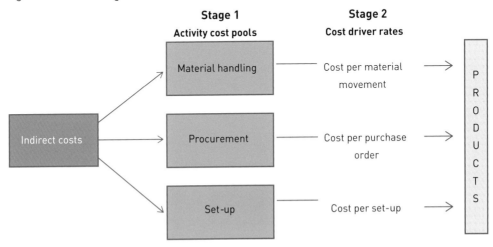

Source: Adapted from CIMA, 2005, p. 3. Reproduced with permission from CIMA.

This makes ABC look misleadingly simple, but each stage involves a substantial amount of research into the firm's operations and costing procedures. This can be highly beneficial, but can cause disruption to normal production. The implementation of an activity-based costing system involves four main steps:

1. Identify the main *activities* in the organization and classify them into *activity cost centres*. An activity centre is an identifiable unit of the organization that performs an operation that uses the resources. Activities consist of the aggregation of many different tasks, events or units of work that cause the consumption of resources. For most organizations the first activity will be purchasing materials. This will involve several tasks, such as drawing up material specifications, selecting suppliers, placing the order, receiving and inspecting the materials that have been delivered. Other support activities include processing supplier records, processing customers' orders, preparing production schedules, setting up machines, inspecting items, etc. Production process activities include machining products and assembling products.
2. Identify the *cost drivers* associated with each activity centre. A cost driver is any factor that causes a change in the cost of an activity or series of activities that takes

place in the business. For example, with the purchase of materials, it would be the number of orders placed. If we were looking at the costs of operating a customer support hotline, it might be the number of calls answered; for a quality control activity, it might be the number of hours of inspection conducted. Some activities have multiple cost drivers and it is important to note that cost drivers are not confined to a specific department.

3. Calculate the *cost driver rate*. This is the cost per unit of an activity. For example, in purchasing it would be the cost per order placed.

4. Assign costs to the products by multiplying the cost driver rate by the volume of the cost driver units consumed by the product. With purchasing, the cost driver rate will be calculated on the basis of orders placed. If Product A requires 15 orders to be placed in January, the cost of purchasing activity for Product A will be 15 times the cost driver rate.

Figure 15.2 contrasts the main stages in absorption costing with those involved in ABC.

Figure 15.2 Main stages in absorption costing and ABC compared

Absorption costing	ABC
Identify cost centres according to their function	Identify activities and group into activity cost centres
Collect indirect costs in cost centres on the basis of allocation or apportionment	Collect indirect costs in activity cost pools
Determine an overhead absorption rate (OAR) for each production cost centre	Determine a cost driver rate for each activity cost pool
Charge indirect costs to products using the OAR and a measure of the product's consumption of those costs	Charge indirect costs to products according to the product's demand for the activity that drives the costs

15.4 Activities and cost drivers

In general, the more complex the production process is, the greater the number of different activities and cost drivers. A business making a simple product is likely to find that any differences have little impact on overhead costs.

Activity

List the various activities that the owner of a takeaway pizza business has to undertake in order to make and deliver pizzas to customers.

You may be surprised at the number of activities you have been able to list, even if you omit all the administration and advertising. You will probably have identified some of the following activities, depending on the assumptions you made about the size of the business.

- Ordering raw materials, such as flour, meat and vegetables (usually referred to as procurement)
- Preparation of raw materials and disposal of waste
- Cooking
- Cleaning and maintenance of kitchen equipment
- Employment of delivery staff
- Receiving orders from customers
- Dealing with complaints.

With complex productions and a wide range of products, there are likely to be a great many activities, but companies usually restrict their analysis to the key activities. Any major activity is likely to have several overhead costs associated with it, which are grouped together to form an *activity cost pool*. Then the cost pool is charged to the product using a common *cost driver*.

Activity

Buoys and Gulls Ltd manufactures sailing and boating equipment. The company makes three products (Products A, B and C). The following information is available for the year.

	Product A	Product B	Product C	Total
Direct material	£95,000	£120,000	£785,000	£1,000,000
Direct labour	£116,000	£145,000	£239,000	£500,000
Number of purchase orders	3,000	8,000	89,000	100,000
Number of machine set-ups	12	18	270	300
Number of quality inspection hours	350	180	4,470	5,000
Number of machine hours	6,000	5,500	88,500	100,000
Number of units produced	1,000	2,000	17,000	20,000

The following table shows the budgeted overheads for each activity cost pool and the associated cost drivers. It also shows the budgeted cost driver rate, which is calculated by dividing the overhead by the budgeted cost driver volume.

Activity	Cost driver	Overhead £	Cost driver volume	Cost driver rate
Purchasing	Number of purchase orders	400,000	100,000 orders	£4 per order
Machine setups	Number of machine setups	300,000	300 setups	£1,000 per setup
Quality control	Number of inspection hours	500,000	5,000 hours	£100 per hour
Power	Number of machine hours	250,000	100,000 hours	£2.50 per hour
Total		1,450,000		

As you can see, the business anticipates the annual production overheads will be £1,450,000. You need to remember that this is in addition to the direct costs (direct materials, direct labour and direct expenses). Using the information provided, calculate (a) the production cost per unit for each product and (b) the total production cost for each product and the total production cost for the period.

At this stage in your studies, you should have had little difficulty in activity-based costing procedures. Check your calculations against the following model answers.

(a) Cost per unit

	Product A £	Product B £	Product C £
Direct material	95.00	60.00	46.18
Direct labour	116.00	72.50	14.06
Prime cost	211.00	132.50	60.24
Production overheads			
Purchasing	12.00	16.00	20.94
Machine set-up	12.00	9.00	15.88
Quality control	35.00	9.00	26.29
Power	15.00	6.88	13.01
Production cost per unit	285.00	173.38	136.36

(b) Total production cost

	Product A	Product B	Product C	Total
	£	£	£	£
Direct material	95,000	120,000	785,000	1,000,000
Direct labour	116,000	145,000	239,000	500,000
Prime cost	211,000	265,000	1,024,000	1,500,000
Production overheads				
Purchasing	12,000	32,000	356,000	400,000
Machine set-up	12,000	18,000	270,000	300,000
Quality control	35,000	18,000	447,000	500,000
Power	15,000	13,750	221,250	250,000
Total production cost	285,000	346,750	2,318,250	2,950,000

15.5 Costing for administrative and marketing overheads

Many firms that use traditional absorption costing to calculate the total cost of a product tend to concentrate on production costs. *Administrative and marketing overheads* are often added to the total production cost using a *blanket rate* for the factory as a whole, which replaces the need to calculate a separate rate for each production cost centre.

Activity

What are the advantages and disadvantages in using a blanket rate?

A key advantage is that it is simple to calculate and apply. The accountant only needs to collect all the overheads together and then select one allocation base. The allocation base is normally related to volume so it could be number of products, direct hour rate or machine hour rate. A blanket rate may be acceptable in a very simple organization with very few products, but there are disadvantages. One main disadvantage is that if there is more than one activity, the blanket rate may distort the total cost. For example, if there are two products and the marketing department is spending most of its time in promoting one of them, it would not be equitable to charge the other product the same overhead rate. Firms using absorption costing will attempt to achieve a better allocation of costs by identifying separate departments and different rates. It will take more time and effort to collect the information and make the calculations, but the resulting costing data will be more informative for management decision making.

In complex organizations, management may decide it is worth the additional costs to implement ABC. In such cases, this cost accounting system can be used to break down the costs involved in marketing and administration by applying the same principles as used for production costs. This enables management to make decisions about the operation of marketing and administration and determine whether it is possible to add value.

We will demonstrate this by applying the principles to Photoprint Ltd, a small company that designs and prints glossy calendars. One of the products is a wildlife calendar, which features photographs and information on endangered species. Each calendar costs £20 to print and it has been the firm's practice to add 15% to cover the cost of advertising, postage and packaging (£20 × 15% = £3.00). Advertising has been by sending leaflets to a large customer mailing list that the company has built up over the years.

However, management is concerned that the price it charges for the calendar to make a profit is not sufficiently competitive and that its existing customer database contains a substantial amount of out-of-date information. In addition, the accountant has looked at the marketing side of the operation and has identified the following activities that give rise to costs:

- Sending out leaflets to potential customers
- Taking orders by post, telephone or through the Internet
- Sending calendars to customers who have ordered them
- Dealing with customer queries (for example, non-deliveries and complaints about damaged goods).

These activities are shown in the first column of the following table and the second column identifies the cost driver. The third column shows an estimate of the annual costs for each activity and the fourth column gives details of the estimated annual driver volume. The final column calculates the cost driver rate by dividing the estimated annual cost of each activity by its estimated driver volume.

Activities	Cost drivers	Estimated annual costs	Estimated driver volume	Cost driver rate
		£		£
Leaflet printing	Customer mailing list	80,000	100,000	0.80
Leaflet dispatch	Customer mailing list	23,000	100,000	0.23
Taking orders	Number of orders	6,000	10,000	0.60
Calendar dispatch	Number sent	4,410	9,800	0.45
Customer complaints	Customer complaints	300	200	1.50
Total cost				3.58

At first glance, the blanket marketing cost of £3.00 per calendar does not look very different from the cost driver rate of £3.58 shown in the above table. However, the reality is that the operation is costing £3.58 per calendar and this is reducing predicted profit by 58p per calendar. It also means that as the market is competitive, management needs to make decisions about the future of the operation.

With the above information, management can consider each activity and determine whether savings can be made. For example, instead of sending leaflets to an existing customer mailing list, it may be more effective and less costly to have advertisements in appropriate magazines. As far as taking orders is concerned, management may decide to accept Internet orders only or even outsource the entire operation.

15.6 Advantages and disadvantages of ABC

Managers considering whether to adopt ABC will need to weigh up the advantages and disadvantages. The example in the previous section simplifies the process greatly; in real life there are likely to be many problems that must be resolved.

Activity

What do you consider are the main advantages and disadvantages to adopting an activity-based costing system?

The main *advantages* of ABC are as follows:

- The cost information should be more accurate and reliable than traditional costing.
- Because it does not distinguish between production overheads and general overheads, it overcomes the problem of finding a meaningful relationship between these non-production overheads and the production activity.
- It provides better information about the costs of activities, allowing managers to make more informed decisions. For example, it takes account of the length of the production run and product complexity. This could lead to some products being eliminated and changes in the market price of other products.
- It improves cost control by identifying the costs incurred by specific activities.

The main *disadvantages* of ABC are:

- A more detailed analysis of cost pools and cost drivers is required and substantial IT costs may be required with skilled staff to carry this out.
- It may be difficult to implement. Success depends on teamwork between accounting, production, marketing and other functions in the company.
- The different basis for assigning costs to products is likely to result in a different total cost per unit. This can have important consequences for decision making and strategy in the company.
- It uses budgeted rates and therefore *under absorption* or *over absorption* of overheads will still occur as they do under absorption costing.
- Managers may not find the information useful.

We can conclude from this analysis that the main advantages of ABC relate to having more accurate cost information, and the main disadvantages relate to the costs incurred in order to acquire it. Therefore, management must conduct a cost/ benefit analysis before adopting an ABC system. If the business already produces product costing information that meets its needs, there is little inducement to make the substantial changes required to introduce ABC. Even if the business is not entirely satisfied with absorption costing, unless the expected benefits of ABC are greater than the costs, the firm should not change from its present system. ABC is probably best suited to businesses that operate in highly competitive markets and have many different products that require complex production processes. In such organizations the arbitrary process of traditional absorption costing does not generate sufficiently specific information to aid managers in planning, controlling and decision making.

Information about the use of ABC internationally is relatively scarce. There is some evidence that adoption is more widespread in the UK and the USA than elsewhere, with growing use in continental Europe (CIMA, 2009).

In the UK, a survey of 176 large firms (Al-Omiri and Drury, 2007) found that 29% had adopted ABC systems and most of these firms were in the financial and commercial sector (see Table 15.1). The majority of firms in the manufacturing sector used absorption costing and firms in the retail sector tended to use direct costing systems. Those that did not have a costing system tended to be the smaller firms responding to the survey.

Table 15.1 **Analysis of costing systems used in the UK**

Sector	ABC (%)	Absorption costing (%)	Direct costing (%)	No costing system (%)	N
Manufacturing	20	52	21	7	91
Financial and commercial	68	9	9	14	22
Retail and other	22	26	35	17	23
Service	33	17	28	22	40
All sectors	29	35	23	13	176

Source: Adapted from Al-Omiri and Drury, 2007, p. 413. Reproduced with permission from Elsevier.

CIMA (2009) conducted a survey of 439 of its international members, 50% of whom were employed in the service sector, 31% in the manufacturing sector and 19% in the public, education, retail, trade and other sectors. The majority of respondents (61%) were located in the UK. The main findings were that only 22% of small firms use ABC as it is resource intensive, whereas 46% of large organizations use ABC. There was also evidence that ABC is more widespread in the UK and USA, but use in continental Europe is growing.

15.7 Conclusions

Activity-based costing has emerged as an alternative to absorption costing because of changes in manufacturing operations. The greater use of technology, the use of techniques such as JIT and the reduction and change in the nature of direct labour have meant that traditional costing methods are not providing sufficiently accurate information for decision-making purposes.

ABC is a costing system in which costs are first assigned to activities and then to products based on each product's use of activities. The principal assumption is that products consume activities and activities consume resources. There are four stages in implementing an activity-based costing system. These appear simple, but in practice they are complex and time-consuming. One of the major problems for companies is identifying those activities that consume resources and keeping this to a workable number. Once the activities have been identified and the costs assigned to them, a cost rate can be calculated by using the cost driver.

ABC offers the advantage of more accurate information than absorption costing because it looks for a closer relationship between overheads and the cause of these indirect costs. However, it suffers from the disadvantage that it is costly to implement and operate. It is most suitable for complex organizations with a range of products where absorption costing fails to provide costing information that is useful to management.

References

Al-Omiri, M. and Drury, M. (2007) 'A survey of factors influencing the choice of product costing systems in UK organizations', *Management Accounting Research*, 18, pp. 300-424.

CIMA (2005) *Management Accounting Official Terminology*, London: Chartered Institute of Management Accountants.

CIMA (2009) *Management Accounting tools for Today and Tomorrow*, London: Chartered Institute of Management Accountants. Available from: www.cima-global.com/Documents/Thought_leadership_docs/CIMA%20Tools%20and%20 Techniques%2030-11-09%20PDF.pdf (Accessed 11 June 2016).

Johnson, H.T. and Kaplan, R.S. (1987) *Relevance Lost: The Rise and Fall of Management Accounting*, Boston: Harvard Business School Press.

Discussion questions

1 Discuss the reasons why accountants have developed ABC as an alternative to the traditional method of absorption costing for charging overheads to products or services.

2 Discuss the advantages and disadvantages of ABC and the types of business that might benefit from implementing this type of cost accounting system.

Practice questions

3 Describe the four main stages in implementing a system of activity-based costing, defining all terms used.

4 Write a list of the activities that take place in the department of the college or university where you study. Decide the most appropriate cost drivers for each activity and how each one should be measured.

5 Continental Communications Ltd manufactures two products: Classico and Moderno. The budget for the next financial year is as follows:

	Classico	Moderno
Production output	100,000	50,000
	£	£
Direct labour	200,000	100,000
Direct materials	50,000	20,000

The indirect overheads have been identified with three cost drivers as follows:

Cost driver	Cost assigned	Activity level Classico	Activity level Moderno
Number of production runs	£150,000	40	10
Quality test performed	£40,000	8	12
Deliveries made	£20,000	80	20

Required

(a) Calculate the total cost per unit produced for each product.

(b) Prepare a presentation to be given to the board demonstrating the calculations and interpreting the results.

6 Perfums de Paris AG has a factory in France producing two aromatherapy oils. Sweet Pea is intended for the younger market and Allure is aimed at the more mature customer. The most significant costs incurred by the company relate to the packaging and advertising of the two products. The chief accountant has attended a seminar on ABC and has decided that it would be beneficial to implement it. The following information relates to the production in the current period:

	Sweet Pea	Allure
Number of litres produced	20,000	4,000
Number of purchasing orders	150	60
Quality inspection hours	1,000	750
Number of batches of materials	2,000	1,000
Cost of direct materials	€35,000	€12,000
Cost of direct labour	€25,000	€16,000

The budgeted cost pools and drivers for the year are as follows:

Activity	Cost driver	Budgeted overheads	Budgeted cost driver volume	Budgeted cost driver rate
		€		
Purchasing	No. of orders placed	180,000	15,000 orders	12 per order
Quality control	No. of inspection hours	50,000	12,500 hours	4 per hour
Material handling	Batches of materials	20,000	10,000 hours	2 per hour

Required

(a) Calculate the cost per unit for each of the two products.

(b) Discuss the decision of the chief accountant to implement the system in the context of the available information.

7 Krafton Kitchens Ltd is a small manufacturing company that makes two styles of kitchen: Country and Urban. The directors have decided to use activity-based costing to account for indirect costs of production. The following table shows the budget for the next financial year.

	Country	Urban
Production output (units)	150,000	50,000
Direct labour	£300,000	£100,000
Direct materials	£100,000	£30,000

The indirect overhead costs have been identified with three cost drivers as shown below.

Cost driver	Cost assigned	Activity level	
		Country	Urban
Number of production runs	£150,000	50	10
Quality tests performed	£40,000	12	12
Deliveries made	£20,000	60	8

Required

(a) Using activity-based costing, calculate the total cost for each product.

(b) Calculate the cost per unit produced for each product.

(c) Critically evaluate the advantages and disadvantages of adopting an activity-based costing system.

8 London Bikes Ltd manufactures two types of bicycle: the roadster and the racer. The budgeted production output and costs for the next financial year are as follows:

- Roadster: The production volume will be 100,000 units; the costs of direct materials will be £50,000 and labour costs will be £200,000.

- Racer: The production volume will be 50,000 units; the costs of direct materials will be £20,000 and labour costs will be £100,000.

The indirect overhead costs have been identified with the following three cost drivers:

	Cost assigned	Activity levels	
		Roadster	Racer
Number of production runs	£150,000	30	20
Number of quality tests performed	£40,000	8	12
Number of deliveries made	£20,000	80	20

Required

(a) Using activity-based costing, prepare a total cost statement for management to show the budgeted costs for each product and the total budgeted costs for next year.

(b) Then calculate the cost per unit produced for each of the two products.

(c) Explain the four main stages in implementing an activity-based costing system, defining any accounting terms you use.

 # Suggested research questions for dissertation students

Students interested in activity-based costing (ABC) may wish to investigate one or more of the following research questions:

- What are the factors that affect the choice of ABC in [industry or country]?

- Does ABC enhance profitability?

- Is ABC appropriate for SMEs?

- Do business relationships influence the firm's adoption of ABC?

- Does the adoption of ABC support or constrain the development of business relationships?

Preliminary reading

Al-Omiri, M. and Drury, M. (2007) 'A survey of factors influencing the choice of product costing systems in UK organizations', *Management Accounting Research*, 18, pp. 300–424.

CIMA (2009) *Management Accounting tools for Today and Tomorrow*, London: Chartered Institute of Management Accountants. Available from: www.cima-global.com/Documents/Thought_leadership_docs/CIMA%20Tools%20and%20 Techniques%2030-11-09%20PDF.pdf (Accessed 11 June 2016).

Hakansson, H. and Lind, J. (2004) 'Accounting and network coordination', *Accounting, Organizations and Society*, 29, pp. 51–72.

Innes, J. and Kouhy, R. (2011) 'The activity-based approach', in Abdel-Kader, M.G. (ed.), *Review of Management Accounting Research*, Basingstoke: Palgrave Macmillan.

Masschelein, S., Cardinaels, E. and Van den Abbeele, A. (2012) 'ABC information, fairness perceptions, and interfirm negotiations', *Accounting Review*, 85, pp. 951–973.

Mitchell, F. and Reid, G. (2000) 'Problems, challenges and opportunities: Small business as a setting for management accounting research', *Management Accounting Research*, 11(4), pp. 385–390.

Mouritsen, J. and Thrane, S. (2006) 'Accounting, network complementarities and the development of inter-organizational relations', *Accounting, Organizations and Society*, 31, pp. 241–275.

Nandan, R. (2010) 'Management accounting needs of SMEs and the role of professional accountants: A renewed research agenda', *Journal of Management Accounting Research*, 8(1), pp. 65–78.

Perren, L. and Grant, P. (2000) 'The evolution of management accounting routines in small businesses: A social construction perspective', *Management Accounting Research*, 11(4), pp. 391–411.

16 Marginal costing

Learning objectives

When you have studied this chapter, you should be able to:

- Explain the main purposes of marginal costing
- Construct a marginal cost statement and associated profit statement
- Conduct a breakeven analysis and a cost-volume-profit analysis
- Conduct a limiting factor analysis
- Describe the limitations of marginal costing

16.1 Introduction

In Chapter 14 we explained that absorption costing takes account of the direct costs plus a share of the indirect costs when calculating the cost per unit. This chapter examines a costing technique known as marginal costing, which only takes account of the variable costs of production when calculating the cost per unit. The fixed costs for the period are written off in full, without attempting to charge them to the cost units. The advantage of this is that marginal costing recognizes that costs behave differently as activity changes. Therefore, whereas absorption costing requires costs to be classified as direct or indirect costs, marginal costing requires costs to be classified as variable or fixed costs.

Although it has some limitations, marginal costing is a widely used technique and the principles are simple to understand and easy to apply. In this chapter we explain how to construct a marginal cost statement to calculate the contribution made by the production and sale of a cost unit towards covering the fixed costs and, hence, profit. We also examine how breakeven analysis and cost-volume-profit analysis using planned or actual figures can provide useful information to management for a number of short-term decisions.

16.2 Classifying costs by behaviour

The *purpose* of *marginal costing* is to meet the need for detailed information about costs in a business where production levels fluctuate. This costing method requires revenue expenditure to be classified into either *variable costs* or *fixed costs* according to their behaviour when the level of production or sales activity changes. The variable cost incurred in producing one unit is known as the *marginal cost*.

Key definitions

The marginal cost is the total cost per unit of production. It represents the additional cost of producing one more unit of production.

A variable cost is an item of expenditure, such as the direct costs and any variable overheads, that in total varies directly with the level of production or sales activity.

A fixed cost is an item of expenditure that is unaffected by changes in the level of production or sales activity.

The variable costs per unit are usually regarded as the direct costs plus any variable overheads and are assumed to be constant in the short term. Therefore, a characteristic of a variable cost is that it is incurred at a constant rate per unit; for example, the cost of direct materials will tend to double if output doubles. In view of its focus on the variable costs of production, marginal costing is also known as *variable costing*.

From these definitions we can deduce that product direct costs will always be variable costs, while indirect costs tend to be fixed costs. Some indirect costs can be described as *semi-variable costs*. This means that they contain a variable element and a fixed element, each of which must be identified so that the variable element can be added to the other variable costs and the fixed element can be added to the other fixed costs. For example, the cost of electricity used to power machinery in a factory may consist of a standing charge (the fixed cost) plus a charge per kilowatt used (the variable cost).

Activity

Classify the following costs for a manufacturing business into variable and fixed costs.

- Depreciation on machinery
- Direct materials
- Direct labour
- Factory rent and rates
- Factory manager's salary
- Commission paid to the sales team.

Even if you have no experience of working in a manufacturing environment, you should have been able to identify these from the definitions of fixed and variable costs. Depreciation, rent and rates, and salaries (unless part of pay is related to productivity levels) are all examples of fixed costs. Direct materials, direct labour and commission paid to the sales team are usually considered as variable costs, because they change in accordance with changes in the level of production or sales activity.

In Chapter 12 we looked at Sam Reeves' taxi business, where the average mileage by a taxi in one quarter of the year was 15,000 miles and the quarterly costs, analyzed by nature, were as follows:

Expense	Cost per quarter £
Driver's salary	2,670
Petrol and oil	1,050
Annual service	450
Tax and insurance	1,110
Depreciation	870

Sam wants to tender for a special job that will involve an additional 500 miles per quarter. This mileage can be done in the driver's current time allowance, so no additional salary will be incurred. Sam needs to know the cost of the additional 500 miles per quarter, so that he can submit a quotation for the job.

Activity

Which of the following figures is the correct cost of the additional 500 miles?

(a) £205
(b) £116
(c) £35

You need to start by deciding which of Sam's quarterly costs is a variable cost and divide it by 15,000 to calculate the cost per mile. Then you can multiply it by 500 to arrive at the cost of the additional 500 miles. The following table shows the cost per mile for all the costs.

Expense	Cost per quarter £	Cost per mile £
Driver's salary	2,670	0.178
Petrol and oil	1,050	0.070
Annual service	450	0.030
Tax and insurance	1,110	0.074
Depreciation	870	0.058
Total cost	6,150	0.410

Answer (a) is the result of multiplying the mileage of 500 miles by the total cost per mile of 41p. However, we know that no additional wages for the driver will be incurred, so it would be incorrect to take £205 as the cost of the additional 500 miles. The driver's wages, in this example, can be considered as a fixed cost. In our example, activity is measured in miles.

Answer (b) has been calculated by multiplying the 500 miles by 23.2p (the total cost per mile less the driver's element), but this is not the correct answer. If you look at the list of costs, you will see that the driver's salary is not the only fixed cost. Certain other costs will not increase because of the additional 500 miles per quarter. Taking them in the order in which they are listed, the costs for petrol and oil will obviously rise with the increased mileage, so they are not fixed. With regard to servicing and repairs, some routine servicing will be carried out regardless of the mileage and this is therefore a fixed cost. However, other servicing and repair costs depend on the mileage. Clearly, tax and insurance are fixed costs and, like the driver's salary, should be excluded from our calculations of the cost for the additional 500 miles. Depreciation, to some extent, is influenced by the amount of mileage, but in a taxi business, depreciation depends mainly on the passage of time.

The above identification of fixed costs should help you with answer (c). The answer of £35 has been calculated by multiplying the 500 miles by 7p, the cost of petrol and oil per mile. In view of the information we have available, this is the best answer. If we are to be more precise, we will need more details of the service and repair costs so that we can identify which are fixed.

Activity

Circle the correct answer in the following statements:

(a) If activity increases, total fixed costs will increase/decrease/stay the same.
(b) If activity increases, the fixed costs per unit will increase/decrease/stay the same.
(c) If activity decreases, total fixed costs will increase/decrease/stay the same.
(d) If activity decreases, the fixed costs per unit will increase/decrease/stay the same.

You should have had little difficulty in deciding the answers to (a) and (c). These are drawn straight from the definition and in both cases the total fixed costs stay the same regardless of changes in the level of activity. You may have found the answers to (b) and (d) a little more difficult, and some simple figures may help. We will take as our example a factory where the rent is £8,000 per annum, a fixed cost. The output of the factory each year is 1,000 units. The cost for rent per unit is therefore £8. If the factory makes 1,500 units one year, what is the rent per unit? The total rent cost will stay the same at £8,000, so the cost per unit for rent will decrease to £5.33. Therefore, the answer to (b) is that if activity increases, the fixed cost per unit will decrease. The reasoning is similar with statement (d), if activity decreases the fixed cost per unit will increase.

Activity

Circle the correct answer in the following statements:

(a) If activity increases, total variable costs will increase/decrease/stay the same.
(b) If activity increases, the variable cost per unit will increase/decrease/stay the same.
(c) If activity decreases, total variable costs will increase/decrease/stay the same.
(d) If activity decreases, the variable cost per unit will increase/decrease/stay the same.

This should have been fairly straightforward after the earlier example. The answer to statements (b) and (d) is that if activity increases or decreases, the variable cost per unit will stay the same. The answer to statement (a) is that when activity increases, the total variable cost will increase. Similarly, with statement (c), when activity decreases, the total variable cost decreases.

16.3 Calculating contribution

We saw in the previous section that in total the *variable costs* tend to increase or decrease in line with production or sales activity, while the *fixed costs* tend to remain the same, despite changes in the level of activity. *Semi-variable costs* contain both variable and fixed elements and must be analyzed so that the variable elements can be added to the other variable costs and the fixed elements can be added to other fixed costs.

Under marginal costing, only the variable costs are charged to the cost unit. The difference between sales revenue and the variable costs is not the profit, since no account has been made for the fixed costs incurred; the difference between sales revenue and variable costs is the *contribution* towards fixed costs and hence, profit.

Key definition

Contribution is the difference between the sales value and the variable costs. It is based on the assumption that both will be constant.

Contribution can be calculated for one unit or for any chosen level of sales. The *contribution per unit* is the selling price less the variable costs per unit. The *total contribution* is the contribution per unit multiplied by the number of units produced. Once the total fixed costs are exceeded by the total contribution, the business starts making a profit.

We will examine the concept of contribution by looking at an example. Mementos Ltd is planning to make ceramic models of Westminster Abbey for the tourist trade. The selling price will be £4.60 per unit and the variable costs will be: direct materials 60p per unit, direct labour £1.20 per unit and packaging (each model is packed in a presentation box) 15p per unit. The fixed costs are the overheads for the business, which will be £2,800 per week. The planned weekly production and sales volume is 1,200 units. With this information we can draw up a *marginal cost statement* that calculates the contribution per unit for the Westminster Abbey model.

Mementos Ltd	
Marginal cost statement	
	Westminster Abbey
	1 unit
	£
Sales revenue	4.60
Direct materials	(0.60)
Direct labour	(1.20)
Packaging	(0.15)
Contribution	2.65

The marginal cost statement forms the basis for a profit statement for the period. The profit statement below shows that if 1,200 units are produced and sold, the business will make a small profit of £380 per week.

Mementos Ltd	
Profit statement for one week	
	Westminster Abbey
	1,200 units
	£
Sales revenue	5,520
Direct materials	(720)
Direct labour	(1,440)
Packaging	(180)
Contribution	3,180
Fixed costs	(2,800)
Profit for the period	380

Marginal costing forms the basis of a number of useful techniques for making short-term decisions and can be based on budgeted or actual costs. The theory is simple to understand and easy to apply.

16.4 Breakeven analysis

Marginal costing principles are used in *breakeven analysis* to identify the *breakeven point*, which gives management further useful information. The breakeven point is where the organization makes neither a profit nor a loss. It can be expressed as:

$$\text{Sales revenue} - \text{Variable costs} - \text{Fixed costs} = 0$$

or

$$\text{Sales revenue} = \text{Variable costs} + \text{Fixed costs}$$

or

$$\text{Contribution} = \text{Fixed costs}$$

Key definition

The breakeven point (BEP) is the level of activity at which the entity makes neither a profit nor a loss. It can be measured by volume of production or sales, percentage of production capacity or level of sales revenue.

The breakeven point (BEP) can be measured in a number of different ways, which we will illustrate with the data for the Westminster Abbey model manufactured by Mementos Ltd.

The management accountant can calculate the level of production and sales activity in terms of the number of *units* needed to break even by using the following formula:

$$\text{BEP (units)} = \frac{\text{Fixed costs}}{\text{Contribution per unit}}$$

We now need to insert the relevant figures into the formula using the data we have for the Westminster Abbey model:

$$= \frac{£2,800}{£2.65} = 1,057 \text{ units}$$

This confirms that in order to cover the total weekly costs, the company needs to sell 1,057 units per week. Note that we have rounded the final number of units to the nearest whole number, because the business can only sell whole units.

Once you have found the breakeven point in units, you can use it to calculate the *sales revenue* at the breakeven point. The formula is:

$$\text{BEP (sales revenue)} = \text{BEP in units} \times \text{Selling price} = 1,057 \text{ units} \times £4.60 = £4,862$$

We now know that the breakeven point will be reached when the company sells 1,057 units, which is a sales revenue of £4,862. Note that we have rounded the answer to the nearest pound but you would not lose marks if you showed it to the nearest penny. However, with large figures like this, knowing the number of pence is not essential for decision making and you need to remember that in most cases, marginal costing is based on budgeted figures for the forthcoming period.

Further useful information can be gained by calculating the breakeven point as a percentage of capacity using the following formula:

$$\text{BEP (percentage of capacity)} = \frac{\text{BEP in units}}{\text{Capacity in units}} \times 100 = \frac{1,057}{1,200} \times 100 = 88\%$$

So we now know that the breakeven point will be reached when the company sells 1,057 units, which is a sales revenue of £4,862 and represents 88% of production and sales capacity. If the business has set a *target profit*, the level of activity needed to achieve the target profit can be found by using the following formula:

$$\text{Level of activity to achieve target profit} = \frac{\text{Fixed costs} + \text{Target profit}}{\text{Contribution per unit}}$$

Using the formula, we can work out how many models the company needs to sell to make a target profit of £500 per week:

$$\text{Level of activity to achieve target profit of £500} = \frac{£2,800 + £500}{£2.65} = 1,245 \text{ units}$$

The difference between the level of activity to achieve the target profit (in this case, 1,245 units) and the breakeven point (in this case, 1,057 units) is known as the *margin of safety*. This means that Mementos Ltd could miss its target of 1,245 units by 188 units before it goes below the breakeven point and starts making a loss. All this information can be shown graphically. The procedure for constructing a *breakeven graph* is as follows:

1. Draw a horizontal axis to measure activity (in units).
2. Draw a vertical axis to measure costs and the sales revenue (£).
3. Plot a fixed costs line that will be parallel to the horizontal axis.
4. Plot the total costs line by adding the variable costs to the fixed costs, remembering that at nil activity there will be no variable costs, but there will be total fixed costs.
5. Plot the sales revenue line. The breakeven point will be where the revenue line and the total costs line intercept.

Activity

Using graph paper, draw a breakeven graph for Mementos Ltd. Assume that the maximum level of activity is 1,500 units (models).

If you have drawn your graph accurately, you should have obtained the same break-even point as you calculated using the formula, and your graph should look like Figure 16.1. Although the breakeven point can be calculated by applying a formula or constructing a graph, the advantage of using a formula is that it permits a greater degree of accuracy with more complex data.

Figure 16.1 Breakeven graph for Mementos Ltd

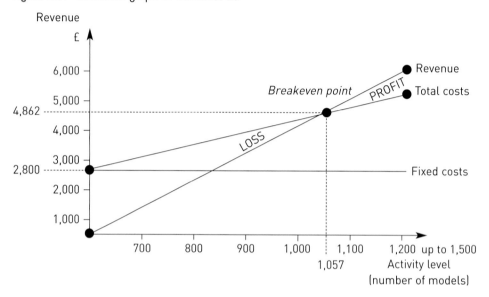

16.5 Cost-volume-profit analysis

Marginal costing principles can also be used for calculating the profit at different levels of activity. This is known as *cost-volume-profit analysis* and focuses on what will happen to the financial results if the level of activity (such as the volume of products produced and sold) fluctuates. This analysis aids management with short-term decisions, such as:

• setting the minimum selling price of a product, particularly in times when the market is depressed and when introducing new products
• evaluating the proposed closure or temporary cessation of part of the business
• assessing whether to accept a special contract or order
• comparing the cost implications of different methods of manufacture
• choosing which of a range of products to make.

We will examine these decisions by looking at some examples. Perhaps the business wants to know the minimum selling price that could be set for its products. The managers might be tempted to think that it should be the total variable costs per unit because anything lower would mean that they would not recover the costs incurred in making the model. However, if the selling price was set at that level, there would be no contribution towards the fixed costs and hence, no profit. In the next activity we explore this and the difficult decision that must sometimes be made to close part of the business or temporarily cease making certain products.

Activity

Icetreats Ltd makes three types of ice lolly and shares its fixed overheads equally over the three types. A summary profit statement for last month is shown below.

Icetreats Ltd
Profit statement for the month

	Fruit Ice	Choc Ice	Kool Ice	Total
Volume	11,200 units	9,000 units	6,000 units	
	£	£	£	£
Sales revenue	5,500	4,500	2,400	12,400
Variable costs	(2,400)	(1,800)	(1,300)	(5,500)
Contribution	3,100	2,700	1,100	6,900
Fixed costs	(2,000)	(2,000)	(2,000)	(6,000)
Profit/(loss) for the period	1,100	700	(900)	900

The sales director has suggested that as sales of all ice lollies are expected to decrease by 10% next month, production of Kool Ice should be stopped until demand picks up. Redraft the above statement showing what will happen if (a) there is a 10% decrease in demand for all three products and alternatively (b) if production of Kool Ice is halted but there is no decrease in demand for the other two products.

Check your answer to (a) against the following solution.

Icetreats Ltd
Profit statement for the month

	Fruit Ice	Choc Ice	Kool Ice	Total
Volume	10,080 units	8,100 units	5,400 units	
	£	£	£	£
Sales revenue	4,950	4,050	2,160	11,160
Variable costs	(2,160)	(1,620)	(1,170)	(4,950)
Contribution	2,790	2,430	990	6,210
Fixed costs	(2,000)	(2,000)	(2,000)	(6,000)
Profit/(loss) for the period	790	430	(1,010)	210

The above profit statement shows the impact that the 10% decrease in sales will have on profit, as well as the fact that Kool Ice is making a contribution to fixed costs. Check your answer to (b) against the following redrafted statement of profit or loss, which shows what will happen if the production of Kool Ice is stopped for the month, but there is no decrease in demand for the other two products.

Icetreats Ltd

Profit statement for the month

	Fruit Ice	Choc Ice	Total
Volume	11,200 units	9,000 units	
	£	£	£
Sales revenue	5,500	4,500	10,000
Variable costs	(2,400)	(1,800)	(4,200)
Contribution	3,100	2,700	5,800
Fixed costs	(3,000)	(3,000)	(6,000)
Profit/(loss) for the period	100	(300)	(200)

If Kool Ice is discontinued despite making a contribution of £1,100, the outcome will be an overall loss of £200 instead of an overall profit of £900. This is because the total fixed costs of £6,000 remain unchanged and must now be covered by the total contribution made by the two remaining products. Therefore, we can conclude that, in general, if a product (or service) makes a contribution towards fixed costs, it is worthwhile producing it. Of course, there may be other business reasons for dropping it, or management may think it would be more profitable to direct the activities of the organization in another direction.

We will now look at a scenario where management needs to decide whether to accept a special contract or order. Imagine that a large hotel has approached Icetreats Ltd and offered to place an order for 600 Kool Ices per month, as long as the price is reduced from 40p to 30p per lolly. The order would restore demand, but should the company accept it in view of the low price offered? The general rule is that, if the business has spare production capacity, it is worthwhile accepting a special order, as long as it makes a contribution. The key figures for Kool Ice, calculated to the nearest penny, are as follows:

	Per unit £		Per unit £
Current selling price	0.40	Proposed selling price	0.30
Variable costs (1,300 ÷ 6,000)	(0.22)	Variable costs (1,300 ÷ 6,000)	(0.22)
Contribution	0.18	Contribution	0.08

As the special price will still give a contribution of 8p, it is worthwhile accepting, but there may be other factors that must be considered before making a final decision, such as the reaction of other customers who may learn of this discounted price.

Now the production manager says he can change the production method so that up to 12,000 Fruit Ices can be produced each month for an additional fixed cost of £500 per month. He estimates that this will save variable costs of 4p per unit of Fruit Ice. Do you think this plan should be implemented? There is no need to do a full calculation again, but look instead at the maximum possible savings in variable costs and compare them with the fixed costs. The maximum savings will be 4p × 12,000 = £480. Since this is lower than the £500 additional fixed costs incurred, the proposal is not financially worthwhile.

16.6 Limiting factor analysis

The information provided by marginal costing also allows us to use contribution to rank products when there is a *limiting factor*. So far, we have assumed that there is nothing that will prevent the business from achieving the level of activity required to break even or reach the desired level of profit. In reality, this is rarely the case as there is nearly always a resource constraint. Examples include shortages of materials or labour, a restriction on the sales demand at a particular price and a limit on the production capacity of machinery. In such circumstances, a decision needs to be taken as to how the available resources can be best utilized.

> **Key definition**
>
> A limiting factor is a constraint that prevents the entity from achieving higher levels of performance and profitability.

Even when a business occupies a very specialist market, it is unlikely to rely on a single product as there is a strong demand in the developed world for a choice of products. Therefore, it is likely that the business will have more than one product at some stage. If there are limiting factors, management will need information to aid decisions about which product is the most profitable. This will then lead to a decision to concentrate production on the most profitable product until demand for that product has been met, and then the next most profitable and so on.

16.6.1 Calculating the contribution per limiting factor

In limiting factor analysis, it is assumed that any production and sales constraints are short-term problems and that the objective of the business is to maximize profit with the resources available. If there is a limiting factor, we need to modify the general rule that decisions are based on whether a product makes a contribution to fixed costs, to using the contribution the product makes per limiting factor. To explain how the contribution per limiting factor is used to rank products, we will return to the example of Mementos Ltd.

Activity

You will remember that Mementos Ltd was planning to make only one product: a model of Westminster Abbey. This product uses 1 kg of direct materials at 60p per kg, which is a cost of 60p per unit. The cost of direct labour will be £1.20 per unit, packaging will cost 15p per unit and each model will sell for £4.60. However, the directors are not happy that the budgeted profit of £380 per week based on a production and sales volume of 1,200 units. Therefore, they are planning to make a second product: a model of Windsor Castle. This will use 1.25 kg of the same direct materials as Westminster Abbey at 60p per kg, resulting in a cost of 75p per unit. Direct labour will cost £1.20 per unit, packaging will cost 15p per unit and the selling price will be £6.00. The fixed costs remain at £2,800 per week. Construct a marginal cost statement showing the marginal cost for 1 unit of each product and a separate profit statement for the week based on the planned volume of 1,200 units of each product.

If you can remember the correct formats for the marginal cost statement and the profit statement, you should have little problem with this activity. Compare your answers with the following solutions.

Mementos Ltd

Marginal cost statement

	Westminster Abbey 1 unit £	Windsor Castle 1 unit £
Selling price	4.60	6.00
Direct materials	(0.60)	(0.75)
Direct labour	(1.20)	(1.20)
Packaging	(0.15)	(0.15)
Contribution per unit	2.65	3.90

Profit statement for 1 week

	Westminster Abbey 1,200 units £	Windsor Castle 1,200 units £	Total £
Volume			
Sales revenue	5,520	7,200	12,720
Direct materials	(720)	(900)	(1,620)
Direct labour	(1,440)	(1,440)	(2,880)
Packaging	(180)	(180)	(360)
Contribution	3,180	4,680	7,860
Fixed costs			(2,800)
Profit for the period			5,060

Looking at the results, we can recommend that the company produces and sells both products because the marginal cost statement shows that the contribution per unit for each model is positive. We can see from the profit statement for the week that if normal sales volumes are achieved, the company will make a production profit of £5,060. However, if there is a limiting factor, management will need further information.

The first step is to identify the limiting factor and arrange production so that the contribution per limiting factor is maximized. The purchasing manager at Mementos Ltd is concerned about a constraint on the supply of direct materials used in Westminster Abbey and Windsor Castle models, due to industrial action at the docks. It looks as though the strike will mean no further supplies for a week and stores manager says that the total inventory of direct materials is only 1,500 kg. Consequently, the management accountant is concerned that there may not be sufficient revenue to cover the fixed costs of £2,800. In addition, the sales forecast is disappointing and the sales manager says that demand for each model is restricted to only 1,000 units of each product next week.

The next step is to calculate the contribution per limiting factor. The general formula is as follows:

$$\text{Contribution per limiting factor} = \frac{\text{Contribution per unit}}{\text{Limiting factor per unit}}$$

Activity

Using the above formula, calculate the contribution per kg of direct materials for each model and rank the products according to your results.

You should have found this straightforward once you have looked up the figures to insert into the formula. Check your answer against the following solution.

	Westminster Abbey	Windsor Castle
Contribution per limiting factor	$\frac{£2.65}{1.00 \text{ kg}} = £2.65$	$\frac{£3.90}{1.25 \text{ kg}} = £3.12$
Ranking	2nd	1st

The results show that Windsor Castle generates a higher contribution per kg of direct materials (£3.12) than Westminster Abbey (only £2.65). Therefore, we can recommend that under the constraint of only 1,500 kg of direct materials, the company should prioritize meeting the demand for the Windsor Castle model, then use the remaining direct materials to produce and sell the Westminster Abbey model.

Activity

Calculate the quantity of direct materials (in kg) each model would require if 1,000 of each model were to be produced and sold. Then allocate the 1,500 kg of direct materials available between the two models, prioritizing Windsor Castle.

Check your answer against the following workings.

	Westminster Abbey	Windsor Castle
Direct materials required	1 kg x 1,000 = 1,000 kg	1.25 kg x 1,000 = 1,250 kg
Allocation of 1,500 kg available	250 kg	1,250 kg
Production and sales volume	1 kg/250 kg = 250 units	1.25 kg/1,250 kg = 1,000 units

We now have all the information we need to prepare a profit statement for the week that takes account of the constraint on sales demand, the limited availability of direct materials and the fact that Windsor Castle will give a higher contribution per kg of direct materials.

Profit statement for one week (with constraints)			
	Westminster Abbey 250 units	Windsor Castle 1,000 units	Total
	£	£	£
Sales revenue	1,150.00	6,000.00	7,150.00
Direct materials	(150.00)	(750.00)	(900.00)
Direct labour	(300.00)	(1,200.00)	(1,500.00)
Packaging	(37.50)	(150.00)	(187.50)
Contribution	662.50	3,900.00	4,562.50
Fixed costs			(2,800.00)
Profit for the period			1,762.50

If you compare the profit for the week when there are no limiting factors (£5,060) with the profit statement when there is a constraint on sales demand and the availability of direct materials is limited (£1,762.50), there is a decrease of £3,297.50. Even if the shortage of direct materials is remedied the following week, the company still faces reduced demand for its products and there may be other constraints on resources in the future, as yet unknown. Returning to the current problems faced by Mementos Ltd, we can use the data we have generated in our analysis to provide some additional information to aid decision making:

- If an extra 5 kg of direct material became available, the company could produce 5 extra units of Westminster Abbey as there is a remaining unsatisfied demand for this product. This would contribute £2.65 for every 1 kg of direct material used, making a total of £13.25 for the five additional units produced and sold.
- Conversely, if 5 kg less of direct materials were available, the company would be unable to produce and sell five units of Westminster Abbey and would lose £13.25 in contribution.
- If 500 kg less of direct materials were available, the company would lose £662.50 in contribution from being unable to produce 250 units of Westminster Abbey (£2.65 x 250 units) and lose £780 in contribution from being unable to produce 200 units of Windsor Castle (£3.90 x 200).
- If the company had an opportunity to introduce a third model, that product would need to contribute at least £2.65 per kg (the contribution per limiting factor made by the Westminster Abbey model) or less than £3.12 per kg (the contribution per limiting factor made by Windsor Castle) to be included in a future production plan. If it contributed more than £3.12 per kg, it would be ranked first.

As you can see, the information provided by limiting factor analysis is very useful in helping managers establish the optimum product mix when there are scarce resources and other constraints on activity.

16.6.2 Internal and external opportunity cost

When conducting a limiting factor analysis, it is important to consider internal and external opportunity costs before making decisions. The opportunity cost of a resource is simply the maximum economic benefit that could be obtained if it were used for an alternative purpose. In the case of a scarce resource, the opportunity cost is likely to be greater than its cost.

> **Key definition**
>
> The opportunity cost is the value of the benefit sacrificed when one course of action is chosen in preference to an alternative. It represents the forgone potential benefit from the best alternative course of action that has been rejected.

In the case of Mementos Ltd, we know that 1 kg of direct material is needed to make 1 unit of the Westminster Abbey model. We also know that because there is unsatisfied sales demand for this model, an additional 1 kg of direct materials at a cost of 60p per kg would generate an additional contribution of £2.65. Therefore, if the purchasing manager could buy further supplies of the direct materials needed during this time of constraint, the company might be willing to pay a maximum of 60p (the external opportunity cost) in addition to £2.65 (the internal opportunity cost) to obtain an extra 1 kg. This is because if the company were able to obtain additional supplies of direct materials during this period of shortage for up to £3.25 per kg, the contribution made by this product would increase and hence so would profit. The analysis of the opportunity cost of direct materials is summarized below.

	£ per kg
External opportunity cost	0.60
Internal opportunity cost	2.65
Total opportunity cost of direct materials	3.25

We can examine this by imagining that Mementos Ltd is able to obtain a further 750 kg of direct materials at an increased price of £2 per kg. This would allow the company to make 750 more units of Westminster Abbey and satisfy the total sale demand for 1,000 units under the present constraints. The total contribution made by Westminster Abbey is shown below.

	Westminster Abbey 1,000 units
	£
Sales revenue	4,600
Direct materials	(1,650)
(60p x 250 kg + £2 x 750 kg)	
Direct labour (£1.20 x 1,000)	(1,200)
Packaging (15p x 1,000)	(150)
Contribution	1,600

As you can see, by paying more than the external opportunity cost of 60p per kg for direct materials, but less than the internal opportunity cost of £2.65, and fully satisfying demand, the Westminster Abbey model now contributes £1,600 towards fixed costs and hence profit.

Activity

Show the total contribution the Westminster Abbey model would make if the company costed all the direct materials used to produce the 1,000 units at the full opportunity cost of £3.25 per kg.

You may have been surprised by your answer. Check yours against the following solution.

	Westminster Abbey 1,000 units
	£
Sales revenue	4,600
Direct materials (£3.25 x 1,000)	(3,250)
Direct labour (£1.20 x 1,000)	(1,200)
Packaging (15p x 1,000)	(150)
Contribution	0

As you can see, if the company paid the total opportunity cost of £3.25 per kg for additional direct materials, the product would not make any contribution towards fixed costs. Therefore, we would not recommend this course of action. From all the examples we have looked at now, we can conclude that the information provided by limiting factor analysis also helps decision making when examining the profitability of other opportunities.

16.7 Limitations of marginal costing

The principles of marginal costing are based on assumptions about the behaviour of fixed and variable costs, but these rarely hold true over a complete range of activities or for any length of time. This leads to a number of limitations:

- Marginal costing is based on the assumption that variable costs will vary in direct proportion to changes in the level of activity, but they may also vary for other reasons. For example, variable costs may rise steeply in the early stages because production is not very efficient and rise again at the peak of activity due to pressure of work causing inefficiencies; a special discount on the price of direct materials for a short period may cause variable costs to fluctuate, while production levels remain constant.
- It is based on the assumption that fixed costs are not affected by changes in the level of activity, but they may change for other reasons. For example, the cost of electricity used to power machines used in the production process may decrease in steps as the level of consumption increases; other fixed costs may increase in steps as additional facilities, such as another machine, more factory space, etc., become necessary as activity levels expand.
- Management may find it difficult to identify the variable and fixed elements of cost within semi-variable costs.
- Care must be taken when making decisions based on contribution since, in the longer term, the business will also need to recover the fixed costs.
- Like other accounting techniques, marginal costing does not take account of non-financial factors, such as changes in the motivation, skills and experience of employees, that might affect activity levels.

In breakeven analysis, the limited range of activity over which the assumptions about the behaviour of costs hold true is known as the *relevant range*, and decisions should be restricted to this range unless investigations are conducted.

Key definition

The relevant range refers to the range of activity levels between which assumptions about cost behaviour in breakeven analysis remain valid. Outside this range, the linear relationships between fixed costs, variable costs and revenue do not apply.

16.8 Conclusions

Marginal costing is a cost accounting technique that only takes account of the variable costs of production when calculating the cost per unit. In this chapter we have explained how a marginal cost statement and an associated profit statement are drawn up. We have calculated the breakeven point using a number of formulae and shown you how cost-volume-profit analysis is used to aid other short-term decisions. Finally, we have discussed the importance of limiting factors, which may constrain the profitability and growth of an organization. We have also explained the general rules for calculating which product will be more profitable to produce when limiting factors are present.

The principles upon which marginal costing techniques are based rest on the assumption that variable costs are not incurred unless production activity takes place, while fixed costs are incurred irrespective of the level of activity. These assumptions apply in breakeven analysis, cost-volume-profit analysis and limiting factor analysis. However, assumptions about the behaviour of variable and fixed costs in relation to changes in the level of activity are only reliable in the short term and over the relevant range of an activity.

 ## Common problems to avoid

Common mistakes students make when using marginal costing are:

- Not showing the name of the business
- Forgetting to include the currency symbol
- Not stating the period covered by the profit statement or the number of units produced
- Classifying fixed and variable costs incorrectly
- Failing to calculate the contribution
- Forgetting that fixed costs can only be subtracted from the total contribution for the period
- Forgetting the formulae for conducting a breakeven analysis and the contribution per limiting factor

Discussion questions

1 Discuss the purposes of marginal costing and the importance of contribution.

2 Discuss the impact of limiting factors and how they affect decisions regarding the product mix.

 ## Practice questions

3 Fill in the missing figures in the following table.

	Product A	Product B	Product C	Product D	Product E
	£	£	£	£	£
Sales revenue	650	1,324	?	643	?
Variable costs	?	(388)	(229)	?	(321)
Contribution	490	?	525	456	590

4 Funfair Engineering Ltd manufactures fairground equipment. The company uses absorption costing and has been experiencing falling demand for its products due to an economic recession. Steve Wrench, the production manager, is worried because the total cost per unit is increasing, despite strict cost controls. Diane Flowers, the marketing manager, is complaining that selling prices will have to be reduced to maintain sales levels. At a recent meeting they found that the selling price suggested by Diane is lower than the total cost per unit calculated by Steve and they concluded that lowering the selling price to increase sales will only lead to even larger losses.

Required

Write a report addressed to Mr Wrench and Ms Flowers that explains:

(a) Why the total cost per unit increases as production decreases.
(b) Why marginal costing may be more appropriate than absorption costing for decision making in times of economic recession.

5 Edward & Co Ltd manufactures teddy bears. The company's bears are in demand all year round and in the next financial year the sales manager plans to sell 12,000 teddies. The management accountant collects cost information for 1 unit of production (1 teddy bear). Based on last year's figures, each unit will sell for £10 and the variable costs will consist of direct materials, which will cost £1.00 per unit, and direct labour, which will cost £5.00 per unit. The fixed costs for the year are expected to be £32,000.

Required

You have been asked to provide information that will help the managing director consider the effect on profitability of changes in the level of sales activity next year.

(a) Draw up a marginal cost statement that calculates the contribution per unit.
(b) Draw up a marginal cost statement on the basis that 12,000 units will be sold and calculate the net profit or loss.

(c) Briefly explain what is meant by the breakeven point.

(d) Using the contribution per unit you have calculated in (a), calculate the following, showing the formulae in words and your workings:

(i) The breakeven point in number of units.
(ii) The breakeven point in terms of total sales value.
(iii) The level of sales activity to reach a target profit of £20,000.
(iv) Calculate the margin of safety in units at the level of sales activity you have computed in (iii).

6 Audiomax Ltd manufactures three models of audio systems: Premier, Deluxe and Superior. When planning next year's production, the management team wants to make sure the most profitable mix of models is produced. The following table shows the selling price and variable costs per unit for each model.

	Premium	Deluxe	Superior
	£	£	£
Selling price	100	150	240
Direct materials	30	40	50
Direct labour	30	50	120
Direct expenses	10	25	24

Required

(a) Construct a marginal cost statement that calculates the contribution per unit for each model.

(b) Calculate the contribution per limiting factor for each model on the assumption that the supply of direct materials is limited and rank the products accordingly. In addition, interpret your results by making a brief recommendation on the action management should take regarding prioritizing the production of these products.

(c) Calculate the contribution per limiting factor for each model on the assumption that the supply of direct labour is limited and rank them accordingly. In addition, interpret your results by making brief recommendations on the action management should take regarding prioritizing the production of these products.

7 You are working as an intern at Falcon Fabrication Ltd, which manufactures two high quality steel products: Product A, which sells for £50 per unit, and Product B, which sells for £65 per unit. The sheet steel used to make both products costs £10 per kg. Product A requires 2 kg of sheet steel per unit and Product B requires 3 kg per unit. The cost of direct labour per unit is £15 for Product A and £20 for Product B. There is also packaging, which costs £2 per unit for Product A and £3 per unit for Product B. The fixed costs are £2,500 per week.

Required

The management accountant asks you to help provide information that will help management make a series of short-term decisions.

(a) Construct a marginal cost statement that calculates the contribution per unit for each product.

(b) Construct a profit statement for the week that shows how much profit the business will make during a normal week if 180 units of each product are produced and sold.

(c) Conduct a breakeven analysis showing the formulae in words, your workings and providing a brief interpretation in each case:
  (i) The breakeven point in number of units.
  (ii) The breakeven point in terms of total sales value.
  (iii) The breakeven point as a percentage of capacity during a normal week.

8 Continuing to use the data for Falcon Fabrication Ltd, the management accountant now asks you to conduct the following limiting factor analysis.

(a) Calculate the contribution per limiting factor for each product on the basis that the supply of sheet metal is limited. Show the formula in words and all your workings. Make brief recommendations on the action management should take regarding prioritizing the production of the two products.

(b) Prioritizing the product indicated by your answer above, construct a revised profit statement for the week on the basis that the supply of sheet metal is limited to 600 kg per week and only 150 units of each product can be sold. Show all your workings.

(c) Discuss the limitations of marginal costing that management should bear in mind when taking decisions based on your analysis.

 Suggested research questions for dissertation students

Students interested in marginal costing may wish to investigate one or more of the following research questions:

- Does marginal costing enhance profitability?
- What are the factors that affect the choice of costing systems in [industry or country]?
- Is marginal costing appropriate for SMEs?

Preliminary reading

Al-Omiri, M. and Drury, M. (2007) 'A survey of factors influencing the choice of product costing systems in UK organizations', *Management Accounting Research*, 18, pp. 300–424.

CIMA (2009) *Management Accounting Tools for Today and Tomorrow*, London: Chartered Institute of Management Accountants. Available from: www.cima-global.com/Documents/Thought_leadership_docs/CIMA%20Tools%20and%20Techniques%2030-11-09%20PDF.pdf (Accessed 11 June 2016).

Johnson, H.T. and Kaplan, R.S. (1987) *Relevance Lost: The Rise and Fall of Management Accounting*, Boston: Harvard Business School Press.

Mitchell, F. and Reid, G. (2000) 'Problems, challenges and opportunities: Small business as a setting for management accounting research', *Management Accounting Research*, 11(4), pp. 385–390.

Nandan, R. (2010) 'Management accounting needs of SMEs and the role of professional accountants: A renewed research agenda', *Journal of Management Accounting Research*, 8(1), pp. 65–78.

Perren, L. and Grant, P. (2000) 'The evolution of management accounting routines in small businesses: A social construction perspective', *Management Accounting Research*, 11(4), pp. 391–411.

17 Budgetary control

Learning objectives

When you have studied this chapter, you should be able to:

- Explain the purpose of budgetary control
- Describe the main stages in budgetary control
- Discuss the requirements for an effective system
- Differentiate between fixed and flexible budgets
- Discuss the advantages and disadvantages of budgetary control

17.1 Introduction

In this chapter we introduce a major technique for planning and controlling income and expenditure known as budgetary control. Financial control is exercised by preparing detailed budgets for all aspects of the organization's activities, monitoring them against actual performance and taking any action necessary to address any unfavourable deviations from the plan. There are very few managers who do not encounter a budgetary control system during their careers. Budgetary control is used in service and manufacturing businesses, as well as in the public sector (entities under state control) and the voluntary sector (public benefit entities such as charities and other not-for-profit entities). In addition to government budgets, some of the most publicly announced budgets are those of major films, where the accountant's name is included in the credits.

In this chapter we explain the purpose of budgetary control and the procedures for setting up a budgetary control system. We also describe how it is used to generate valuable information that helps managers with the task of planning and controlling activities, and making decisions that ensure the business achieves its financial objectives.

17.2 Purpose of budgetary control

The *purpose* of *budgetary control* is to help managers to plan and control the use of the resources they manage. There are no rules and regulations governing management accounting because the information is intended for internal users. One advantage of this is that management accounting information can be produced about future accounting periods. In the previous chapters on cost accounting, you will have seen that costs are based on budgeted or predetermined figures, which can be compared with the actual figures. However, budgetary control focuses on income as well as expenditure and the need of the organization to meet its financial objectives.

Key definition

Budgetary control is the process by which financial control is exercised by managers preparing budgets for income and expenditure for each department or function of the entity in advance of an accounting period. Continuous comparison of actual performance against the budget by the departmental or functional manager helps ensure that objectives are achieved or provides a basis for revising the budget.

We will examine the importance of planning and control by looking at an example. Cascade plc manufactures bathroom fittings. Based on last year's production records, the production manager believes that 15,000 shower units will be needed and buys all the materials and stores them in a warehouse. The marketing manager has heard that the water companies are considering changing their charging methods from rates based on the value of the property where the water is used to a metered system based on the amount of water used. As a result, he has launched a large sales campaign and believes that 30,000 shower units will be sold. The financial accountant has received a letter from the bank stating that overdraft facilities will be withdrawn and has decided to stop any expenditure that is not absolutely necessary. The designer has come up with a new design that incorporates recycling waste water from the shower unit. The personnel manager believes the economic recession will get worse and has started issuing redundancy notices to the workforce. This illustrates how a lack of co-ordination of the various activities and managers following their own ideas can lead to resources not being matched to the demands made on them, which results in waste and inefficiency.

All this can be avoided if the business adopts a system of budgetary control to help them meet their financial objectives. Budgetary control is a major technique used in a wide range of organizations for planning and control. Traditionally, it took the form of a centralized and bureaucratic system of cost control, but it has evolved to meet the needs of modern business. In many organizations, it is a participative exercise that also involves managers at lower levels and the use of budgets to contribute directly to value creation. Cash flow forecasts (see Chapter 2) and financial year forecasts are among the most widely used tools for budgetary planning and control (CIMA, 2009).

In budgetary control, responsibility for monitoring and controlling items of income and expenditure is devolved to the managers of the budget centres. The management accounting system provides information to these managers on a regular basis (often monthly) that gives details of the budgeted figures and the actual figures achieved, so that they can compare their performance against the plan and take any actions deemed necessary. The provision of information to all levels of an organization based on the responsibility of the individual managers is known as *responsibility accounting*.

Key definition

Responsibility accounting is a system that provides income and expenditure information to all management levels, based on the responsibility each departmental or functional manager has for particular items of income or expenditure. Examples of responsibility accounting systems include budgetary control and standard costing.

A formal system of budgetary control enables an organization to carry out its planning in a systematic and logical manner. Control can be achieved only by setting a plan of what is to be accomplished in a specified time period and regularly monitoring progress against the plan. This allows managers time to take corrective action where possible if actual performance deviates from the plan. By setting plans, the activities of the various functions and departments can be co-ordinated. For example, the production manager can ensure that the correct quantity of each product is manufactured to meet the requirements of the sales team, or the accountant can obtain sufficient funding to make adequate resources available to carry out the task, whether this is looking after children in care or running a railway network.

A budgetary control system is a communication system. It informs managers of the objectives of the organization and the constraints under which it is operating. The regular monitoring of performance helps keep management informed of the progress of the organization towards its objectives. Communicating detailed targets to individual managers can enhance motivation, as it gives them a clear sense of direction. By setting separate plans for individual departments and functions of the business, the managers of those departments and functions can make decisions within their budget responsibilities and this avoids the need for every decision to be made at the top level.

By comparing actual activity for a particular period of time with the original plan, any variance (difference), expressed in financial terms, is identified. This enables managers to assess their performance and decide what corrective action, if any, needs to be taken. By predicting future events, managers are encouraged to collect all the relevant information, analyze it and make decisions in good time. An organization is made up of a number of individuals with their own ambitions and goals. The budgetary control process encourages consensus by modifying personal goals and integrating them with the overall objectives of the organization. Managers can see how their personal aims fit into the overall context and how they might be achieved.

17.3 Main stages in budgetary control

The process of preparing budgets for each of the functions and departments in the business, and drawing up a master budget can take several months. The first step is for management to set out their assumptions and predictions about what is going to happen to the firm's markets and business environment.

Activity

Make a list of the factors that management should consider when arriving at their assumptions about what is going to happen to their markets and the business environment.

Depending on the type of organization you are thinking of, the sort of factors you may have included are as follows:

- changes in the size of the organization's market and its market share
- competitors' strategies
- changes in interest rates or sources of funding
- increases in costs and availability of energy, materials and labour
- changes in legislation or social pressures that will affect the organization
- the effects of the activities of other related organizations
- changes in climate, consumer demographics, social and environmental factors, etc.

It is also important to identify any foreseeable limiting factor, such as shortage of materials or a constraint on production capacity. As we saw in Chapter 16, this can prevent the business from achieving higher levels of financial performance in the budget period.

Key definition

A limiting factor is a constraint that prevents the entity from achieving higher levels of performance and profitability.

Having set out their assumptions, management can then start making predictions about what is likely to happen in the year ahead. However, if they were to leave it at that, they would not be discharging their managerial responsibilities. For example, perhaps they forecast that the business will become insolvent and unable to pay its debts when they fall due. Although this might be an accurate prediction, they must take steps to avoid it. Therefore, management must find ways of minimizing all threats to the organization and taking advantage of opportunities. By setting out their financial strategies and the actions that must be taken in view of their predictions, they are making business plans that will help them meet their financial objectives.

The next step requires detailed plans (the *budgets*) to be drawn up with specific financial plans for each designated part of the business (the *budget centres*), thus covering every aspect of the organization's activities.

Key definitions

A budget is a quantitative or financial statement that contains the plans and policies to be pursued during a future accounting period.

A budget centre is a designated part of an entity for which budgets are prepared and controlled by a manager.

The budget period is usually one year and the budget is normally broken down into monthly figures. Initially, it may be expressed in quantitative terms (for example, the numbers of each type of product to be made and the quantity of materials to be ordered), but it will be converted into financial terms for the budgetary control system. A budget centre is typically a department or function in the business, a cost centre, an individual or any combination of these that management wishes to treat as a budget centre.

 Activity

Give an example of a budget using the knowledge you have gained from your studies so far.

A cash flow forecast is a good example of a budget (see Chapter 2). A cash flow forecast is a statement that shows the amount of cash expected to come in and go out during some period in the future. It is usually drawn up for each month over a 12-month period, and shows the monthly cash inflows and outflows, the net cash flows and the cumulative cash position at the end of each month. A cash flow forecast is not a tool for control because it is only a plan. In order to achieve control, comparison must be made with the actual figures.

The next stage involves translating the detailed plans into actions for each manager to pursue.

Activity

Both the production manager and the marketing manager of Cascade plc need to know how many shower units they plan to sell in the coming year, so they can ensure that the number of shower units to be made will meet the anticipated demand. What suggestions would you make if either of the following circumstances arose?

(a) Many more shower units are made than can be sold.
(b) Many more orders are received than the number of shower units made.

In situation (a) you may have decided that it is necessary to cut back severely on production. This could lead to redundancies, with machines and other resources not being used to their full capacity. Alternatively, you may have suggested that production continues at the same level and the excess production is stored, which could be very expensive. Finally, you may consider that the organization should boost sales through price reductions or increased marketing. Both these options could also be very expensive. Although you may think that situation (b) is a good position for the business to be in, it can lead to considerable problems. If the company attempts to boost production, it may need overtime working at a higher wage rate. More machines and larger premises may be required, which may require taking out a loan to pay for them. If the company fails to meet the orders, customers will become dissatisfied and the firm's reputation will be harmed; customers may go to competitors where the service is better.

Whichever of the above alternatives the company chooses, the policy will have to be communicated to all managers. This will ensure that detailed plans can be drawn up which minimize the potential damage to the company's financial performance. However, even if detailed plans are made available to all managers so that activities are co-ordinated, it does not mean that there is control. Because the plans are based on predictions, it is very likely that events such as the following may occur that prevent the plans from being achieved:

• Prices of direct materials, labour or expenses may rise unexpectedly
• New competitors may enter the market and offer cheaper products
• Machines may break down
• Suppliers may not be able to deliver materials on time.

Once the period has commenced, regular financial statements are usually produced comparing actual performance with the budget. This is the final stage, where the individual managers responsible for the budget centres are expected to remedy any controllable adverse *variances* (differences) or revise the plan if necessary.

> **Key definition**
>
> In budgetary control, a variance is the difference between the budgeted cost and the actual cost, or the difference between the budgeted income and the actual income. Individual budget centre managers are responsible for the controllable costs in their budgets and are expected to take action to remedy adverse variances that are considered to be excessive.

Assumptions and predictions about what is going to happen to the firm's markets and business environment are normally made at the highest level, following consultation throughout the organization. Collecting information to measure actual performance is part of the accounting function and accountants are also responsible for issuing financial statements that compare the actual performance with the plan. At this stage, most managers find that they have a role in explaining any variances between the planned and actual figures, and in suggesting the appropriate course to pursue. If there is no formal system of planning and control, there will probably be an informal system. In a very small business, the owner-manager may be responsible for all the stages. In larger businesses, there is likely to be a formal system, with a greater division of responsibility at each stage. Figure 17.1 summarizes the main stages in budgetary control.

Figure 17.1 Main stages in budgetary control

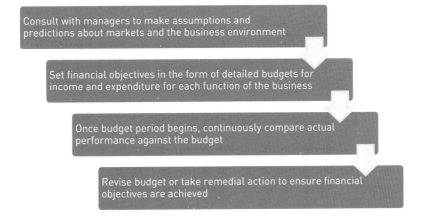

Consult with managers to make assumptions and predictions about markets and the business environment

Set financial objectives in the form of detailed budgets for income and expenditure for each function of the business

Once budget period begins, continuously compare actual performance against the budget

Revise budget or take remedial action to ensure financial objectives are achieved

17.4 Setting budgets

The traditional method for setting budgets is known as *incremental budgeting*. Under this approach, management adds a percentage to the current year's income and expenditure to take account of predicted changes in prices. However, this means that the budget will include non-recurring income or expenditure and it will not be tailored to the conditions expected to prevail during the forthcoming budget period. *Zero-based budgeting* developed to address this problem. As its name suggests, management ignores the current year's figures and starts from a zero-base, justifying each budget figure from the policies and conditions that are likely to exist. This makes the budget much more relevant to the particular conditions expected in the budget period than incremental budgeting.

The budgets give details of the planned income and expenditure during a financial period that will achieve the given financial objective. In the first instance, the budgets may be measured in quantitative terms, such as the number of cost units to be produced or sold, the quantity of materials required or the number of employees needed. However, they will be converted into financial terms for the budgetary control system. Therefore, both *financial budgets* and *non-financial budgets* are normally prepared. Figure 17.2 shows an example of typical budgets prepared for a sales and marketing department (a budget centre).

Figure 17.2   Examples of non-financial and financial budgets

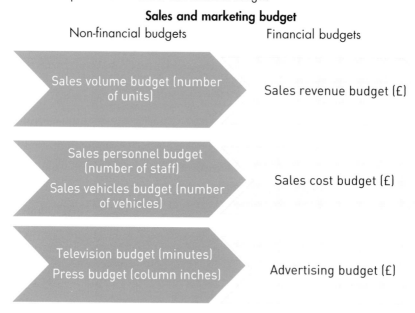

Budgets are drawn up for individual departments and functions, as well as for capital expenditure, inventory and cash flow. Therefore, both *functional* and *non-functional* budgets are needed. Non-functional budgets are not the responsibility of a specific functional manager, but require contributions from various managers and the accountant. Non-functional budgets include the capital expenditure budget, which gives details of planned capital expenditure analyzed by asset, project, functional area and budget period, the cash flow budget, the budgeted statement of profit or loss and other comprehensive income and the budgeted statement of financial position. The master budget incorporates all the budgets and is the final co-ordinated overall budget for the period.

We can illustrate the setting of budgets by looking at Solar Lighting Ltd, a small start-up company that makes only one product: Portalite, a portable solar lighting system. We will start with the *sales budget* as this forms the basis of all the other budgets. It shows the estimated sales volume, the selling price of the product and the budgeted revenue for the period. The company plans to sell 8,500 units of Portalite and each unit will have a selling price of £100.

Sales revenue budget

$$8,500 \text{ units to be sold} \times £100 = £850,000 \text{ sales revenue}$$

The next stage is to prepare the *production budget*. The budget is expressed in quantity only and is the responsibility of the production manager. The objective is to ensure that production is sufficient to meet sales demand for the period. Like all the figures in budgets, the opening and closing inventory figures are based on estimates.

Production budget	
Sales volume	8,500
Closing inventory	1,870
Total units required	10,370
Opening inventory	(170)
Production volume	10,200

The managers of the departments that produce Portalite then prepare the *direct materials usage budget*. This estimates the direct materials required to meet the production budget. In this case, each Portalite uses 10 units of metal alloy.

Direct materials usage budget for metal alloy

10,200 production budget x 10 units of metal alloy = 102,000 units of metal alloy

The next budget is the *direct materials purchase budget*, which is prepared by the purchasing manager to ensure that enough materials are purchased to meet production requirements. The purchase price of metal alloy is £1.50 per unit. As already mentioned, the opening and closing inventory figures are based on estimates.

Direct materials purchase budget for metal alloy	
Direct materials usage budget	102,000
Closing inventory	23,040
Total units required	125,040
Opening inventory	(9,600)
Units of material to be purchased	115,440
Total cost (115,440 x £1.50)	£173,160

The *direct labour budget* is the responsibility of the managers of the departments which produce the product. They will prepare estimates of the labour hours required by the department to meet the planned production. Each Portalite uses 1½ hours of direct labour and the wage rate is £10 per hour.

Direct labour budget for the Assembly Department
10,200 production budget x 1½ hours x £10 = £153,000 direct labour

The *factory overhead budgets* are the responsibility of the relevant departmental managers and show the assignment of overheads to each department, as well as indicating whether they are controllable or non-controllable for reporting purposes. The following simple example illustrates the principles. It is a simple example because Solar Lighting Ltd only makes one product. As the title of the budget suggests, in practice it would be factory wide.

Overhead budget for the Production Department	
	£
Controllable overheads	
Indirect materials	30,600
Indirect labour	15,300
Power	5,100
	51,000
Non-controllable overheads	
Depreciation	25,000
Supervision	25,000
Power (fixed proportion)	10,000
Maintenance	11,400
	71,400
Total overheads	122,400
Total labour hours	15,300
Budgeted overhead rate per direct labour hour	£8.00
(£122,400 ÷ 15,300 hours)	

In practice, separate *administration, sales and distribution budgets* will be produced by the relevant managers of those functions.

For cost control purposes the direct labour, material usage and factory overheads budgets are combined into separate *departmental budgets*. For responsibility accounting purposes, these budgets are compared with the actual results at the end of the period to assess how effective the departmental managers are in controlling the expenditure for which they are responsible.

The objective of the *cash budget* is to ensure that sufficient funds will be available throughout the period to cover the level of operations outlined in the various budgets. The cash budget may be prepared on a weekly, monthly or quarterly basis, as necessary to identify any cash surplus or deficit as early as possible. The following example illustrates a cash budget for the first six months of the year. The following simple example shows a cash budget for one month.

Cash budget for January	Week 1 £	Week 2 £	Week 3 £	Week 4 £
Opening balance	2,850	3,350	(1,000)	(7,750)
Cash inflows from sales	25,500	20,150	18,250	45,250
	28,350	23,500	17,250	37,500
Cash outflows				
Purchase of materials	(12,000)	(8,000)	(10,000)	(18,000)
Wages	(10,000)	(10,000)	(10,000)	(10,000)
Other costs	(3,000)	(6,500)	(5,000)	(4,000)
	(25,000)	(24,500)	(25,000)	(32,000)
Closing balance	3,350	(1,000)	(7,750)	5,500

The *budgeted statement of comprehensive income* and the *budgeted statement of financial position* are constructed to provide the overall picture of the planned financial performance for the budget period and the predicted financial position at the end of the budget period. These are prepared in accordance with financial accounting requirements but will be based on budgeted information.

When all the functional budgets, the capital budget, the cash flows budget, the budgeted statement of comprehensive income and the statement of financial position have been prepared, they form the *master budget*. The master budget is submitted by the accountant to the budget committee, together with a number of budgeted profitability, liquidity and gearing ratios. If the figures are acceptable, the budget will be approved.

Key definition

A master budget is the final co-ordinated budget for the whole entity that brings together the functional budgets and the non-functional budgets. The non-functional budgets include the capital expenditure budget, the budgeted statement of cash flows, the budgeted statement of profit or loss and other comprehensive income, and the statement of financial position.

We can illustrate the interrelationship of budgets by looking at the case of Portalite again, which is the sole product made by Solar Lighting Ltd. The sales director has estimated that the following quantities will be sold over the next 6 months.

	January	February	March	April	May	June
Forecast sales volume	1,000	1,200	1,500	1,600	1,600	1,750

The production department will manufacture the product in the month before the sales take place and it has been agreed that a buffer inventory of 200 units of product will be maintained. On 1 December of the previous year there is an opening inventory of 100 units.

Activity

Calculate the number of units that must be manufactured each month.

The best way to tackle this problem is to draw up a table giving all the information.

	December	January	February	March	April	May	June
Opening inventory	100	1,200	1,400	1,700	1,800	1,800	1,950
Production	1,100	1,200	1,500	1,600	1,600	1,750	
Sales		1,000	1,200	1,500	1,600	1,600	1,750
Closing inventory	1,200	1,400	1,700	1,800	1,800	1,950	

We know that the opening inventory on 1 December was 100 units. To find out how many units need to be manufactured in December, you need to consider how many are expected to be needed to cover the sales volume of 1,000 in January and ensure that there is a buffer inventory of 200 units on 31 December (1,000 + 200 = 1,200). Therefore, the December production volume needs to be the closing inventory less the opening inventory (1,200 – 100 = 1,100). You will remember that the closing inventory at the end of one month becomes the opening inventory at the beginning of the next. Therefore, on 1 January the opening inventory is the same as the closing inventory on 31 December (1,200 units). We continued to use these principles to calculate the forecast production volumes for the rest of the period.

Having calculated the number of units that must be produced, we now need to consider the decisions the production manager must take and which budgets will be affected. The most immediate decision concerns whether there is sufficient machine capacity and labour to make the product. It may be that more machines and labour are required in the busy months and more space will be required in the factory. If so, it will affect all these budgets. The accountant will be concerned with the cash requirements for any changes and will want to ensure that the implications of these decisions are shown in the cash budget. It is because of the interrelated nature of budgets that a change in any one budget can affect the other budgets.

The process of preparing budgets for each of the functions and other activities in an organization and drawing up a master budget can take a number of months. The budgets must be communicated to managers before the start of the appropriate financial period, called the *budget period*, so they know what the plans are for their own departments and can implement them. Some organizations adopt a 'top-down' approach to budget setting, where the owners or senior management decide the individual plans for each department and function, and these plans are given to the individual managers to implement. Other organizations use a 'bottom-up' approach to budget setting, where individual managers construct their own budgets, which are given to the owners or senior managers, who then co-ordinate the individual budgets into a master budget. These are the two extremes, and most organizations fall somewhere between the two policies.

A *budget committee* may be formed, made up of the functional or departmental managers and chaired by the chief executive. The management accountant usually occupies the role of committee secretary, and he or she co-ordinates and assists in the preparation of the budget data provided by each manager. The budget committee reviews the budgets submitted by individual managers and ensures that each has the following characteristics:

- It conforms to the policies formulated by the owners or directors.
- It shows how the objectives are going to be achieved, and recognizes any constraints under which the organization will be operating.
- It is realistic.
- It integrates with the other budgets.
- It reflects the responsibilities of the manager concerned.

If a budget does not display all these characteristics, it will need to be revised. This may affect other budgets and there may need to be negotiations between the managers concerned to introduce the necessary budget changes. When the budgets have been approved by the budget committee, they are submitted to the directors for approval prior to the commencement of the budget period. If the directors accept the budget, it is then adopted by the organization as a whole and becomes the working plans.

17.5 Fixed and flexible budgets

A *fixed budget* is a budget that is not changed once it has been established, even though there may be changes in the level of activity. It may be revised if the situation so demands, but not merely because the actual activity level differs from the planned level of activity. This can be a considerable disadvantage, because a fixed budget may show an adverse variance on costs which is simply due to an increase in variable costs because activity is higher than anticipated. As you will remember from Chapter 16, total variable costs increase or decrease in proportion with changes in activity level.

On the other hand, a *flexible budget* is designed to change with the level of activity. Therefore, in a flexible budget, any cost variance can be assumed to be due to an increase or decrease in fixed costs. A flexible budget may be used at the planning stage to illustrate the impact of achieving different activity levels. It can also be used at the control stage at the end of a month to compare the actual results with what they should have been.

Key definitions

A fixed budget is a budget that is not changed merely because the actual levels of activity differ from the budgeted levels of activity. Therefore, the budgeted cost allowances for each cost item are not changed for the variable items.

A flexible budget is a budget that is changed in accordance with actual levels of activity and reflects the different behaviour of the fixed and variable costs. The adjusted budget is known as a flexed budget.

We will illustrate the importance of flexible budgeting by returning to the example of Solar Lighting Ltd. The budget for January is based on an output of 1,000 Portalite systems. The following budget report shows the budgeted and actual figures for the month when 1,100 units were sold.

Portalite
Budget report for January

	Fixed budget £	Actual £
Sales revenue (£1.50 × 1,000)	1,500	1,650
Variable costs (75p × 1,000)	(750)	(880)
Variable overheads (25p × 1,000)	(250)	(260)
Fixed overheads	(200)	(200)
Profit for the period	300	310

The managing director has been sent the above budget statement and is delighted that the actual profit is £10 above the budget.

Activity

Write a brief report to the managing director explaining why he should not be so pleased with the results. Support your report with calculations.

After all the work you have done on marginal costing in Chapter 16, the words 'variable costs' should immediately have alerted you to the problem of comparing the actual results with the original budget when there has been a change in activity level. In this case the number of units sold was 1,100 compared with the planned amount of 1,000 units. Although the sales department must be congratulated on achieving increased sales, the company needs to construct a flexible budget to see if they have controlled their variable costs. This is done by multiplying the planned variable costs per unit by the actual level of production.

The variable costs were originally set at £750 for 1,000 torches, which is 75p per unit. The variable overheads were originally set at £250 for 1,000 units, which is 25p per unit. If we assume that as the number of torches manufactured increases, the total variable costs increase, the flexible budget compared with the actual results is as follows.

	Flexible budget	Actual
Portalite		
Budget report for January		
	£	£
Sales revenue (£1.50 × 1,100)	1,650	1,650
Variable costs (75p × 1,100)	(825)	(880)
Variable overheads (25p × 1,100)	(275)	(260)
Fixed overheads	(200)	(200)
Profit for the period	350	310

The flexible budget shows that at an output level of 1,100 units, a profit of £350 should have been made, but the business has only made a profit of £310. A comparison of the figures shows that although variable overheads have been reduced, there is an overspend on variable costs that must be investigated. This demonstrates the advantages of using a flexible budget, where the budget is amended if the actual activity level is not the same as planned. By comparing the actual results with what should have been achieved at that level of activity, a more accurate measure is given.

17.6 Variance analysis

Variance analysis is the investigation of the factors that have caused the differences between the actual and the budgeted figures (the differences are known as variances). Actual progress is measured from the beginning of the budget period (usually one year). At the end of each month, the actual figures for all items of income and expenditure are compared with the plan and reported to the managers responsible. If actual income is higher than the budgeted income, there will be a favourable variance. On the other hand, if actual income is lower than budgeted income, there will be an adverse variance. There may also be cost variances. If actual costs are lower than the budgeted costs, there will be a favourable variance. If actual costs are higher than the budgeted expenditure, there will be an adverse variance. Unless they can be remedied, adverse variances will result in reduced profits.

Activity

Richard Pillinger manages a farm that produces early crops by growing them in large polythene tunnels. Complete the following budget report for May by calculating the variances and indicating whether they are favourable or adverse.

Early Crops Ltd
Budget report for May

	Budget £	Actual £	Variance £
Income			
Cucumbers	25,000	24,500	
Peppers	18,000	17,200	
Tomatoes	19,000	19,600	
	62,000	61,300	
Expenditure			
Salaries	28,400	29,000	
Expenses	12,500	12,000	
Administration	1,800	1,700	
Miscellaneous	700	300	
	43,400	43,000	
Profit for the period	18,600	18,300	

You should not have had too much difficulty with this, as it is simply a matter of subtracting the actual figures from the budgeted figures and remembering that an adverse variance is where actual revenue is lower than planned or actual costs are higher than planned. Compare your answer with the completed budget report below.

Early Crops Ltd

Budget report for May

	Budget	Actual	Variance	
	£	£	£	
Income				
Cucumbers	25,000	24,500	(500)	Adverse
Peppers	18,000	17,200	(800)	Adverse
Tomatoes	19,000	19,600	600	Favourable
	62,000	61,300	(700)	Adverse
Expenditure				
Salaries	28,400	29,000	(600)	Adverse
Expenses	12,500	12,000	500	Favourable
Administration	1,800	1,700	100	Favourable
Miscellaneous	700	300	400	Favourable
	43,400	43,000	400	Favourable
Profit for the period	18,600	18,300	(300)	Adverse

The budget report shows that the business made a profit in May, which was £300 lower than planned. This was due to lower income from sales of cucumbers and peppers than planned, combined with higher salaries paid. If you had any problems with the calculations, look at the spreadsheet formulae shown in Figure 17.3.

Figure 17.3   Early Crops Ltd Budget Report for May

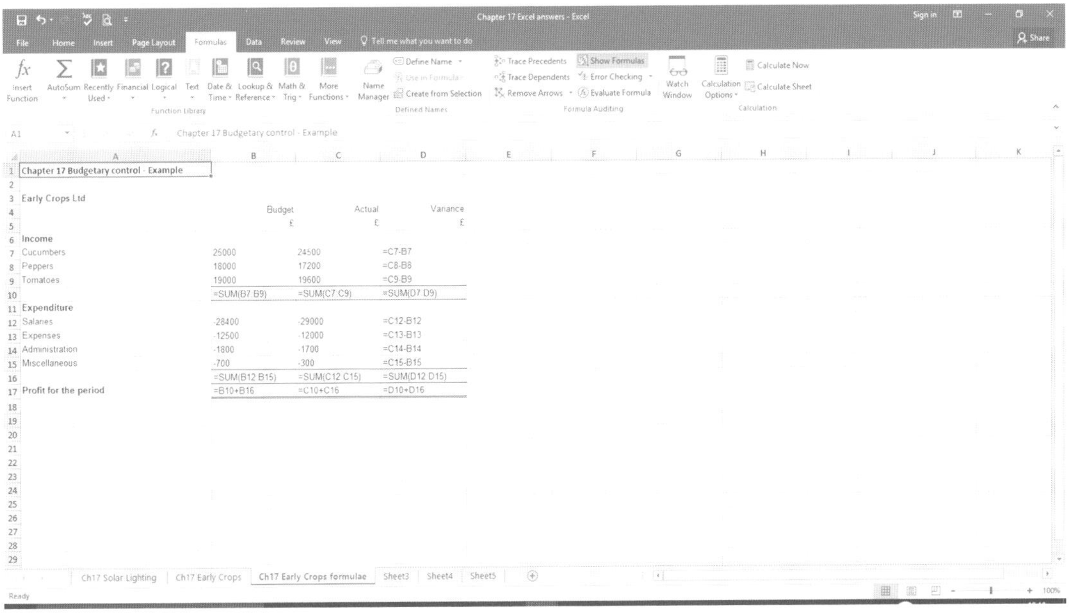

Now Richard must decide whether the adverse variances require any action on his part. The salary increase may not have been planned but is nevertheless necessary. The lower sales income may be due to factors beyond his control, such as unexpected bad weather affecting yield. Most businesses experience peaks and troughs during the year, especially where there are seasonal factors affecting production and demand. Therefore, these variations need to be reflected in the monthly budget figures. On the other hand, Richard may discover it is due to poor marketing or distribution problems. Therefore, before he can make any decision, he must first investigate the causes.

17.7 Advantages and disadvantages

There is no single model of a perfect budgetary control system and each organization needs a system that meets its own particular needs. The following list summarizes the main requirements for an effective system of budgetary control:

- A sound and clearly defined organization with the managers' responsibilities clearly indicated.
- Effective accounting records and procedures which are understood and applied.
- Strong support and the commitment of top managers to the system of budgetary control.
- The education and training of managers in the development, interpretation and use of budgets.
- The revision of the original budgets where circumstances show that amendments are required to make them appropriate and useful.
- The recognition throughout the organization that budgetary control is a management activity and not an accounting exercise.
- The participation of managers in the budgetary control system.
- An information system that provides data for managers so that they can make realistic predictions.
- The correct integration of budgets and their effective communication to managers.
- The setting of reasonable and achievable budgets.

Sometimes management implements a system of budgetary control, but becomes disillusioned with it because the disadvantages seem to outweigh the advantages.

Activity

When an organization has a budgetary control system, internal planning and control should be improved, which must be a considerable advantage. What other advantages might there be, and what are the disadvantages of a budgetary control system?

An effective system of budgetary control will benefit from the following *advantages*:

- Co-ordination – All the various functions and activities of the organization are co-ordinated.
- Responsibility accounting – Accounting information is provided to the managers responsible for income and expenditure budgets to allow them to conduct variance analysis.
- Utilization of resources – Capital and effort are used to achieve the financial objectives of the business.
- Motivation – Managers are motivated through the use of clearly defined objectives and the monitoring of achievement.
- Planning – Planning ahead gives time to take corrective action, since decisions are based on the examination of future problems.
- Establishing a system of control – Control is achieved if plans are reviewed regularly against performance.
- Transfer of authority – Authority for decisions is devolved to the individual managers.

There are quite a number of potential drawbacks associated with budgetary control systems. How serious these drawbacks are depends on the way the system is operated. An ineffective system of budgetary control may suffer from the following *disadvantages*:

- Set in stone – Managers may be constrained by the original budget and not take effective and sensible decisions when the circumstances warrant it (for example, they might make no attempt to spend less than the maximum or make no attempt to exceed the target income).
- Time-consuming – Time spent on setting and controlling budgets may deflect managers from their prime responsibilities of running the business.
- Unrealistic – Plans may become unrealistic if fixed budgets are set and the activity level is not as planned. This can lead to poor control.
- Demotivating – Managers may become demotivated if budgets are imposed by top management without consultation or if fixed budgets cannot be achieved due to lower levels of activity beyond their control.

The first letters of the above list of advantages and disadvantages of budgetary control form two mnemonics (CRUMPET and STUD) which some students find useful for remembering these points.

17.8 Conclusions

Budgetary control involves the preparation of detailed business plans for the forthcoming financial period. These plans take the form of *budgets* for income and expenditure, which are the responsibility of the managers of each *budget centre*.

Financial control is achieved by these managers monitoring the actual performance of the budget centre against the budget on a regular basis, and taking whatever action is considered necessary to correct any adverse variances that are within their control.

In this chapter we have looked at the need for business planning and the cycle of planning and control in an organization. We have examined the way in which budgets are established for separate functions and how they are integrated into a master budget. We have seen how variance analysis is conducted and considered what organizational factors are required to operate an effective system of budgetary control. Finally, we have looked at the benefits of using flexible rather than fixed budgets in a business where activity levels are likely to fluctuate and examined the general advantages and disadvantages of budgetary control.

References

CIMA (2009) *Management Accounting Tools for Today and Tomorrow*, London: Chartered Institute of Management Accountants. Available from: www.cima-global.com/Documents/Thought_leadership_docs/CIMA%20Tools%20and%20 Techniques%2030-11-09%20PDF.pdf (Accessed 11 June 2016).

Discussion questions

1 Discuss the purpose of a budgetary control system and the main stages in budgetary control.

2 Discuss the advantages and disadvantages associated with systems of budgetary control.

Practice questions

3 Explain the difference between a fixed budget and a flexible budget, using an example to illustrate your answer.

4 The managing director of Leisure Magazines Ltd has recently introduced a budgetary control system. The accountant drew up budgets for the advertising and editorial departments based on the actual results for the last three years. At the end of the first month of the new financial period, the actual income was higher than planned, but the actual total advertising department costs were higher than budgeted. The actual costs for the editorial department were the same as those budgeted and the actual profit for the period was higher. On receiving the first month's results, the managing director threatened to dismiss the advertising manager for exceeding the budgeted costs. The advertising manager responded by saying that he would resign unless the budgetary control system was scrapped. The accountant left to join another company.

You work for the firm of consultants that has been asked to advise the company. Prepare a preliminary report covering the following:

(a) An analysis of the problems, and how you think they have arisen.
(b) Guidelines for the operation of a successful and effective budgetary control system.
(c) Recommendations as to what action the managing director of the client company should take.

5 The following information is available from the accounting records of Hadrill Ltd.

Invoices paid in the month after sale	60%
Invoices paid in the second month after sale	25%
Invoices paid in the third month after sale	12%
Bad debts	3%

Invoices are issued on the last day of each month. Customers paying in the month after sale are entitled to deduct a 2% discount. Credit sales for September to December next year are budgeted as follows.

September	October	November	December
£35,000	£40,000	£60,000	£45,000

Required

Calculate the amount budgeted to be received from credit sales in December next year.

6 Tooting Tools Ltd has a budgeted production level of 500 units per month and does not want the inventory level to fall below 1,000 units. The sales budget shows the following figures.

	January	February	March	April	May	June
Units	400	400	600	800	1,000	600

Required

(a) Using the following pro-forma, calculate the opening and closing inventory for each month.

	January	February	March	April	May	June
Opening inventory	1,000	?	?	?	?	?
Production	500	500	500	500	500	500
Total	?	?	?	?	?	?
Sales	(400)	(400)	(600)	(600)	(800)	(800)
Closing inventory	?	?	?	?	?	?

(b) Comment on whether the opening inventory of 1,000 units in January is sufficient to ensure that the level of closing inventory in any month does not fall below 1,000 units. If it does fall below 1,000 units in any month, recalculate the opening inventory needed in January to prevent this.

7 Julia Walker is planning to use £50,000 she has inherited to open a business called
Chelsea Trekkers Ltd, which will sell designer label clothing and footwear for country pursuits. She will rent a shop in Chelsea which will cost £25,000 per quarter,
payable on the first day of the quarter. The overheads are expected to be £10,000
per month, payable the month after the month in which they are incurred. Julia will
pay her part-time sales assistant £5,000 per month. The budgeted sales and purchases for the first three months are as follows.

	Sales	Purchases
	£	£
January	100,000	60,000
February	120,000	70,000
March	180,000	100,000

Julia must pay her suppliers in the month in which the purchase is made. Half her
customers will pay cash and the remainder will receive one month's credit and pay in
the month after the month of the sale.

Required

Using the above information, construct a budgeted cash flow statement for the
first quarter. You may wish to refresh your knowledge of the layout by referring to
Chapter 2.

8 John Murphy is planning to start a business selling bicycles on 1 January 2018.
He has £25,000 capital to invest in the business and has arranged a bank loan of
£25,000 over five years with a fixed interest rate of 6% per annum. Details of the
anticipated income and expenditure for John's Bikes Ltd are as follows:

Cash sales	£30,000 per month
Credit sales	£5,000 per month (1 month's credit)
Purchases	£10,000 per month (2 months' credit)
Rent	£24,000 per annum payable in full on 1 January
Insurance	£6,000 per annum payable monthly
Advertising	£1,000 quarterly, starting in January
Telephone and Internet	£100 per month
Salaries	£6,100 per month
Lighting and heating	£200 per month
Equipment	£12,000 payable in full on 1 January
Fixtures and fittings	£20,000 payable in full on 31 January

Interest on the bank loan will be paid in instalments at the end of each month. The
equipment will be depreciated over four years and the fixtures and fittings over five
years; neither is expected to have any residual value at the end of their respective
useful economic lives. At the end of the first quarter, John expects to have £10,000 of
inventory.

Required

Using a spreadsheet, construct the following budgeted financial statements for the first quarter:

(a) Cash flow budget for the three months 1 January to 31 March 2018.
(b) Budgeted statement of profit or loss for the three months 1 January to 31 March 2018.
(c) Budgeted statement of financial position at 31 March 2018.

You can refresh your knowledge of the layouts of these financial statements by referring to Chapters 2, 6 and 7.

 # Suggested research questions for dissertation students

Students interested in budgetary control may wish to investigate one or more of the following research questions:

- Does a system of budgetary control enhance profitability?
- What factors influence the introduction of a budgetary control system?
- Is budgetary control appropriate for SMEs?

Preliminary reading

CIMA (2009) *Management Accounting Tools for Today and Tomorrow*, London: Chartered Institute of Management Accountants. Available from: www.cima-global.com/Documents/Thought_leadership_docs/CIMA%20Tools%20and%20Techniques%2030-11-09%20PDF.pdf (Accessed 11 June 2016).

Dugdale, D., Jones, T.C. and Green, S. (2006) *Contemporary Accounting Practices in UK Manufacturing*, Oxford: Elsevier/CIMA.

Dugdale, D. and Lyne, S.R. (2010) *Budgeting Practice and Organisational Structure*, Oxford: Elsevier/CIMA.

Dugdale, D. and Lyne, S.R. (2011) 'Beyond budgeting', in Abdel-Kader, M.G. (ed.), *Review of Management Accounting Research*, Basingstoke: Palgrave Macmillan.

Mitchell, F. and Reid, G. (2000) 'Problems, challenges and opportunities: Small business as a setting for management accounting research', *Management Accounting Research*, 11(4), pp. 385–390.

Nandan, R. (2010) 'Management accounting needs of SMEs and the role of professional accountants: A renewed research agenda', *Journal of Management Accounting Research*, 8(1), pp. 65–78.

Perren, L. and Grant, P. (2000) 'The evolution of management accounting routines in small businesses: A social construction perspective', *Management Accounting Research*, 11(4), pp. 391–411.

Ryan, B. (2011) 'Control, budgets and shareholder value: Shifting boundaries of influence', in Abdel-Kader, M.G. (ed.), *Review of Management Accounting Research*, Basingstoke: Palgrave Macmillan.

18 Standard costing

Learning objectives

When you have studied this chapter, you should be able to:

- Describe the technique of standard costing
- Calculate the direct materials variances
- Calculate the direct labour variances
- Describe the advantages and disadvantages of standard costing

18.1 Introduction

This chapter introduces a method of financial control known as standard costing in which predetermined standard costs and standard revenues are compared with actual costs and actual revenues. Standard costing is closely associated with budgetary control, which we looked at in the previous chapter. Although each can be used without the other, it is unusual to find standard costing being used without a budgetary control system also being present.

We have already seen that budgetary control is applied to budget centres and the organization as a whole, and can be used in any type of organization. However, standard costing is mainly applied to products and processes, and therefore, it is more commonly used in manufacturing organizations. As in a budgetary control system, it allows the comparison of predetermined costs and income with the actual costs and income achieved. Any variances, or differences, can then be investigated. Managers within the organization can be held responsible for these variances and, by analyzing the reasons for the variances, control can be achieved.

In this chapter we explain the principles that underpin standard costing and how the different variances associated with total direct costs are calculated. We also discuss the typical causes of any variances and describe the general advantages and disadvantages of standard costing.

18.2 Purpose of standard costing

The *purpose* of *standard costing* is to help managers to control costs. Like budgetary control, there is an emphasis on variance analysis. In a standard costing system, control is achieved by comparing predetermined *standard costs* and *standard revenues* with the actual costs and actual revenues to identify the variances. Any adverse variances can then be investigated and remedied where possible. The variances can also be used to assess whether the business is achieving its financial objectives and also the performance of the cost centre managers. The standard cost can also be used as an alternative to FIFO and AVCO as a method for valuing inventories.

Standards are set in defined working conditions and represent a benchmark of resource usage. They can be set on the following bases (CIMA, 2005):

- an *ex ante* estimate (before the event) of expected performance
- an *ex post* estimate (after the event) of attainable performance
- a prior period level of performance by the same organization
- the level of performance achieved by comparable organizations
- the level of performance required to meet organizational objectives.

> **Key definition**
>
> Standard costing is a system of control in which predetermined standard costs and standard income are compared with the actual costs and the actual income to identify any variances.

Standards can be set at an ideal level or an attainable level, depending on the philosophy of the business. *Ideal standards* are based on the best possible working conditions, but *attainable standards* are more widely used because they are based on realistic efficient performance and allow for such problems as machine breakdowns, materials wastage, etc. Although ideal standards are useful for management decision making, there is some risk that employees will be demotivated by the impossibility of achieving them.

The standard cost is the planned unit of cost that is calculated from technical specifications. These specify the quantity of materials, labour and other elements of cost required, and relate them to the prices and wages that are expected to be in place during the period when the standard cost will be used. It is usual to measure the time in which it is planned to complete a certain volume of work in standard hours or standard minutes. This means that a standard hour is a measure of production output, rather than a measure of time.

Activity

A company has set 1 standard hour's production at 500 units. In a 7-hour day, 4,000 units are produced. What is this output in standard hours?

To answer this question, you will have needed to make the following calculation:

$$\frac{4,000 \text{ units}}{500 \text{ units per standard hour}} = 8 \text{ standard hours' production}$$

18.3 Variance analysis

You will remember from the previous chapter that *variance analysis* is the periodic investigation of the factors that have caused the differences between the actual and the budgeted figures. As in budgetary control, these differences are known as *variances*. At the end of each month of the budget period, the actual figures for all items of revenue and cost are compared with the plan and reported to the managers responsible. Timely reporting gives the opportunity for any *adverse variances* to be remedied, if this is possible.

Any variances are analyzed to reveal their constituent parts, so that sufficient information is available to permit investigation by management. Favourable variances are those which improve the predetermined profit and adverse variances are those which reduce the predetermined profit.

Activity

In the Stitching Department of Jarvis Jackets Ltd 100 pockets can be made in 1 standard hour. In an 8-hour day, 950 pockets are produced. Determine whether this will give rise to a favourable or adverse variance.

The first step is to calculate how many pockets should be made in an 8-hour day:

100 units per standard hour × 8 actual hours = 800 standard hours' production

Next you should have calculated the variance by subtracting the standard hours' production (800) from the actual production (950) to arrive at a figure of 150. This is a favourable variance because 150 more pockets are produced than the 800 planned. Now we are ready to make this part of the standard costing system, by expressing the variance in financial terms.

In a manufacturing business the direct costs associated with each cost unit are normally direct materials and direct labour. The reasons for overspending or underspending on either of these costs are based on the following simple concept:

Total cost of direct materials/labour = Quantity used × Unit price

Any variance in the total direct costs will be due to differences in the quantity used, the price per unit or a combination of both these factors, as shown in Figure 18.1.

Figure 18.1 Total direct costs variance

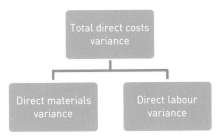

We will now look at the direct materials variance and the direct labour variance in a little more detail.

18.4 Direct materials variance

The above principles are applied to the cost of direct materials. Predetermined standards are set both for the usage level of direct materials for a given volume of production and the price allowed per unit of direct materials. The price standard is based on the price per unit expected to be paid or budgeted for the level of purchases projected over the period for which the standard is to be applied. In general, any price variance is considered to be the responsibility of the buyer or purchasing manager and any variation in the volume or quantity of materials consumed is considered to be the responsibility of the production manager. However, due to the interdependence of price and usage, it may be difficult to assign these responsibilities.

The *direct materials variance* is based on the following formula:

Total cost of direct materials = Quantity used × Price per unit

Standards are set for the quantity of materials to be used for a specific volume of production and the price to be paid per unit of direct materials. The *total direct materials variance* can be calculated using the following formula:

(Standard quantity used × Standard price per unit) − (Actual quantity used × Actual price per unit)

Activity

Jarvis Jackets Ltd has decided to extend its range to include denim jackets. One jacket requires a standard usage of 3 metres of direct materials which has been set at a standard price of £2.20 per metre. In the period, 80 jackets were made and 260 metres of materials consumed at a cost of £1.95 per metre. Using the above formula, calculate the total direct materials variance.

The first stage is to calculate the standard quantity of materials for the actual level of production. As 80 jackets were made and the company planned to use 3 metres of denim per jacket, the standard quantity for that level of production is 240 metres. Inserting the appropriate figures into the formula, the total direct materials variance is:

(240 metres × £2.20) – (260 metres × £1.95) = £528 – £507 = £21 favourable

The difference of £21 between the planned cost and the actual cost is a favourable variance because we have spent less on our materials than we planned for that level of production. Although this information is useful, it needs to be more precise to enable the management to take any action required. The reason why the actual cost of materials can differ from the planned cost of materials for a given level of production is due to two factors. Either we have used more or less materials than planned and/or we have paid more or less per unit of materials than we planned.

The total direct materials variance can be divided into a usage variance and a price variance, as shown in Figure 18.2.

Figure 18.2 Total direct materials variance

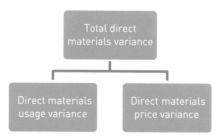

The *direct materials usage variance* is the difference between the standard quantity specified for the actual production and the actual quantity used at standard price per unit. The formula is:

(Standard quantity × Standard price per unit) – (Actual quantity × Standard price per unit)

If data are available, you may find it more convenient to shorten this to:

(Standard quantity – Actual quantity) × Standard price per unit

Activity

Calculate the direct materials usage variance from the data for Jarvis Jackets Ltd.

Inserting the appropriate figures into the formula, the direct materials usage variance is:

(240 metres – 260 metres) × £2.20 = (£44.00) adverse

In this instance, there is an adverse variance because the company has used more materials than planned for that level of production.

The final stage is to find out the *direct materials price variance*. This is the difference between the standard and actual purchase price per unit for the actual quantity of materials purchased or used in production. The formula is:

(Standard price per unit × Actual quantity) – (Actual price per unit × Actual quantity)

If data are available, you can use the following shortened formula:

(Standard price per unit – Actual price per unit) × Actual quantity

Activity

Calculate the direct materials price variance from the data for Jarvis Jackets Ltd.

Inserting the appropriate figures in the formula, the direct materials price variance is:

(£2.20 – £1.95) × 260 metres = £65.00 favourable

The variance is favourable because the business has paid less for the materials than planned for that level of production. If you deduct the adverse usage variance of £44.00 from the favourable price variance of £65.00 you will arrive at the total direct materials variance of £21 favourable. Thus, the first two variances explain the last one you have calculated.

Of course, working out the figures is not the end of the task. Managers need to investigate the reasons for the variances and determine whether any corrective action is required. There are a number of reasons for the adverse usage variance. Perhaps inferior materials were used and this led to higher wastage than planned, or the labour force was inexperienced and this led to high levels of wastage. Alternatively, some materials may have been lost or stolen. One strong possibility for the price variance is that the company has used lower quality and therefore less expensive materials. This would tie in with the possible reason for the adverse usage variance. Other reasons may be that the business is using a different supplier than originally intended or has negotiated a bulk discount.

18.5 Direct labour variance

The same principles are applied to the cost of direct labour. Standards are established for the rate of pay to be paid for the production of particular products and the labour time taken for their production. The standard time taken is expressed in standard hours or standard minutes and becomes the measure of output. By comparing the standard hours allowed and the actual time taken, labour efficiency can be assessed. In practice, standard times are established by work, time and method study techniques.

The *direct labour variance* is based on the following formula:

$$\text{Total labour cost} = \text{Hours worked} \times \text{Rate per hour}$$

The total direct labour variance is calculated by using the following formula:

$$(\text{Standard direct labour hours} \times \text{Standard rate per hour}) - (\text{Actual direct labour hours} \times \text{Actual rate per hour})$$

Activity

The management of Jarvis Jackets Ltd decides that it takes 6 standard hours to make 1 denim jacket and the standard rate paid to labour is £8.00 per hour. The actual production is 900 units and this took 5,100 hours at a rate of £8.30 per hour. Calculate the total direct labour hour variance.

With your knowledge of the calculation of materials variances, this activity should have caused you few problems. The first stage is to calculate the standard direct labour hours for this level of production:

$$900 \text{ jackets} \times 6 \text{ standard hours} = 5,400 \text{ standard hours.}$$

The total direct labour hour variance can then be calculated as follows:

(5,400 standard hours × £8.00) – (5,100 actual hours × £8.30) =
£43,200 – £42,330 = £870 favourable

The variance is favourable because the actual total labour cost is less than the planned cost for that level of production.

The total direct labour variance can be divided into an efficiency variance and a rate variance, as shown in Figure 18.3.

Figure 18.3   Total direct labour variance

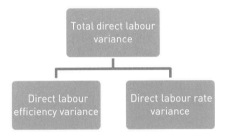

The *direct labour efficiency variance* (sometimes referred to as the labour productivity variance) is the difference between the actual production achieved, measured in standard hours, and the actual hours worked, valued at the standard labour rate. The formula is:

(Standard hours × Standard rate per hour) – (Actual hours × Standard rate per hour)

If data are available, it may be more convenient to shorten the formula to:

(Standard hours – Actual hours) × Standard rate per hour

Activity

Calculate the direct labour efficiency variance from the data for Jarvis Jackets Ltd.

Inserting the appropriate figures into the formula, the direct labour efficiency variance is:

(5,400 standard hours – 5,100 actual hours) × £8.00 = £2,400 favourable

The *direct labour rate variance* is the difference between the standard and actual direct labour rate per hour for the actual hours worked. The formula is:

(Standard rate per hour × Actual hours) – (Actual rate per hour × Actual hours)

If data are available, you can use the following shortened formula:

(Standard rate per hour – Actual rate per hour) × Actual hours

Activity

Calculate the direct labour rate variance from the data for Jarvis Jackets Ltd.

Once again, all you need to do is insert the appropriate figures into the formula and the direct labour rate variance is:

(£8.00 – £8.30) × 5,100 actual hours = (£1,530) adverse

The variance is adverse because employees have been paid more than planned for that level of production. If you deduct the adverse direct labour rate variance of £1,530 from the favourable efficiency variance of £2,400, you arrive at the favourable total direct labour variance of £870. Therefore, the first two variances explain the last one you have calculated.

The most likely reason for the labour rate and efficiency variances is that the company has used more highly skilled labour than originally planned. Therefore, the rate paid was higher and in addition the output was higher than planned. There are other possible reasons, such as the business may have given a pay rise or employees may have had to work overtime and been paid at higher rates. Further investigation would be required to identify the actual reasons and to determine whether any corrective action is required.

18.6 Advantages and disadvantages

As with budgetary control, many of the benefits of standard costing are associated with the processes of planning. Control is improved and it compels managers to make decisions, co-ordinate activities and communicate with one another.

Activity

Make a list of advantages and disadvantages of standard costing.

With your knowledge of budgetary control, you should not have had many problems with this activity. The main *advantages* of standard costing are:

• Standard setting establishes a benchmark against which actual costs can be compared.

- The technique permits a thorough examination of the organization's production and operations activities.
- As the standards are based on future plans and expectations, the information provided to management is much more accurate than that based merely on past performance.
- By examining the reasons for any variances between standard and actual costs and income, management needs to concentrate only on the exceptions to the planned performance. This leads to greater managerial efficiency.
- Variance analysis may result in cost reductions, and control of costs is improved.

The main *disadvantages* of standard costing are:

- It may be difficult to set standards, particularly in a new or dynamic organization.
- The standard costing system may be expensive to maintain and the additional record keeping may become a burden to busy managers.
- Standards will naturally become out of date and require revision. In a very dynamic organization this may happen so quickly that managers lose confidence in the system.
- Information provided by the system is of value only if it is used by managers for control purposes. If the information has no credibility or is not understood, it has no value.

18.7 Conclusions

Standard costing is a method of financial control that is often used in organizations that have a system of budgetary control. Standard costing is mainly applied to products and processes and for this reason it is more commonly used in the manufacturing sector, but it can also be used in the service sector. Financial control is achieved by the individual responsible managers receiving accounting information on a regular basis that allows them to monitor actual performance against the standard performance. They must then investigate the cause of any adverse variances that are considered to be excessive and take action to correct any that are within their control. This is necessary to ensure that the business achieves its financial objectives.

In this chapter we have looked at standard costing and the calculation of variances. We have described how to calculate variances for both total materials costs and total labour costs. We have also examined the calculation of the sub-variances and considered the reasons why they have occurred. Finally, we have examined the advantages and disadvantages of a standard costing system.

References

CIMA (2005) *Management Accounting Official Terminology*, London: Chartered Institute of Management Accountants.

Discussion questions

1 Discuss the purpose of standard costing.

2 Debate the merits of ideal standards versus attainable standards.

3 Discuss the advantages and disadvantages of standard costing.

Practice questions

4 Calculate and suggest possible reasons for the direct materials price variance from the following data:

Standard price is £4 per kilo
Standard usage is 5 kilos per unit
Actual price is £3 per kilo
Actual usage is 5 kilos per unit

5 Calculate and suggest possible reasons for the direct materials usage variance from the following data:

Standard price is £50 per tonne
Standard usage is 1,000 tonnes
Actual price is £50 per tonne
Actual usage is 995 tonnes

6 A manufacturing company has set a standard price for direct materials at £100 per kilo and anticipates that it will make 4 units from 1 kilo of materials. The actual production is 200 units and 52 kilos of materials are used at a price of £98 per kilo.

Required

Calculate all the direct materials variances and discuss the possible reasons for them.

7 A company plans to make 1 unit every 10 hours and the standard rate per hour is set at £9. In a financial period 50 units are made and this takes 460 hours. The total direct labour cost for the period is £5,060.

Required

Calculate all the direct labour variances and discuss the possible reasons for them.

8 Four years ago, your cousin Nikos, who lives in Cyprus, set up Aphrodite Ltd, a small manufacturing company that manufactures shower screens. The business makes two models: Larnaca is the standard model and Paphos is the deluxe model. Both are made from frosted glass and have aluminium frames and fittings. Larnaca has plain glass and silver finish to the frame and fittings, whereas Paphos has an attractive design etched on the glass and a gold finish to the frame and fittings.

Once a year Nikos comes to the UK to spend Christmas with the family. This year, knowing that you are studying management accounting as part of your course, he asks for your advice. He explains that despite a buoyant market and excellent sales figures, his profits have been very disappointing and he wants to embark on a cost-cutting exercise. After discussions, you find that he does not operate a standard costing system and does not seem to know what it is. However, he is very keen to learn, but he is only staying a few days, so he asks you to write to him in Cyprus with full details.

Required

Write a letter to Nikos explaining the advantages of a standard costing system, how it can be implemented and the information he can expect to obtain.

 ## Suggested research questions for dissertation students

Students interested in standard costing may wish to investigate one or more of the following research questions:

- Does standard costing enhance profitability?
- What factors influence the introduction of a standard costing system?
- Is standard costing appropriate for SMEs?

Preliminary reading

CIMA (2009) *Management Accounting Tools for Today and Tomorrow*, London: Chartered Institute of Management Accountants. Available from: www.cima-global.com/Documents/Thought_leadership_docs/CIMA%20Tools%20and%20 Techniques%2030-11-09%20PDF.pdf (Accessed 11 June 2016).

Dugdale, D., Jones, T.C. and Green, S. (2006) *Contemporary Accounting Practices in UK Manufacturing*, Oxford: Elsevier/CIMA.

Dugdale, D. and Lyne, S.R. (2010) *Budgeting Practice and Organisational Structure*, Oxford: Elsevier/CIMA.

Dugdale, D. and Lyne, S.R. (2011) 'Beyond budgeting', in Abdel-Kader, M.G. (ed.), *Review of Management Accounting Research*, Basingstoke: Palgrave Macmillan.

Mitchell, F. and Reid, G. (2000) 'Problems, challenges and opportunities: Small business as a setting for management accounting research', *Management Accounting Research*, 11(4), pp. 385–390.

Nandan, R. (2010) 'Management accounting needs of SMEs and the role of professional accountants: A renewed research agenda', *Journal of Management Accounting Research*, 8(1), pp. 65–78.

Perren, L. and Grant, P. (2000) 'The evolution of management accounting routines in small businesses: A social construction perspective', *Management Accounting Research*, 11(4), pp. 391–411.

Ryan, B. (2011) 'Control, budgets and shareholder value: Shifting boundaries of influence', in Abdel-Kader, M.G. (ed.), *Review of Management Accounting Research*, Basingstoke: Palgrave Macmillan.

19 Strategic management accounting

Learning objectives

When you have studied this chapter, you should be able to:

- Discuss the need for strategic management accounting
- Apply the principles of market-orientated accounting
- Produce target costing information for managerial decision making
- Use the balanced scorecard to make strategic decisions
- Apply the principles of total quality management

19.1 Introduction

In Part III of this book we have looked at how traditional cost and management accounting methods can be used to provide detailed information for cost control and managerial decision making. However, we have pointed out that some techniques can be criticized for their lack of relevance to modern business. For example, in Chapter 15 we explained how the limitations of absorption costing led to the development of activity-based costing and the need for other techniques that will provide information for managing the competitive, strategic and operational issues that businesses face.

Management accounting continues to evolve and in this chapter we describe a group of techniques that analyze management accounting data to provide a forward looking model that assists management in making strategic business decisions. We start by discussing the need for strategic management accounting and describe a range of techniques that can be used to produce strategically relevant financial information. We then discuss the role of management accounting as an aid to managing quality and reducing the impact of the business on the environment.

19.2 Need for strategic management accounting

A strategy is a plan of action devised by management to achieve the financial objectives of the business. Choices are made about what products and services to produce and/or sell, how they will be priced and marketed, what technologies, resources, organizational structures and supply arrangements are needed. *Strategic management accounting (SMA)* is a management accounting system that supplies the information for the strategic management decisions needed to achieve the long-term goals of the business. For management accounting to play a role in strategic management, the system must not only provide information that focuses on internal operations, but also information about the external business environment such as information about competitors' products that will assist in the pricing strategy of new products and decisions relating to expansion.

Key definition

Strategic management accounting provides the information needed for long-term strategic decision making, in contrast to the traditional focus on short-term costs.

The three main stages of SMA are:

- Assess the current position of the business through techniques such as value chain analysis.
- Evaluate the current position of the business through techniques such as an analysis of strengths, weaknesses, opportunities and threats (SWOT), the balanced scorecard and benchmarking.
- Make a strategic choice for the future direction of the business based on factors such as the strength of its existing products or customer base, or diversification of products and markets.

Activity

Consider whether any of the management accounting techniques described in this book could be used to provide information about a business's competitive environment. Do any of these techniques provide non-financial information?

There are a number of problems with using traditional management accounting methods for strategic management purposes because they focus on the internal operations of the business and do not consider factors such as the production costs of competitors or whether products or services are competitive in the market. Although traditional management accounting methods are useful for measuring and controlling costs, and helping to improve internal decision making, they fail to provide benchmarks for comparing the organization's performance with that of its competitors. Table 19.1 compares the characteristics of traditional management accounting techniques with those of SMA.

Table 19.1 **Characteristics of traditional and strategic management accounting**

Traditional management accounting	Strategic management accounting
Historical information	Future-orientated information
Internal focus on entity performance	External focus on market positioning and comparative performance
Considers data from a single period	Considers data from multiple periods
Focuses on a single decision	Focuses on links between decisions
Manufacturing focus	Competitive focus
Focuses on existing activities	Focuses on strategic possibilities
Financial information	Financial and non-financial information
Information from existing systems	Flexible information, unconstrained by existing systems
Exact data	Forecast data and information

For more details see Lord, 2007.

Traditional management accounting adopts an internally focused historical perspective where the focus is on single decisions, single periods and single products. Most of the information is financial in nature and therefore its techniques fail to consider performance that cannot be measured in monetary terms, such as the number of defective products or the level of customer satisfaction. By contrast, SMA is future orientated and has an external focus on the strategic and competitive position of the business and its products in the market. SMA provides subjective non-financial information as well as objective financial information, and its prime focus is on providing information about the success or failure of the entity's business strategy.

In addition to requiring external information about customers, suppliers and competitors, strategic management requires internal information relating to what Porter (1985, p. 48) describes as the firm's *value chain*. This value chain consists of a set of value-creating primary and support activities that are necessary to provide a competitive product or service to customers. Support activities include the firm's infrastructure (e.g. its organizational structure and management control systems), human resource management, research and development processes and procurement. The firm's primary activities are a chain of business activities in which value is added to the product or services of the organization. These may include:

- Inbound logistics, which involve handling the delivery, warehousing and distribution of raw materials.

- Operations, which are the activities needed for producing a product or delivering a service.
- Outbound logistics, which involve the storage and distribution of finished goods to customers.
- Marketing and sales, which comprise activities to identify the product or service attributes that customers require and to generate sales.
- Customer service, which is the support offered to customers after products and services are sold.

A firm's profit margin depends on its ability to perform these activities efficiently, so that the price that a customer is willing to pay for the product or service exceeds the cost of the activities within the value chain. Thus, a firm must focus on only incurring expenditure on those 'value added' activities for which customers will pay. For example, there is little point marketing a laptop computer with a three-year warranty and customer service package if customers are only willing to pay for a computer with a one-year warranty.

Understanding the links within the value chain of activities is critical, since identifying the relationships between the way one activity is performed and the cost of performing another provides opportunities for improving efficiency by redesigning or re-engineering these activities. As an organization's own value chain is linked to the value chains of suppliers and customers, it is also important for SMA to investigate ways in which collaborations between suppliers and customers may reduce costs and increase value added for all parties. For example, an organization may obtain cost savings from having suppliers deliver components to its site with less polystyrene packaging, as such protective materials are costly and after use must be sent for disposal.

As SMA supports strategic decision making, it must provide information to help the business determine its strategic position in the market and analyze whether its position is sustainable in the level of competition in the market. Porter (1985) describes strategy as an analytical process which calculates and selects the optimum strategic position for an organization by balancing the competitive forces within an industry against the distinctive internal abilities of the firm. *Porter's five forces model* (1985, p. 5) can be used to determine the level of competition in an industry, which reflects its attractiveness in terms of the likelihood of being able to achieve above-normal profits. The five forces that drive competiveness are:

- the threat of new entrants to the market
- the threat of substitute products or services
- the bargaining power of customers
- the bargaining power of suppliers
- the intensity of rivalry among existing firms in the industry.

As you can see, the first and the last of these competitive forces are external sources of competition. Government intervention is not included as a competitive force, but government can limit or prevent new entrants to a market through state controls.

SMA techniques can be used to support this positioning process by analyzing the strengths and weaknesses of the business, its opportunities and the threats it faces (SWOT analysis). This may involve monitoring the cost and pricing policies of competitors, comparing the performance of the business with its competitors, analyzing the barriers to entry in its product markets and evaluating the net cost of strategic options such as establishing long-term relationships with suppliers. Some of the SMA information required will be based on estimates (for example, data used to assess whether the costs of competitors are higher than those of the business) and industry benchmarks may be available.

When an organization has found a sustainable strategic position within a market, it must develop a strategy for securing a sustainable competitive advantage over its rivals. According to Porter (1985), an organization can choose between the following options, which can be applied to an entire market or a niche area within a market.

- A product differentiation strategy is where the business provides unique products that offer value not found in competing products and competitive advantage is secured through being able to charge a high market price and to innovate in a cost-effective manner.
- A cost leadership strategy is where the business produces its products at a lower cost than its competitors.

Activity

Identify some well-known companies that adopt product differentiation or cost leadership strategies.

Apple Inc is a good example of a company that adopts a product differentiation strategy, as demonstrated by its unique products such as the Mac computer, the iPhone and the iPad, which are sold at premium prices to a loyal customer base. On the other hand, Tesco Plc and Wal-Mart Stores Inc are examples of companies that have adopted a cost leadership strategy.

We will now look at a case study that will help you understand the importance of SMA information. Euro Cars GmbH was founded in 2003 and operates in a niche market manufacturing three models of car for the European car market. The company's long-term strategy has been to design and make high quality cars and simply price above total cost using cost-plus pricing. For many years this approach has proved profitable and allowed the company to win at least one annual consumer award for best motor vehicle.

The company prides itself on being the most cost efficient in the European motor industry, but cost management has never been a primary strategic or operational concern. The company's managers have never undertaken a comparative analysis with competitors' cost structures and believe they are already following best practice in terms of cost control and operational efficiency. As a result of its reputation for engineering excellence and its perceived cost advantage over its rivals, Euro Cars

GmbH has always adopted a cost-plus pricing policy. Each car is routinely priced at approximately 7% above its total variable production cost.

Since the start of 2016, Euro Cars GmbH has faced strong market competition for the first time, and revenue fell sharply. Further analysis revealed that sales of their Cyclone model had suffered most. Cyclone is a sleekly styled sports car aimed at the professional person market. The company anticipated producing and selling 2,000 Cyclones during 2016, but the actual figures showed sales were 25% below this target. Further bad news came when the company failed to win the 2016 European Car of the Year Award.

Prior to this crisis, Euro Cars GmbH had established a competitive advantage by selling the Cyclone at a lower price than similar models produced by rival companies. However, two low cost competitors entered the market in 2016: China Motors with the SU4 sports car and Indian Cars with the Chita sports car, both with a selling price of €28,000, which was €2,000 less than Euro Car's Cyclone. Furthermore, the SU4 won the 2016 European Sports Car of the Year Award. The following table compares the specifications for the Cyclone and three competing models.

Specifications of Cyclone and competing models

	Cyclone	SU4	Chita	Audi TT
Engine size (litres)	3.2	3.2	3.2	3.2
Engine power in kilowatts (kW)	201	200	199	203
Top speed: kilometres (km) per hour (km/h)	252	248	248	250
0-100 km/h acceleration (seconds)	5.5	5.6	5.7	5.5
Litres of fuel per 100 km	9.7	9.4	9	9.4
CO_2 emissions (grams per km)	179	169	165	175
Insurance group (1-50)	36	34	34	38
Last award won	2011	2012	None	2011
Automatic gearbox	Yes	Yes	No	Yes
Automatic roof	Yes	Yes	Yes	Yes
Leather upholstery	Yes	Yes	Yes	Yes
ABS anti-lock brakes	No	Yes	Yes	Yes
Satellite navigation system	No	No	No	Yes
Premium Sound system	Yes	No	No	Yes
Warranty	5 years/ 140,000 km	4 years/ 120,000 km	4 years/ 120,000 km	2 years/ 100,000 km
Selling price	€30,000	€28,000	€28,000	€36,518

Activity

(a)   Decide whether the company is following a product differentiation strategy or cost leadership strategy and describe any problems associated with following such a strategy.

(b)   Explain how Euro Cars GmbH could use Porter's (1985) model of strategic positioning to assess the current strategy and competitive advantage of the firm.

(c)   Identify the types of financial and non-financial information that could be used to improve strategic decision making at the company.

The company appears to be pursuing a product differentiation strategy for the Cyclone, but has failed to assess its current strategic position in the context of new entrants into the market or the relative value of its product compared with competing products. The comparative table of product attributes suggests that Euro Cars GmbH is charging a premium price of €30,000 for the Cyclone, which is €2,000 more than competing products, which have similar attributes.

Management could use Porter's five forces model to assess the company's current strategic position and how it could secure competitive advantage over its new rivals. The case study contains no information about suppliers, but many car manufacturers try to establish long-term contracts with suppliers to obtain lower prices and/or higher quality materials, components and services.

Due to the threat posed by the low cost competitors, Euro Cars GmbH urgently needs to obtain SMA information such as data on competitor's costs, volumes, market shares and customer satisfaction. Furthermore, the efficiency of the production operations needs to be compared with competitors' or industry benchmarks. Such an exercise will allow the standard costs to be revised in line with best practice. Finally, if the company is to continue its product differentiation strategy, the management accounting system should focus on the marketing costs and establishing the value-added activities that customers are willing to pay for in respect of the Cyclone model.

Whichever strategy is chosen, the exact functioning and content of a supporting SMA system will reflect this choice. A cost leadership strategy will require an SMA system that emphasizes the role of standard and product costs in assessing performance and pricing decisions and the SMA system will emphasize marketing costs and benchmark products on a continuous basis. Research shows that many of the techniques for generating and using this information are already part of the operational management of firms without the involvement of the management accountant or a need for accounting data (Lord, 2007). This also applies to environmental management accounting which we discuss later in the chapter.

The debate over the need for SMA has led to a range of new and modified accounting techniques. We will now review three of the main approaches: market-orientated accounting, target costing and the balanced scorecard.

19.3 Market-orientated accounting

Market-orientated accounting (MOA) is a form of SMA that provides information about the specific attributes that products and services offer customers and monitors how these benefits contribute to securing a competitive advantage. This approach was developed by Bromwich (1990) who suggests that economic goods are desired for the underlying bundle of product attributes they provide rather than their price, as these are the characteristics that give the products their market value. They include a variety of quality elements, such as operating performance variables, reliability and warranty arrangements, physical items (such as the degree of finish and trim), and service factors (such as the assurance of supply and after-sales service. Once the bundle of attributes desired by customers has been identified, the success of the business depends on its ability to produce goods that provide those attributes at a competitive cost level.

Activity

Identify the product attributes of a tube of toothpaste. Hint: Think about the benefits that consumers require.

You may have thought of some of the following attributes:

- Protection from plaque and decay
- Reduced sensitivity
- Stain removal and whitening
- Fresher breath
- Pleasant smell, taste, texture and colour.

The following cost information for a 100ml tube of toothpaste is taken from a traditional absorption costing system:

	£
Direct materials	0.50
Direct labour	0.05
Overhead allocated	0.95
Total cost	1.50
Profit	0.15
Selling price	1.65

This information has little value from a SMA perspective as it is cannot be used to benchmark the relative efficiency of the product's manufacture or whether its price is competitive. In addition, there is no information about the attributes that the toothpaste provides or the cost of including them in the product. The detailed strategic cost analysis shown in the following table addresses these deficiencies. With the help of the marketing, production and engineering staff, the accountant has been able to identify and allocate £1.35 of the total production cost to the product attributes identified by consumers. It was not possible to allocate the remaining £0.15.

Strategic cost analysis for a 100ml tube of toothpaste

	Cost £	% of total cost	Importance to consumers (%)	Strategic cost index
Product attributes				
Protection from decay	0.23	15.33	26.00	1.70
Protection from plaque	0.11	7.33	23.00	3.14
General teeth cleaning	0.10	6.67	17.00	2.55
Whitening capability	0.20	13.33	12.00	0.90
Breath freshening	0.10	6.67	8.00	1.20
Reduced sensitivity	0.11	7.33	4.00	0.55
Taste/texture	0.05	3.33	7.00	2.10
Appearance/colour	0.10	6.67	1.00	0.15
Use of organic ingredients	0.18	12.00	0.80	0.07
Other attributes				
Ethical and green production	0.12	8.00	1.00	0.13
Advertising	0.05	3.33	0.20	0.06
Costs attributable to consumer benefits	1.35	90.00	100.00	
Costs not attributable to consumer benefits	0.15	10.00		
Total cost	1.50	100.00		

The analysis of costs is extremely useful from a benchmarking perspective, and is extended by the analysis of the relative importance of the attributes to consumers, taken from a customer survey. The results show that protection from decay was the most important attribute and the use of organic ingredients was the least important. By comparing the percentage cost of providing the attribute with the percentage importance it is given by consumers, the management accountant can determine whether the cost is justified. The table suggests that protection from decay is inexpensive and consumers consider it to be the most important factor in their buying decision. However, the cost of providing organic ingredients outweighs the benefits. The final column in the table shows the *strategic cost index* (SCI), which is calculated as the relative importance of the attribute divided by the cost of providing that attribute (column three divided by column two). Management should redesign or re-engineer products to focus on the attributes with the highest SCI results and consider ways of eliminating attributes with very low SCI scores.

Thus, the aim of MOA is to determine the cost of providing product features to consumers given operating conditions which continuously seek improvement. For survival in a competitive market, a firm must offer a product which is not dominated by other products, so the business must offer the cheapest way for a consumer to obtain the bundle of characteristics being offered, or yield at least the same amount of each characteristic as its competitors unless it generates sufficient extra of one or more characteristics to offset the lower amount of one or more of the other characteristics. The cost structure of the business relative to that of its actual and potential rivals is the key factor in assuring the sustainability of the firm's market strategy. It must possess cost advantages over rivals and expect to retain these in the future. For example, even a product differentiator must adopt a cost leader-like pursuit of cost containment. As a result, a better understanding of cost behaviour within the firm is a fundamental goal of SMA.

Returning to the case of Euro Cars GmbH, imagine that the management accountant has been given the results of a customer survey that show the important product attributes of a sports car and their relative importance:

- safety 25%
- comfort 20%
- economy 5%
- performance 20%
- styling 30%

This enables the accountant to construct the next table, which estimates how the different components of the car contribute to the product attributes.

Importance index for components of a sports car

Component group	Safety 25%	Comfort 20%	Economy 5%	Performance 20%	Styling 30%	Importance to consumers (%)
Chassis and wheels	0.45	0.20	0.10	0.15	0.15	23.25
Engine, suspension and brakes	0.35	0.30	0.50	0.75	–	32.25
Electrical systems	0.05	–	0.10	0.05	0.05	4.25
Interior fittings	0.05	0.25	–	–	0.30	15.25
Air conditioning	–	0.10	–	–	–	2.00
Other systems	0.10	0.15	0.30	0.05	0.50	23.00
Total	1.00	1.00	1.00	1.00	1.00	100.00

The importance index in the last column incorporates the customer survey data and measures the relative importance of each component in providing the desired product attributes. For example, if you look at the first component group (the chassis and wheels), the importance index is calculated by multiplying the line item value by the weighting of the product attribute from the consumer survey and summing the results:

$$(0.45 \times 0.25) + (0.20 \times 0.20) + (0.10 \times 0.05) + (0.15 \times 0.20) + (0.15 \times 0.30)$$
$$= 0.2325 \times 100 = 23.25\%$$

This tells us that the chassis and wheels provide 23% of the characteristics of the product that consumers consider are important. Together with the engine, suspension and brakes, these components provide nearly 56% of highly rated characteristics, whereas the air conditioning system provides only 2%.

The management accountant has also prepared the following statement of total standard costs for each component group.

Statement of total standard costs	
Component group	% of total standard cost
Chassis and wheels	22.4
Engine, suspension and brakes	23.7
Electrical systems	6.7
Interior fittings	7.9
Air conditioning	6.4
Other systems	32.9
Total	100.0

Activity

Prepare a strategic cost index for each component group of the Cyclone car and suggest how the company could redesign it to make its attributes more appealing to customers.

Your answer should reveal some interesting results about the product. As you can see from the following solution, the air conditioning is the function that is relatively costly to provide (6.4% of the total cost of the Cyclone) when one compares it to the relative importance it has to consumers (only provides 10% of the comfort attribute). A recommendation is for the company to source a less expensive air conditioning unit or even offer a less expensive version of the Cyclone without this function. Other key component groups that require investigation during the product redesign are the electrical and other systems, as they also have an SCI below one. By contrast the interior fittings have an SCI of 1.94, indicating that they provide a required product attribute in a cost-effective manner.

Strategic cost analysis for car component groups

Component group	Importance to consumers (%)	% of total standard cost	Strategic cost index
Chassis and wheels	23.25	22.40	1.04
Engine, suspension and brakes	32.25	23.70	1.36
Electrical systems	4.25	6.70	0.63
Interior fittings	15.25	7.90	1.93
Air conditioning	2.00	6.40	0.31
Other systems	23.00	32.90	0.71
Total	100.00	100.00	

While the costing of product attributes that market-orientated accounting requires can be complex and time-consuming, this type of analysis provides an invaluable source of strategically-relevant information about the relative competitiveness of products. The provision of this type of accounting information may require input from many functional areas within an organization, most notably the marketing and production departments and requires a strategic dialogue between accountants and non-accountants.

19.4 Target costing

Target costing is a strategic technique that relies on market data to provide an externally orientated approach to pricing, profit planning and cost management. It was developed in the Japanese car industry and is now used extensively by US and European manufacturing companies (Ansari et al., 2007). In a target costing framework, the selling price of a product or service is constrained by the product market and is determined by analysis of the entire industry value chain and across all functions in the organization. In contrast to cost-plus pricing, the cost of producing the product or service does not dictate the selling price. Instead, the target cost is the goal that an organization must achieve to meet its strategic objectives. The notion can be expressed mathematically as follows:

$$\text{Target cost} = \text{Target price} - \text{Target profit}$$

In this equation, market price and profit are independent variables as both are determined by competitive forces within the product and capital markets. As illustrated by MOA, price is determined by what customers are willing to pay for the attributes that the product or service offers, and profit is determined by what financial markets expect as a return from operating in a particular industry. The dependent variable is cost, which implies that an organization must manage its costs to meet the external market constraints that it faces.

Key definition

Target costing is a product costing method in which a target cost is determined by subtracting the desired profit margin from a competitive market price that customers are willing to pay.

The main steps in target costing are as follows:

1. Develop a product that satisfies the needs of customers. As we illustrated in the last section on MOA, it is vital that each product or service provides attributes that consumers demand. When designing a new product, it is essential that it offers a bundle of attributes superior to the market competition.
2. Determine an appropriate target price for the product based upon customers' perceived value of its attributes and the price of competing products, and the target profit per unit. For each product, an assessment is needed of the market price that is appropriate for the bundle of attributes it offers and the competition it faces.
3. Calculate the target cost after allowing for target profit (target price − target profit). An organization must provide a return that is appropriate for the level of risk inherent in the business. This target profit per unit can be calculated in a number of different ways, but it is deducted from the target price to obtain the target cost per unit.
4. Use value engineering and SMA techniques to achieve the target cost per unit.

Value engineering is an activity that creates products that meet customer needs at the lowest cost. It supports the target costing process by evaluating the value chain of business functions, with the objective of identifying cost reduction opportunities that help to achieve each product's target cost per unit while still satisfying customer needs. If the actual cost of production exceeds this target cost, products can be re-engineered or redesigned to reduce cost. Target costing is an incremental process that must be repeated on a continuous basis over a product's life cycle.

We will return to the case of Euro Cars GmbH to illustrate the principles for establishing a target cost for the Cyclone sports car that will allow it to survive against its rivals, the SU4 and the Chita. You will remember that both rival cars have the same product attributes as the Cyclone, but the SU4 and the Chita have a selling price of €28,000, whereas the Cyclone has a premium selling price of €30,000. Unless the Cyclone can be redesigned to offer extra attributes or features, its target price must match that of its competitors.

The accountant predicts that the company needs to make a target profit of 10% or €2,800 per unit in order to cover the cost of capital for running the production operation. As a result, the target cost per Cyclone sold is €25,200 (€28,000 – €2,800), which is substantially lower than the Cyclone's existing unit cost. During the last production period, the total standard cost for production of a Cyclone was €28,500 per unit, which included €28,000 of variable production costs and €500 of fixed manufacturing overheads. The challenge for Euro Cars GmbH is to achieve the target cost of €25,200 through value engineering and finding ways to save costs totalling €3,300 per unit (current standard cost per unit – target cost per unit).

Activity

Explain how Euro Cars GmbH could reduce the cost of the Cyclone through value engineering and improved cost efficiency.

You may have decided that the company should investigate the potential for cost saving opportunities in its manufacturing operations and processes. However, any cost reduction exercise must target those costs that do not provide value to the customer, whether these are located within the firm's value chain of business functions or the functions of the car itself. As was identified in the strategic cost analysis for the Cyclone in section 19.3, the firm could reduce the expenditure on the air conditioning and electrical systems without harming customer satisfaction levels. In addition, the management accountant should investigate the waste tolerances and allowable variances contained within the standard cost estimates in order to ascertain whether they reflect attainable best practice in the industry. After completing its value engineering process, the company was able to match the target cost of €25,200 per Cyclone through achieving cost reductions by entering into long-term contracts for the supply of utilities and materials, sourcing a cheaper air conditioning unit of the same quality and retraining the staff to reduce the assembly time required.

The main strength of target costing is that it considers the pricing of products and services in terms of their relative market desirability, and forces an organization to focus on identifying cost saving opportunities that enhance and sustain its competitive advantage over rivals. Its other advantages include the following:

- It reduces the total time for product development, through improved co-ordination of design, manufacturing and marketing.
- It promotes a culture of cost awareness throughout an organization.
- It increases customer satisfaction, as design is focused on customer values.
- It improves product quality, as design is carefully developed and manufacturing issues are considered explicitly in the design phase.
- It creates cross-functional teams that enhance the dialogue about product development and cost control.
- It can be combined with MOA techniques.

19.5 Balanced scorecard

The *balanced scorecard* (BSC) was developed by Kaplan and Norton (1992, 1996) as a strategic performance measurement system and is now widely used in organizations of all sizes throughout the world (CIMA, 2009). Its popularity stems from its ability to translate an organization's vision and strategy into a comprehensive set of performance measures that provides a framework for implementing and monitoring its strategy.

> **Key definition**
>
> The balanced scorecard (BSC) is an approach to the provision of information to management that integrates both financial and non-financial performance measures into a framework that aids strategic policy formulation and achievement.

In contrast to traditional performance measurement systems that solely focus on the achievement of financial objectives, the BSC attempts to balance or integrate financial and non-financial performance measures to evaluate both short-run and long-run performance measures in a single combined report. As a result, the technique focuses on the non-financial objectives that an organization must achieve in order to meet its financial objectives. The logic for this is that non-financial and operational indicators can capture improvements in performance that cannot be found in short-term financial measures. For example, a customer survey in 2012 shows a 20% increase in highly satisfied customers compared with 2011. While this improvement in non-financial performance may lead to increased sales in the future, it is unlikely to have any impact on the income reported for 2012. Because of this assumed relationship between non-financial and financial performance, a BSC incorporates two different types of performance measures:

- *leading drivers of performance*, which are non-financial performance indicators that drive future financial performance (e.g. order execution/fulfilment time)
- *lagging measures of performance*, which are financial measures of outcomes (e.g. revenue or operating profit from growth).

The BSC model shown in Figure 19.1 uses an appropriate mix of these leading and lagging performance indicators to measure performance across four key perspectives:

- Financial – What are the financial goals of our strategy?
- Customer – What customers do we intend to serve and how are we going to win and retain them?
- Internal business processes – What internal processes are critical to providing value to customers?

- Learning and growth – What capabilities and skills must we excel at to achieve superior internal business processes that create value for customers and shareholders?

Figure 19.1 Four perspectives of the balanced scorecard

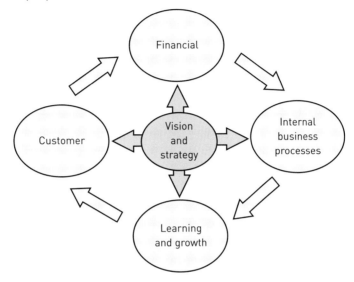

Source: Adapted from Kaplan and Norton, 1996, with permission from Harvard Business School Publishing.

Internal business processes are the activities an organization undertakes to satisfy its customers. For example, in a manufacturing organization, assembly of a product is an internal business process. For an airline, baggage handling is an internal business process. For each of the perspectives within its BSC, an organization must establish specific objectives, performance measures, targets and initiatives that help it to achieve its overall strategy.

A key assumption of the BSC is that each performance measure is part of a cause-and-effect relationship involving a link from strategy formulation to financial outcomes. Improved learning and growth performance is necessary for improving internal business processes, and these in turn drive performance measures within the customer perspective. Finally, improved measures of customer satisfaction will eventually lead to increased financial returns. Figure 19.2 illustrates the cause-and-effect relationship for a delivery company whose strategic objective is to grow by obtaining additional orders from existing customers. If the company invests in enhanced training of its delivery staff, these improvements should result in higher levels of on-time deliveries which should lead to increased customer satisfaction and extra orders from existing customers. Whether the cause-and-effect relationship implicit within the BSC always applies is open to debate and will be discussed later in the critique of the technique.

Figure 19.2 Cause-and-effect relationships within the balanced scorecard

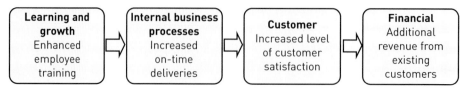

The measurements used to monitor performance within each of the four perspectives in the BSC typically include:

- *Financial*: revenue growth, revenue from new products, cost reductions in key areas, profit increase from productivity gains, operating profit changes from price recovery (i.e. the net impact of changes in input costs and output prices from the previous period).
- *Customer*: market share of a specific type of customer or market, customer satisfaction levels.
- *Internal business processes*: innovation process: number of new products, operations process: yield, defect rate, on-time deliveries, after-sales service: time taken to replace defective product.
- *Learning and growth*: employee education and skill level, employee satisfaction and retention rates, percentage of processes using advanced controls.

Figure 19.3 illustrates the BSC used by Southwest Airlines. As the company operates within the low-cost sector of the market, its strategic theme was to increase its operating efficiency. For each of the perspectives within the BSC that company undertook an investigation as to how each influenced its overall operating efficiency. The following issues were discovered and used to produce a strategy map of the cause-effect relationship between each perspective:

- *Financial*: operating efficiency and profitability were influenced by having increased passengers on fewer planes.
- *Customer*: customers desired the lowest prices and on-time arrival, and it was these factors that were critical to attracting new customers.
- *Internal business processes*: through faster turnaround of aircraft it was possible to reduce the number of aircraft needed for a daily schedule of flights. Aircraft turnaround was also found to be the major driver of on-time arrivals and departures and directly influenced the price per ticket.
- *Learning and growth*: fast ground turnaround was found to require a motivated and committed ground-crew. Through dialogue with the ground-crew, management established that these workers could be 'aligned' towards the achievement of strategy if they were educated and compensated in an appropriate manner.

Figure 19.3 Balanced scorecard for Southwest Airlines

Strategic theme: Operating efficiency	Objectives	Measures	Targets	Initiatives
Financial	Profitability	Market value	30% CAGR*	
	More customers	Seat revenue	20% CAGR*	
	Fewer aircraft	Plane lease cost	5% CAGR*	
Customer	Flight on time	On-time rating	Be number 1	Quality management
	Lowest price	Customer ranking	Be number 1	Loyalty scheme
Internal	Fast ground turnaround	On-ground time	30 minutes	Cycle time optimization
		On-time departure	90%	
Learning and growth	Ground crew aligned with strategy	% ground crew trained	Year 1: 70% Year 2: 90% Year 3: 100%	Training programme
		% ground crew shareholders	Year 1: 70% Year 2: 90% Year 3: 100%	Employee share scheme

* Compound annual growth rate

Source: Adapted from Kaplan and Norton, 2004, with permission from Harvard Business School Publishing.

The strategic map for Southwest Airlines shown in the first column of Figure 19.3 illustrates the key role of ground crew alignment in driving operating efficiency at the airline. Using this, management devised objectives for each of the four BSC perspectives and formulated performance measures for tracking their achievement. Target performance measures were then established in order to benchmark periodic performance, and a range of initiatives introduced to further encourage performance improvements. The BSC for Southwest Airlines shows that employing well-trained ground crews who are shareholders in the company leads to faster turnaround and more on-time flights, which lead to higher customer satisfaction, lower costs and greater profits. This example clearly shows the power of a well designed and implemented BSC.

We will now use the example of Euro Cars GmbH to illustrate the preparation of a BSC. Since the low cost competitors entered the sports car market, the company's market share has fallen from 15% to 10%. As a response, the company has devised a new strategy for the Cyclone, which is to restore its share of the sports car market and profitability by producing a market-leading product with world-class levels of operating efficiency. In order to measure the success of this strategy, the company wants to create a BSC from the following information.

- In terms of the learning and growth perspective, it was discovered that each of the plant's thirty production processes could be improved by implementing advanced software systems. In addition, current levels of employee training were found to be deficient. Production employees currently attend an average of two hours of training seminars and meetings per month. If training is increased to five hours per month, it is believed that both product quality and operational efficiency will increase. This increased training should also raise awareness of the need for continuous improvement and encourage employees to provide suggestions for cost reductions or product redesign.
- Following an audit of its internal business processes, the company discovered the following problems that must be corrected before the Cyclone can be a competitive and profitable product:

  - In terms of raw materials (i.e. aluminium, steel, plastic, glass, rubber and paint), the company only achieves an average yield of 85%, with the 15% of waste being sent to landfill. With increased training, recycling and process improvements, materials yield could be increased to 96%.
  - The company only uses virgin sources of raw materials. The vast majority of vehicle manufacturers utilize at least 40% recycled materials in their products and these can be purchased for 20% less than virgin quality materials.
  - During the last production year, Euro Cars GmbH used 1,980kWh of electricity to manufacture each Cyclone. The target for energy use is to be reduced to 1200kWh per car.
  - Average production downtime due to machine breakdowns is currently 30 minutes per day and the aim is to reduce this to 5 minutes. Average production time per car is currently 80 hours and the new target is 70 hours.
  - Typically, 10% of Cyclones produced fail the quality inspection and require rework. The target is to reduce this to zero failure and reduce warranty claims from an average of 50 per month to 10.
  - On average, two of the Cyclone's main components are redesigned every three months. The new target is to re-engineer a minimum of five components per quarter in order to further differentiate the product from its competition.
- From a customer perspective, to restore its market share to the original 15%, the company must win industry awards for quality, reduce customer complaints and improve customer satisfaction rates. Yearly targets include winning two awards, receiving less than 20 complaints and having a customer satisfaction level of 96%.

- From a financial perspective, the company's new strategy should eventually lead to increased shareholder returns through increased operating profit from sales growth, price recovery (i.e. the profit impact of changes in input and output prices from the prior period) and enhanced operational efficiency. The company has established three-year targets for increased operating profit of €800,000 from growth, €200,000 from price recovery and €300,000 from enhanced operating efficiency.

Activity

Using the above information, design a BSC for Euro Cars GmbH that provides suitable objectives, performance measures, targets and initiatives that support the company's strategy.

Your BSC may differ from the example below, but should share the main features. You will see that it suggests that employing well trained production staff and using improved production processes lead to increased operational efficiency and a better designed car. In turn, this leads to higher customer satisfaction, increased market share, lower costs and increased operating profit.

Objectives	Measures	Targets	Initiatives
Financial Increase shareholder value	Operating profit changes from growth	€800,000	
	Operating profit changes from price recovery	€200,000	Long term contracts with suppliers
	Operating profit changes from operating efficiency	€300,000	
Customer Reclaim market share	Market share of the sports car market	15%	Owners club
	Number of customer complaints	20	Customer hotline
	Customer satisfaction level	96%	
	Number of industry awards	2	Media day at plant
Internal	Average yield on raw materials	96%	
Improve operational efficiency	Use of recycled materials	40%	Review and audit of procurement, production and quality control procedures

(Continued)

Objectives	Measures	Targets	Initiatives
	Energy use per vehicle	1200kWh	
	Average production downtime per day	5 minutes	
	Average production time per vehicle	70 hours	
	Output failing final inspection	0%	
	Number of warranty claims	10	
Improve product design	Components redesigned per quarter	5	Quarterly audit of product design
Learning and growth Increase employee alignment and training	Average number of training hours per employee per month	5 hours	Training schemes
	Number of employee suggestions received	10	Bonus paid if suggestion implemented
Improve production processes	Production processes using advanced software systems	100%	

As we identified in our earlier discussion of strategy and SMA, a BSC must be appropriately designed and modified for the specific strategy that an organization chooses to adopt. For example, a *product differentiation strategy* will require a BSC that includes:

- A financial perspective that isolates the operating income that comes from charging for a premium product.
- A customer perspective that measures the percentage of revenue from new products or customers.
- An internal perspective that measures an organization's ability to develop technologies or processes for producing custom products.
- A learning and growth perspective that measures the number of employee suggestions for new or re-engineered products.

For a BSC to operate effectively, it must be designed to:

- Use objectives, measures, initiatives and targets that link each of the four perspectives to the achievement of strategic objectives.
- Communicate strategy to employees by translating it into performance measures that they understand and can influence.
- Provide an appropriate balance and linkage between non-financial and financial performance measures.

- Prevent suboptimal trade-offs and inappropriate cost cutting (i.e. cutting R&D expenditure during a recession).
- Focus solely on the key measures of performance (i.e. do not use too many measurements).

There has been much debate about whether a cause-and-effect exists between each of the four perspectives. For example, the production of high quality products does not always result in increased profit, especially when customers are unwilling to pay for such improvements. Furthermore, in many instances, a loyal and highly satisfied customer may not be a profitable one, as they may require many hours of costly support and customer service time. A further criticism of the BSC surrounds the choice about the number of performance measures to be used. Using too many may result in a BSC that produces confusing performance measurement data that may increase the risk of corporate failure as attention may focus on incorrect measures and provide a distorted view of strategy. Other limitations of the BSC include:

- As managers are normally evaluated using financial measures of performance, they may attach less importance on improving non-financial performance.
- Certain perspectives, such as other stakeholders, suppliers and the employees are excluded from Kaplan and Norton's BSC.
- As with any technique, a BSC needs to fit the adopting organization's culture.
- It can be costly to implement in terms of resources and management time.

Despite these potential limitations, widespread use of the BSC in Europe and the USA is evidence of its value to many different types of organization (Bhimani and Bromwich, 2009).

19.6 Total quality management

In this chapter we have highlighted that providing customers with desirable products and services is a primary strategic objective. Quality is an essential element of a product's desirability and it is important that management accounting provides information that supports the management of quality. Quality refers to factors such as the product's fitness for use and the degree to which it satisfies customer needs and conforms to design specification requirements. For example, a business customer buying an iPhone would expect it to offer a wireless connection to the internet, fast processing, sufficient memory, a long-life rechargeable battery, an operating system and application software.

Total quality management (TQM) is an approach to managing people and business processes that emphasizes the importance of customer satisfaction and sees continuous improvement as the means by which this is achieved (Law, 2010). For example, washing machine manufacturers can save money by continuously improving the quality of their products to reduce the number of faulty goods returned for repair. Some companies even have specific quality management systems certified by the International Organization for Standardization (ISO) under the ISO 9001 Quality Management Systems programme (see BSI, 2015). As quality-related costs can often equal 20% of revenue, quality improvement programmes may result in substantial savings and help increase customer demand (Bhimani and Bromwich, 2009). From a strategic perspective, if competitors are improving their quality, an organization has no choice but to do the same or lose customers. Management accounting can help an organization to achieve its quality goals by providing a variety of reports and performance measures that motivate and evaluate managerial efforts to improve quality. As with the collection of SMA information, such information may include non-financial and financial information. Managers need to know the costs of quality and how they are changing over time. The costs of quality represent the costs incurred in defect prevention and appraisal activities, and the losses from the internal and external failure of a product or service to meet agreed quality requirements (Bromwich and Bhimani, 1994).

Key definition

Total quality management (TQM) is an integrated and comprehensive system of planning and controlling all business functions so that products or services are produced which meet or exceed customer expectations.

Source: CIMA, 2005, p. 54. Reproduced with permission from CIMA.

A *cost of quality report* can be prepared to measure the total cost to the organization of producing products or services that do not conform to quality standards. Four categories of costs are typically reported:

- Prevention costs – costs incurred in preventing or reducing the production of defective products that do not conform to specification. These may include the cost of undertaking supplier reviews, field trials, quality training or investments in new production technology.
- Appraisal costs – costs incurred on monitoring and inspecting products and material to ensure that they meet quality conformance standards. Examples include the cost of measurement equipment, inspection, testing and audits.
- Internal failure costs – costs that arise from the production of products and components that fail to meet internal quality standards. These may include rework costs, and the net cost of scrap and disposal costs.
- External failure costs – costs incurred when the product or service fails to conform to requirements after it is supplied to the customer. These may include the cost of dealing with warranty claims, product recalls and the cost of lost sales.

Many of the items within a cost quality report have to be estimated and such documents typically exclude the opportunity costs associated with poor quality, such as the lower prices that result from a lack of quality.

We will use the example of Euro Cars GmbH to illustrate the preparation of a cost of quality report. It is now the end of 2016, and a year has passed since the low cost competitors entered the market. The total revenue for 2016 was €48,000,000 (€50,000,000 in 2015), and the company has made a considerable effort to strengthen its quality control system in the hope that enhanced quality will restore the company's competitive position and reduce warranty and servicing costs. Costs relating to quality management and control for 2016 and 2015 are shown in the following table.

Quality management costs	2016	2015
	€	€
Depreciation of testing equipment	133,000	86,000
Disposal of defective products	296,000	211,000
Field servicing	468,000	702,000
Inspection	468,000	296,000
Net cost of scrap	484,000	335,000
Product recalls	320,000	1,326,000
Product testing	624,000	382,000
Quality engineering	312,000	218,000
Rework labour	780,000	546,000
Supplies used in testing	23,000	16,000
System development	413,000	250,000
Warranty repairs	546,000	1,638,000
Warranty replacements	70,000	234,000

Activity

Decide whether the quality management costs in the above table should be classified as prevention, appraisal, internal failure or external failure cost and use your analysis as the basis for a cost of quality report for 2016 and 2015.

Check your report against the following solution where each cost category has been expressed as a percentage of revenue for 2016 and 2015 to aid comparison with previous periods.

Cost of quality report for Euro Cars GmbH

	2016 €	2016 % of revenue	2015 €	2015 % of revenue
Prevention costs				
Systems development	413,000		250,000	
Quality engineering	312,000		218,000	
Total	725,000	1.51%	468,000	0.94%
Appraisal costs				
Product testing	624,000		382,000	
Supplies used in testing	23,000		16,000	
Inspection	468,000		296,000	
Depreciation of testing equipment	133,000		86,000	
Total	1,248,000	2.60%	780,000	1.56%
Internal failure costs				
Rework labour	780,000		546,000	
Net cost of scrap	484,000		335,000	
Disposal of defective products	296,000		211,000	
Total	1,560,000	3.25%	1,092,000	2.18%
External failure costs				
Warranty repairs	546,000		1,638,000	
Field servicing	468,000		702,000	
Warranty replacements	70,000		234,000	
Product recalls	320,000		1,326,000	
Total	1,404,000	2.93%	3,900,000	7.80%
Total cost of quality	4,937,000	10.29%	6,240,000	12.48%

Activity

Compare the costs of quality for the two years. What do the results reveal about the management of quality at Euro Cars GmbH?

During 2016 the company significantly increased its expenditure on prevention costs and appraisal costs. This has led to considerably lower costs related to external failure costs and total quality costs have declined. Despite this improvement, the company still has a poor distribution of quality costs and most costs are identified with internal and external failure, rather than prevention and appraisal. However, as continued emphasis is given on prevention and appraisal activities in the future, this situation should improve and internal and external failure costs should reduce.

Due to the increased spending on prevention and appraisal activities this year, internal failure costs have increased. The reason internal failure costs have gone up is that, through increased appraisal activity, defects are being caught and corrected before products are shipped to customers. Thus, the company is incurring more cost for scrap and rework, but is saving considerable amounts on warranty repairs, field servicing and product recalls. External failure costs have fallen considerably and represented only 3% of revenue in 2016. If the company continues to focus on prevention activities in future years, then appraisal costs and internal failure costs should begin to decline. As quality is built into products through better engineering and design, and process control is improved, the number of defects should decrease. Thus, internal failures and the need to detect these failures through appraisal activities should also decrease.

19.7 Conclusions

In this chapter we have highlighted a number of emerging issues in management accounting. Traditional management accounting practices and techniques have a long history and are subject to frequent criticism for failing to provide relevant information for decision making in the modern business environment. We commenced this chapter by describing how strategic decision making requires a management accounting system that provides not only financial information that focuses on internal operations, but also information, both financial and non-financial in nature, about the environment and markets in which the organization operates. From this starting point, we explained the concept of strategy and the case for developing SMA.

While many organizations now use some form of SMA, the techniques used vary widely and often have differing levels of management accounting involvement. In certain organizations, SMA information is produced by management accountants with the assistance of cross-functional expertise, while in others, non-accountants are chiefly responsible for the generation of market-orientated and strategic information about products or services. Regardless of how and where this SMA information is generated within an organization, its provision is essential for managerial decision making in today's ever changing markets. As a result, SMA techniques and practices continue to evolve as organizations, markets, production technologies and customer demands change.

References

Ansari, S., Bell, J. and Okano, H. (2007) 'Target costing: Uncharted research territory', in Chapman C., Hopwood, A. and Shields, M. (eds), *Handbook of Management Accounting Research*, Amsterdam: Elsevier, pp. 507–529.

Bhimani, A. and Bromwich, M. (2009), *Management Accounting: Retrospect and Prospect*, London: CIMA Publishing.

Bromwich, M. (1990) 'The case for strategic management accounting: The role of accounting information for strategy in competitive markets', *Accounting, Organizations and Society*, 15(1/2), pp. 27–46.

Bromwich, M. and Bhimani, A. (1994) *Management Accounting: Pathways to Progress*, London: CIMA Publications.

BSI (2015) *ISO 9001 Quality Management Systems – Requirements*, Chiswick: BSI.

CIMA (2005) *CIMA Official Terminology*, Oxford: CIMA Publishing.

CIMA (2009) *Management Accounting Tools for Today and Tomorrow*, London: Chartered Institute of Management Accountants. Available from: www.cimaglobal.com/Documents/Thought_leadership_docs/CIMA%20Tools%20and%20Techniques%2030-11-09%20PDF.pdf (Accessed 11 June 2016).

Kaplan, R. and Norton, D. (1992) 'The balanced scorecard – Measures that drive performance', *Harvard Business Review*, 70(1), pp. 71–79.

Kaplan, R. and Norton, D. (1996) 'Using the balanced scorecard as a strategic management system', *Harvard Business Review*, 74(1), pp. 75–85.

Kaplan, R. and Norton, D. (2004) *Strategy Maps: Converting Intangible Assets into Tangible Outcomes*, Boston: Harvard Business School Press.

Law, J.L. (2010) *Dictionary of Accounting*, 4th edn, Oxford: Oxford University Press.

Lord, B. (2007) 'Strategic management accounting', in Hopper, T., Northcott, D. and Scapens, R. (eds), *Issues in Management Accounting*, 3rd edn, Harlow: Prentice Hall.

Porter, M. (1985) *Competitive Advantage: Creating and Sustaining Superior Performance*, New York: Free Press.

Discussion questions

1 Discuss the limitations of traditional management accounting techniques and the main features of strategic management accounting information.

2 Compare the benefits of target costing with the merits of a cost-plus approach to product or service pricing.

3 Explain the purpose of market-orientated accounting and how it can be used to assist in the design of competitive and cost-effective products.

Practice questions

4 Explain what a cost of quality report aims to achieve. In your answer explain how the cause-and-effect relationship between the four types of quality cost can be used to reduce overall costs.

5 Stunt Ltd manufactures stunt scooters that are used for performing tricks and stunts in skate parks. A customer survey reveals that customers look for the following product attributes when purchasing a stunt scooter:

	Relative importance %
Safety	10
Style	40
Performance	50
Total	100

The company is designing a new model called the Slammer. Each Slammer requires the following three components, whose target costs are estimated below.

	Target cost per unit £	% of total cost
Handlebars and steering column	20	33.33
Painted aluminium footplate	30	50.00
Wheels and suspension	10	16.67
Total	60	100.00

With the help of the production and design staff, the management accountant uses the above information to construct the following matrix of the product attributes. This shows how each component of the Slammer contributes to the supply of product attributes.

	Attributes supplied by a stunt scooter		
	Safety (10%)	Style (40%)	Performance (50%)
Handlebars and steering column	40%	20%	40%
Painted aluminium footplate	40%	60%	20%
Wheels and suspension	20%	20%	40%
Total	100%	100%	100%

Required

(a) Calculate an importance index for each of the Slammer scooter's three components. What does it indicate about the relative im]portance of each component in providing the attributes that customers require?

(b) Using the target cost information, prepare a strategic cost index for each of the Slammer's three components. Discuss whether this design incurs too much expenditure on any component.

6 Contain Ltd produces aluminium containers for the airline industry. The company faces intense competition from three competitors whose containers offer identical product attributes. As from 1 January 2016, the strategic objective of Contain

Ltd has been to increase shareholder value through increased market share and reduced production costs. It is thought that new customers can be attracted by producing low-price, high quality containers that are delivered within 10 days of receipt of order. To achieve this objective, the company must strive to increase customer satisfaction, product quality, productivity and employee training and retention. The following events occurred during 2015:

- 20% of employees underwent training in total quality management techniques.

- 15% of employees resigned and left the company's employment during the year.

- It took an average of 12 days to process and fulfil customer orders.

- The yield on the usage of aluminium was 85% and 800 containers were produced per employee.

- 10% of containers were returned by consumers due to defective hinges.

- A survey revealed that 18% of customers were dissatisfied with the company's products during 2015.

- No new customers were recruited during 2015. The company's share of the low-price container market fell by 1% to 9%. Its share of the total container market fell by 5% to 6%.

- Annual turnover fell by 2% to £8,000,000 and total operating income for the year fell by 2% to £600,000.

- The company has targeted productivity and process improvements equal to £150,000 of operating profit by 2019. Furthermore, it plans to obtain cost reductions equal to £50,000 per year from increasing its yield on the factory's usage of aluminium.

- The company has also established a five-year financial target to achieve a total of £300,000 of additional operating income from growth.

Required

(a) Identify the type of strategy that Contain Ltd plans to implement during 2016.

(b) Design a balanced scorecard for Contain Ltd for 2016 that is consistent with the company's strategy and which identifies two performance measures for each of the four perspectives on the scorecard.

(c) Briefly explain the cause-and-effect relationship between the eight performance measures in your balanced scorecard.

(d) Discuss the benefits and problems in implementing and using a balanced scorecard performance measurement system.

7 Norbridge City Football Club is a professional football club with a team that competes in the English Premier League (EPL). The Club has 27,000 season ticket holders and its policy is to develop young, home-grown players. However, only a small proportion of the Club's revenue comes from ticket sales (10%), catering and sponsorship (20%); the majority of revenue is from broadcasting. Not long ago, the Club had heavy debts, but recent wins mean that it is now debt free. Now the directors' main strategic aim is to remain in the EPL with a competitive team of players. However, the directors also want to safeguard the Club's future by adopting a prudent financial approach. As a result, the Club has a rigid wage structure for its players and only a small budget for buying new players. The finance director aims for a wages to revenue ratio of 70% and tries to avoid reporting an annual loss.

Required

You are working as an intern at Norbridge City Football Club and the accountant asks you to contribute to help prepare a report for the directors.

(a) Explain the main strategic aims of Norbridge City Football Club.
(b) Identify the customers of Norbridge City Football Club and design a balanced scorecard for the Club. Identify at least one strategic objective and two performance measures for each of the four perspectives on the scorecard.
(c) Briefly explain the cause-and-effect relationship between the eight performance measures identified in your balanced scorecard.
(d) Discuss the characteristics that make the introduction of the balanced scorecard as a strategic performance measurement system effective.

8 Electro Ltd manufactures a single electronic circuit board for the telecommunications industry. At the end of December 2015 the company received a letter of complaint from its largest customer, Telecom International PLC, about the poor quality of a recent consignment of components. As a result, the directors of Electro Ltd introduced a TQM system in January 2016 and this has been used to estimate the following revenue and costs of quality for 2016. Comparative figures for 2015 are also shown.

	2016 £	2015 £
Revenue	62,000,000	56,700,000
Cost of quality:		
Customer complaints department	270,000	480,000
Depreciation of test equipment	370,000	270,000
Inspection	150,000	80,000
Contribution forgone from lost sales	823,000	1,790,000
Product recall	360,000	920,000
Product testing	670,000	700,000
Quality engineering	770,000	520,000
Quality training	1,100,000	700,000
Retesting	480,000	1,250,000
Rework	580,000	770,000
Supplier reviews	200,000	50,000
Cost of warranty repairs	240,000	320,000

Required

(a) Decide whether the quality management costs above should be classified as prevention, appraisal, internal failure or external failure cost and use your analysis as the basis for preparing a cost of quality report for 2016 and 2015.

(b) Compare the costs of quality for the two years. Comment on what the results reveal about quality management at Electro Ltd.

 ## Suggested research questions for dissertation students

Students interested in strategic management accounting may wish to investigate one or more of the following research questions:

- What are the factors that affect the choice of SMA techniques in [industry or country]?

- How useful are SMA techniques in helping firms achieve their strategic targets?

- Are SMA techniques appropriate for SMEs?

Preliminary reading

CIMA (2009) *Management Accounting Tools for Today and Tomorrow*, London: Chartered Institute of Management Accountants. Available from: www.cima-global.com/Documents/Thought_leadership_docs/CIMA%20Tools%20and%20 Techniques%2030-11-09%20PDF.pdf (Accessed 11 June 2016).

Johnson, H.T. and Kaplan, R.S. (1987) *Relevance Lost: The Rise and Fall of Management Accounting*, Boston: Harvard Business School Press.

Lopez, O. and Hiebl, M. (2015) 'Management accounting in small and medium-sized enterprises: Current knowledge and avenues for further research, *Journal of Management Accounting Research*, 27(1), pp. 81–119.

Lucas, M., Prowle, M. and Lowth, G. (2013) 'Management accounting practices of UK SMEs', *Improving SME Performance through Management Accounting Education*, 9(4). Available from: www.cimaglobal.com/Thought-leadership /Research-topics/Management-and-financial-accounting/Management-accounting-practices-of-UK-SMEs/ (Accessed 12 June 2016).

Ma, Y. and Tayles, M. (2009) 'On the emergence of strategic management accounting: an institutional perspective', *Accounting and Business Research*, 39(5), pp. 473–495.

McLellan, J. (2014) 'Management accounting theory and practice: Measuring the gap in United States businesses', *Journal of Accounting, Business and Management*, 21(1), pp. 53–68.

Nixon, B. and Burns, J. (2012) 'The paradox of strategic management accounting', *Management Accounting Research*, 23(4), pp. 229–244.

Perren, L. and Grant, P. (2000) 'The evolution of management accounting routines in small businesses: A social construction perspective', *Management Accounting Research*, 11(4), pp. 391–411.

Tayles, M. (2011) 'Strategic management accounting', in Abdel-Kader, M.G. (ed.), *Review of Management Accounting Research*, Basingstoke: Palgrave Macmillan.

20 Environmental management accounting

Learning objectives

When you have studied this chapter, you should be able to:

- Discuss the limitations of traditional management accounting
- Explain the need for environmental management systems
- Apply the principles of environmental management accounting
- Explain the importance of greenhouse gas accounting
- Discuss the benefits of enterprise resource planning

20.1 Introduction

In Chapter 11 we explained the statutory obligations of public companies to provide corporate social responsibility information and the growing use of integrated reporting. In order to disclose information about the environmental costs and impact of business operations, companies need to develop internal management and costing systems to collect the relevant data. As we discussed in Chapter 19, traditional management accounting systems adopt an internally focused historical perspective, which fails to provide strategically relevant information. As most of the data collected by such systems is financial in nature, traditional management accounting systems also fail to consider performance that cannot be measured in monetary terms.

In this chapter we extend the discussion of the limitations of traditional management accounting and the ways in which environmental management accounting addresses some of those limitations by providing information on the environmental costs and environmental impact of a company's operations. We explain the need for environmental management systems, the importance of greenhouse gas accounting and the benefits of enterprise resource planning.

20.2 Limitations of traditional management accounting

Due to increasing stakeholder and customer pressure for information about a company's environmental performance, businesses have a growing need to collect information about the environmental impact of their operations, products and services. However, the majority of the information collected by traditional management accounting systems is financial in nature and fails to consider environmental issues that cannot be measured in monetary terms (e.g. use of natural resources and energy). In addition, traditional management accounting systems do not identify environment-related costs, such as expenditure on environmental regulatory compliance and monitoring, making it difficult to manage and control these costs. For example, many of the environmental costs associated with producing products and providing services are included as part of general overheads, rather than being allocated to the cost objects to which they relate. Therefore, it appears that traditional management accounting has two specific limitations in terms of its usefulness in the management of environmental issues:

- It provides a misleading and incomplete account of environmental costs.
- It fails to provide non-financial information about an entity's physical use of natural resources and waste generation.

In addition to the environmental costs that are hidden or misallocated by traditional management accounting, other less tangible environmental costs, such as those related to having a poor environmental image and potential future environmental regulatory costs, are typically ignored by traditional management accounting systems. Providing a clear account of a company's environmental costs is crucial for their management and reduction, but this information may also help to identify other environmental benefits, such as increasing revenues through the development and sale of 'green' products.

In traditional management accounting, the focus is on providing cost information for decision making by analyzing the cost drivers within the company (e.g. machine time and labour hours). However, effective environmental management also requires information about the physical flow of materials and energy through the company, including data about resource usage (e.g. use of energy and raw materials) and waste generation (e.g. volume of carbon dioxide or waste water generated). Physical flow information is crucial for the management of environmental issues, as it helps management understand the environmental impact of business decisions and identify the corporate activities that drive environmental costs. As traditional management accounting systems typically do not provide the physical flow information necessary for the effective management and control of environmental impacts, it is no surprise that companies are now seeking new forms of accounting and management information to address this gap.

Activity

Could any of the management accounting techniques you have studied so far be used to provide information about a company's environmental costs and impact?

As traditional management accounting techniques focus on the management and control costs, they do provide some information about a company's use of certain environmental resources, such as energy, raw materials and water. However, the information collected is normally superficial and lacks connectivity and integration. As a result, it does little to help the internal control and management of a business's environmental costs. In addition, although traditional management accounting methods are useful for measuring and controlling certain environmental costs, they fail to provide benchmarks for comparing the organization's environmental performance with that of its competitors.

Some of the strategic management accounting (SMA) approaches discussed in Chapter 19 could be modified to produce some environment-related benchmarking information. SMA provides non-financial information as well as financial information, and its focus on the value chain may allow companies to improve their efficiency in terms of the use of environmental and natural resources. Although there are some ways in which traditional management accounting and SMA could be used to provide environment-related information for management, they still fail to provide sufficient transparency about the environmental impacts of corporate operations. As a result, there is a need for new forms of management information about the environmental costs and impact of a company's operations.

20.3 Need for environmental management systems

Many internal and external stakeholders are now interested in the environmental performance of companies. For example, internal stakeholders include employees affected by pollution in the workplace. As we discussed in Chapter 11, external stakeholders include environmental pressure groups, investors, suppliers, customers and government regulators. While these environmental pressures vary from country to country and between different business sectors, companies are increasingly seeking new forms of accounting to manage and minimize environmental impacts. For UK companies, important environmental pressures include:

- Supply chain pressures, such as customers requiring suppliers to provide information about their environmental management systems and performance. In many industries, suppliers must now possess an EMS certified to ISO 14001 standards before they are eligible to bid for customer contracts.
- Stakeholder pressure for companies to publicly report environmental performance in the annual accounts and report or in voluntary reports.

- Environmental regulatory and tax pressures, such as the requirements for UK quoted companies to report on greenhouse gas (GHG) emissions, landfill taxes and the obligation for UK producers to recycle packaging.
- The growing importance of socially responsible investment funds, which will only invest in companies with high levels of environmental and social performance.
- Potential for adverse publicity from environmental pressure groups, such as Greenpeace and Friends of the Earth.

As these pressures increase, the internal costs associated with environmental performance also grow. For example, a new environmental regulation may result in additional environmental compliance costs, such as having to purchase new pollution prevention and monitoring equipment. In order to manage these environmental pressures and costs, companies must generate new forms of management information to support internal decision making.

As we discussed in the previous chapter, many companies now have specialized total quality management (TQM) systems to control and manage product quality. In addition, a large number of manufacturing firms have dedicated *environmental management systems* and *energy management systems*. An environmental management system helps the organization identify, manage, monitor and control environmental issues in a holistic manner. Using energy efficiently helps organizations save money as well as helping to conserve resources and tackle climate change. The International Organization for Standardization (ISO) has published two internationally agreed voluntary standards, which we discuss next.

ISO 14001 Environmental Management Systems (BSI, 2015) is suitable for organizations of all types and sizes. It requires the entity to consider all environmental issues relevant to its operations (e.g. air pollution, water and sewage issues, waste management, soil contamination, climate change mitigation and adaptation, and resource use and efficiency). It helps organizations improve their environmental performance through more efficient use of resources and reduction of waste, gaining a competitive advantage and the trust of stakeholders. Revisions to the standard in 2015 increased the prominence of environmental management in the organization's strategic planning processes. They also required greater input from leadership and a stronger commitment to proactive initiatives that boost environmental performance. ISO 14001 helps to:

- Demonstrate compliance with current and future statutory and regulatory requirements.
- Increase leadership involvement and engagement of employees.
- Improve company reputation and the confidence of stakeholders through strategic communication.
- Achieve strategic business aims by incorporating environmental issues into business management.
- Provide a competitive and financial advantage through improved efficiencies and reduced costs.
- Encourage better environmental performance of suppliers by integrating them into the organization's business systems.

ISO 14001 requires the environmental management system to manage the 'elements of an organization's activities, products and services that can interact with the environment' (BSI, 2015, p. 2). Companies must identify the aspects that impact the environment, and assign a level of significance to each one. As financial considerations often play an important role in determining which environmental aspects are tackled first, it is important that businesses have a clear understanding about the environmental cost structure of their processes, products and services (Burritt, 2004; Schaltegger et al., 2013). Many companies currently lack a clear understanding of environmental costs, but new forms of *environmental management accounting (EMA)* could be used to calculate these costs and trace them to their origins in the business. As a result, environmental costs could then be associated with specific environmental aspects, thus helping to establish priorities, targets and objectives within an environmental management system.

*ISO 50001 Energy Management System*s (BSI, 2011) supports organizations in all sectors to use energy more efficiently, through the development of an energy management system. It provides a framework of requirements for organizations to:

- develop a policy for more efficient use of energy
- fix targets and objectives to meet the policy
- use data to better understand and make decisions about energy use
- measure the results
- review how well the policy works
- continually improve energy management.

Both ISO 14001 and ISO 50001 are based on the management system model of continual improvement. This makes it easier for organizations to integrate energy management into their overall efforts to improve quality and environmental management. While environmental management and energy management systems are normally managed by non-accountants (e.g. the production manager or the health and safety manager), they provide additional non-financial and financial information about the environmental impact of the organization's operations. In order to operate effectively, these systems must be integrated within the organization's traditional management system. In this way, the new information they provide can overcome the deficiencies of traditional management systems in respect of environmental issues.

The successful internal use of environmental management systems and environmental energy systems has strengthened calls for the accounting profession to increase its interest in environmental issues. It has also highlighted the need to develop new EMA techniques that aid the identification, control and management of environmental costs and impacts. This will help environmental managers justify investment in environmental improvement projects and identify new ways of improving environmental performance.

20.4 Development of environmental management accounting

In Chapter 19 we explained how traditional management accounting techniques fail to provide strategically relevant information, but many of these conventional practices are also criticized for their deficiencies in providing internal information about an organization's environmental costs and impacts. As a result, the literature is full of competing ideas for developing a form of *environmental management accounting* (EMA). There is no single universally accepted definition of EMA, but it is generally viewed as focusing on the identification, collection, analysis and use of non-financial and financial information for managing the environmental costs and impacts of business operations. As a result, EMA provides and uses two types of information (UNDSD, 2001, p. 2):

- physical information on the use, flows and destinies of energy, water, and materials (including wastes)
- monetary information on environment-related costs, earnings and savings.

While most sectors may benefit from the use of EMA, companies within the manufacturing sector have been its chief adopters, due in part to their heavy reliance on materials, energy and other natural resources. While there is no standard approach to EMA, this new form of accounting overcomes the environmental limitations of traditional management accounting by providing transparent and useful information about an organization's environmental costs and impacts. As such, it focuses on tracking, allocating and attributing environmental costs within the organization, and also provides information about the physical flow of natural resources through the business. By providing this environmental information, EMA allows management to take actions to minimize environment-related costs and impacts, thereby improving an organization's efficiency and its environmental reputation image with stakeholders.

Key definition

Environmental management accounting is the identification, collection, analysis and the use of two types of information for internal decision making:

- physical information on the use, flows and destinies of energy, water, and materials (including wastes) and
- monetary information on environment-related costs, earnings and savings.

Based on UNDSD, 2001.

The regular internal reporting of environmental costs and their causes provides the potential for them to be reduced by redesigning processes in order to reduce hazardous materials used or pollutants emitted to the environment. The information draws management's attention to the possibility of reducing environmental costs by a wiser allocation of costs within the company. The environmental cost information should be used as an attention-directing device to make top management aware of how much is being spent on environmental costs and help to identify those areas that have the greatest potential for cost reduction.

Table 20.1 illustrates the three types of interrelated benefits that a company may obtain from using EMA. At its most basic level, EMA information will assist a company's environmental compliance efforts. EMA data can also be used to improve eco-efficiency and provide information for strategic decisions about an entity's current and future environmental position. This more strategic use of EMA is similar to the benefits achieved from adopting SMA, which we discussed in Chapter 19. For example, EMA data could be used to help identify strategic opportunities for improving an entity's market positioning and image, and identify the impact that future environmental legislation may have on an entity's business model.

Table 20.1 Benefits of environmental management accounting

Eco-compliance	Eco-efficiency	Strategic position
Provides cost-efficient compliance with environmental regulation and a company's own environmental policies	Promotes the reduction of environmental costs and impacts via the efficient use of energy, water and materials in internal operations and final products	Helps identify cost-effective and environmentally sensitive strategies for maintaining and enhancing an organization's long-term strategic position
Examples	Examples	Examples
1. Planning and implementing pollution control investments	1. Tracking the flow of energy, water, materials and wastes	1. Working with suppliers to design products and services for green markets
2. Identifying cost-effective substitutes for toxic materials	2. Planning and implementing energy, water and materials efficiency projects	2. Estimating the internal costs of future environmental regulations
3. Reporting environmental waste and emissions to regulatory authorities	3. Assessing the viability of environmental improvement projects	3. Identifying strategies for improving environmental image and market positioning
4. Providing information for environmental and integrated reporting		4. Reporting environmental performance to external stakeholders

Source: IFAC, 2005. This table is an extract from *International Guidance Document: Environmental Management Accounting*, published by the International Federation of Accountants (IFAC) in August 2005 and is reproduced with permission from IFAC.

An array of different EMA techniques have been developed and used to provide information about a company's environmental costs and impacts, including those that apply existing management accounting techniques to the management of environmental issues. Examples include the following:

- Activity-based costing
- Balanced scorecard
- Total quality management
- Strategic cost analysis
- Environmental management systems
- Life cycle costing
- Input/output analysis.

We have discussed most of these techniques in previous chapters. Life cycle costing is an approach to costing that attempts to identify all of the costs associated with a product during its entire life cycle, including environmental disposal costs. Input/output analysis records the physical flow of materials, such as energy and water, through the company and converts them into monetary amounts. Now that we have identified what EMA is, we will explain the types of information that EMA aims to provide in more detail, along with how this form of accounting defines and classifies environmental costs and impacts.

Activity

Look at the example of Euro Cars GmbH, which we used in Chapter 19, and identify five costs related to the production of motor vehicles that could be classified as environmental costs. Are these costs borne by the company, by society in general or by the local community in particular?

You have probably identified a range of environmental costs as a subset of the costs of operating a business. In terms of manufacturing costs, such as the usage of electricity and materials, the manufacturer pays a market price for these commodities. However, such costs are also environmental in nature as their total stock in the natural environment may be limited and their use may cause social cost externalities in the form of environmental pollution to the local community. Other types of environmental cost include:

- Regulatory compliance costs associated with purchasing testing and monitoring equipment for effluent.
- Environmental taxes payable on waste materials sent to landfill and GHG emissions.
- Fines payable for non-compliance with environmental legislation.

- Back-end costs associated with decommissioning a plant that uses hazardous materials.
- Image and relationship costs associated with producing an environmental report for the local community.
- Social costs resulting from the impact of manufacturing activity, including the impact on human life and environmental degradation.

IFAC (2005) suggests that companies define environmental costs differently, depending on how they intend to use the cost information, management's view of what is environmental and their environmental goals. Based on a review in 2009 of environmental cost guidelines from around the world, IFAC developed the following six cost categories commonly used with EMA:

- Materials costs of product outputs
- Materials costs of non-product outputs
- Waste and emission control costs
- Prevention and other environmental management costs
- Research and development costs
- Less tangible costs.

Materials costs of product outputs include the purchase costs of any natural resources that are converted into products, by-products and packaging. For a manufacturing organization, these would typically include the cost of any direct materials and water used to make a product.

Materials costs of non-product outputs include the purchase and processing costs of energy, water and other materials that do not become part of a final product. For manufacturing companies, any output that is not part of a final product is classified as a non-product output. In contrast, for service sector entities, such as a car wash, all energy, water and materials must eventually leave the organization as non-product outputs. Within many organizations, these non-product output costs are already monitored as part of TQM and quality management systems; they are also environment-related as they may be reduced through investments in new pollution prevention technology.

Waste and emission control costs include the costs of handling, treating and disposing of waste and emissions. This category also includes the costs associated with complying with environmental regulations, such as environmental inspections and permitting costs.

Prevention and environmental management costs include the costs of running a company's EMS and EMA systems, communicating environmental information to stakeholders and the routine measurement of a company's environmental impacts. Research and development costs include a company's expenditure on activities related to environment-related issues and initiatives, such as projects to develop more energy-efficient products.

Less tangible costs include the internal and external costs that are not typically found within a company's cost accounting system. These costs can be significant, as they include environmental liabilities from damage to the natural environment, costs associated with complying with future environmental regulation, image and relationship costs and social externalities.

As well as information about environmental costs, EMA must identify any environment-related earnings and savings, such as the revenues from scrap and any reduced waste disposal costs. It is important to measure these environmental savings correctly within decision making, as they can be used to justify investments in new pollution prevention equipment.

Activity

The accountant of Euro Cars GmbH is thinking about implementing an EMA, and needs your assistance. Using IFAC's six categories of environmental cost, classify each of the following operational costs into an appropriate cost category:

- Depreciation of pollution monitoring equipment
- Cleaning supplies used by the janitor
- Water used to flush the factory's toilets
- Cost of the metal used to make a car chassis
- Costs of sending waste products for recycling

Check your answer against the following solution.

Cost	Cost category
Monitoring equipment depreciation	Waste and emission control costs
Cleaning supplies used by the janitor	Materials cost of non-product output
Water used to flush the factory's toilets	Materials cost of non-product output
Cost of metal used to make a car	Materials cost of product output
Waste recycling costs	Waste and emission control costs

In addition to monetary information about environmental costs and benefits, EMA should also provide physical information about the use and flows of energy, water, materials and waste within an organization. Table 20.2 shows the types of physical EMA information typically provided by manufacturing companies.

Materials inputs include any energy, water or other materials that enter an organization. Outputs are any products, wastes or other materials that leave an organization during its operations. These physical flow categories are consistent with those used within ISO 14001 certified EMS, which ensures that EMA and environmental management systems both report on physical flow environmental inputs and outputs in the same manner, thereby improving the potential for environmental collaboration between a company's accounting and environmental management teams.

Table 20.2   **Types of physical EMA information provided in the manufacturing sector**

Materials inputs	Outputs
Raw and auxiliary materials (e.g. metal and glue used in car production)	Product outputs:
Packaging materials	Products (including packaging)
Merchandise (e.g. inventory bought for resale)	By-products (including packaging)
Operating materials (e.g. production materials not part of the final product, such as office supplies)	Waste and emissions:
	Solid waste
	Hazardous waste
Water	Waste water
Energy	Air emissions

Source: Reproduced from IFAC, 2005, p. 33. This table is an extract from *International Guidance Document: Environmental Management Accounting*, published by the International Federation of Accountants (IFAC) in August 2005 and is used with the permission of IFAC.

20.5 Implementing environmental management accounting

Chapter 11 outlined the way that certain businesses publish reports on their environmental and social impacts. EMA may play a role in providing some of the information needed for disclosure purposes, but its primary focus is on the internal management and control of environmental impacts of the organization. There is no agreed conceptual framework for the scope and extent of EMA, so the term is used to describe many different techniques and practices, including those already practised as part of traditional management accounting. It is unclear as to whether EMA is seen as an entirely new system or simply integrated within traditional management accounting. While this is a problem, the more pressing problem may be how this environmental information is generated and used within decision making, and whether management accountants are the ones to supply this information. While it is clear that traditional management accounting techniques, such as activity-based costing, could be used to manage environmental costs, there is some debate over the need to develop specific techniques for measuring environmental performance. Part of this debate is the argument that management accounting is the cause of the environmental problem by making issues such as manufacturing profit and standard cost visible and the social costs of pollution invisible.

A critical issue that is often overlooked by proponents of EMA is that traditional management accounting should be actively managing many environmental costs as part of normal efficient management. The creation of excess waste and the inefficient use of energy have resulted in costs to manufacturing organizations long before they were given an additional environmental dimension through concern for the preservation of the natural environment. However, the management accounting systems of many organizations fail to systematically manage or reduce these types of costs. It is through increased social interest in environmental issues that accountants are encouraged to focus on the control of costs that should already be part of everyday cost management. Furthermore, despite calls for EMA, evidence suggests that management accountants and accounting are normally uninvolved in the day-to-day management of environmental issues.

Corporate responses to green pressures largely involve the use of non-accounting expertise and non-financial information systems. Indicative of the current use of non-accounting methods to tackle internal environmental issues is the way that many organizations have implemented environmental management systems certified to ISO 14001 (BSI, 2015). Such EMS are typically structured as an extension of existing TQM or health and safety systems, rather than becoming a routine part of the finance function. Furthermore, the manager in charge of the EMS is very rarely, if ever, a qualified accountant. Unsurprisingly, EMA information is typically generated with little direct input from management accountants, and, at best, is used in an ad hoc manner by accountants within decision making. For example, it is only when there is a major environmental problem that the management accounting function needs to refer directly to the environmental management unit, seeking its help as a specialized consultant.

While corporate interest in EMA has grown in recent years, many companies have yet to develop dedicated environmental management systems. In the UK, many large manufacturing companies possess environmental management systems, but the role of accountants and accounting within such systems is largely ad hoc, and often limited to providing cost information for special environmental improvement projects (Perez et al., 2007; Nath and Ramanathan, 2016). Furthermore, while companies are actively using EMA information to reduce their environmental costs and impacts, much of this activity is being driven by environmental managers using information from non-accounting environmental management systems (Bouten and Hoozee, 2013). As a result, many companies are still some way from having an environmental management system that is fully integrated with its traditional management accounting information system.

We will now use the Euro Cars GmbH to illustrate the use of EMA. Production takes place in three departments: Assembly 1, Assembly 2 and Quality Control. Each department uses water that is transformed into special waste during operations. The special waste is collected by tanker on a regular basis by a local waste management firm. During the last production period, the total charge for special waste collection at the site was €500,000. Site overheads are currently apportioned to departments based on area. The total area occupied by the three departments is 25,000 square metres (m²) and the overhead apportionment rate for special waste is €20 per m² occupied. The following table provides further details.

	Area (m²)	Total overhead apportionment for special waste (€)	Total Cyclones processed (units)	Other products processed (units)
Assembly 1	4,500	90,000	1,500	0
Assembly 2	10,500	210,000	0	3,500
Quality control	10,000	200,000	1,500	3,500
Total	25,000	500,000		

Using new metering equipment, assume that the site's environmental manager can provide a detailed EMA analysis of special waste generation at the site. The following information is made available:

	Meter reading for special waste generation (m³)	% of special waste
Assembly 1	300	3
Assembly 2	7,700	77
Quality control	2,000	20
Total	10,000	100

Activity

(a) Using the original overhead apportionment basis, calculate the total amount of special waste overhead that would be allocated to the unit cost of a Cyclone.

(b) Discuss whether the EMA information prepared by the company's environmental manager helps to improve the management and control of special waste costs at the site.

(c) Use the EMA information to recalculate the amount of special waste allocated to each Cyclone.

Under the original apportionment basis, each Cyclone product will be charged with a proportion of the special waste overhead allocated to Assembly 1 and Quality Control. In total, each Cyclone should be charged with €100 of special waste overhead, with €60 per unit in Assembly 1 (€90,000 total overhead/1,500 units of output) and €40 in Quality Control (€200,000 total overhead/5,000 total vehicles processed).

The EMA metering data reveals invaluable information for the management and control environmental overheads. The special waste overhead is clearly influenced by the amount of waste generated in each building rather than its total size. Once the metering equipment was operational, the site accountant no longer had to estimate cost causality and could identify the buildings and products that created the most waste. As 77% of special waste was generated by Assembly 2, the work undertaken there should be allocated €385,000 of special waste overhead (77% of €500,000). As only non-Cyclone products are produced in Assembly 2, it is clear that these models, rather than the Cyclone, are the biggest generators of special waste. Ultimately, a decision could be made to switch production towards more environmentally-friendly models. If overhead allocation is based on the EMA metering data, each Cyclone will be allocated only €30 of special waste overhead, with €10 per unit in Assembly 1 (3% x €500,000 total overhead/1,500 units of output) and €20 in Quality Control (20% x €500,000 total overhead/5,000 total vehicles processed).

This example illustrates just one of the ways that EMA information can also be used to supplement existing managerial accounting information in decision making situations. EMA can be used in a variety of ways, and can provide additional information about costs and strategic opportunities. In the next two chapters we will review a range of techniques used for assessing capital investment opportunities, and EMA information is often used to identify the costs and benefits from investments in new technology or equipment aimed at reducing pollution or increasing production efficiency.

20.6 Greenhouse gas accounting

Under the *Companies Act 2006 (Strategic Report and Directors' Reports) Regulations 2013*, all listed companies in the UK must report on the greenhouse gas (GHG) emissions for which they are responsible. Other companies are encouraged to report their GHG emissions on a voluntary basis. While listed companies are not required to use a specific approach to measuring and reporting GHG emissions, they are advised to use a systematic process in order to provide transparent and reliable data. Requiring companies to report on their carbon footprint should improve the corporate management of GHG emissions, resulting in reduced energy costs, higher internal efficiency, and increased customer loyalty. EMA and environmental management systems can be used to capture the required GHG emissions data, and this information is then used for external reporting purposes in the annual report and accounts.

Most large UK companies use an EMS to collect GHG emissions data and adopt the accounting and reporting guidance provided by *The Greenhouse Gas Protocol: A Corporate Accounting and Reporting Standard* (GHG Protocol, 2013). Formed in 1998, the Greenhouse Gas (GHG) Protocol is a partnership of businesses, non-governmental organizations (NGOs), governments, and others convened by the World Resources Institute (WRI) and the World Business Council for Sustainable Development (WBCSD). The GHG Protocol develops internationally accepted GHG accounting and reporting standards to promote low emissions worldwide. The GHG

Protocol Corporate Standard provides guidance for preparing an inventory of GHG emissions and covers the accounting and reporting of seven greenhouse gases:

- carbon dioxide (CO_2)
- methane (CH_4)
- nitrous oxide (N_2O)
- hydrofluorocarbons (HFCs)
- perfluorocarbons (PFCs)
- sulphur hexafluoride (SF_6)
- nitrogen trifluoride (NF_3).

The GHG Protocol Standard was designed to:

- help companies prepare a GHG inventory that represents a true and fair account of their emissions, through the use of standardized approaches and principles
- simplify and reduce the costs of compiling a GHG inventory
- provide business with information that can be used to build an effective strategy to manage and reduce GHG emissions
- increase consistency and transparency in GHG accounting and reporting among various companies and GHG programmes.

In order to differentiate between direct and indirect emission sources, the GHG Protocol Standard defines three scopes for GHG accounting and reporting purposes:

- Scope 1: Direct GHG emissions, which occur from sources that are owned or controlled by the company. Examples include the emissions from combustion in owned or controlled boilers, vehicles, and the emissions from chemical production in owned or controlled production equipment.
- Scope 2: Electricity indirect GHG emissions, which account for GHG emissions from the generation of purchased electricity consumed by the company. Purchased electricity is purchased or otherwise brought into the company. Scope 2 emissions physically occur at the facility where electricity is generated.
- Scope 3: Other indirect GHG emissions. This is an optional reporting category accounting for all other indirect emissions. Scope 3 emissions result from the activities of the company, but occur from sources not owned or controlled by the company. Examples include the extraction and production of purchased materials; transportation of purchased fuels; and use of sold products and services.

When measuring GHG emissions, companies should use the most accurate calculation approach that is available to them and appropriate for their reporting context. Direct measurement of GHG emissions by monitoring concentration and flow rate is relatively uncommon. Most companies calculate GHG emissions through the application of documented emission factors. These factors are calculated ratios that relate GHG emissions to a proxy measure of activity at an emissions source. As a result, a company reporting on the GHG emissions from its activities must convert 'activity data' such as distance travelled, litres of fuel used or tonnes of waste disposed into carbon emissions. In order to help this conversion process, the UK government provides an online conversion tool for company reporting of GHG emissions (DEFRA, 2016).

The process of GHG accounting requires a company to set objectives and targets for managing its GHG emissions. It normally includes the following nine steps:

1. Set the relevant business objectives.
2. Determine whether to include all or part of the business.
3. Identify the business activities that are responsible for GHG emissions and those to be accounted for.
4. Decide on the start and periodicity of data to be collected.
5. Set up systems for data capture, processing and reporting.
6. Collect primary data for the base period and convert it to carbon dioxide equivalents.
7. Evaluate the outcome and decide future emissions reduction targets.
8. Take steps to achieve the targets.
9. Monitor progress by evaluating outcomes against base period.

Many UK companies have made significant progress towards reducing their GHG emissions. A review by Carbon Clear (2015) of carbon reporting by the FTSE 100 companies found that:

- 99 companies reported on carbon emissions
- 55 companies reported some form of Scope 3 data, 40 of which provided Scope 3 information that went beyond reporting on business travel
- 74 companies set carbon reduction targets
- 55 assessed the risks that future climate change may pose to the business
- 38 purchased green electricity.

The study analyzed each company's published information on GHG emissions and identified that among the best reporters were BT Group, Marks & Spencer Group, Sky, Kingfisher and Unilever. The study also observed that organizations that perform well in all areas of environmental impact also have a strong commitment to their carbon performance. This indicates the need for companies to develop EMA in order to improve the routine management of environmental costs and impacts.

20.7 Enterprise resource planning

In this chapter we have explored the types of EMA information that companies now use to manage their environmental impacts. You must remember that this is just a fraction of the total accounting information generated, and in the other chapters we have discussed a variety of other accounting techniques used to generate information for internal decision making and external financial reporting. In addition to accounting information, companies must also collect non-accounting information to manage functions such as administration, distribution, human resource management, marketing, procurement, and operations in the form of production and/or services. In the past, these different types of information were provided by individual computer systems within a company, which was inefficient due to:

- their individual data storage costs;
- the cost of reformatting data from one system for use in another; and
- having to program links between systems for data transfer.

While these costs can be significant, the main problem with having fragmented information systems is that management cannot easily use performance data obtained from one area of the business to help manage another. For example, if a company's sales system is incompatible with its cost accounting system, management must make sales decisions without any information about product or customer profitability. As a result of these technological problems, many companies have invested in an *enterprise resource planning (ERP)* system, such as *SAP* or *Oracle*. An ERP system is a process management software that allows the organization to use a system of integrated applications to manage the business. ERP software integrates business functions and data into one shared system that provides real-time information for enhanced levels of communication within the organization. ERP was originally created for production planning within the manufacturing industry, but is now used for the organization-wide management of an increasing range of business functions, including accounting, human resources, customer relations, and supply chain management.

Key definition

Enterprise resource planning (ERP) is the management of all the information and resources involved in a company's operations by means of an integrated computer system.

Source: Stevenson, 2010, p. 595.

Although the implementation of an ERP system is often costly and time-consuming, it can provide a range of benefits that are felt in several areas (Staehr et al., 2012):

- operations – reduced costs and improved efficiency
- management – better decision making, management of resources and performance control
- strategy – support for growth planning, alliances, innovation and product positioning
- IT – reduced costs and increased flexibility and capability
- organization-wide – support for change management and goal congruence.

An ERP system automates and streamlines operational processes, thereby improving productivity, reducing costs, improving quality, and enhancing the daily management of customer relations. The centralized databases and real-time information provided by the ERP can also improve managerial decision making. The ERP system can also help to identify strategic opportunities for the market positioning of product or services in a similar way to SMA, as we discussed in Chapter 19. ERP systems can also increase IT efficiency and flexibility, support organizational change, improve learning and growth, improve employee communication, and promote a shared understanding of the entity's culture, goals and vision.

We will now examine how the introduction of an ERP system can result in some or all of these potential benefits. Within an ERP system, all employees use the same information system which provides greater opportunities for collaboration between different functional areas, thereby improving the efficiency of internal business processes and creating a more flexible and adaptable company. When new data are entered in the ERP system, related information is automatically updated elsewhere in the system. As a result, a company's management is able to instantly assess the overall impact of a change within a certain functional or business unit. Tasks that may benefit from the integration provided include:

- tracking customer orders from acceptance through to delivery
- sales forecasting and inventory management
- tracking materials purchases against materials usage and cost.

Although implementing an ERP system can be costly in terms of time and resources, such systems are now widely used by many large and medium-sized companies throughout the world (Ngai et al., 2008). Many ERP systems are now offered via cloud computing, whereby employees can access the software and data by the Internet using a web browser. These developments in cloud-based technology have also enabled ERP systems to be used for information sharing with suppliers and customers (Granlund and Malmi, 2002).

In theory, a company's ERP system could be used to provide and distribute EMA information throughout the business. EMA requires computerized data collection, data processing and data supply in order to provide an information database about a company's environmental costs and impacts. While ERP systems typically contain the essential financial and non-financial data required for EMA, such systems are not designed to track and trace environmental costs, and as a result, the information they provide is insufficiently detailed for environmental management (IFAC, 2005). As cost allocation based upon material and energy flows is insufficiently supported by most ERP systems, most companies will need to modify their system before it can be used to provide EMA information (Moller et al., 2006). Modifications may include implementing EMA as a new ERP application module or implementing it as a new feature within existing accounting-related ERP components. Such changes can be costly, so companies often choose to provide their electronic EMA information databases independently of their ERP system.

20.8 Conclusions

In this chapter we have highlighted the limitations of traditional management accounting in controlling and managing environmental costs and impacts. While traditional management accounting practices and techniques are widely used, they are increasingly criticized for failing to provide environmental information for decision making in the modern business environment. Environmental decision making requires a management accounting system that provides not only financial information that focuses on internal operations, but also information, both financial and non-financial in nature, about the environmental impact of business operations. As a result, a range of EMA techniques and perspectives have been developed that illustrate how management accountants, with the assistance of cross-functional expertise from non-accountants, can be involved in the provision of environmental information for decision making.

While the development and use of EMA is still at an early stage, many companies have ERP systems that can function alongside EMA to manage environment costs and impacts. As UK quoted companies must now report on their GHG emissions in their annual report and accounts, and there is growing interest in integrated reporting, companies must have some form of environmental management system that can provide the information needed for these new forms of reporting. From the developments discussed in this chapter, it is clear that management accounting techniques and practices continue to evolve as stakeholder demands for environmental information increase over time.

References

BSI (2011) *ISO 50001: 2011 Energy Management Systems – Requirements with Guidance for Use*, Chiswick: BSI. Available at: www.iso.org/iso/catalogue_detail?csnumber=51297 (Accessed 23 July 2016).

BSI (2015) *ISO 14001: 2015 Environmental Management Systems – Requirements with Guidance for Use*, Chiswick: BSI. Available at: www.iso.org/iso/catalogue_detail?csnumber=60857 (Accessed 23 July 2016).

Bouten, L. and Hoozee, S. (2013) 'On the interplay between environmental reporting and management accounting change', *Management Accounting Research*, 24(4), pp. 333–348.

Burritt, R. (2004) 'Environmental management accounting: Roadblocks on the way to the green and pleasant land', *Business Strategy and the Environment*, 13(1), pp. 13-32.

Carbon Clear (2015) *Carbon Reporting Performance of the FTSE 100*, Carbon Clear, September 2015. Available at: www.carbon-clear.com/files/FTSE_100_Report_2015.pdf (Accessed 23 July 2016).

DEFRA (2016) *Government Emission Conversion Factors for Greenhouse Gas Company Reporting*, London: DEFRA. Available at: www.ukconversionfactorscarbonsmart.co.uk/ (Accessed 23 July 2016).

GHG Protocol (2013) *The Greenhouse Gas Protocol: A Corporate Accounting and Reporting Standard (Revised Edition)*, The Greenhouse Gas Protocol. Available at: www.ghgprotocol.org/standards/corporate-standard (Accessed 23 July 2016).

Granlund, M. and Malmi, T. (2002) 'Moderate impact of ERPS on management accounting: A lag or permanent outcome?', *Management Accounting Research*, 13(3), pp. 299–321.

IFAC (2005) *International Guidance Document: Environmental Management Accounting*. New York: IFAC. Available at: www.ifac.org/publications-resources/international-guidance-document-environmental-management-accounting (Accessed 23 July 2016).

Moller, A., Prox, M. and Viere, T. (2006) 'Computer support for Environmental Management Accounting', in Schaltegger, S., Bennett, M. and Burritt, R. (eds) *Sustainability Accounting and Reporting*, New York: Springer Publishing, pp. 605–624.

Nath, P. and Ramanathan, R. (2016) 'Environmental management practices, environmental technology portfolio, and environmental commitment: A content analytic approach for UK manufacturing firms, *International Journal of Production Economics*, 171(3), pp. 427–437.

Ngai, E., Law, C. and Wat, F. (2008) 'Examining the critical success factors in the adoption of enterprise resource planning', *Computers in Industry*, 59(6), pp. 548–564.

Perez, E., Ruiz, C. and Fenech, F. (2007) 'Environmental management systems as an embedding mechanism: A research note', *Accounting, Auditing and Accountability*, 20(3), pp. 403–422.

Schaltegger, S., Gibassier, D. and Zvezdov, D. (2013) 'Is environmental management accounting a discipline? A bibliometric literature review', *Meditari Accountancy Research*, 21(1), pp. 4–31.

Staehr, L., Shanks, G. and Seddon, P. (2012) 'An explanatory framework for achieving business benefits from ERP systems', *Journal of the Association for Information Systems*, 13(6), pp. 424–465.

Stevenson, A. (2010) *Oxford Dictionary of English*, Oxford: Oxford University Press.

UNDSD (2001) *Environmental Management Accounting, Procedures and Principles*, New York: United Nations Division for Sustainable Development. Available at: https://sustainabledevelopment.un.org/content/documents/policiesandlinkages.pdf (Accessed 23 July 2016).

Discussion questions

1 Discuss the reasons why traditional management accounting techniques typically fail to manage and control environmental costs.

2 Discuss the purpose of environmental management accounting and how it can be used to assist in the management and control of environmental costs.

3 Debate whether management accountants alone can provide the necessary information for managing a company's environmental costs and impacts.

Practice questions

4 Identify four types of environmental cost that a manufacturing company may typically have, and explain how they would be classified in a traditional management accounting system.

5 Explain the potential benefits of an ERP system, and discuss why such a system may fail to provide sufficiently detailed EMA information.

6 Explain the difference between EMA and environmental reporting. Discuss whether EMA information is used in environmental and integrated reporting.

7 Classify the following operational costs using IFAC's six categories of environmental cost:

- The salary of the manager who runs the company's EMS
- The cost of purchasing freshwater for cooling the company's finished products
- The disposal costs for the waste water
- The costs of preparing the company's voluntary external environmental report
- Cost of direct materials used to build the company's products. 10% is eventually converted into waste products and send to landfill.

8 Zoom SA assembles motorcycle engines for the commercial motorcycle industry. The company produces two engine models, the Standard and the Super, in a largely automated factory in France. The company's accountant provides the following budgeted production costs for 2019.

	Standard	Super
	€	€
Direct materials per unit	200	100
Direct labour per unit	50	50
Total direct costs per unit	250	150

	Standard	Super
Total units produced	2,000	2,000
Power to make 1 unit (kwHs)	8	16
Water to make 1 unit (litres)	–	10
Total power needed (kwHs)	16,000	32,000
Total water needed (litres)	–	20,000

The budgeted utility costs are €0.50 per kwH of electricity and €0.30 per litre of water. The budgeted factory overheads for 2019 are as follows:

	€
Utilities – water usage	6,000
Utilities – power usage	24,000
Toxic waste disposal costs	150,000
Materials handling costs	50,000
Supervisors' salaries	60,000
Factory insurance	10,000
Total overheads	300,000

The company allocates overheads to products using a predetermined overhead allocation rate based on the total direct materials used in production. The company plans to produce 2,000 units of each product. The budgeted total direct materials for 2019 are shown below.

	€
2,000 Standard engines x €200 direct materials per unit	400,000
2,000 Super engines x €100 direct materials per unit	200,000
Total direct materials costs	600,000

Based on this information, the company's overhead allocation rate is 50% of the cost of direct materials (€300,000 total overhead/€600,000 total direct materials). The accountant has used this rate to calculate the following total cost per unit.

	Standard	Super
	€	€
Direct materials per unit	200.00	100.00
Direct labour per unit	50.00	50.00
Overhead per unit	100.00	50.00
Total cost per unit	350.00	200.00

Although the accountant is relatively satisfied with these costings, the company's environmental manager suggests that they inadequately allocate environmental costs between the two types of engine. The environmental manager provides the following information about overheads:

- Due to its complex design, the Super engine must be rinsed with cooling water during its construction. The Standard engine has no need for rinsing.

- The pistons of the Super engine must be sprayed with a special coating. This coating is toxic and any waste material must be sent to a third party for disposal. Disposal costs for 2019 are estimated at €150,000. The Standard engine does not require this coating.

- Based on prior tests, production of the Super engine requires twice as much power and energy as the Standard engine.

Required

(a) From an environmental perspective, describe any problems you see with the company's current approach to allocating overheads to products.
(b) Identify any of the company's overheads that would be classified as environmental costs under EMA and describe how they should be directly attributed or allocated to the two products in 2019.
(c) Calculate a revised cost per unit for each product. Discuss whether your alternative accounting figures provide more useful information for the environmental management of the company's operations.

Suggested research questions for dissertation students

Students interested in environmental management accounting may wish to investigate one or more of the following research questions:

- Which EMA techniques are most widely used in [industry]?
- What factors influence the adoption of EMA techniques?
- Do small companies use environmental management accounting techniques?
- How do companies manage and account for environment-related costs?
- How can EMA techniques be adapted to support their use in developing countries?
- What role do non-accountants play in the provision of EMA information?

Preliminary reading

Bennett, M., Schaltegger, S. and Zvezdov, D. (2011) 'Environmental management accounting', in Abdel-Kader, M.G. (ed.) *Review of Management Accounting Research*, Basingstoke: Palgrave Macmillan.

Bouten, L. and Hoozee, S. (2013) 'On the interplay between environmental reporting and management accounting change', *Management Accounting Research*, 24(4), pp. 333–348.

Burritt, R. (2004) 'Environmental management accounting: Roadblocks on the way to the green and pleasant land', *Business Strategy and the Environment*, 13(1), pp. 13–32.

Christ, K. and Burritt, R. (2013) 'Environmental management accounting: The significance of contingent variables for adoption', *Journal of Cleaner Production*, 41(July), pp. 163–173.

CIMA (2010) *Accounting for Climate Change: How Management Accountants can Help Organisations Mitigate and Adapt to Climate Change*, London: CIMA.

Hartmann, F., Perego, P. and Young, A. (2013) 'Carbon accounting: Challenges for research in management control and performance measurement', *Abacus*, 49(4), pp. 539–563.

Henri, J., Boiral, O. and Roy, M. (2014) 'The tracking of environmental costs: Motivations and impacts', *European Accounting* Review, 23(4), pp. 647–669.

Lopez, O. and Hiebl, M. (2015) 'Management accounting in small and medium-sized enterprises: Current knowledge and avenues for further research', *Journal of Management Accounting Research*, 27(1), pp. 81–119.

Nath, P. and Ramanathan, R. (2016) 'Environmental management practices, environmental technology portfolio, and environmental commitment: A content analytic approach for UK manufacturing firms', *International Journal of Production Economics*, 171(3), pp. 427–437.

Ratnatunga, J., Balachandran, K. and Kashi, R. (2009) 'Carbon business accounting: The impact of global warming on the cost and management accounting profession', *Journal of Accounting, Auditing and Finance*, 24(2), pp. 333–355.

Schaltegger, S., Gibassier, D. and Zvezdov, D. (2013) 'Is environmental management accounting a discipline? A bibliometric literature review', *Meditari Accountancy Research*, 21(1), pp. 4–31.

PART IV

Capital investment appraisal

21 Payback period and accounting rate of return

Learning objectives

When you have studied this chapter, you should be able to:

___

- Explain the purpose of capital investment appraisal
- Calculate the payback period for an investment project
- Calculate the accounting rate of return for an investment project
- Discuss the advantages and disadvantages of these two methods

21.1 Introduction

In this part of the book we focus on techniques that provide information to aid managers in making decisions about capital expenditure. The process of appraising projects that involve the investment of large sums of capital is known as capital investment appraisal and a number of techniques have been developed to provide information that will help management choose between different long-term projects. For example, a business may want to invest capital in extending its premises, buying new delivery vehicles or adopting new technologies. In any major project that requires capital investment, there are a number of decisions that management needs to make. Some are important organizational and personnel decisions, but it is crucial that the financial implications of any such decisions are considered.

In this chapter and the next, we look at the different approaches to capital investment appraisal and some of the commonly used techniques. We start with the payback period, which is a simple method that considers the project purely from the point of view of how long it takes to recover the initial capital invested. We then go on to examine the accounting rate of return, which focuses on profit rather than cash. In order to evaluate the usefulness of these methods, we also discuss the advantages and disadvantages of each. The next chapter examines techniques based on discounted cash flows.

21.2 Purpose of capital investment appraisal

The *purpose* of *capital investment appraisal* is to provide information to management that will help them decide which of several proposed capital investment projects is likely to yield the highest financial return. Capital expenditure is the outlay of a considerable amount of money on a project such as the purchase of a new non-current asset (e.g. buying a new factory), the enhancement of an existing non-current asset (e.g. extending the existing factory) or investment in a new business venture. Non-current assets are assets the business owns and plans to keep in the long term in order to generate future streams of revenue.

Key definition

Capital investment appraisal is the evaluation of proposed investment projects with a view to determining which is likely to give the highest financial return.

Capital investment decisions are among the most important decisions made by management and are critical not only for the owners and managers of the business, but at the macro level they are also important for the country's economy. Research in innovative small, medium and large firms (Chittenden and Derregia, 2004) shows that some of these entrepreneurial businesses bypass the investment decision-making process by using operating leases, rental or hire contracts to obtain some of the non-current assets they require, such as land, buildings and capital equipment. This reduces the effect of uncertainty on decisions and increases the resources available to the business for a much lower initial outlay. However, not all non-current assets can be obtained like this and some are only available for outright purchase; hence the continuing need for methods to help management choose between different capital investment projects.

Capital investment decisions are very important to the long-term survival of the business and focus on strategic issues, such as whether to build or buy a new factory. The investment project is likely to span two or more years and require a high level of expenditure. External factors, such as interest and inflation rates, are very important. On the other hand, short-term decisions focus on operational issues, such as whether to discontinue a product (see Chapter 16). When a business is considering investing capital in a long-term project, management needs to be sure that the amount of money received during the life of the project will be higher than the initial amount invested; at the very least, management needs to know that the business will get its money back. The annual profit and the distinction between fixed and variable costs is therefore of less importance than the timing and amount of the cash coming into the business (cash inflows) and the cash going out of the business (cash outflows). In some cases, an investment is made to make a saving on costs, rather than to generate more cash. For example, a business may be deciding whether to replace an old machine with the latest model that will be less expensive to run. The question that the managers of the business need to answer is whether the saving on costs is likely to be sufficiently high that they make the investment worthwhile. Once again, cash is the most important factor.

Activity

The directors of the Cheddar Cheese Company Ltd are considering investing in a new packing machine. They have a choice of three suitable machines, each of which would cost £150,000 and each of which would have an estimated useful economic life of five years with no residual value. However, the annual net cash flows (the difference between the cash inflows and the cash outflows) are expected to vary over the period. The following table shows the budgeted annual net cash flows.

Year	Machine 1	Machine 2	Machine 3
	£	£	£
1	60,000	20,000	10,000
2	50,000	30,000	20,000
3	40,000	40,000	30,000
4	30,000	50,000	40,000
5	20,000	60,000	150,000

Which machine should the company purchase?

One way to make the comparison is to total the annual net cash flows for each machine:

Year	Machine 1	Machine 2	Machine 3
	£	£	£
1	60,000	20,000	10,000
2	50,000	30,000	20,000
3	40,000	40,000	30,000
4	30,000	50,000	40,000
5	20,000	60,000	150,000
Total	200,000	200,000	250,000

Both Machine 1 and Machine 2 are expected to give a total net cash flow of £200,000 over the five-year period, which suggests that perhaps either would be a worthwhile investment. However, you may decide that Machine 1 is preferable because the cash comes in more quickly. Machine 3 looks better than the other two because the total net cash flow is £50,000 more than the other two machines. However, the directors would have to wait until Year 5 before the business generates most of the cash and this means increased risk. Indeed, the net cash flows are forecast figures for all three machines and the further into the future the estimate is, the more unreliable the prediction is likely to be.

As you can see, it is difficult to decide which machine would be the best to buy, but accountants have developed a number of different investment appraisal techniques that can provide useful information to aid the decision. The main methods can be classified into the non-discounting methods and the more sophisticated methods where future cash flows are discounted to take account of the time value of money. In this chapter we are going to focus on the two non-discounting methods: simple payback period method and the accounting rate of return (see Figure 21.1). We will discuss the discounted cash flow methods in the next chapter.

Figure 21.1   Non-discounting methods of investment appraisal

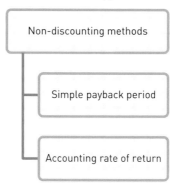

21.3 Simple payback period

The simple *payback period* method is widely used as it is easy to apply and is easily understood by non-accountants. The *purpose* of the payback period method is to calculate the time required for the amount invested to be repaid by the net cash outflow generated by the investment project and is a simple way to evaluate the investment risk. The payback period is expressed in years and fractions of years. When comparing potential investment projects, the payback period is a key factor in determining which project should be undertaken: the project with the shortest payback period is preferred, as longer payback periods are not desirable for investment positions.

Key definition

The payback period method calculates the time required for the predicted net cash flows to equal the capital invested in a proposed capital investment project.

The payback period can be calculated using the following formula:

$$\text{Payback (years)} = \frac{\text{Initial capital invested}}{\text{Annual cash inflows}}$$

The following estimates are needed:

- the amount of capital required for the investment
- the annual cash inflows (based on the predicted cash inflows and outflows, including repayments of capital)
- the timing of the movements of cash.

We will illustrate the method with an example. Jimmy Chang is considering investing £15,000 in a hot dog van that will have an estimated useful economic life of five years, with no residual value after that time. He would employ someone to operate it from a single site in the marketplace in the centre of town. His accountant has done some research and estimates that annual cash flows will be as follows:

	£
Cash inflows	
Sales revenue	20,000
Cash outflows	
Purchases	(5,000)
Employee's salary	(8,000)
Motor expenses	(2,000)
	(15,000)
Net cash flow	5,000

We can now calculate the payback period:

Year	Cash flow	Cumulative cash flow
	£	£
0	(15,000)	(15,000)
1	5,000	(10,000)
2	5,000	(5,000)
3	5,000	0
4	5,000	5,000
5	5,000	10,000

Depreciation of the van is not included because depreciation is an accounting adjustment rather than a cash flow. The cash flow relating to the van is the cash paid when the van was bought, but there are several other things in this table which need explaining:

- Year 0 is a conventional way of referring to the start of Year 1. Year 1, 2, 3, etc. mean the end of Year 1, 2, 3, etc.
- It is customary to assume that cash flows during a year will be received evenly throughout the year. Of course, this is not likely to be true, but it is one way of simplifying the calculation. It is possible to estimate cash flows on a quarterly or monthly basis, but this is seldom done in payback calculations, because forecasting to this degree of refinement is rarely possible.
- Cash outflows are shown in brackets.

The cumulative cash flows are shown as zero at the end of Year 3. This means that at the end of Year 3, the net cash flowing in from the investment has reached the figure of £15,000, which is the same as the initial cash outflow in payment for the van at the start of Year 1. Therefore, we can tell Jimmy that, based on his estimates, the payback period for this project will be exactly three years.

If the projected cash flows after the initial investment are constant annual sums, as in the above scenario, then you can also use a simple formula to calculate the payback period:

$$\frac{\text{Initial capital investment}}{\text{Annual cash inflows}} = \frac{£15,000}{£5,000} = 3 \text{ years}$$

However, this formula cannot be used when the projected annual cash flows vary from one year to another. We will illustrate this by continuing the example of our entrepreneur, Jimmy Chang.

Activity

As well as considering the hot dog van business, Jimmy is also considering investing £15,000 in the purchase of a fish and chip van. The van is expected to have an economic life of five years with no residual value after that time. The operator will drive the van around the main suburban areas of town and Jimmy's research suggests that it will take some time to build up a customer base. The following table shows how the estimated net cash flows for this project are expected to gradually build up over the period.

Year	Cash flow
	£
0	(15,000)
1	3,000
2	4,000
3	5,000
4	6,000
5	7,000

Calculate the simple payback period for the fish and chip van project.

The first step is to work out the cumulative net cash flows over the period. Check your answer against the following table.

Year	Cash flow	Cumulative cash flow
	£	£
0	(15,000)	(15,000)
1	3,000	(12,000)
2	4,000	(8,000)
3	5,000	(3,000)
4	6,000	3,000
5	7,000	10,000

The cumulative cash flows show that the payback period lies somewhere between three years (when the cumulative position is expected to be a cash deficit of £3,000) and four years (when the cumulative position is expected to be a cash surplus of £3,000). Assuming the cash flow is regular throughout the year, we can calculate the part year by dividing the figure for the earlier year by the sum of the two years (ignoring the negative sign on the earlier year):

$$\frac{3,000}{3,000 + 3,000} = 0.5 \text{ of a year or six months}$$

Therefore, the payback period for the investment in the fish and chip van is three years and six months, compared with only three years for the hot dog van. Each project requires the same capital outlay, but on the basis of the time it will take to break even, Jimmy would be best advised to choose the hot dog van since he will recover his investment six months earlier.

21.4 Accounting rate of return

Whereas the payback period method is concerned with cash flows, the *accounting rate of return (ARR)* focuses on profit. Not only is this a more conventional measure of success in business than cash, but it also takes account of depreciation, which spreads the capital cost of acquiring or enhancing tangible non-current assets (such as plant and machinery) over their useful life. ARR is an accounting ratio and its *purpose* is to measure the relationship between profit (return) and capital employed (equity plus non-current liabilities). The investment project with the highest ARR is the one preferred.

As there are a number of different ways in which profit and capital employed can be defined, we can only compare ratios that have been calculated on the same basis. We will define *profit* as the average annual profit before interest and tax that is expected to be generated over the life of the project. We will define *capital employed* as the average capital employed to finance the project. The formula is:

$$\frac{\text{Average profit before interest and tax}}{\text{Average capital employed}} \times 100$$

Key definition

The accounting rate of return (ARR) is an accounting ratio that measures the predicted average profit before interest and tax as a percentage of the capital employed in a proposed capital investment project.

We will illustrate the ARR with an example. The owners of Cut Above Hairdressing are considering refurbishing the salon and are trying to decide between two different projects. Project A will require an initial investment of £19,000 (Year 0) but at the end of Year 1 the capital employed in the project will have increased to £21,000. Project B is more ambitious and will require an initial investment of £40,000 (Year 0) and by the end of Year 1 the capital employed in the project will have increased to £50,000. After a good deal of careful budgeting, the accountant has produced the following table showing the annual profits before interest and tax that the two projects are expected to generate.

Year	Project A £	Project B £
1	5,000	12,000
2	4,500	10,000
3	4,000	8,000
4	3,500	8,000
5	3,000	6,000

Before we can work out the accounting rate of return for the two projects, we need to calculate the averages.

	Year	Project A £	Project B £
Profit before interest	1	5,000	12,000
and tax (PBIT)	2	4,500	10,000
	3	4,000	8,000
	4	3,500	8,000
	5	3,000	6,000
		20,000	44,000
Average PBIT (÷ 5 years)		4,000	8,800
Capital employed (CE)	0	19,000	40,000
	1	21,000	50,000
		40,000	90,000
Average CE (÷ 2 years)		20,000	45,000

$$\frac{\text{Average PBIT}}{\text{Average CE}} \times 100 \qquad \frac{4,000}{20,000} \times 100 \qquad \frac{8,800}{45,000} \times 100$$

ARR		20%	20%

You can see from the results that although the average annual profit for Project B is a little more than twice as much as the average for Project A, both projects give a similar rate of return. This is because this technique also takes into account the average capital employed in the project, which for Project B is slightly more than twice the amount needed for Project A. However, both projects appear to be worthwhile and offer an accounting rate of return of 20%, which seems satisfactory when compared to an alternative, non-risky investment.

However, the accounting rate of return has not helped the owners of Cut Above Hairdressing choose between the two projects and they will need to take other factors into consideration, such as the cost of raising the larger sum of capital for Project B and the length of time that business will be disrupted by this more ambitious refurbishment. The most important thing to remember is that the calculation of the accounting rate of return is based on projected figures. Therefore, the technique relies on assumptions and best estimates and, however careful the accountant is in preparing the figures, it is difficult to predict future profits with accuracy.

Activity

Robbie Oliver already owns a successful restaurant in London. He is now considering opening a second restaurant in either Richmond or in Hampton. Property is slightly cheaper in Hampton, but sales are likely to be lower than in Richmond. The following table shows financial estimates for the two locations.

	Richmond £	Hampton £
Average sales revenue	872,000	500,000
Average costs and expenses	656,000	340,500
Average capital employed	1,440,000	800,000

Calculate the ARR for each restaurant, and decide which investment is the more favourable of the two.

Before you can use the formula, you need to calculate the average profit. Drawing on your knowledge of financial accounting you should remember that profit is sales less all the costs of sales and expenses. Check your answer against the following:

	Richmond £	Hampton £
Average sales revenue	872,000	500,000
Average costs and expenses	(656,000)	(340,500)
Average PBIT	216,000	159,500

	Richmond	Hampton
$\dfrac{\text{Average PBIT} \times 100}{\text{Average CE}}$	$\dfrac{216,000}{1,440,000} \times 100$	$\dfrac{159,500}{800,000} \times 100$
ARR	15%	20%

If we rank these projects by their ARR, the Hampton restaurant is ranked first, as the rate of return is 20% compared with 15% for the Richmond restaurant. However, Robbie would be well advised not to base his decision purely on this method of investment appraisal. For example, it would be useful to know what the payback period for each project would be. We cannot use this technique because the cash flow information is not available. Also, you can see that the Richmond restaurant requires more capital (an average of just under £1.5m compared with £800,000 for the Hampton restaurant), but the Richmond restaurant is likely to give a significantly higher average annual profit in absolute terms (£216,000 compared with £159,500 for the Hampton restaurant).

Assuming that the capital required for the Richmond restaurant is available for investment, and since the Hampton restaurant requires considerably less, what is Robbie going to do with the difference? He could deposit it in a bank or building society, but the return would be likely to be much less than the 15% for the Richmond restaurant. He might want to consider investing in a similar project, but this might not be possible.

Robbie may find it useful to calculate the ARR for each year of the project and examine the incremental effects. In the early years, a project tends to have a lower ARR (because revenues are growing and assets are new), whereas in later years, the ARR is likely to be higher (because revenues are higher but the net book value of assets is lower).

21.5 Advantages and disadvantages

21.5.1 Simple payback period

The calculation of the payback period is very simple, the results are easily understood by managers who are non-accountants and it allows different investment projects to be compared. The other main *advantages of the simple payback period method* are:

- It is useful for comparing risky projects where the prediction of cash flows after the first few years is difficult, due to possible changes in the business environment. For example, changes in technology could make a product obsolete in a year or so, although the current market seems assured.
- It is useful where short-term cash flows are more important than long-term cash flows. For example, if the business has insufficient capital to sustain long-term objectives, it is little use aiming for long-term profitability if the business becomes insolvent six months later.
- It is useful if borrowing or gearing is a concern.

The main *disadvantages of the simple payback period method* are:

- It is difficult to estimate the amount and timing of future cash flows.
- It ignores cash flows after the payback period.
- It ignores profitability. Therefore, the project with the shortest payback period might be chosen, even though an alternative project with a longer payback period might be more profitable.
- It ignores the size of the investment; therefore, the project with a smaller initial investment may have a shorter payback period than an alternative project that requires a larger investment but is more profitable in the long term.

- It ignores the time value of money because it gives net cash flows in later years the same importance as those in Year 1, even though cash received this year is worth more than the same amount at a later date.

Activity

Returning to the example of the Cheddar Cheese Company Ltd, which packing machine would you recommend the directors purchase on the basis of the payback period method?

Your answer should be Machine 1, because this has a payback period of only three years compared with more than four years for the other two machines. Check your calculations against the following workings.

Year	Machine 1		Machine 2		Machine 3	
	Net cash flow	Cumulative net cash flow	Net cash flow	Cumulative net cash flow	Net cash flow	Cumulative net cash flow
	£	£	£	£	£	£
0	(150,000)	(150,000)	(150,000)	(150,000)	(150,000)	(150,000)
1	60,000	(90,000)	20,000	(130,000)	10,000	(140,000)
2	50,000	(40,000)	30,000	(100,000)	20,000	(120,000)
3	40,000	0	40,000	(60,000)	30,000	(90,000)
4	30,000	30,000	50,000	(10,000)	40,000	(50,000)
5	20,000	50,000	60,000	50,000	150,000	100,000

Payback period:

$$4 \text{ years} + \frac{10,000}{10,000 + 50,000} \qquad 4 \text{ years} + \frac{50,000}{50,000 + 100,000}$$

3 years   4.17 years   4.33 years

However, if the directors relied solely on the payback period and chose Machine 1, they would not be taking account of the fact that Machine 3 is likely to give the greatest return of cash, which is what we observed when we looked at this example in section 21.2. This illustrates the disadvantage we mentioned that the simple payback period ignores any cash flows that occur after the initial investment has been recovered.

We used Microsoft® Excel to calculate the payback period for the Cheddar Cheese Company Ltd and Figure 21.2 shows you the formulae we used.

Figure 21.2 Cheddar Cheese Company Ltd payback period formulae

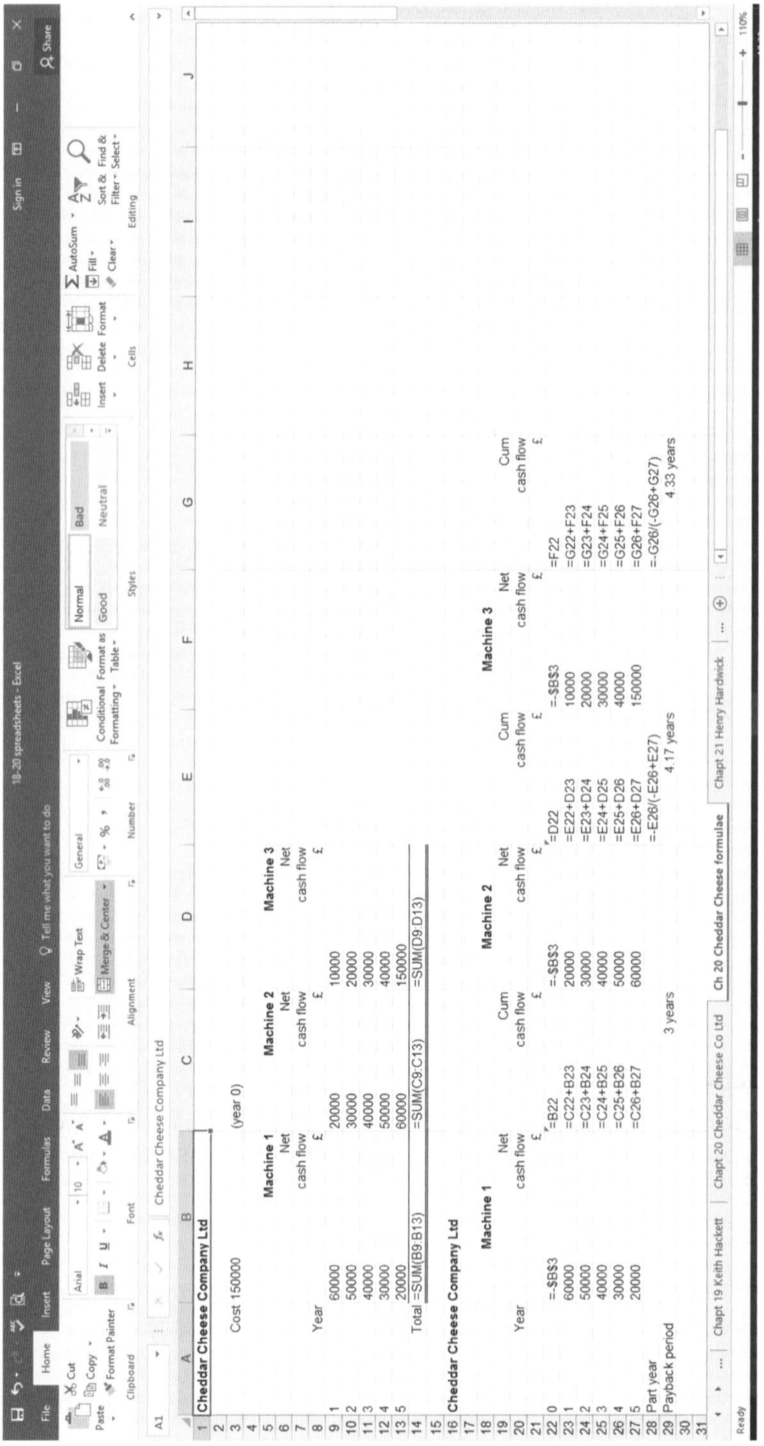

Cheddar Cheese Company Ltd

Cost 150000 (year 0)

	Machine 1	Machine 2	Machine 3
	Net cash flow £	Net cash flow £	Net cash flow £
Year			
1	60000	20000	10000
2	50000	30000	20000
3	40000	40000	30000
4	30000	50000	40000
5	20000	60000	150000
Total	=SUM(B9:B13)	=SUM(C9:C13)	=SUM(D9:D13)

Cheddar Cheese Company Ltd

	Machine 1		Machine 2		Machine 3	
	Net cash flow £	Cum cash flow £	Net cash flow £	Cum cash flow £	Net cash flow £	Cum cash flow £
Year						
0	=-B3	=B22	=-B3	=D22	=-B3	=F22
1	60000	=C22+B23	20000	=E22+D23	10000	=G22+F23
2	50000	=C23+B24	30000	=E23+D24	20000	=G23+F24
3	40000	=C24+B25	40000	=E24+D25	30000	=G24+F25
4	30000	=C25+B26	50000	=E25+D26	40000	=G25+F26
5	20000	=C26+B27	60000	=E26+D27	150000	=G26+F27
Part year				=E26/(-E26+E27)		=-G26/(-G26+G27)
Payback period		3 years		4.17 years		4 33 years

Chapt 19 Keith Hackett | Chapt 20 Cheddar Cheese Co Ltd | Ch 20 Cheddar Cheese formulae | Chapt 21 Henry Hardwick | ...

21.5.2 Accounting rate of return

Like the simple payback period, the calculation of the ARR is very simple, the results are easily understood by managers who are non-accountants and it allows different investment projects to be compared. The other main *advantages* of the ARR are:

• The entire life of the project is taken into account.
• The technique is compatible with ROCE, a similar ratio used in financial accounting for assessing the financial performance of the business.

However, ARR leaves many questions unanswered and is not sufficient on its own for making capital investment decisions. The other main *disadvantages* of the ARR are:

• There is no standard definition of terms used in the formula, which makes comparison of ratios that have not used the same definitions unreliable.
• Averages can be misleading as they are hypothetical values; the actual figure in any year may be higher or lower.
• It does not take into account the benefit of earning a larger proportion of the total profit in the early years of the project.
• It is based on profit, yet the crucial factor in investment decisions is cash flow.
• It does not take account of the timing of profits or cash.
• There is no guidance on what is an acceptable rate of return.
• It ignores the time value of money.

21.6 Investment decisions based on both methods

So far, we have implied that capital investment decisions are based on only one method. However, this is not the case as the disadvantages of one particular method can be offset by the information provided by an alternative method. We will illustrate this by returning to our example of the Cheddar Cheese Company.

Activity

The directors of the Cheddar Cheese Company Ltd have a choice of three cheese packing machines, each of which would cost £150,000 and have an estimated useful economic life of five years, with no residual value. Estimate the annual profits for each machine by deducting the annual depreciation charge from the annual cash flows, using the straight-line method. Then calculate the ARR for the three machines and consider this information with the payback periods you calculated in section 21.5.

The first step is to calculate the annual depreciation charge. You will remember that the formula for the straight-line method is:

$$\frac{\text{Cost}}{\text{Useful life}} = \frac{£150,000}{5 \text{ years}} = £30,000$$

The following table shows the deduction of the annual depreciation charge of £30,000 from the annual cash flows to calculate the annual profit or loss for each machine.

Year	Machine 1		Machine 2		Machine 3	
	Cash flow	Profit/(loss)	Cash flow	Profit/(loss)	Cash flow	Profit/(loss)
	£	£	£	£	£	£
1	60,000	30,000	20,000	(10,000)	10,000	(20,000)
2	50,000	20,000	30,000	0	20,000	(10,000)
3	40,000	10,000	40,000	10,000	30,000	0
4	30,000	0	50,000	20,000	40,000	10,000
5	20,000	(10,000)	60,000	30,000	150,000	120,000
Total		50,000		50,000		100,000
Average (÷ 5 years)		10,000		10,000		20,000

$\frac{\text{Average PBIT}}{\text{Capital employed}} \times 100$	$\frac{10,000}{150,000} \times 100$	$\frac{10,000}{150,000} \times 100$		$\frac{20,000}{150,000} \times 100$
ARR	7%	7%		13%
Payback period	3 years	4.17 years		4.33 years

In section 21.2 we noted that both Machine 1 and Machine 2 are expected to give a total net cash flow of £200,000 over the five-year period, which suggests that perhaps either would be a worthwhile investment. However, cash is not the same as profit and you can now see that although both machines will generate an average profit of £10,000 over the life of the project, averages can be misleading. In the case of Machine 1, this project will stop making profits after Year 3 (breaking even in Year 4 and making a loss of £10,000 by Year 5). In the case of Machine 2, the project will make a loss of £10,000 in Year 1, break even in Year 2 and not start generating profits until Year 3. These differences are not revealed by the ARR, which shows the same low return over the life of the project for both machines.

The ARR for Machine 3 suggests that this would be the most favourable investment as it offers almost twice the return of either Machine 1 or Machine 2. However, when we calculated the payback periods in section 21.5, we ranked Machine 3 last because it would take the longest to recover the initial investment (four years and four months compared to three years for Machine 1 and four years and two months for Machine 2). The directors of the Cheddar Cheese Company Ltd may want to take this into consideration when making a decision, as a short payback period is important if liquidity is a problem, gearing is a concern or borrowing is involved. For example, if debt finance is being used, a short payback period means less interest to pay and lower risk to the lender that the business will not be able to repay the loan.

Table 21.1 summarizes the key characteristics of the two methods we have examined in this chapter.

Table 21.1   Comparison of non-discounting methods of investment appraisal

Characteristic	Simple payback period method	Accounting rate of return
Focus	Cash flows	Profits
Nature	Measures time taken to recover investment	Assesses profitability of investment
Assumptions	Value and amount of cash flows	Reliability of annual profits

21.7 Conclusions

Capital investment appraisal provides accounting information that helps managers choose between different long-term projects that involve the investment of large sums of money. In a business context, owners and managers need to evaluate potential projects carefully and select the investment that is likely to give the highest financial return. One of the main features of capital investment decisions is the difficulty in predicting events that could affect the future returns from an investment project; both financial and non-financial factors need to be considered.

In this chapter we have examined two methods that provide information for capital investment appraisal. The simple payback period method focuses on early cash flows and gives information on how soon the capital invested is likely to be recovered by calculating the number of years it is expected for the project to break even. The accounting rate of return method focuses on profitability over the life of the project by expressing average profit as a percentage of the average capital employed. These methods offer a number of different advantages and disadvantages, but the main drawback is that they do not take account of the time value of money. In the next chapter we will be looking at discounted cash methods that address this deficiency.

It is important to remember that the usefulness of the results of the different methods for evaluating potential investment projects depends on whether the figures are based on realistic predictions. The further into the future the estimate is, the higher the level of uncertainty. We have mentioned a number of times in this book that accounting is not an exact science and you should be aware by now that a considerable amount of accounting information is based on estimated figures.

References

Chittenden, F. and Derregia, M. (2004) *Capital Investment Decision-Making: Some Results from Studying Entrepreneurial Businesses*, Briefing paper, London: ICAEW.

Discussion questions

1 Discuss the purpose of capital investment appraisal.

2 Discuss the advantages and disadvantages of the payback period method.

3 Discuss the advantages and disadvantages of the accounting rate of return.

Practice questions

4 Explain the purpose of the payback period method and the accounting rate of return.

5 The managing director of Stuart's Boatyard Ltd has £500,000 to invest in a new marine project and has asked you to provide information that will help him choose which is the more favourable of two potential projects. Details of the annual net cash flows are as follows:

Year	Project 1	Project 2
	£	£
1	80,000	90,000
2	100,000	110,000
3	180,000	190,000
4	140,000	110,000
5	100,000	80,000

Required

(a) Calculate the payback period for each project.

(b) Recommend which of the two projects is likely to be the better investment, giving reasons to support your advice.

(c) Comment on any limitations of the method you have used.

6 Henry Hardwick is planning to buy a bed-and-breakfast business in the South of France. He finds two potential businesses. Business A is located in a popular area where demand has been increasing, whereas Business B is in an area where demand has been falling. The vendors of the two businesses have provided the following estimates for the next three years.

	Business A	Business B
	€	€
Initial capital required	400,000	400,000
Pre-tax profit Year 1	60,000	100,000
Pre-tax profit Year 2	80,000	80,000
Pre-tax profit Year 3	100,000	60,000

Required

(a) Calculate the accounting rate of return for each project.

(b) Comment on your results and determine which of the two projects would be the better investment, giving reasons to support your advice.

(c) Comment on any limitations of the method you have used.

7 The owners of Film Animation Ltd wish to expand the business by investing in new technology. They have the necessary capital and have identified two potential projects, only one of which can be financed. The details are as follows:

	Project A	Project B
	£	£
Average sales	318,500	358,000
Average cost of sales including expenses	240,500	264,400
Average capital employed	650,000	780,000

(a) Calculate the accounting rate of return for each project.

(b) Recommend which of the two projects is likely to be the better investment, giving reasons to support your advice.

(c) Comment on any limitations of the method you have used.

8 Wren Electronics Ltd has capital available for investment in new equipment and the directors are considering two five-year projects, only one of which can be financed. Details of the annual net cash flows are as follows:

Year	Equipment 1	Equipment 2
	£	£
1	5,000	20,000
2	17,000	30,000
3	42,000	20,000
4	30,000	20,000
5	10,000	20,000

In both cases, the project will require an average investment of £50,000. Annual profit before interest and tax will be based on net cash flows less annual depreciation on the equipment. This will be based on the straight-line method over five years with no residual value at the end of the project. You should assume that the annual cash flows shown in the above table arise evenly throughout the year.

(a) Calculate the payback period for each project.

(b) Calculate the accounting rate of return for each project.

(c) Recommend which of the two projects is likely to be the better investment, giving reasons to support your advice.

(d) Comment on any limitations of the methods you have used.

 Suggested research questions for dissertation students

Students interested in capital investment appraisal may wish to investigate one or more of the following research questions:

- What factors influence the choice of capital investment appraisal technique?
- Are capital investment appraisal tools based on a large company template appropriate for SMEs?
- How do firms make capital investment decisions in developing countries?

Preliminary reading

Alkaraan, F. and Northcott, D. (2006) 'Strategic capital investment decision-making: A role for emergent analysis tools? A study of practice in large UK manufacturing companies', *British Accounting Review*, 28(2), pp. 149–173.

Chittenden, F. and Derregia, M. (2004) *Capital Investment Decision-Making: Some Results from Studying Entrepreneurial Businesses*, Briefing paper, London: ICAEW.

CIMA (2009) *Management Accounting Tools for Today and Tomorrow*, London: Chartered Institute of Management Accountants. Available from: www.cimaglobal.com/Documents/Thought_leadership_docs/CIMA%20Tools%20and%20Techniques%2030-11-09%20PDF.pdf (Accessed 11 June 2016).

Harris, E.P. and El-Massri, M. (2011) 'Capital investment appraisal', in Abdel-Kader, M.G. (ed.), *Review of Management Accounting Research*, Basingstoke: Palgrave Macmillan.

Mitchell, F. and Reid, G. (2000) 'Problems, challenges and opportunities: Small business as a setting for management accounting research', *Management Accounting Research*, 11(4), pp. 385–390.

Nandan, R. (2010) 'Management accounting needs of SMEs and the role of professional accountants: A renewed research agenda', *Journal of Management Accounting Research*, 8(1), pp. 65–78.

Perren, L. and Grant, P. (2000) 'The evolution of management accounting routines in small businesses: A social construction perspective', *Management Accounting Research*, 11(4), pp. 391–411.

Verbeeten, M. (2006) 'Do organizations adopt sophisticated capital budgeting practices to deal with uncertainty in the investment decision? A research note', *Management Accounting Research*, 17(1), pp. 106–120.

22 Discounted cash flow methods

Learning objectives

When you have studied this chapter, you should be able to:

- Explain the purpose of discounted cash flow techniques
- Calculate and interpret the net present value for an investment project
- Calculate and interpret the internal rate of return for an investment project
- Calculate and interpret the discounted payback period for an investment project
- Describe the advantages and disadvantages of these three techniques

22.1 Introduction

In the previous chapter we looked at the usefulness of the simple payback period method and the accounting rate of return as tools for providing information when a long-term capital investment decision has to be taken. However, we concluded that both techniques suffer from the serious limitation that they do not take account of the time value of money. Since decisions concerning the investment of large amounts of capital in potential projects are crucial in business, discounted cash flow methods have been developed to provide managers with sophisticated discounting techniques. The principle of discounting is now so important that it is also used in financial accounting.

We start by explaining the concept of the time value of money. This is a fairly straightforward principle and, once you have mastered it, you will find the calculations in this chapter relatively simple. We introduce you to three discounted cash flow methods used in investment appraisal. All three methods take account of the time value of money.

22.2 Time value of money

In the previous chapter we looked at two of the main methods used to support capital investment decisions. The simple payback period method focuses on early cash flows and calculates the time it is expected to take to recover the capital invested. The accounting rate of return is an accounting ratio that expresses the average profit over the life of the project as a percentage of the average capital employed in the investment. One of the main criticisms of these techniques is that they do not take account of the *time value of money*. In this chapter we are going to look at three *discounted cash flow* techniques that address this deficiency: the net present value, the internal rate of return and the discounted payback period (see Figure 22.1).

Figure 22.1   Main methods of investment appraisal

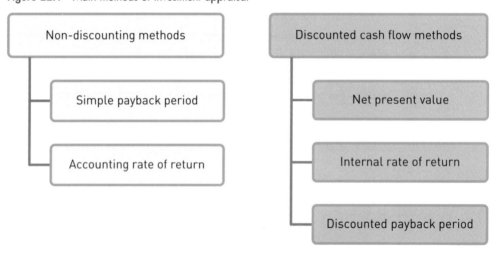

The *time value of money* is the concept that cash received at an earlier date is worth more than a similar amount of cash received later. This is because the cash received earlier can be invested to earn interest in the intervening period. The interest forgone in this way is known as the *opportunity cost of capital*. Similarly, because the cash paid out later is not available for investment today, it is worth less than a similar amount received at an earlier date.

Key definitions

The time value of money is the concept that cash received today is worth more than a similar sum received at a later date because of the opportunity cost of capital.

The opportunity cost is the value of the benefit sacrificed when one course of action is chosen in preference to an alternative. It represents the forgone potential benefit from the best alternative course of action that has been rejected.

The longer we have to wait for the money, the less it is worth. For example, supposing someone wanted to borrow money from you now and promised to pay you £100 in a year's time, how much would you be willing to lend them if the usual interest rate is 10%? One concern you may have is whether you are likely to be paid the £100. If you consider it is doubtful, you may decide not to lend the money or you may decide to charge a high rate of interest because of the risk. If you consider the loan is very safe, you may be willing to lend £90.90. In a year's time this would give interest of £9.10 to make the sum of £100 which you are repaid.

Activity

How much would you be willing to lend now, if the interest rate is 15% and the borrower promises to repay £500 in 3 years' time?

You have probably had to make some complex calculations to arrive at the correct answer of £329. However, there is an easy method that makes use of the *present value table* in the Appendix, which shows the present value factors for future years at a range of different interest rates. For convenience, Table 22.1 shows an extract.

Table 22.1   Present value table for £1 at compound interest (extract)

Future years	Interest rate			
	1%	5%	10%	15%
1	0.990	0.952	0.909	0.870
2	0.980	0.907	0.826	0.756
3	0.971	0.864	0.751	0.658
4	0.961	0.823	0.683	0.572
5	0.951	0.784	0.621	0.497
6	0.942	0.746	0.564	0.432
7	0.933	0.711	0.513	0.376
8	0.923	0.677	0.467	0.327
9	0.914	0.645	0.424	0.284
10	0.905	0.614	0.386	0.247

The question we are trying to answer is: What is the present value of £500 received in 3 years' time, if the interest rate is 15%? Look down the left-hand column until you reach future Year 3 and then look along the row to the 15% interest column. The discount factor is 0.658, which is the discount factor for £1. It means that the present value of £1 received in 3 years' time is only £0.658. If you multiply £500 by the discount factor of 0.658, the result is £329, which is the amount you would be willing to lend now. You can check this by working out 15% compound interest on £329 for 3 years.

Year		£
0	Principal	329.00
1	Interest 15%	49.35
		378.35
2	Interest 15%	56.75
		435.10
3	Interest 15%	65.27
	Total	500.37

The time value of money underpins all discounted cash flow (DCF) techniques, which makes them much more sophisticated tools for appraising capital investment projects. The *purpose* of DCF techniques is to convert future cash flows into present-day values.

Key definition

Discounted cash flow (DCF) is a method that predicts the stream of cash inflows and outflows over the estimated life of a capital investment project and discounts them to present values using a cost of capital or hurdle rate.

The basic assumptions of discounted cash flow (DCF) are as follows:

- Cash is invested at the start of the year (Year 0).
- Future annual cash flows are certain (but in reality they are estimates).
- There is no inflation.
- Interest rates for lending and borrowing are the same.
- The interest rate is constant throughout the period.

We are now ready to look at the first method.

22.3 Net present value

The *net present value (NPV)* method uses discounting to convert the future cash flows of a project into present-day values. The *discount factor* is chosen on the basis of the required interest rate. Therefore, the net present value tells us how much better the return on a capital investment project will be than an alternative low risk investment.

Key definition

Net present value (NPV) is the difference between the total discounted values of the predicted net cash flows and the capital invested in a proposed capital investment project. When comparing capital investment projects, the project with the largest positive NPV is the one preferred.

Activity

Keith Hackett is considering whether to buy computer-aided design equipment that will improve his cash flows by £30,000 per annum for the next 5 years. At the end of this time, the equipment will have reached the end of its useful economic life as it will be out of date and have no residual value. The equipment will cost £75,000 and will be bought for cash. The cost of capital (the interest rate) that Keith is using as the discount factor is 15%. Calculate the NPV of this investment project using the following pro forma and the present value factors in the Appendix.

Year	Cash flow	Discount factor	Present value
	£	15%	£
0	(75,000)	1.000	(75,000)
1			
2			
3			
4			
5			
		NPV	

If you had problems with this activity, you may find the following comments helpful:

- The initial investment takes place in Year 0, which refers to the start of Year 1. It is shown in brackets because it is a negative cash flow.
- Cash flow x Discount factor = Present value
- The discount factor in Year 0 is 1.000 because this is the present year, not a future year.
- The NPV is the difference between the total of the present value (PV) of the future cash flows expected from the project (the discounted cash flows) and the initial capital invested. ('Net' always means something has been deducted.)

Check your answer against the following solution.

Year	Cash flow	Discount factor	Present value
	£	15%	£
0	(75,000)	1.000	(75,000)
1	30,000	0.870	26,100
2	30,000	0.756	22,680
3	30,000	0.658	19,740
4	30,000	0.572	17,160
5	30,000	0.497	14,910
		NPV	25,590

The results show that the NPV of the project is a positive £25,590, which means that Keith will be getting a return on his investment of 15% plus this amount. If the NPV had been 0, his return would be 15%. If the project had shown a negative NPV, the return would be less than 15%. If 15% represented the return on an alternative low risk investment, a negative NPV would indicate that the project under consideration would not be worthwhile. Therefore, the decision rule is to accept the project with the highest positive NPV.

22.4 Internal rate of return

The *internal rate of return* (IRR) uses the same principles as the NPV method, but the aim is to find the interest rate which gives a NPV of zero for the project. This is the rate at which the sum of the discounted values of the predicted cash flows is equal to the capital invested in a proposed investment project. The IRR allows us to show the return on the investment entirely as a percentage instead of measuring it partly as a percentage and partly as a financial figure.

Key definition

The internal rate of return (IRR) is the interest rate at which the total discounted values of the predicted net cash flows are equal to the capital invested in a proposed capital investment project. When evaluating a single project, the IRR will be chosen when it is higher than the cost of capital. When comparing projects, the project with the highest IRR is preferred.

Activity

In the previous example we concluded that at an interest rate of 15%, a positive NPV of £25,590 made Keith's investment worthwhile. In other words, Keith would be getting a return on the project in excess of 15%. Using the following pro forma and the present value factors in the Appendix, calculate the net present value for the project using interest rates of 20%, 25% and 30%.

Year	Cash flow	Discount factor	Present value	Discount factor	Present value	Discount factor	Present value
	£	20%	£	25%	£	30%	£
0	(75,000)	1.000	(75,000)	1.000	(75,000)	1.000	(75,000)
1	30,000						
2	30,000						
3	30,000						
4	30,000						
5	30,000						
		NPV	_____		_____		_____

Check your answer against the following solution.

Year	Cash flow	Discount factor	Present value	Discount factor	Present value	Discount factor	Present value
	£	20%	£	25%	£	30%	£
0	(75,000)	1.000	(75,000)	1.000	(75,000)	1.000	(75,000)
1	30,000	0.833	24,990	0.800	24,000	0.769	23,070
2	30,000	0.694	20,820	0.640	19,200	0.592	17,760
3	30,000	0.579	17,370	0.512	15,360	0.455	13,650
4	30,000	0.482	14,460	0.410	12,300	0.350	10,500
5	30,000	0.402	12,060	0.328	9,840	0.269	8,070
		NPV	14,700		5,700		(1,950)

We can summarize the information we now have as follows:

- Using an interest rate of 15%, the NPV is a positive £25,590.
- Using an interest rate of 20%, the NPV is a positive £14,700.
- Using an interest rate of 25%, the NPV is a positive £5,700.
- Using an interest rate of 30%, the NPV is a negative (£1,950).

We can conclude from this that the higher the interest rate used to discount the future cash flows, the smaller the NPV becomes, until it eventually becomes negative somewhere between 25% and 30%. The IRR lies at the point where the net present value changes from positive to negative, which is where the NPV is 0. This is illustrated in Figure 22.2 by plotting the NPVs on a graph against the appropriate interest rates. The interest rates are marked on the x axis, and net present values on the y axis.

Figure 22.2   Keith Hackett: internal rate of return

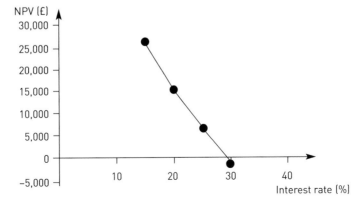

You will see that the line joining the four points is a slight curve, but for all practical purposes, we can assume that it is a straight line, provided the points are not too far apart. We shall use the data at 25% and 30% interest rates. The interest rate at which the line crosses the x axis, where NPV is 0, is somewhere between 25% and 30%; in other words, 25 + a number between 0 and 5 (30 – 25). The calculation of the IRR involves linear interpolation (linear, because it assumes a straight line) and the formula is as follows:

$$\text{Positive rate} + \left(\frac{\text{Positive NPV}}{\text{Positive NPV} + \text{Negative NPV}} \times \text{Range of rates} \right)$$

$$= 25 + \left(\frac{5,700}{5,700 + 1,950} \times (30 - 25) \right)$$

$$= 25 + (0.745098 \times 5) = 28.73\%$$

As you can see, Keith will get a return of 28.73% on the project. The figures in brackets represent the proportion of 5 that we require to be added to 25. The difference between the two NPVs (£5,700 positive and £1,950 negative) is actually the sum of the two figures, because we are ignoring the fact that the second figure is negative. If you find this difficult to understand, the following explanation may help. If you had £100 in the bank yesterday (a positive figure), and today find that you have an overdraft of £50 (a negative figure), how much money have you drawn out of the bank since yesterday? The answer is:

$$£100 + £50 = £150$$

22.5 Discounted payback period

In the previous chapter we explained that the simple payback period is widely used because it is important for the owners and managers of a business who are considering an investment project to know how long it will take before the capital invested has been recovered and the project begins to pay for itself. However, the drawback of the simple method is that it ignores the time value of money. This can be overcome by discounting the future cash flows.

> **Key definition**
>
> The discounted payback period method calculates the time required for the predicted discounted net cash flows to equal the capital invested in a proposed capital investment project. The project taking the shortest possible time is the one preferred.

Activity

In the previous chapter, we looked at the example of the Cheddar Cheese Company Ltd where we compared the simple payback period for three projects that involved investment in a packing machine. Using a spreadsheet and the following layout, calculate the discounted payback periods for each project. Then compare them with your earlier results and make recommendations to the directors.

Year	Cash flow	Discount factor	Present value	Cumulative cash flow
	£	10%	£	£
0				
1				
2				
3				
4				
5				

Check your calculations against the following:

Machine 1

Year	Cash flow	Discount factor	Present value	Cumulative cash flow
	£	10%	£	£
0	(150,000)	1.000	(150,000)	(150,000)
1	60,000	0.909	54,540	(95,460)
2	50,000	0.826	41,300	(54,160)
3	40,000	0.751	30,040	(24,120)
4	30,000	0.683	20,490	(3,630)
5	20,000	0.621	12,420	8,790

$$\text{Discounted payback period} = 4 \text{ years} + \frac{3,630}{3,630 + 8,790}$$

$$= 4.29 \text{ years}$$

Simple payback period   = 3 years

Machine 2

Year	Cash flow	Discount factor	Present value	Cumulative cash flow
	£	10%	£	£
0	(150,000)	1.000	(150,000)	(150,000)
1	20,000	0.909	18,180	(131,820)
2	30,000	0.826	24,780	(107,040)
3	40,000	0.751	30,040	(77,000)
4	50,000	0.683	34,150	(42,850)
5	60,000	0.621	37,260	(5,590)

Discounted payback period = Investment not recovered
Simple payback period   = 4.17 years

Machine 3

Year	Cash flow	Discount factor	Present value	Cumulative cash flow
	£	10%	£	£
0	(150,000)	1.000	(150,000)	(150,000)
1	10,000	0.909	9,090	(140,910)
2	20,000	0.826	16,520	(124,390)
3	30,000	0.751	22,530	(101,860)
4	40,000	0.683	27,320	(74,540)
5	150,000	0.621	93,150	18,610

$$\text{Discounted payback period} = 4 \text{ years} + \frac{74,540}{74,540 + 18,610}$$

= 4.8 years

Simple payback period   = 4.33 years

This exercise illustrates the difference it makes to the choice of project when the time value of money is taken into consideration in the calculation of the payback period. With an interest rate of 10%, you can see that the investment in Machine 1 will not be recovered at the end of Year 3 after all; instead, the directors will have to wait for 4 years and 3½ months (4.29 years), which is into the second quarter of Year 5. If you look at the results for Machine 2, the simple payback period was 4 years and 2 months (4.17 years), but now you can see that once the annual cash flows are discounted, the capital will not be recovered at all. Finally, the results for Machine 3 show that instead of being paid back in 4 years and 4 months (4.33 years), the discounted payback period shows it will not be paid pack for 4 years and 9½ months (4.8 years) and the company will have to wait until the last quarter of Year 5 to recover the capital.

You should have recommended Machine 1 as being the most favourable project in terms of its discounted payback period. Not only does this method consider the time value of money, but it also takes account of more of the future cash flows, since the discounted payback period is always longer than the payback period using the simple method.

22.6 Advantages and disadvantages

Like non-discounting methods of investment appraisal, discounted cash flow methods allow different investment projects to be compared. The other main *advantages* of discounted cash flow methods are:

- They use the concept of the time value of money.
- The NPV and IRR methods take account of the entire life of the project (the discounted payback period only considers the project up to the payback period).
- They permit comparisons with other opportunities to be made.

Although we have suggested that discounted cash flow methods have been developed to overcome the limitations of the simple payback method and the accounting rate of return, they are not without their limitations. The main *disadvantages* of discounted cash flow methods are:

- It is difficult to determine the appropriate interest rate to use and predict the cash flows over the life of the project.
- The calculations are complex.
- They do not take account of non-financial factors such as the flexibility of plant and equipment purchased.
- Some managers may have difficulty in understanding the results.

We can conclude from this analysis that although the net present value, internal rate of return and discounted payback period are useful methods, they are also complex and managers with little knowledge of accounting may have difficulty in understanding them. The main purpose of management accounting is to help managers by providing information that will help them carry out their responsibilities of planning, controlling and decision making. Therefore, giving information that is hard to interpret makes it less useful.

Activity

What sort of problems do you think might be associated with investment appraisal techniques based on discounted cash flows?

As well as the management team having problems in understanding the results of the calculations, the accountant may have difficulty in obtaining the figures to do the calculations. Indeed, this is a problem that is common to all investment appraisal techniques. As far as DCF methods are concerned, the difficulty lies in predicting the amount of cash inflows and outflows over the life of the project. Some projects last for many years and it will not be possible for the accountant to forecast the amounts with any certainty. For this reason, many firms prefer the payback period, because it is based on the earliest cash flows. One cash flow that can arise at the end of a project is the sale of the machinery and equipment that was originally purchased for the project. With a large investment in machinery, the *residual value* (the second-hand or scrap value) may be very high, even after many years of use. The expected proceeds from the sale of such assets must be shown as a cash inflow in the calculations.

Another problem is the choice of *discount factor*. In this chapter we have used a number of different rates as illustrations, but management (with advice from the accountant) must decide which rate to use. You will appreciate that the choice of discount factor is critical to the results. Most commonly, businesses base their choice on the current rate of return received on capital employed, the current cost of capital, the return on other projects available or the rate that could be received if the business were to invest the capital externally. When answering questions on capital appraisal, it is easy for students to concentrate on the calculations and forget these other aspects. The calculations are relatively easy, but the above issues make capital investment appraisal techniques complex. However, it is vital that the management accountant makes use of them, as they assist management in determining the likely return they will get from a long-term project and deciding whether it is acceptable in view of the risks involved.

Table 22.2 summarizes the key characteristics of the methods we have examined in this chapter.

Table 22.2 Comparison of discounted cash flow methods used for investment appraisal

Characteristic	Net present value	Internal rate of return	Discounted payback period
Focus	Cash flows	Cash flows	Cash flows
Nature	Measures the present value of cash flows	Determines the rate of return at which the investment breaks even	Measures the time taken to recover the investment
Assumptions	Value and amount of cash flows and the interest rate	Value and amount of cash flows, and the interest rate	Value and amount of cash flows, and the interest rate

In the past it was argued that the investment appraisal methods emphasized by academics were not widely used in practice. However, a study by Arnold and Hatzopoulos (2000) combined the results of a survey of firms in the UK with data collected over a 22-year period and found a substantial narrowing of the gap between theory and practice. More recently, a survey of the UK and international members of CIMA

(2009) shows that of the range of methods we have discussed in this chapter and the last, the most widely used methods are ranked as follows:

1. Net present value
2. Simple payback method
3. Internal rate of return
4. Discounted payback method
5. Accounting rate of return.

The CIMA survey found that the use of leasing, renting, outsourcing and subcontracting reduces the effect of uncertainty on decisions and increases the resources available for a much lower initial outlay. In some cases, it avoids capital investment decisions altogether.

22.7 Incorporating environmental management accounting information in capital investment decisions

A further limitation of the capital investment appraisal methods we have described is that they overlook the benefits and/or cost savings that cannot be quantified easily in monetary terms. As a result, managers must conduct a careful and detailed investigation of project opportunities to ensure that all the financial and non-financial benefits have been identified before conducting a capital investment appraisal.

In Chapter 20 we explained how *environmental management accounting (EMA)* information can also be used to improve the decisions companies make about the environmental impacts of their operations. As EMA recognizes all the environmental costs and benefits associated with an investment project, it helps support capital investment decisions in environmentally efficient equipment and technology.

To illustrate the importance of using EMA information when taking capital investment decisions, we will return to the example of Euro Cars GmbH. The company has just received a letter from its waste management agent about a forthcoming increase in the waste water treatment fees, and management is seeking ways to reduce the creation of waste water at the company. As part of the manufacturing process, each vehicle's chassis is sprayed with a special anti-rust paint. To create the paint, fresh water is pumped to the factory, specially heated in a storage tank and mixed with paint chemicals. The paint in the storage tank is then fed into a special coating machine. Any excess paint from the coating process is classified as white water and collected by the machine's waste water collection system. Once the waste water has cooled in the collection system, it is pumped directly to a waste water treatment facility.

The company is considering investing in a new filtration machine that would allow most of the waste water to be recycled. The filtration machine will receive the waste water from the coating machine, filter it and feed most of the still warm, treated water immediately back into the painting process. It is estimated that the filtration machine will recover 50% of the paint chemicals and 90% of the water. Based on an estimated annual usage of 800,000 kg of paint chemicals and 400,000 litres of fresh water, the company's accountant predicts that the filtration machine will incur the following costs and cost savings over its useful life of four years.

Investment appraisal for filtration machine

	Year 0	Year 1	Year 2	Year 3	Year 4
	€	€	€	€	€
Cost of new equipment	(1,300,000)				
Chemical agents for paint/water separation		(10,000)	(10,000)	(10,000)	(10,000)
Power costs for new equipment		(5,000)	(5,000)	(5,000)	(5,000)
Staff costs for new equipment		(30,000)	(30,000)	(30,000)	(30,000)
Waste water treatment fees avoided		55,000	55,000	55,000	55,000
Paint chemicals recovered from waste water		360,000	360,000	360,000	360,000
Annual savings (costs)	(1,300,000)	370,000	370,000	370,000	370,000
Discount factor (10% cost of capital)	1.000	0.9091	0.8264	0.7513	0.6830
Present value	(1,300,000)	336,367	305,768	277,981	252,710

$$\text{NPV (total of the present values)} = (€127,174)$$

The accountant estimates that the filtration machine will allow the annual recovery of 400,000 kg of paint chemicals and prevent 360,000 litres of waste water having to be sent to the waste water treatment facility. The company expects all projects to pay back the original investment within three years and achieve an IRR of 12%. The company's cost of capital or interest rate is 10%. Based on the figures in the above table, the project has a negative NPV of €127,174, which indicates that it should be rejected under this method of investment appraisal. We can use Microsoft® Excel's inbuilt IRR formula to find the interest rate at which the project's NPV is zero. We do this by entering the data for the yearly undiscounted annual savings and then entering the IRR function in cell A2.

	A	B	C	D	E	F
1	Annual savings (costs)	(1,300,000)	370,000	370,000	370,000	370,000
2	=IRR(B1:F1,0.1)					

You must enter the IRR formula by entering the formula exactly as shown in cell B2. The IRR for the filtration project is approximately 5.40% which is below the company's target IRR rate of 12%. We can also calculate the project's simple payback period using the following table.

Year	Cash flow	Cumulative cash flow
	€	€
0	(1,300,000)	(1,300,000)
1	370,000	(930,000)
2	370,000	(560,000)
3	370,000	(190,000)
4	370,000	180,000

The cumulative cash flows show that the payback period lies somewhere between Years 3 and 4, and we can calculate the part year by dividing the cumulative cash flow for Year 3 by the sum of the figures for Year 3 and Year 4 (ignoring the negative sign on Year 3).

$$3 \text{ years} + \frac{190,000}{190,000 + 180,000} = 3.51 \text{ years}$$

The simple payback period for the investment in the filtration machine is approximately three years and six months, which is beyond the company's maximum period of three years.

Based on the results of our investment appraisal, management should reject the filtration project as it does not provide a suitable return according to the company's target NPV, IRR or payback criteria.

Activity

Do you think the management of Euro Cars GmbH should reject the opportunity to invest in the filtration project? Assess whether the company's management accountant has considered all the environmental financial and non-financial costs and benefits associated with the investment project.

Although the accountant has considered most of the more obvious direct costs and benefits, he has failed to consider all of the environmental costs and benefits that result from the project, including its impact on the company's annual indirect utility overheads:

- The cost savings from reducing the company's usage of fresh water. As fresh water costs €0.12 per litre and the filtration will reduce the annual need for fresh water by 360,000 litres (400,000 litres x 90% is recycled), the company will save €43,200 per year.
- A reduction in energy use for pumping fresh water (i.e. the company can effectively reuse 90% of the fresh water in the next period, saving on pumping costs).

It costs €0.01 per litre to pump fresh water to the paint storage tank and 360,000 recycled litres will no longer require pumping, saving €3,600 in energy costs per year.
- A reduction in energy use for heating fresh water for the painting process. It costs €0.02 per litre to heat fresh water for paint mixing and 360,000 recycled litres will not require heating, saving €7,200 per annum in energy costs.
- A reduction in energy use for pumping waste water to the waste treatment facility. It costs €0.03 per litre to pump waste water to the treatment facility and the 360,000 litres of recycled water will not require disposal, saving €10,800 in disposal costs per annum.
- The reduction in regulatory compliance, inspection and permit costs (if necessary). Let us assume that these are zero in this case.

Non-financial environmental factors that may be relevant include:

- The reduced risk of environmental liability from waste water accidents and spillage.
- The increased reputational impact from the investment.
- The learning and experience obtained from undertaking the environmental project. This may allow management to identify other opportunities for environmental improvement within the company.

Once these additional environmental costs and benefits are taken into consideration, the filtration investment becomes a much more attractive investment as shown below.

	Year 0	Year 1	Year 2	Year 3	Year 4
	€	€	€	€	€
Original annual costs or savings	(1,300,000)	370,000	370,000	370,000	370,000
Additional environmental costs:					
Reduced usage of fresh water		43,200	43,200	43,200	43,200
Reduced fresh water heating costs		7,200	7,200	7,200	7,200
Reduced fresh water pumping costs		3,600	3,600	3,600	3,600
Reduced waste water pumping costs		10,800	10,800	10,800	10,800
Total annual savings (costs)	(1,300,000)	434,800	434,800	434,800	434,800
Discount factor (10% cost of capital)	1.000	0.9091	0.8264	0.7513	0.6830
PV	(1,300,000)	395,277	359,319	326,665	296,968

Revised NPV (total of the present values) = €78,229

Rather than providing annual cost savings of €370,000, the revised environmental cost analysis shows that the filtration project results in annual savings of €434,800, an increase of 64,800 per year. Using the revised figures in the above table, the project now generates a positive net present value of €78,229. The project's IRR is now approximately 12.75%, which exceeds the company's target rate of return on projects.

	A	B	C	D	E	F
4	Annual savings (costs)	(1,300,000)	434,800	434,800	434,800	434,800
5	=IRR(B4:F4,0.1)					

Using the revised figures, the filtration project's simple payback period is calculated as follows.

Year	Cash flow	Cumulative cash flow
	€	€
0	(1,300,000)	(1,300,000)
1	434,800	(865,200)
2	434,800	(430,400)
3	434,800	4,400
4	434,800	439,200

The cumulative cash flows now show that the payback period lies somewhere between Year 2 and Year 3:

$$2 \text{ years} + \frac{430{,}400}{430{,}400 + 4{,}400} = 2.99 \text{ years}$$

Therefore, the simple payback period for the investment in the filtration machine is now just under 3 years, which is within the company's target period.

Regardless of the non-financial benefits from the filtration project, based on the results of our revised investment appraisal incorporating the environmental costs and benefits, we can now advise management to accept this project. We can conclude from this example that traditional approaches to investment appraisal do not take account of the full costs and benefits associated with environmental improvement projects.

22.8 Conclusions

There are a number of different investment appraisal methods that can provide useful information to aid capital investment decisions. In the last chapter we introduced the simple payback period method and the accounting rate of return. In this chapter we have described three techniques that are based on discounted cash flows: net present value, internal rate of return and discounted payback period. Each method provides different information and each method has its advantages and disadvantages.

The specific information required for discounted cash flow methods presents some problems, but if available these more sophisticated methods offer the advantage of incorporating the time value of money in the calculation of return. Guided by the accountant, management will have to decide which methods are appropriate to aid decisions. In many companies, multiple methods are used to overcome the individual weaknesses inherent in the individual methods.

References

Arnold, G.C. and Hatzopoulos, P.D. (2000) 'The theory-practice gap in capital budgeting: Evidence from the United Kingdom', *Journal of Business Finance and Accounting*, 27(5–6), pp. 603–626.

CIMA (2009) *Management Accounting Tools for Today and Tomorrow*, London: Chartered Institute of Management Accountants. Available from: www.cima-global.com/Documents/Thought_leadership_docs/CIMA%20Tools%20and%20Techniques%2030-11-09%20PDF.pdf (Accessed 11 June 2016).

Discussion questions

1 Discuss the advantages and disadvantages of using discounted cash flow methods for capital investment appraisal.

2 Compare the net present value method with the internal rate of return.

Practice questions

3 Using the present value tables in the Appendix, and assuming a discount rate of 20%, answer the following questions:

(a) What will £68,000 invested now be worth in 2 years' time?
(b) What will £102,000 invested now be worth in 3 years' time?
(c) What will £153,000 invested now be worth in 4 years' time?
(d) What will £204,000 invested now be worth in 5 years' time?
(e) What will £306,000 invested now be worth in 10 years' time?

4 Using the present value tables in the Appendix, select the correct answer to the following questions:

	(i)	(ii)	(iii)	(iv)
(a) PV of £1 received in 5 years' time with a 10% discount rate	£0.909	£0.683	£0.621	£0.565
(b) PV of £100 received in 10 years' time with a 15% discount rate	£150.00	£247.00	£500.00	£185.00

		(i)	(ii)	(iii)	(iv)
(c)	PV of £1,000 received in 20 years' time with a 20% discount rate	£500.00	£200.00	£40.00	£26.00
(d)	PV of £100 received at the end of each year for the next 5 years with a 12% discount rate	£360.50	£500.00	£567.00	£600.00
(e)	PV of £750 received at the end of each year for the next 3 years with an 18% discount rate	£2,174.00	£1,630.50	£405.00	£135.00

5 Kerry Melrose is considering an investment in audio visual equipment costing £10,000 for her business, Melrose Events. With the help of her accountant, Kerry has done her calculations on a cash basis and is assuming that the following annual cash flows will take place evenly throughout the year. She anticipates that the project will require the business to spend £5,000 on advertising in the first year, but it should generate £1,000 in revenue. The advertising costs are expected to reduce to £3,000 in the second year and generate £2,000 worth of business. In the third and fourth years, no advertising will be required and the revenue generated is expected to be £3,000 in Year 3 and £6,000 in Year 4. In Year 5 the project will generate £8,000 worth of business, but by the end of the year she expects the equipment will be obsolete, with no residual value.

Required

(a) Calculate the simple payback period and the net present value for the project using an interest rate of 12%.

(b) Interpret your results and recommend whether Kerry should go ahead with the project, giving reasons to support your advice.

(c) Comment on any financial considerations Kerry should bear in mind.

6 The managing director of Stuart's Boatyard Ltd has £500,000 to invest in a new marine project and has asked you to provide information that will help him choose which is the more favourable of two projects. Details of the annual cash flows are as follows and these are assumed to arise evenly throughout the year:

Year	Project 1 £	Project 2 £
1	80,000	90,000
2	100,000	110,000
3	180,000	190,000
4	140,000	110,000
5	100,000	80,000

Required

(a) Calculate the discounted payback period for each project and the net present value of each project using an interest rate of 6%.

(b) Recommend which of the two projects should be chosen, giving reasons to support your advice.

(c) Comment on any limitations of the techniques you have used.

7 Your Aunt Laura owns Bloomfield Laundry Ltd and has £50,000 to invest in new dryers. She has asked you to advise her on the financial viability of the project and tells you that she requires a 15% rate of return. The following projected annual cash flows are expected to be spread evenly throughout each year.

Year	£
1	10,000
2	25,000
3	25,000
4	20,000
5	10,000

Required

(a) Calculate the following in relation to the investment in the new dryers:
  (i) Net present value
  (ii) Discounted payback period
  (iii) Internal rate of return.

(b) Interpret your results and advise your aunt.

(c) Comment on any limitations of the techniques you have used.

8 Eagle Engineering Ltd is considering buying a hydraulic machine press that will improve cash flows by £60,000 per annum over the next five years. The cost of the machine is £150,000 to be paid in cash. At the end of the period, it will be obsolete and have no residual value. The company requires a return of 20%.

Required

(a) Calculate the NPV of the proposed investment in the machine using discount factors of 20%, 25% and 30%.

(b) Using data from your answer to (a) above, calculate the IRR of the investment project and interpret your results.

(c) Comment on the strengths and weaknesses of the capital investment appraisal method you have used.

Suggested research questions for dissertation students

Students interested in capital investment appraisal may wish to investigate one or more of the following research questions:

- What factors influence the choice of capital investment appraisal technique?
- Are capital investment appraisal tools based on a large company template appropriate for SMEs?
- How do firms make capital investment decisions in developing countries?

Preliminary reading

Alkaraan, F. and Northcott, D. (2006) 'Strategic capital investment decision-making: A role for emergent analysis tools? A study of practice in large UK manufacturing companies', *British Accounting Review*, 28(2), pp. 149–173.

Chittenden, F. and Derregia, M. (2004) *Capital Investment Decision-Making: Some Results from Studying Entrepreneurial Businesses*, Briefing paper, London: ICAEW.

CIMA (2009) *Management Accounting Tools for Today and Tomorrow*, London: Chartered Institute of Management Accountants. Available from: www.cima-global.com/Documents/Thought_leadership_docs/CIMA%20Tools%20and%20Techniques%2030-11-09%20PDF.pdf (Accessed 11 June 2016).

Harris, E.P. and El-Massri, M. (2011) 'Capital investment appraisal', in Abdel-Kader, M.G. (ed.), *Review of Management Accounting Research*, Basingstoke: Palgrave Macmillan.

Mitchell, F. and Reid, G. (2000) 'Problems, challenges and opportunities: Small business as a setting for management accounting research', *Management Accounting Research*, 11(4), pp. 385–390.

Nandan, R. (2010) 'Management accounting needs of SMEs and the role of professional accountants: A renewed research agenda', *Journal of Management Accounting Research*, 8(1), pp. 65–78.

Perren, L. and Grant, P. (2000) 'The evolution of management accounting routines in small businesses: A social construction perspective', *Management Accounting Research*, 11(4), pp. 391–411.

Verbeeten, M. (2006) 'Do organizations adopt sophisticated capital budgeting practices to deal with uncertainty in the investment decision? A research note', *Management Accounting Research*, 17(1), pp. 106–120.

Appendix: Present value tables

Table 1. Present value of £1 at compound interest rates

Future years							Interest rate								
	1%	2%	3%	4%	5%	6%	7%	8%	9%	10%	11%	12%	13%	14%	15%
1	0.990	0.980	0.971	0.962	0.952	0.943	0.935	0.926	0.917	0.909	0.901	0.893	0.885	0.877	0.870
2	0.980	0.961	0.943	0.925	0.907	0.890	0.873	0.857	0.842	0.826	0.812	0.797	0.783	0.769	0.756
3	0.971	0.942	0.915	0.889	0.864	0.840	0.816	0.794	0.772	0.751	0.731	0.712	0.693	0.675	0.658
4	0.961	0.924	0.888	0.855	0.823	0.792	0.763	0.735	0.708	0.683	0.659	0.636	0.613	0.592	0.572
5	0.951	0.906	0.863	0.822	0.784	0.747	0.713	0.681	0.650	0.621	0.593	0.567	0.543	0.519	0.497
6	0.942	0.888	0.837	0.790	0.746	0.705	0.666	0.630	0.596	0.564	0.535	0.507	0.480	0.456	0.432
7	0.933	0.871	0.813	0.760	0.711	0.665	0.623	0.583	0.547	0.513	0.482	0.452	0.425	0.400	0.376
8	0.923	0.853	0.789	0.731	0.677	0.627	0.582	0.540	0.502	0.467	0.434	0.404	0.376	0.351	0.327
9	0.914	0.837	0.766	0.703	0.645	0.592	0.544	0.500	0.406	0.424	0.391	0.361	0.333	0.308	0.284
10	0.905	0.820	0.744	0.676	0.614	0.558	0.508	0.463	0.422	0.386	0.352	0.322	0.295	0.270	0.247

Future years							Interest rate								
	16%	17%	18%	19%	20%	21%	22%	23%	24%	25%	26%	28%	30%	40%	50%
1	0.862	0.855	0.847	0.840	0.833	0.826	0.820	0.813	0.806	0.800	0.794	0.781	0.769	0.714	0.667
2	0.743	0.731	0.718	0.706	0.694	0.683	0.672	0.661	0.650	0.640	0.630	0.610	0.592	0.510	0.444
3	0.641	0.624	0.609	0.593	0.579	0.565	0.551	0.537	0.524	0.512	0.500	0.477	0.455	0.364	0.296
4	0.552	0.534	0.516	0.499	0.482	0.467	0.451	0.437	0.423	0.410	0.397	0.373	0.350	0.260	0.198
5	0.476	0.456	0.437	0.419	0.402	0.386	0.370	0.355	0.341	0.328	0.315	0.291	0.269	0.186	0.132
6	0.410	0.390	0.370	0.352	0.335	0.319	0.303	0.289	0.275	0.262	0.250	0.227	0.207	0.133	0.088
7	0.354	0.333	0.314	0.296	0.279	0.263	0.249	0.235	0.222	0.210	0.198	0.178	0.159	0.095	0.059
8	0.305	0.285	0.266	0.249	0.233	0.218	0.204	0.191	0.179	0.168	0.157	0.139	0.123	0.068	0.039
9	0.263	0.243	0.225	0.209	0.194	0.180	0.167	0.155	0.144	0.134	0.125	0.108	0.094	0.048	0.026
10	0.227	0.208	0.191	0.176	0.162	0.149	0.137	0.126	0.116	0.107	0.099	0.085	0.073	0.035	0.017

Table 2. Cumulative present value of £1 at compound interest rates

Interest rate

Future years	1%	2%	3%	4%	5%	6%	7%	8%	9%	10%	11%	12%	13%	14%	15%
1	0.990	0.980	0.971	0.962	0.952	0.943	0.935	0.926	0.917	0.909	0.901	0.893	0.885	0.877	0.870
2	1.970	1.942	1.913	1.886	1.859	1.833	1.808	1.783	1.759	1.736	1.713	1.690	1.668	1.647	1.626
3	2.941	2.884	2.829	2.775	2.723	2.673	2.624	2.577	2.531	2.487	2.444	2.402	2.361	2.322	2.283
4	3.902	3.808	3.717	3.630	3.546	3.465	3.387	3.312	3.240	3.170	3.102	3.037	2.974	2.914	2.855
5	4.853	4.713	4.580	4.452	4.329	4.212	4.100	3.993	3.890	3.791	3.696	3.605	3.517	3.433	3.352
6	5.795	5.601	5.417	5.242	5.076	4.917	4.767	4.623	4.486	4.355	4.231	4.111	3.998	3.889	3.784
7	6.728	6.472	6.230	6.002	5.786	5.582	5.389	5.206	5.033	4.868	4.712	4.564	4.423	4.288	4.160
8	7.652	7.325	7.020	6.733	6.463	6.210	5.971	5.747	5.535	5.335	5.146	4.968	4.799	4.639	4.487
9	8.566	8.162	7.786	7.435	7.108	6.802	6.515	6.247	5.995	5.759	5.537	5.328	5.132	4.946	4.772
10	9.471	8.983	8.530	8.111	7.722	7.360	7.024	6.710	6.418	6.145	5.889	5.650	5.426	5.216	5.019

Interest rate

Future years	16%	17%	18%	19%	20%	21%	22%	23%	24%	25%	26%	28%	30%	40%	50%
1	0.862	0.855	0.847	0.840	0.833	0.826	0.820	0.813	0.806	0.800	0.794	0.781	0.769	0.714	0.667
2	1.605	1.585	1.566	1.547	1.528	1.509	1.492	1.474	1.457	1.440	1.424	1.392	1.361	1.224	1.111
3	2.246	2.210	2.174	2.140	2.106	2.074	2.042	2.011	1.981	1.952	1.923	1.868	1.816	1.589	1.407
4	2.798	2.743	2.690	2.639	2.589	2.540	2.494	2.448	2.404	2.362	2.320	2.241	2.166	1.849	1.605
5	3.274	3.199	3.127	3.058	2.991	2.926	2.864	2.803	2.745	2.689	2.635	2.532	2.436	2.035	1.737
6	3.685	3.589	3.498	3.410	3.326	3.245	3.167	3.092	3.020	2.951	2.885	2.759	2.643	2.168	1.824
7	4.039	3.922	3.812	3.706	3.605	3.508	3.416	3.327	3.242	3.161	3.083	2.937	2.802	2.263	1.883
8	4.344	4.207	4.078	3.954	3.837	3.726	3.619	3.518	3.421	3.329	3.241	3.076	2.925	2.331	1.922
9	4.607	4.451	4.303	4.163	4.031	3.905	3.786	3.673	3.566	3.463	3.366	3.184	3.019	2.379	1.948
10	4.833	4.659	4.494	4.339	4.192	4.054	3.923	3.799	3.682	3.571	3.465	3.269	3.092	2.414	1.965

Glossary

Absorption costing	A costing method that, in addition to direct costs, assigns production overheads to cost units through the process of absorption. Costs are first allocated or apportioned to the cost centres, where they are absorbed into the cost unit using absorption rates
Accountability	A duty or obligation to give an account
Accounting	The process of identifying, classifying, measuring, recording and communicating the economic transactions of the entity
Accounting principles	The basic theoretical concepts that guide financial accounting
Accounting rate of return (ARR)	An accounting ratio that measures the predicted average profit before interest and tax as a percentage of the capital employed in a proposed capital investment project
Accounting standard	An authoritative statement on how a particular type of transaction or other event should be reflected in the financial statements. In the UK, compliance with accounting standards is normally necessary for the financial statements to give a true and fair view
Accrual	An estimate of a liability that is not supported by an invoice or a request for payment at the time the accounts for the period are being prepared
Accrual accounting	Accounting based on the principle that revenue and costs are recognized as they are earned and incurred irrespective of when cash (or its equivalent) is received or paid (the *realization principle*), and they are matched with one another (the *matching principle*) and dealt with in the income statement of the period to which they relate (the *period principle*)
Activity cost pool	A collection of all the indirect costs associated with a particular activity
Activity-based costing (ABC)	A method of costing in which overheads are assigned to the activities that take place within the entity and cost drivers are used to attach the activity cost pools to the cost units
Allowance for doubtful receivables	An amount charged against profit and deducted from receivables to allow for the estimated non-recovery of a proportion of debts

Asset	A present economic resource controlled by the entity as a result of past events (Exposure Draft Conceptual Framework for Financial Reporting, 2015 [4.4])
Associate	An entity over which the investor has significant influence (IAS 28, 2014 [3])
Audit	An independent examination of the accounting systems and records, and the subsequent expression of opinion on whether the financial statements give a true and fair view
Bad debt	An amount owed to the entity that is considered to be irrecoverable. It is written off as a charge against profit or against an existing allowance for doubtful receivables
Balanced scorecard (BSC)	An approach to the provision of information to management that integrates both financial and non-financial performance measures into a framework that aids strategic policy formulation and achievement
Breakeven point (BEP)	The level of activity at which the entity makes neither a profit nor a loss. It can be measured by volume of production or sales, percentage of production capacity or level of sales revenue
Budget	A quantitative or financial statement that contains the plans and policies to be pursued during a future accounting period
Budget centre	A designated part of an entity for which budgets are prepared and controlled by a manager
Budgetary control	The process by which financial control is exercised by managers preparing budgets for income and expenditure for each department or function of the entity in advance of an accounting period. Continuous comparison of actual performance against the budget by the departmental or functional manager helps ensure that objectives are achieved or provides a basis for revising the budget
Business combination	A transaction or other event in which an acquirer obtains control of one or more businesses (IFRS 3, 2013, Appendix A)
Capital	The money contributed by the owner(s) of the business to enable it to function
Capital investment appraisal	The evaluation of proposed investment projects with a view to determining which is likely to give the highest financial return
Cash	Comprises cash on hand and demand deposits (IAS 7, 2017 [6])

Cash deficit	The cash position when the cash outflows exceed the accumulated cash in the business
Cash equivalents	Short-term, highly liquid investments that are readily convertible to known amounts of cash and which are subject to an insignificant risk of changes in value (IAS 7, 2017 [6])
Cash inflows	The cash receipts of the business
Cash outflows	The cash payments of the business
Cash surplus	The cash position when the accumulated cash in the business exceeds the cash outflows
Comprehensive income	The total of all profits and gains made over the period
Conceptual framework	A statement of theoretical principles that provides guidance for financial accounting and reporting
Consolidated financial statements	The financial statements of a group in which the assets, liabilities, equity, income, expenses and cash flows of the parent and its subsidiaries are presented as those of a single economic entity (IFRS 10, 2011, Appendix A)
Contribution	The difference between the sales value and the variable costs. It is based on the assumption that both will be constant
Control of an investee	Achieved when the investor is exposed, or has rights, to variable returns from its involvement with the investee and has the ability to affect those returns through its power over the investee (IFRS 10, 2011, Appendix A)
Convergence of accounting standards	The reduction of differences in the accounting standards issued in different countries, especially as a result of adopting International Financial Reporting Standards (IFRSs)
Corporate governance	The system by which companies are directed and controlled by the directors, and the nature of their accountability to the investors
Cost	The amount of expenditure on goods and services that are needed to carry out the economic activities of the entity
Cost accounting	The process of collecting, processing and presenting financial and quantitative data to ascertain the cost of designated cost centres and cost units within the entity
Cost centre	A designated area, function or activity for which costs are collected within the entity
Cost driver	Any factor that drives the cost of a particular activity. An activity may have multiple drivers, such as the number of transactions and the duration of the transactions

Cost unit	A designated unit of production for which costs are collected within the organization
Cumulative cash brought forward (b/f)	The cash surplus or deficit at the start of the accounting period that has been brought forward from the previous period
Cumulative cash carried forward (c/f)	The cash surplus or deficit at the end of the accounting period that is carried forward to the next period
Depreciable amount	The cost of an asset, or other amount substituted for cost, less its residual value (IAS 16, 2014 [16.6])
Depreciation	The systematic allocation of the depreciable amount of an asset over its useful life (IAS 16, 2014 [16.6])
Differential reporting	The idea that different reporting entities should follow different accounting regulations
Direct costs	Costs that can be traced directly to a product or cost unit
Discounted cash flow (DCF)	A method that predicts the stream of cash inflows and outflows over the estimated life of a capital investment project and discounts them to present values using a cost of capital or hurdle rate
Discounted payback period method	Calculates the time required for the predicted discounted net cash flows to equal the capital invested in a proposed capital investment project
Double-entry bookkeeping	An accounting system based on the principle that every financial transaction involves the simultaneous receiving and giving of value and therefore needs to be recorded in at least two accounts
Economic resource	A right that has the potential to produce economic benefits (Exposure Draft Conceptual Framework for Financial Reporting, 2015 [4.4])
Enterprise resource planning (ERP)	Enterprise resource planning (ERP) is the management of all the information and resources involved in a company's operations by means of an integrated computer system (Stevenson, 2010, p. 595)
Environmental and social reporting	The process of communicating the social and environmental effects of organizations' economic activities to particular interest groups within society and to society at large (Gray, Owen and Maunders, 1987, p. ix)
Environmental management accounting	The identification, collection, analysis and the use of two types of information for internal decision making: physical information on the use, flows and fates of energy, water, and materials (including wastes) and monetary information on environment-related costs, earnings and savings (UNDSD, 2001, p. 2)

Equity	The residual interest in the assets of the entity after deducting all its liabilities (Exposure Draft Conceptual Framework for Financial Reporting, 2015 [4.4])
Ethics	The moral principles that guide behaviour. They may form a code of conduct for a specific group.
Expenses	Decreases in assets or increases in liabilities that result in decreases in equity, other than those relating to distributions to holders of equity claims (Exposure Draft Conceptual Framework for Financial Reporting, 2015 [4.4])
Fair value	The price that would be received to sell an asset or paid to transfer a liability in an orderly transaction between market participants at the measurement date (IFRS 13, 2013, Appendix A)
Finance	1. The money involved in a project, especially the capital needed to start a business
	2. A loan of money for a particular purpose, especially a loan provided by a bank or other financial institution
Financial accounting	The branch of accounting concerned with classifying, measuring and recording the economic transactions of an entity in accordance with established principles, legal requirements and accounting standards. It is primarily concerned with communicating a true and fair view of the financial performance and financial position of an entity to external parties at the end of the accounting period
Financial reporting	The statutory disclosure of general purpose financial information by limited liability entities via the annual report and accounts
Financing activities	Activities that result in changes in the size and composition of the contributed equity and borrowings of the entity (IAS 7, 2017 [7.6])
First in, first out (FIFO) cost	A method of valuing units of direct materials that uses the price of the earliest consignment received for all issues to production until all inventory at that price has been used up. Then the next latest price is used, and so on. The valuation of closing inventory is based on the same FIFO basis
Fixed budget	A budget that is not changed merely because the actual levels of activity differ from the budgeted levels of activity. Therefore, the budget cost allowances for each cost item are not changed for the variable items

Fixed cost	An item of expenditure that is unaffected by changes in the level of production or sales activity in the short term
Flexible budget	A budget that is changed to reflect the actual levels of activity. Therefore, it reflects the different behaviour of fixed and variable costs. The adjusted budget is known as a flexed budget
Goodwill	An asset representing the future economic benefits arising from other assets acquired in a business combination that are not individually identified and separately recognized (IFRS 3, 2013, Appendix A)
Gross profit	The difference between the revenue and the cost of goods sold during the period
Harmonization in financial reporting	The reduction of differences in the regulatory frameworks of different EU Member States, especially as a result of EU Directives
Income	Increases in assets or decreases of liabilities that result in increases in equity, other than those relating to contributions from holders of equity claims (Exposure Draft Conceptual Framework for Financial Reporting, 2015 [4.4])
Indirect costs	Costs that cannot be traced directly to a product or cost unit and are therefore classified as overhead expenses
Integrated report	A concise communication about how an organization's strategy, governance, performance and prospects, in the context of its external environment, lead to the creation of value in the short, medium and long term (IIRC, 2013, p. 7)
Integrated reporting <IR>	Promotes a more cohesive and efficient approach to corporate reporting and aims to improve the quality of information available to providers of financial capital to enable a more efficient and productive allocation of capital (IIRC, 2013, p. 4)
Internal rate of return (IRR)	The interest rate at which the total discounted values of the predicted net cash flows are equal to the capital invested in a proposed capital investment project
Inventory	The unsold goods in a trading business, or the raw materials, components, work-in-progress and finished goods in a manufacturing business
Investing activities	The acquisition and disposal of long-term assets and other investments not included in cash equivalents (IAS 7, 2017 [7.6])

Joint control	The contractually agreed sharing of control of an arrangement, which exists only when decisions about the relevant activities over an economic activity require the unanimous consent of the parties sharing control (IFRS 11, 2014, Appendix A)
Joint operation	A joint arrangement whereby the parties that have joint control of the arrangement have rights to the assets, and obligations for the liabilities, relating to the arrangement (IFRS 11, 2014, Appendix A)
Joint venture	A joint arrangement whereby the parties that have joint control of the arrangement have rights to the net assets of the arrangement (IFRS 11, 2014, Appendix A)
Liability	A present obligation of the entity to transfer an economic resource as a result of past events (Exposure Draft Conceptual Framework for Financial Reporting, 2015 [4.4])
Limited liability	The extent to which members of a limited company or limited liability partnership are liable for payment of the debts of the business
Limiting factor	A constraint that prevents the entity from achieving higher levels of performance and profitability
Management accounting	The branch of accounting concerned with collecting and analyzing financial and other quantitative information. It is primarily concerned with communicating information to management to help effective performance measurement, planning, controlling and decision making
Marginal cost	The total variable cost per unit of production. It represents the additional cost of producing one more unit of production
Master budget	The final co-ordinated budget for the whole entity that brings together the functional budgets and the non-functional budgets. The non-functional budgets include the capital expenditure budget, the budgeted statement of cash flows, the budgeted statement of profit or loss and other comprehensive income, and the statement of financial position
Materials	Raw materials, components or sub-assemblies purchased from a supplier for use in the manufacture of a product
Net cash flow	The difference between the cash inflows and the cash outflows

Net present value (NPV)	The difference between the total discounted values of the predicted net cash flows and the capital invested in a proposed capital investment project
Net realizable value (NRV)	The sales value of the inventory minus any additional costs likely to be incurred in getting it to the customer
Non-controlling interest	The equity in a subsidiary not attributable, directly or indirectly, to a parent (IFRS 3, 2013, Appendix A)
Operating activities	The principal revenue generating activities of the entity and other activities that are not investing or financing activities (IAS 7, 2017 [7.6])
Operating profit	The difference between the operating income and revenue expenditure for the period
Opportunity cost	The value of the benefit sacrificed when one course of action is chosen in preference to an alternative. It represents the forgone potential benefit from the best alternative course of action that has been rejected
Other comprehensive income (OCI)	Items of income and expense (including reclassification adjustments) that are not recognized in profit or loss as required or permitted by other IFRSs (IAS 1, 2014 [1.7])
Overhead absorption rate (OAR)	A predetermined rate that is used in absorption costing to charge the production overheads to the cost units
Parent	An entity that controls one or more entities (IFRS 10, 2011, Appendix A)
Payback period method	Calculates the time required before the predicted net cash flows are equal to the capital invested in a proposed capital investment project
Power	The existing rights [of the investor] that give the current ability to direct the relevant activities [of the investee] (IFRS 10, 2011, Appendix A)
Prepayment	A payment made for goods or services that will be received in the next accounting period
Profit or loss	The total of income less expenses, excluding the components of other comprehensive income (IAS 1, 2014 [1.7])
Property, plant and equipment (PPE)	Tangible assets that are held for use in the production or supply of goods or services, for rental to others, or for administrative purposes, and are expected to be used during more than one period (IAS 16, 2014 [16.6])

Protective rights	Rights designed to protect the interest of the party holding those rights without giving that party power over the entity to which those rights relate (IFRS 10, 2011, Appendix A)
Ratio analysis	A technique for evaluating the financial performance and financial stability of an entity through the use of accounting ratios. Comparisons are made with previous periods, other companies and industry averages
Relevant activities	Activities of the investee that significantly affect the investee's returns (IFRS 10, 2011, Appendix A)
Relevant range	The range of activity levels between which assumptions about cost behaviour in breakeven analysis remain valid. Outside this range, the linear relationships between fixed costs, variable costs and revenue do not apply
Reporting entity	An entity that chooses, or is required, to prepare general purpose financial statements. It is not necessarily a legal entity and can comprise a portion of an entity, or two or more entities (IASB, 2015 [3.11])
Residual value	The estimated amount that an entity would currently obtain from disposal of the asset, after deducting the estimated costs of disposal, if the asset were already of the age and in the condition expected at the end of its useful life (IAS 16, 2014 [16.6])
Responsibility accounting	A system that provides income and expenditure information to all management levels, based on the responsibility departmental or functional managers have for particular items of income or expenditure. Examples of responsibility accounting systems include budgetary control and standard costing
Significant influence	The power to participate in the financial and operating policy decisions of the investee but is not control or joint control of those policies (IAS 28, 2014 [3])
Standard costing	A system of control in which predetermined standard costs and standard income are compared with the actual costs and actual income to identify any variances
Stewardship	The responsible management of resources entrusted to the care of an agent (such as a director) and the obligation to provide relevant and reliable financial information relating to the resources to the principal (such as an investor)

Strategic management accounting	Provides the information needed for long-term strategic decision making, in contrast to the traditional focus on short-term costs
Target costing	A product costing method in which a target cost is determined by subtracting the desired profit margin from a competitive market price that customers are willing to pay
Time value of money	The concept that cash received today is worth more than a similar sum received at a later date because of the opportunity cost
Total comprehensive income	The change in equity during a period resulting from transactions and other events, other than those changes resulting from transactions with owners in their capacity as owners (IAS 1, 2014 [1.7])
Total quality management (TQM)	A comprehensive system for planning and controlling all business functions with a view to improving the quality of products and services through ongoing refinements in response to continuous feedback
Trial balance	A list of the balances on all the accounts that shows the debit balances in the left-hand column and credit balances in the right-hand column. If the principles of double-entry bookkeeping have been followed and the records are accurate, the totals of each column should be the same
UK GAAP	The regulatory framework for financial reporting in the UK, which comprises company law, accounting standards and stock exchange rules
Useful life	The period over which an asset is expected to be available for use by an entity... or the number of production or similar units expected to be obtained from the asset by the entity (IAS 16, 2014 [16.6])
Variable cost	An item of expenditure that varies directly with the level of production or sales, such as the direct costs and any variable overheads
Variance in budgetary control	The difference between the budgeted cost and the actual cost, or the difference between the budgeted income and the actual income. Individual budget centre managers are responsible for the controllable costs in their budgets and are expected to take action to remedy adverse variances that are considered to be excessive

Variance in standard costing	The difference between the standard cost and the actual cost, or the difference between the standard income and the actual income
Weighted-average cost (WAC)	A method of valuing units of direct materials based on the weighted-average price, which is recalculated after each new consignment is received. The valuation of closing inventory is based on the same WAC basis

Index